# Expert SharePoint 2010 Practices

Steve Wright, Dan Bakmand-Mikalski,
Razi bin Rais, Darrin Bishop, Matt Eddinger,
Brian Farnhill, Ed Hild, Joerg Krause,
Cory Loriot, Sahil Malik, Matthew McDermott,
David Milner, Ed Musters, Tahir Naveed,
Mark Orange, Doug Ortiz, Barry Ralston,
Ed Richard, Karthick Sethunarayanan,

Apress®

**Expert SharePoint 2010 Practices**

ISBN-13 (pbk): 978-1-4302-3870-6

ISBN-13 (electronic): 978-1-4302-3871-3

Trademarked names, logos, and images may appear in this book. Rather than use a trademark symbol with every occurrence of a trademarked name, logo, or image we use the names, logos, and images only in an editorial fashion and to the benefit of the trademark owner, with no intention of infringement of the trademark.

The use in this publication of trade names, trademarks, service marks, and similar terms, even if they are not identified as such, is not to be taken as an expression of opinion as to whether or not they are subject to proprietary rights.

President and Publisher: Paul Manning
Lead Editor: Jonathan Gennick
Technical Reviewer: Jeff Sanders
Editorial Board: Steve Anglin, Mark Beckner, Ewan Buckingham, Gary Cornell, Morgan Ertel, Jonathan Gennick, Jonathan Hassell, Robert Hutchinson, Michelle Lowman, James Markham, Matthew Moodie, Jeff Olson, Jeffrey Pepper, Douglas Pundick, Ben Renow-Clarke, Dominic Shakeshaft, Gwenan Spearing, Matt Wade, Tom Welsh
Coordinating Editor: Anita Castro
Copy Editor: Mary Behr and Tiffany Taylor
Compositor: Bytheway Publishing Services
Indexer: SPI Global
Artist: SPI Global
Cover Designer: Anna Ishchenko

Distributed to the book trade worldwide by Springer Science+Business Media, LLC., 233 Spring Street, 6th Floor, New York, NY 10013. Phone 1-800-SPRINGER, fax (201) 348-4505, e-mail orders-ny@springer-sbm.com, or visit www.springeronline.com.

For information on translations, please e-mail rights@apress.com, or visit www.apress.com.

Apress and friends of ED books may be purchased in bulk for academic, corporate, or promotional use. eBook versions and licenses are also available for most titles. For more information, reference our Special Bulk Sales–eBook Licensing web page at www.apress.com/bulk-sales.

The information in this book is distributed on an "as is" basis, without warranty. Although every precaution has been taken in the preparation of this work, neither the author(s) nor Apress shall have any liability to any person or entity with respect to any loss or damage caused or alleged to be caused directly or indirectly by the information contained in this work.

Any source code or other supplementary materials referenced by the author in this text is available to readers at www.apress.com. For detailed information about how to locate your book's source code, go to www.apress.com/source-code/.

*I would like to dedicate this book to my mother Zahida Rais and sister KhaizranSiddiqui for both standing beside me throughout my career and while I was writing this book.*

*Razi bin Rais*


*I dedicate my chapter to Dan and June Eddinger for raising a son they can be proud of, Marcy Eddinger for supporting me when I needed it most, and my nephews, Daniel and William, who inspire me to teach future generations every day.*

*Matt Eddinger*


*For my daughter Vanessa, who always makes me smile, and for the whole SharePoint community—especially the Australian guys and girls, whose motivation and talent are a constant inspiration for me.*

*Brian Farnhill*


*I want to dedicate this book to my father (Abdul Sattar Nadeem) and my mother (Zahida Sattar), without them I wouldn't be where I am today.*

*Tahir Naveed*

# Contents at a Glance

v

# Contents

# About the Authors

**Steve Wright** is a senior manager and SharePoint solution lead for Sogeti USA in Omaha, Nebraska. For more than 20 years, Steve has worked on air-traffic control, financial, insurance, and a multitude of other types of systems. He enjoys writing and speaking at user-group meetings and MSDN events, and he holds more than 45 Microsoft certifications. Steve has contributed to and performed technical reviews for several previous titles covering Microsoft products, including SharePoint, Access, Windows, SQL Server, and BizTalk Server. For the past several years, he has focused on building highly customized SharePoint solutions.

**Dan Bakmand-Mikalski** works with research and development at the global Danish company SurfRay Inc., a market leader in search technology on the SharePoint platform. Firsthand experience with customers and SharePoint professionals has given him a unique insight into the core challenges you are likely to face when doing advanced customizations and extensions to native SharePoint search. He specializes in understanding the SharePoint search engine characteristics and the search interfaces, and his experience offers relevant insights for newcomers as well as experienced SharePoint administrators and developers about how to take advantage of unused potential in SharePoint. Dan has an academic background as a civil engineer in the fields of computer science and mathematical modeling from the Technical University of Denmark. He was born in Copenhagen, Denmark in 1978, where he also currently lives and works. Although Dan has written several articles on SharePoint and search technology, this book is his debut as a published author and professional writer. Dan can be contacted by e-mail at bakmand@gmail.com.

**Razi bin Rais** works as a Microsoft SharePoint SME for a global IT firm based in New York. He is also a Microsoft SharePoint Server MVP. He has authored numerous technical articles and also worked with Microsoft Learning (MSL) as a SharePoint subject matter expert for several Microsoft courses and certifications. He has been a speaker for the International .NET Association (INETA) and the Global IT Community Association (GITCA) and has led sessions during several conferences, including the SharePoint Conference SEA 2010, Microsoft TechDays, Microsoft ISV Innovation Days, Singapore Community Technology Updates, and SharePoint Saturdays. He maintains a blog at http://razirais.wordpress.com, is on Twitter @razibinrais, and can be reached at razibinrais@live.com.

▪ **Darrin Bishop** is a speaker, author, and developer who has focused on Microsoft SharePoint Technologies since the release of SharePoint Portal Server 2001. Lately, Darrin has branched out to Azure and Windows Phone development projects. He frequently writes, blogs, and speaks about SharePoint, Azure, and Windows Phone. Darrin is an international speaker and speaks at many SharePoint conferences, SharePoint Saturdays, MOSS Camps, and user groups. Darrin is a director of Aptillon, a company focused on high-quality SharePoint, Azure, and Windows Phone architecture, design, and development. Contact Darrin via his blog at www.darrinbishop.com/blog or via www.aptillon.com.

▪ **Matt Eddinger** has more than 15 years of experience in several areas of the information technology field. He works for Microsoft Consulting Services, where he specializes in SQL Server and SharePoint engagements. With a bachelor's degree from Shepherd University and a master's in strategic leadership from Mountain State University, Matt is especially adept at mapping business strategy to technical solutions. He received his first Microsoft Certified Professional recognition in 1999. He has been an MCSE, MCSD, MCDBA, and MCAD. His current certifications include seven MCTSs, five MCITPs, and MCT.

▪ **Brian Farnhill** is an experienced SharePoint expert with a passion for the technology. He has received recognition by Microsoft with the SharePoint Server Most Valuable Professional Award. With a strong technical background, he has delivered a wide range of successful projects for many clients. Brian is involved with many SharePoint community projects, such as SharePoint Saturday events and the Canberra SharePoint user group, and he loves being able to share his passion for SharePoint with the world.

▪ **Ed Hild's** first job after college was as a math and computer science teacher at Walt Whitman High School in Bethesda, Maryland. After upgrading the curriculum, he decided to practice what he was teaching and moved into consulting. Ed soon felt the teaching itch again, and took a position teaching MCSD and MCSE courses for a technical education center as well as developing the software that would run the franchise. Ed gained most of his development experience at his next position as director of technology at e.magination, a Microsoft partner in Baltimore. There, he worked for several years building web applications for a wide variety of customers using Microsoft technologies. He was then lured to Microsoft and now works as the collaboration technology architect in the Microsoft Technology Center in Reston, Virginia.

▨ **Joerg Krause** has been working with software and software technology since the early 1980s, starting with a ZX-81 and taking the first steps using BASIC and assembler language. He studied information technology at Humboldt University Berlin, Germany, but left early to start his own operation in the 1990s. He is the author of several books about online marketing, PHP, ASP.NET, and SharePoint. He's MCP for .NET technology and SharePoint development. He currently works as a freelance consultant and software developer for Microsoft Technologies. Joerg can be reached at joerg@krause.net, and you can get more information at www.joergkrause.de.

▨ **Cory Loriot** has been working with SharePoint as an administrator, architect, and developer since January 2007, beginning with SharePoint Portal Server 2003, continuing with Microsoft Office SharePoint Server 2007, and most recently with SharePoint Server 2010. Cory works for Computer Technology Solutions, Inc. as a senior consultant, designing and implementing Microsoft SharePoint 2010 and ASP.NET solutions.

▨ **Sahil Malik** is the founder and principal of Winsmarts.com and has been a Microsoft MVP and INETA speaker for the past 10 years. He has authored many books and numerous articles in the .NET and SharePoint space. Sahil has architected and delivered SharePoint-based solutions for extremely high-profile clients, and he talks at conferences internationally. Sahil has authored two books for Apress on SharePoint 2010.

▨ **Matthew McDermott** is a founder and director at Aptillon, Inc, a five-time Microsoft SharePoint Server MVP, and a part-time trainer for Critical Path Training. Matthew specializes in SharePoint integration, strategy, and implementation consulting, helping his clients solve business problems with SharePoint. Matthew is a content author, blogger, and specialist in SharePoint technologies focused on web content management, collaboration, search, and social computing. He speaks regularly at SharePoint conferences internationally, including the Microsoft SharePoint Conference, TechEd, the European SharePoint Best Practices Conference, and other local and regional events. Matthew blogs regularly at www.ablebleue.com/blog. Matthew spends his free time as a canine handler for K9 Search Austin, a volunteer K9 search team serving the FBI and Austin and San Antonio police departments. An accomplished cook and bartender, in his spare time Matt spends as much time with his wife as his dogs will allow. (Photo credit: Carlos Austin, Austin Photography)

**Dave Milner** is a senior SharePoint architect and the products lead at ShareSquared, where he builds SharePoint products and helps companies implement their SharePoint solutions. Dave is a technology professional with a deep understanding of Microsoft technologies, including 19 years of IT experience and experience with Microsoft technologies spanning more than a decade. Dave holds a master's in business administration with a technology management focus, and he is a Microsoft Certified Trainer. He has also obtained other advanced Microsoft certifications in the .NET and SharePoint areas. In addition, he is a certified Scrum Master, having successfully implementing Scrum methodologies with several application-development and solution teams. In the technology community, Dave is a frequent speaker and trainer at local and national SharePoint- and .NET-related events. He serves on the leadership team of the Colorado SharePoint User Groups (COSPUG) and helps run the local branch in Colorado Springs; he's also involved in other local technology groups. When he's not working on technology, Dave enjoys the outdoors of Colorado Springs, where he lives with his wife and two children.

**Ed Musters** is a SharePoint Most Valuable Professional and a SharePoint architect for Infusion. He has taught the exclusive Critical Path Training SharePoint courses for many years, and he holds all certifications in SharePoint 2010. He has been a featured speaker at DevReach in Sofia, Bulgaria; Time for SharePoint in Poland; SharePoint Summit in Montreal; Great Indian Developer Summit in Bangalore, India; DevTeach; SharePoint Saturdays; Microsoft TechDays; and various Code Camps. Ed also enjoys speaking to user groups across the world.

**Tahir Naveed** is a Microsoft Technology Specialist with focus on Microsoft SharePoint products and technologies. He has extensive experience in designing and implementing IT solutions using Microsoft SharePoint and .NET platforms. Tahir's core skills are architecture, design, development, and support. He also contributes to SharePoint blogs and sites with articles, tips, and best practices. Tahir holds a bachelors degree in software engineering from Bahria University and is currently working as a technology consultant in the New York/New Jersey region where he is leading a team of software specialists to deliver IT solutions. Tahir can be reached at tahir.naveed@gmail.com.

**Mark Orange** is a practicing consultant at Knowledge Cue and a SharePoint trainer for 3grow based in Wellington, New Zealand. Mark has specialized in implementing SharePoint solutions since early 2007 for numerous New Zealand government agencies, state-owned enterprises, and private companies. Prior to this, he designed and architected intranet and Internet solutions on early versions of SharePoint and the good-old Microsoft Content Management Server. To complement his technical SharePoint expertise, Mark brings significant experience in business processes, creative design, and information architecture to ensure that SharePoint solutions are fit for the required purpose, easy to use, and able to deliver value to the business. Much of his time is spent supporting clients in establishing enterprise strategies for SharePoint and information management, and training people so they can get the most out of SharePoint.

**Doug Ortiz** is an independent consultant whose skill set encompasses multiple platforms such as .Net, SharePoint, Office, and SQL Server. He possesses a master's degree in relational databases and has more than 20 years of experience in information technology; half of those years have been in .Net and SharePoint. His roles have included architecture, implementation, administration, disaster recovery, migrations, development, and automation of information systems, in and outside of SharePoint. Doug is the founder of Illustris, LLC. When possible, he blogs at: http://dougortiz.blogspot.com. He can be reached at dougortiz@illustris.org.

**Barry Ralston** is the chief architect for business intelligence with Birmingham-based ComFrame Software. Barry is also Microsoft's Virtual Technical Specialist (VTS) for business intelligence, responsible for assisting in Alabama, Mississippi, and northwest Florida in sales efforts including customer meetings, software demonstrations, and proof-of-concept efforts. Barry's client successes include American Cast Iron Pipe Company, Georgia Tech Research Institute, Bank of Hawaii, Honda Manufacturing of Alabama, and Aflac.

**Ed Richard** is a Microsoft SharePoint MVP (awarded three years in a row), is a Microsoft Virtual Technology Specialist for Visio, and has been involved with and actively developing with Microsoft SharePoint since its inception in 2001. Ed recognized the platform's potential early on and has been researching and developing integrated Office and SharePoint solutions over the past ten years. As a business-focused professional running e-Agility, Ed's focus has been on getting the most out of Microsoft Visio and Microsoft SharePoint 2010, building business process visualization solutions.

**Karthick Sethunarayanan** runs an independent IT solutions, products, consulting, and training company based in India with clients around the globe. His company specializes in delivering Microsoft SharePoint-based document management systems portals, workflow, eForms, and business intelligence solutions. Having also worked with Microsoft and various other organizations, Karthick has been one of the early starters with SharePoint 2010 and has implemented notable projects including a major SharePoint 2010 CMS implementation for Bahrain's government, designed to handle more than 50TB of data. He has been part of over 25+ SharePoint implementations as an architect, consultant, and trainer and is currently also working on launching cloud-based applications built on SharePoint 2010. With his passion for Microsoft technologies, Karthick also provides training and consulting to leading companies in India, the Middle East, the United States, and Australia. His blog is at http://karthickmicrosoft.blogspot.com, and he can be reached at skarthick6@gmail.com.

# About the Technical Reviewer

**Jeff Sanders** is a published author, technical editor, and accomplished technologist. He is currently employed with Avanade as a group manager and senior architect. He is a coauthor of SharePoint Server Standards and Best Practices for the US Department of Defense.

Jeff has years of professional experience in the field of IT and strategic business consulting, leading both sales and delivery efforts. He regularly contributes to certification and product-roadmap development with Microsoft, and he speaks publicly on Microsoft enterprise technologies. With his roots in software development, Jeff's areas of expertise include collaboration and content management solutions, operational intelligence, digital marketing, distributed component-based application architectures, object-oriented analysis and design, and enterprise integration patterns and designs.

Jeff is also the CTO of DynamicShift, a client-focused organization specializing in Microsoft technologies, specifically Office365/BPOS, SharePoint Server, StreamInsight, Windows Azure, AppFabric, Business Activity Monitoring, BizTalk Server, and .NET. He is a Microsoft Certified Trainer, and he leads DynamicShift in both training and consulting efforts.

Jeff enjoys non-work-related travel and spending time with his wife and daughter, and he wishes he had more time for both. He can be reached at jeff.sanders@dynamicshift.com.

# Acknowledgments

Many thanks to Bob Wallace and Beau Bertke, my teammates at Microsoft, for helping me figure some of this stuff out.

Matt Eddinger

I would like to give thanks to my wife of nearly ten years, Mandy, whose love, inspiration and no-nonsense attitude have kept me grounded. You truly are the complement to my life; I love you. To my parents, Cliff and Becky, who through careful instruction and loving discipline guided me, gave me wisdom, and encouraged me to honor God in all I do. To my family, for your love. To my Gulf Coast friends, you gave me your unguarded friendship for many years, and I miss you all. To Apress publishing for giving me a chance and patiently bearing with me in my first publication endeavor. To you, the reader, without whom this book would be needless; I hope you enjoy it. Finally, to the Eternal Living God that has granted me life to live, a mind to learn, a heart to listen, and a mouth to speak the words "Thank you."

Cory Loriot

Any acknowledgment for my success has to begin with my wonderful wife, Mary Jane. Through my many different occupations, you have never wavered in your support. For that I am blessed. You never complain when I have to push through a weekend to complete a chapter and add that one last thing to make it perfect. Thank you for raising two amazing dogs! I became an MVP though the help and guidance of many friends and colleagues who guided my technical education through the years. To my friends in the MVP community, I want to say thank you for your patience with my many questions. My friends at Microsoft, who are my sounding board when the path to success is unclear, I appreciate you listening and helping to make the product better so that everyone can benefit from what great software you have produced.

Matthew McDermott

I would like to thank Ted and Andrew of Critical Path Training for starting me on my SharePoint journey, the folks at Telerik for their fantastic support of my community work, and finally my loving wife Gala for her unwavering support for this project.

Ed Musters

I want to thank Pradeep Thekkethodi at Orion who encouraged and supported me to become a part of this book.

Tahir Naveed

I would like to dedicate this book and thank my family for all their help and support, alongside Apress, which made the publishing of the chapter a reality.

Doug Ortiz

First and foremost, I would like to thank my parents, sister, and family for providing me all the support, motivation, and encouragement required for me to attain success in entrepreneurship. I also thank my friends Sudarshan and Anand for always being there to advise, guide, and help me throughout my career. I would also like to thank my team for working with me (and tolerating my quest for speedy perfection) and helping us win customer confidence and trust all these years. Last and most important, I would like to express my gratitude to all my clients. The have been partners who have provided a wonderful opportunity for me to work with them, learn their problems and objectives, and collaboratively provide suitable and acceptable solutions. Without those learning experiences, being a part of this book would not have been possible.

Karthick Sethunarayanan

# CHAPTER 1

# Workflows

These days organizations have two possible ways to get ahead of each other. One is by working harder and the other is by working smarter. Now we all know how much working hard gets you ahead, not much! So it all boils down to working smarter. Working smarter simply means achieving more by doing less. This means finding someone else to do your work, so you don't have to do it, conventionally referred to as outsourcing. Interestingly, we know that doesn't go too far either! Therefore, the only long term and viable alternative that organizations have discovered to better productivity is to automate. Automate more and more processes. Automation in an office environment means creating software that supports business processes that involve numerous roles, people, and perhaps, even external systems.

As a result of following those automated processes, there is never a confusion on whose turn it is next to approve a certain project proposal so it can be efficiently routed to a customer. In contrast, when a serious exception occurs based on predefined rules, appropriate people can be emailed so human intervention can be involved where necessary. By following these processes in a system setup, you can be assured that no particular step was missed. There is no need to double check, because the computers are doing that double-checking for you. Finally, by working through the process defined in a computer system, you are also collecting historical information that can be looked at later or archived using one of the many ways to manage SharePoint data as you have already seen in this book.

To support this endeavor, a new player was introduced in .NET 3.0 called as the Workflow Foundation! SharePoint 2007 and SharePoint 2010 leverage Workflow foundation to provide the capability of authoring and running workflows in SharePoint as well. In other words, SharePoint can act as a workflow host.

Now you might argue that everything I described so far about creating automated business processes in software can be hand-coded from scratch. You'd find me agreeing with you—not everything needs workflow foundation. In fact, using workflow foundation introduces some additional complexity and also ties you down to a certain way of doing things. But, it gives you so much other stuff on top, that maybe in some instances it makes sense to represent complex long-running business processes using workflow foundation. In terms of SharePoint 2010, the following interesting facilities become available to you should you choose to author your business processes in SharePoint Workflows.

- Everything that workflow foundation gives you, such as the reliability of long-running processes to last across machine reboots, is made available to you, if you represent your business processes as workflows in SharePoint.

- Ability to visualize the workflow graphically, so the end users can view the current flow. The running progress of a workflow is made available using Workflow Visualization using Visio if you use Workflow in SharePoint 2010.

- Business users can craft up workflows in tools such as Visio or SharePoint Designer in a very easy-to-use graphical way. These graphical views of the workflow can then show running workflows in SharePoint; reporting analysis tools can be written on the log history of the running workflow instances which can allow you to perform improvements on the running workflow.

- The same workflows that have been written by business users can then be exported to Visual Studio, where developers can extend the workflows and integrate them with custom logic, third party products, and make them interact with proprietary algorithms or systems. Of course, you do have the capability of writing a workflow from scratch in Visual Studio as well.

Given an enterprise processes problem, when should you choose to implement it as a workflow and when should you just write custom code representing that business process? I hope once you have examined all of the preceding scenarios in this chapter, you will be able to answer this question very well.

In this chapter, I will start by demonstrating out of the box workflows that come with SharePoint, so you get an idea of what workflow foundation in SharePoint gives us. Once you have a solid understanding of the basics, then I will enhance it further by involving tools such as Visio and SharePoint Designer. Finally, I will wrap up by involving Visual Studio in authoring complex logic that SharePoint Designer and Visio are unable to express. Let's get started with using out of the box workflows in SharePoint 2010.

# Out of the Box Workflows

SharePoint 2010 comes with several workflow templates out of the box. These are generally installed as features, and are available for you to associate with lists or at the site level. In SharePoint 2007, you could only associate workflows with lists. Therefore, step one of having a workflow available for use is for it to be installed as a feature. Once it is available for use, you can then create "Associations" of the workflow with existing lists or sites. At this point, you can optionally ask the user associating the workflow some questions, usually presented as an "Association Form". An association form is what allows the workflow to interact with the user when the workflow is first associated with a list.

Once you have created an association of a workflow template, you can then choose to run the workflow on individual list items (or run it on the site if you had chosen to associate it). When you start a workflow, it can ask more questions by showing yet another form called as the initiation form. Thus, the "initiation form" is what allows the system to ask questions when a workflow is first initiated/instantiated.

As the workflow is running, it can ask further questions of the users. In asking those questions, the workflow can create tasks for users, and those tasks can then be performed by the end users. Those tasks go in a list, and can be represented as yet another kind of form, called as the "Task Form". Note that a workflow can have zero or one association forms, it can have zero or one initiation forms, but it can have many task forms.

Similar to task forms, the workflow can also be altered midcourse by end-users by using yet another kind of form called a "Modification form". Just like the task form, there can be zero or many modification forms on a workflow.

Let's pick an out of the box workflow and understand the usage of all these forms and the workflow lifecycle in general. The workflow I intend to use here is the "Approval" Workflow, which comes out of the box in paid versions of SharePoint.

In your SharePoint site, go ahead and create a new list based on the Custom List Template and name it "Items to be Approved". Then visit the list settings page of this list and view the versioning settings. Under versioning settings, choose to "require content approval for submitted items". By choosing this option, you just enabled the ability to have draft items available in the list. Draft items mean items that are currently a work in progress and should not be seen by everyone. They can be seen only by the author or by people who have the ability to view and approve draft items. This is controlled by the "manage lists" permission, which is one of the permission settings that you can give any particular SPPrincipal. An SPPrincipal can be an SPGroup or SPUser. I will talk more about security in Chapter 12 where these object names will make more sense.

Next, back under lists settings visit the workflow settings link. Here you will find the various workflow associations you can create with this particular list. If you are using the enterprise version of SharePoint, the various workflow associations available to you are the following:

- Disposition approval

- Three state

- Collect signatures

- Approval

- Collect feedback

For this example, you will use the approval workflow. Therefore, select the approval workflow template and give it a name of "Approval". Then, click the next button. Clicking the next button brings up the association form, which is an out of the box InfoPath form. If you have used this workflow in SharePoint 2007, you would note that this form has been redone. Fill out the form as shown in Figure 1-1.

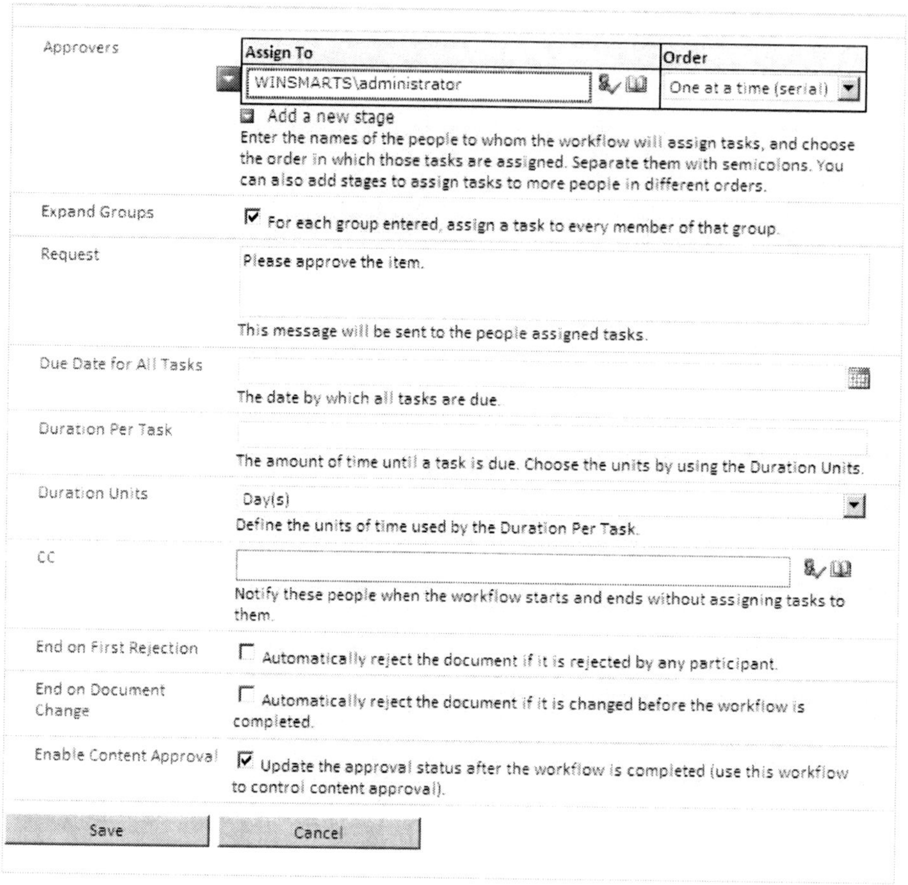

***Figure 1-1.*** *The Association form created in InfoPath*

Notably, I have checked the check box for "Enable Content Approval". This means that the completion of this workflow will approve the associated list item that this workflow is running upon. Once you've filled out the form, click the save button. You will then be presented with a screen, as shown in Figure 1-2.

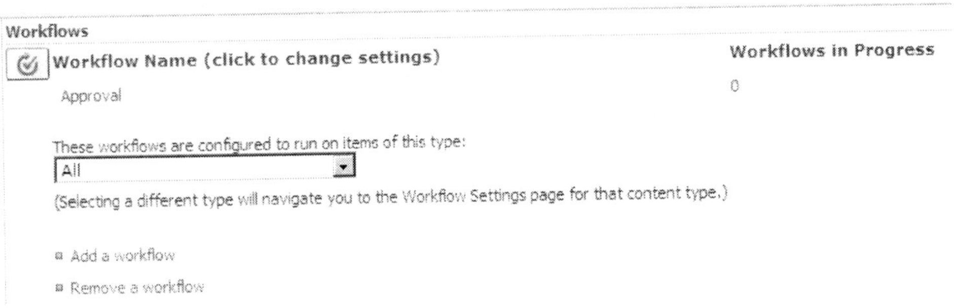

**Workflows**

☑ **Workflow Name (click to change settings)**          **Workflows in Progress**

   Approval                                                  0

These workflows are configured to run on items of this type:

[All                              ▾]

(Selecting a different type will navigate you to the Workflow Settings page for that content type.)

▪ Add a workflow

▪ Remove a workflow

***Figure 1-2.*** *The associated workflows with a list*

This screen informs you of all the associated workflows with this particular list. If you have used workflows in SharePoint 2007, you would note a notable difference here. Even within a list, you now have the ability to configure to run a particular workflow with a particular content type.

Now add an item into the list and put "Test Item" in the Title. Note that SharePoint informs you that the items in this list require content approval, and that your items will not appear in public views, unless they are first approved by someone with proper rights. This can be seen in the Figure 1-3.

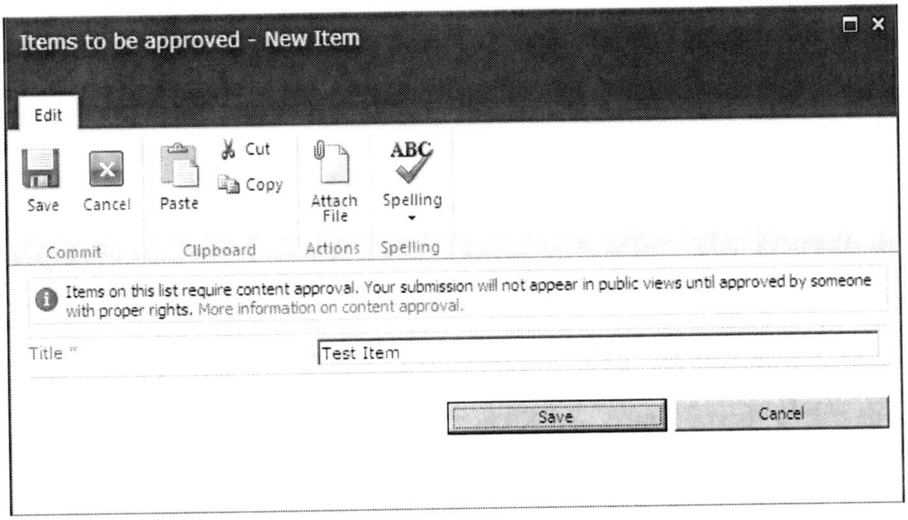

**Items to be approved - New Item**                                        ▫ ✕

| Edit |

| 💾 Save | ✕ Cancel | 📋 Paste | ✂ Cut  📋 Copy | 📎 Attach File | ABC✓ Spelling |
|---|---|---|---|---|---|
| Commit | | Clipboard | | Actions | Spelling |

ⓘ Items on this list require content approval. Your submission will not appear in public views until approved by someone with proper rights. More information on content approval.

Title *          [Test Item                                              ]

                         [      Save      ]          [     Cancel     ]

***Figure 1-3.*** *You are being informed that items on this list will require content approval.*

Once you have created this item you would also note that the default view now contains a column called "Approval Status" and the approval status as of now is "Pending". Select the item and from the ribbon under the items click the workflows button. Alternatively, you can also choose to access the workflow screen from the ECB menu. Click the approval workflow association that you had created earlier to initiate the workflow. Initiating the workflow will present you with the initiation form. This form can be seen in Figure 1-4.

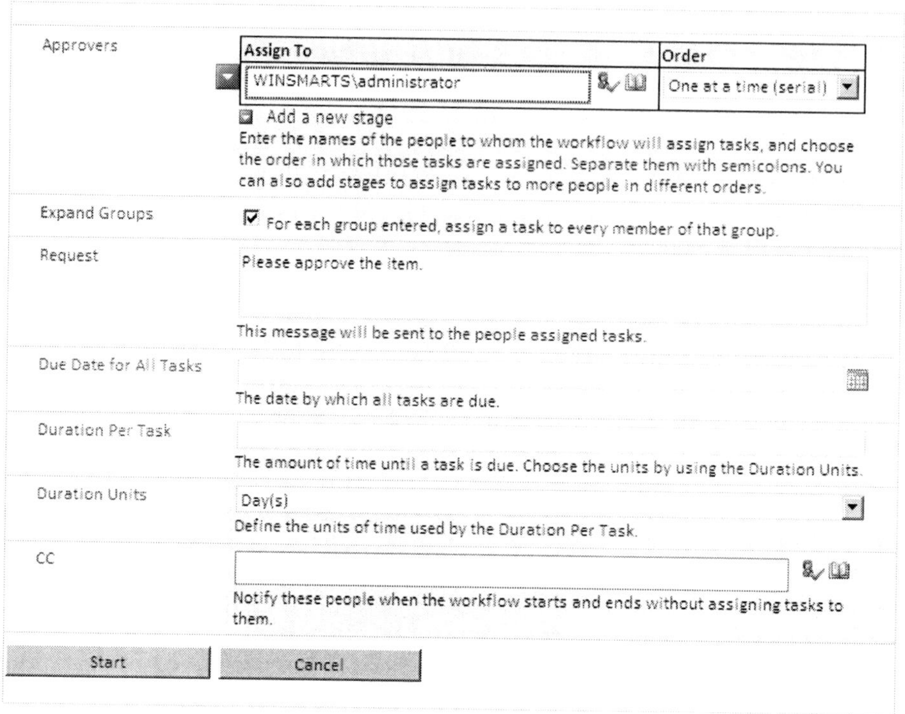

**Figure 1-4.** *The initiation form for the workflow*

Click the start button to start the workflow. By starting the workflow, the specified approver will be sent an e-mail message, and a task will be created for them requesting to come and approve the item. This task presents itself as yet another InfoPath form and can be accessed directly from either their e-mail or from the SharePoint site. In the SharePoint site, the task is created in a list called "Tasks". You specified this list name right before association form. There is another list you specified when creating this association, called "Workflow History". This is a hidden list and will store all the history activities of the running workflows.

Now visit the tasks list at http://sp2010/Lists/Tasks, and you will see a task created for the administrator. Clicking on this task brings up another form, which is the task form. This can be seen in Figure 1-5.

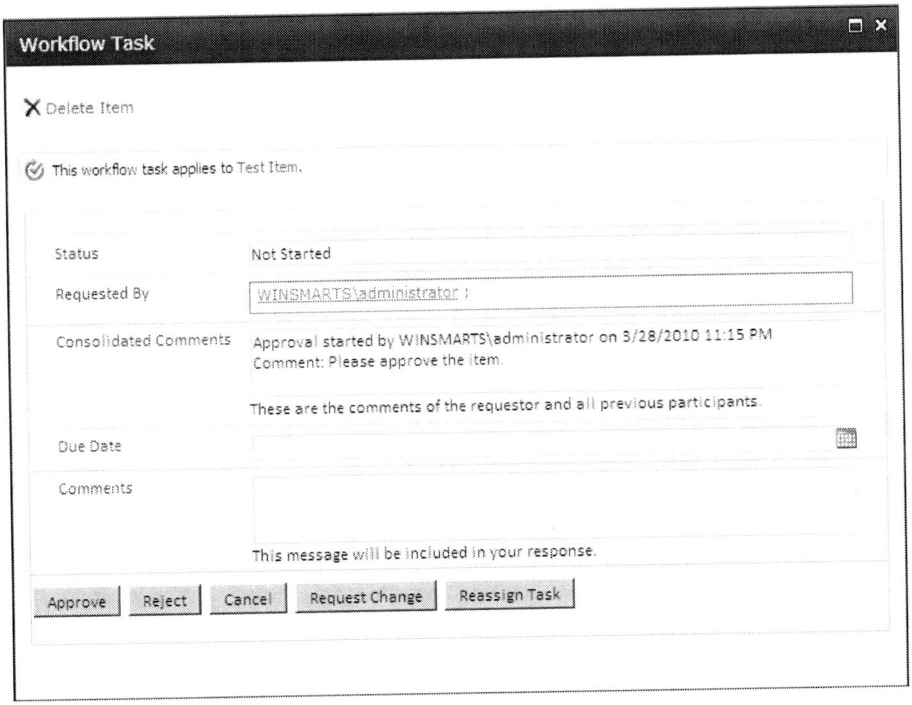

**Figure 1-5.** *Task form for the workflow*

At this point, clicking on the request change or reassigned task will bring up the necessary modification forms as well. For now, go ahead and click the approve button and then visit the "items to approve" list one more time. You would note that the item that the workflow was running upon has now been approved. This can be seen in Figure 1-6.

**Figure 1-6.** *Approval Status and Workflow Status on the list item*

Now, let me show you something really cool! Click the "Approved" link under the "Approval" column. This should take you to a page that informs you of the status of the current workflow. Assuming that you have office web applications installed in the current site collection you're working in, and you have activated the "SharePoint Server Enterprise Site Collection features", and that Visio

Services of configured on your web application, you should see a graphical view of the current workflow instance as shown in Figure 1-7[1].

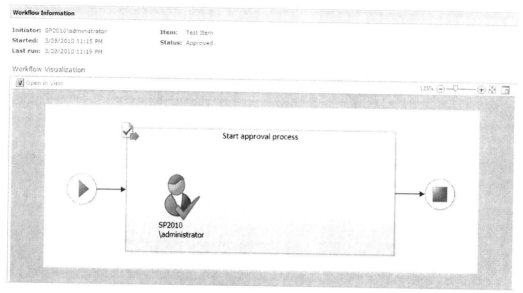

***Figure 1-7.*** *Visio Visualization of your workflow*

This is really amazing because it gives the user a friendly graphical view of the current workflow instance with the necessary values populated. On the same page, you would also see the historical tasks, and the workflow history associated with this instance of the workflow. This is information that most organizations would find extremely helpful.

Now that Visio services picture was pretty cool! Wouldn't it be helpful if end user's could also craft up a Visio diagram to display their workflow, and perhaps that same visio diagram could be used to give life to an actual running workflow in SharePoint 2010? Exactly this scenario is possible.

# Customizing Out of the Box Workflows

Out of the box workflows are great, and the biggest reason they are so great is because you don't have to write them. However, if you have business users like the ones I deal with, there will always request a minor tweak to an out of the box workflow, and then they give me puzzled looks when I give them a time estimate in weeks. In SharePoint 2007, out of the box workflows were pretty much sealed. They were what they were and you could not change them. In SharePoint 2010, however, you have the ability to tweak out of the box workflows and change them to your heart's content.

---

[1] Note that in Figure 1-7, I took the screenshot on a machine with domain name "SP2010", your domain will be "Winsmarts" or whatever you choose.

Let's take the example of the out of the box workflow. Say that you want to perform a minor tweak to an out of the box workflow. Specifically, the tweak you wish to do is that you don't want to display the CC Field in the initiation form. Also, since I'm not too fond of the colors used on the initiation form let's also change the colors of the inititiation form.

You have the ability of customizing out of the box workflows using SharePoint Designer. Open your site collection in SharePoint Designer and look at all the workflows available within this site. You should see the "Approval - SharePoint 2010" workflow available and you can double-click it and start editing it right through SharePoint Designer. What I like to do is to right-click an existing out of the box workflow definition, choose to make a copy, and then modify the copy. This way the original workflow definition remains intact, so someone else can use it later.

Therefore, right-click the "Approval - SharePoint 2010" workflow template and choose "Copy and Modify". By doing so, SharePoint Designer will ask you for a name of the copy, call it "Approval Copy". Also, SharePoint Designer will ask you which content type you want to limit this workflow to. This can be seen in Figure 1-8.

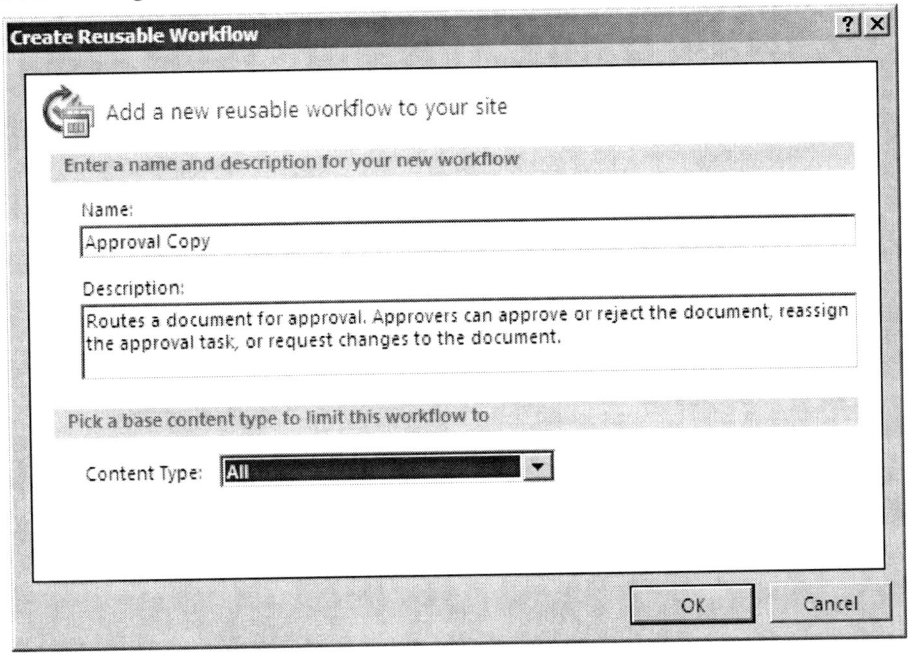

**Figure 1-8.** *Associating the workflow to a particular content type*

What you're doing here is creating a reusable workflow. This reusable workflow can be exported as a solution package. It can be imported into Visual Studio for further tweaking or it can be deployed across various other farms. When you create a reusable workflow through SharePoint Designer, you associate it with a content type. By associating a reusable workflow to a content type, you are essentially defining the structure of information that this workflow can always assume will be present. Therefore, if you associate the workflow with announcements, you can be sure that there will be a field called "Expires" because every announcement has an "Expires" field in it.

Any content type that inherits from announcement will be able to use your reusable workflow. Therefore, in order to create a globally reusable workflow, you should associate with the item content type. By doing so, you can be guaranteed that only the title field is present. This workflow can then be associated with any content type, since every content type eventually inherits from the item content type.

For this example, choose the content type to be "All" and click OK. The next screen will show you the workflow logic written out as a series of logical steps and conditions. This can be seen in Figure 1-9.

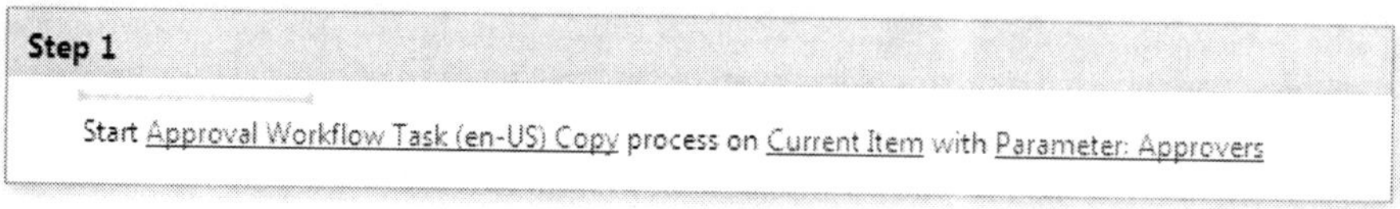

> **Step 1**
>
> Start <u>Approval Workflow Task (en-US) Copy</u> process on <u>Current Item</u> with <u>Parameter: Approvers</u>

*Figure 1-9. Workflow design in SharePoint Designer 2010*

Let's say that at the very end of this workflow you wish to log to the history list that the workflow has finished executing. If you pay close attention to this logic tree, you will see an orange horizontal blinking cursor. By either using your cursor keys or by clicking the mouse left button, you have the ability to move that orange cursor. Take that cursor to the very end of the workflow, as shown in Figure 1-10.

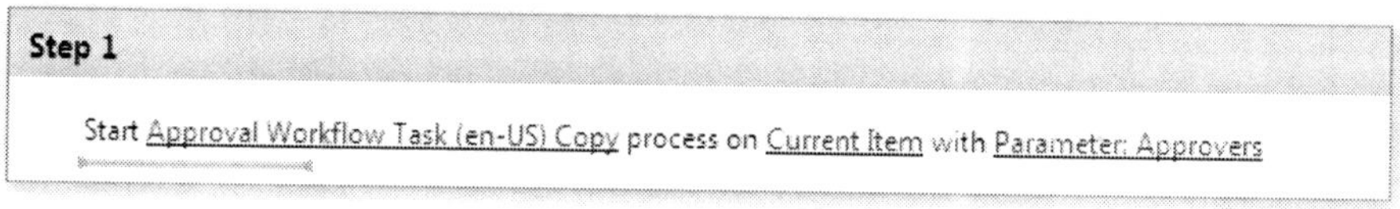

> **Step 1**
>
> Start <u>Approval Workflow Task (en-US) Copy</u> process on <u>Current Item</u> with <u>Parameter: Approvers</u>

*Figure 1-10. I just moved my cursor to the end of the workflow.*

With the cursor double-click it using the left button of your mouse. After a text box appears prompting you to start typing to search. Start typing "Log" and you will see that SharePoint Designer has narrowed your search to the Log to History list activity, as shown in Figure 1-11.

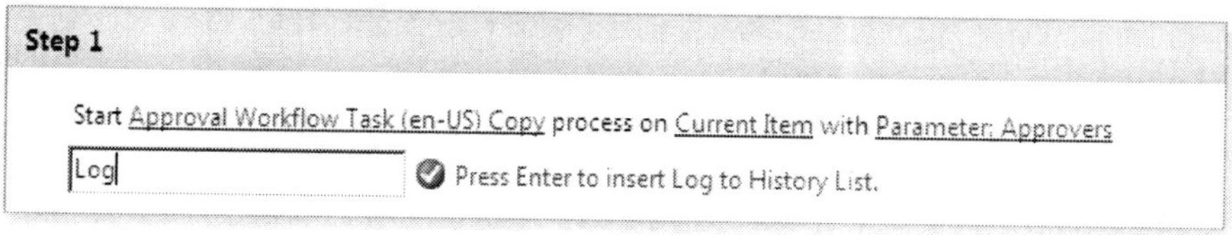

> **Step 1**
>
> Start <u>Approval Workflow Task (en-US) Copy</u> process on <u>Current Item</u> with <u>Parameter: Approvers</u>
>
> Log    ● Press Enter to insert Log to History List.

*Figure 1-11. Picking a workflow activity in SharePoint Designer 2010*

As prompted, hit enter to insert the necessary activity and then configure it to log a suitable message into the workflow history list. This can be seen in Figure 1-12.

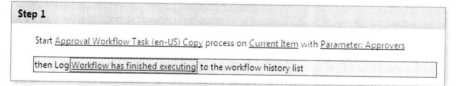

> **Step 1**
>
> Start <u>Approval Workflow Task (en-US) Copy</u> process on <u>Current Item</u> with <u>Parameter: Approvers</u>
>
> then Log <u>Workflow has finished executing</u> to the workflow history list

*Figure 1-12. A configured workflow activity in SharePoint Designer 2010*

Go ahead and save this workflow. Now draw your attention to the ribbon, which shows a button that says "Export to Visio". Clicking on this button will allow you to export a .vwi file. Save this .vwi file at a convenient location on the disk.

Next, start Visio and create a new diagram under the flowchart category, based on the "Microsoft SharePoint Workflow" stencil. This visio diagram allows a business analyst to craft up an entire workflow from scratch entirely in Visio. This can be imported/exported back and forth from SharePoint Designer as many times as you please. You can experiment by creating a brand new workflow yourself using the Visio stencil, but I'm going to import the .vwi file you had exported from SharePoint Designer earlier. In Visio, go to the flowchart category and create a new diagram based on "Microsoft SharePoint Workflow". Once the diagram is created, in the ribbon under the process tab, look for the import and export buttons, as shown in Figure 1-13.

**Figure 1-13.** *The import/export buttons for the SharePoint workflow*

Click import and choose to import the .vwi file you had exported from SharePoint Designer earlier. You should see a graphical representation of your workflow in Figure 1-14.

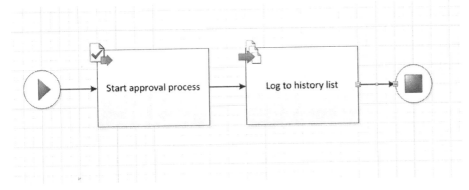

**Figure 1-14.** *Your created workflow depicted graphically in Visio*

For a moment, I'd like you to stop here and compare this graphical representation with the Visio Services representation you saw earlier. You will see that the log to history list block is new. Therefore, this diagram accurately reflects my intent.

Again, I leave it up to you to experiment with this Visio stencil and the various workflow actions and conditions you can use in Visio and give those SharePoint flowcharts life as SharePoint workflows with SharePoint Designer.

Now come back to SharePoint Designer and let's make some additional tweaks to the approval copy workflow you were working on. There are two additional things I'd like to do to this workflow. I'd like to tweak the look of the infopath form and I'd like to eliminate the CC Field from the initiation form. In order to do so, open the approval copy workflow in SharePoint Designer and click the Initiation Form

Parameters button in the ribbon. This form will allow you to add, modify, or remove various parameters for the workflow, and also choose which ones appear in the initiation form, association form, and which appear in both. Select the CC variable and choose to modify it by having it appear only in the association form. This can be seen in the Figure 1-15.

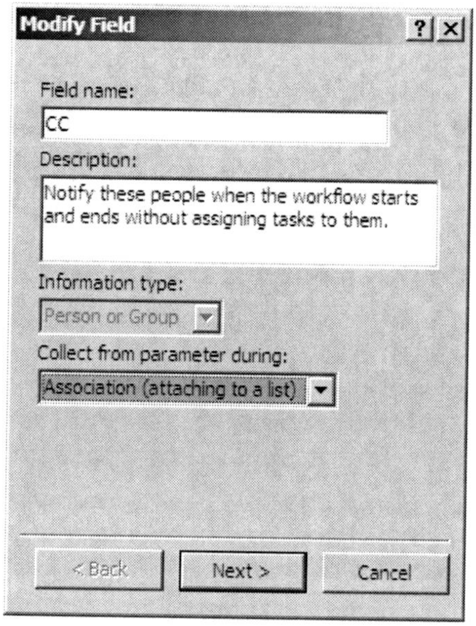

**Figure 1-15.** *Modifying an out of the box workflow*

The variables specified over here will also automatically generate the necessary InfoPath forms for you. Now double-click the InfoPath form under the "Forms" section of the workflow and make some modifications to the InfoPath form. Your modified infpath form should look like Figure 1-16.

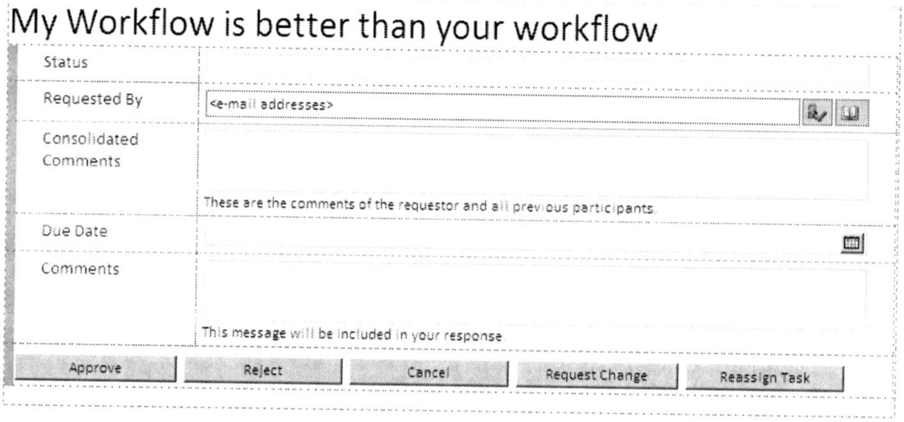

**Figure 1-16.** *Modified InfoPath form*

Save this infopath farm anywhere on your machine. Then, publish it by clicking on the quick publish button next to the save button in the title bar of InfoPath.

Your modifications to the workflow are now complete. Click the edit workflow link one more time and from the ribbon choose to save and publish. Publishing the workflow will process all the necessary files, including the workflow visualization and the solution package, and will make the workflow available on the SharePoint site.

Just like before, create a new association to the "Approval Copy" workflow and run the workflow. Note the following:

- The CC Field is no longer being asked for in the initiation form.

- The workflow visualization now shows a log to history list activity at the end of the workflow.

- The task form reflects the changes you had made previously.

- In the workflow history, you should see a new comment saying "Workflow has finished executing", as shown in Figure 1-17.

**Workflow History**

The following events have occurred in this workflow.

| | Date Occurred | Event Type | User ID | Description | Outcome |
|---|---|---|---|---|---|
| ☐ | 3/29/2010 12:08 AM | Workflow Initiated | WINSMARTS\administrator | Approval Workflow Task (en-US) Copy was started. Participants: WINSMARTS\administrator | |
| | 3/29/2010 12:08 AM | Task Created | WINSMARTS\administrator | Task Created for WINSMARTS\administrator. Due by: 1/1/0001 12:00:00 AM | |
| | 3/29/2010 12:08 AM | Error | System Account | The e-mail message cannot be sent. Make sure the outgoing e-mail settings for the server are configured correctly. | |
| | 3/29/2010 12:08 AM | Error | System Account | The e-mail message cannot be sent. Make sure the outgoing e-mail settings for the server are configured correctly. | |
| | 3/29/2010 12:08 AM | Task Completed | WINSMARTS\administrator | Task assigned to WINSMARTS\administrator was approved by WINSMARTS\administrator. Comment: | Approved by WINSMARTS\administrator |
| | 3/29/2010 12:08 AM | Workflow Completed | WINSMARTS\administrator | Approval Workflow Task (en-US) Copy was completed. | Approval Workflow Task (en-US) Copy on Test Item has successfully completed. All participants have completed their tasks. |
| | 3/29/2010 12:08 AM | Comment | System Account | Workflow has finished executing | |

*Figure 1-17. The workflow history of the approval copy workflow*

# Writing Workflows with SharePoint Designer

Just like you have the ability to edit out of the box workflows, using SharePoint Designer you can also craft up brand new workflows. In order to do so, open your site collection and SharePoint Designer and click the workflows section. From the ribbon, you will see three possibilities as shown in Figure 1-18.

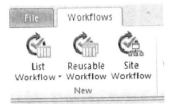

*Figure 1-18. The kinds of workflows you can create*

A list workflow is associated with an individual list. This is very similar to how it used to be authoring workflows in SharePoint Designer 2007 with the concept of association when an initiation was merged. Compared to SharePoint Designer 2007, SharePoint Designer 2010 offers significant improvements such as a completely redesigned workflow editor, the ability to export workflows as .wsp's, and so forth.

The second button, "Reusable Workflow", is very similar to the customization of the out of the box workflow that you just did in the previous section of this chapter. Creating a reusable workflow simply means that you're targeting the workflow to a particular content type. Once you have crafted up such a workflow definition, you can then associate this workflow with the source content type or any content types that inherit from the source content type.

The last button is rather interesting. It allows you to target the workflow to the site. This is something you were not able to do in SharePoint 2007. Frequently, you will be presented with enterprise processes that don't really tie to a list item. In fact, they don't even tie to a document set. In those instances, it is helpful to run the workflow on a container that is not exactly an individual list item. SharePoint 2010 allows you to run workflows on a site collection. These are referred to as site workflows. Let's create a site workflow.

The workflow I am about to set up adds the facility of users being enabled to add simple reminders for themselves in the site. Similar to a calendar, by starting a workflow, the user would be able to enter a title, a description, and a date and time at which an e-mail would be sent to the user with the title and description with a reminder.

Start SharePoint Designer, and under workflows, click site workflow in the ribbon. Call your new Workflow "Remind Me". Add the following initiation form parameters to this workflow:

- *Remind title*: Single line of text, visible on the initiation form only.

- *Remind description*: Multiple Lines of text, visible on the initiation form only.

- *Remind time*: Date and Time. The form should ask for both date and time, visible on the initiation form only.

Next, craft up the workflow, as shown in Figure 1-19.

**Step 1**

Pause until Parameter: Remind Time

then Email Workflow Context:Current User

***Figure 1-19.*** *Your workflow structure in SharePoint Designer 2010*

Now go back to the main workflow page within SharePoint Designer and check the check box for "Show workflow visualization on status page". Save and publish the workflow. If you get any errors during publishing, make sure that you followed all the previous steps, including populating the subject and body of the email.

Next, visit your site collection in the web browser and visit all site content and click the "Site Workflows" link. Here you should see the option to start the "Remind Me" workflow. Start this workflow but note that by starting up this workflow SharePoint prompts you with the initiation form, as shown in Figure 1-20.

| Remind Title | Eat Lunch | |
| Remind Description | Don't forget to eat! | |
| Remind Time | 3/29/2010 | 12:30:15 AM |

Start    Cancel

**Figure 1-20.** *The initiation form for your workflow*

Fill out the form as shown and click the start button. Note that the workflow visualization clearly tells you exactly where the workflow is at the given point. This can be seen in Figure 1-21.

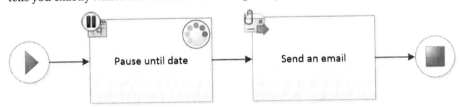

**Figure 1-21.** *Visio Visualization of your workflow*

Once the workflow has finished, and assuming that you have your SMTP server configured, you should receive an e-mail with the necessary reminder.

# Writing Workflows with Visual Studio

So far you have seen that you can take a workflow between Visio and SharePoint Designer multiple times, and allow the business user to express their workflow desires to a great length. However, there will be situations where you will need to involve a developer. The situations are twofold, either you need to use an activity that you cannot find in SharePoint Designer, in which case you will have to author a custom activity in Visual Studio 2010 and use it in your workflows. Alternatively, your workflow involves crazy proprietary calculations or integration with external systems, stuff that you cannot expect SharePoint to provide out of the box.

In either of these scenarios, you have the ability to use Visual Studio. Visual studio has the ability to import a .wsp package, which was in turn exported from SharePoint Designer, and could contain workflow definitions. Or you can use Visual Studio to craft up a brand new workflow from scratch!

In order to write a brand new workflow in Visual Studio, start Visual Studio and create a new project called "RollOfDiceWF" based on the empty SharePoint project template. Since this project will contain workflow templates, you need to make this a farm solution. What I intend to do in this workflow, is begin by rolling dice. Rolling dice should give me a random number between one to six and that randomly generated number will be updated in the title of the list item the workflow is running upon.

Thus, right-click the project and choose to add a new SPI of type "Sequential Workflow". You could also choose to add a state machine workflow. Any process can be represented as either a sequential workflow, or a state machine workflow. However, it is generally easier to represent machine involving tasks that you can easily think of as flowcharts as sequential workflows. It is generally easier to represent workflows that go through various states have long pauses between them and involve human being or external system interaction as state machine workflows.

As soon as you choose to add a new sequential workflow, Visual Studio will ask you a couple of questions.

- It will ask if this is supposed to be a site workflow or a list workflow. In this case, choose to make it a list workflow.

- The second and optional step here is to automatically associate this workflow to a list and also specify a tasks and workflow history list. This is a convenience that Visual Studio provides you which facilitate easy debugging; you could assign a workflow yourself manually if you wished. However, associate the workflow with a list called "Test" based on the custom list template. Also, if your site collection currently doesn't have a tasks and workflow history list, just create an association to any out of the box workflow through the browser, and that will give you an option to create the tasks and workflow history list.

As you will note, once the sequential workflow has been added the first activity in the workflow is the onWorkflowActivated activity. This can be seen in the Figure 1-22.

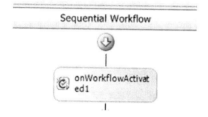

**Figure 1-22.** The onWorkflowActivated activity

The first activity in any SharePoint workflow has to be the onWorkflowActivated activity. The responsibility of this activity is to set the various context variables, such as the list item you are operating upon, the user that started the workflow, etc. Therefore, when you're adding more activities into your workflow you must always ensure that your activities fall below the onWorkflowActivated activity.

Also, note that in the toolbox you have the ability to add activities from workflow foundation 3.0, workflow foundation 3.5, and SharePoint workflow activities. .NET activities are also usable within SharePoint workflows, but you must be careful of not using certain activities in SharePoint workflows such as TransactionScope activity, CompensatableTransactionScope activity, SynchronizationScope activity etc.

At this point, drag and drop a code activity and place it below the onWorkflowActivated1 activity in your sequential workflow. As soon as you drag and drop the activity, you would see a red exclamation mark on the code activity, which is informing you that further work needs to be done before this workflow is complete. Double-click the code activity to create its MethodInvoking event handler, and add the code shown in Listing 1-1 into this event handler.

**Listing 1-1.** MethodInvoking event handler for codeActivity

```
private int diceRoll = 0;

private void codeActivity1_ExecuteCode(object sender, EventArgs e)
{
    Random rnd = new Random();
```

```
    diceRoll = rnd.Next(1, 6);
    workflowProperties.Item["Title"] = diceRoll;
    workflowProperties.Item.Update();
}
```

As you can see from Listing 10-1, you're generating a random number between one and six and updating the items title with the generated number. Next, build and deploy your workflow, and then run the workflow on a new list item that you create in the test list you created earlier. Note that the title of the list changes at random between one to six.

Since you're rolling dice, let's make this a little bit more interesting. The idea here is that anytime you get a number greater than two, a task should be created for you allowing you to win a prize. In order to do so, drop an ifElseActivity under the code activity. This ifElseActivity will have two ifElse branches. You need only one, so go ahead and delete one of those branches. Inside the ifElse branch that is left, drag and drop the createTask activity from under the SharePoint workflow, workflow activities category. Your newly added section in the sequential workflow should look like Figure 1-23.

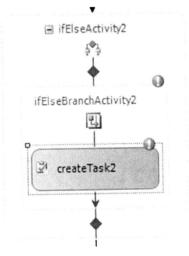

**Figure 1-23.** *Red exclamation marks on my activities. I have more work to do.*

The red exclamation marks signify that there is some additional work that needs to be done on those activities to properly configure them. Specifically, the if else branch activity needs a condition supplied on it. Select the if else branch activity and in its properties choose to specify a declarative condition. Give the condition name as "isWinner", and the Expression as "this.diceRoll > 2".

By specifying the condition in this manner, you will cause the create task activity to be called whenever the diceRoll value is greater than two. The next thing you need to do is to configure the create task activity.

The createTask activity requires a correlation token. Correlation tokens are an integral concept to workflows. Workflows run in a workflow host, and a number of instances of the workflow are multiplexed in a single running instance of an in-memory workflow class. Between various activity executions the workflow can be paused and persisted back to the persistence database, in this case the content database, and then rehydrated as necessary in the future. For the workflow host to keep everything straight between multiple workflow instances but a single in-memory instance of the workflow, workflow foundation relies on correlation tokens. Note that you already have a correlation token for the entire workflow. Since there can be many tasks within a single workflow, you need to create a new correlation token for the task. Therefore, edit the properties of the create task activity, and under the correlation token, type the new correlation token and call it "taskToken". You will also have to specify an owner activity name. At this point, you can really pick any other activity name that is at the parent level of the createTask activity, but choose to make the workflow itself as the owner activity name.

The next thing you need to do is to specify values for the TaskID and TaskProperties of the create task activity. To do so, click the ellipse by each one of these, and go to the "bind to a new member" tab then choose to create a field, as shown in Figure 1-24.

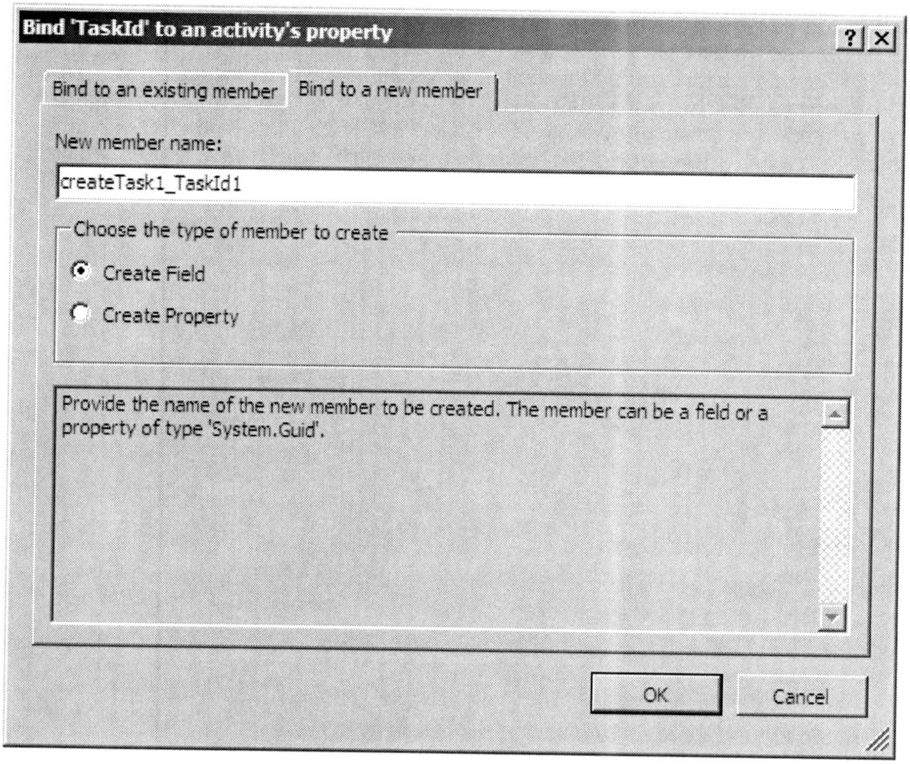

**Bind 'TaskId' to an activity's property**                                    ? | X

Bind to an existing member | Bind to a new member

New member name:

createTask1_TaskId1

Choose the type of member to create

   ⊙ Create Field

   ○ Create Property

Provide the name of the new member to be created. The member can be a field or a property of type 'System.Guid'.

OK     Cancel

**Figure 1-24.** *Creating a field for TaskID*

Repeat this procedure for TaskProperties. Once you have configured the create task activity, the properties pain should look like Figure 1-25.

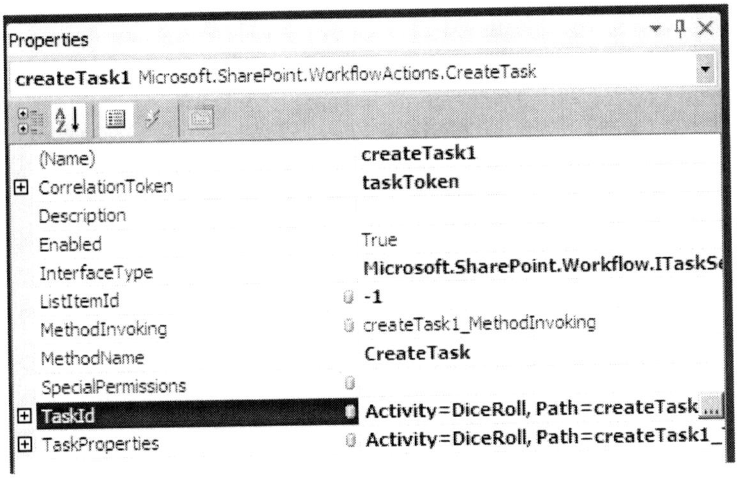

*Figure 1-25.* *Properties of my CreateTask activity*

Next, double-click the create task activity to create a MethodInvoking event handler for it. The MethodInvoking event handler is a great opportunity for you to set properties on the task before the task actually gets created. In this event handler, put the code as shown in Listing 1-2.

*Listing 1-2.* *Code for the createTask MethodInvoking Event Handler*

```
private void createTask1_MethodInvoking(object sender, EventArgs e)
{
    createTask1_TaskId1 = Guid.NewGuid();
    createTask1_TaskProperties1.AssignedTo = workflowProperties.Originator;
    createTask1_TaskProperties1.Title = "Congratulations!!";
    createTask1_TaskProperties1.Description =
        "You have won!!! Now go and claim your prize";
    createTask1_TaskProperties1.SendEmailNotification = true;
}
```

As you can see in the MethodInvoking event handler for the create task activity, you're specifying the task title to task descriptions and sending an e-mail and and assigning the task to the user that originated the workflow.

Rebuild and redeploy this workflow and execute it on a list item again. Run the workflow a couple of times, until you get a value greater than two. Note that whenever you get a value greater than 2, a task is created for you in the tasks list.

Now let's make this workflow even more interesting. What if at the beginning of each workflow you could pick, "On whose behalf I'm playing this game". In other words, when the workflow is started you could present an initiation form with a dropdown prepopulated with the list of users in the site.

In order to add an initiation form in the workflow, first add the layouts mapped folder in your project. Once the layouts folder has been added, right-click your project and choose to add the new SPI. When prompted to pick the kind of SPI you're adding choose to add a workflow initiation form. Add this workflow initiation form at _layouts\RollOfDiceWF\WFInitiationPlayer.aspx.

Your workflow initiation form has been added to the project. It will now be deployed with the project. But you need to do three things to actually make it work with your workflow.

1. You need to edit the initiation form so it presents the user with a dropdown with the list of users in the site.

2. You need to tell the workflow that the workflow needs to present an initiation form to the end user whenever the workflow is instantiated.

3. Finally, in the MethodInvoking event handler off your createTask activity, instead of assigning the POS to the workflow originator you need to assign the task to whoever the user picked in the initiation form.

Let's go implement the previous three steps one by one. Step one is to edit the initiation form so it presents the user with the dropdown list of users in the site. In order to do so in the placeholdermain ContentPlaceHolder of your initiation form, add the code shown in Listing 1-3.

**Listing 1-3.** *Code Necessary to Present the User with the Dropdown with a List of Users*

```
<asp:Content ID="Main" ContentPlaceHolderID="PlaceHolderMain" runat="server">

    <SharePoint:SPDataSource runat="server" ID="usersList" DataSourceMode="List"
    SelectCommand="<Query><OrderBy><FieldRef Name='Title'
Ascending='true' /></OrderBy></Query>">
        <SelectParameters>
            <asp:Parameter Name="ListName" DefaultValue="User Information List" />
        </SelectParameters>
    </SharePoint:SPDataSource>

On whose behalf are you playing?

<br />
<asp:DropDownList ID="userName" runat="server" DataSourceID="usersList"
    DataTextField="Title" DataValueField="Account">
</asp:DropDownList>

    <asp:Button ID="StartWorkflow" runat="server" OnClick="StartWorkflow_Click" Text="Start
Workflow" />
          
    <asp:Button ID="Cancel" runat="server" OnClick="Cancel_Click" Text="Cancel" />
</asp:Content>
```

As you can see from Listing 1-3, you're creating an SPDatasource object bound to the "User Information List". The "User Information List" is a hidden list present in any site collection that gives me a list of users in the site collection. You're then data binding that data source to a simple DropDownList.

The second thing you need to do is to tell your workflow that the initiation form needs to be popped up whenever the workflow is instantiated. To do so, you need to edit the workflow element in the element.xml that defines your workflow. The workflow element in the elements.xml is shown in Listing 1-4. Note that my workflow name is DiceRoll, and you need to appropriately reflect the CodeBesideClass attribute in your code.

*Listing 1-4.* The Edited Workflow Element

```
<Workflow
    Name="RollOfDiceWF - DiceRoll"
    Description="My SharePoint Workflow"
    Id="05b3d065-ad8a-4a9b-b808-aa32eab22057"
    InstantiationUrl="/_layouts/RollOfDiceWF/WFInitiationPlayer.aspx"
    CodeBesideClass="RollOfDiceWF.DiceRoll.DiceRoll"
    CodeBesideAssembly="$assemblyname$">
```

As you can see from Listing 1-4, you have added a new attribute called InstantiationUrl. At this point, play with the intellisense offered by the xml schema for elements.xml and try to discover how you will specify an association form a modification form and a task form. Note that all of these details are specified in a manner similar to InstantiationURL.

You've done the first two steps, which will pop open an instantiation form and show the appropriate drop down. The last thing you need to do is to assign the picked value from the dropdown in the create task MethodInvoking method handler. This last step actually involves two steps. The first step is to populate the initiation data. This is done in the code behind of the initiation form in a method called GetInitiationData. The code for this method is as follows:

```
private string GetInitiationData()
{
    return userName.Text;
}
```

You're simply returning the picked username text. If you add multiple initiation variables perhaps it is a good idea to return an xml formatted string.

Next, in MethodInvoking event handler of the create task activity comment out the following line:

```
// createTask1_TaskProperties1.AssignedTo = workflowProperties.Originator;
```

Instead, replace it with the following code line:

```
createTask1_TaskProperties1.AssignedTo = workflowProperties.InitiationData;
```

As you can see, instead of assigning the task to the user that originated the workflow, you are assigning the workflow to the user that was picked in the drop down list.

Your workflow changes are now complete so go ahead and rebuild and redeploy the workflow. Run a workflow instance on a list item, and you will note that an initiation form, as shown in Figure 1-26.

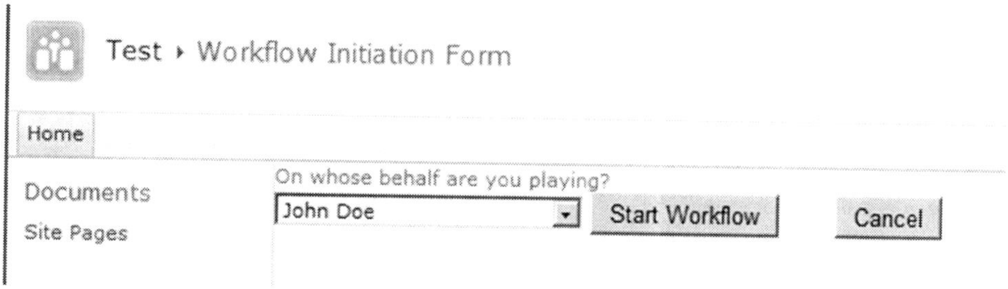

**Figure 1-26.** *Your inititiation form shows up at the start of the workflow.*

Pick a user other than the logged in user and click the start workflow button. Keep playing this game until you get a value greater than two. Once you get a value greater than two, visit the tasks list and look at the task created by this workflow. Note that the task has been created for the user that you picked in the dropdown in the initiation form. This can be seen in Figure 1-27.

| | |
|---|---|
| Title | Congratulations!! |
| Predecessors | |
| Priority | (2) Normal |
| Status | Not Started |
| % Complete | |
| Assigned To | John Doe |
| Description | You have won!!! Now go and claim your prize |
| Start Date | 3/29/2010 |
| Due Date | |
| Workflow Name | RollOfDiceWF - DiceRoll |

**Figure 1-27.** *Task created if you win the dice roll.*

This is how you can write workflows in Visual Studio 2010 and add forms into those workflows allowing them to interact with the user.

## Summary

Workflows are an important topic of SharePoint. In this chapter, you familiarized yourself with the basic concepts of authoring and using workflows in SharePoint. You saw that there are certain out of the box workflows. You saw that those out of the box workflows can be visualized using Visio visualizations or they can be tweaked further using SharePoint Designer. You also saw that business users can author the workflows directly inside Visio by using the SharePoint sequential workflow stencil. Also, workflows can be imported and exported back and forth between SharePoint Designer and Visio as many times as you wish.

A huge improvement over SharePoint 2007 workflows is that SharePoint Designer workflows are now much more usable and they can be exported as solution packages. Therefore, they can be moved between farms and environments. Also, when they are exported as solution packages they can be imported right inside Visual Studio and a project can be created out of them.

You can then choose to customize such a workflow in Visual Studio, or you can write a workflow from scratch in Visual Studio, including various kinds of forms associated with the workflow. Obviously when you begin customizing a workflow using Visual Studio, your customizations can include anything, and therefore such highly customized workflows cannot be imported back into SharePoint Designer. Therefore, the move from SharePoint Designer to Visual Studio is one way!

# Bridging the Office-SharePoint Gap

In previous versions of SharePoint and Office there was always a clear divide between client- and server-based capabilities. Although Microsoft introduced the term "Microsoft Office System"in 2007,the true integration has been a challenge. Even today, when using the 2010 wave of the product cycle, I'd argue that true integration works in some scenarios but leaves a lot to be desired in many others. However, the landscape is changing and the role of the client environment and operating system is slowly changing to a model where users canuse many different devices on a common server or even a cloud-based set of services and data. To support that model, Microsoft has made sure users can use server- or browser-based versions of the popular client applications such as Word, OneNote, PowerPoint,Excel, and Outlook Web Access.

Features or capabilities more suited to operate within the server-based environment can really benefit from the infinite scalability of the cloud-based model, such as Excel Services for storing and executing server-based calculation logic. Building on the popularity of Excel Services, the 2010 wave of SharePoint introduces a new set of server-based facilities in line with the client applications. Examples include Word Services for creating and formatting data-driven documents that can be saved in the Word file format or as PDFs or XPS files; Access Services for providing data entry and reporting capabilities using the Access client as the development tool but the SharePoint server for delivery and storage; and Visio Services, a server-based engine that enables businesses to display and interact with powerful dynamic diagrams through the browser without the need to install the Visio client application for users other than the authors of the diagrams. This chapter will focus on Visio Services and will briefly touch on Access Services and Word Services;services such as Excel are already extensively documented in other publications

This chapter will discuss some common business scenarios and explore how they can be approached by providing examples of solutions or directions on how to build solutions that leverage these capabilities. The discussions will be relatively generic, pointing out the useful options. There's not much use in adding heaps of screenshots describing the numerous options and steps you may or may not use; that approach would be better suited to a book on Visio and SharePoint.

## Visio Services

Visio Services is part of the Enterprise feature set of Microsoft SharePoint 2010. It has to be enabled by the site owner of a SharePoint site by activating the SharePoint Server Enterprise Site features. Doing this will make the Visio Web Access page and Web Part available for use on the site. This Web Part will render a Visio diagram in the browser by either using a Silverlight component or, if Silverlight is not available on the client, it will render the Visio diagram using a .png format; see Figure 2-1. If you want to make the most of the interactivity, you will need to use the Silverlight approach as that will enable advanced scenarios such as overlaying of graphics or textand zooming and selecting of shapes.

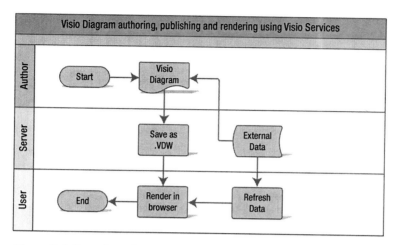

***Figure 2-1.*** *Overview of creating, rendering, and consuming a Visio diagram using Visio Services*

The Visio Services engine is not only capable of rendering the drawings, it also refreshes data graphics used in the drawing; this can be a user-initiated event or can be set to refresh the data at given intervals. A third interesting capability is the interaction with shapes on the drawing. A shape can be associated with one or more hyperlinks to allow navigation in a drawing by navigation to a different page in the drawing, to a different page in another drawing, or to external URLs. This last option is particularly useful in business process modeling scenarios where a shape could trigger filling out a form that is deployed to a SharePoint environment using InfoPath Forms services. Lastly, the provided Mashup API allows a developer to react to events by adding JavaScript functions to a page that hosts a Visio Services Web Part. This can trigger code that overlays graphics on the drawing or communicates with other Web Parts on the page. You'll explore these options later in this chapter.

## Basics

The following sections cover the basics of getting started.

## Save to SharePoint

To start using Visio Services effectively, you need to take care of some basics first. A diagram created in the Visio Client application needs to be saved in the Visio Web Drawing format (.vdw). To do this, from the File menu in Visio, pick Save & Send, Save to SharePoint, and on the bottom right of that pane, make sure the Web Drawing File Type is selected (see Figure 2-2).

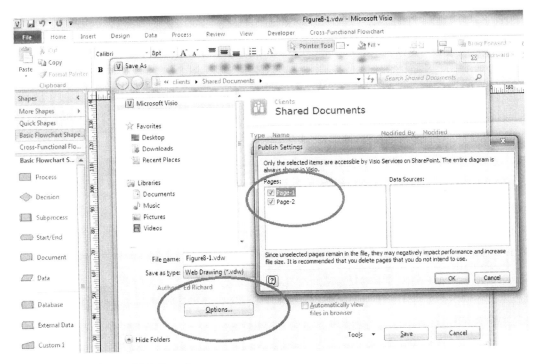

*Figure 2-2. Saving as Web Drawing*

Note that the Options button on the Save dialog allows an author to limit the pages that will be visible through the Web Part rendering; however, the .vdw file is still full fidelity and, when opened in Visio, will still have all information available. It's not required to keep files in the original.vsd format; you can author and save all drawings in the .vdw format if you want.Once a file is saved in SharePoint, all the normal SharePoint document management facilities become available to the authors.

## Display of a Diagram on a SharePoint Page

Embedding a Visio diagram on a page is done by adding the Visio Web Access Web Part to a page. This can be Wiki page in your team site or a standard SharePoint Web Part page. The Web Part is found in the Business Data category and is called Visio Web Access, as shown in Figure 2-3.

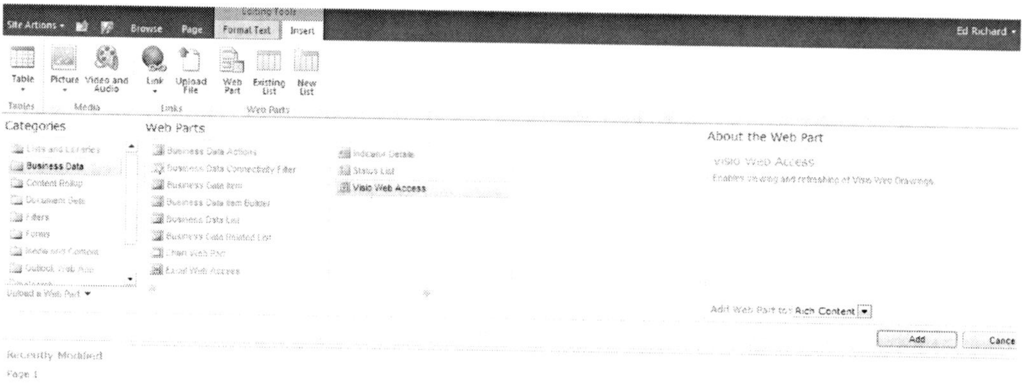

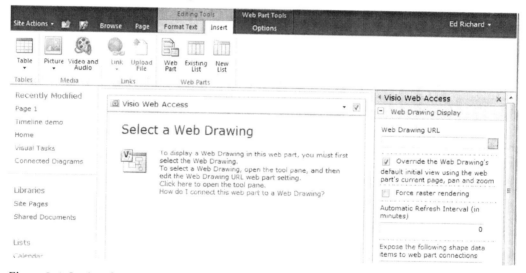

*Figure 2-3. Insert the Visio Web Access Part*

After adding the Web Part, it's just a matter of pointing the part to the correct Web Drawing URL using the toolpane, as shown in Figure 2-4.

*Figure 2-4. Setting the URL using the toolpane*

Thankfully SharePoint provides a nicely integrated asset picker so navigating to the correct drawing file is a breeze, as you can see in Figure 2-5.

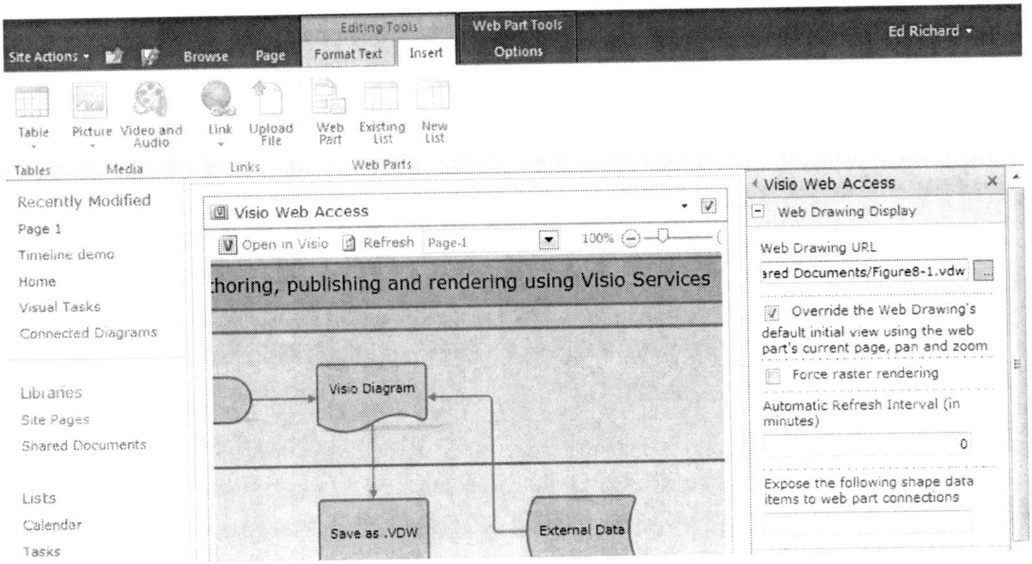

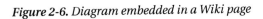

**Figure 2-5.** *The display after selecting the .vdw file URL*

Figure 2-6 shows the end result on a Wiki page after tweaking some of the other options of the Web Part settings. You'll look into those specific settings in a bit more detail later on.

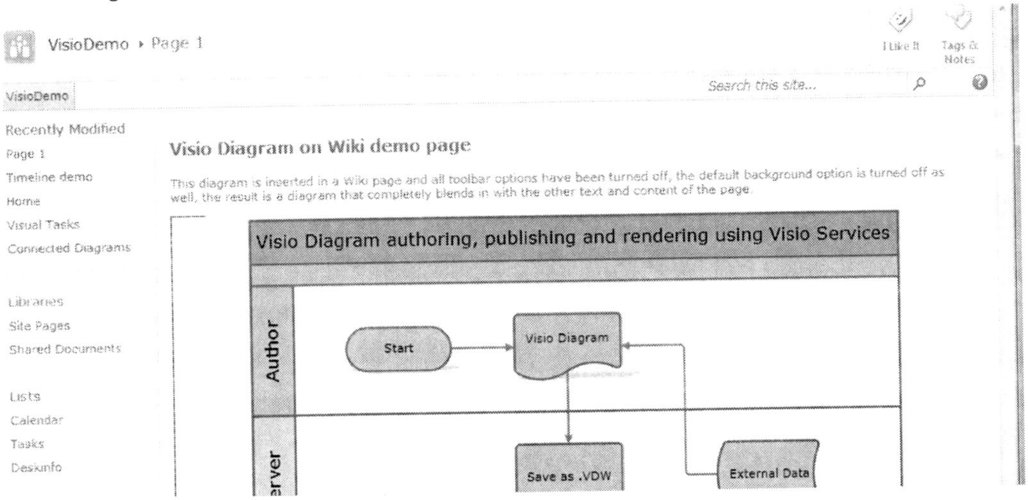

**Figure 2-6.** *Diagram embedded in a Wiki page*

If there's a need for the connected Web Part functionality or JavaScript functions to interact with the drawing or shapes, you should use a regular SharePoint Web Part page; the Wiki page doesn't fully support the Web Part zone and Web Part Manager infrastructure. A new Web Part page can be created by going to All Site Content, selecting Create, filtering by page, and selecting Web Part page.

# Advanced Configuration Settings for the Visio Web Access Web Part

The Visio Web Access Web Part has a whole range of settings to configure not only the way the diagram looks on the page, but also what options the users has to interact with the diagram. This allows for the end result to be highly interactive and adaptive—or very static and "by design." There's definitely a need for both in real world scenarios.

The settings are divided in three categories: Display, Toolbar, and Interactivity. You've already seen the use of the first, which is the URL of the diagram to display. The second option offers a choice: is the initial display of the diagram determined by what the author picks as the display properties when saving the drawing file, or is it driven by the values for zoom and pan as entered in Edit Page mode?I usually don't check that checkbox. I also make sure that the viewing dimensions set in Visio when drawing the diagram are suited for display on a web page; it takes some experimenting to find out what works best. Something to take into consideration is the size of the page canvas in Visio. When a diagram is meant for display in a web page, make sure the canvas is as small as possible in Visio. This is done by selecting the Fit to drawing option under the Size button in the Design tab.You're probably accustomed to consuming diagrams through Visio or as printed documents. Visio Services changes that and the diagrams should be designed with the browser in mind, not a printer.

The Force Rastering checkbox, when checked, forces the Web Part to use .png rendering even when Silverlight is installed. The automaticrefresh interval speaks for itself; when using external data connections (explained later) it will refresh the data loaded into the diagram at the entered interval in minutes. Note that setting it to 0 disables automatic refresh. Also, don't set the interval to small—on busy servers the process of refreshing diagrams, depending on where the data comes from, can take a fair bit of time. Last in this category is the Shape Data Item textbox, which takes a comma-separated list of strings reflecting the names of the Shape Data items that will be exposed to the Web Connections dialogs. In Visio, shapes can have multiple data name/value pairs attached to them so basically any number of metadata items can be available for interaction and setting up Web Part connections or by making them available to the JavaScript object model. You'll explore the use of this later in the section discussing various business scenarios.

The checkboxes in the other categories should be self-explanatory. The only one that is really interesting at this point is the Show Default Background option. By default, this is a grey background. Switching this option off makes the diagram use the page background, which in Web Part page usages usually turns out more appealing.

That's really all there is to make your diagrams available to your SharePoint users. The remainder of this chapter provides additional ways of building visually appealing solutions with Visio as engine behind them.

## The Repository

As you will understand by now, authors creating and modifying Visio diagrams can benefit from the collaboration and versioning features SharePoint offers. When you create a new site in SharePoint you'll see a site template called Visio Process Repository. What this template provides is a simple team site with a special document library called Process Diagrams that has a range of diagram content types defined that support some of the Visio Process Management or Workflow templates, as shown in Figure 2-7.

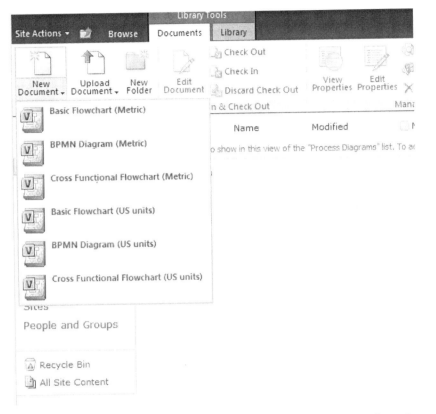

*Figure 2-7. Visio Process diagram content types in Visio Process Repository site template*

These content types are a good start for those authors that want to embrace what SharePoint has to offer. When using the content types and templates in this site template you'll see that Visio provides some synchronization between the metadata for tags (keywords) and category as edited through the document properties pane in Visio.

## SharePoint Workflows in Visio

Once used to the idea of using SharePoint to collaborate on Visio diagrams, users will soon start thinking about automating processes relating to their own daily work, such as reviewing diagrams or assigning specific tasks. This is where typical users of Visio, such as the business analysts using Visio for process modeling, meet the SharePoint developers—or they become SharePoint developers themselves! One of the new templates available in Visio is SharePoint Workflow. This template has all the standard SharePoint workflow actions and conditions that are available for developing workflows in SharePoint Designer 2010, and it enables you to export the diagram to SharePoint Designer or import it back retaining all information added by the developer in SharePoint Designer. This makes it possible to have a full fidelity workflow design ➤ develop ➤ deploy ➤ use process in place for those workflows that can be developed using the range of new activities and conditions available in SharePoint Designer out of the box. At this point, you are probably thinking of all kinds of future projects were you could use this; be aware that the model breaks when using custom activities so it needs to be handled with care and can only be used in scenarios where the out of the box activities and conditions suffice. Note that a whole range of activities and conditions are available in 2010, so you should have plenty of opportunities to make good use of this great capability.

After providing a diagram designed in Visio and deployed through SharePoint Designer, SharePoint can also use this diagram to render the running workflow instances and provide visual feedback of the workflow status to the end users by rendering status icons as overlays over the process steps, as shown in Figure 2-8.

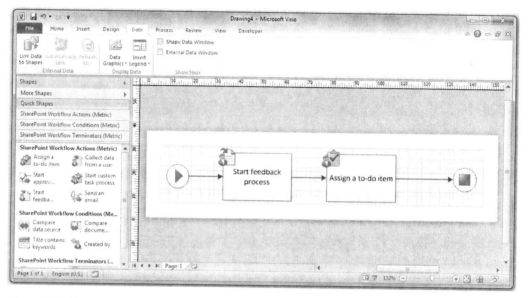

*Figure 2-8. SharePoint workflow in Visio*

The intricacies of this functionality probably warrant a chapter of its own, but for the purpose of this book I'll just leave you with this high level explanation. It's certainly worthwhile to research this more and see if using a Visio for SharePoint Workflow design is a viable approach in your business scenarios. A learning video to get you started is available from MSDN at http://msdn.microsoft.com/en-us/Office2010DeveloperTrainingCourse_VisioSharePointDesignerWorkflow.aspx and some good instructions are available on the Office Online help site at http://office2010.microsoft.com/en-us/visio-help/import-and-export-sharepoint-workflows-HA010357165.aspx?CTT=1.
That last site, Office2010.microsoft.com, deserves a plug. The documentation team is doing a great job and this site is a really good resource for Office-related tasks. For example, you may have worked up an appetite for Visio and decided to brush up on your diagramming skills. Here's a good source for BPMN diagramming in Visio 2010: http://office.microsoft.com/en-us/visio-help/bpmn-diagramming-basics-RZ102712773.aspx; note that there are five videos in seven pages of content.

# Data Linkage

In Visio 2007, Microsoft introduced the ability to link data to your diagrams and connect the rows in your data source to shapes. With SharePoint 2010 and Visio Services now in the picture, this opens up a range of opportunities, in particular because you are able to setup an automatic refresh for diagrams displayed using the Visio Services Web Part. There is a range of available data source types, including the use of an existing .odc file stored in SharePoint; see Figure 2-9.

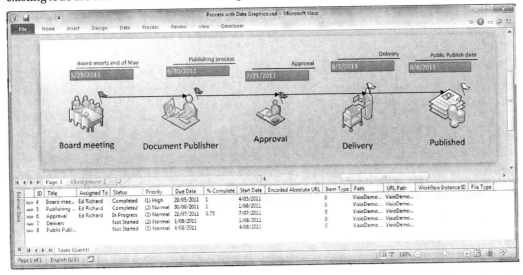

*Figure 2-9. Example of a simple process diagram linked to a SharePoint list showing icons, due date, and title*

As a default, Visio Services uses the identity of the currently logged on user to access the connected data source. For example, when a diagram is connected to an Excel spreadsheet stored in your SharePoint site, the user needs rights to view that Excel file. When using data sources external to SharePoint, the data source requires more configuration for using the SharePoint Secure Store Service or the Unattended Service Account, which typically is done by your administrator who configures the Visio Graphics Service through Central Admin or using PowerShell. This Service also allows the configuration of trusted providers, which allows the administrator to configure what types of data sourcedata sourcesdata sources the diagrams areallowed to connect to. Note that this does not limit the available options in the Visio Client for the author of the diagram. The diagram just displays an error when viewed through the browser while the data is being refreshed.

When none of the datasource options work for your scenario, there is also the option to write your own custom data provider. MSDN provides a good walkthrough covering that process.(at http://msdn.microsoft.com/en-us/library/ff394595.aspx).

The actual process of attaching a data source to a diagram and linking the shapes is supported by a wizard that can be accessed through Visio's Data tab, as shown in Figure 2-10.

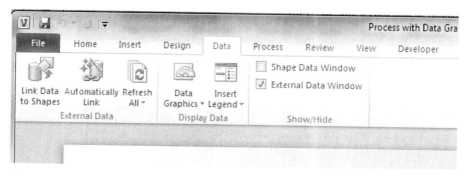

*Figure 2-10. Data Tab in Visio 2010 Premium*

The Link Data to Shapes button launches the wizard, which is pretty straightforward. Depending on the chosen data source, there are different configuration steps. For example, when connecting to a SharePoint List there's an option to link to a specific view. This results in an extra step to select the appropriate view. After connecting to a data source, the external data pane opens, showing the rows available in the data source (see Figure2-9). You can connect a diagram to multiple data sourcedata sourcesdata sources.

By default, the rows aren't linked to any shapes. This can be done through the Automatically Link wizard or by manually selecting a row and dropping it on the relevant shape in the diagram. Typically, when a row is dropped on a shape for the first time, Visio creates a default Data Graphic that will be used for all shapes that have a linked row. It's this Data Graphic definition that determines which data items are displayed on the shape and what the data item looks like. Visio provides a range of options to display data items (fields in the rows) as text, data bars, or icons; the value can also be used to set the color of the shape. All of these data items in the data graphic definition have extensive configuration options that allow good control over what and where the items are displayed. The Data Graphic configuration is accessed by right-clicking a linked shape and selecting Data➤ Edit Data Graphic from the Context menu. Figure2-11 shows one of the configuration options—in this case the definition of a data item that will show a colored flag based on the value of the Status field. In this example, the data source is a Task list in SharePoint and the connection just points to the Gantt view, a custom view that filters based on a Yes/No field called Gantt (see Figure2-9).

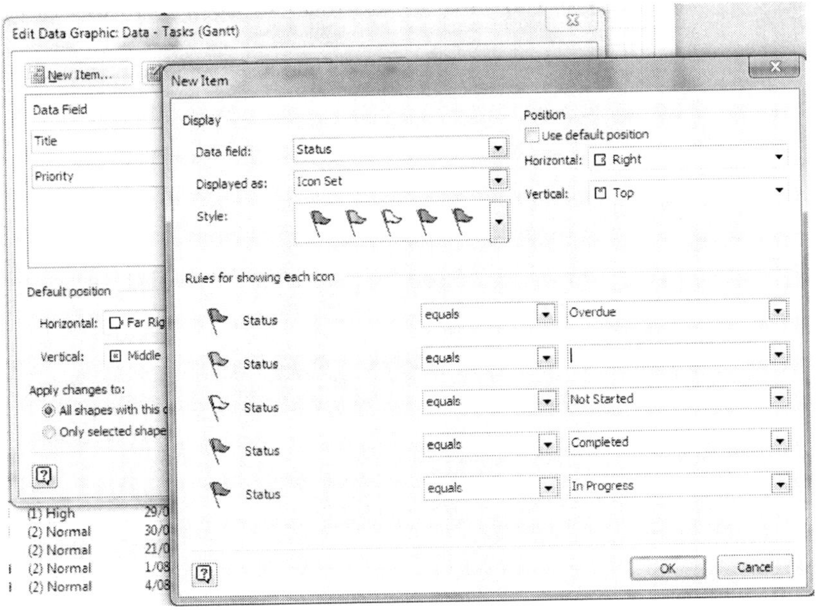

*Figure 2-11. Configuration of a Data Graphic item using icons mapping to status values*

## Refresh

The most exciting bit about these linked data sources is that Visio Services can be setup to automatically refresh the data when rendering a published diagram. The configuration settings can be set by using the Refresh Dataoption under the Refresh All button in the Data tab. This type of visualization offers some powerful functionality to your solutions. Typical examples of this type of use are to monitor the status of network, hardware, or even software components. Microsoft itself uses Visio dashboards in Microsoft System Center Operations Manager at `http://visio.microsoft.com/en-us/Templates_And_Downloads/Software_Add-ins/Pages/Visio_2010_Add-in_for_System_Center_Operations_Manager_2007_R2.aspx`. It's also used in the workflow visualization in SharePoint to make the icons on the steps render dynamically. I personally have used it to indicate status of workflow processes and workload for a loan origination solution and as a status indicator against SQL Server Integration packages when processing large amounts of data in multiple steps. It's most useful in longer running processes as the typical refresh interval should be set to minutes (as opposed to tasks that take seconds) because connecting to an external data source, refreshing the data, and rendering the results will take multiple seconds by nature (see Figure 2-12).

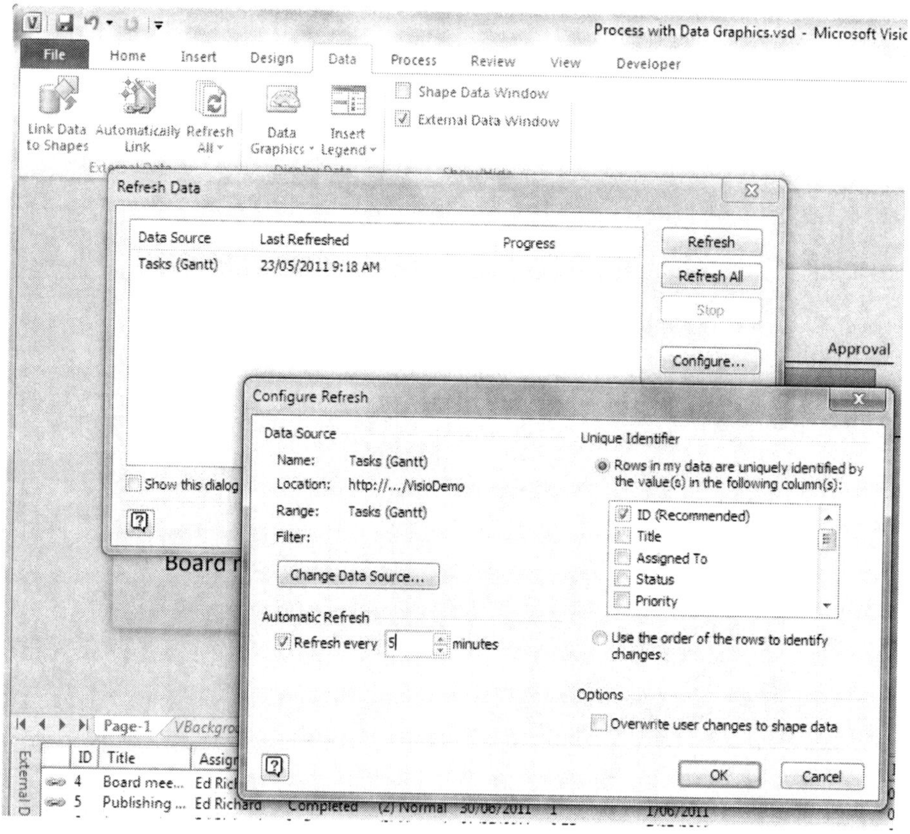

*Figure 2-12. Configuring the Data Refresh settings*

Note that Visio needs to know which field is the unique identifier. There is a limit to the interval that can be used for the refresh. On most production environments, it can take a bit of time to verify access to a data source and run the query to get to the data. On top of that, the rendering engine has some work to do figuring out all the linked shapes and iterating through the dataitems for each shape, so it often takes a little bit of time to render a refresh. This is why the smallest interval that can be set is a minute. I recommended you test your scenario and determine the appropriate value by taking into account the number of linked data sourcesand users who will be looking at the diagram concurrently. I found it reassuring that Microsoft has actually published results and recommendations around the research they have done on Visio Services performance and capacity planning and I'd like to point out that I found the same results in my projects; see http://technet.microsoft.com/en-us/library/gg193020.aspx. Obviously you need to look carefully at your environment and make sure that making the dataconnections doesn't cause bottlenecks in these cases.Remember, the SharePoint Developer Dashboard is an excellent tool to analyze what is going on in your dashboard pages.I recommendconnecting to SharePoint external lists over direct connections because SharePoint cleverly caches the dataso the refreshes will typically be faster.

The data refresh interval value can also be set on the Visio Web Access Web Part that renders the diagram on the page in SharePoint. This value can be edited through the Web Part properties (see Figure2-13).

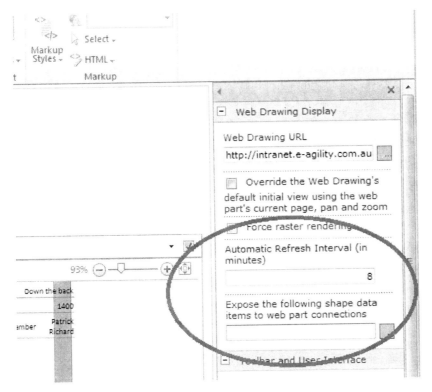

*Figure 2-13. Setting the refresh interval in SharePoint*

Looking at the Web Part settings in SharePoint reveals another interesting feature that provides good extensibility options for further customization scenarios. The "Expose the following shape data items to web part connections"option allows full flexibility over what information hidden inside the diagrams can be exposed to the connected Web Parts interface the Web Part framework uses. This is where things get exciting because it allows you to use the published diagram in the context of data stored in SharePoint or exposed through SharePoint. This means you can use data, selections, or filters to drive the behavior of the diagram, or you can use the diagram and user selections to drive what happens on the rest of the page.

I have used this option to build pages that show a business process map and provide contextual information based on the user selecting a step in the process. Imagine, for example, showing all policy and procedure documents that are relevant to a particular step in a process. I'll use this scenario in the next section to explain how to approach this type of solution.

## Connected Web Parts

Conceptually, SharePoint supports connecting Web Parts out of the box and the Visio Web Access Web Part exposes some shape data, such as the name, by default. There are multiple sample on the Web that explain how,for example, to link two diagrams where the parent diagram drives the selection of pages in the child diagram to provide a dynamic master-detail relationship view. In reality, however, there are challenges with dealing with the out-of-the-box configuration and making sure the right naming conventions and data types are used. This is why I have adopted the approach of setting it up manually so I have complete control over the parameters that make these connections work.

In order to do this, I make use of the Visio feature to add custom data items using the Define Shape data dialog. You can find this by choosing the Data option in the Context menu of a Shape and selecting the second option in that sub-menu. This lets you specify the name you need, the type of item, and the value. This uses the same principle as the data linkage described previously, but this time it provides manual control over which items are created for each shape. Take good note of the name for the relevant data item—it's the same name you'll need to use in the previously mentioned "Expose the following shape data items to web part connections" property for the Visio Web Access Web Part.

Follow these steps:

1. Define a new data item for the relevant shapes. Please note the use of the name, ProcessStepID, to make setting up the connections and filtering easy. You need to add a column of the same name and data type of the document library you will be displaying. Use 3.1 as the example value. See Figure 2-14.

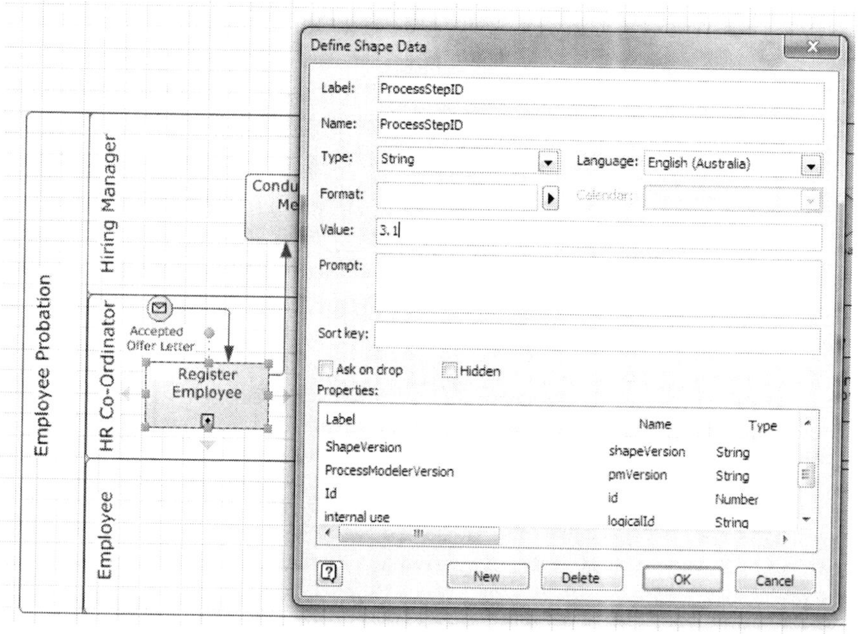

*Figure 2-14. Adding a new DataItem for the Register Employee Shape*

2. Save the diagram as a Web Drawing in your SharePoint site.

3. Create a new Web Part page. (Best practice is to use a regular Web Part page, not a Wiki page, as the Web Part connections don't work in Wiki pages).

4. Add a Visio Web Access Web Part and make it display the web drawing. In the Web Part properties, make sure that you add ProcessStepID for the Shape Data Items to expose.

5.  Add a column to your document library with the same name (ProcessStepID) of type singlelineedit.

6.  Make sure there's at least one document in the Document library with the value 3.1 in the ProcessStepID column.

7.  Add another Web Part to the Web Part page to display the content of the Document library.

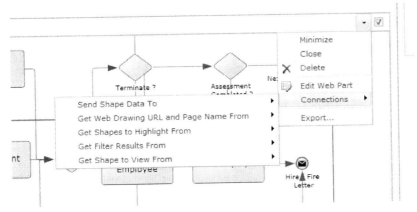

*Figure 2-15. Setting up a Web Part connection*

8.  While still in Edit mode on the Web Part Page, select Connections➤Send Shape Data To from the Context menu of the Visio Web Access Web Part and configure the connection to use the ProcessStepID column (see Figure 2-15). Note how the Provider Field Name drop-down now has ProcessStepID as an option because you have exposed that data item through the Web Part Settings (see Figure 2-16).

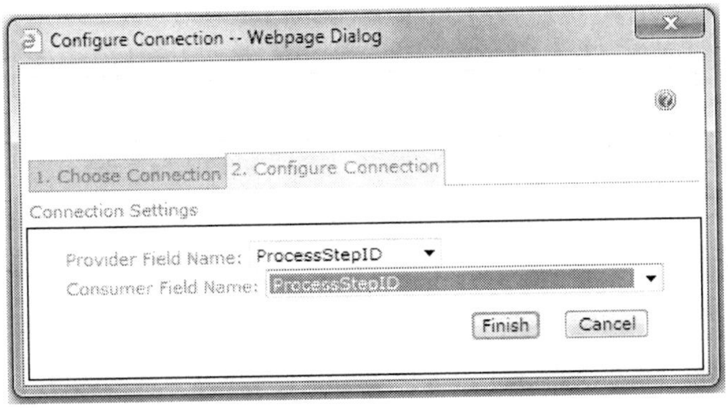

*Figure 2-16. Configuring the Web Parts connection to use ProcessStepID*

9.  Save the page and test the filter by clicking on the shape where you have set the ProcessStepID value (see Figure 2-17).

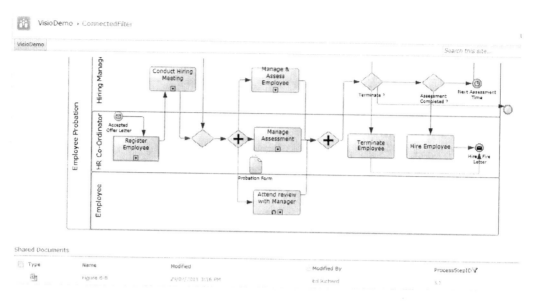

**Figure 2-17.** *The result. Note that Visio Services renders the selected shape using a blue border and SharePoint filters the Document library content indicated by the Filter icon next to the ProcessStepID column.*

Another way this functionality could be usedis by creating a custom list with a multi-line edit column configured to accept HTML content. If used in a similar way, the user can see contextual HTML content that is changing and relevant depending on the selected shape. Linking data to shapes also creates data items on each shape, so by setting those data items as being exposed, the same approach can work for data-linked shapes and data item values. This offers a genuine advantage over displaying linked data using Data Graphics because when using Data Graphics, all data is always visible on all shapes so it's easy to create a very crowded and messy diagram. Using the connected Web Part approach, you can just display the contextual information you need for each selected shape.

## Mashup API

You are not restricted to using the connected Web Part framework to add interaction and dynamics to the diagram displayed using the Visio Web Access part. The Visio 2010 developers have added an object model to Visio Services that allows developers to respond to events in JavaScript and even draw additional information on top of the rendered diagrams. The API is fully documented on MSDN and there are some great articles on the Visio team blog called Visio Insights. You will find the URLs to these important resources in the "References and Links" section.

I am often asked to include a pop-up screentip associated with a shapethat is launched when the user hovers the mouse over the shape. Visio has that option, but diagrams published to SharePoint and rendered in the browser lose that ability. This is great example of something you can add using this JavaScript API Library.

As with any other client script addition to a SharePoint page, you can add some JavaScript functionality on a page by adding a content Web Part that point to a .js file. (I'm assuming that you're familiar with that concept; if not, try a simple search on the Web for more information.)

Listing 2-1 shows the JavaScript code to display a pop-up message. The first step in the process is setting up some variables and the event handlers. All Visio-Mashup-JavaScript solutions follow this basic pattern.

*Listing 2-1. JavaScript for Pop-up Message*

```
Sys.Application.add_load(onApplicationLoad)

//  Declare global variables for the application
var webPartElementID = "WebPartWPQ3";          // The HTML tag id of the Visio Web Access part.
var vwaControl;                                 // The Visio Web Access
Web part.
var vwaPage;                                     // The current page.
var vwaShapes;                                   // The collection of all
the shapes on the current page.
var currentlyAnnotatedShape;                    //   The currently highlighted
shape.

function onApplicationLoad() {
        try{
                vwaControl= new Vwa.VwaControl(webPartElementID);
                vwaControl.addHandler("diagramcomplete", onDiagramComplete);
                vwaControl.addHandler("shapemouseenter", onShapeMouseEnter);
            vwaControl.addHandler("shapemouseleave", onShapeMouseLeave);
        }
        catch(err){
        }
}
```

The onDiagramComplete function is typically used to initialize the variables:

```
function onDiagramComplete() {
        try{
                vwaPage = vwaControl.getActivePage();
                vwaShapes =  vwaPage.getShapes();
                vwaShapeCount = vwaShapes.getCount();
                vwaPage.setZoom(-1);            // Set a default zoom level
            }
        catch(err){       }
}
```

Generally, I also use this function to set a default zoomlevel. I've left this in Listing 2-1 to show you how to do it, but it's optional. The value -1 means "Fit to page" where the context page is the area occupied by the Visio Web Access Web Part.

Listing 2-2 shows how to implement the MouseEnter and MouseLeave events.

*Listing 2-2. MouseEnter and MouseLeave Events*

```
onShapeMouseEnter = function(source, args)
{

        try
        {
        var shape = vwaShapes.getItemById(args);      // Grab the selected shape

        // Add a XAML Overlay but add text found in the shape's data item called 'Status'
        // this shows a shapedata field called status if found
        var shapeData = shape.getShapeData();
        var c = "Status Not Found";

        for (var j=0; j<shapeData.length; j++)
        {
                if (shapeData[j].label.toLowerCase().indexOf("status") !=-1)
                {
                        c = shapeData[j].value.toLowerCase();
                }
        }
        var xaml = "<TextBlock>"+c+"<\/TextBlock>";


        shape.addOverlay(
                        "Overlay",
                        xaml,
                        0,
                        0,
                        shape.getBounds().width-50,
                        shape.getBounds().height-40);

        }
        catch(err){}
        }
}
```

This function should be easy to understand. It looks for the selected shape and loops through the data items in that shape for one called Status. It constructs an XAML element and passes that into the addOverlay function of the API, which takes care of the rendering. As content of the textblock, it uses the value of the found data item.

Listing 2-3 shows how to remove the screentip.

*Listing 2-3. Removing the Screen Tip*

```
onShapeMouseLeave = function(source, args) {
        try{
 var shape = vwaShapes.getItemById(args);
                        shape.removeOverlay("Overlay");
        }
        catch(err)
```

```
        {
        }
}
```

Not too complicated, but very powerful and flexible because you have many options in the way you build the XAML fragment. How is this different from the standard behavior of displaying a data item's value using Data Graphics? In this case, the data only displays when the mouse is over the shape, which keeps the diagram nice and tidy yet adds many options for displaying information. This JavaScript function could get fairly complicated in the way it implements business rules and interprets data item values. Because it's XAML, you also have a full arsenal of user interface controls at your disposal.

## Hyperlinks

Visio comes with some behavior that can make shapes do things. Visio allows authors to specify one or more hyperlinks on shapes; when rendered through Visio Services, those hyperlinks still work. You can hyperlink to external URLs so clicking a shape could start an InfoPath form, navigate to a page in your site, or simply link to anther page in the diagram itself. If multiple links have been defined on a shape, holding the control button while clicking renders a list of the hyperlinks that can subsequently be clicked like a menu.

There's an important thing to keep in mind, though, when deciding to make use of hyperlinks in this way: the previously discussed interaction using connected Web Parts stops working. In other words, you can't have hyperlinks and connected Web Parts based on shape selection working on the same page. This is an important design consideration you have discuss when designing a user experience for you solution. Users can get excited by all the options, but in this case you can't have them all at once.

## Business Scenarios Enabled by Visio Services

I hope by now you've got some ideas on how Visio Services is going to fit your business needs. One of the solutions I recently built using Visio Services for multiple clients was in the space of Business Process Visualization.

## Business Process Modeling

In Visio 2010 Premium, Microsoft included functionality and templates for drawing Business Process Models using the BPMN 1.2 notation standard as well as some others. When combined with SharePoint 2010, this adds another dimension to publishing Business Process Models and contextual information. Many organizations are currently reviewing their policies, procedures, and processes and already have SharePoint available. Visio Services and SharePoint provide a great platform for integrating all that information, collaborating on the review effort, and publishing the results in a multi-dimensional, easy-to-discover way.

## Document Sets

SharePoint 2010 Document Sets are a good example of this. I call them "folders on steroids." They add behavior (workflows), metadata, and a user interface (Welcome page) to the mix. The Document Set could be used as a container for all policy and procedure documents in a business process so they can all be managed and versioned together in a consistent container. The Document Set Welcome page is a SharePoint Web Part page, so it can easily be customized to display the process map developed in Visio, including drill-down functionality by implementing detail process maps as pages in a Visio diagram. It might be too hidden of a hidden feature, but customizing the Welcome page is an option that can be accessed via the Document Set Settings page; there's a link all the way on the bottom of that page. It opens up the Welcome page and from there you can use the normal Edit Page functionality in the ribbon. Keep in mindthat when modifying the Welcome page, if you do it on the Document Set content type, you'll modify the page for all sets that are based on that content type. If you want different diagrams for each process, the correct approach is to create a new Document Set content type for each process you want to visualize.

## Shape Highlights Depending on Roles

Using the Mashup API you could highlight the steps in the process that are most relevant to the userby providing a dynamic view those steps. The approach to take is to store the information linking roles to process steps somewhere; you could just store the information in a custom dataitem on the shapes or you could use a SharePoint list and link the relevant items using a Process Step ID field that you define. I found the latter approach a good one as it provides the business users with an easy way to change the roles that apply to a step without having to re-publish the diagram. I have then used the Mashup API and JavaScript to lookup the relevant roles and overlay the information on the selected shape. This provides a nice interface where the diagram doesn't get cluttered up with information but just shows the relevant information on selection.

These are just a few features that the combination of Visio Services and SharePoint 2010 offer you. I'm sure you'll discover many more once you start exploring the power of Visio and SharePoint.

# Word Services

Word services is another one of the service applications Microsoft has added to the arsenal of tools in SharePoint. The key application of this service is those scenarios where you would in the past have used Word, possibly installed on a server (by the way, this scenario is not supported!) to generate documents such as invoices or letters (typically templates) merged with business data. I've done it myself and I felt the pain of having to debug such implementations. It's no fun having to re-start servers every so often because of some hidden dialog Word has popped up because it could open a file or something like that. In batch scenarios this can quickly open up hundreds of Word instances that never go away until you re-start the server or kill them manually one by one.

Many customers have a need for this scenario which is why Microsoft has basically created a server version of Word, without a UI that can process or create Word documents really fast. Combined with the power of the .docxXML file format and an SDK to access those files from code, this forms a framework for very flexible business scenarios for generating or manipulating Word documents. One use could be to insert business data in Wordtemplates or convert Word documents into .pdf or .xps files.

Andrew Coates, a developer evangelist for Microsoft Australia, has posted some very good instructions on his blog that deal with Word Services, SharePoint, and the OpenXML SDK (http://blogs.msdn.com/b/acoat/). I highly recommend that you read them before you get your feet wet with these types of solutions.

# Access Services

When it comes to Access Services, I have often wondered where it would fit in typical business scenarios. There's the obvious one: the ability to rapidly build applications that can be deployed and accessed through SharePoint. Of course, there are also the powerful reporting capabilities Access provides, such as reporting on data stored in SharePoint. By the way, did you know in some cases you can also create some sophisticated visually appealing reports using Visio? Go into a tasks list in SharePoint; on the List tab you will find a Create Visio Diagram option in the Connect & Export group. Try it out!

One of the really cool business uses for Access that I recently discovered is to do batch operations on SharePoint list data—something you can't easily do any other way without resorting to third party tools. In Access 2010 you can create a new query against a SharePoint list, effectively creating a local copy of the data inside Access that can be manipulated using SQL queries in Access. Sync the list back to SharePoint and voila, you've got a very capable batch processing solution for your SharePoint data.

## Summary

At the end of the day, all these solutions provide business users with dynamic, powerful tools that typically make them work smarter, not harder. It's all about the Business Agility the platform enables. That's the true business value that SharePoint solutions deliver.

## References and Links

- Visio custom dataprovider

  http://msdn.microsoft.com/en-us/library/ff394595.aspx

- TechNet Visio Graphics Service configuration

  http://technet.microsoft.com/en-us/library/ee524061.aspx

- MSDN Visio Vwa Namespace for JavaScript

  http://msdn.microsoft.com/en-us/library/ff394600.aspx

- The Visio Team blog, Visio Insights

  http://blogs.msdn.com/b/visio/

- The Author's blog; check it out for more hands-on examples of Office and SharePoint integration.

  http://EdonOffice.blogspot.com

**CHAPTER 3**

# Leveraging Content Types

"A better place to put our content" is the most common and fundamental reason that organizations give when implementing SharePoint. For all of SharePoint's rich capabilities, a SharePoint solution is of very little value without good content. An event in a calendar, a policy document in a library, a news article in a pages library—these are all first and foremost content, and they are each defined and managed within SharePoint using content types. This chapter explores the importance of content types and the role of managed metadata to ensure that SharePoint can become that "better place"—not just a glorified file system and content dumping ground.

## The Importance of Content Types and Metadata

Both the greatest strength and greatest weakness of modern information management systems is the ease at which users can create information—vast amounts of information. There is no question we are well into the Information Age with the Internet providing the distributed backbone. But the Internet is so often just an *information black hole*—information goes in and is never seen again.

Like the Internet, SharePoint can become an information black hole within an organization, much in the same way that file systems and filing rooms were in the past. The key difference with SharePoint is the wide range of information and formats that it can accommodate—wiki pages, contact lists, Key Performance Indicator (KPI) data, video files, and stock standard documents, to name a few. Nearly everything an information worker does within an organization can be easily created or put into SharePoint; this is both the solution and the problem.

For SharePoint to be "a better place to put our content" it needs to be designed, implemented, and managed to be that better place. This all starts with an understanding of the roles played by content types and metadata.

---

**Note** Content types are the fundamental building blocks for managing information and data within SharePoint.

---

A content type is an item template for a specific style of information asset, such as an event or a policy document. Like site columns within SharePoint, content types are defined independent of any specific lists and libraries and can therefore be used across many lists and libraries. This allows you to manage information assets by *what* they are rather than just *where* they are—a change from the traditional system of physical filing cabinets and rooms.

To function as an item template, a content type defines a collection of metadata, properties, rules, and behaviors that are enforced for items of that type regardless of the list or library in which they are stored. This collection can include the following:

- Workflows, such as approval or feedback

- Information management policies, such as expiry or auditing

- Columns and metadata, such as Author or Topic

- Document templates, such as a word.dot file

- Document Information Panel settings

## Out of the Box Content Types

Within SharePoint 2010, many out of the box (OOB) content types are implemented to support standard types of information and to allow some of SharePoint's rich functionality. For example, a *Post* content type defines the properties needed to be a blog post.

For those not yet familiar with content types, Table 3-1 will at first read like a list of the standard lists and libraries; this is because each list and library under the hood has a content type to support its type of information and functionality.

*Table 3-1. A Selection of OOB Content Types*

| Item | Event | Message | Basic Page | Video |
|------|-------|---------|-----------|-------|
| Announcement | Comment | Folder | Web Page | Image |
| Post | Contact | Document | Picture | Audio |
| Issue | Link | Wiki Page | Rich Media Asset | Page |

When a site is provisioned using the standard Team Site template, a document library called Shared Documents and an announcements list called Announcements are created and each has an underlying content type. Shared Documents has a content type of *document* and Announcements has a content type of *announcement.*

## Showing the Content Types of a List or Library

By default, content types are not shown in the settings page of a list or library, but it is easy to make them visible so you can understand what content type or types are being used by each list or library. You can do this for any list or library but here we will refer to the Shared Documents library in a standard Team Site (it's assumed you have full control permissions for the site).

1. Navigate to the Shared Documents library.

2. From the Library tab in the ribbon, select Library settings.

3. Select Advanced settings.

4. The first option is to allow the management of content types; set this to Yes.

5.  Select the OK button at the bottom of the advanced settings page and you will be returned to the main Library.

6.  On the Settings page you should now see a new section called content types, as shown in Figure 3-1.

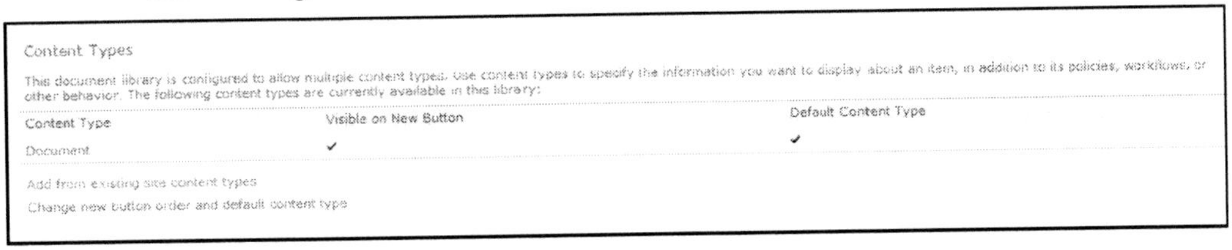

Content Types

This document library is configured to allow multiple content types. Use content types to specify the information you want to display about an item, in addition to its policies, workflows, or other behavior. The following content types are currently available in this library:

| Content Type | Visible on New Button | Default Content Type |
|---|---|---|
| Document | ✓ | ✓ |

Add from existing site content types

Change new button order and default content type

*Figure 3-1. The content types section on SharePoint library settings page*

You can now do this for any list or library to see what content types are being used; I recommend you find a calendar and a discussion board to explore what content types they use by default.

---

▪ **Note**  This chapter will not step through the details of configuring or developing custom content types. This is a common activity that is already well documented by Microsoft, community blogs, and existing publications. I recommend these MSDN articles:

"Create Custom Content Types in SharePoint 2010" at http://msdn.microsoft.com/en-us/library/ff630942.aspx and "Walkthrough: Create a Custom Field, Content Type, List Definition, and List Instance" at http://msdn.microsoft.com/en-us/library/ee231593.aspx.

An important concept to understand is that each content type you see in a list or library is actually a local instance that has been provisioned when the specific list or library was created. This allows you to extend these local content types within the context of this list or library without impacting on the site content types. The site content types are managed in the site content types gallery within each site in a site collection, and they are not bound directly to any list or library.

---

Each site has a content types gallery that is used to manage the collection of content types that are available for use within that site (see Figure 3-2). The gallery actually displays all content types from all sites above it within a site collection hierarchy; this is why each content type has a source property indicating which site it is managed in. This means that most content types are actually managed within the root site of a site collection and only custom configured or deployed content types will be managed within a local site.

| Site Content Type | Parent | Source |
|---|---|---|
| **Business Intelligence** | | |
| Excel based Status Indicator | Common Indicator Columns | Team Site |
| Fixed Value based Status Indicator | Common Indicator Columns | Team Site |
| Report | Document | Team Site |
| SharePoint List based Status Indicator | Common Indicator Columns | Team Site |
| SQL Server Analysis Services based Status Indicator | Common Indicator Columns | Team Site |
| Web Part Page with Status List | Document | Team Site |
| **Content Organizer Content Types** | | |
| Rule | Item | Team Site |
| **Digital Asset Content Types** | | |
| Audio | Rich Media Asset | Team Site |
| Image | Rich Media Asset | Team Site |
| Rich Media Asset | Document | Team Site |
| Video | Rich Media Asset | Team Site |
| **Document Content Types** | | |
| Basic Page | Document | Team Site |
| Document | Item | Team Site |

*Figure 3-2. Standard SharePoint site content types*

# Viewing Content Types in the Site Content Types Gallery

To view the site content types within any given site, follow these steps:

1. Navigate to the site you want to view.

2. From the site actions menu, select Site Settings.

3. From the Galleries group, select Site content types.

4. Use the drop-down box on the right to view a specific group of content types.

---

■ **Note** The site content types displayed within a site can vary for a number of reasons including custom content types that have been configured or deployed, SharePoint Foundation vs. SharePoint Server, activated features, and third party products.

---

# What vs. where

My favorite analogy to illustrate this concept is the rules around renovating a house in New Zealand, as this was a project I was tackling when I started trying to explain the value of content types to my customers.

New Zealand has laws that specify how a house must be built and these are defined in the National Building Code. Regardless of where you build a house in New Zealand, you must comply with this code because of *what* is being constructed. Then, depending on where the house is built, further local bylaws apply that cover specific location variations such as very high winds or very cold temperatures relating to *where* the house is being constructed (see Figure 3-3).

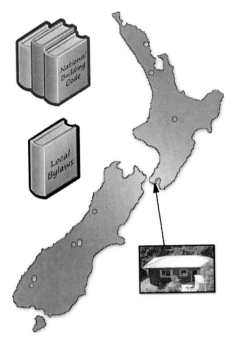

*Figure 3-3. What vs. where for a house in New Zealand*

Content types are like the SharePoint Building Code specifying the rules to which content must comply. Lists and libraries are like the SharePoint local bylaws that specify further rules that content must comply with when stored in a specific List or Library because of where it is.

The first two versions of SharePoint contained no content types within the architecture of the SharePoint platform, so a solution could only drive rules based on *where* an item was located.

For example, if you wanted to manage different behaviors for Books and Reports, you needed to create a specific list or library for each. But with the addition of content types in SharePoint 2007 and in SharePoint 2010, you have the flexibility to have a single list or library that contains both Books and Reports by leveraging a content type for each document type that can apply specific rules to each content type even though they are in the same location.

By leveraging content types to consolidate different types of information into a single location, while still preserving specific properties and behaviors for each type, you can provide a much simpler OOB user experience for both content contributors and content consumers (see Figure 3-4).

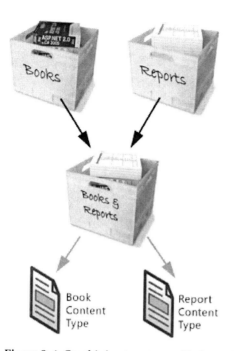

*Figure 3-4. Combining two types of information into a single library using content types.*

In this Books and Reports example, you can easily provide a list or library view to your users of just Books or just Reports, and you can easily provide a consolidated view of Books and Reports. For content authors, you can easily apply a specific approval workflow to just Reports, a different approval workflow to just Books, and then apply an expiry policy to all documents in the Library.

---

■ **Note** Content types apply rules, behaviors, and metadata based on *what* an item is. Lists and libraries apply rules, behaviors, and metadata based on *where* an item is.

---

In the next example, each office has a library and can apply rules and behaviors for all content relating to that office. At the same time, content types can be leveraged to apply rules and behaviors for specific types of information regardless of what office library they are located in. Content types can also be easily leveraged for the legal team to see all contracts by creating views in the document libraries that provide an aggregated view using a Content Query Web Part or by using an advanced search filtered by Contracts content type (see Figure 3-5).

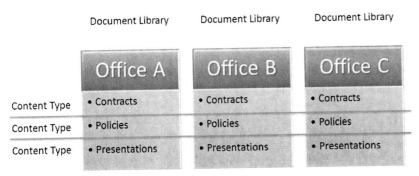

*Figure 3-5. Example library and content type relationship for three offices*

# Inheritance

There are many places within SharePoint where inheritance is an important pattern, such as for the management of user permissions, applying site themes, or controlling available site templates. Inheritance is also a critical concept for the creation and management of content types; all content types inherit from a parent content type, other than the underlying content type called System (see Figure 3-6).

This content type inheritance pattern can be used to an organization's advantage by creating parent content types that include any properties that are required across all items and documents of a particular type. Then, as the organization evolves, further properties can be added to the parent content type and therefore can be inherited automatically to all the descendent content types.

*Figure 3-6. Parent child relatiohship from system content type to Web Part page content type*

Figure 3-6 shows the child parent hierarchy from the OOB Web Part page content type down to the System content type, which is the foundation content type of all content types. The OOB content types also leverage this exact same inheritance pattern; this can be explored by navigating to the parent of each content type from the content type Settings page, as illustrated in Figure 3-7.

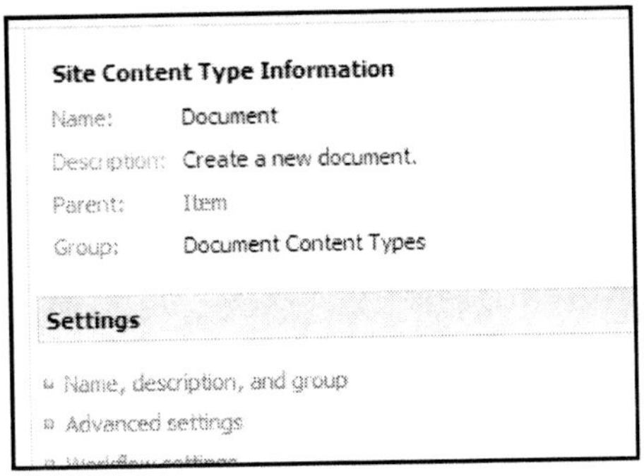

**Site Content Type Information**

Name: Document

Description: Create a new document.

Parent: Item

Group: Document Content Types

**Settings**

▫ Name, description, and group

▫ Advanced settings

*Figure 3-7. The Settings page of a content type*

Figure 3-8 illustrates a simple scenario for an organization with three types of documents: Contracts, Policies, and Presentations. Each type of document has a specific content type with two unique metadata columns and three generic metadata columns that are inherited from the parent content type called Document Base. If another column was added to the parent content type, all the child document types could inherit that new column. Further unique columns can be added to just the Contract content type to extend it to meet specific business requirements for managing contract documents.

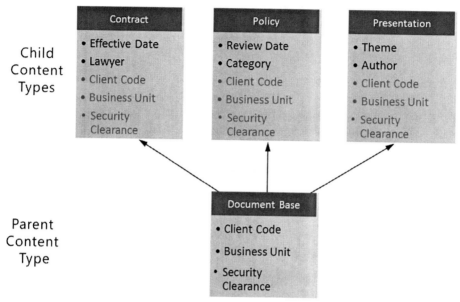

**Figure 3-8.** *Three types of documents modeled as three specific content types*

# Creating Custom Content Types

One of the great opportunities for organizations when managing information in SharePoint is the creation of custom content types. Figure 3-5 and Figure 3-8 illustrate three custom content types that are not provided OOB when SharePoint is installed; Contract, Policy, Presentation. Other than very simple SharePoint environments that just leverage the OOB content types or simply add a few columns to some lists or libraries, the activity of designing and creating custom content types is an important step in extending SharePoint to meet an organization's specific information needs.

---

■ **Note** It is a best practice to <u>not</u> add columns directly to an OOB content type. It is a best practice to create a custom content type that inherits from the OOB content type that needs to be extended.

---

As SharePoint is used to deliver business solutions across areas such as document management, team calendars, team contacts, and publishing pages, you will probably discover a need for many custom content types. The content types for a publishing web site will be quite different than those of a document management repository or a team calendar.

One of the small but useful features SharePoint provides to support a vast number of content types is the ability to group content types. The OOB content types are grouped as illustrated in Figure 3-2; this pattern should be followed for custom content types by creating custom groups to help with sorting and usability of working with content types. An effective grouping approach is solution-centric grouping; Project Site Content Types, Public Web Site Publishing Content Types, Intranet Publishing Content Types, or Platform Content Types.

The most important part of a custom content type is the definition of the columns that define the data it manages. Designing a content type and the columns it needs is a fairly traditional business analyst activity that starts with understanding the lifecycle of the information, the people who interact with the information, and the way people need to find and experience the information. This analysis will inform the requirements and purpose of each column (and will be discussed in more detail shortly).

Once a content type is designed and understood, the approach for creating them is usually very straightforward (see Table 3-2). Once created, they can be assigned to a list or library.

*Table 3-2. Custom Content Type Creation Steps*

| Step | Contract Document Example |
| --- | --- |
| Determine the OOB content type that will be the parent content type. | As this is a type of document that is managed in the business as a Microsoft Word file, the parent content type will be Document. |
| From the site content types gallery in the root site of the site collection, create a new site content type. | Create a new custom content type named Contract. |
| Assign the content type to a group or create a new group. | This is the first document centric-content type being created, so create a new group named Legal Document Content Types. |
| Add existing site columns or create new site columns for the content type. | Create custom site column named Effective Date that is a Date Time column. Create a custom site column named Lawyer that is a lookup over a contact list that contains all associated lawyers. |
| Add any other settings such as a document template, workflows, and information management policies. | Specify the existing Microsoft Word template that is used to create contracts. Specify a document retention policy based on 24 months after the contract Effective Date. |

There are no hard and fast rules or best practices around the number of columns in the design of custom content types because it's so specific to an organization's requirements. But here are some usability-centric guidelines that can help with realistic and useable boundaries:

- Aim for 12 or less columns in list content types used for storing data.
- Aim for 5 or less columns in library content types used for storing files.

- Aim for 5 or less content columns, supported by 5 or less metadata columns on a Publishing content type used for creating publishing web pages.

- If a column is not mandatory, remove it; then really justify why it needs to come back.

- Give columns default values for types such as dates or current user, but avoid pick lists as many users will be lazy or simply in a hurry and just stick with the default.

- Keep column names unique, short, and descriptive as they are displayed at the top of every standard list and library view.

- Create three simple and specific content types rather than one complicated yet flexible content type.

- Test your content types with real business users as part of your design and build process.

While lots of columns may look great when the design is on paper and provide amazing future proofing and flexibility, end users will simply not respond well to lots of boxes to populate when creating or uploading information. Many business users will give up and not use the system at all or they will simply populate poor quality values just to get through the process quickly. Either way, the design might be great but the solution won't be a success.

## Columns Need a Purpose

One of the significant risks of content types and the inheritance pattern is that enthusiastic architects create such a complex hierarchy of granular content types that it becomes difficult to use and impossible to manage. Any good system design should be as simple as possible. Everything in that system should have a distinct and describable purpose. The same applies in SharePoint 2010 for content types—particularly for columns.

---

■ **Note** The columns in a content type define the different content elements and metadata needed to manage that type of information.

---

It is a best practice that each column has a well-defined and communicated purpose. If a column doesn't have at least one purpose that can be described succinctly, that column shouldn't exist. In many instances, columns will actually have more than one purpose, because the data they hold may help with a number of scenarios. For example, date columns help with searching and retrieving the content. They can also help define an audit of activity against content for records management purposes. Column purposes can be grouped under four types to help describe the role or roles a column performs; see Table 3-3.

---

■ **Note** It is a best practice that each column has a well-defined and communicated purpose.

---

*Table 3-3. The Four Purposes of Columns*

| Group | Purpose | Description |
| --- | --- | --- |
| Content | Information to be displayed to end users. | The column contains information such as text and images that is the content or part of the content that is to be displayed to end users. Examples include the headline or body of a web page item or the name or phone number of a contact item. |
| Metadata Record | Information as captured at a specific point in time and retained as a record. | The column contains content or data that relates to a SharePoint item, such as a document or a task, which is an important record of a business transaction, activity, or process. The column may contain the content that was published or provide context about who edited the content and at what time. |
| Metadata Findability | Information to allow the discovery, sorting, filtering, and grouping of items. | The column is leveraged by end users for advanced search, content query Web Parts, data view Web Parts, or views to create lists of SharePoint items based on the information within the column, such as all SharePoint items that are customer documents created after a certain date by a certain user. |
| Metadata Activity | Information to support an activity, process, or function. | The column contains information that is used programmatically to support an activity such as a workflow, routing of items, or integration with another business system such as K2 or SAP. |

Figures 3-9 and 3-10 show two tables in a style that can be used to document each column. The specific columns in these examples illustrate an interesting scenario relating to the challenges of names and the fact that names can change over time.

| Column Display Name: | Client Full Name | |
|---|---|---|
| Column Purpose:<br>• Content<br>• Record<br>• Findability<br>• Activity | Primary | Findability |
| | Secondary | Activity |
| | Tertiary | NA |
| | The purpose of this column is to maintain a relationship to the clients current full name they actively use, this value will update in the case of a change in their name due to marriage or other circumstances. | |
| Column Name: | ClientFullName | |
| Column Description: | Full name of client that they currently use. | |
| Column Group: | Client Document Columns | |
| Column Type: | Text | |
| Default Value: | NA | |
| Status: | Requried | |

*Figure 3-9. Example documentation of a column called Client Full Name*

| Column Display Name: | Client Full Name Record | |
|---|---|---|
| Column Purpose:<br>• Content<br>• Record<br>• Findability<br>• Activity | Primary | Record |
| | Secondary | Findability |
| | Tertiary | Activity |
| | The purpose of this column is to record the clients full name at the **point in time** the document was captured. This value will not change in the case of a change in their name due to marriage or other circumstances. | |
| Column Name: | ClientFullNameRecord | |
| Column Description: | Full name of client at time document is captured into the system. | |
| Column Group: | Client Document Columns | |
| Column Type: | Text | |
| Default Value: | NA | |
| Status: | Requried | |

*Figure 3-10. Example documentation of a column called Client Full Name Record*

# The Platform vs. the Solution

To design and govern SharePoint effectively, one of the most important concepts to understand is that the SharePoint platform is distinct from the solutions that exist on that platform. A single SharePoint platform can technically manage an Internet web site solution, an intranet web site solution, and a corporate records center solution (see Figure 3-11). While each of these solutions will function differently and possibly be managed independently by different business teams, they all coexist on a single platform and therefore share common platform architecture. A critical part of that platform architecture to understand is the role of content types and managed metadata. In this scenario, will content that is a *document* have metadata and behaviors that are consistent across all three solutions, or will each solution define a *document* in a unique way?

*Figure 3-11. Three solutions implemented on a shared platform*

Often a large corporate intranet is actually a collection of solutions with numerous web applications, site collections, and areas of functionality for end users. These solutions might feel and behave like a single intranet experience, but architecturally they are likely to be different site collections managed by different teams and performing very different functions. However, when it comes to defining specific types of content that will exist across the intranet, you want to them behave in a consistent way regardless of the solution.

Take, for example, project documents. An organization may provision many sites within a projects area of their intranet with each site having the specific purpose of supporting a single project. Some of these projects use a waterfall methodology and some use an agile methodology. Therefore, depending on the project methodology, there are certain metadata columns that support describing documents to suit that methodology, (such as a metadata column called Stages within waterfall and a metadata column called Sprints within agile) but there are also common metadata columns, such as Owner and Project Code.

The organization decides to develop a custom site definition for provisioning waterfall projects and another custom site definition for provisioning agile projects. Based on the size and lifespan of these project sites, it is decided there will be a site collection for all waterfall projects and a site collection for all agile projects. So the organization now has a solution for provisioning sites to manage waterfall projects and a solution for provisioning sites to manage agile projects (see Figure 3-12).

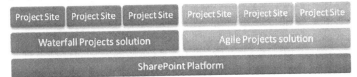

*Figure 3-12. Two solutions implemented on a shared platform.*

# The Role of the Content Type Hub

Once a SharePoint environment is described as being a platform with solutions, then the role of the content type hub becomes easy to explain: to manage common platform content types that can be used by different solutions (see Figure 3-13).

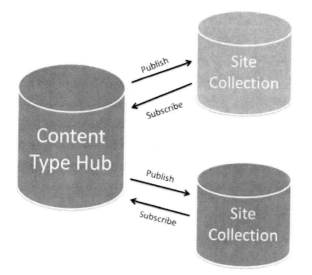

*Figure 3-13. The relationship betweem content type hub and site collections*

The content type hub is a new feature provisioned as part of the managed metadata service (commonly known as MMS) within SharePoint 2010. A hub provides a place to centrally create and manage content types that need to be leveraged across many site collections or Web Applications. Each site collection that needs to leverage content types from a hub can subscribe to the hub. When a hub publishes its content types, all subscribed site collections will get the content types or any updates to content types.

Take the previous example about the organization with the waterfall projects solution and the agile projects solution each with their own specific site collection. Each site collection will have a specific type of project document represented by a content type, but what content type should the project document inherit from?

Figure 3-14 illustrates a logical approach to leveraging content type inheritance to have a common content type called Project Document that extends from the standard Document content type. The Project Document content type then adds two columns generic to all project documents. Then each of the project methodologies has a specific content type that extends Project Document to add the required methodology specific column.

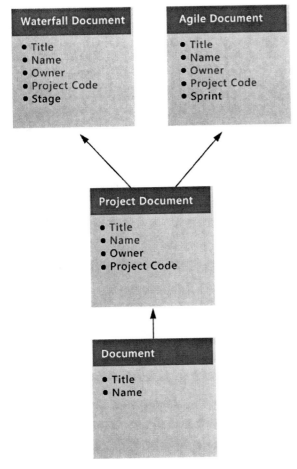

*Figure 3-14. Inheritance of two types of project document*

Because the project methodology content types are each specific to their own site collection but the parent Project Document content type is common to both, it's clear in this scenario that the Project Document content type should be managed in a central content type hub so that both site collections can leverage it. One of the great future benefits is if the Project Document content type is updated in the future, both Waterfall Document and Agile Document content types can be automatically updated also.

Once a content type hub is being used in an environment, the content types at the destination site collections are automatically made read-only. This ensures that the intent of centralized management of content types is actual preserved; therefore, if the site collections need different content types that can be configured at the site collection level, don't subscribe them to the hub or don't even have a hub. Once committed to a content type hub, it's best practice to leave content types at the destination site collections as read-only and make all future updates through the hub.

■ **Note** Once committed to a content type hub, it is best practice to leave content types at the destination site collections as read-only and make all future updates through the hub.

If you browse the blogs posts and forum threads that relate to the content type hubs, a common theme or comment you will find is something along the lines of "The CTHub can become a real nightmare if you don't get your design right the first time round." This is because it is much easier to add and extend columns on content types through the content type hub than it is to change or remove columns. This is, in fact, not just about the content type hub because the same issues arise when trying to change and remove columns within the context of a site collection. It all relates to the way SharePoint is designed and architected to provide a level of isolation and preservation for content once it is created. Once a content type is leveraged to create content, data is stored against the columns; therefore, for areas such as audibility, version history, and records management, this data (and also the columns) most likely need to be preserved. Just like changing a database schema (which is what changing columns on content types is essentially doing), there are potentially serious implications if the system has been in use for some time and already has significant volumes of content reliant on that schema.

If a new column is added to a content type in the content type hub and published, the outcome is as straightforward as the destination site collections. However, if you want to change or remove an existing column, you first have to untangle the relationships the site column has with any content types within the content type hub; then you have to publish the updated content type. This will remove the read-only state on the destination site column so that you can untangle the relationships the site column has with any content types within each site collection. However, if you have content you need to keep and preserve within a site collection, this needs to be done with due care and consideration.

■ **Note** While many SharePoint platforms won't have a content type hub (or maybe only one hub), a SharePoint environment can actually have multiple content type hubs if the architecture of the enterprise environment and business requirements necessitate this model.

In the Project Document content type scenario, for this content type to be updated in the future, the content type hub and the role it plays will require a level of governance. This governance will be required to protect the platform content types from misuse or inappropriate change and to ensure that they are used across the solutions on the platform in the appropriate way. When a new solution is being designed for implementation on the SharePoint platform, one of the critical activities is to understand which of the available platform content types the solution should leverage, extend, or add to. (Later in this chapter, I talk more about this design activity.) If this level of governance can't be maintained within an organization as an operational activity for their SharePoint platform, then a content type hub could create more problems than benefits. While in many scenarios with many site collections the content type hub can provide a simple solution to shared content types, it also adds a level of complexity to the architecture and the governance that could outweigh the benefits. This is an important concept for SharePoint capabilities in general; just because SharePoint can doesn't mean you should.

While I don't feel there is a best practice statement I can make around this topic, I can offer some general guidance based on an organization's size and capabilities. These hopefully read like common sense, but we all know that it is not always so common.

- If an organization can't design the information architecture relating to columns and content types in-house and needs to bring in an external party, then they are unlikely to be able to manage that architecture over time and should avoid the complexity that managing content types in a content type hub may introduce in their context.

- If an organization doesn't have a recognized information architecture discipline in-house that can provide guardianship and governance of a complex columns and content types hierarchy, then they should avoid the complexity that managing content types in a content type hub may introduce in their context.

- If an organization has a small team looking after their information management architecture within SharePoint (and often it is just one of the many hats they are wearing), then they need to consider if they can realistically ensure continuity of the expertise and understanding necessary to provide guardianship and governance of a complex columns and content types hierarchy.

To sum up with a slightly left-field analogy: if you don't have the resources to staff, service, repair, fuel, and dock a super yacht, you should seriously consider a less complex, more manageable power boat.

# The Role of Managed Metadata

Content types are the building blocks for managing information within SharePoint 2010, but it is the metadata users define and manage against content that brings many solutions and benefits for end users to life. Many people understand the potential benefits of metadata and most have experienced metadata in action through online systems such as Amazon and eBay, but many organizations struggle to implement and leverage metadata effectively within their internal information management systems. There is no travelling medicine man selling a guaranteed magic solution to good metadata because it is a technical issue, a governance issue, and an end user issue. However, SharePoint 2010 does provide some great features for creating, managing, and defining metadata that can help organizations to succeed with leveraging metadata.

---

■ **Note** Metadata is the glue for joining related information and data within SharePoint.

---

When an organization and its users are moving to SharePoint from storing content in network drives and folders, they often struggle to see beyond using folders to organize their content. A simple and effective approach to help them see the role and benefits of metadata is to present the following scenario.

An organization writes many reports about endangered animals and environmental impacts of mining and logging on animals. They currently store reports in a hierarchy of folders using animal's names and different types of mining and logging. If a report is written on the impacts of copper mining around the world on endangered animals, the report is put into the Copper Mining folder. If a report is written on the environmental impacts on tigers, it's put into the Cats folder. So how do you file a report on the impact of copper mining on tigers and panda bears in Asia?

This scenario sets the scene for introducing a better approach of leveraging metadata to organize information. If this organization creates a single SharePoint library for reports and then takes the names of the different types of animals, types of mining, and types of logging and makes them available as metadata, then the report called "Impact of Copper Mining on Tigers and Panda Bears in Asia" can go into the Reports library and be tagged with Copper Mining, Tigers, and Panda Bears. Then, using filtering, views, or search on this library, a user can be presented with reports on Copper Mining, Tigers, or those that include Copper Mining and Tigers. Keep in mind, however, that in very large situations the scale and security for all reports may require multiple libraries or even multiple site collections, and then search can leverage the metadata to create consolidated views from all sources.

The managed metadata service that enables the content type hub capability also provides significantly improved capabilities for managing metadata, as its name implies! The service provides a term store feature, an enterprise keywords feature, a managed metadata feature, and some smart end user controls for defining metadata values for content items. If used wisely these features can help metadata succeed.

The first point to make is that the name managed *metadata service* is not supposed to trick you into thinking it will manage your metadata. It provides the tooling to enable the management of metadata, but without good design and governance of metadata values and how metadata is used, the benefits will not be realized or will be short lived.

The second point to make is that the discipline of designing and managing taxonomies, ontologies, controlled vocabularies, lookup lists, data dictionaries, and metadata is a large and potentially complex field. Being able to install and configure SharePoint does not instantly make you a metadata master, so be realistic about what can be achieved with the available skills and resources. The tooling provided by the managed metadata service will not reduce complexity. Situations with multiple levels relationships between terms might be too complex to be managed effectively so more specialist taxonomy modeling tools may be required. That said, there are many organizations that don't need or aren't ready to leverage an exhaustive taxonomy or complex metadata. Doing the basics with managed metadata could be a small step for a SharePoint administrator but a giant leap for the organization.

---

■ **Note** Doing the basics with managed metadata could be a small step for a SharePoint administrator but a giant leap for the organization.

---

The two primary types of metadata commonly used in content management solutions are *controlled* and *uncontrolled*. The more technical terms often used to describe these are *taxonomies* and *folksonomies*. Taxonomy is commonly a collection of hierarchical terms that is designed and managed by an information architect and made available for end users to select values from to define metadata against content. In contrast, a folksonomy is commonly a naturally evolving and changing collection of values that users can add to and select from. SharePoint 2010 supports both these approaches through the enterprise keywords feature and the managed metadata feature that through open or closed allows either read-only or read and write.

## Enterprise Keywords

To support a semi-controlled approach to metadata, SharePoint 2010 provides the enterprise keywords feature that includes:

- a standard column called Enterprise Keywords that can be added to content types, lists, and libraries.

- an enterprise keywords control for users to interact with when editing the properties of an item.

- an enterprise keywords term set which is a bucket of non-hierarchical terms that via the term store that administrators can use to view and manage the enterprise keywords that have been created.

What makes this solution semi-controlled is the way the enterprise keywords control provides a list of existing terms as the user types. When a user starts to type in the control, a list of existing terms is displayed based on the characters that have been entered. By displaying existing terms, a user is highly likely to find the term they want to add and select that existing term rather than adding a new term. Obviously the longer enterprise keywords have been in use, the more chance that the term will already exist. The list also includes any managed keywords, further increasing their chance of being able to select an existing term. If the user doesn't see the term they need, they are able to add a new term, which will be added to the enterprise keywords term set and will be available to them and any other users next time.

But wait, there's more! Not only do they get existing terms, the terms are displayed relative to their location in the term set hierarchy. Therefore if *design* is a keyword, they can qualify if they want to select *design* relative to *user interface design* or *system infrastructure design* or *landscape design*. Exposing existing terms in this contextual way creates a semi-controlled keywords solution that encourages users to leverage existing terms while also allowing them to freely expand the terms over time.

## Managed Terms

To support a more controlled approach to metadata, SharePoint 2010 provides managed terms that includes:

- a type of column called Managed Metadata that can be added to content types, lists, and libraries.

- a managed metadata control for users to interact with when editing the properties of an item.

- term sets that via the term store administrators can use to view and manage hierarchical collections of terms.

While enterprise keywords is just a big non-hierarchical bucket of terms, managed terms allow the use of hierarchies to organize and control the context of terms. If a term needs to appear in different parts of different hierarchies, this can be accommodated by reusing terms. For example, in the reports scenario earlier I introduced Tiger as a term for the organization, but Tiger may need to be described in relation to being a large cat or in relation to being an Asian animal. The reuse term capability allows the single term of Tiger to exist in different contexts. If the animal's term set is a closed and therefore doesn't allow users to add terms when they are adding metadata to a content item, then the user will have to select one of the existing terms such as Tiger. This forces a controlled set of terms and removes data quality issues relating to bad spelling or slang terminology.

## The End Goal: Finding Content Using Metadata

While managed metadata and the related controls support better population of metadata for content items, metadata doesn't return any business value until users leverage it to find the content they need. The activity of finding content, particularly searching, often relies on users knowing what they are looking for by using familiar keywords and terminology. A user may not be familiar with the metadata terms that have been populated against content items for a number of reasons: they may use different terminology to describe the same concepts or they may be new to the concepts and not have any terminology to use. To support these users, there are two managed metadata capabilities in particular provided by SharePoint 2010.

- Synonyms : In addition to synonyms at the search level you can provide synonyms on terms within term stores; therefore when a user searches using a term that is a synonym of primary term, they will get results back for the primary term.

- Metadata Navigation: Turning on the metadata navigation control for a library provides a tree view of the related term store that the user can navigate through to see if any documents are tagged with the term they are interested in.

■ **Note** In order to turn on metadata navigation, the site feature called *metadata navigation and filtering* must be activated.

While the managed metadata service and the capabilities it provides can be leveraged very effectively, they also add a level of complexity that needs to be considered. An organization should only activate and leverage these rich capabilities if they have the resources and capacity to manage them; keeping it simple with choice columns and lookup lists might still be the most realistic solution. The same applies to the other extreme where an organization has large taxonomy management needs. In these situations the term store can be a very frustrating tool to populate and maintain terms so an additional tool could well be justified to help extend the native capabilities of the managed metadata service to improve the management experience of the taxonomy.

## Visualizing the Complexity of Content Types

One of the many challenges in solution design within any enterprise is achieving a shared understanding of what exists within the enterprise systems and platforms that provide boundaries and opportunities for new solutions (as in, what type of search capabilities are available, what web services can be leveraged, what authentication is in place, and what content types can be used or extended?). The first step in achieving a shared understanding is that the people involved need to be made aware of what exists, and one of the most powerful tools for giving visibility to systems and platforms are diagrams and pictures that can capture and visualize the important elements in a single view.

■ **Note** If you can print a diagram on an A3 sized piece of paper and sit around a table, point to it and discuss it with a team, then you have a greater chance of achieving shared understanding than just talking or referring to words in a design document.

A SharePoint content types model can be used is to illustrate and describe the relationships, context, and purpose of all content types within the different layers of the Enterprise SharePoint Platform. This model is an important information asset for the operational management of content types. As new SharePoint-based solutions and information needs are identified across the organization, this model must be used to design and define how additions and changes to the model happen to support the constant evolution of the SharePoint Platform and the information managed within it.

# The Model: Layers

The SharePoint content types model is defined by four layers with each layer representing a logical layer within the Enterprise SharePoint Platform, as shown in Figure 3-15.

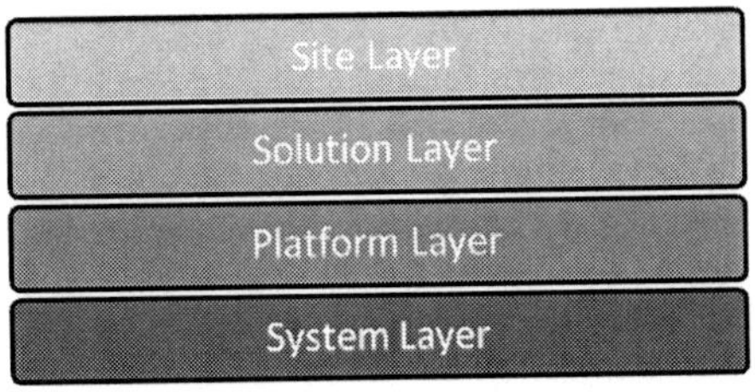

*Figure 3-15. Model layers*

## System Layer

**Owned and managed by: Microsoft**

The system later contains the generic foundation elements of SharePoint that are created by the Microsoft development team that builds the SharePoint product. These are the elements that are automatically provisioned when SharePoint is installed in any organization. The system layer is extended by the platform layer to provide the organization-specific SharePoint platform elements.

## Platform Layer

**Owned and managed by: Enterprise Architecture**

The platform layer contains the global elements that are configured or developed for the organization and are consumed by solutions that are built on the platform or integrate with the platform. The content type hub is an important feature for the centralized management of global content types in the platform layer. As existing solutions evolve and new solutions are created, new global elements will be identified as part of the solution design that need to be provisioned and managed as part of the platform layer.

## Solution Layer

**Owned and managed by: Enterprise Architecture and Solution Design**

The solutions layer contains elements that are configured and developed for specific business solutions that are deployed on the platform. These solutions are often developed by a Project team and then handed over to the Business as Usual team on completion of the project and the solution. Most solutions will be described as SharePoint solutions; however some solutions may be other systems or applications that need to integrate with the SharePoint platform in some way. A critical part of the solution design process is to identify elements within a solution that will consume platform layer elements, extend platform layer elements, are new platform layer elements, or new solution-specific elements.

## Site Layer

**Owned and managed by: Site Collection Administrators, Site Owners and End Users**

The site layer contains elements that are provisioned and configured for a specific SharePoint site collection and/or site that is being used by business users on the SharePoint platform. Sites are the end user experience of the SharePoint platform and the solutions delivered upon it. A critical part of provisioning a site is understanding, communicating, and managing the type of site it is within the organization, relative to the type of solution and the platform. For example, a centralized enterprise search center or enterprise records center is a very different type of site than a Project Collaboration site or a person's blog site. There are "one off" sites and there are "stamp out lots of sites" sites; these are all valid SharePoint solutions and sites but should be understood, designed, and managed appropriately.

## Illustrating the Model

The diagrams that follow, Figure 3-16 for libraries, Figure 3-17 for lists and Figure 3-18 for an actual project site, illustrate a content types model for a SharePoint 2010 platform. These were created using Microsoft Visio but could be created in any number of tools or simply hand drawn on a whiteboard or piece of paper. The example model captured in these diagrams is an enterprise view for a relatively small and simple SharePoint 2010 environment that currently supports three solutions.

- **Solution One**: Management of customer documents within the Lending Services department of the organization.

- **Solution Two**: Management of customer documents within the Credit Services department of the organization.

- **Solution Three**: SharePoint site definition for provisioning sites for managing agile projects within the organization.

Reviewing the diagrams that follow for this model, you should be able to clearly identify the four layers and the content types that are defined within each. You should also be able to find the following:

- The system layer content types that are intended to be available for use within sites within this environment.

- The platform layer content types for documents that define the global document content types that will be used across the currently defined solutions within this environment.

- The platform layer content types for tasks and stakeholders that define both these types of content as global types that will be used across the currently defined solutions within this environment.

- The solution layer content types that define the solution-specific content types needed for the three currently defined solutions within this environment.

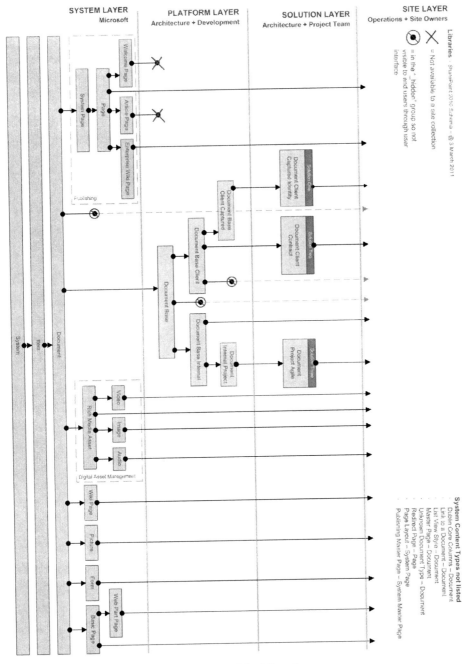

*Figure 3-16. Enterprise Content Types Model—Libraries*

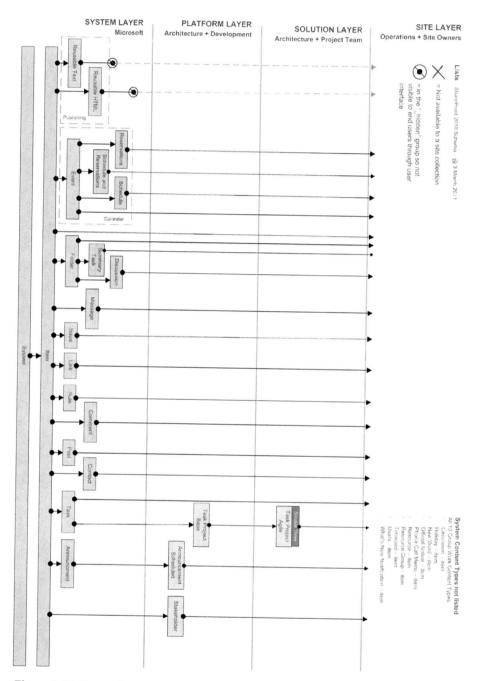

**Figure 3-17.** *Enterprise Content Types Model— Lists*

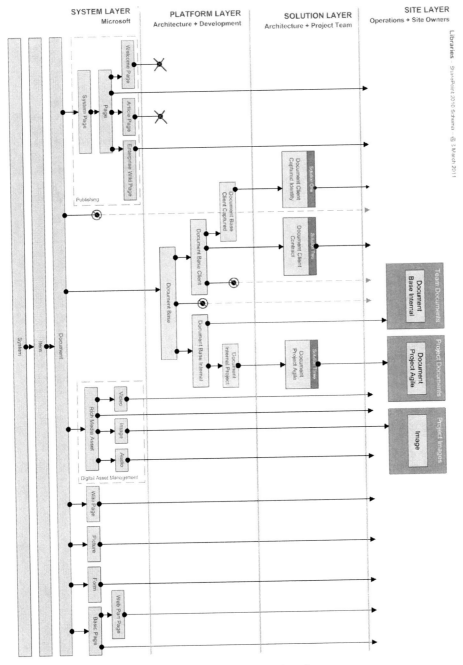

*Figure 3-18. Provisioned libraries in an actual project site*

# Summary: Designing for Complexity and Growth

The goal is not to create a complex design, but many organizations and their required information architecture are inherently complex. The real goal is to keep the model as simple as possible yet still meet the business requirements.

Planning for an appropriate level of evolution and change within the model is important, and deciding when to create platform level or solution level content types to support potential future requirements is an important design decision. As discussed earlier, it's much easier within SharePoint to extend content types than to change or remove them. This is particularly true in relation to inheritance. Therefore, it is a best practice to create platform-level content types that provide a parent between the system content types and solution content types. This approach makes it easier to add branching in the model to support future solutions that need to leverage the same content type but with solution specific columns and behaviors. When planning for potential growth, platform content types will often have no specific columns or behaviors when they are first created, but they are ready for them should a future business need require it.

---

■ **Note** Empty platform content types make it easier to add columns and behaviors in the future and create branching to support solution-specific child content types.

---

The down side to this approach is the risk of over-engineering and trying to predict every future possibility. An overly enthusiastic analyst can easily create a very complex collection of content types that risks being very difficult to manage over time and difficult for site administrators and business users to leverage. It is critical to keep the end users of the model in mind and balance designing very specific content types that restrict what users can do with flexible content types. Flexible content types provide an opportunity to reduce the overall number of content types in the model to reduce complexity; however, flexibility also increases the opportunity for the end user to use the content types incorrectly when populating content and data into SharePoint.

As highlighted already in this chapter, how much complexity an organization needs vs. how much they can govern and maintain overtime is an important consideration that will influence the approach to content types, metadata, and information architecture within SharePoint.

# Automating Document Assembly

Windows SharePoint Services provides an enhanced storage system that facilitates collaboration. This system improves upon old collaboration techniques of simply e-mailing documents back and forth or dropping them in a file share. Relying on e-mail is awkward, as team members are never sure they have the most up-to-date version of the document, and consolidating the changes becomes an ongoing, laborious task. File shares are also limited in that the files may be difficult to find, users have no idea if they are currently being edited by another team member, and versioning is reduced to Save As/Rename operations. In contrast, SharePoint's system of Web-enabled content databases provides a rich experience for the team working on the document. The environment provides check-in/check-out functionality, versioning, metadata, search, and an entire web site for storing lists of data related to the creation of the document.

However, even this system becomes strained in scenarios in which the team's documents are really collections of separate components. Frequently, these components are independent and different team members are responsible for different pieces. Under these circumstances, team members ideally should be able to submit their contributions whenever completed. Yet this work often takes place serially because the file in a SharePoint library can be checked out by only one user at a time. In this chapter, we will detail how, as a developer, you can enhance this experience to provide an automated method of document assembly. We will have a master document that a user may markup with requests for supplemental contributions by other team members. This will result in tasks being created in a SharePoint team site. Contributors can then attach their contributions to the task and when they mark it complete, we will merge their contribution back into the correct place of the master document.

## Real-World Examples

The key identifier that makes this solution applicable to an organization is any process in which different team members work on specific sections of a document. Consulting firms often have a sales resource, a project manager, and a development lead working on distinct portions of a proposal. The sales resource focuses on background information on the company, case studies, and pricing. The project manager is responsible for documenting the project lifecycle, creating a high-level project plan, and detailing the change/review mechanisms. Meanwhile, the developer is taking the customer's functional requirements and outlining a proposed solution. You also typically have individual résumés that need to be collected from specific members of the organization. All of these pieces have to be put together to complete the proposal. This problem is rather generic and can be found across many different customer types. In the construction industry, different team members are often responsible for certain sections of a contract. Even in the military, different organizations or levels are tasked with completing specific sections of a deliverable, such as in a policy review from different functional areas of the organizational branch. By allowing the team to divide and conquer the work, the solution in this chapter enables an efficient process that reduces the amount of time and level of effort it takes to complete an entire document.

# Solution Overview

To provide some context for our automated document assembly solution, we've focused on a scenario in which a sales person in an organization is constructing a proposal that requires updated résumés from key individuals in the company. We will give this sales person a tool that will help identify the correct people to include, as well as mark up the document with placeholders for their contributions. This tool will be a Visual Studio Tools for Office (VSTO) Microsoft Word 2010 template. By extending a Word template with VSTO, we will be able to add an actions pane specific to the document where we can place additional controls for the sales person to use. These controls will let the sales person search for individuals in the company, using functionality that leverages SharePoint 2010's search web service to look through the profile repository for matching individuals. (This is the same profile repository that surfaces in the enterprise's My Sites and People search functionality.) Once a desired person is found, the actions pane will enable the sales person to insert a placeholder for the employee's résumé and specify a due date by which it must be provided.

After the sales person has marked up the proposal document with résumé placeholders, she will save it to a Proposals document library in a SharePoint site. When the proposal lands in this library, several things will happen. First, we will leverage SharePoint 2010's Document ID service to assign a unique identifier to the document. We will use this in several ways—to allow us to easily find the file, but also in the body of the document, a practice in many enterprises that lets users relate a printed document back to its electronic counterpart.

Besides assigning the Document ID, we will also develop an event handler that will parse the document looking for the résumé placeholders. For each of these résumé requests, we will create a corresponding task in the SharePoint site. This task will be for the identified person, have the delivery date indicated by the sales person, and contain information so that we can relocate the document and specific placeholder in the proposal once the contribution has been submitted.

Our scenario then shifts from the sales person to the individual identified as needing to provide an updated résumé. This person will be notified that a new résumé has been requested. Completing the task involves attaching a Microsoft Word document containing the updated résumé, along with marking the task as complete. An event handler monitoring the task list will see that the task has been completed and merge the attachment into the correct location of the proposal document. This merge won't just be text; we will incorporate other embedded items such as pictures and smart art. It is important to realize that when we are working on the Word documents on the server, this is made possible by the Open XML file format. In both cases, we are able to perform these operations on the server—interacting with streams and XML documents. At no time are we automating Microsoft Word on the server. In fact, Microsoft Word doesn't even need to be installed on the server for this solution to work.

Lastly, it isn't really appropriate for our proposal VSTO solution to be the end result that we would send directly to a customer. This is because the document has references back to our custom VSTO assembly that would then require installation and trust outside of our enterprise. Therefore, we will enable the organization to convert the constructed proposal from Microsoft Word to PDF format. This conversion will be done on the server using SharePoint 2010's Word Automation Services.

# Solution Walkthrough

The following section will detail the major elements of the solution and the decisions that were made in coding it. The walkthrough will show you how we set up the SharePoint site to support the proposals and their corresponding tasks. We will demonstrate how to turn on the Document ID service and how to take the default document library's Word template as a starting point to a Word 2010 template project in Visual Studio 2010. We will explain how content controls can be used to surface metadata properties of the file into the body of the document, as well as to how to add them dynamically as content placeholders. With the Visual Studio Tools for Office solution, we will show you how to build a document actions pane and how to have that pane interact with SharePoint's search web service. Our VSTO solution will also extend the backstage interface so that a user can easily check on the status of the tasks from the proposal document. When the proposal template tool is complete, we will demonstrate how to deploy it so it is available as the default document template of the site's document library.

We will also walk you through the creation of the two event handlers that will use the Open XML file format to operate on the proposal. The first event handler will be responsible for parsing the proposal and creating tasks for each résumé request. The second one will respond to a completed résumé submission, merging the contents of the résumé back into the proposal. The walkthrough will also show you how to provide a workflow that converts the final proposal from a Word format to PDF using SharePoint's Word Automation Services. As in most of our chapters in the book, not every line of code will be explained. Since there are so many moving pieces to this chapter, we want to focus on the major elements of the solution design. We highly recommend you download the accompanying code for this chapter from Apress's site in order to follow along and reuse some of the objects.

## Setting up the SharePoint Site and Document ID Service

For the solution, you will need a site for building out the components. In our environment, we chose the root web of a site collection. Its URL is http://edhild3/sites/sales. It is this site that will contain the document library and task list we will discuss in just a bit. Within your SharePoint environment you will also need a Search center. Most enterprises have their search center deployed as part of their root intranet site collection or as a site collection unto itself. In our environment, the enterprise search center is located at http://edhild3/search. If you don't have a search center, take the time to create one. If you are going to add it to an existing site collection, just be sure to activate the SharePoint Server Publishing Infrastructure site collection feature before creating the search center.

You also need to make sure you have some individuals in the profile repository. In our environment, we have two accounts that we will request résumés from: northamerica\edhild and northamerica\chadwach. These accounts exist in Active Directory and have been granted access to the site where we will be creating the tasks and proposal. They also have profiles in the profile repository. You can have SharePoint import attributes from AD or simply go the User Profile Service Application and create the accounts there. If you have not seen this interface, use the following steps to navigate there to either create or confirm your user data. Of course, with the user data in place, make sure you perform a new search crawl and that you can actually find a person by performing a people search through your search center.

1. Open SharePoint's Central Administration site.

2. Under the Application Management heading, click **Manage service applications**.

3. Locate the User Profile Service Application and click it to highlight that application. Click the **Manage** button in the ribbon.

4. Under the People heading, click **Manage User Profiles**.

5. From here, you should be able to search through existing profiles. Clicking the **New Profile** button lets you to manually create profiles for your accounts. Be sure to define something worth searching for. For example, for Ed Hild we used the title of **Development Team Lead** with a description that he likes **Visual Basic and C#**.

Getting back to the sales site where we'll be developing the proposals solution, one of the first things we will want to do is turn on the Document ID service. If you go to the site's settings and look at the Site

Collection's features, you'll find a Document ID Service feature that needs to be activated. You can see this option in Figure 4-1.

**Document ID Service**
Assigns IDs to documents in the Site Collection, which can be used to retrieve items independent of their current location.

Deactivate    Active

*Figure 4-1. Activating the Document ID Service*

Activating this feature extends the Document and Document Set content types with additional capability. Mainly, there is a new Document ID column that for each new file (or each new document set) will hold a unique value that can be used to retrieve the file through a static URL, regardless of where the file is located. You have some out-of-the-box influence on the format of these identifiers and even more if you want to code your own document ID provider. Once the Document ID Service has been turned on, the Site Collection settings will have a new option entitled Document ID Settings. Figure 4-2 shows some of the options there. Notice that you can determine what characters you want the identifiers to begin with.

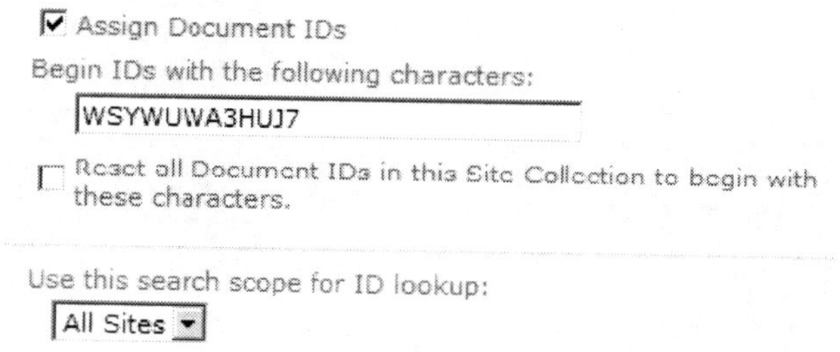

☑ Assign Document IDs

Begin IDs with the following characters:

WSYWUWA3HUJ7

☐ React all Document IDs in this Site Collection to begin with these characters.

Use this search scope for ID lookup:
All Sites ▾

*Figure 4-2. Document ID settings*

The word "begin" here is important as SharePoint will append an identifier for the list as well as the list item, leaving your complete identifiers to look something like: WSYWUWA3HUJ4-1-12. This means that the document could be retrieved through a static URL in the format of http://edhild3/sites/sales/_layouts/DocIdRedir.aspx?ID=WSYWUWA3HUJ4-1-12. The following URL gives you more detail on Document IDs, including what happens when you move or copy files: http://msdn.microsoft.com/en-us/library/ee559302(office.14).aspx.

Now in your development site, create a new document library called **Proposals**. To this library, add a new column named **ProposalID** that will hold a single line of text and make sure it is placed in the default view. You may be wondering why we would need a ProposalID when the Document ID Service has already added a Document ID column to the Document content type. The reason is that the Document ID column is a bit locked down internally within the product. For example, you won't actually see it in the definition of site columns or in use in the content types. It also is not available as a quick part in Microsoft Word, which is what we normally would use to get the identifier into the body of the document unless there's already a value assigned. This won't work with our approach of providing a template tool, since no Document ID would be present until the file is saved to the library and we don't want our sales person to have to know how to place quick parts onto a document. We will therefore use the ProposalID column for most of our work, and add a bit of code later to make sure its value stays in sync with the Document ID.

We will also need a tasks list. Create one in the site named **ResumeTasks**. Extend this list by adding **ProposalID** and **RequestID** columns. Both of these are single lines of text and present in the default view. The ProposalID in the task list will help us remember which proposal document the task is referring to. The RequestID column will contain a GUID value that matches a placeholder control inside the proposal document where the résumé content is to be placed.

## Preparing the Document Template

Now let's turn our attention to the document template of the Proposals library; this will be the central part of the tool for the sales person working on the proposal. By default, each document library has a blank Word template that we can modify to represent a typical proposal. Use the following steps to open the document template so you can enter the boilerplate text along with a content control for the value of the ProposalID field.

1. Click on the **Proposals** library in the left-hand navigation of your site.

2. Open up the Library tab in the ribbon and click on the **Library Settings** button.

3. In the General Settings section, click **Advanced Settings**.

4. In the Document Template setting, click the (**Edit Template**) link. This will launch Microsoft Word so you can edit the template and save the changes back to the library.

We want to enter some boilerplate text, a control to hold the value of the ProposalID field, and a Résumés heading that will be the beginning of the section where the résumé contributions will be inserted. The boilerplate text can really be anything. Make sure the Résumés heading is the last paragraph in the document as we will use that as a marker when we write some code a bit later. Use the following steps to insert the control for the ProposalID field. The end result should look like Figure 4-3.

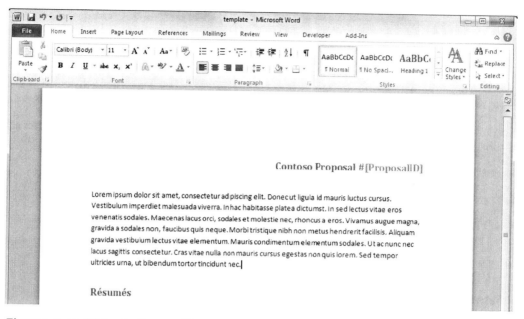

**Figure 4-3.** *Modifying the Proposal Document Template*

5.  Place your cursor where you want the ProposalID field control to be placed and make sure you have any styles you'd like applied selected. In our example, the first line is right-aligned and uses the Heading 1 style.

6.  Click the **Insert** tab in the ribbon.

7.  In the Text group, click the down-arrow to access the options of the **Quick Parts** button. Quick Parts are already configured content controls in Microsoft Word that enable you to surface the file's data (in this case, properties) in the body of the document.

8.  Choose the **Document Property** menu option.

9.  Select ProposalID.

10. Now just click **Save** to commit your changes so this document becomes the template for the document library. You can test this out by going to the Proposals library and from the Document tab, choosing **New Document**.

This completes the non-code portion of preparing the document template. We now want to export the template from the SharePoint site so we can use it as the starting point for our Visual Studio solution in the next section. An easy way to export this file is to use SharePoint Designer. Simply open your site in SharePoint Designer and choose the **All Files** option in the Navigation menu. Browse to the Proposals library and open its **Forms** folder, where you'll see our `template.dotx` file. Select it and choose the **Export Files** button in the ribbon. Save the exported `template.dotx` file to your local Documents folder. Figure 4-4 shows this export option in SharePoint Designer.

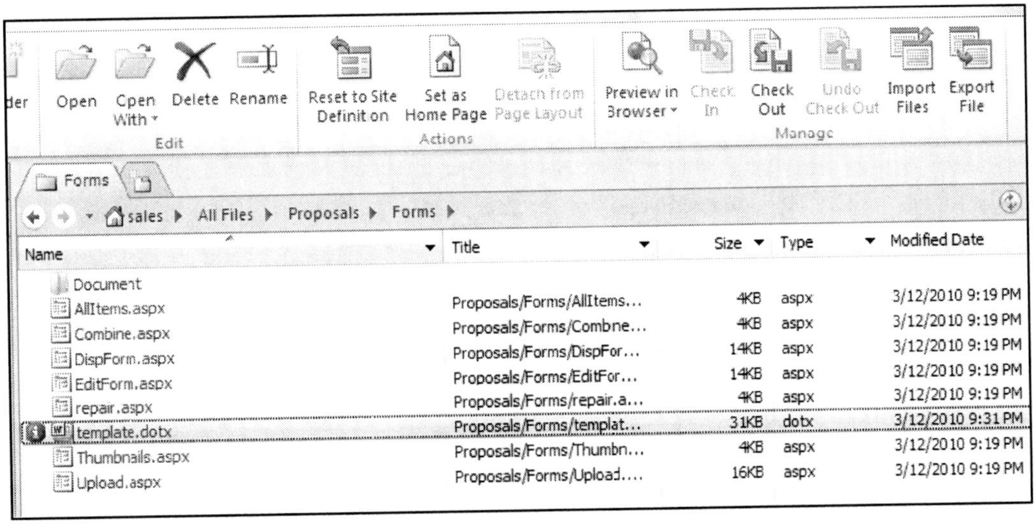

*Figure 4-4. Exporting the Document Template using SharePoint Designer*

# Creating the Visual Studio Tools for Office Solution

In this section of the walkthrough, we will move over to Visual Studio and create a document-level Visual Studio Tools for Office project out of the Microsoft Word template. Start Visual Studio and choose to create a **New Project**. Under the C# language node, select Office and then 2010 to display the VSTO project templates.

From the listing of Visual Studio installed templates, select Word 2010 Template. Name the project **templateProject**. Leave the default option of creating a new solution and confirm that the .NET framework drop-down at the top of the dialog is set to .NET Framework 4. As we discussed in Chapter 4, there are several advantages to using version 4 of the framework for Office development, such as C# support for optional parameters. We want to make sure that these advantages are available to us. Your New Project dialog should look like Figure 4-5.

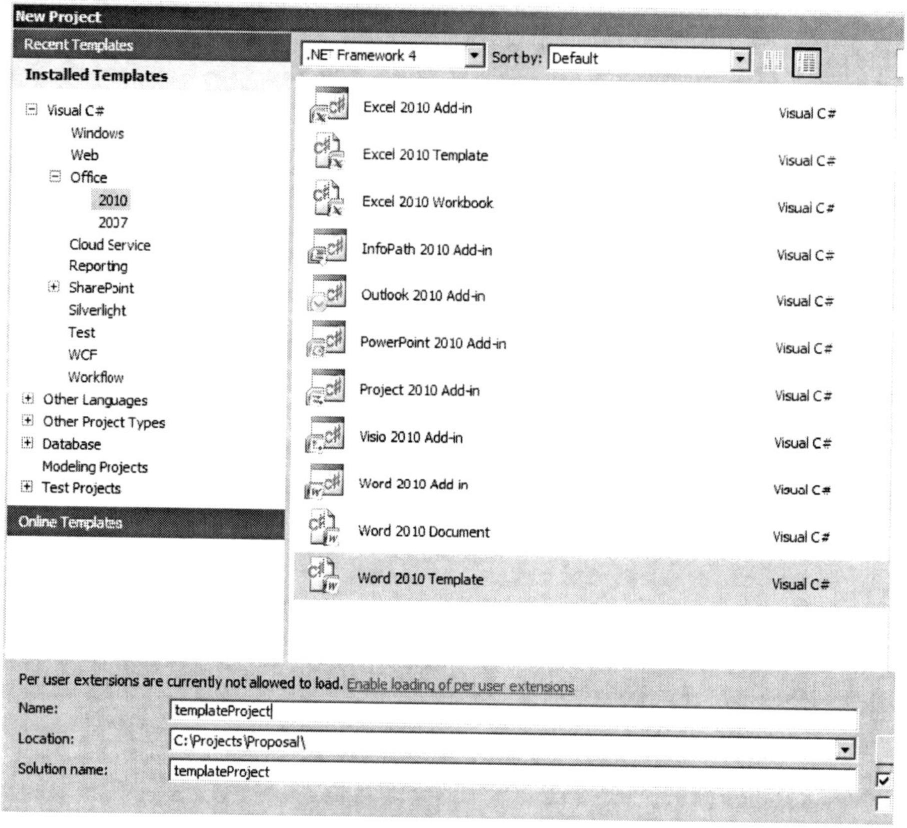

*Figure 4-5. Creating the VSTO solution for the proposal template*

Clicking OK starts a project wizard that asks if you wish to create a brand new Word template for the basis of the project or use a copy of an existing template. Choose **Copy an existing document** and browse to the `template.dotx` file that you exported from the site earlier.

When the new project is created, your solution will contain a few files by default. These are visible in the Visual Studio Solution Explorer window. You'll find a `template.dotx` node with a code file named `ThisDocument.cs`, which is the main entry point for document-level projects. This file is where developers can write code for events and where we will wire up our actions pane in the next section. You can go ahead and close the designer that is surfacing Microsoft Word. Our work in Visual Studio will supplement the work we have already done inside the document.

Before we get to coding away, let's take care of one other item at the project level. We will need a web service reference to the SharePoint search functionality since our document will be remote from the server (on the user's desktop) when it is being used. SharePoint 2010 contains a `search.asmx` web service that will be our entry point for issuing a remote search query and getting results. This search API remains unchanged from SharePoint 2004—good news for developers who built solutions leveraging it in the previous release. This also means that most of the references and examples you find describing this web service for SharePoint 2004 will be useful in building solutions for the 2010 version. You interact with `search.asmx` using the ASP.NET 2.0 style of web services, so it will take us a few steps to get the appropriate reference into our Visual Studio 2010 project. Follow the steps below to set the web service reference.

1.  Right-click on the templateProject and choose **Add Service Reference**.

2.  Click the **Advanced** button in the bottom left-hand corner of the dialog.

3.  Click the **Add Web Reference** button in the bottom left-hand corner of the dialog since we need to add an ASP.NET 2.0 asmx style reference.

4.  Enter the URL for the search.asmx web service, which should be off the Search center you identified earlier in the chapter. In our environment the URL is http://edhild3/search/_vti_bin/search.asmx.

5.  Click the green arrow.

6.  Once you can see the operations of the web service in the window, name the service reference **SPQueryService** in the textbox to the right.

7.  Click the **Add Reference** button. Your project structure in Visual Studio's Solution Explorer should look like Figure 4-6.

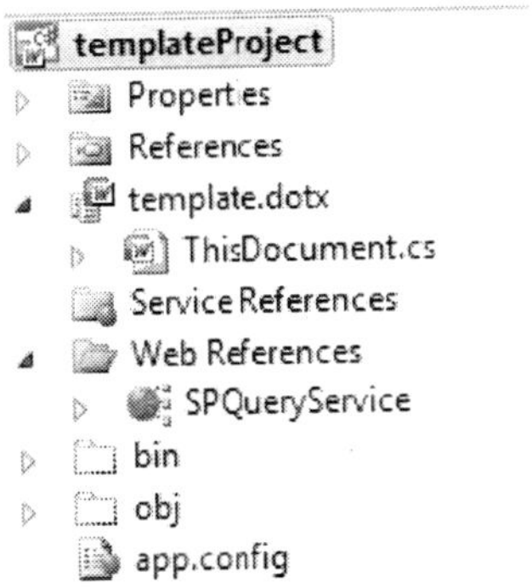

- templateProject
  - ▷ Properties
  - ▷ References
  - ▲ template.dotx
    - ▷ ThisDocument.cs
    - Service References
  - ▲ Web References
    - ▷ SPQueryService
  - ▷ bin
  - ▷ obj
  - app.config

*Figure 4-6. The templateProject solution structure*

In the next few sections, we will walk through the major elements of the VSTO solution, which creates a tool out of the Microsoft Word proposal template. As in our other chapters, we won't detail every line of code so we highly recommend you download the code for this chapter from the Apress web site and follow along.

## The Document Actions Pane

Most people are familiar with the task pane in Microsoft Office applications. In Microsoft Word, the Research pane is an example of a task pane that enables a user to search registered repositories for more information without having to leave the Word application. Task panes provide another surface (usually located to the right of the document) for a developer to build additional user interface elements that add capability to the Word application. While task panes are application-level and can be called on regardless of the document that is open, document actions panes present similar user interface options but are available only for a specific document or document template. This is exactly why we chose to create a document-level project in the last section. Our pane makes sense only if the user is working with the proposal template. You can create a custom document actions pane using a Windows Forms user control. Figure 4-7 shows the design surface of the ProposalPane user control.

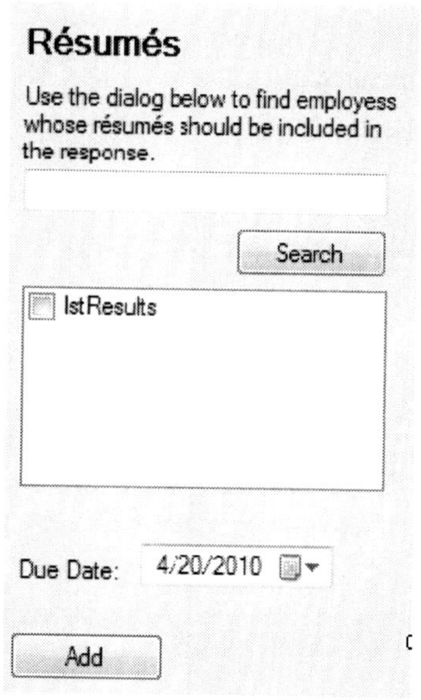

*Figure 4-7. Designing the ProposalPane control*

The ProposalPane user control contains some labels at the top for instructions. The txtKeywords textbox will enable the user to enter a search query that will perform the people search against the profile repository. The search button is responsible for executing the web service call and populating the CheckedListBox control below with results. Our sales person user can then select the desired individuals, choose a due date using the DateTimePicker control and click the Add button. This button will dynamically place a content control at the end of the document, below the Résumés heading, for each checked individual. The content of this control will specify whose résumé is requested along with the due date so we can create the correct tasks. With the user control created, the code in Listing 4-1 in the ThisDocument class loads it up as a document actions pane when our template is opened.

*Listing 4-1. Adding the ProposalPane as a Document Actions Pane*

```
private ProposalPane proposalPane = new ProposalPane();

private void ThisDocument_Startup(object sender, System.EventArgs e)
{
    this.ActionsPane.Controls.Add(proposalPane);
}
```

The next bit of code we want to draw attention to is the code that runs in response to the user clicking the Search button. The initial portion of this code is presented in Listing 4-2. First, the proxy for SharePoint's search web service is configured with the URL of the search center, the current user's credentials, and a timeout value of 20 seconds in case the server is too busy for our request. Next, a queryPacketTemplate string variable shows the structure of the XML envelope our query must be wrapped in that we pass to the web service. The most important attribute here is that the query type is set to MSSQLFT. There are two types of search queries we could submit through this API—a keyword style and a style that resembles SQL Select statements, which is the style we will use here. We won't delve into all of the options here and turn this into a reference on search query syntax; if this is an area of interest, you'll find some reference links in the Further Reading section at the end of this chapter.

*Listing 4-2. Building the Search Request*

```
private void btnSearch_Click(object sender, EventArgs e)
{
  SPQueryService.QueryService service = new SPQueryService.QueryService();
  service.Url = "http://edhild3/Search/_vti_bin/search.asmx";
  service.PreAuthenticate = true;
  service.Credentials = System.Net.CredentialCache.DefaultCredentials;
  service.Timeout = 20000; //wait 20 secs

  string queryPacketTemplate = "<?xml version=\"1.0\" encoding=\"utf-8\" ?>"
    + "<QueryPacket xmlns=\"urn:Microsoft.Search.Query\">"
    + "<Query domain=\"QDomain\"><SupportedFormats>"
    + "<Format>urn:Microsoft.Search.Response.Document.Document</Format>"
    + "</SupportedFormats>"
    + "<Context><QueryText language=\"en-US\" type=\"MSSQLFT\">"
    + "{0}</QueryText></Context>"
    + "</Query></QueryPacket>";
```

In the next section of code shown in Listing 4-3, you can see our actual SQL statement in the sqlQueryTemplate string variable where we ask for the PreferredName and AccountName of any person who has the user-entered keyword in any of the indexed properties of the profile repository. The next two lines simply package everything together as one XML string. You may wonder how we came to know about the PreferredName and AccountName properties. The answer to that lies in the User Profile Service Application you accessed earlier in this chapter. Using the Manage User Properties option in the service application takes you to a listing of the properties in the profile store. Note that the display name you see here is not always the internal property name. Edit the property to see its internal name. This listing of profile properties is shown in Figure 4-8.

*Listing 4-3. The SQL Search Query*

```
string sqlQueryTemplate = "SELECT PreferredName, AccountName FROM SCOPE() "
    + "WHERE \"Scope\" = 'People' AND CONTAINS(*,'{0}') ";

string enteredText = txtKeywords.Text.Replace(' ', '+');
string sqlQuery = string.Format(sqlQueryTemplate, enteredText);string queryXml =
string.Format(queryPacketTemplate, sqlQuery);
```

---

**Note** Pay particular attention to the fact that we are replacing any space character with a plus symbol. There are several characters the user can enter that would present a problem for our code. We are accounting for the spaces, but, for example, a query for a user with the last name of O'Brian would also be a problem because of the apostrophe. Use the links in the Further Reading portion of this document to get a fuller explanation of characters that cause problems and how you can handle for them.

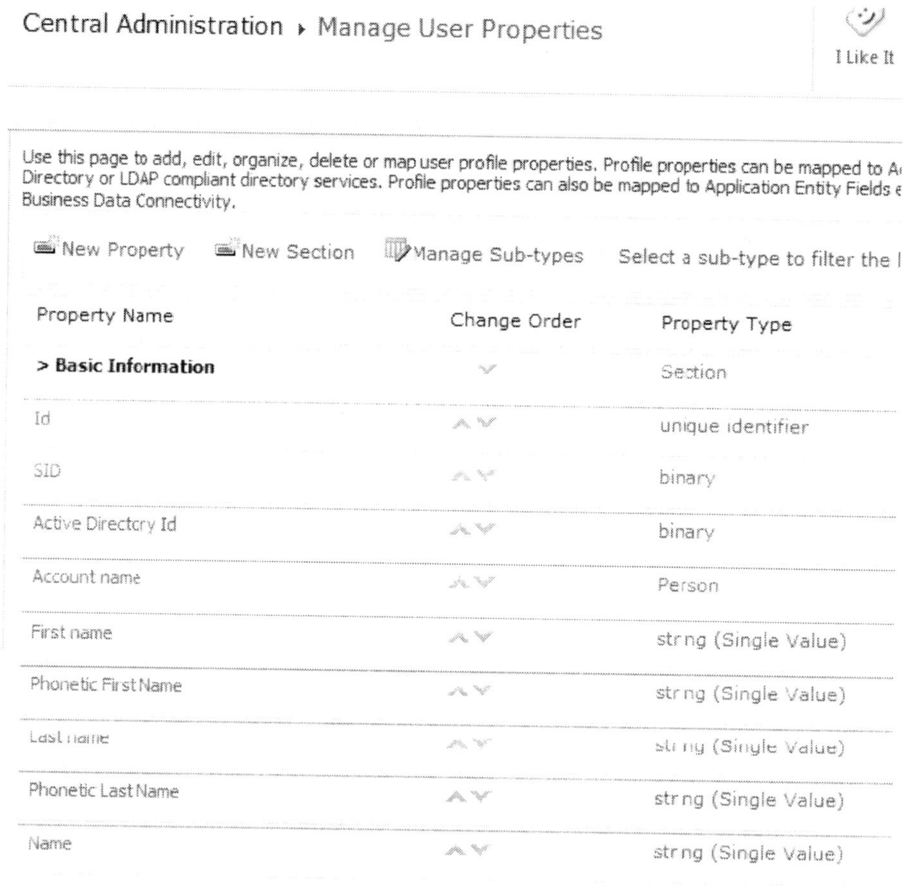

**Central Administration ▸ Manage User Properties**

I Like It

Use this page to add, edit, organize, delete or map user profile properties. Profile properties can be mapped to A Directory or LDAP compliant directory services. Profile properties can also be mapped to Application Entity Fields a Business Data Connectivity.

New Property    New Section    Manage Sub-types    Select a sub-type to filter the l

| Property Name | Change Order | Property Type |
| --- | --- | --- |
| **> Basic Information** | | Section |
| Id | | unique identifier |
| SID | | binary |
| Active Directory Id | | binary |
| Account name | | Person |
| First name | | string (Single Value) |
| Phonetic First Name | | string (Single Value) |
| Last name | | string (Single Value) |
| Phonetic Last Name | | string (Single Value) |
| Name | | string (Single Value) |

*Figure 4-8. Discovering profile properties*

Before we look at the section of the search button's click event handler where we process the results, we wanted to call out a helper class we constructed simply to make placing the people in the results list easier. The PersonResultItem class we placed at the bottom of the code-behind of the user control is just a class that contains the returned PreferredName and AccountName information for a specific search result (see Listing 4-4). The reason we created the class was to be able to specify the ToString() method that will be used by the CheckedListBox for the display value of the item. In this case, we want the PreferredName, which is the display name for the account.

*Listing 4-4. The PersonResultItem Helper Class for Reading Results*

```
internal class PersonResultItem
{
  public string PreferredName { get; set; }
  public string AccountName { get; set; }
  public PersonResultItem(string preferredName, string accountName)
  {
    PreferredName = preferredName;
    AccountName = accountName;
  }
  public override string ToString()
  {
    return this.PreferredName;
  }
}
```

So the last piece of code for our Search button, shown in Listing 4-5, executes the query and adds the results to the list box. In this instance, we are using the QueryEx method of the search web service, which returns the results as a dataset with a table named RelevantResults. We are using a WaitCursor here to keep things simple; a more advanced approach would be to make an asynchronous web service call.

*Listing 4-5. Executing the Query and Processing the Results*

```
this.UseWaitCursor = true;
DataSet ds = service.QueryEx(queryXml);
DataTable tbl = ds.Tables["RelevantResults"];
lstResults.Items.Clear();
foreach (DataRow r in tbl.Rows)
{
  lstResults.Items.Add(new PersonResultItem(↵
      r["PreferredName"].ToString(),↵
      r["AccountName"].ToString()));
}
this.UseWaitCursor = false;
}
```

So far, our ProposalPane enables the sales person to perform a people search from within the Word template. Once the results have been gathered and the user selects which people to request résumés for, the control needs to place résumé requests into the document in the Résumés section. To accomplish this, the code in Listing 4-6 finds the Résumés section by knowing that it is the last paragraph in the document. For each selected individual, we insert a paragraph containing a rich-text content control. When this control is created, we name it with the string Resume along with a GUID so we can guarantee uniqueness. The control is titled **Resume Request** and the same GUID is placed in its tag property for us to retrieve later. This tag value allows us to tell the résumé requests apart and relate the corresponding tasks we need to create in the SharePoint site later. Lastly, we place some formatted text in the control so that it will fit the format of "Resume request for northamerica\edhild due by 4/20/2010". Figure 4-9 shows the end result running in Microsoft Word.

*Listing 4-6. Inserting Content Controls for Resume Requests*

```
foreach (PersonResultItem person in lstResults.SelectedItems)
{
  Microsoft.Office.Interop.Word.Paragraph last =
    Globals.ThisDocument.Paragraphs[Globals.ThisDocument.Paragraphs.Count];
  last.Range.InsertParagraphAfter();

  Globals.ThisDocument.Paragraphs[Globals.ThisDocument.Paragraphs.Count]
    .Range.Select();
  Microsoft.Office.Tools.Word.RichTextContentControl ctl;
  Guid id = Guid.NewGuid();
  ctl = Globals.ThisDocument.Controls.AddRichTextContentControl(
    "Resume " + id.ToString());
  ctl.Title = "Resume Request";
  ctl.Tag = id.ToString();
  ctl.PlaceholderText = string.Format("Resume request for {0} due by {1}",
    person.AccountName, dtDueDate.Value.ToShortDateString());
}
```

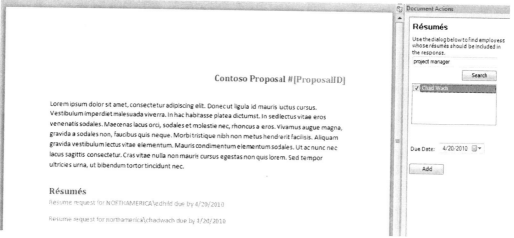

*Figure 4-9. Résumé request as dynamic content controls*

# Extending Backstage

As described in Chapter 4, Microsoft Office 2010 provides a new extension point for developers called the *backstage*. This interface replaces the old-style, drop-down file menu, bringing a ribbon-like treatment to operations users will perform on their documents, or a way to present information about the document. The new interface opens up a lot of real-estate for providing useful information. Our solution will provide a click link to the SharePoint site's résumé tasks list, filtering the list for the tasks specific to the open proposal. We point out in the Extensions section of this chapter how you could make this much more elaborate by actually bringing the task details into this interface. The Further

Reading section also includes links for more details about advanced options, and more controls you could utilize in the backstage environment.

To get started with our customization, add a new project item to the Visual Studio templateProject. Choose the Ribbon (XML) item template and name the file backstagecustomization.cs. As mentioned in Chapter 4, there is no designer for backstage customizations; however, these extensions leverage the same ribbon infrastructure as the ribbon items the user sees while authoring the document. When the new project item process completes, two files will have been added—an xml file and a class file. Both of these in concert will be used to build our backstage extension. Let's start with the XML file, which is shown in Listing 4-7.

*Listing 4-7. The Backstage Customization Ribbon XML*

```xml
<?xml version="1.0" encoding="UTF-8"?>
<customUI xmlns="http://schemas.microsoft.com/office/2009/04/customui"
          onLoad="Ribbon_Load">
  <backstage>
    <tab idMso="TabInfo">
      <firstColumn>
        <group id="ProposalInfoGroup"
               label="Proposal Information"
               helperText="Use the link provided to get details on resume
                           tasks for this proposal. Note that document must
                           be saved to SharePoint initially for this link to
                           work.">
          <topItems>
            <hyperlink id="taskLink" label="View tasks"
                       getTarget="GetHyperLink"/>
          </topItems>
        </group>
      </firstColumn>
    </tab>
  </backstage>
</customUI>
```

Notice that this ribbon XML uses a different namespace than the one that was added by default. In the backstage, the tabs are listed vertically on the left-hand side of the screen. By specifying the idMso of TabInfo, we are telling Word to place our customization on the out-of-the-box Info tab. We then define a new Group that will be placed in the first column of that tab. This group has a label, description, and an inner hyperlink control. The text for this hyperlink will always be "View Tasks", but the URL for the hyperlink will be dynamically determined using a ribbon callback technique. This is because we want the URL to filter the résumé tasks list for tasks specific to this proposal. Since this will be different for different proposals, we add a callback method into the backstagecustomization.cs file named GetHyperLink, which will return the correct URL string. Use the following URL for more details on building ribbon customizations and, in particular, for figuring out what controls can be loaded there and the method signature of callbacks for their properties: http://msdn.microsoft.com/en-us/library/ee691833(office.14).aspx. Listing 4-8 shows our GetHyperLink callback method.

*Listing 4-8. The GetHyperLink Ribbon Callback*

```csharp
public string GetHyperLink(Office.IRibbonControl control)
{
    string url = "http://edhild3/sites/sales/Lists/ResumeTasks/AllItems.aspx";
```

```
string filterTemplate = "?FilterField1=ProposalID&FilterValue1={0}";
string id = Globals.ThisDocument.plainTextContentControl1.Text;
if (id != string.Empty)
{
  return url + string.Format(filterTemplate, id);
}
else
{
  return url;
}
}
```

The GetHyperLink method builds a URL to the résumé tasks list in the SharePoint site. Assuming the proposal has been saved to the site at least once, it will have a Document ID and therefore a ProposalID. We will show you later how to synchronize those values. If a ProposalID exists, we can access its value through the quick part content control that we added in the very beginning. We didn't name the control, so it is referenced here as plainTextContentControl1. Notice how we can filter the list for the user by specifying both the field to filter by as well as the filter value as query parameters in the URL. If this ProposalID content control does not have a value, we need our hyperlink to do something so we send the user to the résumé tasks default all items view.

Last but not least, we need to inform Word of our ribbon customization when the document-level project loads. This is accomplished with the code in Listing 4-9 which is placed in the ThisDocument.cs file. Figure 4-10 shows the end result of our customization alongside the versioning group on the Info tab.

*Listing 4-9. Loading the Backstage Customization for the Document*

```
protected override Microsoft.Office.Core.IRibbonExtensibility⏎
    CreateRibbonExtensibilityObject()
{
  return new backstagecustomization();
}
```

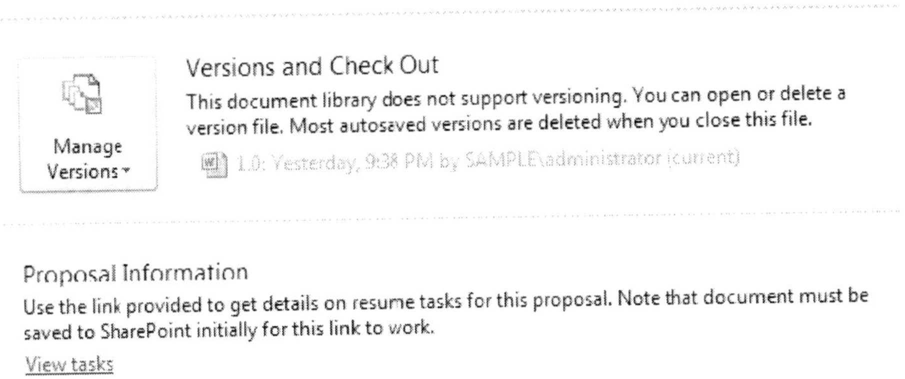

**Versions and Check Out**

This document library does not support versioning. You can open or delete a version file. Most autosaved versions are deleted when you close this file.

Manage Versions ▾

1.0: Yesterday, 9:38 PM by SAMPLE\administrator (current)

**Proposal Information**

Use the link provided to get details on resume tasks for this proposal. Note that document must be saved to SharePoint initially for this link to work.

View tasks

*Figure 4-10. The Proposal Information Backstage Customization*

# Deploying the Proposal Template Tool

Now that the proposal template tool is complete, we want to deploy it so that is available as the default template of the Proposals SharePoint library. Remember, though, since this is a document-level project, we are really talking about deploying the `template.dotx` file along with the assembly that has our VSTO customizations. Visual Studio Tools for Office solutions are usually deployed using ClickOnce, which means the user accesses the solution from a central location such as a web site or a file share. The solution installs the first time the user accesses the document, and then the application has the ability to reach back to this installation point to check for updates.

You may be skeptical about SharePoint as a deployment destination. SharePoint is not your typical web application and we really don't want assemblies treated as content in its databases. Storing the assembly outside of the content database is not a requirement, just more of a general practice. A more accurate description of what we are going to do is to deploy the solution through ClickOnce to a file share, but distribute the `template.dotx` file via SharePoint. This approach is valid since the template file maintains a reference to where its VSTO components were deployed. So our users will be able to access the document as they normally would and if it is the first time the file is accessed, it will reach back to the deployment file share to install the solution. This also increases the flexibility of the solution, as you could deploy the document to many different sites, but have a single point of maintenance for the code-behind assembly.

To get started, we need to first get our templateProject solution deployed. Right-click on the project and choose **Properties**. Within the Visual Studio dialog, as seen in Figure 4-11, select the **Publish** tab.

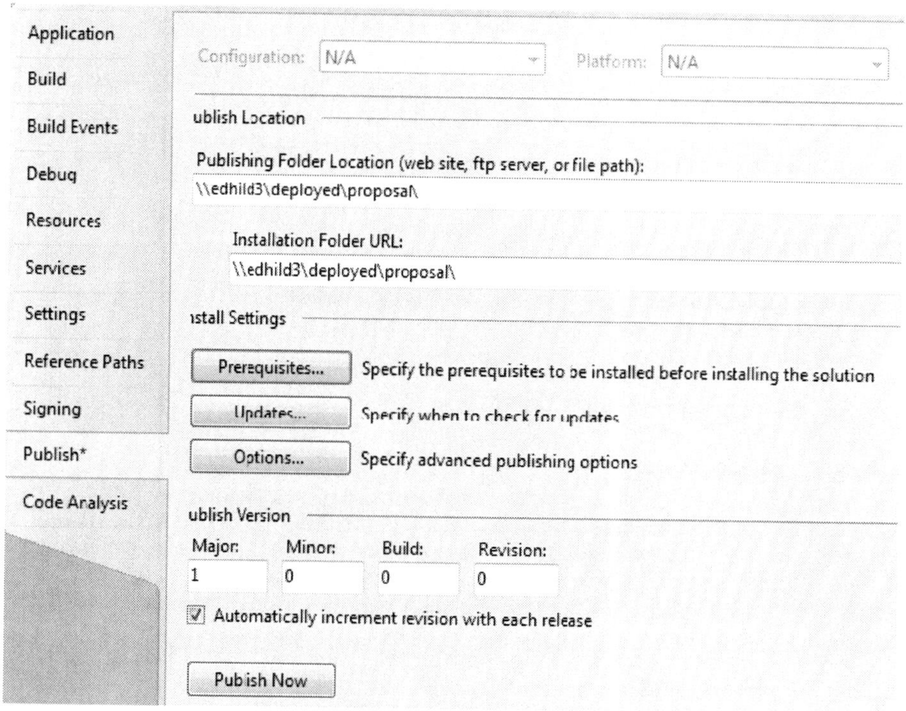

*Figure 4-11. Publishing the VSTO Solution*

Now ClickOnce deployment is a topic that goes far beyond the scope of this book, so we include some references for you to do more research in the Further Reading section of this chapter. For now, we will just explain enough to get this project integrated with your SharePoint environment. In Figure 4-11, notice that we have specified a file share for the publishing location and the installation folder. For our approach of using the SharePoint library to deploy the solution, these should be the same. Please make sure this is actually a valid path in your environment. You will likely also want to change the default Updates option. Clicking the Updates button lets you set the application to check for updates every time it is loaded. This is useful if you expect to still be doing some debugging. Finally, click the Publish Now button to publish the VSTO solution, `template.dotx` file, and other application settings information to the shared folder.

Remember when we used SharePoint Designer to export the library's template file so we could use it to create the Visual Studio project? Use the same technique now, but import the `template.dotx` file that was placed in the deployment shared folder.

Chances are you need to adjust the Trust Settings in Microsoft Word before it will even attempt to load the solution. There are many different ways to establish trust, such as by location or publisher (using a signing certificate). Since location is the easiest to set up in a development environment, we will take that approach. Launch Microsoft Word and use the following steps to set up the trust settings.

1. Launch a new instance of Microsoft Word.

2. Click the File menu and choose **Options**.

3. Click **Trust Center** in the left-hand navigation.

4.   Click Trust Center Settings button.

5.   Click **Trust Locations** in the left-hand navigation.

6.   Check the checkbox at the bottom of the dialog to **Allow Trusted Locations on My Network**.

7.   Click the **Add New Location** button.

8.   Enter your deployment file share location (for our environment, this was `\\edhild3\deployed`). Choose the checkbox so that **Subfolders of this location are also trusted**.

9.   Repeat the previous step for the SharePoint location where the `template.dotx` file is deployed. We simply added the root of the site collection `http://edhild3/sites/sales` and selected to trust all the subfolders.

10.  Click **OK** twice.

Depending on your environment, you may also want to disable opening the document in Protected View. This is also done in the Trust Center settings of Microsoft Word. You should now be able to go to the SharePoint site and choose **New Document**, which will retrieve the template. Since this is the first time you are launching the customization from its deployment location, the installer for the customization will be launched. You will only see this step the first time. Subsequent requests simply check for updates. Your proposal template should now load along with your document actions pane.

---

**Note** A few issues have surfaced in our development environment, making us have to run the setup.exe in the deployment folder as an additional step. From a clean client machine, this doesn't appear to be a problem, but just in case you are using a single virtual machine as both server and client, we thought it worth mentioning. Again, please look to the Further Reading section of the chapter if you want more ClickOnce and SharePoint deployment details.

---

## Using SPMetal

In the next two sections of this chapter we'll focus on the event handlers that will respond to proposal documents being stored in the library and the résumé task requests being completed. Since we will be writing code against the lists in our SharePoint site, we will take a moment to generate a helper class to streamline the amount of code we need to write. SPMetal is a command line tool that generates code that is an alternative to the SharePoint object model. By default, the tool is located at `C:\Program Files\Common Files\Microsoft Shared\Web Server Extensions\14\BIN`. Simply point it at a SharePoint team site and the resulting code file will contain strongly-typed entity classes for all of the site's lists and libraries as they are configured at the moment in time that you run the tool. This code is often easier to use than the SharePoint object model equivalents. The best example of this is querying the list for a specific item. Using the SharePoint object model, you could issue a query for specific items of a list using an XML-formatted CAML query such as the one in Listing 4-10. Notice that the query is just in the form of a string with no IntelliSense provided for structure, field names, or possible values.

*Listing 4-10. Querying for Specific List Items using CAML*

```
SPList list = m_web.Lists["ResumeTasks"];
SPQuery query = New SPQuery();
query.Query = "<Where><Eq><FieldRef Name='ProposalID'/><Value
                        Type='Text'>12345</Value></Eq></Where>";
SPListItemCollection items = list.GetItems(query);
```

Instead, the entity classes created by SPMetal support LINQ. So the query in Listing 4-10 becomes less code to write, even easier to understand, and definitely less prone to spelling a field or value incorrectly. Listing 4-11 shows the transformed query, which also gets only the collection of the title fields we're interested in.

*Listing 4-11. Query for Specific List Items using SPMetal and Linq*

```
using (EntitiesDataContext dc = new EntitiesDataContext(webUrl))
{
    var q = from resumetask in dc.ResumeTasks
            where resumetask.ProposalID == "12345"
            select resumetask.Title;
```

A developer would typically use SPMetal during the coding phase, running the tool and adding the generated file into the Visual Studio project. To run the tool, launch a command window and type a command similar to SPMetal /web:http://edhild3/sites/sales /code:ProposalEntities.cs /language:csharp. In this command we have specified three parameters. The first, *web*, specifies the site you'd like to use as the source. The generated code file will contain classes for working against a similarly structured site. In this case, we chose our team site where we are building the solution. The second parameter, *code*, specifies the name of the file you want the generated code to be placed in. This file will be placed in the same directory as the SPMetal tool. Once you have it, copy it and add it to the Visual Studio project we will create in the next section. The last parameter, *language*, specifies the .NET language you'd like the generated code to be in. There are many more parameters to this file and if you are going to be spending a lot of time coding against SharePoint data sources, we recommend spending some time to get to know all of its options. We have added a link in the Further Reading section of this chapter.

---

**Note** It is important to realize that this code runs in the context of the developer running the command unless another user is specified as a parameter. Since SharePoint security trims what a user has access to, make sure the user running this tool actually has access to the data you are planning to code against.

---

## The Proposal Document Event Handler

In this next section of the walkthrough, we will add a new Visual Studio SharePoint project to the solution that will contain the event handlers that run in response to both the proposal being saved to the document library as well as a user completing her résumé task. With Visual Studio select to add a new project to the current solution. Under the C# language node, select SharePoint and then 2010 to display the SharePoint 2010 project templates.

From the listing of Visual Studio installed templates, select EventReceiver. Name the project **ProposalEvents**. Leave the default option of creating a new solution and confirm that the .NET framework drop-down at the top of the dialog is set to .NET Framework 3.5. Your New Project dialog should look like Figure 4-12.

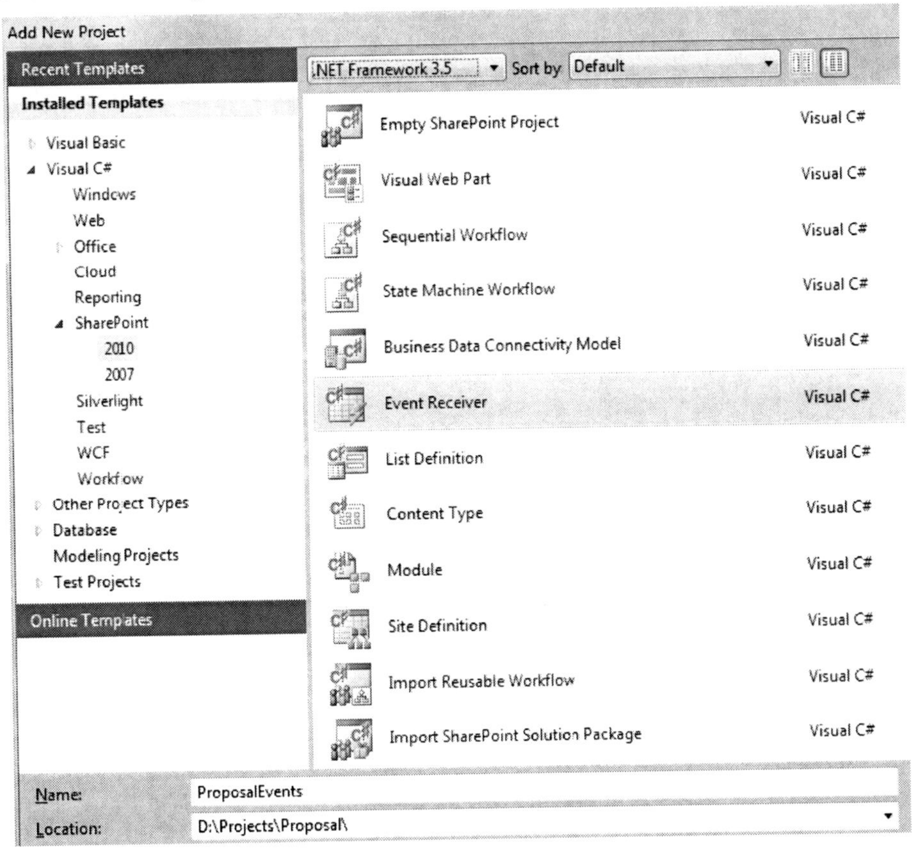

*Figure 4-12. Creating the ProposalEvents Solution*

Clicking OK will start the SharePoint Customization Wizard, which will ask a few questions about the solution you are going to build. The first dialog in this wizard asks for the SharePoint site you want Visual Studio to deploy to when you debug your code. Stick with the same site you used earlier in the chapter, `http://edhild3/sites/sales`.

You are also asked whether your solution is a farm or sandboxed solution. This alludes to security restrictions that will be placed on your solution and whether it is a part of the enterprise (farm) or a customization for a specific site collection (sandboxed). Since our code will be operating on files using Open XML, it falls outside the typical restrictions of sandboxed solutions, so choose the **farm level** option. The wizard's next screen asks how to bind your event handler. We will be starting with the code that generates the résumé tasks when the proposal is saved. In this case, we want to bind it to a List, so choose **List Item Events**. We then get to pick a particular list type—choose **Document Library**.

---

▒ **Note** You might be curious why we are not asked to specifically pick the Proposals document library. This is because, declaratively, we can only bind an event handler to a list type or content type. So our event handler will actually run in response to this action for any document library in the site. If you wanted to scope this down to a specific list or library, you would write code in a feature receiver so that upon activation, the feature binds the specific list and event handler. Another option would be to define the proposals as their own content type and bind the receiver that way. This approach is an Extension Point for the chapter.

---

Lastly, we get to select which events we wish to respond to. You will notice that most of these events either have "is being" or "was" in their description. This refers to whether you want your event handler to be called synchronously with the action or asynchronously after it has taken place. Since the generation of résumé tasks can happen after the document is saved, select both the **An item was added** and **An item was updated** options. Click **Finish**.

Once the new project is created, your solution will already have a few files by default, including an event receiver named EventReceiver1. Right-click and rename this to **ProposalDocumentReceiver**. When you expand this node, you will see an Elements.xml file, which has the registration information that this SharePoint customization is an event handler, the class that contains the code that should be run, and the events it is responding to. The class EventReceiver1.cs already has the ItemAdded and ItemUpdated events stubbed out for you.

Before jumping into the actual code that will parse the document and create the résumé tasks, let's get a few other things out of the way. First, don't forget to add the ProposalEntities class we created with SPMetal earlier. Also, there are a few assemblies we need to add references to:

- **WindowsBase:** This assembly gives us access to the System.IO.Packaging namespace, which is used to open up Office files that use the Open XML file format.

- **DocumentFormat.OpenXml:** This assembly is provided by the Open XML Format SDK 2.0. For this chapter we are using the March 2010 release, which you can download and install from: http://msdn.microsoft.com/en-us/office/bb265236.aspx. DocumentFormat.OpenXml allows us to manipulate the content of the presentation without having to write XML nodes directly. The SDK provides an object model that is an abstraction from the actual XML, making our code easier to read and write.

- **Microsoft.SharePoint.Linq:** This assembly is included in the SharePoint install, though you may have to browse to it when adding the reference. Its default location is C:\Program Files\Common Files\Microsoft Shared\Web Server Extensions\14\ISAPI\Microsoft.SharePoint.Linq.dll. Microsoft.SharePoint.Linq allows us to query the list for specific items using LINQ instead of the old CAML used in previous versions of SharePoint. It is used by the SPMetal class we generated earlier.

Now that the appropriate references have been added, you can add the using statements into the event receiver code file we will be modifying. These statements are the key namespaces we will use in the code, and they keep us from having to fully qualify their class names. If you notice that the namespaces are not resolving, you may have missed adding a reference to an assembly. Listing 4-12 details the using statements that need to be added to the code-behind file of the class EventReceiver1.cs.

*Listing 4-12. Using Statements*

```
using DocumentFormat.OpenXml.Wordprocessing;
using DocumentFormat.OpenXml;
using DocumentFormat.OpenXml.Packaging;
using System.Linq;
using System.Collections.Generic;
using System.Text;
using System.IO;
```

The code in the ItemAdded and ItemUpdated methods is almost identical. Looking at Listing 4-13, you see that we first make sure it is the Proposals library that we are working with. Had you bound the event handler with a content type or through a feature receiver, this would not have been necessary. We then retrieve a reference to the file and web we are working with and call the method where most of the work will happen—ProcessFile.

*Listing 4-13. Handling the ItemAdded Event for the Proposal Library*

```
public override void ItemAdded(SPItemEventProperties properties)
{
    if (properties.List.Title != "Proposals") return;
    SPFile file = properties.ListItem.File;
    SPWeb web = properties.ListItem.Web;
    ProcessFile(file, web);
    base.ItemAdded(properties);
}
```

The ProcessFile method begins by addressing the fact that we really want the Document ID to be synchronized with our ProposalID field. You might think that, ideally, this should have happened as part of a synchronous event; however, the Document ID field simply isn't available for you to retrieve at that moment. Therefore, we have to perform this action in the after event, being very careful that we don't cause any events to run again as part of the change, or trigger the creation of any new versions. Listing 4-14 contains this part of the ProcessFile method. We determined this property's internal name by attaching Visual Studio's debugger and looking at the properties collection.

*Listing 4-14. Syncing the ProposalID and Document ID fields*

```
if (!file.Name.EndsWith(".docx")) return;
this.EventFiringEnabled = false;
file.Item.Properties["ProposalID"] = file.Properties["_dlc_DocId"].ToString();
file.Item.SystemUpdate(false);
this.EventFiringEnabled = true;
```

Listing 4-14 starts by confirming that we are operating on a Microsoft Word document that has been saved using the Open XML file format. Using the EventFiringEnabled property allows us to make sure that this update of properties will not cause any new events to be raised. Notice that instead of updating the file, we are focused on the file's SharePoint item. This is because we are not changing the file itself, just its metadata. Using the SystemUpdate method with a false parameter tells the system not to create a new version as a result of the update. It is important to realize that we are only updating the property of the proposal document and not its body. This property will be retrieved by Microsoft Word upon opening and then displayed in our content control, but if the property isn't saved again, its value isn't really part of the document. This isn't much of an issue in this solution as we expect our sales person would still be working on the file as the résumés are coming in, but we wanted to make sure you clearly got the action that was being performed here.

The next portion of the ProcessFile method is going to tackle finding those content controls we placed under the Résumés heading so that we can create the correct tasks. The fact that we have saved this document using the Open XML file format allows us to perform this action without having to have Microsoft Word on the server. As explained in Chapter 4, the Microsoft Office desktop tools have switched from proprietary binary-formatted files to formats based on Open XML specifications. Now each file—whether it be a spreadsheet, presentation, or document—is really a package of parts and items. Parts are pieces of content for the file, whereas items are metadata describing how the parts should be assembled and rendered. Most of these pieces are XML files, making it possible for them to be manipulated through code. You can gain insight into the structure of an Open XML–based file by replacing its file extension with .zip, since the file is really an ordinary Zip archive. Figure 4-13 shows the root of the archive for a test proposal document.

| Name | Type |
| --- | --- |
| rels | File Folder |
| customXml | File Folder |
| docProps | File Folder |
| word | File Folder |
| [Content_Types].xml | XML Document |

*Figure 4-13. Examining the archive of a Word document*

The XML file in the root is named [Content_Types].xml and it stores content-type directives for all the parts that appear in the archive. A content type contains metadata about a particular part or groups of parts and, more importantly, contains a directive about how the application should render that part. For example, Listing 4-15 shows just a few lines from the file, but clearly delineates how the file tells the rendering application which parts are styles, relationships, settings, and even the main document.

*Listing 4-15. The Document's Content Types*

```
<Default Extension="rels" ContentType="application/vnd.openxmlformats-↵
    package.relationships+xml"/>
<Default Extension="xml" ContentType="application/xml"/>
<Override PartName="/word/document.xml" ContentType="application/vnd.↵
    openxmlformats-officedocument.wordprocessingml.document.main+xml"/>
<Override PartName="/word/settings.xml" ContentType="application/vnd.↵
    openxmlformats-officedocument.wordprocessingml.settings+xml"/>
<Override PartName="/word/styles.xml" ContentType="application/vnd.↵
    openxmlformats-officedocument.wordprocessingml.styles+xml"/>
```

Pay particular attention to the Override element for the part named /word/document.xml. This file contains the document's contents, and by inspecting it we can see the impact of tagging the document with the custom schema elements. Figure 4-14 shows the document.xml file in Visual Studio. We have collapsed a few of the XML nodes to focus in on one of the résumé request controls.

```
    <w:t>Résumés</w:t>
  </w:r>
</w:p>
<w:sdt>
  <w:sdtPr>
    <w:alias w:val="Resume Request"/>
    <w:tag w:val="f0116752-a5c8-4936-8556-44d08a231e31"/>
    <w:id w:val="1732124448"/>
    <w:placeholder>
      <w:docPart w:val="95AE5564C16E4459A363747CDE5F3560"/>
    </w:placeholder>
    <w:showingPlcHdr/>
  </w:sdtPr>
  <w:sdtContent>
    <w:p w14:paraId="3BF2D2DC" w14:textId="77777777" w:rsidR="00074F9C" w:rs
      <w:r w:rsidRPr="00E365EA">
        <w:rPr>
          <w:rStyle w:val="PlaceholderText"/>
        </w:rPr>
        <w:t>Resume request for NORTHAMERICA\edhild due by 4/21/2010</w:t>
      </w:r>
    </w:p>
  </w:sdtContent>
</w:sdt>
```

*Figure 4-14. An Open XML Look at the Resume Request Content Control*

Notice that the entire portion of the control we are interested in is wrapped with an sdt (structured document tag) element, which is how the text content control is persisted in XML. There are a series of properties (sdtPr), which includes our name of the control (alias) as well as our tag. Later on, the actual content of the control is specified; this includes a paragraph containing our formatted text indicating whose résumé we want and the due date.

Now the good news is that if all this XML is making your eyes glaze over, help is on the way. Remember that the Open XML Format SDK we installed earlier is going to provide an object model that moves us up a layer from manipulating this XML directly. In addition, we will get LINQ support to make finding these nodes in the document relatively painless.

Moving back to the ProcessFile method, the code in Listing 4-16 opens the proposal document as a stream and uses the Open XML classes to declare a Word-processing document, letting us find the main document part. By using the alias property in the XML, we use a LINQ query to generate the list of résumé request controls. This LINQ query is looking for SdtBlocks within the document that have an alias property with the value of "Resume Request".

*Listing 4-16. Finding the Resume Requests in the Proposal*

```
using (Stream stream = file.OpenBinaryStream())
{
  using (WordprocessingDocument wpDoc = WordprocessingDocument.Open(stream, true))
  {
    MainDocumentPart docPart = wpDoc.MainDocumentPart;
    DocumentFormat.OpenXml.Wordprocessing.Document doc = docPart.Document;
```

```
//find all resume requests
string alias = "Resume Request";
List<SdtBlock> requests = new List<SdtBlock>();
requests = (from w in doc.Descendants<SdtBlock>()
            where w.Descendants<SdtAlias>().FirstOrDefault() != null &&
            w.Descendants<SdtAlias>().FirstOrDefault().Val.Value == alias
            select w).ToList();
```

Once we have the list of controls, we then want to enumerate through them. For each one, we need to retrieve the GUID that was the unique identifier we put in the tag property of the control. We will use this as a RequestID for the tasks so we can tell if we already created a corresponding task in the résumé tasks list. The code in Listing 4-17 retrieves the tag property, then uses the SPMetal-generated ProposalEntitiesDataContext to look for any list items in the task list that may have that RequestID.

*Listing 4-17. Looking to See if a Resume Task Already Exists*

```
foreach (SdtBlock request in requests)
{
 //get the tag for this request
 string tag = request.GetFirstChild<SdtProperties>().GetFirstChild<Tag>().Val.Value;

//is there a task list item with that GUID as a RequestID field
using (ProposalEntitiesDataContext dc = new ProposalEntitiesDataContext(web.Url))
{
  var resumeTasks = dc.GetList<Item>("ResumeTasks").Cast<ResumeTasksTask>();
  var foundTasks = from task in resumeTasks
                   where task.RequestID == tag
                   select task;
  if (foundTasks == null || foundTasks.Count<ResumeTasksTask>() == 0)
  {
```

If we don't find a task with the corresponding RequestID, then this is the first time we are seeing it in the proposal document and a task should be created. The code in Listing 4-18 creates a new task item, sets its properties, and persists it back to the ResumeTasks list. We perform some string manipulation to parse the text of the control in order to set the task properties appropriately. Notice that to resolve the user accounts, we simply look at the AllUsers collection of the web. This means that the users must have visited the site or been explicitly granted permission in order for this code to work. There are several different ways to try to resolve user accounts. Chapter 11 provides alternatives if you are interested.

*Listing 4-18. Creating a Resume Task*

```
SPList resumeTaskList = web.Lists["ResumeTasks"];
SPListItem newTask = resumeTaskList.Items.Add();
newTask["Title"] = "Your resume is requested";
newTask["Body"] = "Please attach your latest resume for inclusion in a proposal";
//parse current content for assigned person and date
string instruction = request.GetFirstChild<SdtContentBlock>().↩
  GetFirstChild<Paragraph>().GetFirstChild<Run>().GetFirstChild<Text>().Text;
// Resume request for sample\administrator due by 12/12/2009
string account = instruction.Substring(19, instruction.IndexOf(" ", 19) - 19);
string dateDue = instruction.Substring(instruction.LastIndexOf(" ") + 1,
  instruction.Length - instruction.LastIndexOf(" ") - 1);
```

```
SPUser person = web.AllUsers[account];
newTask["AssignedTo"] = person;
newTask["DueDate"] = dateDue;
newTask["ProposalID"] = file.Properties["_dlc_DocId"].ToString();
newTask["RequestID"] = tag;
//save the task
newTask.Update();
}
}
}
```

You have completed enough now to go ahead and deploy the ProposalEvents project. You can just right-click on the project and choose Deploy. Or, just running the project will deploy the feature to your site, activate it, and attach the debugger. Remember that your code will run for a brief period after a proposal has been successfully saved to the site. Be sure to check for résumé tasks as well as the setting of the ProposalID. Figure 4-15 shows the ResumeTasks list for the two requests we made in a test run.

| | | | | | | | |
|---|---|---|---|---|---|---|---|
| ▯ | Your resume is requested ⊙ NEW | Ed Hild | Completed | (2) Normal | 1/5/2010 | 100 % | WSYWUWA3HUJ7-3-3 | 6aa9494d-46e4-4735-b454-ccb99tb412a1 |
| ▯ | Your resume is requested ⊙ NEW | Chad Wach | Completed | (2) Normal | 1/6/2010 | 100 % | WSYWUWA3HUJ7-3-3 | fd361e5a-e5f2-453e-aff5-703feb8b38e2 |

*Figure 4-15. Generated Resume Tasks*

## The Résumé Tasks Event Handler

Using what you learned in the previous section. Add an additional SharePoint 2010 event receiver to the ProposalEvents project named **ProposalTaskReceiver**. You can do this through the add new item option of the project. This event handler will be tied to the ItemUpdated event of task lists in the site. We only need the updated event this time since our earlier code is responsible for adding the task. We now need to respond when the user completes the task and attaches a résumé in the form of an Open XML-based Word document. Since much of code is concerned with checking to make sure the task is related to a proposal, the task is complete, and there is indeed a Word attachment, we won't include every line of code here. Again, please download the accompanying code for this chapter so you can follow along.

The code in Listing 4-19 starts the heavy lifting by retrieving the attached résumé as a stream and then uses the ProposalID field to query the Proposals library for the corresponding proposal document.

*Listing 4-19. Retrieve the Attachment and Find the Proposal Document*

```
//retrieve attachment
string resumeAttachment = String.Empty;
resumeAttachment = properties.ListItem.Attachments.UrlPrefix +
                   properties.ListItem.Attachments[0];
SPFile resumeFile = properties.Web.GetFile(resumeAttachment);
//make sure it is a word document
if (resumeAttachment.EndsWith(".docx"))
{
  //get the proposal document
  SPFile proposalFile = null;
  using (ProposalEntitiesDataContext dc = new ProposalEntitiesDataContext(↵
    properties.WebUrl))
```

```
{
    Microsoft.SharePoint.Linq.EntityList<ProposalsDocument> proposals =
        dc.GetList<ProposalsDocument>("Proposals");
    var found = from doc in proposals.ToList()
                where doc.DocumentIDValue ==
                    properties.ListItem["ProposalID"].ToString()
                select doc.Name;
    string name = found.First<String>();
    proposalFile = properties.Web.Folders["Proposals"].Files[name];
}
```

Next, the method opens the proposal document as a stream and uses the Open XML Format SDK classes to access the main document part. The LINQ query shown in Listing 4-20 is then used to find the résumé request using the alias and the tag property, which needs to match the RequestID field of the task.

*Listing 4-20. Finding the Corresponding Resume Request Control in the Proposal*

```
//find the resume request
string alias = "Resume Request";
List<SdtBlock> requests = new List<SdtBlock>();
requests = (from w in doc.Descendants<SdtBlock>()
            where w.Descendants<SdtAlias>().FirstOrDefault() != null &&
            w.Descendants<SdtAlias>().FirstOrDefault().Val.Value == alias &&
            w.Descendants<Tag>().FirstOrDefault() != null &&
            w.Descendants<Tag>().FirstOrDefault().Val.Value ==
                properties.ListItem["RequestID"].ToString()
            select w).ToList();
```

Once we have found the correct location for the résumé, we prepare for the insertion by creating an AltChunk. An AltChunk in Word is a way of inserting additional content without having the merge all the XML yourself. This is even more time-saving when you consider that the posted résumé might contain embedded object like images, smart art, and so forth that would only be referred to using relationships in the document part's XML. AltChunks do all the hard work for you. As you can see in Listing 4-21, we create a new AltChunk with a unique name, feed it the résumé using the résumé's stream, and then remove the request content control we had as a placeholder. This is the line of code that calls the Remove method. Since the résumé has been provided, there is no need to keep the placeholder around that told us of the request. The last two lines simply commit the changes we have made back to the stream of the proposal document.

*Listing 4-21. Inserting the Résumé into the Proposal*

```
//build the addition
string chunkId = String.Format("AltChunkId{0}", properties.ListItemId.ToString());
AlternativeFormatImportPart chunk = docPart.AddAlternativeFormatImportPart↵
    (AlternativeFormatImportPartType.WordprocessingML, chunkId);
chunk.FeedData(resumeFile.OpenBinaryStream());
AltChunk altChunk = new AltChunk();
altChunk.Id = chunkId;
SdtBlock newBlock = new SdtBlock();
newBlock.AppendChild(altChunk);
requests[0].InsertBeforeSelf(newBlock);
```

```
//remove the request content control
requests[0].Remove();
//save the result
doc.Save();
wpDoc.Close();
```

Finally, we need to save the modified stream back to document in the proposals library. There is a bit of an issue in that the document could be locked while we are trying to make this change. The possibilities are: no lock at all, a shared lock, or an exclusive lock. An exclusive lock is placed on the file if a user has explicitly checked it out. A shared lock occurs if, say, the sales person still has the proposal open in Microsoft Word, but hasn't checked out the file. The reason for the shared lock is that Microsoft Word actually supports co-authoring. This is new functionality to the 2010 stack that allows multiple users to work on a Word document at the same time and, as they save back to the library, they pick up each other's changes. In this scenario, co-authoring is not really happening with another user, but rather with our code running on the server. It is worth pointing out that in a production system, you should probably code this portion as a workflow so you can set a timer and retry if there is an exclusive lock. This chapter is complex enough already, though, so let's go with the assumption that are sales people are trained not to check out proposals exclusively. (See Listing 4-22.) Redeploy the ProposalEvents project. Figure 4-16 shows a résumé merged back into the proposal.

*Listing 4-22. Saving the Changed Proposal Document*

```
if (proposalFile.LockType != SPFile.SPLockType.Exclusive)
{
  proposalFile.CreateSharedAccessRequest();
  proposalFile.SaveBinary(stream);
  proposalFile.RemoveSharedAccessRequest();
}
```

Contoso Proposal #WSYWUWA3HUJ7-5-1

Lorem ipsum dolor sit amet, consecteturadipiscing elit. Donec ut ligua id mauris luctus cursus.
Vestibulum imperdiet malesuada viverra. In hac habitasse platea dictumst. In sed lectus vitae eros
venenatis sodales. Maecenas lacus orci, sodales et molestie nec, rhoncus a eros. Vivamus augue magna,
gravida a sodales non, faucibus quis neque. Morbi tristique nibh non metus hendrerit facilisis. Aliquam
gravida vestibulum lectus vitae elementum. Mauris condimentum elementum sodales. Ut ac nunc nec
lacus sagittis consectetur. Cras vitae nulla non mauris cursus egestas non quis lorem. Sed tempor
ultricies urna, ut bibendum tortor tincidunt nec.

### Résumés

**Ed Hild** is a Technology Architect at the Microsoft Technology
Center in Reston, VA specializing in Portal and Collaboration
solutions. At the MTC, he meets daily with both commercial- and
public-sector customers to discuss business requirements and map
them to the Microsoft platform. He helps customers understand
product features, best practices, and necessary customizations for
them to realize SharePoint's full potential. Ed has previously
presented at Microsoft Dev Days, Tech Ed, and Microsoft SharePoint
Conference events as well as many local area user groups. He
published an advanced SharePoint developer book through Apress
entitled: Pro SharePoint Solution Development and was included in
the MSPress Microsoft Office SharePoint Server 2007 Best Practices
book. Ed's previous experiences include a high school teacher,
government contractor, Microsoft Certified Trainer and lead
developer at a Microsoft partner.

*Figure 4-16. The Merged Proposal Document*

# Incorporating Word Automation Services

Since our scenario involves sending this constructed proposal to a customer, we have to address the fact
that it isn't appropriate to send the Word document because of its relationship to the VSTO solution.
Even if we could strip away the assembly, it is not a given that the destination customer has the ability to
read our Open XML-formatted file. Though it's possible to detach a VSTO customization
(http://msdn.microsoft.com/en-us/library/bb442099(VS.100).aspx), it requires some more code and
only solves half of the problem. Instead, we are going to use this opportunity to build a SharePoint
workflow that leverages the new SharePoint 2010 Word Automation Services to create a PDF version of
the document. Word Automation Services is server-side functionality that solves a key problem for
enterprises related to doing bulk format conversions of files. Basically think of the ability to perform Save
As operations on Word documents to other formats. This SharePoint Service is able to do this on sets of
files, and to do it as a background process so it will not have a significant impact on the server. This is, of
course, without having the Microsoft Word desktop application installed. We do need to write some
code, however, to schedule our proposal document for conversion, and in this solution we have decided
to encapsulate this functionality in a workflow. The choice of a workflow is a bit arbitrary, but looking at

the big picture, this conversion would likely be the last step of a human-oriented approval process. We will add this workflow project to the solution that contained our other projects earlier. So right-click on the solution and choose to add a new project. Under the C# language node, select SharePoint and then 2010 to display the SharePoint 2010 project templates. From the list of Visual Studio installed templates, select the Sequential Workflow template. Name the project **PublishToPDF**. Your New Project dialog should look like Figure 4-17.

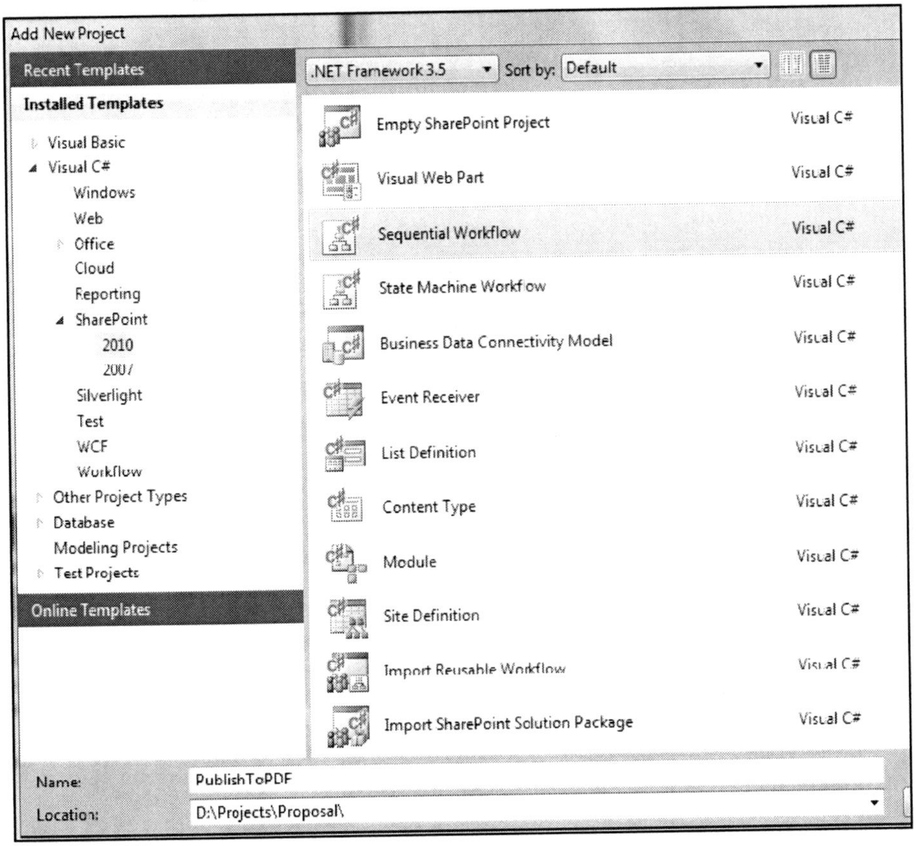

*Figure 4-17. Creating the PublishToPDF workflow project*

Clicking OK will start the SharePoint Customization Wizard. Specify the SharePoint site we have been working with (such as http://edhild3/sites/sales) and select a farm-level solution. Name the workflow **PublishToPDF** and, since this workflow will be operating on our proposal documents, select a List Workflow. The next screen configures the association of the workflow with the library. Be sure in the first drop-down to choose **Proposals**. The defaults for the other settings are fine. Since we are focused on building the solution in a development environment, on the next dialog, choose to allow the workflow only to be manually started. Click **Finish** and Visual Studio will add the project to the solution.

Once the new project is created, the solution will already have a few files by default. The Workflow1 node will be the focus of most of our attention. Workflows in Visual Studio are really a function of Windows Workflow Foundation and are presented in Visual Studio with a flow-chart type of design experience. There are entire books on Windows Workflow Foundation and, in fact, SharePoint-specific workflows so we will only provide enough information to complete the necessary tasks here. Chapter 11 has a larger focus on workflows and goes into much more detail.

Before jumping into the actual code that communicates with Word Automation Services, let's get a few other things out of the way. There are a few assemblies we need to add references to:

- **Microsoft.Office.Word.Server**: This assembly gives us access Word Automation Services functionality. By default, it is located at C:\Program Files\Common Files\Microsoft Shared\Web Server Extensions\14\ISAPI. You may receive a warning about a version of the .NET Framework and the System.Web.DataVisualization. Just continue adding the reference; we will take care of that warning with the next few references.

- **System.Web**: This assembly is part of the .NET Framework and should show up in the .NET tab of the references dialog. Be sure to choose the version from the 2.0 framework. The runtime version should be version 2.0.50424.

- **System.Web.DataVisualization**: Be careful adding this reference as we do not need the version of this assembly that ships as part of version 4.0 of the .NET Framework. Instead, we need to look for the one tied to version 3.5. It may be listed in your .NET Add Reference tab. If it is not, the good news is that this was part of the prerequisites for your SharePoint installation as it is required for the Chart controls. You should be able to find this assembly at C:\Program Files (x86)\Microsoft Chart Controls\Assemblies. You only need System.Web.DataVisualization.dll, not the additional Design assembly.

Now that the appropriate references have been added, you can add the using statement for Word Automation Services into the code-behind file of Workflow1. This statement is: using Word = Microsoft.Office.Word.Server;

Figure 4-18 shows the design surface of the workflow you need to build. Basically, there are only two shapes that need to be added. A code activity shape will contain our code for communicating to the Word Automation Services functionality. You can find this shape in the Visual Studio toolbox under the Windows Workflow v3.0 heading. The second shape is SharePoint-specific. It is a LogToHistoryListActivity shape and can be found in the toolbox under the SharePoint Workflow heading. This shape allows us to record entries in the history list of the SharePoint site as a form of audit trail. If you look at the example in the code download, you'll see that this shape has a History Description property that we set to "**Document submitted for conversion**" in order to inform users that their request was received and recorded.

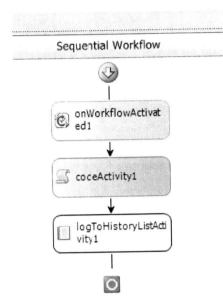

*Figure 4-18. The PublishToPDF Workflow*

Double-clicking on the code activity will create an event handler for the code in Listing 4-23. The code begins by building a URL for the proposal document that we would like converted. A new conversion job object is then configured with a name, user context, and the source and destination file names. You might wonder how the service knows that we want a PDF file. The conversion job can automatically determine the output format by looking at the destination URL, which in our case ends in ".pdf". You can gain finer control over the conversion using a ConversionJobSettings object as described at http://msdn.microsoft.com/en-us/library/microsoft.office.word.server.conversions. conversionjobsettings_properties(office.14).aspx . Lastly, the conversion job is started, which requires us to run as the system account since the current user may not have enough permission to kick it off. Go ahead and deploy your workflow and manually start it on a test proposal.

*Listing 4-23. Code to Schedule Conversion using Word Automation Services*

```
private void codeActivity1_ExecuteCode(object sender, EventArgs e)
{
  string file = workflowProperties.WebUrl + "/" + workflowProperties.ItemUrl;
  //schedule the conversion
  Word.Conversions.ConversionJob conversionJob = new ↩
      Word.Conversions.ConversionJob("Word Automation Services");
  conversionJob.Name = "Proposal Conversion";
  //run under the user that ran the workflow
  conversionJob.UserToken = workflowProperties.OriginatorUser.UserToken;
  conversionJob.AddFile(file, file.Replace(".docx", ".pdf"));
  SPSecurity.RunWithElevatedPrivileges(delegate { conversionJob.Start(); });
}
```

It is important to realize that when this workflow completes, all we have done is successfully scheduled a task that informs Word Automation Services that it has work to do. In fact, you can go ahead and deploy the project and run the workflow on a proposal document. Don't be surprised that the workflow will report a completed status without a new PDF file showing up in your document library. This is because Word Automation Services runs on a schedule (default every 15 minutes) and won't create that PDF until its next execution time. This feature is to help keep this functionality from overwhelming server resources; however, it really impacts demonstrations. The good news is that you can manually tell this timer job to run. Use the following steps to make the job run on demand and you should get your PDF file. You could also do this via code or Windows PowerShell commands. Of course make sure you have Adobe Acrobat Reader installed if you want to open it.

1. Open SharePoint 2010's Central Administration.

2. Under the Monitoring heading, click **Check job status**.

3. Click Job **Definitions** in the left-hand navigation.

4. Locate the Word Automation Services Timer Job which may require you to page through the listing of jobs since they are in alphabetical order. Click the name of the timer job.

5. Click the **Run Now** button to force this service to process your conversion request.

6. You should be able to see this job execute by looking at either the Running Jobs or Job History portions of this administration tool. When it is complete, you should have the PDF file shown in Figure 4-19.

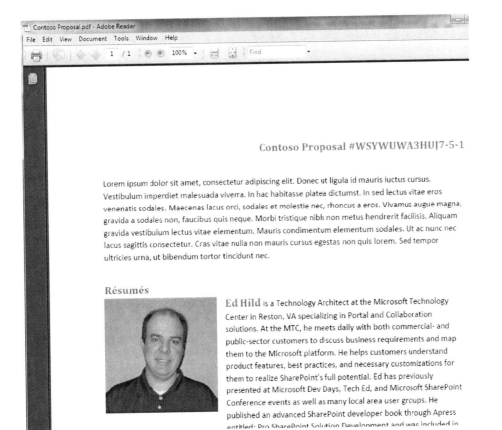

*Figure 4-19. PDF version of the proposal*

# Important Lessons

This proposal document-assembly solution incorporated several key techniques that are worth highlighting as they can easily be reused in other projects.

**Content controls in the body of a document:** Content controls are a Microsoft Word feature that allow you to promote data into the body of the document. In this case, we used quick parts, which are already configured content controls for metadata properties of the document.

**VSTO document-level project:** In this solution we extended the document library's Microsoft Word template file with custom functionality that turned the document into a tool for building proposals. Since our extensions only make sense for the specific template, we created the solution as a document-level project. The extensions included a document actions pane as well as new backstage functionality.

**Event handlers that process the document using Open XML:** In this solution, we needed to parse the document on the server to look for résumé request controls whenever the document was saved or modified. SharePoint event handlers enabled us to respond to these events, and the Open XML SDK eased the task of querying through the XML of the file.

**SPMetal:** This solution used the SPMetal tool to construct entity classes for working with SharePoint site data. By using these classes, we were able to make LINQ-style queries on SharePoint lists and refer to fields of list items with IntelliSense. This resulted in fewer lines of code that were less error-prone.

**Merging document chunks into a central document:** This solution needed to be able to take résumés and inject them into the proposal document. This work had to be done on the server. We were able to use the AltChunks technique to streamline the necessary Open XML notation to perform the merge.

**Scheduling document conversions with Word Automation Services:** SharePoint 2010 has a new service that can perform scheduled conversions of Microsoft Word documents. In this solution we used a workflow as the scheduling mechanism.

## Extension Points

While coding this example, we thought of several variations to the solution that we didn't incorporate. Mostly, these were not included because they distracted from the overall objective of the solution. We call them out now as extension points since they may be applicable to a specific project you are working on.

**Convert the résumé task event handler into the workflow:** In our example, we just created another event handler for merging the résumé into the proposal document since we had just taken a large part of the chapter to teach you the details of event handlers. The only issue is that the proposal document could potentially be exclusively locked by a user. You would need a way of waiting and retrying to get a successful shared lock. Changing this part of the solution into a workflow would be a way to accomplish this.

**Make the people-search web service call asynchronous:** Currently, the actions pane only uses a wait cursor as the method to inform the user that work is being performed. Also, all of the work is being performed on the same thread. A better approach would be to use the async version of the web service call and specify a delegate that should be called when the call is complete.

**Incorporate BCS quick parts from an external list:** You may well have some sort of CRM database whose data would be part of this proposal. You can use the business connectivity services functionality of SharePoint to register this repository and create an external list in the SharePoint site. By adding external data columns as metadata properties of the Proposals library, you would gain quick parts for embedding the external customer data into the document. Chapter 10 contains a good starting point for building this extension.

## Further Reading

Here are a number of links to resources we think you'll find useful:

- How to Query Search using the Web Service http://www.dotnetmafia.com/blogs/dotnettipoftheday/archive/2008/04/14/how-to-query-search-using-the-web-service.aspx

- Using SharePoint Web Services http://www.obacentral.com/en/Learn/Recommended%20Reading/Using%20SharePoint%20Web%20Services.pdf

- Adding References for Word Automation Services http://msdn.microsoft.com/en-us/library/ee559644(office.14).aspx

- VSTO Deployment via SharePoint http://www.craigbailey.net/vsto-deployment-via-sharepoint/

- Word Automation Services http://msdn.microsoft.com/en-us/library/ee558248(office.14).aspx

- Brian Jones: Open XML Formats Blog http://blogs.msdn.com/brian_jones/

- Intro to Word XML http://blogs.msdn.com/brian_jones/archive/2005/04/05/435442.aspx

- SPMetal http://msdn.microsoft.com/en-us/library/ee538255(office.14).aspx

- OpenXMLDeveloper.org http://openxmldeveloper.org/

- Introduction to the Office 2010 Backstage View for Developers http://msdn.microsoft.com/en-us/library/ee691833(office.14).aspx

- Customizing the Office 2010 Backstage View for Developers http://msdn.microsoft.com/en-us/library/ee815851(office.14).aspx

- How to Use altChunk for Document Assembly http://blogs.msdn.com/ericwhite/archive/2008/10/24/how-to-use-altchunk-for-document-assembly.asp

# CHAPTER 5

# Practical Document Management with SharePoint 2010

SharePoint has grown to be unanimously acclaimed as the best collaboration platform on the planet. The latest iteration from Microsoft, SharePoint 2010, has seen the fastest adoption rate of any version due to the rich feature set and agile ribbon-based user interface (UI).

SharePoint is a platform that helps move from personal productivity (using the ubiquitous Microsoft Office suite) to organizational productivity. It can seamlessly slide into an organization of any size and become the central window to all common ways of sharing information, be it documents, tasks, images, or videos.

I am repeatedly inclined to call SharePoint a platform, implying that developers and development companies have a huge opportunity (and, in fact, a responsibility) to provide a complete solution to the customer by building and enhancing the features the platform offers. Only then can the technology itself be fully appreciated and consumed.

That is where the challenge really starts looming in front of development companies. Instead of claiming extreme superiority regarding the technology itself, they should think from a customer's standpoint about what solutions would really address their needs, their industry's needs, and help them stay competitive. Some companies have been reasonably successful in creating solutions that have this depth and also a *verticalized* story to share with a customer in a particular industry.

SharePoint's rich feature set across multiple areas (collaboration, portal, content management, search, eForms, workflows, and Business Intelligence) is really its advantage as well as its disadvantage. If a solution is not built around any of these facets, it really becomes very hard for a customer to be convinced to choose SharePoint over anything else.

The solutions could include intranet, extranet, Internet portals, document management systems, content management systems, business process automation solutions, project management solutions, search solutions, and business intelligence solutions. SharePoint can be used to design and develop multiple types of solutions, as shown in Table 5-1.

**Table 5-1.** *Types of SharePoint Solutions*

| | |
|---|---|
| ECM (Enterprise Content Management) | ECM solutions help organizations archive content of many formats and types, such as documents, records, and multimedia content. |
| Document Management (DM) | DM capabilities are usually a subset of ECM solutions where the focus is primarily on document storage, information management policies, permissions, scanning, OCRing, plus search and archival features. |
| Records Management (RM) | RM solutions help organizations to store content that will not be modified anymore. Information management policies can be applied to convert documents to records. |
| Web Content Management (WCM) | WCM is the ability of SharePoint to create portals with dynamic content managed by users themselves instead of requiring web developers. Implementing bilingual portals has been made tremendously easier with SharePoint 2010. |

DM solutions face the stiffest competition of the group because every organization around the globe wants to go paperless; they are all hunting for the most suitable solution that will understand exactly what they do and help them move from heaps of papers lying around to a sleek and efficient electronic way of managing their documents.

This chapter aims to bring to light some of the practical challenges that one would face in positioning, developing, and deploying DM solutions built on Microsoft SharePoint 2010. I want to bring together all that I have learned from being involved in a number of SharePoint implementations centered around DM for customers worldwide. For a SharePoint professional, I have tried to go into as much detail as possible; for a SharePoint implementation company, the end-to-end coverage and comprehensiveness is something that you might favor.

The chapter assumes reasonable knowledge of SharePoint 2007 or 2010, though the uninitiated may find some of these sections compelling enough to join the club.

# Why Use SharePoint for Document Management?

Before you start to appreciate why SharePoint could be a good foundation to build a DM system on, you must first understand what document management is and why there's such a buzz around it.

Document management is more precisely *electronic document management* and it is a solution to help companies store, archive, and locate (search for) documents that they receive or create. Though the volume, type, and source of documents vary, companies in every industry—be it manufacturing, oil and gas, construction, automotive, consulting, high tech, IT, or consumer goods—all need an efficient way to store their electronic documents.

Companies have moved from allowing users to store documents on their local disks to shared folders, but shared folders are little more than shared storage—they don't tie into your business structure or processes. The next evolutionary step is to choose a system that is not just a dump yard for documents but one that has the required intelligence to integrate with your business and business applications—and even external organizations such as vendors and customers (see Figure 5-1).

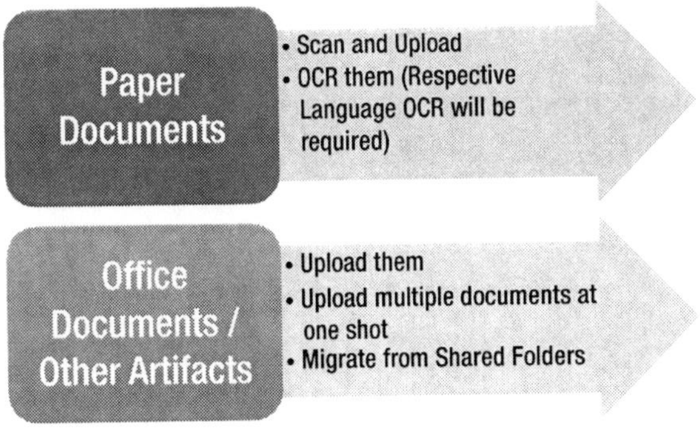

**Paper Documents**
• Scan and Upload
• OCR them (Respective Language OCR will be required)

**Office Documents / Other Artifacts**
• Upload them
• Upload multiple documents at one shot
• Migrate from Shared Folders

*Figure 5-1. Documents source for the DMS*

The following questions arise when it comes to looking for a DMS solution:

- What's the face of the DMS? Can it have an interface through my existing systems?

- Will it be web-based?

- What protocols should/can it use—HTTP, FTP, WebDAV?

- Can it store paper documents by way of integrating with my scanning systems?

- Will I be able to search scanned documents by content?

- Can the security tie into my existing security infrastructure (Active Directory, for example)?

- Will it allow me to attach tags or attributes to the documents, thus making them searchable?

- Will it let me annotate the documents that I upload?

- Will I be able to share comments and thoughts on a document?

- Can I have pre-designed templates attached to certain types of documents?

- Can it scale as my organization and its needs grow?

- Does it tie into my business process?

- Can it integrate with my line of business applications (LOBs) like my ERP or CRM?

- As an IT decision maker, can it tie in/use my existing resources and align itself with my virtualization strategy?

And so on. Happily, for most of us, SharePoint does indeed have the features to cater to most, if not all, of these requests. Compliance to a customer's every requirement comes via a combination of out-of-the-box features (OOB) and configuration/customization. For answers to the specific questions mentioned previously, see Table 5-2.

*Table 5-2. Questions and Answers*

| | |
|---|---|
| 1. What's the face of the DMS? Can it have an interface through my existing systems? | A SharePoint-based portal can be built and the DMS system can be exposed through it. |
| 2. Will it be web-based? | SharePoint is web-based. |
| 3. Can it store paper documents by way of integrating with my scanning systems? | This is tricky and not available OOB. Happily, every scanning company has an integration option where scanned documents can be sent as PDFs straight into SharePoint document libraries. Companies like Websio and KnowledgeLake also have scanner add-ons that integrate with the SharePoint document library interface itself. |
| 4. Will I be able to search scanned documents by content? | OCR solutions can be integrated with scanner add-ons. Microsoft Office Document Imaging is the component used by most scanner add-on companies for providing OCR capabilities. Of course, languages like Arabic require different OCR Solutions and third party companies do exist, like Sakhr and Novodynamics Verus. |
| 5. Can the security tie into my existing security infrastructure (Active Directory, for example)? | SharePoint has OOB support for this. |
| 6. Will it allow me to attach tags or attributes to the documents, thus making them searchable? | Document libraries can have columns that act as metadata for the documents uploaded. Apart from this, SharePoint 2010 introduces the Enterprise Metadata Management or Central Termstore that offers amazing new possibilities. Enterprise Metadata allows you to define Terms at the SharePoint Farm Level and then make it available across all your Web Applications. For example, you can have a Master Term Set such as Countries and this can be re-used in any library or list across all your Web Applications. |
| 7. Will it let me annotate the documents that I upload? | Again, this is tricky; it could fall under document imaging capability requirements. Though few third party add-ons are available from companies like KnowledgeLake, this capability has not reached a high maturity level. |

| | |
|---|---|
| 8. Will I be able to share comments and thoughts on a document? | Absolutely. With Discussion Forums and SharePoint 2010's new NoteBoard capabilities, this can be very straightforward to implement. |
| 9. Can I have pre-designed templates attached to certain types of documents? | Templates can be attached to content types, so you can create new documents based on these templates. This is very handy if a company wants to have a central store of all its templates (like letterheads, memos, circulars, letters to clients, purchase orders, invoices, etc). |
| 10. Can it scale as my organization and its needs grow? | SharePoint 2010's new Services and Service Applications architecture (bye-bye, Shared Services Provider!) allows you to really scale out and scale up the SharePoint architecture, thus providing more resources to any component that will be utilized more. |
| 11. Does it tie into my business process? | With improved OOB Workflows and *much* improved SharePoint Designer Workflows, any type of workflow can be built. |
| 12. Can it integrate with my line of business applications (LOBs) like my ERP or CRM? | With BCS (Business Catalog Services, the new Business Data Catalog), you can pull data from external sources; you can also have a metadata column's value coming from an external source (External Data Column). Microsoft Dynamics CRM 2011 actually integrates OOB with SharePoint 2010—the best part being the on-demand CRM 2011 integrating with your on-premise SharePoint 2010! |
| 13. As an IT decision maker, can it tie in/use my existing resources and align itself with my virtualization strategy? | With Windows Server 2008 R2 being the OS for SharePoint 2010, Hyper-V is fully embraced, so organizations can use some of the exciting features such as snapshots, virtual machine failovers, etc. |

# Is SharePoint OOB a Complete DM Solution?

If you read the previous section, you understand by now that SharePoint is an excellent platform but is not really a full-fledged DM solution unless it is customized or third party add-ons are implemented. To understand this a little better, let's first define the terminologies; see Table 5-3.

*Table 5-3. Document Management Terminologies*

| | |
|---|---|
| Document Management | Document Management refers to the whole solution. |
| Document Storage | Document Storage is just one part of the solution that just stores the documents that are being created, scanned, or uploaded. |
| Document Archive | Document Archive is interchangeably used with the Document Storage term but I use it to refer to the ability to store documents that have exhausted their use in day-to-day business. |
| Document Imaging | Document Imaging refers to capabilities including but not limited to:<br><br>• Scanning<br><br>• OCRing (Optical Character Recognition)<br><br>• Annotating the scanned documents<br><br>• Indexing the scanned documents |
| Document Routing | Documents, once they are created/uploaded, may have to be routed to their correct destination, be it a single user or a department for further processing. |

Table 5-4 lists the features that are not available OOB. I will show you ways to address this missing functionality later in this chapter.

*Table 5-4. Feature Areas and Functionality Not Available OOB*

| Feature Area | What Is Not Available |
|---|---|
| Scanning | Integrated scanning from within the SharePoint interface itself. |
| OCRing | Scanned documents being subjected to a OCR process whereby scanned documents become searchable by content. |
| Cross-Site Lookup | On document libraries residing in a site, the ability to lookup on a master list what is present in another Site. |
| Field Level Permissions | In a document library or a list, field level restrictions are not possible. |
| Column or List validation | The column or list validation that has been introduced in SharePoint 2010 is very basic; customers have much more sophisticated validation requirements and a need for error messages that clearly depict the issue.<br><br>*SharePoint 2010 Column or List validations also have what I believe to be bugs that throw up the actual .NET exception page along with the validation failed message.* |

| Feature Area | What Is Not Available |
|---|---|
| Automatic reference number generation | Though the new Document ID feature can help achieve this to an extent, customers have different requirements in the way the reference numbers should be formed. |
| InfoPath not being supported for a document library | InfoPath customization on a list is a great feature for customizing how forms should look/behave. The same has not been carried over to document libraries, which are the central unit of document storage in SharePoint. |
| Custom Edit forms where specific controls can be disabled | Custom Edit/New forms for a document library can be created from SharePoint Designer, but it would require customization in order to make certain forms enabled or invisible. |
| Linq with Taxonomy columns | If you have ever used SPMetal.exe to generate the LINQ entity classes for use in your SharePoint projects, you will have noticed that Taxonomy columns are not present. |
| Offline access for pages | SharePoint Workspace 2010 (part of Office Professional Plus 2010) allows users to take their documents offline, modify them, and later synchronize them with the SharePoint document libraries. This, however, doesn't work for pages. It would be nice to have the ability to take pages offline so users can read the content published on their intranet portal, for example, at their leisure. |
| Workflows spanning across sites | Workflows in SharePoint can be implemented in three ways: Out of the Box Workflows attached to document libraries or content types; SharePoint Designer Workflows; and Visual Studio Workflows. The first two are most widely used but they don't have the ability for a workflow to span or access objects across multiple SharePoint sites. |
| Document Information Panel validations preventing save functionality | Document Information Panel (DIP) is used to enter the metadata for a document library from within Microsoft Word. This automatically opens up when a new document is opened from a SharePoint document library. DIP can be customized using InfoPath in SharePoint 2010. In the DIP, though you can make use of the excellent validation rules available in InfoPath, they don't really prevent the document from saving into the library—quite strange! Of course, documents can be uploaded without filling out any columns, but they will fall in Checked-Out mode so that users can edit properties later on and provide information for those columns. |
| Word disallowing saving into other locations | Some customers might want the documents opened from SharePoint to only be allowed to be saved back to SharePoint rather than a local disk. |
| Search | Custom Properties-based search must be customized. There are also issues with respect to the dd/mm/yyyy format, for example. |

| Feature Area | What Is Not Available |
|---|---|
| Usable audit reports | Every company wants to have clear auditing on the additions, modifications, and deletions done on SharePoint content. The auditing, though much improved from the 2007 version, still lacks precision. It's too complex to pull the exact information one is looking for. There are excellent third party tools from companies like Muhimbi. |
| Reporting on SharePoint content | All is not well, when we start storing documents in SharePoint, organizations want reports on how their content is being stored, the reports with quite a few filtering criteria as well. For example, you could have Documents Stored with metadata columns such as Country and / or Category and users may want to search by User, by Country, by Category or a combination of these. SSRS (SQL Server Reporting Services) is quite powerful as a reporting tool, but it lacks reporting data from SharePoint libraries and lists. (SSRS 2008 does have the ability to report on a SharePoint list, but it is quite basic). Custom reporting using Web Parts may be the alternative. With SharePoint Lists / Libraries becoming one of the widely used Data Sources, many third party reporting providers have mushroomed in the recent past with their tools designed to work on data stored in SharePoint. |

# Document Management Needs for Organizations

Document management needs for organizations depend on their size, industry, budget, and IT roadmap. Though these are some common parameters, often times it also depends on how strong/IT savvy the organization's IT Department is; many IT departments are so particular about the core business applications that they don't pay much attention to peripheral applications.

As an organization selling SharePoint-based DM solutions, the first real challenge is to attract/create an impression with the IT department of the importance of such systems, if the need or the requirement has not originated from the company. In fact, the need for a DM system is felt/appreciated more by the business users than IT because IT doesn't have to deal with all of the papers lying around!

The matrix in Table 5-5 might help you understand how the requirements vary based on the size of the organization.

*Table 5-5. Organizational Needs*

| Organization Type | Organizational Challenges | Needs in a DM System |
|---|---|---|
| Small (less than 50 employees) | • Preventing users from storing their files on local disks<br><br>• Categorizing the files and storing them centrally | • User-friendly interface<br><br>• Ease of installation and maintenance<br><br>• Low upfront costs, preferably no license fee or heavy hardware requirements (SharePoint Online!)<br><br>• Ability to access from anywhere |
| Medium (50 to 300 employees) | • Migrate from shared folders on the network to a central storage<br><br>• Ability to have a common categorization across the organization instead of each department having its own way of storing documents<br><br>• Easy access for the top management to the documents from anywhere<br><br>• Migrate from existing DM system like previous versions of SharePoint or Lotus Dominos | • Integration with Microsoft Office<br><br>• Common keywords store<br><br>• Scanner integration<br><br>• Clear audit trail records<br><br>• Reports/statistics of document usage<br><br>• Quick implementation time<br><br>• Training for in-house resources post-implementation<br><br>• Branding in alignment with corporate branding standards and guidelines |

| Organization Type | Organizational Challenges | Needs in a DM System |
|---|---|---|
| Large (300+ employees) | • Document process aligned with the business process<br><br>• In an organization spread across multiple locations, decision on whether the system has to be single-instance or multi-instance with replication configured<br><br>• Scalability<br><br>• Better performance | • Support for hardware load balancing<br><br>• Support for WAN (Wide Area Network) optimizers (utilizing less bandwidth across multiple locations is something they look for and many SharePoint compatible WAN optimizers are available)<br><br>• Integration with their LOB applications<br><br>• Integration with their portal<br><br>• Provide extranet access to their customers and suppliers<br><br>• Workflows to span external entities as well<br><br>• Multilingual |

In terms of industries, the needs of DM systems vary. Table 5-6 shows a matrix summarizing the needs for most common industries for which implementing DM Systems will be a priority.

*Table 5-6. Needs by Industries*

| Industry | Nature | Typical Needs |
|---|---|---|
| Construction, Engineering | Documents by projects, subcontractors, clients | • Store documents coming from subcontractors/clients<br>• Store documents created internally<br>• To have a provision to create a project-based document template so that when the actual documents come in, they are mapped against this plan<br>• Versioning is very critical to know exactly who modified this document in this cycle<br>• Generate reports of documents by project, plus project checklist attachments<br>• Track the time spent creating a document<br>• Scan and store large sized documents up to A0 sizes<br>• Files of MS Office formats plus PDFs, AutoCAD files, etc. |
| Manufacturing and Distribution | Documents by departments, plants, factories, products | • With similar needs to Construction/Engineering, but heavy needs for large document storage |
| Consulting | Documents by projects, engagements, services offered | • Map the documents with their process systems<br>• Strong workflows for collecting feedback, review, and approval |
| IT and IT enabled services | Documents for projects; other documents created by each department | • Integration with Outlook<br>• Project-based document storage<br>• Versioning<br>• Documents created by sales teams and sales personnel<br>• Integration with CRM |
| Government | Documents by department, sections, and users | • Heavy scanning requirements with documents being submitted by individuals and organizations on a daily basis<br>• Integration with the core business applications<br>• Security |

| Industry | Nature | Typical Needs |
|---|---|---|
| Defense | Documents by activities and engagements; Associated documents with secure data such as suspect information | • Secure document storage <br><br> • Secure document transmittal <br><br> • Very clear audit trail and reporting on the actions performed <br><br> • Ability of the system to run/upgrade without Internet access <br><br> • Secure interaction with local user machines and the server <br><br> • Integration with other defense and surveillance systems <br><br> • Sophisticated functionality such as facial recognition on photographs scanned and uploaded <br><br> • Integration with GPS where documents can be associated with any physical location, the same being rendered on a map <br><br> • Documents even when they are taken out to be not accessible by users who are not part of your company's active directory / domain |

Apart from the size and industry of the organization, its IT roadmap also plays an important role in deciding on a DM system. This is where I believe SharePoint fits in like nothing else. SharePoint has this positively uncanny ability of growing upon you as you start using it. You could just start with few document libraries and grow up to multiple web applications and site collections spanning thousands of users (of course, subject to the way your SharePoint farm is sized initially). Microsoft's general recommendation of a Content Database size's upper limit has been 200 GB. With SharePoint 2010 Service Pack 1, this limit has been increased to 4 TB, which most times is really ample for an organization of any size.Planning multiple site collections and multiple content databases is a very important design activity for organizations with huge content storage needs.

# A DM Project: Selling to Implementation to Support

We all think about how to execute/deliver a project, but we first need a project to start planning to deliver! As mentioned previously, SharePoint by itself has significant gaps as a DM solution.

If you are from .NET/custom development background, there is a fundamental difference that needs to be understood. In a .NET project, every requirement from the customer is new and needs to be developed from scratch. But in a SharePoint project, the thinking is more along the lines of let's see what's available out of the box and then decide what needs to be customized.

Here's an example to understand the difference: say a customer asks for a place to upload documents with one attribute being a selection of countries. In .NET, you end up creating a table, a UI for the upload process, and classes to do the uploading. The whole exercise might take 30 days to develop. In SharePoint, it would take about 3 minutes!

Now the customer requires that whenever a document is uploaded, a corresponding meeting event is created in a calendar. This will require customization in both .NRT and SharePoint; *though in SharePoint, a no-code solution for this exists using a simple SharePoint Designer workflow.*

# Selling

The pre-sales stage boils down to the following activities:

- Making the right proposal.

- Preparing a customized demonstration of the abilities.

I don't want this to sound like guidance for aspiring sales and marketing professionals, but the proposal for a SharePoint-based DM system can be successfully received only if it is NOT positioned against any other system the customer might be evaluating.

The proposal is going to succeed if it talks about SharePoint as a comprehensive collaboration platform that can grow as needs grow. At the same time, the proposal also needs to talk about how the solution will be built specifically for their industry. This will require research into the industry and interviews with users; it may also require some research on alternative solutions in the marketplace.

The proposal's technology solution ideally should contain the following sections, apart from your company profile and executive summary:

- A custom industry requirements matrix and how your solution is compliant

- A list of DM features you are providing

- The particular SharePoint edition that you recommend (the choice of SharePoint edition is very important)

- The topology being recommended

- Hardware and software requirements

- Phases of implementation

- What is clearly not in scope

- Any integration with external applications

- The migration strategy, if applicable

- Man-hour estimates and calendar duration

- Project team matrix

- Types of training that will be offered

Once the proposal is accepted, you might be required to make a demonstration of your solution; this is where you may have to install certain third party solutions for the demonstration. Simple things like changing the logo and doing a bit of branding will certainly create an excellent impression on the customer. The full functionality obviously may not be present, but it doesn't matter. Make sure the demo looks attractive.

It's also important to set the expectations with the customer. Any ambiguities in the proposal or the requirements should be clarified at this point in time. Lingering open issues could lead to big problems during the implementation.

# SharePoint Project Team

It is very important to assemble the right team as you move towards implementation. The team ideally should comprise the people shown in Figure 5-2 and discussed in Table 5-7.

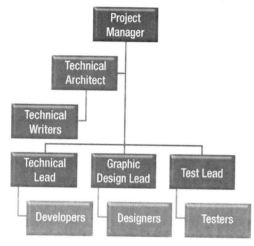

*Figure 5-2. The project team*

*Table 5-7. Implementation Team*

| | |
| --- | --- |
| Project Manager | Every project has one. In case of a smaller team, the Project Manager might also be the Key Technical Architect as well. The key roles and responsibilities are to ensure that the project stays on track and within the given timeline. |
| | Some of the SharePoint projects could be of lower value, thus ensuring there is no extra usage of the resources, which will add to the cost. |
| SharePoint Architect | The key person responsible for planning all technical aspects of the project. This person also has to be very mindful of the project resources, timelines, and expectations set with the client. |
| | The person can double as a Business Analyst on a small project team. |

| | |
|---|---|
| SharePoint Business Analyst | Business Analyst on a SharePoint project varies significantly from a typical business analyst for a custom development project. When a BA interacts with the business users when collecting requirements, he must know the SharePoint OOB functionality well. He should be able to map the customer requirements to what is available OOB and propose new functionality. For instance, customer might want a place to store his meetings and minutes. The BA should be able to immediately map this to the Calendar list events with Attachments functionality. On top of this, he should also propose the possibility of creating a Meeting Workspace for each meeting to store meeting agendas, objectives, attendees, documents, etc. Moreover, the customer wants the ability to send out a meeting request whenever a new meeting is created. This is where the developer folks come into picture. |
| | As you can see, there is OOB capability and there are value-add functions where you can raise the bar with customization. That's really the power of SharePoint! Tools such as Balsamiq and the much-improved Visio 2010 can help the BA demonstrate the functionality required in terms of mockups and static prototypes. |
| Technical Lead | The Technical Lead typically has multiple years of experience in implementing SharePoint projects and leading teams in the process. It should be a person who understands the requirements and can adopt the best approach in carving out a solution. This person has to work closely with the Technical Architect. |
| SharePoint Administrator | Setting up the SharePoint development environment is something that a company has to do immediately upon starting a project. In the past, SharePoint 2007 was a big issue as every developer required a separate instance of Windows Server OS, either installed directly on their machines or in a separate virtual environment dedicated for each developer. |
| | With Windows 7 (remember, this works only with Professional, Enterprise or Ultimate Editions) Support for SharePoint 2010, you can continue to work on the client environment and have SharePoint 2010 and Visual Studio 2010 installed on the same machine. There must also be a common development server where the customizations can be deployed periodically. Source control and configuration management are also very important aspects in a multi-developer environment. Team Foundation Server 2010 can be set up along with Visual Studio 2010. |
| | This is all the responsibility of the Administrator. |
| | Setting up the production environment is something that the Administrator will have to do as well. I will talk about the production environment setup in later in this chapter. |

| | |
|---|---|
| Designer | A SharePoint Designer is one of the toughest species to find: someone who comes with a great graphic design ability, HTML conversion skills, and the ability to create SharePoint master pages/page layouts. You may have multiple people doing all of the above, but if you want to be a serious SharePoint contender in the marketplace, having a good SharePoint designer can make the difference. |
| | As companies grow bigger, images, branding, colors, and fonts become as important as the functionality itself *(Sometimes even more! I have worked with customers who have spent hours creating a few images and adjusting few pixels—and just have couple of document libraries!)* |
| Developer | There used to be a time where there were plenty of VB6 developers and very few .NET developers. SharePoint is slowly but steadily gaining adoption by this finite number of .NET developers. |
| | A SharePoint developer is someone who has a strong foundation in .NET, a good understanding of what SharePoint is, is very good knowledge about OOB features, and has excellent SharePoint customization skills. Most of the development may be around Web Parts; event receivers; application pages; customization of New/Edit forms, libraries, and lists; or integration with third party applications. |
| Tester | Software Testers play an integral role in delivering a quality project. They do the thankless job of reading through the specifications document, creating thousands of test cases, and testing the application against those test cases. With SharePoint-based projects, they are saved quite a bit of hassle. If the technical documentation clearly states which features/functionality have been created using OOB features and which of them have been customized, the testers can focus on testing the later more than the former. This is one important difference between a regular bespoke software development team's tester and a SharePoint tester. |

| Technical Writer | Technical Writers should be involved right from the beginning of the project to create various documentation required for the project, including: |
| --- | --- |

- SRS (System Requirement Specifications) document

- Technical documentation that maps the functional requirements to the technical requirements and the approaches decided.

- Mockups/prototype walkthrough created by working closely with the BA.

- Implementation/solution documentation that clearly describes all features implemented along with screenshots.

- The above can also form part of a User Manual, apart from an Admin Manual that may have to be provided as well.

## Support

Once the solution is implemented, customer support starts. Typically there are two types of clients: companies who have their own IT department with specific skills in SharePoint administration and development, or companies who have their own IT department but would like to only do activities oriented towards content authoring and want the actual technical support to come from the vendor who implemented the application.

In the former case, the support calls to the company will be less; in the later, the support calls may be very high, at least during the initial period of post-launch. Another approach is to install a resident support engineer at the company, thus supplying the vendor company with recurring revenue.

In either case, it will be important to set up an online help desk where the support cases can be logged by the customer. SharePoint itself can be used for this. There is a WSS 3.0 HelpDesk Template, which is just a structure, but in SharePoint 2010, a help desk can be developed in a much better fashion using InfoPath-based Form libraries.

## Critical Architectural Choices

When involved in implementing a SharePoint 2010 project, specifically a DM project, there are some very important architectural choices that the Architect will be expected to make. These can be categorized into the following:

- Physical topology

- Information architecture

- Customization options

# Physical Topology

This is probably one of the most critical architectural decisions and it must be made at the beginning of a project (in fact, even in the proposal stage when the recommended topology has to be specified). The questions that need to be answered are as follows:

- How many servers are in the topology?

- Should we go the virtualization route or not?

- If it's a multi-location organization, what is the connectivity between the locations?

    - Do we go for a single-instance SharePoint setup?

    - Do we go for a multi-instance SharePoint setup in order to save the WAN bandwidth usage? If so, what are the challenges/tools available to replicate data between these instances?

- How do we optimize the SharePoint HTML traffic/document traffic in case of a WAN setup with depleted bandwidth availability?

- If there is a lot of video-based content, what are the options for optimizing the rendering?

## Servers in a Topology

With hardware capacities continuing to soar high, what used to be super computers are now sitting in the form of servers in your own computer network. Obviously, the resource requirements for software applications are continuously on the rise. With this premise, it is important to answer the following questions:

- How many servers are required in our topology?

- How are we going to split our SharePoint roles into these servers?

- What is the response time required by our customer?

- What are high availability needs of our customer?

- What is the toleration time that the company can afford to have in the event of failure?

- What internal skills does the company have?

- What are the current servers and how can they be leveraged?

- Finally, the Big B: Budget!

Before I attempt to answer these questions, it's important to follow distinctive approaches depending on the size of your company; see Table 5-8. For a small-medium sized company, the users typically will be

- Accessing the DMS from within the company's network.

- Accessing the DMS from on the move.

- Letting external parties access the DMS solution.

For a large sized company, the users will be

- Accessing the DMS from within the company's network.

- Accessing the DMS from within the company's WAN connected through MPLS Networks (depending on the country, the expenses for setting up this would vary).

*Table 5-8. Topology Options*

| Options | Topology Options | |
|---------|------------------|---|
| Option 1: Single Instance | Single Server Environment |  Single Server Environment |
| | Two Server Environment |  Front-End / App Server          Database Server |
| | Three Server Environment |  Front-End Server     Application Server     Database Server  Application Server running various services:  • Search Service  • User Profile Service  • Logging |

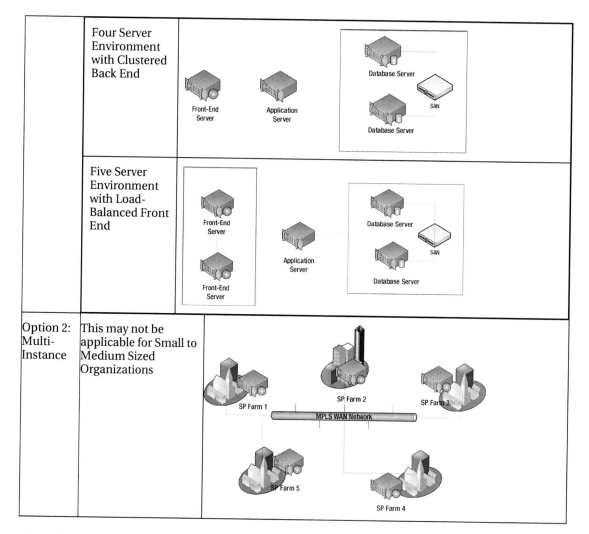

## Single Instance vs. Multi-Instance

These are the pros and cons for a single instance setup.

### Pros:

- Easier to maintain with single instance; reduced dependency on maintaining replication software and upcoming customized codes that may not get replicated in the future.

- Reduced overhead on costlier MPLS links and taking traffic over the cheaper Internet links.

- Reduced expenses on catering for application load balancers at all locations having 1,000+ user base.

- Reduced expenses on remote management when things go wrong (hardware/software replication support).

- Fall back to MPLS in case Internet links go down at any location.

- DR location out of secondary location (using native replication with SharePoint 2010's Content Deployment feature without involving third party solution).

## Cons:

- Need for higher capacity Internet links (depending upon projected usage).

- Initial administrative overhead: Local IT teams need to establish IPSEC tunnels to primary location for bringing in WAN optimization over riverbeds for inbound bound traffic only.

- Initial administrative overhead: Local IT teams need to establish an automatic fallback mechanism to MPLS in case Internet links go down at any location including that to primary DC.

These are the multi-instance pros and cons.

## Pros:

- With multi-instance, the main and key benefit is nearness to the SharePoint environment for each location's users.

- They will be able to access the environment on local LAN speeds.

## Cons:

- Initial installation overhead is high.

- Maintenance of multiple farms.

- The hardware cost/license cost plus the cost of setting up a data center if one doesn't exist at any location.

- The technical challenge of keeping all the environments synchronized.

# Replication Options

When you have a multi-instance SharePoint farm or even intend to keep a primary SharePoint farm and a secondary SharePoint farm for DR purposes, it will be important to keep both farms synchronized. Traditionally, this was done using third party tools or SQL replication (of content databases) or SharePoint backup/restore depending on how "soon" you wanted the other instances to be synchronized.

The new Content Deployment feature is best used in the case of replication from Staging to Production environments. It is important to keep in mind that customizations by way of WSPs always needs to be re-deployed across these environments. Content Deployment takes care of changes across libraries and lists. There are third party solutions from companies like DocAve, Syntergy, and Infonic that also provide excellent replication functionality.

Table 5-9 is a checklist you can use to verify if a particular solution can really fit your requirements.

*Table 5-9. Replication Tools Checklist*

| SNo | Requirement | Compliance |
|---|---|---|
| 1 | Tool has a UI to select the site collections to be replicated. | |
| 2 | Tool has UI to select sites to be replicated. | |
| 3 | Tool has UI to select lists/libraries to be replicated. | |
| 4 | Can replicate page libraries with publishing pages. | |
| 5 | Can replicate changes made in the SharePoint Master Pages. | |
| 6 | Can replicate changes made to Custom Page Layouts. | |
| 7 | Can highlight the differences between the Source and Destination environments before initiating replication. | |
| 8 | Highlights the possible items to be overwritten. | |
| 9 | Automatically pushes the destination item to an older version and creates the source version as the latest. | |
| 10 | Tool has been tried and tested with customers who have intranet portals built on SharePoint 2010 with publishing capabilities. | |
| 11 | Absence of custom Web Parts and custom code in the destination farm is highlighted. | |
| 12 | Maintains a clear history of all replication. | |
| 13 | Incremental setting only pushes the differences and not the whole chunk again. | |
| 14 | Can optimize the use of the available bandwidth across the WAN and if the production/staging are in two different countries. | |
| 15 | The tool has a clear audit trail and log of every synchronization done. | |

| SNo | Requirement | Compliance |
|---|---|---|
| 16 | Ability to synchronize back from the secondary site if the secondary environment is accessed and updated while the primary one is down. | |
| 17 | Local support in our locations. | |
| 18 | Licensing costs | |
| 19 | Pricing: Replication between Staging and Production Replication between Production and two other environments | |
| 20 | Customer References | |

## WAN Optimizers

When you have a multi-instance SharePoint Farm or if you intend to keep a primary SharePoint farm and a secondary farm for DR in a different location, the choice of the tool or methodology largely depends on the type of connectivity and bandwidth available between these locations. You can't have identical methods for companies that have connectivity between 1Mbps and 10Mbps. TechNet has a good article about this at `http://technet.microsoft.com/en-us/library/cc263099(office.12).aspx`.

Some of the popular WAN optimizers include solutions from F5, RiverBed, Packeteer, Citrix, and Cisco; RiverBed and F5 are really popular. F5 also has a hardware-based load balanced solution.

## Topology Options

Table 5-10 shows capacity numbers; these are from my own experience of implementing SharePoint-based DM systems. Some customers may demand high availability with clustering for even smaller number of users, so variations of these numbers are possible.

*Table 5-10. Topology Options*

| Option | Capacity | Remarks |
|---|---|---|
| Single server | Less than 100 users | |
| Two servers (Front-End/App and DB) | Less than 300 users | |
| Three servers (Front-End, App, and DB) | Less than 1,000 users | More processing power for the services that are running. |

| Option | Capacity | Remarks |
|---|---|---|
| Four servers with a two-node active-passive SQL cluster | | High availability for the storage hardware, which is the most critical component of your SharePoint farm. |
| | | The complete farm can be rebuilt if you just have your data (content databases). |
| Five servers with Network load balanced servers, App, and clustered DB servers | Less than 15,000 users | Network load balancing (NLB) provides the ability to load balance your front end, thus providing more processing power to render user requests. |

## Large Farms

SharePoint 2010 farms can typically grow to many more servers that what you have seen in the previous section. At any of the roles, web or application, more servers can be added.

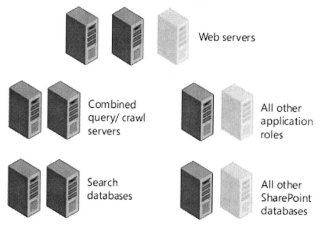

*Figure 5-3. Large farm topology*

The farm in Figure 5-3 really puts a lot of focus towards search with search databases/search roles provided with separate processing power. The environment in Figure 5-4 provides separate processing power for search as well as SharePoint content databases.

Servers to handle all
incoming requests

Dedicated to crawling and
administration

Crawl Servers

Query Servers

All other services

Servers for executing
sandboxed code

Search databases

Content databases

All other SharePoint
databases

*Figure 5-4.* *This environment provides separate processing power for search as well as SharePoint content databases.*

## Information/Storage Architecture

Once you have decided on the topology, the other critical aspect is to plan the information architecture design. This relates to the way you will create your Web Applications, site collections, sites, keywords, and search. Table 5-11 might help in choosing the right direction.

*Table 5-11.* *Choosing Your Information Architecture*

| Question | If Your Answer Is Yes | If Your Answer Is No |
| --- | --- | --- |
| Is the company divided into different locations and each location has with different departments/sections with heavy demand for document storage? | Go for multiple Web Applications with a Web Application for each location. | Go for a single Web Application with each department as separate site collection. |

135

| Question | If Your Answer Is Yes | If Your Answer Is No |
|---|---|---|
| Is the company divided into departments and sections? Does each unit has significant document storage/collaboration requirements? | Go for a site collection for each department and have sites created for sections under them. Also, ensure that a separate content database is created for each site collection. SharePoint is pretty smart in leveling the content sat abases for the site collections. That is, if you create a site collection, it will be created in a content database. Before you create the second site collection, create a content database (which will have zero site collections). Now when the second site collection is created, it will automatically fall in the content database, which has no site collections. | Go for a single site collection and sites/sub-sites, respectively, for departments and sections. |
| Does the company have a great demand for branding/content authoring? | Go for Publishing templates for each site, thus providing these capabilities. | Team sites should do. |
| Does the company require customized pages to be used across multiple Web Applications? | Use application pages (deployed in Layouts folder). | Use site pages where the pages are stored in the Site Pages library itself. |
| Does the company need a robust search feature? | Consider using FAST 2010 Search if the quantity runs to millions and there is some very specific search functionality that is not provided by SharePoint 2010 Search. A comparison is provided in a later section. | The default search should be fine. |
| Is the company looking at "dd/mm" format against the US format? | Regional settings are to be changed to English-UK. Interestingly, this doesn't change the Advanced Search date formats to dd/mm. This is a confirmed issue from Microsoft and is likely to be fixed in the next cumulative update for SharePoint from Microsoft. In the meantime, the browser settings need to be changed to English-German for this work. | The default US format settings should be fine. |

| Question | If Your Answer Is Yes | If Your Answer Is No |
|---|---|---|
| Does the company have custom Search requirements. | Custom properties may have to be created in the Advanced Search screen. This should be mapped to site columns used across site content types; the default date search is only available for "Modified Date." | The default properties should suffice. |
| Is the company using different types of content across multiple sites? | Use site content types at the site collection level and use them across sites. | Use independent content types in each site and map them to templates. |
| Is the company using different content types across the organization (different Web Applications)? | Use the new Content Type Hub feature with SharePoint 2010 and enable content type publishing across Web Applications in your farm. | Use independent content types at the site collection level. |
| Does the company have a number of file shares, and would it like to have them migrated into the DMS, but would like the ability to only search on those contents? | Instead of migrating these files to document libraries, it would be best to create a Search Content Source on these files and enable them only for search. | If the number of shares is not huge, you can have the documents moved into SharePoint document libraries. |
| Is the company is mainly looking at storing large set of documents and access them in a read-only fashion? | Use the Record Center template which is the only template that has the document parsing framework disabled, thus providing quick upload and access functionality. | You can just use any other template |
| Does the company have documents of sizes consistently over 256KB? | Consider using RBS (Remote Blob Storage). | The default SharePoint setup should be fine |
| Does the company do extensive document archiving? Does it have media streaming needs? | Use RBS with FILESTREAM. Tests show that with RBS FILESTREAM Provider, large BLOB objects have better I/O compared with putting everything in the database. | The default SharePoint setup should be fine |

| Question | If Your Answer Is Yes | If Your Answer Is No |
|---|---|---|
| Is the company upgrading from WSS 3.0 on WID (Windows Internal Database) to SharePoint Foundation 2010 with SQL Server Express (4GB limit)? | Microsoft no longer supports Windows Internal Database (WID) with SharePoint Foundation 2010. However, SQL Server Express has a 4GB DB size limit. The direct upgrade of a content DB > 4GB from WID to SQL Server Express is not supported. To get around of this limit, the customer can use RBS FILESTREAM Provider to store all the BLOB content on a file system so the DB size will still remain small. | Other suitable upgrade approaches need to be adopted |

## RBS and FILESTREAM

You are aware that SharePoint stores all its content in SQL content databases. When the DB size crosses a particular limit (Microsoft indicates it's around 200GB), the performance of the SharePoint sites may deteriorate. An architect in this scenario has the option to store SharePoint's content on a remote storage outside the SQL content database. Third party solutions exist for this as there was no native support or native tools with Microsoft. With SharePoint 2010 and SQL Server 2008, RBS is available as an option for architects without the need of any other solutions.

The following set of questions and answers might help you understand these terms better.

### Q: What is RBS?

RBS (Remote Blob Store) is a set of standardized APIs that allow storage/retrieval of BLOBs outside of your main SQL database where a dedicated BLOB store is desirable for various reasons. This uses a provider model for plugging in any dedicated BLOB store that implements these RBS APIs.

### Q: Which version of SQL Server can I use for SharePoint RBS?

SQL Server 2008 and SQL Server 2008 R2 both support RBS. A RBS Library needs to be downloaded and installed on SQL Server to enable the feature. All SQL editions (Express, Standard, and Enterprise) support RBS. Licensing requirements may be involved depending on the scenario.

### Q: What is FILESTREAM?

FILESTREAM is a SQL Server 2008 feature to store BLOB content on to file system.

FILESTREAM integrates the SQL Server Database Engine with an NTFS file system by storing varbinary (max) binary large object (BLOB) data as files on the file system. Transact-SQL statements can insert, update, query, search, and back up FILESTREAM data. Win32 file system interfaces provide streaming access to the data.

FILESTREAM uses the NT system cache for caching file data. This helps reduce any effect that FILESTREAM data might have on Database Engine performance.

The SQL Server buffer pool is not used; therefore, this memory is available for query processing. SQL FILESTREAM feature <u>does not allow you to store content on anything other than local storages</u>. (SMB shares can't be used for store BLOB content.)

**Q: What is RBS FILESTREAM Provider?**

RBS FILESTREAM Provider is a free OOB provider shipped by the Microsoft SQL RBS team that allows a deployment to use a SQL database (local or remote) as a dedicated BLOB store. This provider utilizes the FILESTREAM as the BLOB storage mechanism and ties the two technologies together.

**Q: Is there any benefit in using RBS with SharePoint?**

By using RBS for SharePoint, the customer may be able to leverage cheaper storage, improve performance, and enable better integration stories with third party technology for their SharePoint databases. But be careful; the benefit is different case by case. You need to investigate your scenarios to see if RBS really fits you.

**Q: How does backup and restore get affected when using RBS?**

If you use the local FILESTREAM provider with RBS, you can use built-in SharePoint tools to back up and restore. These operations backup and restore both the metadata and the BLOB store. If you use the remote RBS provider, you must carefully coordinate the backup and restore processes. This is because the backup and restore processes involve both the metadata and the BLOB store. You should take this into account when planning the RBS configuration. Not all RBS providers support backup and restore of BLOB data. You must check with the provider to confirm support.

You can also use the Microsoft System Center Data Protection Manager to back up and restore the RBS environment.

**Q: Can RBS FILESTREAM Provider support SMB shares to store the content, such as a NAS device?**

No. The SQL FILESTREAM feature doesn't allow you to store content on anything other than local storage. Therefore, the RBS FILESTREAM Provider has the same limitation. Third party RBS providers don't have this limitation if they are not leveraging SQL FILESTREAM feature.

# SharePoint 2010 and FAST 2010 Search

Microsoft is heavily pushing for FAST 2010 Search as the Enterprise Search Solution but is it really worth it? What additional features does it offer? Table 5-12 answers these questions. It also has certain possible search requirements that are addressed neither by SharePoint nor FAST.

*Table 5-12. SharePoint and FAST Search Comparison*

| Search Requirement | SharePoint 2010 | FAST 2010 Search | Remarks |
|---|---|---|---|
| When searched in English, if the meaning of the words match content in any other language (Arabic for example), such Arabic results are returned and are translated as well. | No | No | |
| Multimedia content like images and video can be searched using their file size, file format, and in case of videos, the length of the video. | No | Yes | Third party: Autonomy Search |
| Transliteration search (returns an alternative language's equivalent based on literal words) | No | No | Third party: Autonomy Search (to an extent) |
| Faceted search | No | Yes | |
| Search results should display thumbnails of documents | Yes | Yes | |
| Search results should display thumbnails of multi-media content | No | Yes | |
| Relevance search | Yes, limited | Yes | FAST: Conceptual searching, metadata extraction, pipeline control, rules-based relevance, facetted navigation. |
| Search can search within external file shares | Yes | Yes | |
| Search can search within Exchange public folders | Yes | No | |
| Search within Exchange Private Mailboxes | No | No | Third party: Longitude Exchange Connector, http://www.ba-insight.NET/connector-feature-matrix.html |
| Search can crawl external web sites | Yes | Yes | |
| Search allows Boolean logic | Yes | Yes | |

| Search Requirement | SharePoint 2010 | FAST 2010 Search | Remarks |
|---|---|---|---|
| Search allows relational operators to be used | Yes | Yes | |
| Search using properties | Yes | Yes | |
| Find content of a particular language | Yes | Yes | |
| Search using Best Bets (highlights results matching predefined keywords) | Yes | Yes | |
| Visual Best Bets | Yes, limited | Yes | FAST Shows a section of relevant information along with the search results |
| Searches inside e-mail boxes of the currently logged-in user | No | No | |
| Search results are based on relevance | Yes | Yes | |
| Relevancy tuning by document or site promotions | Yes, limited | Yes | Promotes selected documents or sites as highly relevant results for a keyword. Demotes documents or sites to a lower rank. (Limited: promotes documents for a given site, not query-specific.) |
| Search enhancements based on user context | No | Yes | Scopes Best Bets, visual Best Bets, and document promotions and demotions to a subgroup of employees |
| Continuous search (background engine searches for matching results and alerts the user) | No | No | |
| Search events are recorded | Yes | Yes | |
| Similar searches done by others in the recent past are shown | No | No | |

| Search Requirement | SharePoint 2010 | FAST 2010 Search | Remarks |
| --- | --- | --- | --- |
| Based on predefined keywords, matching results to be alerted to the supervisor, who can then decide to retain this or discard it. A log of such discarded items is kept. | To Customize | To Customize | |
| Stop Word Removal | No | Yes | A query for "President of United States" would also match documents mentioning "The President of the United States". |
| Phonetic Search | No | Yes | Phonetic search will detect all possible variants of "Muamar Gadaffi" ( Muammar Al Ghaddafi; Muammar Al Qaddafi; Muammar Al Qaddafi; Muammar El Qaddafi; Muammar Gadaffi; Muammar Gadafy; MuammarGadafy, etc.) |
| Lemmatization (the process of grouping together the different inflected forms of a word so they can be analyzed as a single item. For instance, the word "better" has "good" as its lemma and the word "walk" is the base form for the word "walking.") | No | Yes | |
| Automatic spelling correction | No | Yes | "floghts to London" should be generate responses to a search for "flights to London" rather than having to click on a "did you mean...?" dialog box |
| Similar results | No | Yes | Generates a new search based on the selected search result |

| Search Requirement | SharePoint 2010 | FAST 2010 Search | Remarks |
|---|---|---|---|
| Sort results on managed properties or rank profiles | No | Yes | Sort results based on selected managed properties or by FAST Query Language (FQL) formula. The relevancy of a document with respect to a query is represented by a ranking value. The rank profile concept enables full control of the relative weight of each component for a given query (such as, how important is the title relative to the body of the article?). This enables individual relevance tuning of different query applications. |
| Basic results refinement | Yes | Yes | |
| Deep results refinement (based on metadata) | No | Yes | |
| Document preview and thumbnails | No | Yes | Displays thumbnails of Word and PowerPoint documents. Displays inline (scrollable) previews of PowerPoint files on the Results page. |
| Rich web indexing support | No | Yes | Indexing of wide variety of web content, including JavaScript. |
| Sophisticated property extraction | Yes, limited | Yes | Extracts key information (people names, locations, company names) from unstructured text to use as additional managed properties. (Limited: title, author, and date only.) |
| Morphologic | No | Yes | Including all forms of a given word via linguistic normalization (lemmatization) |
| Results transformation | No | Yes | This is the algorithmic processing of search results. It includes result-set reordering (e.g., duplicate removal), adding navigation information (e.g., clustering/drilldown), and result content conversion or reformatting. |

| Search Requirement | SharePoint 2010 | FAST 2010 Search | Remarks |
|---|---|---|---|
| Lotus Notes, Documentum, JDBC Connectors | No | Yes | |
| Item level scale | 100 million | 500 million | |

## Office Web Apps 2010

Office Web Apps 2010 seamlessly integrates with SharePoint 2010 to allow you to view/edit MS Office documents (Word, Excel, and PowerPoint) within the browser itself. OWA 2010 (sometimes mistaken as Outlook Web Access) should definitely be considered because users generally find it quite easy (and actually fast) to view the documents within the browser itself.

Note that the Excel Web Access (EWA) part of SharePoint 2010 Enterprise allows you to view (without editing) Excel files within the browser even without OWA. EWA also allows users to interact with parameters (parameters can be linked to Excel formulas) and PivotTables.

# Requirements Gathering

In the analysis phase, requirements gathering is done with business users. It can be done with a requirements-gathering template with certain questions. Though these questions can mostly be answered by business users such as department heads, the internal IT team may also help in providing certain required information.

## The Requirements Gathering Team

When performing the requirements gathering, it is important to have the right team on both sides. Figure 5-5 shows an good formula. Each member is expected to provide input of certain nature to help understand the requirements better and provide the most appropriate solution.

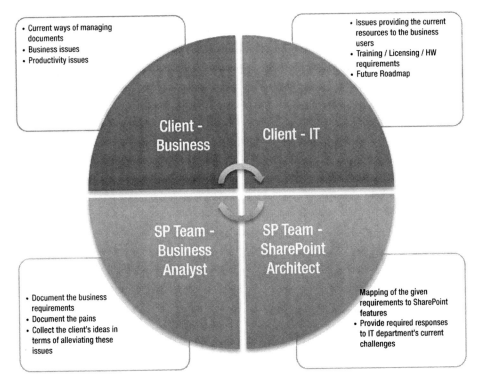

**Figure 5-5.** *The requirements gathering team*

## Requirements Gathering Questionnaire

An requirements gathering questionnaire is presented in Table 5-13.

*Table 5-13. Requirements Gathering Questionnaire*

Department Name:

# of Department Staff:

Department Head:

Sections under this department:

Describe your current ways of storing documents.

How would you like to store documents in the future?

Organization chart:

What kind of workflows would you like to have for your documents?

Do you use any corporate-wide templates for any document types?

Requirement for discussion on documents:

Are you using any paper forms or e-mail exchanges between sections?

Do you have any paper registers that are being used to record any incoming or outgoing documents?

What percentage of your documents are internally created and what percentage are received from the outside?

Do documents received from outside need to be scanned, OCRed, and uploaded into libraries?

What is your security requirement for the content that is being uploaded?

Links to external sites:

Links to internal applications:

Photo Gallery?

Media Gallery? [Videos, audio, etc.]

What kind of keywords do you want to use to locate your content?

Do you use common document/presentation templates?

Is there content that you want to share with the whole organization/executives?

Reports? Policies and Procedures? Updates?

What kind of document statistics would you like to see?

What is the importance in terms of audit trial?

Staff nominated for content management:

You could add more questions as per your client's requirements. The following section with features might also help in adding/modifying any of these questions. It is also important to understand the different types of users and what their expectations might be from the document management system. Table 5-14 is a matrix of the same.

## Type of Users and Expectations

Different levels of users in a company will have different expectations of the DM system. Most, if not all, of the expectations need to be catered to in order for your document management implementation to be called successful.

*Table 5-14. End User Types and Expectations from a DMS*

| S.No | Type of Users | Expectations | Related Features | Availability in SharePoint |
|---|---|---|---|---|
| 1. | End users | • Easier document upload and download<br><br>• Easier search<br><br>• Offline access when not in office<br><br>• Accessing versions<br><br>• Sharing comments | Document library, versioning, SharePoint search, Compare versions in Word, NoteBoard Web Part that allows your messages interaction | All OOB with offline access enabled by SharePoint Workspace |
| 2. | Managers | Controlled access to fields in Edit form | Library Edit form customization | Not available OOB. Can be achieved using JavaScript. Refer the next section. |
| 3. | | Route documents to other sites/site collections | Content Organizer feature | The new Content Organizer feature along with Content Routing rules lets you configure custom menus to route documents to other site collections/Sites in the same Web Application or to a different Web Application. |
| 4. | | Security | Site permissions, library permissions, item level permissions | Available OOB |
| 5. | | Managed metadata validations (same metadata should not be selected again in the same form) | Managed Metadata column | Not available OOB. Can be achieved using JavaScript. Refer the next section. |

| S.No | Type of Users | Expectations | Related Features | Availability in SharePoint |
|---|---|---|---|---|
| 6. | | Document information panel validations | DIP customized in InfoPath | Available when you customize the DIP using InfoPath and apply those validations. (Note that, in spite of these validations not succeeding, Word will still upload the document into SharePoint library—there is no real coordination between DIP validations and SharePoint.) |
| 7. | | Audit trail | Site collection Audit settings | OOB auditing reports are available, but they are not easy to filter/view. Muhimbi's SharePoint Audit especially does a good job here. |
| 8. | Management | Statistics in terms of increasing document usage as Management is keen to understand how the users are moving from traditional ways of storage to the modern DMS. | | Not available OOB, so document library statistics Web Parts may have to be built. |
| 9. | | Common keywords across the organization that can be used in documents | Enterprise Metadata Management, Term Store Management | EMM allows users to create terms and tag them to documents present in any Web Application, site collection, or site in your farm. |
| 10. | Administrators | Backup and restore on a periodic basis | Backup/restore from Central Administration, PowerShell, or StsAdm | Available OOB. It's better to use Task Scheduler to run it automatically. For large content databases, use SQL backup or third party backup solutions (because PowerShell or StsAdm backups dump the site collection as a whole and don't provide incremental functionality). |

| S.No | Type of Users | Expectations | Related Features | Availability in SharePoint |
|---|---|---|---|---|
| 11. | | Service accounts management | Manage Service Accounts in Central Administration | In SharePoint 2007, whenever account passwords were changed by the Server Administrator, it was a big challenge for the SharePoint Administrator to apply this to SharePoint Services running under those identities. With Manage Service Accounts, this can be done effortlessly. |
| 12. | | Viewing and retracting farm level solutions | Central Administration, Farm Solutions | Administrator can deploy/retract/delete solutions (.wsp) from the Central Administration |
| 13. | | Enabling solutions to be deployable by a site collection administrator | Sandbox Solutions | A solution built as a Sandbox Solution can be deployed at a site collection level by a site collection administrator in SharePoint 2010, thus eliminating the need for every developer to possess farm admin credentials. |

# Moving from Traditional Ways of Storage

Table 5-15 outlines the ways users are currently be storing documents/information and the better options offered by SharePoint.

*Table 5-15. Traditional Ways of Storage to SharePoint Ways*

| Storing documents by way of e-mail attachments in their Outlook or Exchange Inbox | These users must be encouraged to use the "Receive e-Mails to Document Library" feature, whereby without leaving the Outlook interface, they can forward that e-mail received along with any attachments to an ID like shareddocs@yourcompany.com. |
|---|---|
| | Another new way is to use add-ons from companies such as Colligo (Contributor) which integrate with Outlook to allow users to just drag and drop e-mails into document libraries. |
| Storing documents on their personal machines | Domain Group Policies can be enabled to prevent saving documents on local machines and have mapped drives to SharePoint document libraries. |

| | |
|---|---|
| Storing documents on Network Shared Folders | These network shared folders have probably grown in a very unorganized manner. So a mapping/cleansing activity must be first carried out to differentiate between documents that are active and will be further used by the company, documents of no worth, and documents that need to be saved for search.

The live documents should be moved into SharePoint document libraries. The non-active documents required for search can be retained in the shared folders with just SharePoint Search crawling it as a content source. |

# Implementation

Once the requirements have been gathered and understood, you can proceed with the actual implementation. The implementation may involve creating the actual structure required by the client. During implementation, apart from the usual requirements, you may also encounter requirements that need to be customized. There are other aspects that need to be considered as well. This section covers them.

## Document Management Features/Customized Functionality

Table 5-16 covers some OOB features and some customization approaches to functionality that are either overlooked or lack a straightforward manner of implementation.

*Table 5-16. Special Features*

| | |
|---|---|
| Compare document versions: Word integrates with SharePoint to provide these dynamically created review menu options. This a very popular feature. | **Major Version** Compare this document with the last major version published on the server.

**Last Version** Compare this document with the last version saved on the server.

**Specific Version...** Compare this document with a specific version saved on the server.

**Compare...** Compare two versions of a document (legal blackline).

**Combine...** Combine revisions from multiple authors into a single document. |
| Accessing validating metadata fields in Edit form using JavaScript: (Refer to the SpUtility section later) Here it checks for the presence of the same value across three different metadata fields. | Save In: PF 101

Copy To: PF 101; PF 102;

Extract To: PF 103; |

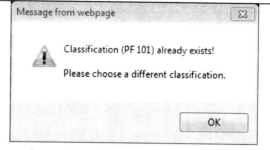

```
<script type="text/javascript">

function PreSaveAction()
    {
        //alert("calling before save")

        var iRef = document.getElementsByTagName("div");

        var arr = new Array();
        var duplicate = false;
        var errors = new Array();

        for (var i = 0; i < iRef.length; i++) {
          if (iRef[i].id.indexOf("editableRegion") >= 0) {
            var itemFound = iRef[i];
            if (itemFound.innerText.length == 1) {
               continue;
            }

            var splitItems = itemFound.innerText.split(";");
            for (k = 0; k < splitItems.length; k++) {
              for (var j = 0; j < arr.length; j++) {

                if (splitItems[k].length > 1) {
                  if (arr[j].indexOf(splitItems[k].replace(/^\s+/, "")) >= 0) {
                     duplicate = true;
                     var foundInArray = false;
                     for (var m = 0; m < errors.length; m++) {
                       if (errors[m] == splitItems[k])
                       { foundInArray = true; }
                     }
                     if (!foundInArray) {
                        errors.push(splitItems[k]);


                  }
                  // return false;
                }
              }
            }

          }
        }
```

Cont

```
arr.push(itemFound.innerText);

        }
    }
    if (duplicate) {
        alert("Classification (" + errors.join(',') + ") already exists! \n\nPlease choose a
different classification.")

        return false;
    }
```

Validating a Date field against the current date in JavaScript. The code assumes that the input is in dd/mm/yyyy format, which you are converting to mm/dd/yyyy for comparison.

| Date of Creation * | 05/05/2011 | 🗓 |

**Message from webpage** ☒

⚠ Date of Creation cannot be greater than Current Date!

OK

```
try {
    var createdate = SPUtility.GetSPField('Date of Creation').GetValue();
    //alert(createdate);
    var createdatestr=createdate.toString();
        var dt1  = createdatestr.substring(0,2);
        var mon1 = createdatestr.substring(3,5);
        var yr1  = createdatestr.substring(6,10);
        temp1 = mon1 + "/" + dt1 + "/" + yr1;
    var dtCr = new Date(temp1);
    var CreatedDateInUTC = dtCr.toUTCString();
    var currentTime = new Date();
    var CurDateInUTC = currentTime.toUTCString();
    var dt3 = new Date(CreatedDateInUTC);
    var dt4 = new Date(CurDateInUTC);
        if(dt3 > dt4){
    alert('Date of Creation cannot be greater than Current Date!');
    return false;
        }
}
catch(ex)
{}
return true;
}       </script>
```

Disabling a field based on a condition

| Date of Creation * | 03/05/2011 | |
| Date Information Received | 07/05/2011 | 🗓 |

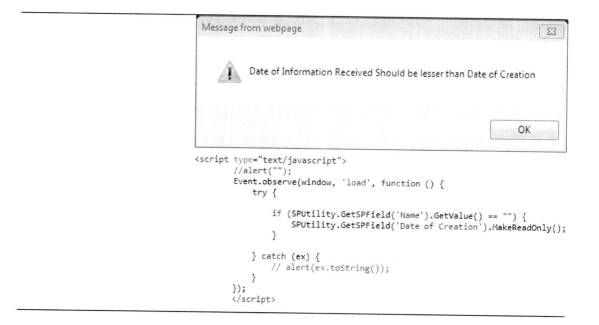

```
<script type="text/javascript">
    //alert("");
    Event.observe(window, 'load', function () {
        try {

            if (SPUtility.GetSPField('Name').GetValue() == "") {
                SPUtility.GetSPField('Date of Creation').MakeReadOnly();
            }

        } catch (ex) {
            // alert(ex.toString());
        }
    });
</script>
```

## PreSaveAction and SpUtility/Prototype JavaScript Libraries

One of the most popular features in the SharePoint document libraries is the ability to disable/enable certain fields in the Edit form (where the Document Library's metadata is captured) once the data has been captured. For instance, you might have the user enter a reference number for a document in the library; the rest of the document can still be edited, but that field must be locked against changes. You may also want to change a field's value based on what is entered in any other fields. This can be done using SPUtility.JS and Prototype.JS, available from CodePlex at http://sputility.codeplex.com/.

SPUtility.js is a JavaScript library used to make modifications to SharePoint's list forms (NewForm.aspx and EditForm.aspx in a survey, custom list, or library). This library depends on Prototype.js (www.prototypejs.org/ is a JavaScript framework). SPUtility.js has been tested in SharePoint 2007 with WSS 3.0 and MOSS. It is primarily written and tested for 2007; however, it works well with SharePoint 2010 and I have used it in few of my projects.

PreSaveAction is a JavaScript function that is called when Save is pressed in a New or Edit form, in which these validations can be performed. You can insert a ContentEditor Web Part into the Edit form or New form and insert your Script section into it using the HTML source.

## Large Document Libraries

Document libraries, being the central container for storing documents, can get quite large. Although you can go as high as 30 million documents per document library, you will feel the document library's performance slow as it crosses the 5,000 or 1,000 item threshold. That is why even a single view threshold is kept at a maximum of 5,000. RBS must be considered for document sizes above 256KB.

# Using Document Sets

If you have started working with SharePoint 2010, Document Sets would not have missed your attention. They are way beyond what a folder has to offer. Document Sets should be leveraged as much as possible when you have to store a set of related files together as a single work unit. The benefits include:

- Customizable Welcome page: A page that opens up when a document set is opened, showing shared metadata and any Web Parts that add to it.

- Shared columns between the Document Set's properties and document's (that reside inside) properties.

- Allowed content types that help you restrict the content types available in the new menu inside the Document Set.

- Capturing versions of the whole Document Set.

# Offline Access

SharePoint 2010 Workspace allows you to take documents offline. Be mindful of limitations such as Workspace not working for Page libraries; also, there is a limit of about 5,000 items that can be taken offline. SharePoint 2010 is part of Office Professional Plus 2010. Figure 5-6 shows a workspace with documents in a library.

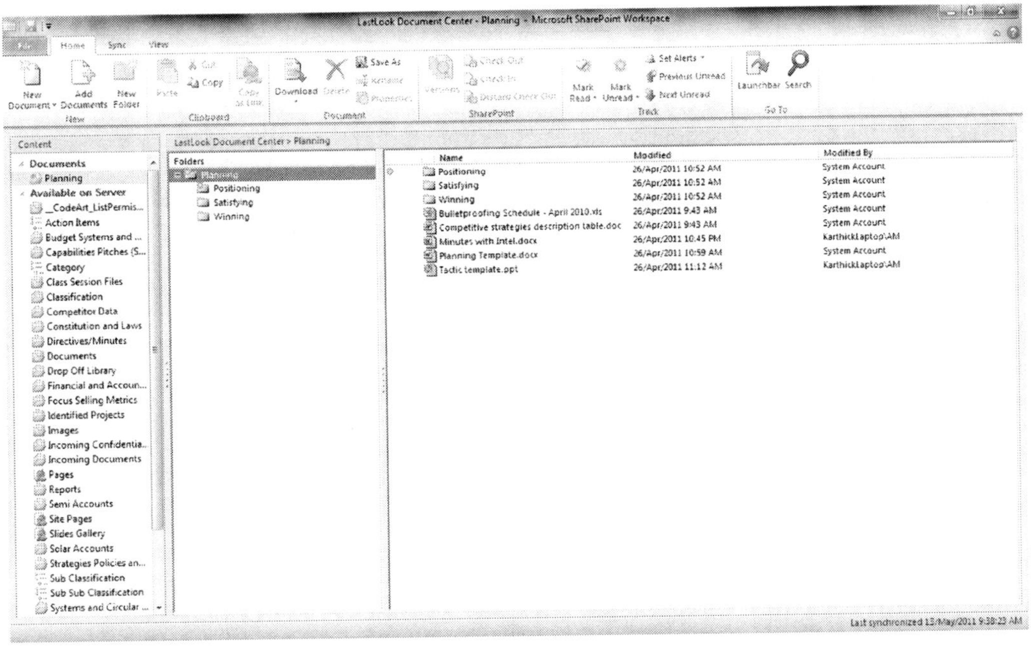

*Figure 5-6. Documents taken offline inside SharePoint Workspace.*

# Multilingual Support

SharePoint 2007's ability to have multilingual sites was limited to using Publishing templates with variations and variation labels. Many SharePoint 2007 professionals completely ignore this portion as it is perceived to be quite cumbersome to set up and maintain; it's also is not available for simple team sites.

SharePoint 2010 brings multilingual capabilities to the commonly used Team Sites itself. It is very easy and straightforward to set up; one of my blog posts has steps with screenshots (http://karthickmicrosoft.blogspot.com/2010/08/arabic-language-on-sharepoint-2010.html ).

There is a difference between customers wanting to store content of different languages and the UI itself being available in different languages. Don't assume that you have to create a web site or a site collection in multiple languages just because a document library contains documents in multiple languages. For example, the document library for an English site collection can contain documents written in French and Japanese. For publishing sites, content can be created in any language.

When you are planning multilingual sites, you should also consider what locales are necessary to support your sites. A locale is a regional setting that specifies the way numbers, dates, and times are displayed on the site. However, the locale doesn't change the language in which the site is displayed. For example, selecting the Thai locale changes the default sort order of list items and uses the Buddhist calendar instead of the default calendar. The locale is a setting that is configured independently of the language specified when a site is created, but unlike the language, the locale can be changed at any time.

It is important to understand the limitations of using the multilingual capabilities in SharePoint. There are few elements in the SharePoint UI that do not support MUI (Multilingual User Interface):

- Shared components—such as Web Parts, lists, and permissions—appear across all site templates. Their functionality is centrally defined, and their behavior is consistent regardless of the site template in which they appear.

- The titles and descriptions are MUI-enabled only for list-based Web Parts. For example, the title and description for Web Parts that display list and library data, such as announcements and shared documents, are displayed in a user's preferred language. By contrast, the title and description for other Web Parts, such as the Content Editor and the Content Query Web Parts, are displayed only in the primary site language. The following properties and features of non-list-based Web Parts are not MUI-enabled. They are always displayed in the language in which they were created.

  - Custom properties: Any custom Web Part properties that are created or edited by the user remain in the language in which they were created.

  - Import error message: The default value of this error message is always displayed in the primary site language. If a user has created a custom error message, that error message is always displayed in the language in which it was created.

  - List views and list items are not MUI-enabled. These user interface elements will continue to display the values that were entered when they were created, regardless of the preferred language selected by the user.

  - Links to list titles in the Quick Launch and the top link bar menu will continue to display the values that were entered when the lists were created.

- Although the Quick Launch and the top link bar menu are MUI-enabled, the list titles that they display are independent of the actual list titles. To work around this issue, the user must edit the list title for the Quick Launch and the top link bar menu.

- The following properties and features of permissions are not MUI-enabled; they are always displayed in the primary site language or the language in which they were created:

  - Permission group names: These include default permission group names and any custom permission groups that were created by a user.

  - Permission level names and descriptions: These include default permissions levels and any custom permission levels that were created or changed by a user.

  - User information: User information such as About Me, Title, and Department.

- Site templates

  - My Site: The following My Site properties and features are not MUI-enabled and are always displayed in the primary site language: Web Parts, Web Part titles, descriptions, custom properties, import error messages, user-generated content, list items, discussions, notes, comments, documents, and HTML content.

  - Blogs: The Blog site template includes many Web Parts and user-generated content that are not MUI-enabled. If additional display languages are enabled on the Blog site settings page, an error message will be displayed.

  - Meeting sites: Meeting site templates include many Web Parts and user-generated content, which are not MUI-enabled. If additional display languages are enabled on the site settings page for any meeting site template, an error message will be displayed.

  - Search: The Search site uses features in addition to the Search Web Part and Search Site templates. Many of the Search site limitations are not actually related to multilingual user interface features but are architectural designs that affect the user interface.

  - The following limitations are a mix of multilingual user interface and architectural limitations for Search sites:

    - Search indexes content in the primary language of the SharePoint Server installation. Even if content is provided in secondary languages, that content is only searchable by using the primary language of the site. For example, if your secondary preferred language is German, but the primary language for the site is English, a search for "Freigegebene Dokumente" returns no results. However, a search for "Shared Documents" does return results.

- Search Web Part properties: Title, description, and custom properties are not MUI-enabled. The default search prompt for the search box will be displayed in a different language when the user changes their secondary preferred language. However, if this prompt is customized, its customized value will be displayed for all languages.

- Web databases

  - Only the Options menu and the Open menu are MUI-enabled for web database sites. Database section tabs correspond to different views for the database, and the labels for these tabs are always displayed in the primary site language. Database content is user-generated content and will always be displayed in the language in which it was originally created.

## SharePoint Mobile Integration

Top executives look for ways in which they can access documents on the move and make approvals from their mobile devices. Though SharePoint OOB has good support for Windows Mobiles and Mobile Views for all pages, there are other mobile platforms and a several interesting add-ons that could be of help. Table 5-17 has a summary.

*Table 5-17. SharePoint Mobile Integration*

| | |
|---|---|
| For Windows Mobile | OOB integration with Windows Mobile Sync and SharePoint 2010 Mobile Workspace for using documents offline |
| For all devices: iPhone, Blackberry, Android, Symbion mobile OS platforms | www.noko.co.uk/what_we_do/solutions_for_sharepoint_2007/ sharepoint_for_smartphones.aspx |
| For iPhone only | www.moprise.com/ |
| For iPhone only | http://itunes.apple.com/gb/app/ishare/id305862898?mt=8 (Spyk Software) |
| For Blackberry only | http://silverdust.softartisans.com/blackberry-sharepoint-mobile-integration-use-cases-457.aspx |
| For Blackberry only | www.wicksoft.com/sharepoint_summary.htm |

## Scanning/OCR

Scanning of documents into SharePoint document libraries can either be done manually by uploading the scanned files or by choosing an add-on that can invoke the scanner interface, perform the scanning, and get the generated file (usually a PDF) into the document library. In the process, OCR can also be applied, thus providing a content-searchable file.

Websio has developed some pretty interesting add-ons. The scanner/OCR add-on achieves the aforementioned sequence of actions. A number of screenshots are available at http://www.websio.com/product.aspx?ID=103

If you are working in the Middle East, you will need Arabic OCR solutions; the leaders in that field are Sakhr (http://international.sakhr.com/index.html) and Verus (from Novodynamics, www.novodynamics.com/verus_pro.htm).

## Launch, Training, Support

Once development is done, the following phases have to be carried out:

- User acceptance testing: This should be done in the client environment itself, so that the application is locally available and won't be quoted as having any performance issues.

- Training

    - Administrators: The users who are going to administer the SharePoint environment need to be trained first.

    - Managers/power users need to be trained next.

    - End users

- Go Live and Support follows training

    - During Go Live, the following aspects need to be monitored:

        - Event Viewer

        - ULS Logs for any critical/high errors

        - Growth of the content databases

        - Errors reported by SharePoint Health Analyzer

## Summary

In this chapter, I used my experience to provide approaches, guidelines, and practices that you can adopt while designing and implementing a SharePoint 2010-based DM system. For a quick reference, the following is a list of the best practices you should follow:

- Size your SharePoint farm appropriately.

- Don't overlook high availability needs even on a small to medium sized farm. You always have option of database mirroring if failover clustering is too expensive.

- In an enterprise, multi-location scenario, consider HTTP accelerators/WAN optimizers to speed up access.

- In a large site collection, RBS is a good option for storing all content inside content databases.

- Use different service accounts for running your services.

- It is very important to keep your search index files on a volume with sufficient size to accommodate growth.

- ULS logs and Event Viewer records have to be checked regularly to ensure there are no errors reported.

- For better control, use Enterprise Metadata Management's terms for keywords tagging for documents across your SharePoint farm, instead of using document library lookup columns.

- Consider using OOB features as much as possible instead of venturing into customization for every business requirement.

- In fact, it's good to categorize your customers or projects into customers who are looking to implement projects using only OOB features in SharePoint; customers who are looking to implement projects using OOB features plus customization with no-code solutions and third party add-ons; and customers who are open to solutions using customization. This categorization will provide boundaries to work within and thus think of solutions within those perimeters.

- Use the Document ID Service to provide unique document identifiers across documents in a site collection.

- Use site content types and site columns instead of document library-specific columns.

- Document Sets are a good way to manage a collection of documents instead of folders in SharePoint 2010.

- Consider using FAST Search Server 2010 for huge volumes of data that needs to be crawled.

- Office Web Apps 2010 lets users view/edit documents within the browser itself.

All the best for your SharePoint 2010 DM Implementation!

# CHAPTER 6

# Forms Services and InfoPath

Exposing forms to the browser empowers users to leverage one of SharePoint's advanced features. Creating simple forms is easy, even for end users. However, creating more complex forms requires higher-level knowledge. This chapter shows how to build and extend a basic form within InfoPath using code, deploy this to a SharePoint server, and make the form available online. Different ways of deploying InfoPath form templates and integrating forms into complex solutions will be described. Taking it further, you will see how to program InfoPath forms and how to add custom code to forms.

These form templates can be published to a SharePoint server, which can render them in a web browser using InfoPath Forms Services. This enables users without an InfoPath client installed on their computers to fill out InfoPath forms.

XmlFormView is a Web Part used to render InfoPath forms in SharePoint and make the form available in the browser. Programming the control extends its behavior and provides enhanced features usually available only to InfoPath clients. In this chapter we explain how to overcome common limitations of the form viewer.

InfoPath uses XML to store user input. With programmatic access to the XML, changes are possible on the fly during the loading and saving processes. Combined with workflows, which are described in the next chapter, this creates powerful applications and makes complex form management possible.

This chapter includes

- How InfoPath files are structured

- How to design browser-enabled forms

- Using data connections to access external data

- Publishing forms to SharePoint and making the forms available in a browser

- Building InfoPath forms with code-behind

- Creating applications with XmlFormView and extending its default behavior

## Internals of InfoPath Forms

Using line-of-business (LOB) applications on browser-based platforms is a solution in high demand, with many advantages for the enterprise. Often one of the core challenges is to provide users with easy-to-use forms. In many cases, such forms must adhere to corporate design stipulations, and their textual information needs to be adjusted regularly.

SharePoint and InfoPath complement one another and offer a solution to many of these issues. InfoPath provides a very intuitive UI for developing form templates, enabling information workers and even business users to develop and customize forms.

Designing solutions for SharePoint in combination with InfoPath Forms Services requires developers to be familiar with InfoPath. This includes a basic understanding of the internal structure of forms, as well as designing form templates using InfoPath. Since many of the wizards integrated into InfoPath are aimed at ad hoc solutions and lack support for professional development solutions, we will examine the internal structure and functionality of InfoPath form templates.

InfoPath separates layout and data. On one hand, an InfoPath form template describes the layout and behavior of the form. This information is stored within a template file with the extension .xsn. On the other hand, the data that is entered by a user into the form's controls is stored in an XML data file. This XML file contains a reference to the corresponding XSN file that is used to display the data. When discussing an InfoPath form, we are generally referring to the form template.

# InfoPath Form Template

Despite the attractive InfoPath UI, developers need to understand the internal structure of InfoPath form templates. The XSN file, created by InfoPath when designing a form template, is essentially a *Windows Cabinet Archive (.cab)* file containing several different files. You can see those files when you use the option Share ➤ Save Form Template As ➤ Source Files. This allows you to save all the files individually in a local folder. Alternatively, you can rename an XSN file as a CAB file and view the files contained within the archive. Figure 6–1 shows the structure of an XSN file.

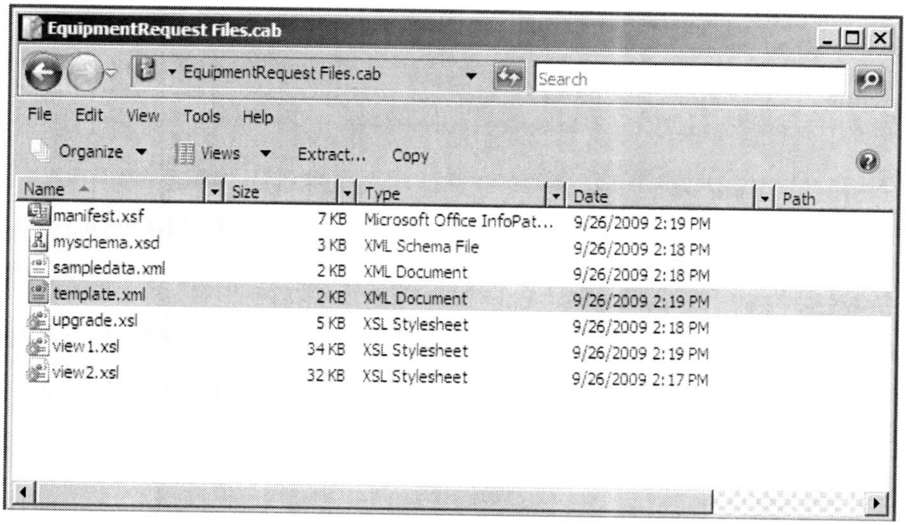

*Figure 6–1. Structure of InfoPath files*

We will describe the constituent files within an InfoPath form template in more detail. The listings and snippets in this chapter are taken from an example form template called Conference Room Booking. Figure 6–2 shows a form that is used to book conference rooms within a company. Users can enter their names and contact information and reserve a room for a specified date and time period. The form consists of two different views: one for editing the form, and another, marked as read-only, that will be displayed after the document has been submitted.

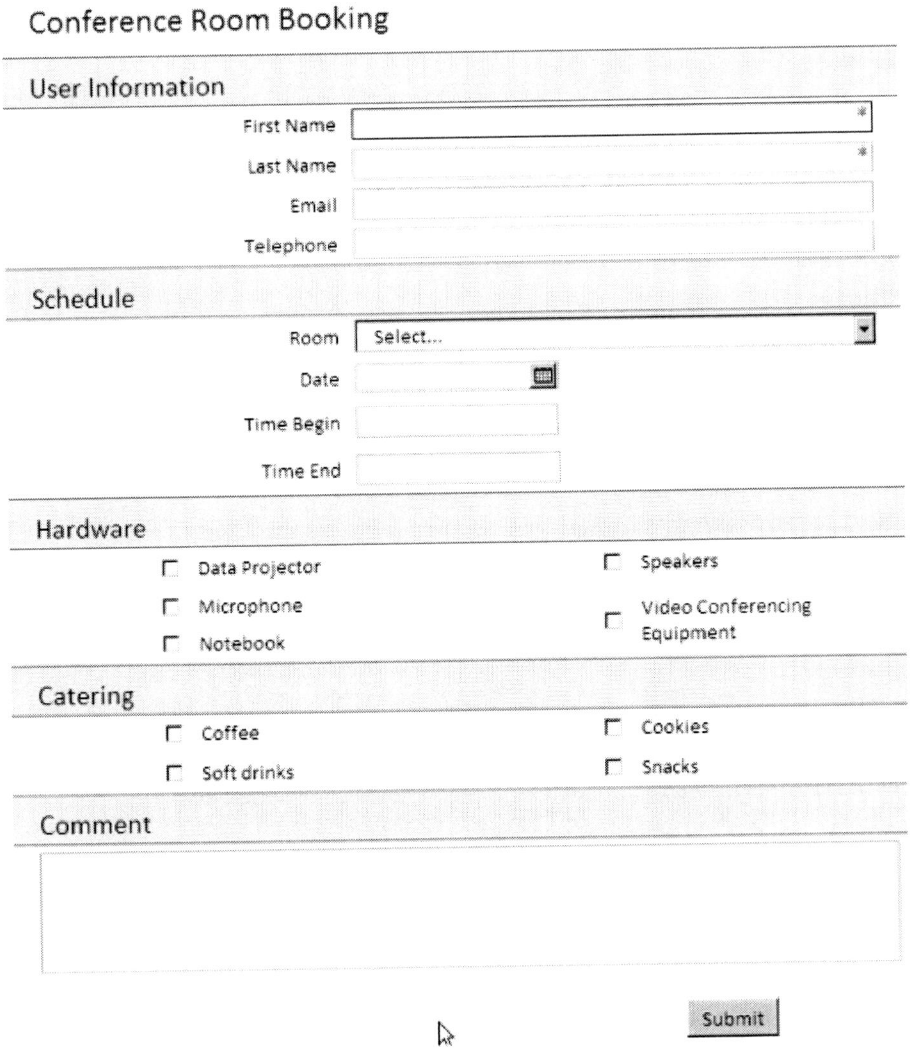

## Conference Room Booking

### User Information

| | |
|---|---|
| First Name | [                                    ] * |
| Last Name | [                                    ] * |
| Email | [                                    ] |
| Telephone | [                                    ] |

### Schedule

| | |
|---|---|
| Room | [ Select...                        ▼ ] |
| Date | [              ] 📅 |
| Time Begin | [              ] |
| Time End | [              ] |

### Hardware

☐ Data Projector          ☐ Speakers

☐ Microphone             ☐ Video Conferencing Equipment

☐ Notebook

### Catering

☐ Coffee                  ☐ Cookies

☐ Soft drinks             ☐ Snacks

### Comment

[                                                          ]

[ Submit ]

*Figure 6–2. Example form template: Conference Room Booking*

## BUILDING XSN FILES FROM SOURCE FILES

In some scenarios it might be necessary to edit the source files manually, such as when there is a problem with the XSN file, or when you want to edit some of the files programmatically. In these situations you need to add the files to a CAB file and rename the extension to `.xsn`. The command-line utility `makecab.exe`, which is included in all Windows versions since Windows 2000, can assemble CAB archives. This tool is located in the `Windows\System32` folder.

To generate a CAB file, take the following steps:

Copy all files to be included in the cabinet into a folder.

Create a cabinet definition file (.ddf) that provides information about the cabinet name, the directory in which the cabinet file should be stored, and a list of files to include, as follows:

```
OPTION EXPLICIT
.Set CabinetNameTemplate=<cabinet filename>.XSN
.set DiskDirectoryTemplate="<directory to save cabinet to>"
.Set Cabinet=on
.Set Compress=on
"<Path to XSN folder> \myschema.xsd"
"<Path to XSN folder>\manifest.xsf"
"<Path to XSN folder>\sampledata.xm"
"<Path to XSN folder>\Template.xml"
"<Path to XSN folder>\upgrade.xsl"
"<Path to XSN folder>\view1.xsl"
"<Path to XSN folder>\view2.xsl"
```

Run the makecab command from the command line:

```
Makecab /f <cabinet definition>.ddf
```

Rename the cabinet file extension to .xsn.

## Form Definition Files

InfoPath stores all the relevant information about a form template in the form definition file, called manifest.xsf. This file is the core file of an InfoPath template and holds information about the document schema, views, business logic, event handlers, form metadata, and deployment information.

When viewing the XML structure of this file in a text editor, you will find many elements that hold information you have entered in InfoPath Designer. Listing 6–1 shows a complete XSF file for the Conference Room Booking example form. Some of the subelements have been omitted to increase readability.

*Listing 6–1. Sample XSF File*

```
<?xml version="1.0" encoding="UTF-8"?>
<xsf:xDocumentClass trustSetting="automatic"
                    trustLevel="restricted"
                    solutionFormatVersion="3.0.0.0"
                    solutionVersion="1.0.0.16" productVersion="14.0.0"
                    publishUrl="C:\Forms\EquipmentRequest.xsn"
                    name="urn:schemas-microsoft-com:office:infopath:
                        EquipmentRequest:-myXSD-2009-09-22T18-21-06"
                    xmlns:xsf="http://schemas.microsoft.com/office/
                            infopath/2003/solutionDefinition"... >
    <xsf:package>
        <xsf:files>
            <xsf:file name="myschema.xsd">
                <xsf:property name="namespace" type="string"
```

```
                    value="http://schemas.microsoft.com/office/
                        infoapth/2003/myXSD/2010_01_20T22:54:17"> </xsf:property>
            <xsf:property name="editability" type="string" value="full">
            </xsf:property>
            <xsf:property name="rootElement" type="string" value="RoomBooking">
            </xsf:property>
            <xsf:property name="useOnDemandAlgorithm" type="string" value="yes">
            </xsf:property>
         </xsf:file>
          <xsf:file name="template.xml"></xsf:file>
          <xsf:file name="sampledata.xml">...</xsf:file>
        <xsf:file name="view1.xsl">...</xsf:file>
        <xsf:file name="view2.xsl">...</xsf:file>
        <xsf:file name="upgrade.xsl"></xsf:file>
    </xsf:files>
  </xsf:package>
<xsf:importParameters enabled="yes"></xsf:importParameters>
<xsf:documentVersionUpgrade>
    <xsf:useTransform transform="upgrade.xsl" minVersionToUpgrade="0.0.0.0"
                    maxVersionToUpgrade="1.0.0.15"></xsf:useTransform>
</xsf:documentVersionUpgrade>
<xsf:extensions>
    <xsf:extension name="SolutionDefinitionExtensions">
        <xsf2:solutionDefinition runtimeCompatibility="client server"
                            allowClientOnlyCode="no">
            <xsf2:offline openIfQueryFails="yes" cacheQueries="yes">
            </xsf2:offline>
            <xsf2:server isPreSubmitPostBackEnabled="no"
                    isMobileEnabled="no" formLocale="en-US">
            </xsf2:server>
            <xsf2:solutionPropertiesExtension branch="share">
                <xsf2:share formName="test"
                        path="C:\Users\Administrator\Documents\test.xsn"
                        accessPath="">
                </xsf2:share>
            </xsf2:solutionPropertiesExtension>
            <xsf2:viewsExtension>
                <xsf2:viewExtension ref="view2" readOnly="yes" clientOnly="no">
                </xsf2:viewExtension>
            </xsf2:viewsExtension>
        </xsf2:solutionDefinition>
    </xsf:extension>
</xsf:extensions>
<xsf:views default="View 1">
    <xsf:view showMenuItem="yes" name=" View 1" caption=" View 1">
    ...
    </xsf:view>
    <xsf:view showMenuItem="yes" name="Readonly" caption="Readonly">
    ...
    </xsf:view>
</xsf:views>
<xsf:applicationParameters application="InfoPath Design Mode">
```

```
    <xsf:solutionProperties
fullyEditableNamespace="http://schemas.microsoft.com/office/infopath/2003/myXSD/2009-09-
22T18:21:06" lastOpenView="view1.xsl"
lastVersionNeedingTransform="1.0.0.15"></xsf:solutionProperties>
    </xsf:applicationParameters>
    <xsf:documentSchemas>
        <xsf:documentSchema rootSchema="yes"
location="http://schemas.microsoft.com/office/infopath /2003/myXSD/2009-09-22T18:21:06
myschema.xsd"></xsf:documentSchema>
    </xsf:documentSchemas>
    <xsf:fileNew>
        <xsf:initialXmlDocument caption="EquipmentRequest" href="template.xml">
        </xsf:initialXmlDocument>
    </xsf:fileNew>
    <xsf:submit caption="Submit" disableMenuItem="no" onAfterSubmit="close"
showStatusDialog="no">
        <xsf:submitToHostAdapter name="Main submit" submitAllowed="yes">
        </xsf:submitToHostAdapter>
        <xsf:errorMessage>The form cannot be submitted because of an error.</xsf:errorMessage>
    </xsf:submit>
    <xsf:ruleSets>
        <xsf:ruleSet name="ruleSet_1">
            <xsf:rule caption="Send" isEnabled="yes">
                <xsf:assignmentAction targetField="my:readonly" expression="&quot;true&quot;">
                </xsf:assignmentAction>
                <xsf:submitAction adapter="Main submit"></xsf:submitAction>
                <xsf:closeDocumentAction promptToSaveChanges="no"></xsf:closeDocumentAction>
            </xsf:rule>
        </xsf:ruleSet>
    </xsf:ruleSets>
</xsf:xDocumentClass>
```

You can find the following important information in the manifest file:

- *Unique identifier for the form*: This identifier is also used within SharePoint to reference the form template. It is provided using the name attribute of the root element <xsf:xDocumentClass>.

- *Global metadata about the form*: The root element <xsf:xDocumentClass> also contains information about document versions, publishing, trust settings, and definitions for the various namespaces that are used within the manifest.

- *Packaging of the XSN file*: The <xsf:package> element lists all the files that are included in the cabinet file using <xsf:files> elements.

- *XML Schema definition of form data*: Within the <xsf:files> section you can see the <xsf:file> element that references the schema XSD file. It contains several <xsf:property> elements, which define the name of the rootElement and whether the schema can be edited. The exact properties that can be specified vary depending on the file type. Later in the manifest file, the element <xsf:documentSchemas> contains a reference to the document schema used in the form.

- *Definition of the different views within the form*: The `<xsf:views>` element contains a child `<xsf:view>` element for each view. Each view element defines the Etensible Stylesheet Language Transformation (XSLT) that is used to display the view. Furthermore, editing components are defined within the `<xsf:editing>` tag. Editing controls are special controls that handle user editing of the nominated data field. In the following example (in Listing 6–2), a calendar control for editing the date field and a control for multiline data are defined. The `<xsf:unboundControls>` element describes additional controls that are not bound to the XML data, such as Button controls.

*Listing 6–2. Definition of Views in XSF*

```
<xsf:view showMenuItem="yes" name="View1" caption="Edit View">
    <xsf:mainpane transform="view2.xsl"></xsf:mainpane>
    <xsf:editing>
        <xsf:xmlToEdit name="Date_7" item="/my:RoomBooking/my:Date">
            <xsf:editWith proofing="no" autoComplete="no" component="xField"></xsf:editWith>
        </xsf:xmlToEdit>
        <xsf:xmlToEdit name="Comment_15" item="/my:ConferenceBooking/my:Comment">
            <xsf:editWith type="plainMultiline" component="xField"></xsf:editWith>
        </xsf:xmlToEdit>
    </xsf:editing>
    <xsf:unboundControls>
        <xsf:button name="CTRL18_6">
            <xsf:ruleSetAction ruleSet="ruleSet_1"></xsf:ruleSetAction>
        </xsf:button>
    </xsf:unboundControls>
</xsf:view>
```

- *Actions and rules*: These are defined within the `<xsf:ruleSets>` element as described in Listing 6–3. They define how the rules are bound to controls and what actions are taken. In the following example, a rule is defined that sets the my:readonly field to true, submits the form using the Main submit data source, and closes the document.

*Listing 6–3. Definition of Rules in XSF*

```
<xsf:ruleSet name="ruleSet_1">
    <xsf:rule caption="Send" isEnabled="yes">
        <xsf:assignmentAction targetField="my:readonly"
                              expression="&quot;true&quot;">
        </xsf:assignmentAction>
        <xsf:submitAction adapter="Main submit"></xsf:submitAction>
        <xsf:closeDocumentAction promptToSaveChanges="no"></xsf:closeDocumentAction>
    </xsf:rule>
</xsf:ruleSet>
```

- *Data validation*: In the section `<xsf:CustomValidation>`, all custom validation rules are expressed using `<xsf:ErrorCondition>` elements as shown in Listing 6–4. These describe the fields that are validated using the match attribute and the expression to be evaluated. The subelement `<xsf:errorMessage>` contains the shortMessage that will be displayed if validation fails.

*Listing 6–4. Validation Rules in XSF*

```
<xsf:customValidation>
    <xsf:errorCondition match="/my:RoomBooking"/my:Schedule/my:Date"
                        expressionContext="."
                        Expression="msxsl:string-compare(.,xdDate:Today()) &lt; 0">
        <xsf:errorMessage type="modeless" shortMessage="Date must be in the future">
        </xsf:errorMessage>
        <?caption Validate Date?>
    </xsf:errorCondition>
...
</xsf:customValidation>
```

# Form Schema File (XSD)

Every form template has a schema file (.xsd) that prescribes the data structure expected by this form template. The schema file is expressed in XML Schema Definition (XSD), as defined by the W3C organization.

InfoPath validates every XML file to be rendered by the specified form template against this schema. This makes designing the schema very important, especially when the XML data files are manipulated outside of the InfoPath and Forms Services environments. If the XML is invalid according to the schema, the form cannot be displayed.

---

■ **Caution** InfoPath does not support all features of XSD! Please check out the MSDN library for a list of XML schema elements that are not supported by InfoPath: http://msdn.microsoft.com/en-us/library/bb251017.aspx.

---

Listing 6–5 shows the schema file from the Conference Room Booking example. The second line contains a very important definition: the target namespace. This is the namespace to which all the elements and attributes belong. During validation of XML data files, InfoPath verifies that all the elements and attributes in the XML instance exist within the declared namespace.

In the example form data file (in Listing 6–8), you will see that the namespace declaration for the namespace my is exactly the targetNamespace of the schema. The other namespaces used in the schema define the XML schema namespace that contains all schema elements and some additional InfoPath schema extensions.

InfoPath uses element references to structure the schema. Starting at the root node, InfoPath creates complexType elements containing all elements at that node. Each element is described using element references pointing to elements, which are defined at the root element of the schema. This enhances readability of the schema and reusability of the elements.

Looking at the elements, you can see that InfoPath created some simpleType definitions, such as requiredString. This is used to implement the "Cannot be blank" check box in the field properties dialog in InfoPath Editor. This string extends the basic string format of XML Schema using a restriction, saying that the element has a minimum length of 1. You need to understand the difference between this and the minOccurs attribute used in the element descriptions. minOccurs tells the XML parser how often an element may be present in the XML. If you define the FirstName element with minOccurs=1, you are only specifying that this XML element is mandatory. However, the value of the element could still be empty.

Another important related attribute is the nillable attribute. This is usually used for date and time fields, as it allows an element to set the attribute nillable=true. Because a date element always requires the content to be a valid date, this is the only way to create empty date fields. Otherwise, if you entered an empty string into the date element, the validation of the XML would fail. An empty date can thus be created in the XML as <my:Date nil='true'></my:Date>.

*Listing 6–5. Example Schema*

```
<?xml version="1.0" encoding="UTF-8" standalone="no"?>
<xsd:schema targetNamespace="http://schemas.microsoft.com/office/infopath/2003/myXSD/2009-09-
29T22:54:17" xmlns:xsi="http://www.w3.org/2001/XMLSchema-instance"
xmlns:my="http://schemas.microsoft.com/office/infopath/2003/myXSD/2009-09-29T22:54:17"
xmlns:xd="http://schemas.microsoft.com/office/infopath/2003"
xmlns:xsd="http://www.w3.org/2001/XMLSchema">
    <xsd:element name="RoomBooking">
        <xsd:complexType>
            <xsd:sequence>
                <xsd:element ref="my:UserInformation" minOccurs="0"/>
                <xsd:element ref="my:Schedule" minOccurs="0"/>
                <xsd:element ref="my:Hardware" minOccurs="0"/>
                <xsd:element ref="my:Catering" minOccurs="0"/>
                <xsd:element ref="my:Comments" minOccurs="0"/>
                <xsd:element ref="my:readonly" minOccurs="0"/>
            </xsd:sequence>
            <xsd:anyAttribute processContents="lax"
                              namespace="http://www.w3.org/XML/1998/namespace"/>
        </xsd:complexType>
    </xsd:element>

    <xsd:element name="UserInformation">
        <xsd:complexType>
            <xsd:sequence>
                <xsd:element ref="my:FirstName" minOccurs="0"/>
                <xsd:element ref="my:LastName" minOccurs="0"/>
                <xsd:element ref="my:Email" minOccurs="0"/>
                <xsd:element ref="my:Telephone" minOccurs="0"/>
            </xsd:sequence>
        </xsd:complexType>
    </xsd:element>
    <xsd:element name="FirstName" type="my:requiredString"/>
    <xsd:element name="LastName" type="my:requiredString"/>
    <xsd:element name="Email" type="xsd:string"/>
    <xsd:element name="Telephone" type="xsd:string"/>

    <xsd:element name="Schedule">
        <xsd:complexType>
            <xsd:sequence>
                <xsd:element ref="my:Room" minOccurs="0"/>
                <xsd:element ref="my:Date" minOccurs="0"/>
                <xsd:element ref="my:TimeBegin" minOccurs="0"/>
```

```xml
                              <xsd:element ref="my:TimeEnd" minOccurs="0"/>
                      </xsd:sequence>
                  </xsd:complexType>
          </xsd:element>
          <xsd:element name="Room" type="xsd:string"/>
          <xsd:element name="Date" nillable="true" type="xsd:date"/>
          <xsd:element name="TimeBegin" nillable="true" type="xsd:time"/>
          <xsd:element name="TimeEnd" type="xsd:string"/>

          <xsd:element name="Hardware">
              <xsd:complexType>
                  <xsd:sequence>
                      <xsd:element ref="my:DataProjector" minOccurs="0"/>
                      <xsd:element ref="my:Microphone" minOccurs="0"/>
                      <xsd:element ref="my:Notebook" minOccurs="0"/>
                      <xsd:element ref="my:Speakers" minOccurs="0"/>
                      <xsd:element ref="my:VideoConferencing" minOccurs="0"/>
                  </xsd:sequence>
              </xsd:complexType>
          </xsd:element>
          <xsd:element name="DataProjector" nillable="true" type="xsd:boolean"/>
          <xsd:element name="Microphone" nillable="true" type="xsd:boolean"/>
          <xsd:element name="Notebook" nillable="true" type="xsd:boolean"/>
          <xsd:element name="Speakers" nillable="true" type="xsd:boolean"/>
          <xsd:element name="VideoConferencing" nillable="true" type="xsd:boolean"/>

    ...

          <xsd:element name="readonly" nillable="true" type="xsd:boolean"/>

          <xsd:simpleType name="requiredString">
              <xsd:restriction base="xsd:string">
                  <xsd:minLength value="1"/>
              </xsd:restriction>
          </xsd:simpleType>

          <xsd:simpleType name="requiredAnyURI">
              <xsd:restriction base="xsd:anyURI">
                  <xsd:minLength value="1"/>
              </xsd:restriction>
          </xsd:simpleType>

          <xsd:simpleType name="requiredBase64Binary">
              <xsd:restriction base="xsd:base64Binary">
                  <xsd:minLength value="1"/>
              </xsd:restriction>
          </xsd:simpleType>
      </xsd:schema>
```

## GENERATING A CLASS FROM A SCHEMA

The schema definition file can be used to generate .NET classes that represent the XML data elements. Using generated classes makes working with the XML files more convenient and reduces errors.

To generate a C# or VB class from an XSD file, you can use the `xsd.exe` command-line utility, which is part of the .NET Framework. The following command generates a C# class from the input `<schemafile>` and places the generated class into the `<output directory>`:

```
> xsd.exe <schemafile>.xsd /classes /language:CS /outputdir:<output directory>
```

To populate an object with data from an XML instance, you can use the `Deserialize` method of the `XmlSerializer` class as follows:

```
using System.Xml.Serialization;
System.IO.StreamReader str = new System.IO.StreamReader("example.xml");
XmlSerializer xSerializer = new XmlSerializer(typeof(ConferenceBooking));
ConferenceBooking res = (ConferenceBooking) xSerializer.Deserialize(str);
```

In this example we assume that we generated a class called `RoomBooking` based on our example form template.

## Form Views (XSL)

Each view in the form template is defined by an XSL stylesheet file, which comprises all the relevant information for displaying the view. To render a view, the selected XML data file will be transformed into an HTML view via XSLT processing.

Listing 6–6 shows the body of such a view definition. For a clearer perspective, the HTML content, style definitions, and namespace definitions have been removed.

*Listing 6–6. Form View Definition in XSL*

```xml
<?xml version="1.0" encoding="UTF-8"?>
<xsl:stylesheet version="1.0" xmlns:"...">
    <xsl:output method="html" indent="no"/>
    <xsl:template match="my:RoomBooking">
        <html>
            <head>
                <meta content="text/html" http-equiv="Content-Type"></meta>
                <style controlStyle="controlStyle">...</style>
                <style themeStyle="urn:office.microsoft.com:themeOffice">...</style>
                <style languageStyle="languageStyle">...</style>
            </head>
            <body style="BACKGROUND-COLOR: #ffffff; COLOR: #000000">
                ...
            </body>
        </html>
    </xsl:template>
</xsl:stylesheet>
```

The stylesheet defines one template rule that applies to the root element of the XSD schema. In the example you can see that the match attribute points to the RoomBooking node, which is the root element in our example. Within this template, HTML defines the display behavior. To insert the XML information from the data file, XSLT instructions are used within the template. The following snippet (in Listing 6–7) demonstrates how the drop-down list for the room is defined as a table element within the HTML layout. An XSLT select element is inserted, and the attributes value and selected are supplied from the XML data using XSLT instructions.

*Listing 6–7. XSLT Transformation in XSL File*

```
<td class="xdTableComponent" style="PADDING-BOTTOM: 1px; VERTICAL-ALIGN: middle; PADDING-TOP:
1px">
    <div>
        <select class="xdComboBox xdBehavior_Select" title="" size="1" tabIndex="0"
xd:xctname="dropdown" xd:CtrlId="CTRL19" xd:binding="my:Schedule/my:Room" xd:boundProp="value"
style="WIDTH: 100%">
            <xsl:attribute name="value">
                <xsl:value-of select="my:Schedule/my:Room"/>
            </xsl:attribute>
            <option value="">
                <xsl:if test="my:Schedule/my:Room=&quot;&quot;">
                    <xsl:attribute name="selected">selected</xsl:attribute>
                </xsl:if>
            </option>
        </select>
    </div>
</td>
```

As you can see, the structure of XSL views is quite easy to follow and allows you to make changes to the layout or the XSL instructions. Nevertheless, manually editing views is very time consuming and requires you to deal with some Microsoft-specific schemas.

## Form XML Template (XML)

Every form template contains two XML files: sampledata.xml and template.xml. The sampledata.xml file contains all the elements of the form with their default values, which were specified when the form was designed. The template.xml file represents an XML template that is used as a template for creating new documents. Although at first sight these files may not seem to be very useful, for developers this is not so. The template file, for example, can be used to create new document instances from custom code. If you wish to dynamically set default values for your forms, you can edit sampledata.xml from within your code.

The structure of the XML files is the same as the structure of form data files, described next.

## InfoPath Form Data

The following snippet (see Listing 6–8) shows an example data file for the InfoPath form used in the Conference Room Booking example. In addition to the standard XML structure that complies with the preceding schema definition, InfoPath has added two special processing instructions. Within them are several attributes that define InfoPath metadata, such as version numbers. The most important attribute is the href attribute in the mso-infoPathSolution processing instruction. It links to the InfoPath form template—which is used to render the form—by specifying its location.

*Listing 6–8. Sample XML Data File*

```
<?xml version="1.0" encoding="UTF-8"?>
<?mso-infoPathSolution solutionVersion="1.0.0.24" productVersion="14.0.0"
PIVersion="1.0.0.0"
href="file:///C:\Users\Administrator\AppData\Local\Microsoft\InfoPath\Designer3\70314fc28
49b4bbc\manifest.xsf" ?><?mso-application progid="InfoPath.Document"
versionProgid="InfoPath.Document.3"?>
<my:ConferenceBooking xmlns:xsi="http://www.w3.org/2001/XMLSchema-instance"
xmlns:my="http://schemas.microsoft.com/office/infopath/2003/myXSD/2009-09-22T18:21:06"
xmlns:xd="http://schemas.microsoft.com/office/infopath/2003" xml:lang="en-us">
    <my:UserInformation>
        <my:FirstName>John</my:FirstName>
        <my:LastName>Smith</my:LastName>
        <my:Email>john@smith.com</my:Email>
        <my:Telephone>01234567</my:Telephone>
    </my:UserInformation>
    <my:Schedule>
        <my:Room>Conference Room 1</my:Room>
        <my:RoomNumber>0001</my:RoomNumber>
        <my:Date>2009-12-31</my:Date>
        <my:TimeBegin>12:00:00</my:TimeBegin>
        <my:TimeEnd>14:00:00</my:TimeEnd>
    </my:Schedule>
    <my:Hardware>
        <my:DataProjector>true</my:DataProjector>
        <my:Microphone>false</my:Microphone>
        <my:Notebook>false</my:Notebook>
        <my:Speakers>false</my:Speakers>
        <my:VideoConferencing>true</my:VideoConferencing>
    </my:Hardware>
    <my:Catering>
        <my:Coffee>false</my:Coffee>
        <my:SoftDrinks>false</my:SoftDrinks>
        <my:Cookies>false</my:Cookies>
        <my:Snacks>false</my:Snacks>
    </my:Catering>
    <my:Comments>
        <my:Comment>Some additional comment</my:Comment>
    </my:Comments>
    <my:readonly>false</my:readonly>
</my:RoomBooking>
```

# Designing Browser-Enabled Form Templates

Having examined the internal structure of InfoPath form templates, we will now take a closer look at the important steps in building form templates that can be used within SharePoint and Forms Services. Most of the wizards, dialogs, and property windows that can be used throughout these steps are identical in InfoPath 2007 and 2010. Many of the changes made to the InfoPath 2010 UI are concentrated in the reorganized menus on to the ribbon bars. You will find some properties that used to be hidden in cascaded dialogs are now directly available in the ribbon bars, which is a great improvement when designing larger forms.

InfoPath 2010 has been divided into two distinct programs: InfoPath Designer and InfoPath Filler. This separation reflects the two different usage scenarios and with it the two different roles for working with InfoPath. InfoPath Designer is targeted at those who create and design form templates. InfoPath Filler is the client application for filling out forms. The split makes it easier for users to understand InfoPath—in the past this difference was not made clear to new users of InfoPath.

## Defining the Data Structure

When using forms in complex business solutions, the most important aspect is the design of your data schema. This is particularly so if you are using the schema throughout a business process where you access the XML contents using custom .NET code or property promotion and demotion in SharePoint lists. Schema design becomes even more complex if you plan to use your schema across different applications (e.g., when using BizTalk to process form data with the BizTalk mapping facilities).

There are two approaches to designing the schema:

- Use the InfoPath client to generate and edit the schema during template design.

- Define your schema first and create a form template based on this schema.

When you begin form creation by selecting a new blank form template, InfoPath will create the schema definition for you. This way you can simply add new controls to your views, or edit the schema in the Fields dialog (see Figure 6–3). Although your control over the schema that is produced is limited in this case, this scenario may be adequate for simple forms.

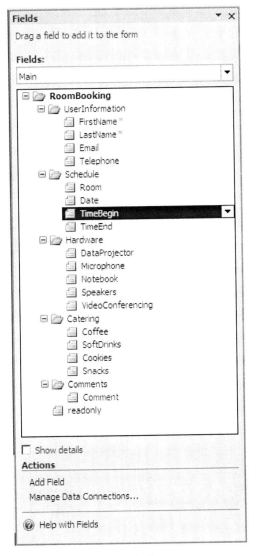

*Figure 6–3. The Fields dialog*

If you need full control over the XSD schema definition (e.g., when planning to use the XML across different applications), you should first build the XSD schema definition yourself and then create a new form template based on this schema. InfoPath provides a wizard to generate a new form by selecting the XML or Schema template. You merely choose your schema and start designing your form based on that schema.

When you design your own schema, you are able to use some advanced mechanisms of XML Schema, but you should keep in mind the following:

- InfoPath does not support the entire XML Schema syntax.

- If you build your form on an existing schema, you will not be able to change the field properties using the Fields dialog. Instead you will have to use the Data ➤ Refresh Fields option to reload the schema.

- You can use data type restrictions in your schema to limit the allowed values in your form. Since InfoPath validates your XML input against the schema, you have only limited control of the errors that are presented to users when they input data that is invalid according to the schema.

- For suitable user feedback, it may be better to validate input data using rules in InfoPath and displaying meaningful messages to the users.

- Very strict schema definitions can prevent Forms Services from displaying your form at all, since invalid XML, according to the schema, will not be opened. This results in a very general "Form has been closed" message in the UI.

- Overly restrictive data types in the schema make modifying "accepted input" more complex, especially if you intend that not only developers but also information workers should be able to make changes to the form design. For example, if your schema is defined to accept any string for user input, rules can be used to constrain the input to certain values. These rules can be changed by anyone capable of working with InfoPath, whereas a change to the schema would necessitate a complex development change scenario.

Overall, you should create your schema with care and weigh the pros and cons of very strict schemas. Use your schema to define the basic data structure but take care when using strong data type restrictions—you might end up spending a lot of time searching for the reason why your forms can't be displayed.

## Designing the Form Templates

To lay out form templates, InfoPath uses different views. Only one view at a time will be displayed when the form is rendered, but users can switch between these views. This allows you to split large forms into different views, which makes it easier to work with the form. Furthermore, views can also be defined as *read-only* or designed with the sole purpose of printing. Read-only views in particular are very useful when forms should be immutable after they have been submitted. To achieve this behavior you simply add a property named readonly to your schema that will be set to true when the form is submitted. Adding a rule into the form load event, which switches the active view to the read-only view, if this readonly property is set to true, will always show the read-only view after the form is submitted.

Within views, layout tables should be used to arrange elements. These layout tables are displayed in InfoPath Editor using dashed lines, but they are not displayed when the form is rendered. These tables result in HTML table elements in the XSL form view. Controls or fields can simply be dragged into the layout table at the desired position. To limit the effort to lay out the form, InfoPath 2010 offers some table and section templates, as shown in Figure 6–4. You can use them to quickly build well-organized form templates.

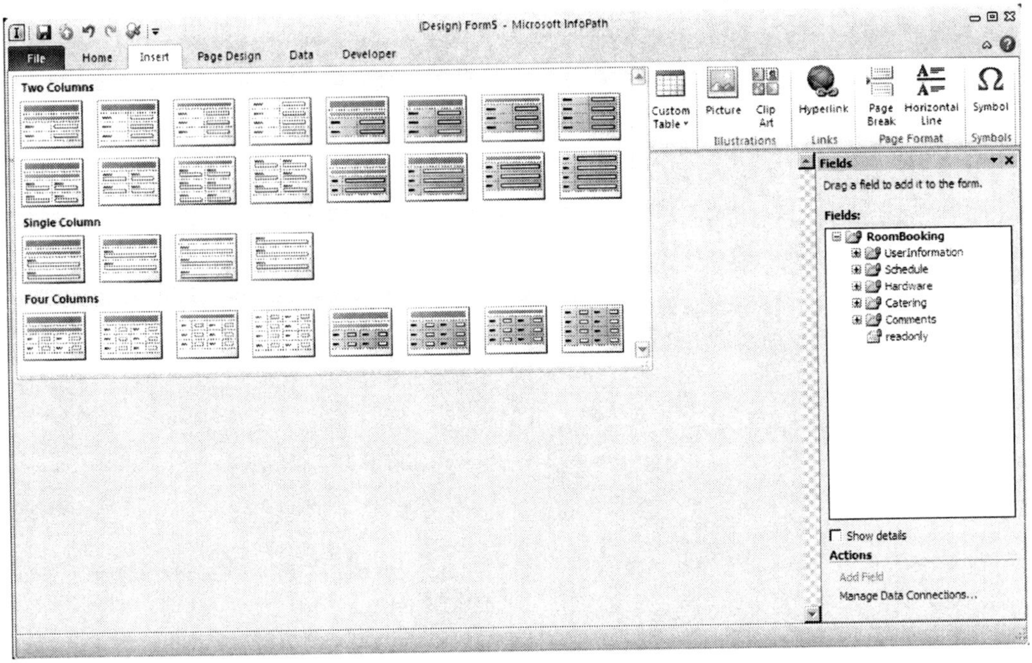

*Figure 6–4. Section templates*

To edit the behavior of control fields you can use either the context menu or the Properties ribbon bar. Depending on the type of control, different properties will be available. Every control is bound to a field in your document schema. The Change Binding option will change the binding target. Selecting the Control Properties window will allow you to specify data properties, display properties, size properties, and some other advanced properties. For special data types such as integers and dates, on the display tab you can configure the output format—for example, to display an integer as a currency.

## Adding Rules and Validation

Rules are used in InfoPath to control form behavior. While in InfoPath 2007 rules are dispersed across multiple menus—rules, data validation, and conditional formatting—InfoPath 2010 merges them together. They can now be action rules, validation rules, or formatting rules, but are all accessible through one editor pane, the Rules dialog (Figure 6–5).

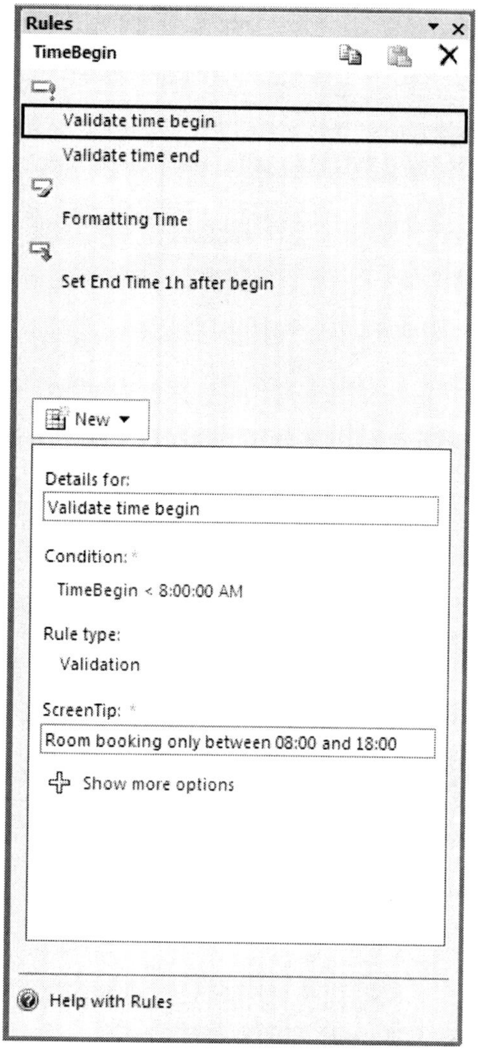

**Figure 6–5.** *The Rules dialog*

Every rule consists of an entry condition, allowing the form template author to define when the rule applies. Formatting rules specify text formatting to apply to the nominated field. Validation rules will result in a form error when the condition is not met, and the data for the particular control will be flagged as invalid. Whenever a user changes the value of a control, InfoPath checks the entry conditions of all the action rules assigned to that control. If the condition for a rule is fulfilled, the specified actions are executed.

■ **Caution** Action rules will only by evaluated when the value in the field actually changes. Loading a default value does not trigger the change event, even when it meets the condition for the action rule. Formatting and validation rules, on the other hand, will always be applied.

To view all the rules within a form, you can use the Rule Inspector. It shows all the dynamic elements (e.g., rules, calculated default values, and managed code). Figure 6–6 shows the Rule Inspector for the Conference Room Booking example. You can see that data validations have been added for the date and time values, aggregated under Alerts. Also note too the interesting rules shown in the Other Actions section. The Programming section will contain the events raised by your code when you add code to your form template.

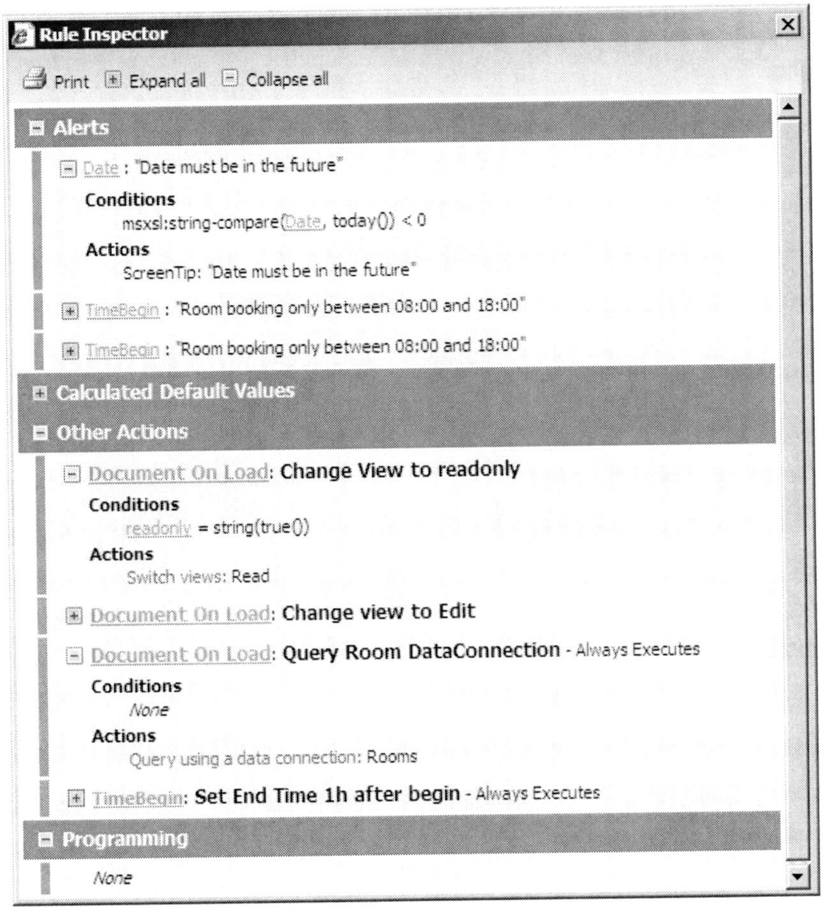

*Figure 6–6. The Rule Inspector*

## Accessing External Data

Designing forms for LOB applications often requires data from external data sources to be included in the form. Typically, such data is retrieved from databases, SharePoint lists, or web services. A drop-down list, for instance, could be populated with values directly within the form. If the values are subject to change, though, you might consider populating them from outside the form. InfoPath accommodates access to external data through the definition of secondary data sources.

Each form consists of one primary data source (also called a data connection) and several secondary data sources. In the previous chapter we described how to define a primary data source using an XSD schema. Data connections can be managed via the Data menu. You can add new data connections using the Data Connection wizard. The wizard will prompt for some specific parameters for the data connection, such as the URL of the SharePoint list and the fields that you want to use. Once the data connection is set up, you need to tell InfoPath to load the data from this connection. This is not done automatically, except when you check the box "automatically retrieve data when the form is opened" in the final step of the Data Connection wizard. Otherwise, you will have to add a rule action that queries the data connection, as shown in Figure 6–7, or execute the connection using code.

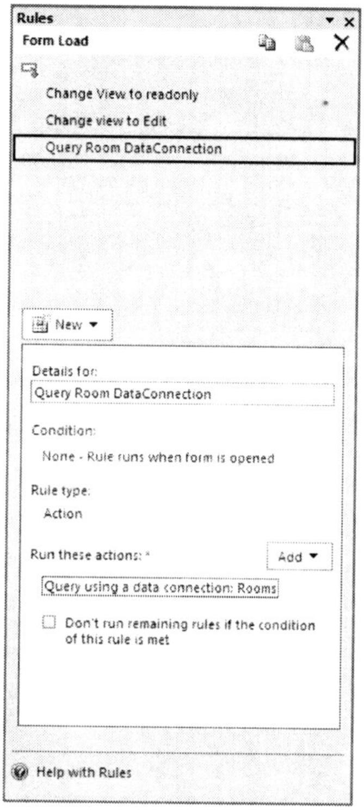

*Figure 6–7. Creating a rule to query a data connection*

When using web service connections that require query parameters, you need to build a rule that sets the query parameter, queries the connection, and finally returns the result of the web service.

Secondary data connections can be employed in the same ways as primary data connections—in rules and formulas or binding to a control. A common scenario for secondary data connections is to fill a drop-down list with dynamic values, as shown in Figure 6–8.

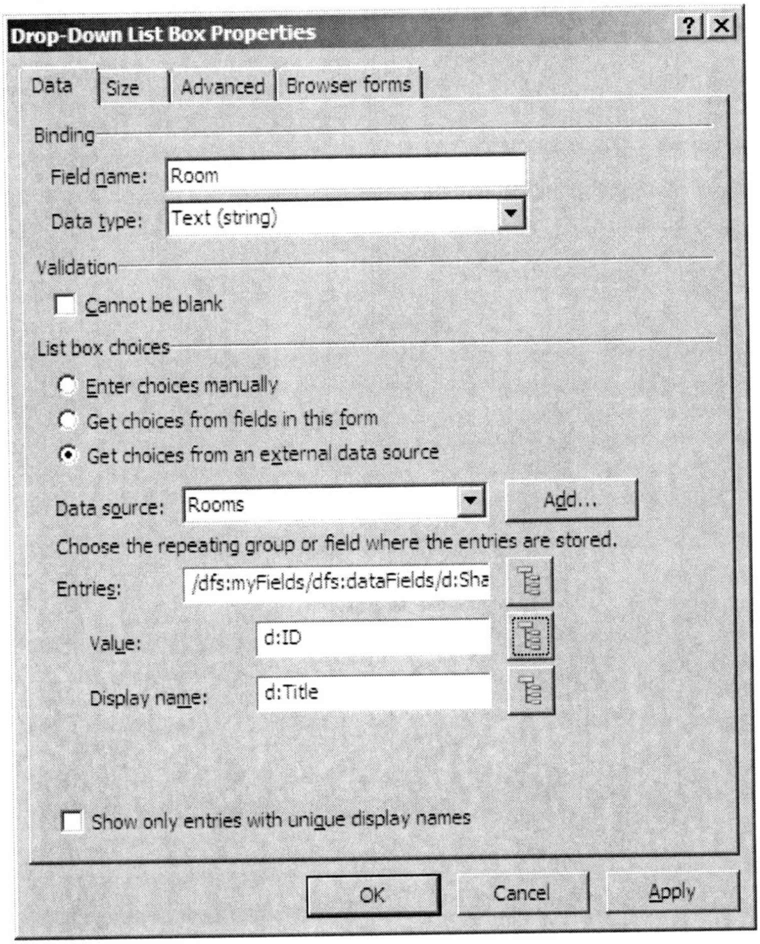

*Figure 6–8. Building a drop-down list from a data connection*

In this example, the Rooms data source is selected to supply the values in the drop-down list. This data source points to a SharePoint list containing all rooms. The Entries field references the repeating item in the resultant data from the connection, and the list ID and Title are used in the Value and "Display name" fields, respectively.

Data connections can be used for querying data from and submitting data to a data repository. The following table shows a list of data sources you can use and whether they can be used for sending or receiving data.

*Table 6–1. Different Types of Data Connections*

| Data Connection | Submit | Receive |
| --- | --- | --- |
| Web service | Yes | Yes |
| SharePoint library or list | No | Yes |
| SharePoint document library | Yes | No |
| E-mail message | yes | No |
| Groove library or list | No | Yes |
| Microsoft SQL Server database | No | Yes |
| XML document | No | Yes |
| Hosting environment | Yes | No |

One very useful data repository is the hosting environment. This can be used to send data to the environment that is hosting the InfoPath form, such as the forms service running on SharePoint or a custom application page. We will discuss this topic in the "InfoPath Forms Services" section later in the chapter.

Using the InfoPath wizard to add a data connection strongly binds the form template to the data connection, since all the information about the connection is stored within the form. When working with SharePoint forms within a multilevel development environment—consisting of a development and production environment—or when creating reusable forms, this solution is very inflexible. To add another layer of abstraction for data connections, you should use data connection libraries in SharePoint. They can easily be created like any other library. Select View All Site Content from the Site Actions drop-down menu. Then click Create and select Data Connection Library to create a new data connection library.

Those libraries can hold *Universal Data Description (UDCX)* files, which are used to store connection information. UDCX files can then be used by InfoPath to reference data connections. This decouples the strong binding between the actual data connection and the form template, and thus allows you to supply the same form template with different UDCX files for different SharePoint environments.

UDCX files are XML files adhering to the UDC schema definition. Listing 6–9 shows an example UDCX file for a data connection to SharePoint, to retrieve the rooms for the Conference Room Booking example.

*Listing 6–9. Example Universal Data Description File*

```
<?xml version="1.0" encoding="UTF-8"?>
<?MicrosoftWindowsSharePointServices
ContentTypeID="0x010100B4CBD48E029A4ad8B62CB0E41868F2B0"?>
```

```
<udc:DataSource MajorVersion="2" MinorVersion="0"
xmlns:udc="http://schemas.microsoft.com/office/infopath/2006/udc">
    <udc:Name>Rooms</udc:Name>
    <udc:Description>Format: UDC V2; Connection Type: SharePointList; Purpose: ReadOnly;
Generated by Microsoft Office InfoPath 2007 on 2009-10-05 at 13:46:53 by
WAPPS\moss_service.</udc:Description>
    <udc:Type MajorVersion="2" MinorVersion="0" Type="SharePointList">
        <udc:SubType MajorVersion="0" MinorVersion="0" Type=""/>
    </udc:Type>
    <udc:ConnectionInfo Purpose="ReadOnly" AltDataSource="">
        <udc:WsdlUrl/>
            <udc:SelectCommand>
                <udc:ListId>{68BB674B-85D9-450A-B394-6FD9F08B6959}</udc:ListId>
                <udc:WebUrl>http://winsrv2008as/</udc:WebUrl>
                <udc:ConnectionString/>
                <udc:ServiceUrl UseFormsServiceProxy="false"/>
                <udc:SoapAction/>
                <udc:Query/>
            </udc:SelectCommand>
            <udc:UpdateCommand>
                <udc:ServiceUrl UseFormsServiceProxy="false"/>
                <udc:SoapAction/>
                <udc:Submit/>
                <udc:FileName>Specify a filename or formula</udc:FileName>
                <udc:FolderName AllowOverwrite=""/>
            </udc:UpdateCommand>
            <!--udc:Authentication><udc:SSO AppId='' CredentialType='' />
</udc:Authentication-->
        </udc:ConnectionInfo>
    </udc:ConnectionInfo>
</udc:DataSource>
```

The preceding listing contains a processing instruction for SharePoint with a ContentTypeID attribute, which specifies the ContentType for data connection files within SharePoint. The DataSource element defines the namespace and the version of the UDCX format. The attributes of the data connection are defined within the ConnectionInfo section. The element Type as a subelement of DataSource has an attribute also called Type, which specifies the type of the connection. It can be one of the following values, which match the data connection option in InfoPath Editor:

- SharePointList

- SharePointLibrary

- Database

- XmlQuery

- XmlSubmit

- WebService

The attribute Purpose specifies the direction of the data connection. ReadOnly is used for receive connections, WriteOnly is used for submit connections, and ReadWrite is used for bidirectional connections. Depending on this parameter, SelectCommand and/or UpdateCommand need to be supplied. Both support all the necessary information to set up the connection.

To create a UDCX file, you can edit an existing UDCX file or let InfoPath create the file as follows:

1. Create a data connection library in SharePoint.

2. Configure your data connection using the InfoPath wizard.

3. Select the Data Connection Manager in InfoPath from Data ➤ Data Connections.

4. Choose the particular data connection and click Convert to Connection File...

5. Enter the path to the data connection library you created in step 1, followed by the file name of the UDCX file you want to create.

6. Choose "Relative to site collection" to cause InfoPath to look for the data connection library relative to the site collection, or choose "Centrally managed data connection" if you intend to manage your data connections in Central Administration.

7. If you choose to manage your UDCX files centrally, you need to download the UDCX file, save it locally, and then add it manually to Central Administration.

8. Now you can use this UDCX file in your forms to create a new data connection by selecting "Search for connections on a Microsoft Office SharePoint Server" and entering the URL to the data connection library.

## Forms Security

InfoPath form templates support three different levels of security. Each security level defines the allowed level of access to external resources from a form. The required security level for your form depends on the scenario in which you want to use your form. These scenarios range from simple data input scenarios where the form is only used for user input with no programming logic or access to external data sources, to very sophisticated forms that make use of programming facilities and aggregate information from various sources.

You can change the security settings in the Form Options dialog, accessible via File ➤ Info ➤ "Advanced form options," as shown in Figure 6–9.

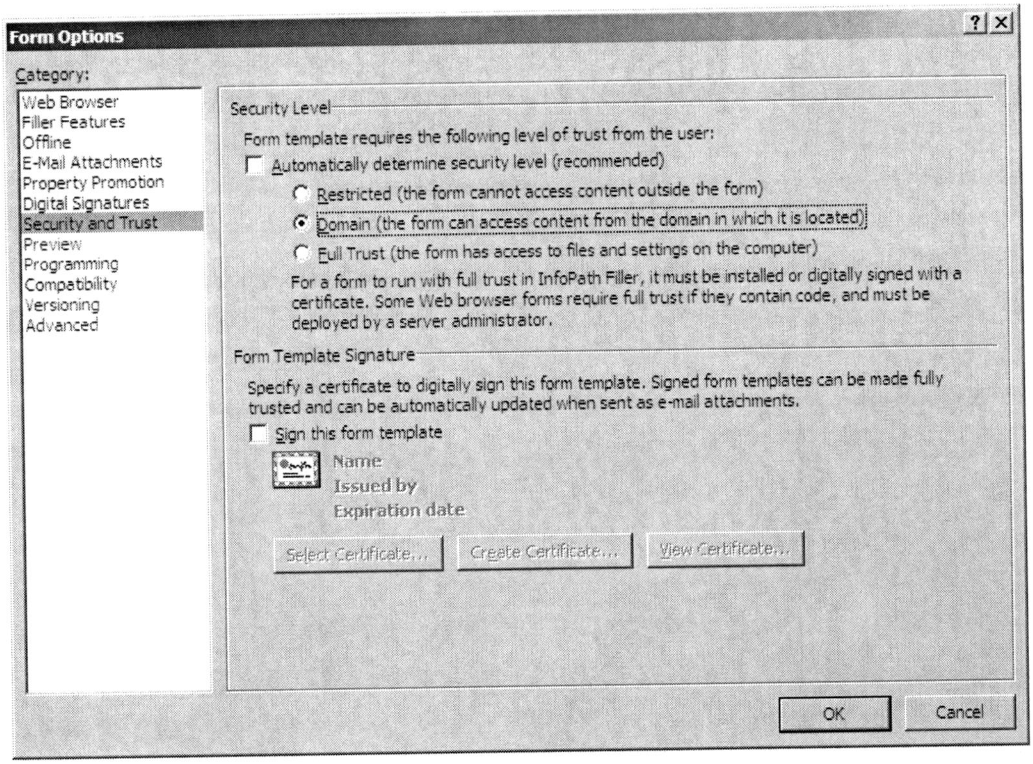

*Figure 6–9. Security options*

By default, the check box "Automatically determine security level" is checked. In this case, InfoPath tries to define the security level based on the features used in the form. Since you should know the scenario for which you are designing the form, it is a good idea to manually select one of the following options. Otherwise, you might run into complications during publishing and deployment, and have to spend extra time searching for the source of your problems.

- *Restricted*: The Restricted security level is used for forms that don't contain any code and don't communicate with external data sources. Forms that are created with restricted access can only be used as a data container to collect information from users. Since communication outside of the form is not permitted and no potentially harmful code can be contained in those forms, restricted forms provide the highest level of security. On the other hand, usage scenarios for these types of forms are very limited. Restricted forms always require InfoPath Filler, because to use them with Forms Services in SharePoint, a minimum security level of Domain is required. However, you could e-mail these forms to the recipients or put them on a network share and have users fill them out with InfoPath Filler.

- *Domain*: The Domain security level restricts the access of a form to a particular domain. The form can contain code and may access data sources within the domain of the form. InfoPath Forms Services requires at least the Domain security level for forms to render in the browser. By default, you will work with this security level when designing browser-based form templates, as they are suitable for most scenarios where the form accesses lists and libraries on the local SharePoint Server but doesn't contain code that accesses local resources. This type of form is also called *sandboxed*, because the form is placed in the local cache while the user is filling it out, and access to system resources is denied.

- *Full Trust*: The Full Trust security level allows the form to access system resources and other components on the computer where the form will be used, or to use cross-domain data connections. For example, fully trusted forms can contain potentially harmful code and use Microsoft ActiveX controls. Having a higher set of permissions requires fully trusted forms to be digitally signed to ensure security when deploying them to SharePoint. Although you could possibly create fully trusted forms without signing the form, this scenario would require you to install the template on each client—not an acceptable solution in most scenarios. We will show you how to sign and deploy fully trusted form templates in the section "Deploying InfoPath Forms to SharePoint." Fully trusted forms in SharePoint need to be approved by a farm administrator.

## Enabling Browser Support

InfoPath allows you to design form templates, targeting different scenarios. The most interesting scenario within the context of SharePoint is the ability to render InfoPath forms in a browser using InfoPath Forms Services. Designing browser-based forms requires some special considerations and settings, and poses some limitations compared to designing forms for the InfoPath client.

### Setting Form Compatibility

When you start to design a new form, you can choose the type of template you want to design. Some advanced templates will require you to enable browser support in your form template. To enable browser support, go to File ➤ Info ➤ "Advanced form options," and select Compatibility from the Category list. Set the form type to Web Browser Form, as shown in Figure 6–10. This tells InfoPath that this form can be rendered in a browser. You can enter your SharePoint URL in the field beneath to allow InfoPath to validate your browser compatibility directly on the SharePoint server using a web service of InfoPath Forms Services.

Depending on the compatibility setting, some features will be hidden or deactivated in the relevant dialogs. For example, the multiline feature of text boxes is limited when you work with browser-enabled forms. Figure 6–11 shows the different options for templates designed for InfoPath Editor (on the left) and InfoPath Forms Services (on the right). Therefore, you should always set the compatibility before starting to design your form template. This way you ensure that you are only using available features.

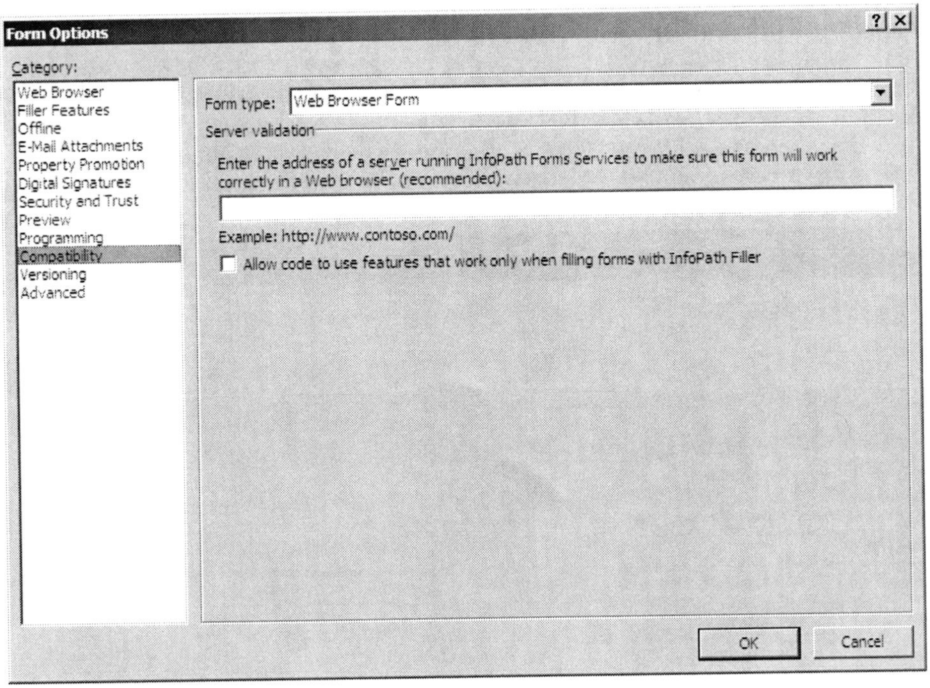

*Figure 6–10. Enabling browser compatibility*

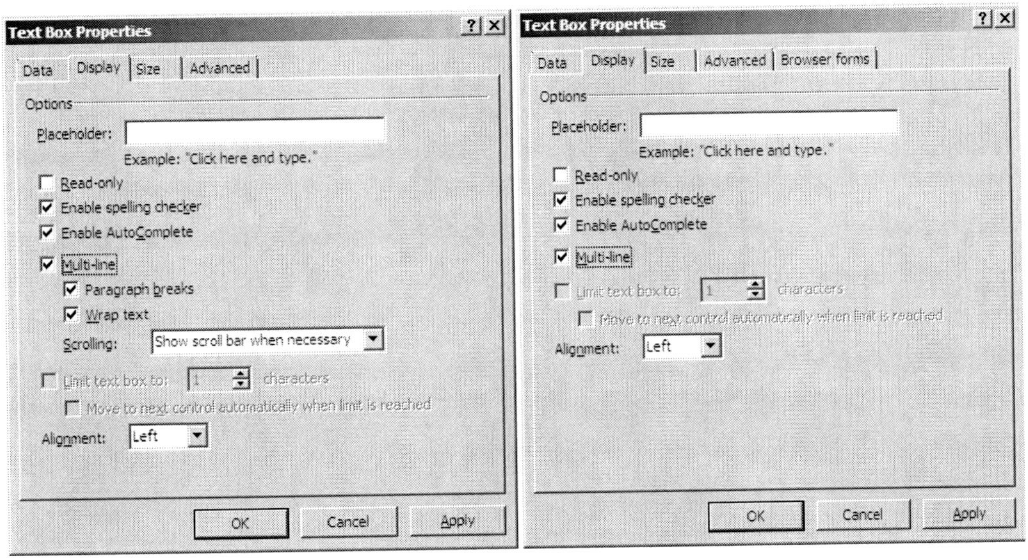

*Figure 6–11. Different properties for InfoPath forms (left) and browser-enabled forms (right)*

## Configuring Interface Options for InfoPath Forms Services

After you have set the compatibility to Web Browser Form, you will find a new category called Web Browser in your Form Options dialog when you reopen it (Figure 6–13). Here you can set advanced options that change the browser interface, which is shown in Figure 6–14. You can select the commands you wish to display to the user when editing the form. Furthermore, you can select alternative toolbars in case the ribbon bar is not available, and set the language that will be used for displaying the commands and dialogs.

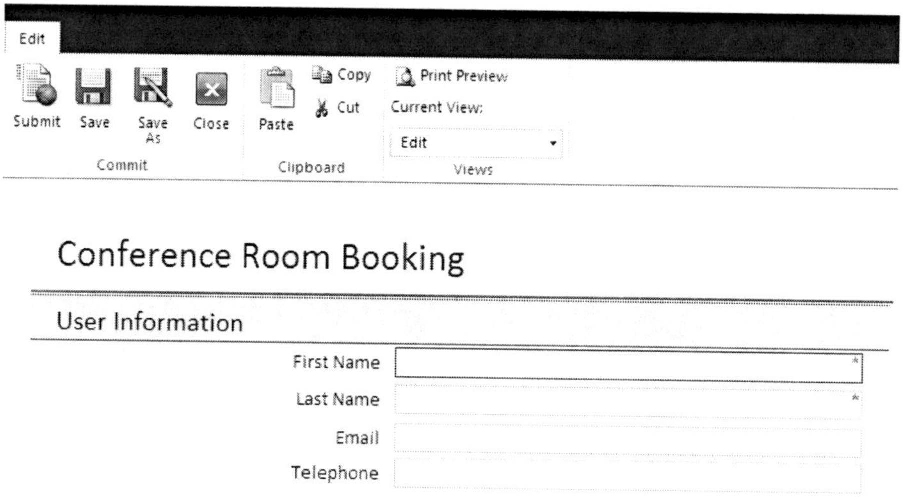

*Figure 6–12. UI in InfoPath Forms Services*

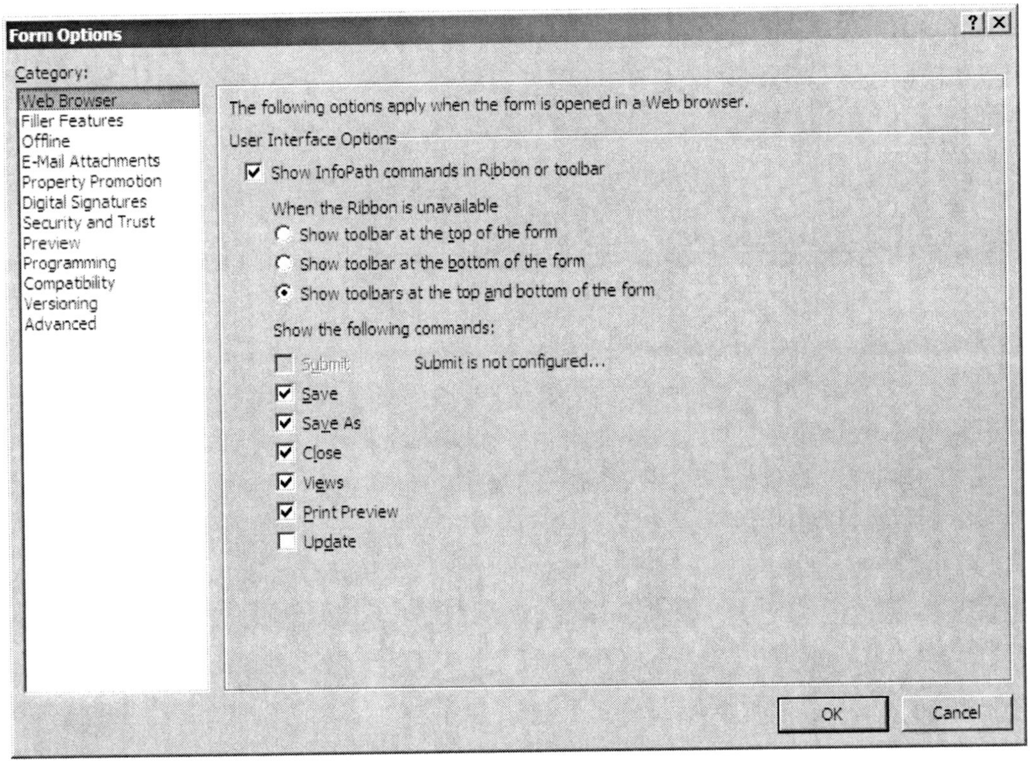

*Figure 6–13. Setting UI options*

## Configuring Submit Options

You need to specify the destination for the data entered into the form. Submitting the form will trigger Forms Services to run the validation checks on the form. All the validation rules must pass before the submit is allowed to proceed.

You can either specify submission using rules (i.e., you can add a button with an action rule and select the submit action) or you can use the submit options from the Data ribbon bar. In either case you need to specify a submit data connection as described previously. Most commonly you will use a connection to a SharePoint library, a SharePoint data connection, or the hosting environment. When specifying a SharePoint library, you need to provide the URL of the library and the file name for saving the form. The file name can be constructed using a formula. The hosting environment will be used when you want to programmatically access the form information from an ASP.NET application such as SharePoint application pages.

The submit options, as shown in Figure 6–14, allow you to specify the submit destination and the corresponding data connection. As an alternative, you could use code to programmatically handle the submit event.

Specifying submit options and using a button with action rules to submit the form differ in the way the submit action will be displayed to the users. If you are using submit options, the submit button will be displayed in the ribbon bar; however, placing a button in the form provides more flexibility and might be more intuitive for many users. You can also make use of the new image buttons, which allow you to customize button layout.

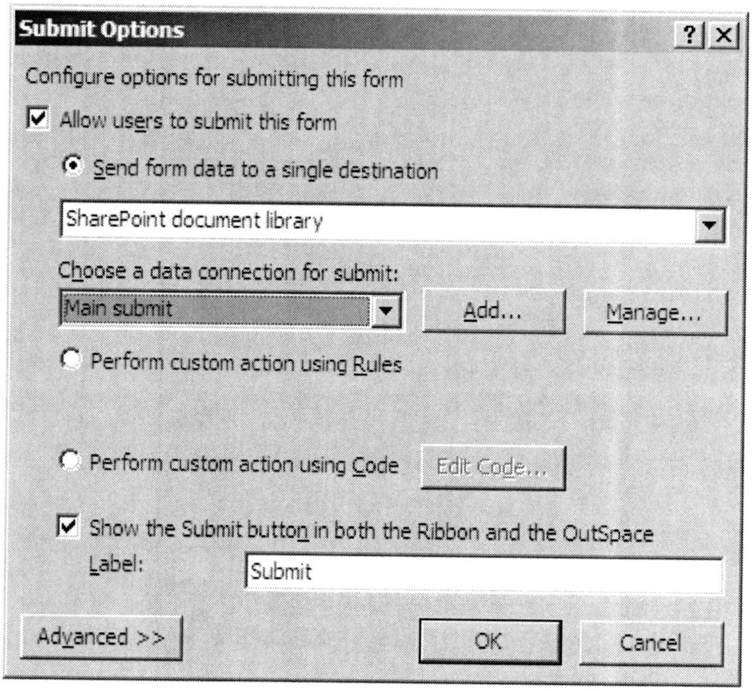

*Figure 6–14. Setting submit options*

To ensure that browser support is configured correctly, use the following checklist:

- Compatibility is set to Web Browser Form.
- The UI options are set correctly.
- The security level is set to Domain or Full Trust.
- Design Checker shows no compatibility errors.
- The Submit option is set to either SharePoint or Hosting environment.

# Deploying InfoPath Forms to SharePoint

Once you have finished designing your InfoPath form template using InfoPath Designer, you need to make the form template available to users so that they can fill out forms based on your form template. Since information about the target location is stored inside the XSN file, you cannot simply copy your form to that location. Instead, InfoPath offers a process called *publishing*, which prepares the form template for its target location. Depending on the targeted scenario, required parameters are set in the manifest.xml file inside the XSN archive.

# Using InfoPath Forms in SharePoint

Before talking about how publishing works, we will take a closer look at the different ways to use InfoPath forms inside SharePoint. (You can also use your InfoPath forms without SharePoint, but such scenarios will not be covered here.)

The following are some scenarios for using InfoPath forms in SharePoint:

- *Forms in document libraries*: This is probably the most common scenario for using InfoPath forms in SharePoint. You simply create a *forms library*—a special type of document library—in SharePoint and attach form templates to this library. Users are then able to fill out forms based on the provided form templates and submit the results to the forms library. You can easily attach SharePoint workflows to these document libraries to implement simple business processes for your forms.

- *Workflow forms*: When building SharePoint workflows you can use InfoPath forms to gather information from users. Workflows allow you to integrate forms at various stages of workflow execution (e.g., association, initiation, or user tasks). Each of these forms can be handled with InfoPath forms instead of custom ASPX pages. In Chapter 16, we describe workflows in more detail and also show how to deploy and integrate InfoPath forms into workflows.

- *Custom application using InfoPath Forms Services*: Of course, you can also develop your own application pages, built on InfoPath forms and InfoPath Forms Services. You can host the XmlFormView control within your own page and use it to display InfoPath forms. We will describe the XmlFormView control in more detail later, in the section "InfoPath Forms Services." Creating your own application pages is the most powerful option for using InfoPath forms, because you are barely limited in the solution you build. On the other hand, you have to do more coding, but you gain a significant amount of control!

- *Integrating forms into SharePoint pages using the InfoPath Form Web Part*: In SharePoint 2010 a new Web Part for displaying forms has been added, allowing users to add a form to a SharePoint page without any additional effort. Simply select Insert ➤ Web Part in the editing mode of a page and select the InfoPath Form Web Part. We will describe this Web Part in more detail in the section "InfoPath Forms Services."

- *List item forms*: SharePoint 2010 increases the integration of InfoPath forms and offers the possibility of customizing all forms for creating, editing, and viewing items in SharePoint lists using InfoPath. If you select Customize Form from the List ribbon bar, as shown in Figure 6–15, InfoPath Designer will open, allowing you to create a custom form for viewing, editing, and creating list items. You can also manage these forms under List Settings ➤ General Settings ➤ Form Settings. The created InfoPath forms will be placed in a subfolder of your list, called Forms.

**Figure 6–15.** *Customizing list forms*

# Publishing and Deploying Using the InfoPath Wizard

The easiest way to publish your form templates is to use the InfoPath Publishing wizard. You can reach the wizard from File ➤ Share ➤ Publish. In the Publish pane, you will be presented with the following four options to publish your form:

- Publish form to current location
- Publish form to SharePoint Library
- Publish form to a list of E-Mail recipients
- Publish form to a network location or file share

The first option is available as soon as you define a publishing location. You can use this option to quickly publish your form with the settings you entered the last time you published the form. The publish button is also available in the Quick Access Toolbar.

Publishing to e-mail recipients requires each user to have InfoPath Filler installed on their computer, to fill out the form.

To deploy forms directly to SharePoint you can select the second option, "Publish form to SharePoint Library." If you are deploying your form using a special deployment method, such as features, command-line scripts, or uploading your form using Central Administration, you can also use the fourth option and publish your form to a network location. All the InfoPath Publishing wizard does is add some parameters and options to your manifest file. These settings can, of course, also be set by the other publishing methods. Nevertheless, the wizard can be used for prototyping and ad hoc solutions, so we will describe the different publishing options using the wizard first. In the next chapter, we will show how you can use other publishing methods.

When you start to publish a form to SharePoint using the Publishing wizard, the first step requires you to enter the URL of your SharePoint server. After InfoPath contacts the SharePoint web services to gather information about the site, the dialog shown in Figure 6–16 will appear. Some of the options might be disabled based on the security settings of the form. For example, fully trusted forms will only allow the last option to be selected. The three options are discussed following.

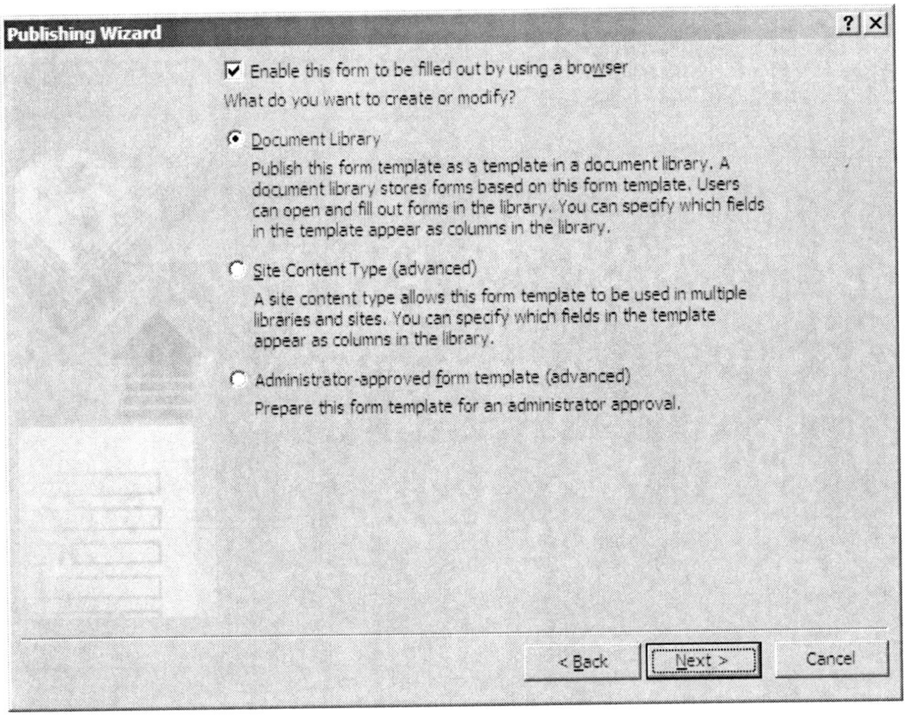

*Figure 6–16. Publishing a form template to SharePoint (basic options)*

---

■ **Tip** After you have entered all the relevant information and finished the wizard, InfoPath will use the Forms Services web service to browser-enable the form template. You can use the same web service for your own deployment scenario. The web service is available at `<web application URL>/_vti_bin/FormsServices.asmx`. This web service offers methods for browser-enabling form templates and design-checking forms, and several other methods that are useful for form template deployment. Detailed information is available at `http://msdn.microsoft.com/en-us/library/bb862916.aspx`.

---

## Publishing Form Templates to Document Libraries

When you choose to publish the form template to a document library, the form template will be stored inside the document library in an invisible folder called `Forms`. The form template itself will be called `template.xsn`, irrespective of its original file name. A content type will then be created based on this XSN file, and assigned as a standard content type for the document library in question.

By default, when creating a new document library, either from the wizard or manually, only one content type is allowed per library. During publishing, InfoPath will overwrite this content type and set the form template as the default content type.

You can create new documents based on the published form template by clicking New Document on the library toolbar. Thus, this publishing option offers a quick method to create a document library with one InfoPath form assigned. This way you can provide a single form template per library, and you cannot reuse the published form template across multiple libraries.

---

■ **Note** Although you can select the "Allow management of multiple content types" option from Form Library Settings ➤ Advanced Settings, publishing a second template to this library using the wizard will still overwrite the existing content type. To publish more than one form to a library, you need to publish the form as a separate content type.

---

## Publishing Form Templates as a Separate Content Type

If you want to use your InfoPath template across multiple libraries, or use multiple form templates within one library, you need to publish your form template as a separate content type. When you do so, InfoPath Forms Services will create a new content type (or update an existing one if you choose this option) based on the form template. You will then be able to select this content type for your library in the list settings page. When you add the new content type to your library, users will be able to create new documents based on this form template by selecting New Document from the Documents ribbon.

In the Publishing wizard you will be asked to specify a location and file name for your form template (Figure 6–17). You can specify any document library within the site to which your content type will be published. However, the best location for your form templates is a library called Form Templates within your site. This library is available in every site and can be accessed by the path <Site URL>/FormServerTemplates.

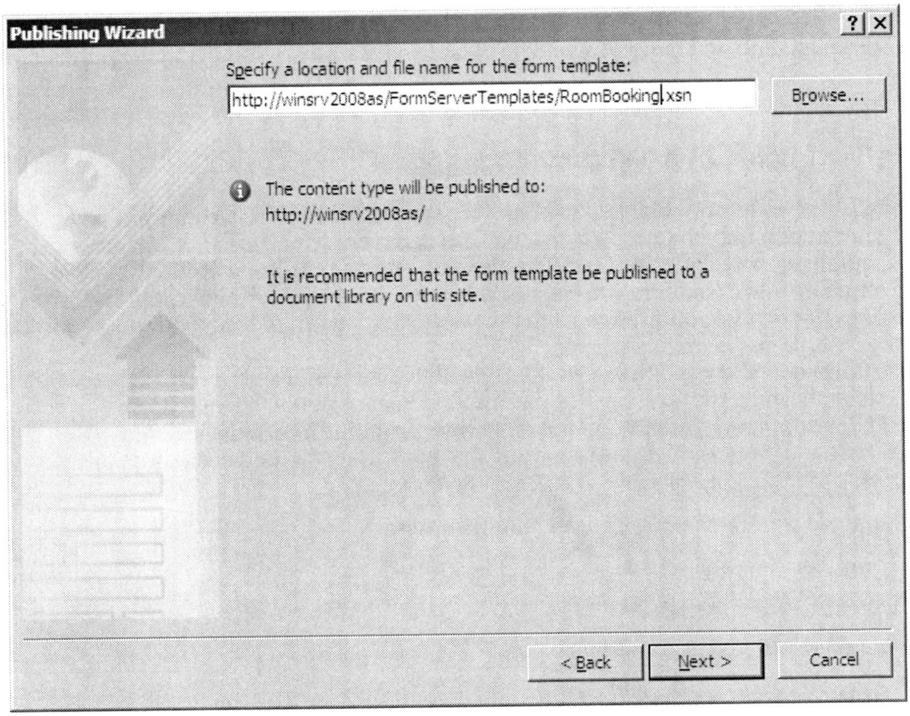

*Figure 6–17. Publishing a form template to SharePoint as a content type*

## Publishing Form Templates as Administrator-Approved Templates

As already mentioned in when talking about forms security earlier, whenever you wish to publish a fully trusted form to SharePoint, the form must be deployed by a farm administrator. Such forms are known as *administrator-approved form templates*. Of course, you can also deploy forms as administrator-approved form templates that don't require administrator approval. You might want to do this to unify your deployment when working with different types of form templates. However, the form templates will have to be deployed by a farm administrator in any case.

During publishing of an administrator-approved template you will be asked to enter the SharePoint URL, which will be saved in the published form template. After that, you must enter a network location or local file name where the template will be saved. A SharePoint administrator can now upload this published form to SharePoint via Central Administration. After uploading, the form must be enabled for the site collections where it is to be used.

In general, using administrator-approved templates requires the following:

- The form template must be published to a location on the network or local file system.

- The template must be uploaded to SharePoint.

- The template must be enabled for a site collection or activated using a script.

In the "InfoPath Forms Services" section we will describe how you can manage form templates in SharePoint Central Administration and how you can deploy and activate your administrator-approved form templates.

## Publishing Form Templates to a Network Location

Instead of directly publishing your form template to SharePoint or publishing it as an administrator-approved template, you can publish your template to a network location. In particular, if you are deploying your form template manually to the SharePoint server, or using any other method, such as including your form template into a solution, you can use this publishing method. Since publishing to a network connection does not require you to connect to the SharePoint server, this method will also work when you don't have access to the SharePoint server.

All the relevant settings that allow you to use your form within SharePoint will be established when you enable your template, meaning that you can use this method instead of the more complex SharePoint wizards. In development scenarios, on the other hand, running a wizard allows you to quickly publish new versions of your form. But when using this publishing method, make sure to take one of the following steps to make your form work in Forms Services:

- Manually upload your form using Central Administration.

- Use the Forms Services web service.

- Use stsadm -activateformtemplate.

- Use the Enable-SPInfoPathFormTemplate cmdlet.

- Use the XSNFeatureReceiver class in your feature definition (described next).

---

■ **Caution** If you are deploying your form to a network location, you must in any case specify no "alternate access path" in the last step of the Publishing wizard (as shown in Figure 6–18). Otherwise, the form will not work, because it will not be browser enabled. When you leave the field empty, InfoPath will show a warning you can ignore by selecting OK.

---

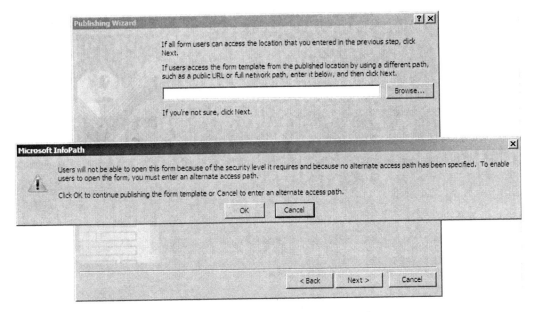

*Figure 6–18. Publishing to a network location: Alternative access path*

# Embedding Forms into SharePoint Features

SharePoint features offer a standardized way to package all the relevant elements of a certain scope together and deploy them to a SharePoint farm. When creating a feature you will probably also want to include your form templates to deploy them along with your other elements.

The example in Listing 6–10 demonstrates how to build a feature to deploy your form templates to the Form Template library of a site collection. The feature definition file contains the following important entries that are particular to form template deployment:

- `ReceiverClass`: This attribute of the feature element points to the `XsnFeatureReceiver` class, which provides an implementation of the `SPFeatureReceiver` and handles events that are raised when a feature is installed, uninstalled, activated, or deactivated. It takes actions on the forms according to the feature event, such as registering a form template when the feature is installed. Essentially, the `XsnFeatureReceiver` class takes care of your XSN files when you include them in a feature.

- `ReceiverAssembly`: This refers to the `Microsoft.Office.InfoPath.Server` assembly, which contains the `XsnFeatureReceiver` class.

- `ElementFile`: The `Location` attribute points to the XSN file of your form template relative to your `feature.xml` file.

- ActivationDependency: To make sure that the InfoPath Forms Services feature is available, it is good practice to add an activation dependency to this feature. This way, an error will be displayed during feature activation if Forms Services is not available. In the following example, you will see an ActivationDependency element referencing the FeatureId of the InfoPath Forms Services feature.

---

■ **Tip** For additional requirements and extreme scenarios, you can also extend the feature receiver and develop your own implementation for deploying XSN files through a SharePoint feature. Please refer to the MSDN documentation for further information: `http://msdn.microsoft.com/en-us/library/microsoft.office.infopath.server.administration.xsnfeaturereceiver(office.14).aspx`.

---

*Listing 6–10. Including a Form Template in a Feature: feature.xml*

```xml
<?xml version="1.0" encoding="utf-8"?>
<Feature  Id="F1C92BB0-61E2-4372-B626-4276BE8A4435"
    Title="RoomBookingFeature"
    Description="RoomBooking form deployed using a feature"
    Version="1.0.0.0"
    Hidden="False"
    Scope="Site"
    DefaultResourceFile="core"
    xmlns="http://schemas.microsoft.com/sharepoint/"
    ReceiverClass="Microsoft.Office.InfoPath.Server.Administration.XsnFeatureReceiver"
    ReceiverAssembly="Microsoft.Office.InfoPath.Server, Version=14.0.0.0,
Culture=neutral,
                    PublicKeyToken=71e9bce111e9429c">

    <ElementManifests>
        <ElementManifest Location="elements.xml"/>
        <ElementFile Location="RoomBookingFeature.xsn" />
    </ElementManifests>

    <ActivationDependencies>
        <ActivationDependency FeatureId="C88C4FF1-DBF5-4649-AD9F-C6C426EBCBF5" />
    </ActivationDependencies>

</Feature>
```

The elements.xml manifest file contains only one Module element (Listing 6–11). Module elements are used to provision files to SharePoint. The Url attribute of the module element denotes the target URL on the SharePoint server. In this case, the form template will be stored in the form template library relative to the site collection. For each file that needs to be provisioned to SharePoint, one File element is required within the Module element. You can also provision a collection of files using one module. See the following link for more details on file provisioning: `http://msdn.microsoft.com/en-us/library/ms441170(office.14).aspx`.

*Listing 6–11. Including a Form Template in a Feature: elements.xml*

```
<?xml version="1.0" encoding="utf-8" ?>
<Elements  xmlns="http://schemas.microsoft.com/sharepoint/">
    <Module Name="RoomBooking" Url="FormServerTemplates" RootWebOnly="TRUE">
        <File Url="RoomBookingFeature.xsn" Name="RoomBookingFeature.xsn"
Type="GhostableInLibrary" />
    </Module>
</Elements>
```

# Deploying Forms Using Command-Line Utilities

When you are developing SharePoint applications in a professional environment, you will probably wish to automate deployment and avoid uploading each form template to each environment by hand using the InfoPath UI. There are two options, both of which are command-line utilities to script SharePoint administration tasks: stsadm.exe and PowerShell cmdlets.

For either to work correctly, you first need to publish your form to a file on a network share or on the local file system. This step needs to be done manually by the form template designer. When referring to a form template to be deployed, we are always talking about a previously published template.

## stsadm.exe

stsadm.exe is the command-line utility used in previous SharePoint versions to administer SharePoint from the command line and for scripting batch files. Although its use will diminish in favor of PowerShell cmdlets, it is still supported by SharePoint 2010. Since it is widely used, we will show the most important commands. stsadm.exe is located in the bin folder of the SharePoint installation path: C:\Program Files\Common Files\Microsoft Shared\Web Server Extensions\14\bin\stsadm. To run the utility, you need to pass the parameter -o followed by the supported operation you wish to execute.

Working with InfoPath forms, the operations described in Table 6–2 are useful for uploading and installing form templates.

*Table 6–2. stsadm Operations for InfoPath Form Templates*

| Operation | Description |
| --- | --- |
| ActivateFormTemplate | Activates a form template for a site collection |
| AddDataConnectionFile | Adds a new instance of a DataConnectionFile to the DataConnectionFiles collection |
| DeactivateFormTemplate | Deactivates a form template for a site collection |
| EnumDataConnectionFileDependants | Enumerates all forms that are dependent on the specified data connection file |
| EnumDataConnectionFiles | Enumerates all of the DataConnectionFiles in the collection |
| EnumFormTemplates | Enumerates all form templates |
| GetFormTemplateProperty | Retrieves properties of a form template |

| | |
|---|---|
| `RemoveDataConnectionFile` | Removes specified data connection files from the collection |
| `RemoveFormTemplate` | Removes the specified form template |
| `SetDataConnectionFileProperty` | Sets a file property to a data connection file |
| `SetFormsServiceProperty` | Sets a configuration property of Form Services |
| `SetFormTemplateProperty` | Sets the properties of an individual form template |
| `UploadFormTemplate` | Uploads a form template to Forms Services |
| `VerifyFormTemplate` | Checks whether it's acceptable for the form template to be uploaded to the server |

Using the preceding operations you could write a script such as the following to upload a new form template after deactivating and removing the prior version of the form. Instead of the file name, you can also use the <formid> to specify the form template.

```
STSADM.EXE -o DeActivateFormTemplate -url http://<servername> -filename <filename.xsn>
STSADM.EXE -o RemoveFormTemplate -filename <filename.xsn>
STSADM.EXE -o VerifyFormTemplate -filename <filename.xsn>
STSADM.EXE -o UploadFormTemplate -filename <filename.xsn>
STSADM.EXE -o ActivateFormTemplate -url http://<servername> -filename <filename.xsn>
```

## PowerShell Cmdlets

As described in Chapter 9, SharePoint 2010 relies heavily on PowerShell cmdlets for administration tasks. The following cmdlets are relevant when working with InfoPath form templates. The table also lists the stsadm commands that have similar functions, to give users familiar with stsadm a quick cross-reference:

*Table 6–3. PowerShell Cmdlets for InfoPath Form Templates*

| Operation Name | Description | stsadm Equivalent |
|---|---|---|
| `Disable-SPInfoPathFormTemplate` | Deactivates a form template for a site collection | `DeactivateFormTemplate` |
| `Enable-SPInfoPathFormTemplate` | Activates a form template for a site collection | `ActivateFormTemplate` |
| `Get-SPDataConnectionFile` | Enumerates all of the DataConnectionFiles in the collection | `EnumDataConnectionFiles` |
| `Get-SPDataConnectionFileDependent` | Enumerates forms that are dependent on the specified data connection file | `EnumDataConnectionFileDependants` |

| Operation Name | Description | stsadm Equivalent |
|---|---|---|
| Get-SPInfoPathFormTemplate | Returns an InfoPath form template and its parameters | GetFormTemplateProperty, EnumFormTemplates |
| Install-SPDataConnectionFile | Installs the provided data connection file | AddDataConnectionFile |
| Install-SPInfoPathFormTemplate | Uploads a form template to Forms Services | UploadFormTemplate |
| Set-SPDataConnectionFile | Sets properties of a data connection file | SetDataConnectionFileProperty |
| Set-SPInfoPathFormsService | Sets parameters for InfoPath Forms Services | SetFormsServiceProperty |
| Set-SPInfoPathFormTemplate | Sets the properties of an individual form template | SetFormTemplateProperty |
| Test-SPInfoPathFormTemplate | Validates that a form template can be browser enabled | VerifyFormTemplate |
| Uninstall-SPDataConnectionFile | Removes specified data connection files from the collection | RemoveDataConnectionFile |
| Uninstall-SPInfoPathFormTemplate | Removes the specified form template from a farm | RemoveFormTemplate |
| Update-SPInfoPathFormTemplate | Upgrades all form templates on the farm | |

By analogy, with the stsadm commands shown in the table, the following script can be used to upload a new version of an InfoPath form, after deactivating and removing the prior version of the form:

```
Uninstall-SPInfoPathFormTemplate -Identity formName.xsn
Install-SPInfoPathFormTemplate -Path C:\Form.xsn
Enable-SPInfoPathFormTemplate -Identity "FormTemplate.xsn" -Site "http://TestSite"
```

# Deploying Forms with Code

When using custom code in your InfoPath form template, as described in the next section, you have two deployment options:

- Deploying your form as a sandboxed solution

• Deploying your form as an administrator-approved form

InfoPath forms that contain code will be deployed as sandboxed by default when you use the Publishing wizard to deploy your form to SharePoint. In this case, the code will be run in a sandbox to avoid harm to your SharePoint farm. This publishing method can be chosen by any site administrator and does not require farm administration privileges. Sandboxed form templates are only available to InfoPath 2010 form templates that do not use Web Part connection parameters.

The second option is to deploy your form as an administrator-approved form template, as described earlier. In this case, the code will be granted full trust, since this deployment method is only available to farm administrators.

---

■ **Tip** To use sandboxed form templates you must ensure that the Microsoft SharePoint Foundation User Code Service is started. This service is responsible for sandboxed solutions. It can be started in Central Administration via System Settings ➤ Manage Services on Server.

---

Table 6–4 compares the two options for deploying forms with code.

*Table 6–4. Comparing Sandboxed and Administrator-Approved Templates*

| Category | Sandboxed Form Template | Administrator-Approved Template |
|---|---|---|
| Permission | Site collection administrator | Farm administrator |
| Publishing | InfoPath Designer wizard | Central Administration |
| Security | Form code run in sandbox, no harm to farm | Code runs with full trust on the server |

# Programming InfoPath Forms

InfoPath Designer 2010 features a convenient UI for designing form templates and adding some basic control logic using rules. But as soon as the complexity of your forms grows and interaction with the environment increases, you should take a closer look at the development facilities in InfoPath. Looking at the Developer tab in the ribbon bar (Figure 6–19), you can get an idea of the variety of events that can be used to integrate managed code into your InfoPath form template.

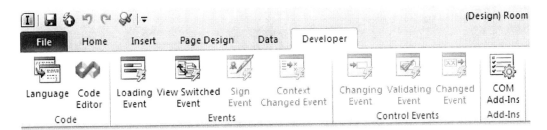

*Figure 6–19. Developer ribbon bar in InfoPath Designer*

# Attaching Managed Code

Before you can begin programming your form template, you need to specify the code language and the location for your code project in the Form Options dialog. You can reach this dialog directly using the Language button on the Developer tab. The managed code language options are C# and Visual Basic. In addition, you can nominate the location where the project for your form code will be stored. For every form, a separate project is created. The assembly that is generated when the project is built will also be included in the resulting XSN file.

---

■ **Note** You can also use InfoPath 2010 to develop forms that are compatible with 2007. You can select "InfoPath 2007 compatible code" from the Form template code language drop-down list. In this case, the project will reference the old library, located by default in `C:\Program files\Microsoft Office\Office14\InfoPathOM\InfoPathFormsServices\InfoPathFormsServicesV12`.

---

After you have configured these basic development settings, a click on the Code Editor button or one of the events on the Developer tab of the ribbon bar will cause Visual Studio Tools for Applications (VSTA) to start. InfoPath 2010 still uses VSTA 2005, and the resulting projects are based on .NET 2.0. However, VSTA will configure all the required settings for you. The project for your form template will open, and you can start programming your form template. Figure 6–20 shows the basic skeleton of a form project.

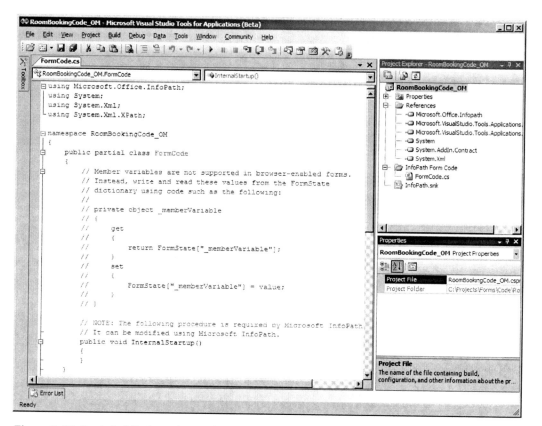

*Figure 6–20. Basic InfoPath project with VSTA*

---

■ **Note** The ability to develop script code using JScript or VBScript has been removed in InfoPath 2010. Instead, form templates can use only managed code.

---

## ADDING AN EXISTING PROJECT TO A TEMPLATE

You can add an existing code project to a form template. This can be useful if you accidentally remove the code in the Programming dialog in Form Options. Since you are not able to select a `.csproj` file in the Programming dialog, and since manually entering it will also fail, follow these steps:

1. 1. In Form Options ➤ Programming, select a temporary project location.

2. 2. Click Code Editor on the Developer tab to create a new project.

3. 3. Save your form and close it.

4. 4. Delete the temporary project location.

5. 5. Reopen your form and click Code Editor.

6. 6. InfoPath will display a dialog saying that your project cannot be found. You can select the project file you want to use.

Now you can work with your project. This location will be stored in your form. The next time you open your form template, this project is used.

Depending on the form type that is selected in the form options, the appropriate InfoPath library will be included into the project. Since Forms Services only supports a subset of functionality when designing web browser forms, a different `Microsoft.Office.InfoPath.dll` is loaded from the subfolder `InfoPathOMFormsServices`.

When accessing the form code for the first time, the necessary project will be created automatically. A class named `FormCode` will be autogenerated. This class is derived from `XmlFormHostItem`, which is an abstract class, acting as a wrapper for an `XMLForm`. The `FormCode` class that you will use for programming is implemented as a partial class. All virtual methods that need to be overwritten are implemented in `FormCode.Designer.cs`. From here, the method `InternalStartup` and all the events you implement will be called. This illustrates the basic paradigm for programming InfoPath forms: everything you do must be associated with an event. The only way to execute your code is in reaction to something that happens in the form, such as loading the form, changing a value, or closing the form.

## InfoPath Object Model

The InfoPath object model offers programmatic access to the views, data connections, and behavior of the form. Using this object model, you can make your forms highly flexible. As stated earlier in this chapter, Forms Services only supports a subset of the InfoPath object model, which is available to InfoPath Filler forms. Since we are focusing on using InfoPath together with SharePoint, the following descriptions are focused on the object model available to Forms Services.

The `Microsoft.Office.InfoPath.XmlForm` class represents the data of the underlying XML document. Thus, it is one of the key objects for interacting with the XML data of the form. However, when working with browser-compatible forms, you will only have access to the properties and methods of the `XmlForm` object that are wrapped by the `XmlFormHostItem` object in the form template code. Since the class that is created for you is a subclass of `XmlFormHostItem`, you can access the relevant members using the keyword `this`.

## Events

For code in your InfoPath project to be called, it needs to be tied to an event. Events can be added by clicking the event buttons in the development ribbon. Each event will be registered as a delegate in the `InternalStartup` method. The class `EventManager` is used to bind event handlers to the different events.

Events are divided into three categories: `FormEvents`, `ControlEvents`, and `XmlEvents`. Each of these categories is represented by an object of the same name. `FormEvents` are events that occur to the form, such as loading and saving. `ControlEvents` are events issued by special controls. For example, the `ButtonEvent` implements the `Clicked` event, which is handled as a control event. Whenever you add a button and want to handle the Clicked event using code, an event handler will be added to the ControlEvents.

Finally, XmlEvents are used for anything that happens to the underlying XML structure of your form—for example, when a field is changed. When changes are made to the XML data, events will be bubbled up through the data structure. Assume your schema has a group element group1 that contains a field element called test. Figure 6–21 shows the simple data schema for this example.

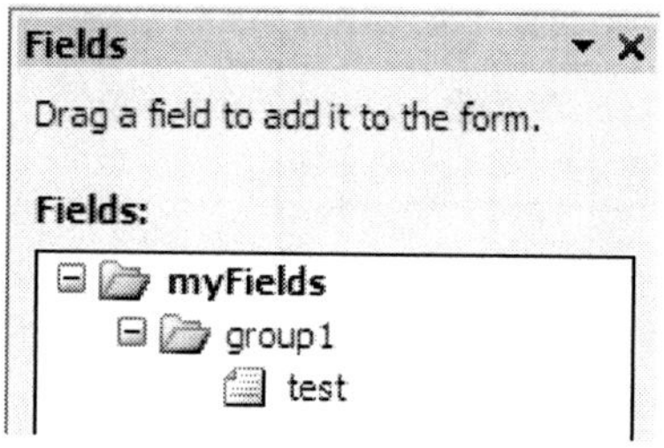

*Figure 6–21. Simple data schema used for the events example*

When you change the content of the field element test, the event handler of the test element will be called. After that, the Changed event of the group1 element will be raised. When working with XmlChange events, the XmlEventArgs object supplies detailed information about the change. You can retrieve the OldValue, which shows the value before the change, and the NewValue, which contains the value after the change. In addition, the member Site returns an XPathNavigator object that points to the element on which the change event is currently being handled. The element that is responsible for the change (in the preceding example, this is the test element) can be accessed using the sender object. This is also an XPathNavigator object that points to the element that was originally changed and caused the event to be passed upward through the hierarchy. Listing 6–12 shows how these events will be thrown. Each event simply displays a MessageBox that outputs the name of the event along with the name of the Site element and the name of the sender object. This example is built with an InfoPath Filler form template to keep it as simple as possible. The MessageBox is not available to web browser forms.

*Listing 6–12. Assigning Events in Form Code*

```
public partial class FormCode
{
    public void InternalStartup()
    {
        // Register events
        EventManager.XmlEvents["/my:myFields"].Changed +=
                            new XmlChangedEventHandler(myFields_Changed);
        EventManager.XmlEvents["/my:myFields/my:group1"].Changed +=
                            new XmlChangedEventHandler(group1_Changed);
        EventManager.XmlEvents["/my:myFields/my:group1/my:test"].Changed +=
                            new XmlChangedEventHandler(test_Changed);
    }

    public void group1_Changed(object sender, XmlEventArgs e)
    {
        // Show a message box about the changes
        MessageBox.Show("group1_Changed: Site=" + e.Site.Name + " sender=" +
```

```
        ((XPathNavigator)sender).Name + "from " + e.OldValue + " -> " +
        e.NewValue);
    }

    public void test_Changed(object sender, XmlEventArgs e)
    {
        MessageBox.Show("test_Changed: Site=" + e.Site.Name + " sender=" +
            ((XPathNavigator)sender).Name);
    }

    public void myFields_Changed(object sender, XmlEventArgs e)
    {
        MessageBox.Show("myFields_Changed: Site=" + e.Site.Name + " sender=" +
            ((XPathNavigator)sender).Name);
    }
}
```

Table 6–5 shows all events that are available in browser-enabled forms. When working with InfoPath Filler, some additional events are available.

*Table 6–5. Events in Form Templates*

| Category | Event | Description |
|---|---|---|
| FormEvents | Loading | Occurs after the form template has been loaded. |
| FormEvents | Submit | Occurs when the form is submitted. |
| FormEvents | ViewSwitched | Occurs after a view has been switched. |
| FormEvents | VersionUpgrade | Occurs when the form needs to be updated, because its version number is older than the form template on which it is based |
| ControlEvents | Clicked | Occurs when a Button control is clicked. The ButtonEvent class implements the Clicked event. |
| XmlEvent | Validating | Occurs when changes have been made to the XML document and after InfoPath has finished validation. |
| XmlEvent | Changed | Occurs after changes have been made to the XML document and after the Validating event. |

## Accessing the Form Data

When discussing events earlier, we encountered a very important class for working with XML data sources: XPathNavigator. This class provides cursor-based access to primary and secondary XML data sources of the InfoPath form and allows modification of the XML data structure. You can use XPathNavigator to navigate over the XML structure using move methods such as MoveToFirstChild or MoveToParent. The cursor of XPathNavigator will then be moved relative to its current node and point to a different node in the XML hierarchy. On the node to which the cursor is currently pointing, you can execute several methods to modify the data or retrieve information about that node. The property Name contains the name of the current node, and OuterXml will return the XML data for the current node from its opening to its closing tags, including its child nodes. InnerXml, on the other hand, returns the XML fragment that is contained within the current node, excluding the node itself. The property Value returns the string of the current node's value item, and the method SetValue allows you to set this value.

When working with InfoPath, navigating through the XML structure along the XPath axes is not very common, since you already know about your data structure. Most of the time you will want to directly select a node or node set to read or write fields in your data source. XPathNavigator offers two very useful methods for selecting nodes: Select and SelectSingleNode. Both methods select nodes according to the given XPath expression, but instead of returning an instance of XPathNodeIterator, SelectSingleNode returns the XPathNavigator object of the first node matching the XPath query. Thus, accessing a node in your form becomes very easy. All you need to do is right-click the node in the Fields pane in InfoPath Designer and select Copy XPath, as shown in Figure 6–22.

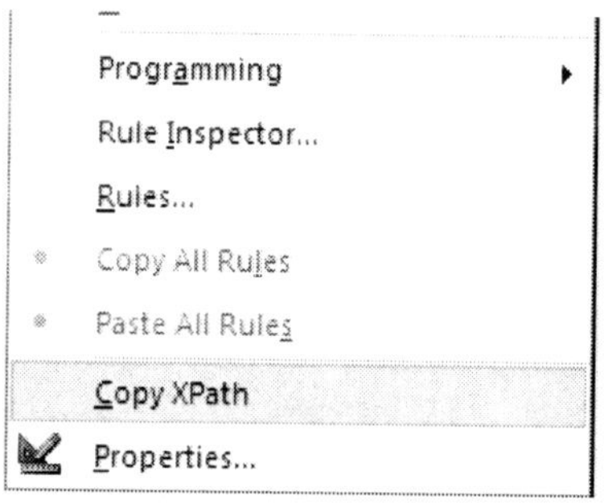

*Figure 6–22. Copying the XPath of a field*

This will create the XPath expression for selecting the node, which can then be copied into the Select method of the XPathNavigator object. To resolve the namespaces used in the form, the select methods also require an element implementing the IXmlNamespaceResolver interface. Fortunately, the NamespaceManager object of the XmlForm already implements this interface, and you can simply use the NamespaceManager property when calling the Select methods.

To access the XML data using XPathNavigator, you first need access to the data sources. XmlForm offers access to a DataSource through its DataSources property. As mentioned earlier, a form consists of one primary and several secondary data sources. The DataSources property contains all the data sources, including the main data source. In addition, MainDataSource provides direct access to the form's main data source. On any DataSource object, you can call the CreateNavigator method to obtain an XPathNavigator that can be used to access and manipulate the data source.

The following example shows a very common scenario, in which data is loaded from a web service into the main data source using XPathNavigator. A data connection to the SharePoint list Rooms was added to retrieve all the room entries in the list and load them into the Room drop-down list on the InfoPath form, which is shown in Figure 6–23.

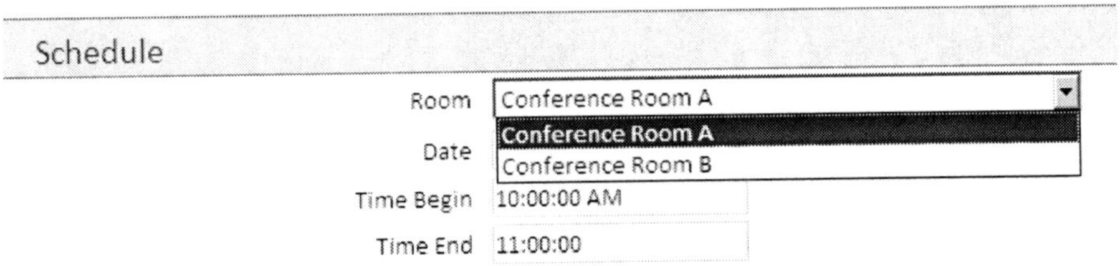

**Figure 6–23.** *Selecting rooms from a SharePoint list*

The web service will be called during form loading, and a second data connection, called GetRoom, will be added. It will be queried when a user selects a room from the drop-down list, and will load the detailed information from the list for the selected room. Then the "RoomNumber" field will be filled from the web service response using XPathNavigator. Calling the "GetRoom" data connection and loading the "RoomNumber" will be done in the changed event that is bound to the Room field. So whenever someone edits the content of the Room field by selecting a room, this code will be executed.

**Listing 6–13.** *Loading Data from a Web Service into a Form*

```
using Microsoft.Office.InfoPath;
using System;
using System.Xml;
using System.Xml.XPath;

namespace RoomBooking_LoadingWebService
{
    public partial class FormCode
    {

        public void InternalStartup()
        {
            EventManager.XmlEvents["/my:RoomBooking/my:Schedule/my:Room"]
                        .Changed += new XmlChangedEventHandler(Room_Changed);
        }

        public void Room_Changed(object sender, XmlEventArgs e)
        {
            XPathNavigator form = MainDataSource.CreateNavigator();

            // Set parameter for web service request and query connection
            DataSources["GetRoom"].CreateNavigator().SelectSingleNode(
                    "/dfs:myFields/dfs:queryFields/q:SharePointListItem_RW/q:ID",
                    NamespaceManager).SetValue(e.NewValue);
            DataSources["GetRoom"].QueryConnection.Execute();

            // Create navigator on web service response
            XPathNavigator roomdata = DataSources["GetRoom"].CreateNavigator();

            // Set fields with values from web service response
            XPathNavigator nodeRoomNumber = form.SelectSingleNode(
                "/my:RoomBooking/my:Schedule/my:RoomNumber", NamespaceManager);
```

```
                nodeRoomNumber.SetValue(roomdata.SelectSingleNode(
                    "/dfs:myFields/dfs:dataFields/d:SharePointListItem_RW/d:RoomNumber",
                    NamespaceManager).Value);
            }
        }
    }
}
```

## Maintaining State in Browser-Based Forms

To maintain global state in browser-enabled forms, you can use the FormState property of XmlForm. Working with browser-enabled forms, this is the only way to persist data during a session. As with web pages, you cannot use member variables to maintain state, since they will not be persisted between requests. The FormState property will keep its values from the time the form is opened until it is closed.

FormState is an IDictionary object that holds user-defined key/value pairs of state variables. Both key and value can be any object, but generally strings are used for the key. The value can store objects that hold complex data. For convenience you might consider introducing a global member variable that leverages FormState by reading from and writing to FormState in the get and set methods. This gives you the ease of use of properties while still persisting data between requests.

Listing 6–14 shows how you can create a member variable using FormState, which can persist information across multiple events.

*Listing 6–14. Maintaining State in Forms Using FormState*

```
public string Username
{
    get
    {
        if (FormState["_username"] != null)
        {
            return (string)FormState["_username"];
        }
        else
        {
            return "";
        }
    }
    set
    {
        FormState["_username"] = value;
    }
}
```

## Accessing Views

Forms are organized using views. You can also work with views in your form code. As described earlier, you can use the ViewSwitched event to react to the change of the current view. The XmlForm object contains useful information about views. First of all, you can use the CurrentView property to get the view that is currently active. In a web-based form template, the resulting View object contains a ViewInfo member with descriptive information about the view. In web forms, you can only access the Name of the view. To access all the available views for a form template, the ViewInfos member returns a list of ViewInfo objects. In addition, it holds the Default and Init properties, which return the default view and the initial view of the form.

If you wish to programmatically switch the view, you can use the SwitchView method of the ViewInfoCollection returned by ViewInfos to switch the view from the current view to the desired view.

## Handling Errors

During validation of a form, several errors in the form data can occur. For example, if you add a validation rule, the field will be displayed in red when the validation fails. In general, errors can arise when a form's XML schema is validated, when a custom validation rule fails, or when the error is added to the collection of errors from code. The XmlForm object keeps in the Errors property a collection of all errors that occurred. You can access individual Error objects from the list of errors, as with any other enumerable collection.

Each Error object contains detailed information about the error, (e.g., in the Name, Message, and DetailedMessage properties). The property FormErrorType specifies how the error was generated: through SchemaValidation, SystemGenerated or, UserDefined. Since an error always belongs to a node in the XML data that caused the error due to a failed validation, the property Site holds an XPathNavigator object that points to the affected node.
You can also add your own errors to the Errors collection using the Add method. This method expects an XPathNavigator pointing to the affected node, a name, and a message. Deleting errors from the list can also be done easily using the Delete method.

Using the Errors collection allows you to manage all the errors in your form that can eventuate during validation.

# InfoPath Forms Services

InfoPath Forms Services is part of Microsoft SharePoint Server 2010. It renders InfoPath forms in the browser and allows users to complete InfoPath forms without InfoPath Filler. This section discusses the basic settings for enabling InfoPath Forms Services on SharePoint 2010, how to manage form templates, and how you can use XmlFormView to customize Forms Services. Finally, different ways to integrate forms with SharePoint are presented.

## Preparing InfoPath Forms Services Support

Before you can start viewing InfoPath forms in SharePoint, several configuration options need to be set, and the form templates have to be managed appropriately. Compared to SharePoint Server 2007, many of the configuration settings have been simplified, especially because the shared service providers have been replaced by service applications in SharePoint 2010. Many of the settings we will demonstrate using Central Administration can also be adjusted using PowerShell. As far as is practicable, we will also mention corresponding cmdlets.

For Forms Services to work properly, you need to do the following:

- Enable the State Service using the Farm Configuration wizard.

- Configure InfoPath Forms Services in the general application settings.

After you are finished with these settings you can start to deploy your forms and integrate them into your SharePoint solution. But first we will show you in more detail what these settings are about.

## State Service

What was a painful configuration hazard in earlier versions of SharePoint has become effortless with SharePoint 2010: configuring the State Service. Since SharePoint relies on service applications to provide shared functionality, you don't have to deal with shared service providers any more. Simply run the Farm Configuration wizard from the Configuration Wizard section. On the second page are many service applications. Select State Service and complete the wizard.

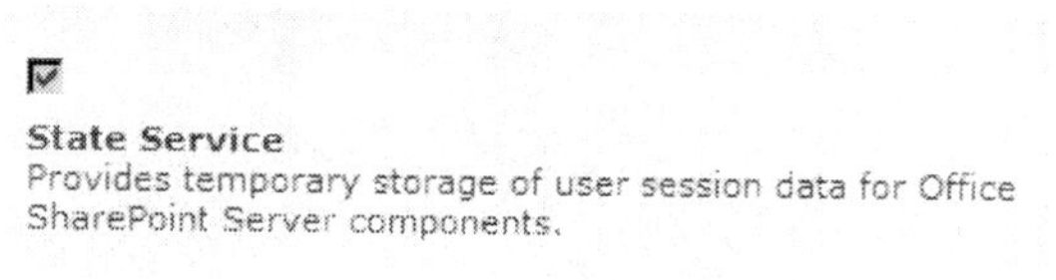

**State Service**
Provides temporary storage of user session data for Office
SharePoint Server components.

*Figure 6–24. State Service configuration*

The State Service is required to store temporary data between related HTTP requests and thus keep the state of your forms. To store the data, a SQL database is used. By default, the data will be stored in the same database as the content database, and a single State Service instance will be shared among all components that require State Service. You can only change those advanced settings using PowerShell. SharePoint Central Administration does not provide any control other than enabling State Service using default settings.

---

### CONFIGURING STATE SERVICE USING POWERSHELL

Use the following cmdlets to perform additional configuration of State Service, or to enable/disable it:

```
Get-SPStateServiceApplication: Gets a list of State Service applications
New-SPStateServiceApplication: Creates a new State Service application
Set-SPStateServiceApplication: Sets parameters on a State Service application
```

There are many additional cmdlets to manage State Service (e.g., for configuring the databases). For a complete list, type **gcm \*spstate\*** into PowerShell.

---

## Configuring InfoPath Forms Services

SharePoint Central Administration contains a separate section for managing InfoPath Forms Services. It is located on the General Application Settings page. Besides management of form templates, data connection files, and a proxy for InfoPath forms, it also contains a link to the "Configuration of InfoPath Forms Services" settings.

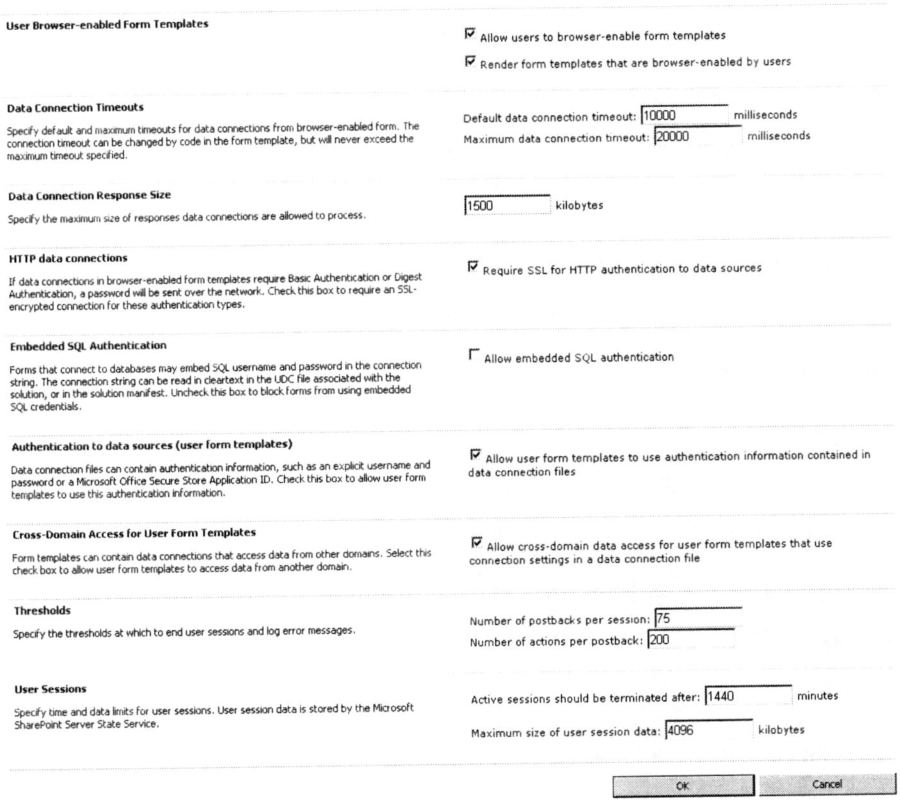

**Figure 6–25.** *Central Administration: Configuring InfoPath Forms Services*

Without going into too much detail, we will briefly describe the most relevant settings in the configuration screen (Figure 6–25). Most of the settings are self explanatory.

The first section defines how browser-enabled forms deployed by users are handled in InfoPath Forms Services. If you select "Allow users to browser-enable form templates," you allow users to deploy browser-enabled forms. The next option allows browser-enabled user form templates to be displayed in the browser. If you don't select "Render form templates that are browser-enabled by users," users will still be able to deploy browser-enabled forms, but the forms will not be displayed in the browser. If you ever have trouble displaying a browser-enabled form, make sure that these options are set correctly.

If you want your users to access data from other domains using data connection files, you should check the "Allow cross-domain data access . . ." check box.

For any other settings, please refer to MSDN for detailed information here:
http://technet.microsoft.com/en-us/library/cc262263(office.14).aspx.

For many common scenarios, the default settings in this dialog are appropriate.

213

## CONFIGURING INFOPATH FORMS SERVICES USING POWERSHELL

Again, you can also use PowerShell cmdlets for these administrative tasks:

```
Get-SPInfoPathFormsService:  Gets the InfoPath Forms Services settings for the farm
Set-SPInfoPathFormsService:  Sets parameters for InfoPath Forms Services settings
```

Set-SPInfoPathFormsService also contains some parameters that are not available to Central Administration.

# Configuring Libraries

Each document library has options for displaying browser-based documents and for managing document templates. In addition, settings concerning content types also need to be considered when deploying forms to form libraries. Figure 6–26 shows the most significant options for configuring forms in document libraries.

You can configure separately for each library whether an InfoPath form will be opened in the browser when adding a new form to the library or selecting an existing form in the list. Go to the Library settings page and select Advanced Settings. Among several others, you will be able to change the "Opening Documents in the Browser" setting. You can choose whether you always want your forms to be opened in the browser or on the client using InfoPath Filler.

Depending on how you deploy your forms, and whether you want to use several different forms in one library, you can specify whether the library in question should allow management of content types. Under the Yes option, different forms can be added to the library via content types. This requires you to deploy your form templates as a content type. If you select No, only one template is allowed at a time.

The Document Template setting allows you to specify the URL of the form template used in this library. This option is only available when management of content types is deactivated. If you have InfoPath Designer installed on your computer, you can use the (Edit Template) link to directly edit the form template.

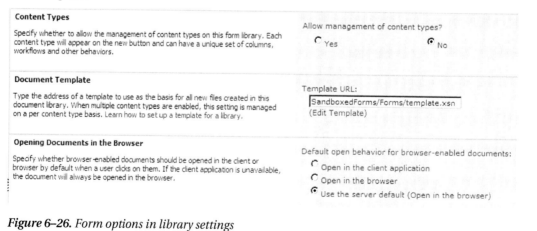

*Figure 6–26. Form options in library settings*

# Managing Form Templates

Deploying InfoPath forms to a SharePoint library can easily be done in InfoPath Designer with the help of the Publishing wizards. But if you need to deploy your form template as an administrator-approved template, you must manually upload your template to SharePoint. This can be done in the Central Administration page. Under *General Application Settings, InfoPath Forms Services* is "Manage form templates." On this page (Figure 6–27) you will find all form templates that are available to the farm, which are templates that are either shipped with SharePoint or have been uploaded by an administrator. Those form templates can be activated to a site collection. Doing so will copy these templates to the Form Templates library in the selected site collection. Naturally, you can also deactivate a form template from a site collection, causing the form template to be removed from the Form Templates library of the site collection.

If you don't need your templates to be approved by an administrator, or if you only want to use your forms in the context of a site collection, you can simply upload your form template to the Form Templates library of the site collection.

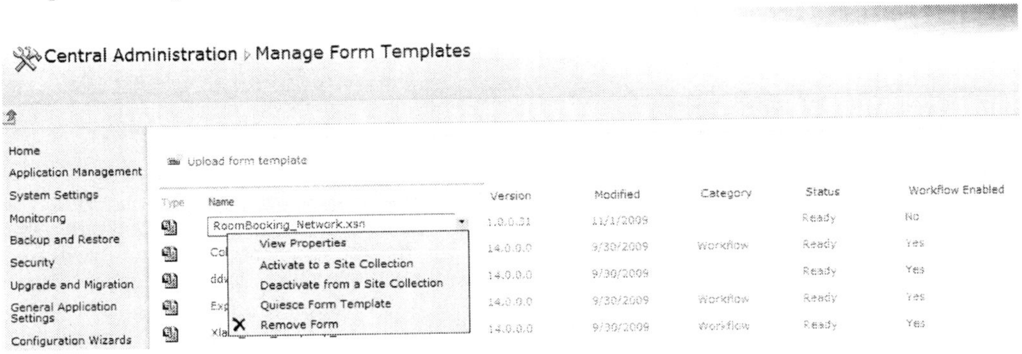

*Figure 6–27. Manage form templates in Central Adminstration*

# Displaying Forms in the InfoPath Form Web Part

Probably the easiest way to display your browser-enabled forms in a web page is by using the InfoPath Form Web Part. This Web Part is new with SharePoint 2010 and allows you to integrate your forms into any page. You can use this Web Part like any other Web Part and simply add it to one of the Web Part zones on your page. Although your influence on form behavior is limited, this Web Part is excellent for rapid prototyping and basic scenarios. For more complex scenarios you might want to look into the possibilities offered by the XmlFormView control, described in the next section.

The InfoPath Form Web Part uses the XmlFormView control to render InfoPath forms. Many options for configuring the Web Part are available, and the Web Part can handle different sources for the form template and the form data, but form rendering is handled by XmlFormView.

To insert the Web Part into your page, you need to switch to Edit mode for the page and select Editing Tools ➤ Insert from the ribbon bar. Now you can select the InfoPath Form Web Part from the Forms category to insert the Web Part, which is shown in Figure 6–28. After you insert the Web Part, a small box is displayed as a placeholder for the InfoPath form. You can now configure your Web Part to display the desired form.

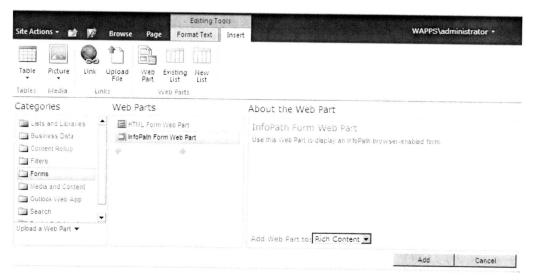

*Figure 6–28. Inserting the InfoPath Form Web Part*

Use the Edit Web Part option to configure the Web Part. You will find the following settings in the Web Part configuration pane, as shown in Figure 6–29. You can specify the source of your form template to display. Essentially, you can select any form template that is published to a list or library, and is thus available as a content type. Opt for the appropriate list or library and then choose the template. You can also specify the default view to display and the behavior after the form is submitted.

You may be wondering where you configure the destination of the form data when it is submitted. Remember that this is already configured within the form template, and therefore there is no configuration required in the Web Part. However, since you don't have full control over the Web Part, the "Submit to the hosting environment" option cannot be used with this scenario.

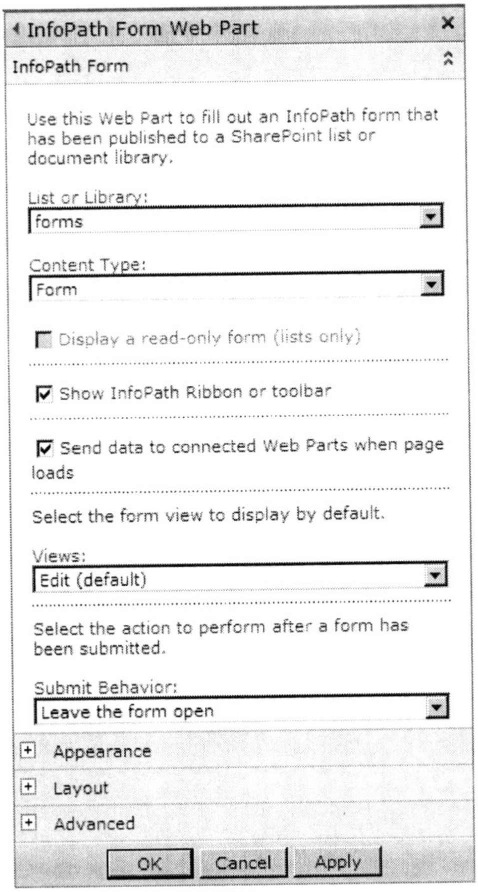

*Figure 6–29. InfoPath Form Web Part configuration dialog*

# Customizing the Browser View Using XmlFormView

To display your browser forms within SharePoint you can use the InfoPath Form Web Part to integrate the form with a page, as described earlier. If a form is opened from a form library, it will be displayed by FormServer.aspx, which is an application page that hosts a control for displaying forms. If you need more control over the way the form will be displayed and want direct access to events, you can use the XmlFormView ASP.NET control in your own application page. This control renders InfoPath forms in the browser and provides several facilities for developers to change its default behavior.

## Integrating XmlFormView in an Application Page

To integrate XmlFormView with your web page, you need to register the assembly Microsoft.Office.InfoPath.Server. Having done that, you can place the XmlFormView control in your ASPX markup, set some important parameters for the control, and bind events. The following listing

217

shows the markup for an application page. The OnSubmitToHost attribute is bound to a method in the code-behind file. This code will be called when the form sends data to the hosting environment, using a submit data connection. Another attribute to note is the EditingStatus. This describes the editing state of the form and has three possible values: Init, Editing, and Closed. Use the Init state to hide the form during loading of the form and set it to Editing later on. In state Editing, the form is visible to the user. This is the only state in which the user can edit or view the form. When the form is closed, the common message "The form has been closed" will be displayed. If you have ever had an error in your form, you will be familiar with this message.

*Listing 6–15. Integrating XmlFormView into the Markup of an Application Page*

```
<%@ Page Language="C#" AutoEventWireup="true" CodeFile="ShowForm.aspx.cs" Inherits="ShowForm"
EnableSessionState="True" %>
<%@ Register tagprefix="fv" namespace="Microsoft.Office.InfoPath.Server.Controls"
assembly="Microsoft.Office.InfoPath.Server, Version=14.0.0.0, Culture=neutral,
PublicKeyToken=71e9bce111e9429c" %>
<%@ Register tagprefix="Server" namespace="Microsoft.Office.InfoPath"
assembly="Microsoft.Office.InfoPath, Version=14.0.0.0, Culture=neutral,
PublicKeyToken=71e9bce111e9429c" %>
<html xmlns="http://www.w3.org/1999/xhtml">
    <head runat="server">
        <title>FormViews</title>
    </head>
    <body style="margin: 0px;overflow:auto;padding:20px">
        <form id="form1" runat="server" enctype="multipart/form-data">
            <fv:XmlFormView ID="formView" runat="server"
                            EditingStatus="Editing"
                            OnSubmitToHost="FormView_SubmitToHost"
                            Width="700px">
            </fv:XmlFormView>
        </form>
    </body>
</html>
```

To correctly display forms, XmlFormView needs to know the location of the form to display, the location of the form template used to render the form, and finally, the location for saved forms to be stored. The properties XmlLocation, XsnLocation, and SaveLocation are used to pass this information to the XmlFormView object.

---

■ **Note** You don't need to specify SaveLocation if you don't use the Save method. This may be the case if you deactivate the Save button in the User Interface Options section of the Form Options dialog (see Figure 15–13), or if you implement your own save method.

---

When opening an existing form, the matching form template is contained in the manifest file and does not need to be specified. But when a new form is created, the form template needs to be specified. You can specify these parameters in the page markup as attributes or set the class properties directly inside your code-behind.

To display an XML form, you can use the following code in the On_Load method in the code-behind file of the previous example. In the following listing, depending on a request parameter, either an existing form will be loaded using the XmlLocation parameter or the template will be assigned by the XsnLocation if the request parameter action equals new.

*Listing 6–16. Code-Behind File of an Application Page Hosting XmlFormView*

```
using System;
using Microsoft.SharePoint;
using Microsoft.SharePoint.WebControls;
using Microsoft.Office.InfoPath.Server.Controls;

namespace com.apress.formviewdemo
{

    public partial class ShowForm : LayoutsPageBase
    {

        protected void Page_Load(object sender, EventArgs e)
        {
            string action = Request.Params["action"];
            if (action == "new")
            {
                // Set the template location for new forms
                String templateLib = "FormServerTemplates";
                String xsnName = "template.xsn";
                formView.XsnLocation = String.Format("{0}/{1}/{2}",
                            SPContext.Current.Web.Url, templateLib, xsnName);
            }
            else
            {
                // Set the XML location for an existing form
                String lib = "TestForms";
                String name = "example.xml";
                formView.XmlLocation = String.Format("{0}/{1}/{2}",
                                    SPContext.Current.Web.Url, lib, name);
            }
        }

        protected void FormView_SubmitToHost(object sender, SubmitToHostEventArgs e)
        {
            // Will be implemented later
        }
    }
}
```

## Accessing the XmlForm Object

Working with XmlFormView, you can access the XmlForm object and thus all the values and settings of the form described in the "Table 6–6 compares the two options for deploying forms with code.

*Table 6–6. Comparing Sandboxed and Administrator-Approved Templates*

| Category | Sandboxed Form Template | Administrator-Approved Template |
|---|---|---|
| Permission | Site collection administrator | Farm administrator |
| Publishing | InfoPath Designer wizard | Central Administration |
| Security | Form code run in sandbox, no harm to farm | Code runs with full trust on the server |

Programming InfoPath Forms" section. Via the XmlForm property you can reach the properties DataSources, ViewInfos, FormState, and such from within the page that is hosting the form. The XmlForm object can be accessed whenever the code is run within one of the following event handlers, which enables a form to communicate with its hosting environment:

*Table 6–7. Events Available in XmlFormView*

| Event | Description |
|---|---|
| Initialize | This is called when the form is loaded. |
| NotifyHost | Notification events can pass a parameter to the hosting environment. Call this.NotifyHost() in your form template code. |
| SubmitToHost | This is called when the form is submitted using a submit to host data connection. |
| Close | This is called when the form is closed. |

If you want to access the XmlForm object from another event on your page, you have to first call the method Data Bind of the XmlFormView object to ensure that the XmlForm object is adequately populated.

You can directly access fields inside your form using the XPathNavigator on the MainDataSource. This may be required when implementing your own OnSubmitToHost event where you wish to store the XML data into a library and build the file name using information within the form. Listing 6–17 shows how this can be done. To keep things clear, we have only implemented the OnSubmitToHost event, which was left blank in the previous example.

*Listing 6–17. Saving a Form to a SharePoint Library Using OnSubmitToHost Event*

```
protected void FormView_SubmitToHost(object sender, SubmitToHostEventArgs e)
{
    SPWeb web = SPContext.Current.Web;
    web.AllowUnsafeUpdates = true;

    // Load the XML and save it as a byte array
    System.Xml.XPath.XPathNavigator navigator =
```

```
                        formView.XmlForm.MainDataSource.CreateNavigator();
    Byte[] formBytes = System.Text.Encoding.UTF8.GetBytes(navigator.OuterXml);

    // Create XmlDocument from the form XML
    XmlDocument doc = new XmlDocument();
    XmlNamespaceManager nsm = new XmlNamespaceManager(doc.NameTable);
    nsm.AddNamespace("my", "http://schemas.microsoft.com/office/infopath/2003/myXSD/2009-09-
29T22:54:17");
    doc.LoadXml(navigator.OuterXml);

    // Load name information from the XML
    XmlNode nodeLastName = doc.SelectSingleNode(
                    "/my:RoomBooking/my:UserInformation/my:LastName", nsm);
    string name = (nodeLastName != null) ? nodeLastName.InnerText : string.Empty;
    XmlNode nodeFirstName = doc.SelectSingleNode(
                    "/my:RoomBooking/my:UserInformation/my:FirstName", nsm);
    string firstname = (nodeFirstName != null) ?
                                    nodeFirstName.InnerText : string.Empty;

    // Generate file name
    string filename = String.Format("{0}{1}_{2}.xml", name, firstname,
                                    DateTime.Now.ToString("yyyyMMdd"));

    // Open library and save XML
    SPFolder formLibrary = web.GetFolder(LIBRARY_NAME);
    formLibrary.Files.Add(filename, formBytes);

    web.AllowUnsafeUpdates = false;
}
```

# Integrating InfoPath Forms with the Environment

InfoPath forms can be developed and designed independently of your SharePoint environment. If you
need to load additional information from external sources into your form, you can call a web service or
use other data connections. But as soon as your form is part of a more complex business process, you
might need some additional information within your form that is provided by the business process, or
you may need information from outside of InfoPath that is entered through a form. In some scenarios
you will have to pass parameters from your SharePoint application to your form, or vice versa.

## Property Promotion and Demotion of XML Documents

Using InfoPath forms in SharePoint and storing the forms in a forms library enables development of
complex browser-based applications with a great user experience. The forms are well-integrated into
SharePoint with the support of Forms Services, but all the information that was entered by the users is
stored within the XML file. There seems to be no easy access from the SharePoint environment to this
data. What if you want to create a view that shows all the room bookings for one particular room? Or
what if you want to change single values in your XML file from SharePoint? Many of the great features
SharePoint offers work with list columns but don't offer extensibility to access information within
XML files.

To solve this problem, SharePoint and InfoPath support features called *property promotion* and *property demotion*. SharePoint allows you to define fields in your InfoPath form that will be automatically provided as a column in your SharePoint document library. SharePoint automatically propagates changes that are made in your document to the SharePoint column and vice versa. Property promotion involves extracting fields from XML documents and writing these values to columns in SharePoint document libraries. Property demotion, on the other hand, involves taking changes to the SharePoint column available in your XML form.

Property promotion and demotion work as follows: whenever a new or existing XML file is saved in the document library, SharePoint invokes a built-in XML parser on the XML file. When the document content type contains a column that maps a field in the XML document to a list column (via an XPath expression that is pointing to the XML field), this value will be promoted to the library. In the other situation, where the column in the library is updated, this XPath expression is used to demote the information to the XML file.

In the description of the XmlFormView earlier in this chapter, we showed a method to directly manipulate the form's XML structure, which could also be used to access form fields, but requires more effort.

---

▪ **Tip** You can find more details on property promotion and demotion on MSDN at
http://msdn.microsoft.com/en-us/library/aa543481(office.14).aspx.

---

## Configuring Promotion/Demotion Using InfoPath

When you are using the InfoPath Publishing wizard to publish your form template to SharePoint, you will encounter the dialog shown in Figure 6–30. In this dialog, you can add property promotion and demotion using the Add... button in the upper area of the wizard. In the upcoming dialog you can select a field from your main data source and specify the column name within the document library. InfoPath Forms Services will then create the necessary columns in the document library and store the XPath link to the referenced nodes in the column definition. The lower area is used for Web Part connection parameters (described next).

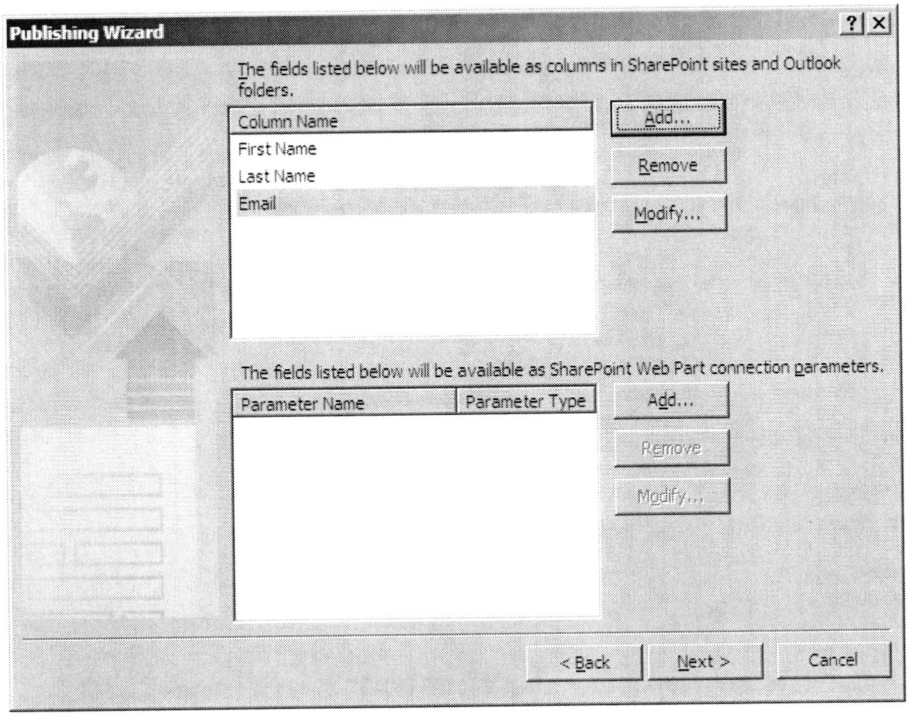

**Figure 6–30.** *Configuring property promotion and demotion*

## Configuring Promotion/Demotion Within a List Feature

When using InfoPath Designer to manage list propagation, the necessary settings and changes will only be made on the list to which the InfoPath file is published. For any other deployment scenario (such as a multistage development and production environment), you can describe list propagation together with your list using the schema.xml file. You can simply nominate the column that should be used for property promotion with an ID and Name attribute. In addition, you merely need to specify the Node attribute. This attribute takes an XPath expression pointing to the field within the XML file. This XPath expression will be used for promotion and demotion of properties. Listing 6–18 shows an example for a list definition that specifies some nodes in the RoomBooking form that will be promoted to the list.

To make sure that you are using the right XPpath expression, you can use InfoPath Designer: right-click the field in the Fields tree and select Copy XPath, which will generate the correct expression for you.

**Listing 6–18.** *Configuring Property Promotion and Demotion in a Feature Definition*

```xml
<?xml version="1.0" encoding="utf-8"?>
<List xmlns:ows="Microsoft SharePoint"
    Title="Order Requests"
    Direction="$Resources:Direction;"
    Url="OrderRequests" BaseType="1"
    EnableContentTypes="TRUE"
    AllowMultipleContentTypes="True"
```

```
xmlns="http://schemas.microsoft.com/sharepoint/">
<MetaData>
    <ContentTypes>
        <ContentType ID="0x01010100B3E78F42234547a580BDE72BCB3E650A" Name="Order Requests"
                     Description="Request a new Order"
                          Group="$Resources:Document_Content_Types" Version="1">
            <FieldRefs>
                <FieldRef ID="{DDC3C6B7-C34A-4d5a-8355-DC4E81885C8D}"
                          Name="Title" />
        ...
                <FieldRef ID="{6CE8A87B-0862-4d8d-891F-5CA9C16833D4}"
                          Name="Room" />
                <FieldRef ID="{05F09611-7D5B-4bae-9FA5-3EC8402F7A00}"
                          Name="Date" />
                <FieldRef ID="{2C1B30B7-AADC-434b-9F82-D70639B59AB1}"
                          Name="TimeBegin" />
                <FieldRef ID="{52BBFDF2-3176-43d7-A4D2-EFFA78CCED33}"
                          Name="TimeEnd" />
            </FieldRefs>
            <DocumentTemplate TargetName="/FormServerTemplates/RoomBooking.xsn"
            />
        </ContentType>
    </ContentTypes>
    <Fields>
    ...
        <Field ID="{6CE8A87B-0862-4d8d-891F-5CA9C16833D4}" ShowInNewForm="FALSE"
Type="Text" Name="Room" DisplayName="Room"
SourceID="http://schemas.microsoft.com/sharepoint/v3" StaticName="Room"
Node="/my:RoomBooking/my:Schedule/my:Room" ></Field>
        <Field ID="{05F09611-7D5B-4bae-9FA5-3EC8402F7A00}" ShowInNewForm="FALSE"
Type="DateTime" Name="Date" DisplayName="Date"
SourceID="http://schemas.microsoft.com/sharepoint/v3" StaticName="Date"
Node="/my:RoomBooking/my:Schedule/my:Date" ></Field>
        <Field ID="{2C1B30B7-AADC-434b-9F82-D70639B59AB1}" ShowInNewForm="FALSE"
Type="DateTime" Name="TimeBegin" DisplayName="TimeBegin"
SourceID="http://schemas.microsoft.com/sharepoint/v3" StaticName="TimeBegin"
Node="/my:RoomBooking/my:Schedule/my:TimeBegin" ></Field>
        <Field ID="{52BBFDF2-3176-43d7-A4D2-EFFA78CCED33}" ShowInNewForm="FALSE"
Type="DateTime" Name="TimeEnd" DisplayName="TimeEnd"
SourceID="http://schemas.microsoft.com/sharepoint/v3" StaticName="TimeEnd"
Node="/my:RoomBooking/my:Schedule/my:TimeEnd" ></Field>
        </Fields>
    </MetaData>
</List>
```

This listing defines common attributes for the list, such as Title and Url. In the <MetaData> section, the content type and fields are specified. The ID of the <ContentType> element starts with 0x01010, which is the parent ID for form libraries. The <FieldRef> elements refer to the <Field> elements that are specified later using their GUIDs. The <Field> elements specify an additional attribute, Node, which contains the XPath to the field in the XML file of the InfoPath form. This node will be used to perform property promotion and demotion.

## Web Part Connection Parameters

Web Parts on a page can be interconnected using connection parameters to pass values between them. Similar to property promotion, InfoPath fields can be promoted as Web Part connection parameters. This allows Web Parts to send data to or get data from a field in an InfoPath form without any further coding. Especially when using the newly introduced InfoPath Form Web Part, these connection parameters enable you to quickly interconnect your form with other SharePoint Web Parts. Figure 6–21, which was already described in connection with property promotion earlier, shows this dialog that allows you to add new Web Part connection parameters.

To specify Web Part connection parameters, you can use the Property Promotion category, accessible either through the Publishing wizard or the Form Options dialog. When adding new Web Part connection parameters, you will be asked to select the field you want to promote and enter a name for the parameter. Finally, you need to choose the parameter type: input, output, or input\output. Input parameters can be used to retrieve data from other Web Parts. Output parameters can send data to other Web Parts. If you want to do both, you must select "input\output."

---

■ **Note** Remember that Web Part connection parameters cannot be used with sandboxed form templates, which contain managed code.

---

## Passing Parameters from SharePoint to InfoPath Forms

When your form already exists, you can use property demotion to set fields in your form. But often you want to preload information in your form when a new form is created. In this case, you can pass parameters to your browser form using request parameters. If you write your own application page that hosts the XmlFormView, you can access the form's XML data and directly write parameters into the XML. But if you don't, request parameters might be the solution for you.

You can pass your additional parameters as so-called input parameters via HTTP request parameters. There are two ways to access these parameters:

- Using the InfoPath InputParameters property
- Directly accessing the HTTP request parameters

InfoPath offers access to input parameters either for InfoPath Filler forms or for browser-based forms. They are handled exactly the same way. In the load event you access the LoadingEventArgs parameter e and select the desired parameter using the [ ] selector:

```
String param = e.InputParameters["param"];
```

In this case, you don't have to deal with HTTP request parameters. But since your form is hosted inside a web page you can also read the HTTP request parameters from within your form template in the form code. All you need to do is add a reference to the System.Web assembly. Then you can access the QueryString collection of the HttpRequest to read all the parameters required to load data into the form. Of course, you can also access the other properties of the request (e.g., Url, Headers, UserAgent, LogonUserIdentity, and anything else that might be useful when programming your form). You can retrieve the browser session to exchange data between SharePoint and InfoPath. The next example demonstrates both ways to load data into your form using a request parameter. Instead of simply writing the value directly into the form, the parameter will be used to call a web service that is responsible for fetching the data that is required in the form.

To begin, add the following reference to your project, along with the using statement, to access the HTTP request:

```
using System.Web;
```

Now you can obtain the request parameters in your form-loading event to retrieve a parameter that identifies an item from the QueryString. With this itemid parameter, the GetItemData web service is called. The results are then stored into the form using XPathNavigator.

*Listing 6–19. Accessing Request Parameters in a Form Template*

```
public void FormEvents_Loading(object sender, LoadingEventArgs e)
{
    // Get the request parameter using InputParameters:
    string itemId = e.InputParameters["itemId"];
    // Get the request parameter directly from the request:
    itemId = HttpContext.Current.Request.QueryString["itemId"];

    XPathNavigator form = MainDataSource.CreateNavigator();

    if (!String.IsNullOrEmpty(itemId))
    {
        // Set the parameter for the web service query
        DataSources["GetItemData"].CreateNavigator().SelectSingleNode(
            "/dfs:myFields/dfs:queryFields/tns:GetItemData/tns:itemId",
            NamespaceManager ).SetValue(itemId);

        // Query web service and create navigator
        DataSources["GetItemData"].QueryConnection.Execute();
        XPathNavigator itemdata = DataSources["GetItemData"].CreateNavigator();

        // Fill the Name field with the value from the web service
        XPathNavigator nodeName = form.SelectSingleNode(
            "/my:ItemForm/my:Name", NamespaceManager);
        nodeName.SetValue(itemdata.SelectSingleNode(
"dfs:myFields/dfs:dataFields/tns:GetItemData/tns:GetItemDataResult/tns:ItemName",
            NamespaceManager).Value);

        // Fill the Price field with the value from the web service
        XPathNavigator nodePrice = form.SelectSingleNode(
            "/my:ItemForm/my:Price", NamespaceManager);
        nodePrice.SetValue(itemdata.SelectSingleNode(
"dfs:myFields/dfs:dataFields/tns:GetItemData/tns:GetItemDataResult/tns:ItemPrice",
            NamespaceManager).Value);
    }
}
```

---

▪ **Caution** As always when working with request parameters, keep in mind that they can be easily modified by users. You must use the same precautions as in any other web page when working with request parameters. Always check the validity of the data passed to your form.

---

## ACCESSING INFOPATH EVENTS IN THE BROWSER

For complex scenarios, working with the NotifyHost event can be very frustrating, since you can only pass a string parameter. If you wish to react to InfoPath events in your hosting environment, you can use the following approach, which lets you directly pass events to your server environment from within InfoPath. For example, you can delegate the ViewSwitched event to SharePoint by following these steps:

1. Create an Interface and define the methods that will handle the event:

```
public interface IInfoPathEvents
{
    void OnViewSwitched(object sender, ViewSwitchedEventArgs e);
}
```

2. Implement the interface in a serializable class.

3. Implement the method that will be called by an InfoPath event.

4. Instantiate your class and store the object into the session within your web page.

5. 5Add a reference to the assembly containing your interface definition to your InfoPath code project.

6. Load your object from the session in the InfoPath event and call the Interface method:

```
void FormEvents_ViewSwitched(object sender, ViewSwitchedEventArgs e)
{
    IInfoPathEvents ev = HttpContext.Current.Session["events"] as
                         IInfoPathEvents;
    if (ev != null)
    {
        ev.OnViewSwitched(this, e);
    }
}
```

7. If the ViewSwitched event is called in the InfoPath form, the events object is loaded from the Session object and the method that is offered through the interface is called.

This extended example shows the flexibility of InfoPath and SharePoint working together to bring InfoPath forms to the Web. You can use .NET code to create complex solutions and overcome existing limitations.

# Summary

This chapter described how InfoPath forms can be used to create professional SharePoint applications that handle complex user input. InfoPath 2010 has greatly improved browser support and is easier to use when designing forms for the SharePoint environment.

Starting with a description about the internals of the InfoPath form templates, this chapter covered all the topics a developer needs to understand when working with InfoPath forms. Although designing form templates may not be a common developer task, basic information on how to design a browser-enabled form template was provided, together with the different ways to deploy the results to SharePoint.

Programming InfoPath form templates offers developers a powerful way to integrate form templates into complex business processes and develop intelligent form templates. However, not only can you use custom code to enrich business logic within InfoPath form templates, but you can also use it to customize form template–hosting inside SharePoint. Along with some basic configuration tasks, this chapter described the possibilities for programmatically changing the behavior of InfoPath Forms Services within SharePoint.

# CHAPTER 7

# The SharePoint 2010 Client Object Model

In previous versions of SharePoint, developers accessed content and performed operations via server side code called Server Object Model and/or used SharePoint Web Services. Now Microsoft has introduced a new way for developers to communicate with SharePoint Foundation 2010; this third way of writing code is known as Client Object Model. (SharePoint Server Object Model and SharePoint Web Services are still options). The Client Object Model (Client OM) API can be used in .NET based applications, Silverlight applications, and in ECMAScript (JavaScript) that executes in the browser. Although the Client OM API is not as rich as the Server Object Model, it has its own benefits, such as an object-oriented way of accessing SharePoint content without the complexities of Server Object Model and SharePoint Web Services, no packaging and deployment hassles, easy access to content stored in SharePoint list/libraries, quick and easy scripting, etc.

This chapter will focus on ECMAScript (JavaScript) to access the Client OM API. The concepts are same if you want to develop a Silverlight or a .NET application.

---

**Note** Silverlight and .NET applications need reference to `Microsoft.SharePoint.Client.dll` and `Microsoft.SharePoint.Client.Runtime.dll` to access the API. These two dlls can be downloaded from the server where SharePoint 2010 is installed.

---

## How It Works

The SharePoint Client OM provides an object-oriented way of retrieving SharePoint data. Developers first need to get the client context object; through this context they can access the client objects of a site (any level in a site collection). The `Client` object's parent class is `ClientObject` and it can be used to get properties of a specific SharePoint object, etc.

Once the client application uses Client OM, the calls are converted into XML request and sent to the SharePoint server. On the server, the XML request is handled by a service called `Client.svc` where it translates the XML request into appropriate Object Model calls (SharePoint Server Object Model) and gets the results. After getting the results, `Client.svc` translates them into JavaScript Object Notation (JSON) and sends back to the Client Managed Object Model. On the client side, the JSON response is translated into ECMAScript objects for ECMAScript. This process is shown in Figure 7-1.

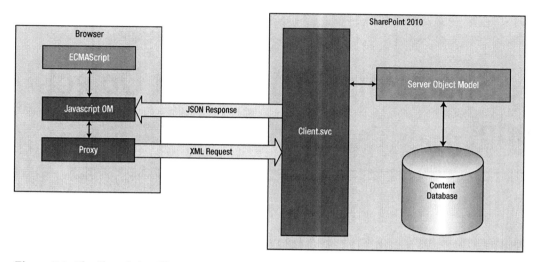

*Figure 7-1. The SharePoint Client OM provides an object-oriented way of retrieving SharePoint data.*

# ECMAScript

ECMAScript is a JavaScript-based client-side scripting language for web pages developed by Ecma International and now supported in SharePoint 2010. The first version of ECMAScript was released in June 1997 and latest version (the fifth) was released in Dec 2009. From a developer's point of view, it's just another version of JavaScript and its SharePoint Class Library can be viewed at `http://msdn.microsoft.com/en-us/library/ee538253.aspx`. Commonly used JavaScript files for Client OM are `CUI.js`, `SP.js`, `SP.Core.js`, `SP.Ribbon.js`, etc. Table 7-1 lists the main classes of ECMAScript for the SharePoint Object Model.

*Table 7-1. The Main Classes of ECMAScript*

| Server Object Model | EMCAScript Object Model |
|---|---|
| `Microsoft.SharePoint.SPContext` | `SP.ClientContext` |
| `Microsoft.SharePoint.SPSite` | `SP.Site` |
| `Microsoft.SharePoint.SPWeb` | `SP.Web` |
| `Microsoft.SharePoint.SPList` | `SP.List` |
| `Microsoft.SharePoint.SPListItem` | `SP.ListItem` |
| `Microsoft.SharePoint.SPField` | `SP.Field` |

# Using Client Object Model

To create a list in SharePoint 2010 site, follow these steps:

1. Go to the site by typing the URL in the address bar.

2. Select Site Actions ➤ More Options from the left top corner, as shown in Figure 7-2.

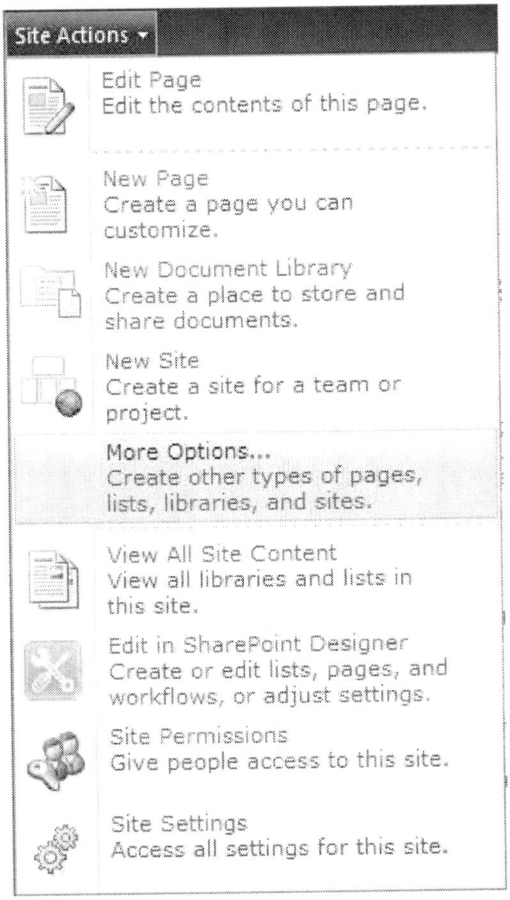

*Figure 7-2. Select Site Actions ➤ More Options*

3. On the Create form, select List from Filter By, then select Custom List and provide a name of the list, such as Product, and hit the Create button, as shown in Figure 7-3.

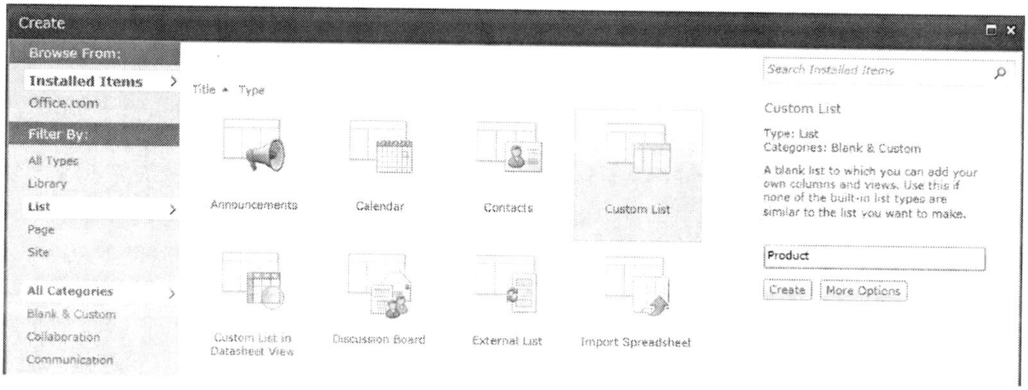

*Figure 7-3. Select the Custom List option*

4.   Select List Tools ➤ List ➤ Create Column, as shown in Figure 7-4.

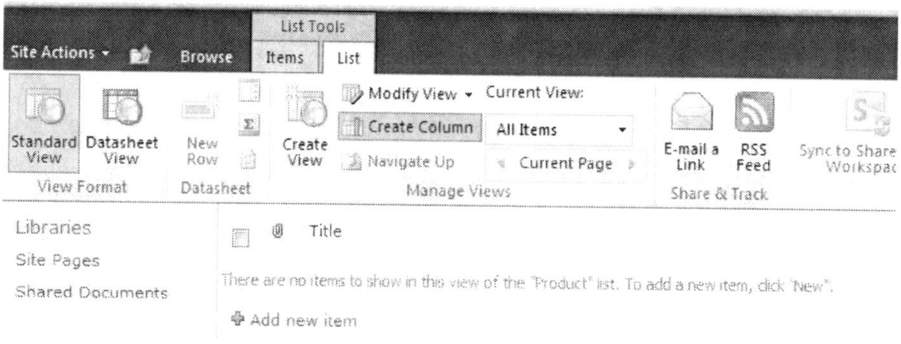

*Figure 7-4. Select List Tools ➤ List ➤ Create Column*

5.   In the Create Column form, provide the column name as Price; Column Type as Currency; Min: as 0; and hit the OK button, as shown in Figure 7-5.

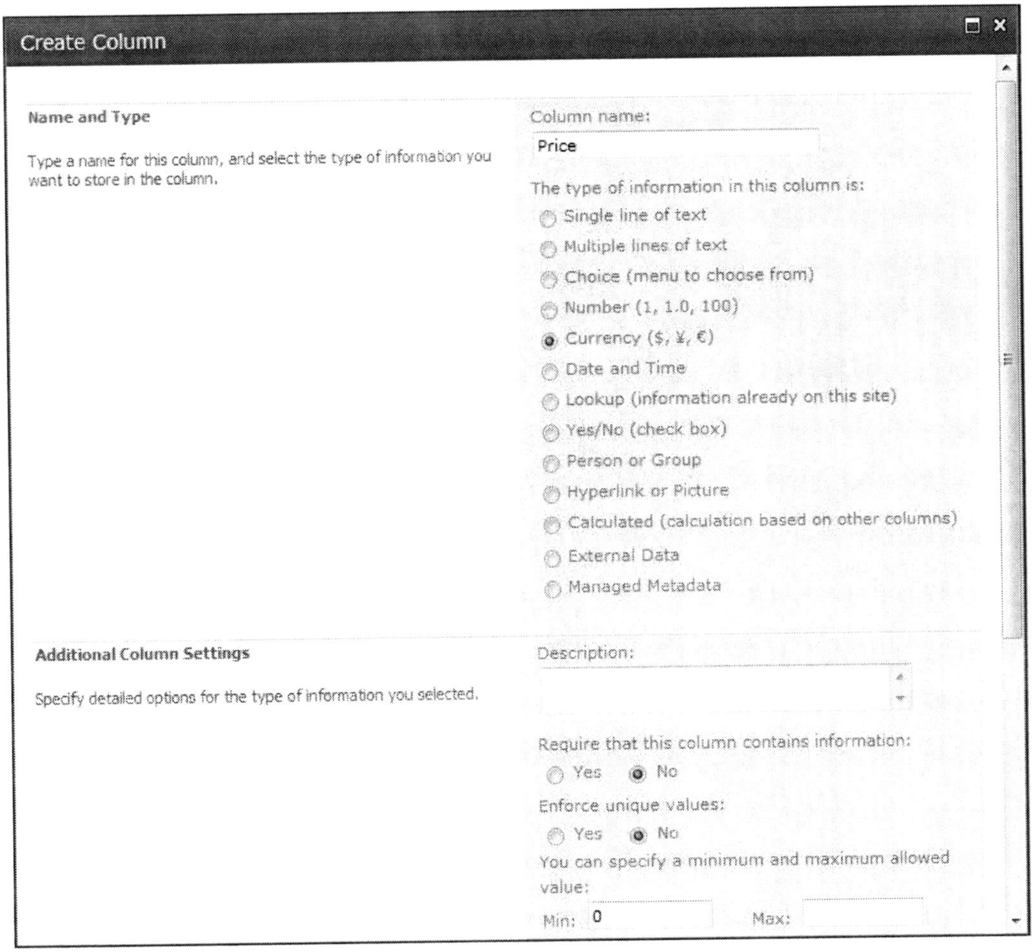

**Create Column**

**Name and Type**

Type a name for this column, and select the type of information you want to store in the column.

Column name:

Price

The type of information in this column is:

- Single line of text
- Multiple lines of text
- Choice (menu to choose from)
- Number (1, 1.0, 100)
- ⦿ Currency ($, ¥, €)
- Date and Time
- Lookup (information already on this site)
- Yes/No (check box)
- Person or Group
- Hyperlink or Picture
- Calculated (calculation based on other columns)
- External Data
- Managed Metadata

**Additional Column Settings**

Specify detailed options for the type of information you selected.

Description:

Require that this column contains information:
- Yes ⦿ No

Enforce unique values:
- Yes ⦿ No

You can specify a minimum and maximum allowed value:

Min: 0          Max:

*Figure 7-5. Fill out the Create Column options*

■ **Note** Now you have a list with column Title (Text) and Price (Currency).

# Creating an Add Form

In this section you will create an ASPX page to add items into the product list using the Client Object Model in ECMAScript. Follow these steps to create an AddItemForm.aspx page.

1. Open the Site in the SharePoint Designer.

2. From the Navigation panel select All Files and then select Lists ➤ Product, as shown in Figure 7-6.

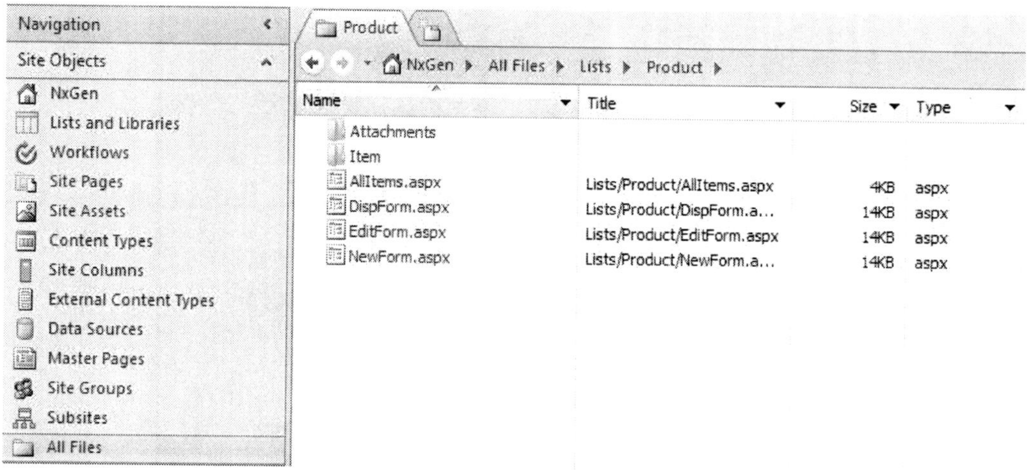

*Figure 7-6. The Product folder*

3. Right-click and point to New ➤ ASPX. Rename the newly created page as `AddItemForm.aspx`, as shown in Figure 7-7.

*Figure 7-7. Rename the file*

4.  Click the AddItemForm.aspx and hit Yes on the warning message, as shown in Figure 7-8.

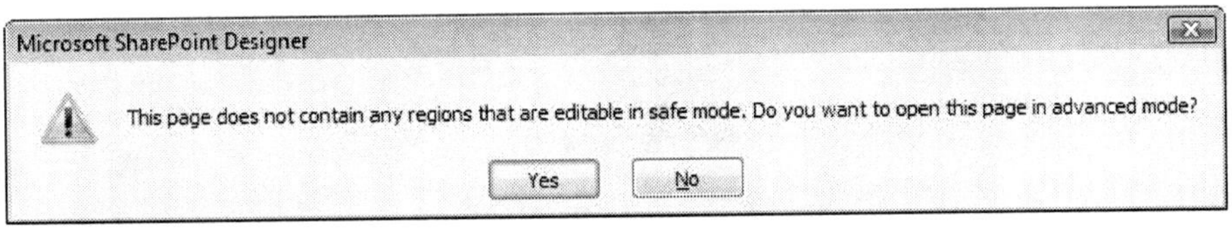

**Figure 7-8.** *Open the page in advanced mode*

5.  Select Split tab from the bottom, as shown in Figure 7-9.

**Figure 7-9.** *The Split tab*

6.  From the Style menu, select Attach ➤ v4.master to apply the default MasterPage on your custom ASPX page.

7.  Click on PlaceHolderMain and select Create Custom Content, as shown in Figure 7-10. It will let you add your custom code into the ASPX page in the main place holder section.

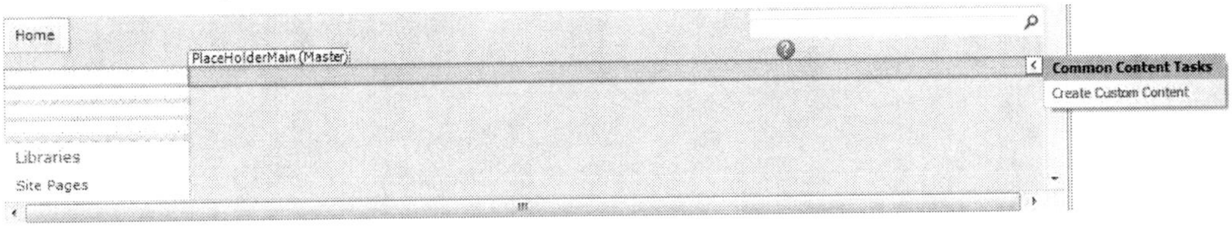

**Figure 7-10.** *Now you can create custom content*

8.  Insert two HTML text boxes (txtTitle and txtPrice) and one HTML button (btnAdd, which will call the JavaScript function AddItem()) inside the PlaceHolderMain, as shown in the following code and in Figure 7-11:

```
<table style="width: 100%">
        <tr>
                <td>Title</td>
                <td><input  id="txtTitle" name="txtTitle" type="text" /></td>
</tr>
        <tr>
                <td>Price</td>
                <td><input id="txtPrice" name="txtPrice" type="text" /></td>
        </tr>
        <tr>
                <td></td>
                <td><input name="btnAdd" type="button" value="Add" onclick=↵
"javascript:AddItem();"/></td>
```

```
        </tr>
    </table>
```

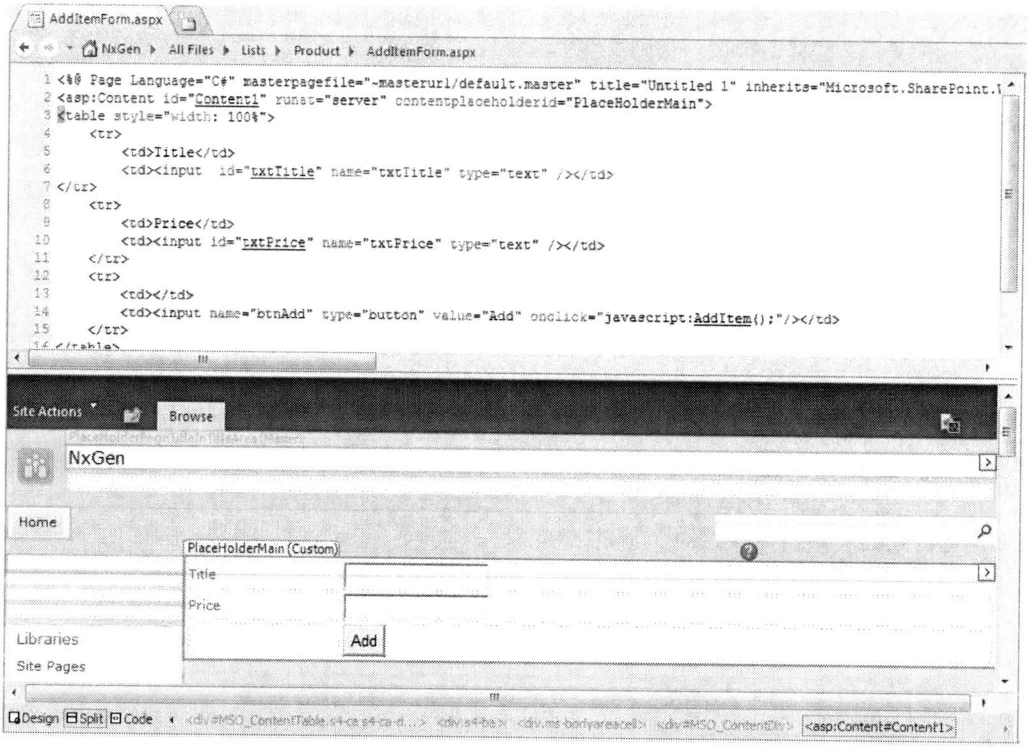

```
1 <%@ Page Language="C#" masterpagefile="~masterurl/default.master" title="Untitled 1" inherits="Microsoft.SharePoint.I
2 <asp:Content id="Content1" runat="server" contentplaceholderid="PlaceHolderMain">
3 <table style="width: 100%">
4     <tr>
5         <td>Title</td>
6         <td><input  id="txtTitle" name="txtTitle" type="text" /></td>
7 </tr>
8     <tr>
9         <td>Price</td>
10        <td><input id="txtPrice" name="txtPrice" type="text" /></td>
11    </tr>
12    <tr>
13        <td></td>
14        <td><input name="btnAdd" type="button" value="Add" onclick="javascript:AddItem();"/></td>
15    </tr>
16 </table>
```

*Figure 7-11. HTML code and resulting text boxes*

    9.    Add the ECMAScript in Listing 7-1 right above the HTML table.

*Listing 7-1. ECMAScript to Add an Item*

```
<script type="text/javascript">

ExecuteOrDelayUntilScriptLoaded(MainFunction, "sp.js");

var objContext = null;
var objWeb = null;
var objList = null;
var objItem = null;
var objListItemCreationInfo = null;


function MainFunction()
{
}
```

```
function AddItem()
{

        var strTitle = document.getElementById('txtTitle').value;
        var strPrice = document.getElementById('txtPrice').value;


        objContext = new SP.ClientContext.get_current();
        objWeb = objContext.get_web();
        objList = objWeb.get_lists().getByTitle("Product");

        objListItemCreationInfo = new SP.ListItemCreationInformation();

        objItem = objList.addItem(objListItemCreationInfo);
        objItem.set_item('Title', strTitle);
        objItem.set_item('Price', strPrice);
        objItem.update();

        objContext.load(objItem);

        objContext.executeQueryAsync(Function.createDelegate(this, this.AddItemSuccess),↵
  Function.createDelegate(this, this.AddItemFail));

        document.getElementById('txtTitle').value = '';
        document.getElementById('txtPrice').value = '';
}

function AddItemSuccess(sender, args)
{
        alert('Item added successfully.');
}

function AddItemFail(sender, args)
{
    alert('Item is not added.');
}
</script>
```

10. Save the code and stop editing the page from SharePoint Designer.

11. Access the AddItemForm.aspx via a browser (e.g. http://sps2k10dev01:5000/
    NxGen/Lists/Product/AddItemForm.aspx). Provide the product title and price,
    and then press the Add button, as shown in Figure 7-12.

**Figure 7-12.** *Product title and price*

12. Access the `AllItems.aspx` page (`http://sps2k10dev01:5000/NxGen/Lists/Product/AllItems.aspx`) of the product list. You should see the newly added item displayed there, as shown in Figure 7-13.

**Figure 7-13.** *The new item*

## Explanation of the Add Code

The first step to using the Client Object Model in ECMAScript is to load the `SP.js` file, which can be loaded by calling the `ExecuteOrDelayUntilScriptLoaded(Func, "sp.js")` method. Along with loading the `sp.js` file, this method also calls the `MainFunction()` which can be used as `OnLoad` or initialized the function on the page.

---

▓ **Note** `SP.js` is referred to in ECMAScript and `Microsoft.SharePoint.Client.dll` and `Microsoft.SharePoint.Client.Runtime.dll` are referred to in .NET code to access the Client Object Model. The two dlls could be located at `C:\Program Files\Common Files\Microsoft Shared\Web Server Extensions\14\TEMPLATE\LAYOUTS\ClientBin` on the server.

---

Once the page is called, the `MainFunction()` executes (which, of course, isn't doing anything in your example). When the Add button is clicked, after filling the text fields, the `AddItem()` method is called. In the `AddItem()` method, the values from two text boxes are stored in the `strTitle` and `strPrice` variables, and then the current context of the site is loaded using `SP.ClientContext.get_current()`, which is used to load the current site using `get_web()` method. Once you have the current site, you can access the lists, document libraries, etc. The current site's lists will be called by the `get_lists()` method, and then the product list will be pointed to by calling `getByTitle(strListName)` method and will pass it the list name.

The `objListItemCreationInfo` object is created to store the information to create the list item and is passed to the `List` object by calling the `addItem()` method. The item object is then populated with the values by calling `set_item(strColumnName, strValue)` method, and the `update()` method is called to add the item to the product list. The current context's load item is called to only load the `item` object and to avoid the performance hit of loading all the objects.

The actual execution will take place when the executeQueryAsync() method of the current context is called. This method executes asynchronously on the server and takes two function names (AddItemSuccess and AddItemFail) as parameters to call them if the execution succeeds or fails respectively. One of the AddItemSuccess() and AddItemFail() functions will be called and will display the success or failure method to show how the execution of executeQueryAsync() went.

## Creating an Edit Form

Creating an Edit form is much like creating the Add form, so I will skip some of the steps and jump directly into the main functionality.

1.  Open the Site in SharePoint Designer and go to your Product list.

2.  Create a new page called EditItemForm.aspx and add two HTML text boxes (txtTitle and txtPrice) and one HTML button (btnUpdate, which will call the JavaScript function UpdateItem()) inside PlaceHolderMain, as shown here and in Figure 7-14:

```
<table style="width: 100%">
    <tr>
        <td>Title</td>
        <td><input  id="txtTitle" name="txtTitle" type="text" /></td>
</tr>
    <tr>
        <td>Price</td>
        <td><input id="txtPrice" name="txtPrice" type="text" /></td>
    </tr>
    <tr>
        <td></td>
        <td><input name="btnUpdate" type="button" value="Update" onclick=↵
"javascript:UpdateItem();"/></td>
    </tr>
</table>
```

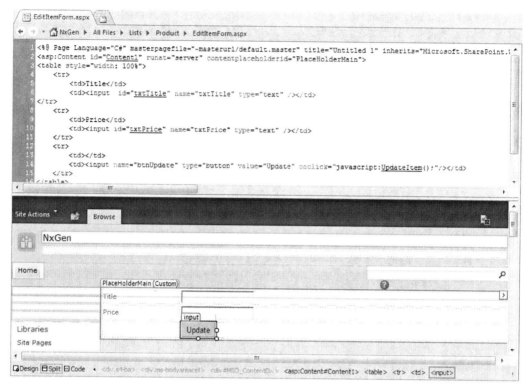

**Figure 7-14.** *Creating an Edit form*

3. Add the ECMAScript in Listing 7-2 right above the HTML table.

*Listing 7-2. ECMAScript for Updating Products*

```javascript
<script type="text/javascript">

ExecuteOrDelayUntilScriptLoaded(MainFunction, "sp.js");

var strID = null;
var objContext = null;
var objWeb = null;
var objList = null;
var objItem = null;
var objCollectionListItem = null;

function MainFunction()
{
        strID = QueryString("ID");

        objContext = new SP.ClientContext.get_current();
        objWeb = objContext.get_web();
```

```
        objList = objWeb.get_lists().getByTitle("Product");

        var objQuery = new SP.CamlQuery();
        objQuery.set_viewXml('<View><Query><Where><Eq><FieldRef Name="ID"/><Value Type=↵
"Number">'+ strID +'</Value></Eq></Where></Query><ViewFields><FieldRef Name="Title"/>↵
<FieldRef Name="Price"/></ViewFields></View>');
        objCollectionListItem = objList.getItems(objQuery);

        objContext.load(objCollectionListItem);

        objContext.executeQueryAsync(Function.createDelegate(this, this.LoadItemSuccess),↵
 Function.createDelegate(this, this.LoadItemFail));

}

function LoadItemSuccess(sender, args)
{
        var listItemEnumerator = objCollectionListItem.getEnumerator();

    //This loop will run only once
    while (listItemEnumerator.moveNext())
    {
        var objTempItem = listItemEnumerator.get_current();

        document.getElementById('txtTitle').value = objTempItem.get_item('Title');
        document.getElementById('txtPrice').value = objTempItem.get_item('Price');
        }
}

function LoadItemFail(sender, args)
{
        alert('Item loading failed.');
}

function QueryString(parameter)
{
        var loc = location.search.substring(1, location.search.length);
        var param_value = false;
        var params = loc.split("&");

        for (i=0; i<params.length;i++)
        {
                param_name = params[i].substring(0,params[i].indexOf('='));
                if (param_name == parameter)
                {
                        param_value = params[i].substring(params[i].indexOf('=')+1)
                }
        }

        if (param_value)
        {
                return param_value;
```

```
        }
        else
        {
                return false;
        }
}


function UpdateItem()
{

        var strTitle = document.getElementById('txtTitle').value;
        var strPrice = document.getElementById('txtPrice').value;


        objContext = new SP.ClientContext.get_current();
        objWeb = objContext.get_web();
        objList = objWeb.get_lists().getByTitle("Product");

        objItem = objList.getItemById(strID);
        objItem.set_item('Title', strTitle);
        objItem.set_item('Price', strPrice);
        objItem.update();

        objContext.executeQueryAsync(Function.createDelegate(this, this.UpdateItemSuccess),↵
    Function.createDelegate(this, this.UpdateItemFail));

        document.getElementById('txtTitle').value = '';
        document.getElementById('txtPrice').value = '';
}

function UpdateItemSuccess(sender, args)
{
        alert('Item updated successfully.');
}

function UpdateItemFail(sender, args)
{
    alert('Item is not updated.');
}
</script>
```

4.  Save the page.

5.  Access the EditItemForm.aspx via browser and pass it a valid ID of the item already existing in the Product list (e.g. http://sps2k10dev01:5000/NxGen/ Lists/Product/EditItemForm.aspx?ID=9).

6.  Loading the page will display the title and price of the item whose ID is passed and hitting the Update button will update the item, as shown in Figure 7-15 and 7-16.

*Figure 7-15. Update the item*

*Figure 7-16. The new Product info*

# Explanation of the Edit Code

As mentioned earlier, the first step to using the Client Object Model in the ECMAScript is to load the SP.js file, which can be loaded by calling the ExecuteOrDelayUntilScriptLoaded(Func, "sp.js") method. Along with loading the sp.js file, this method also calls the MainFunction(), which can be used as OnLoad or to initialize a function on the page.

Once the page is called, the MainFunction() executes, which will call QueryString() to get the value of the querystring ID. The Product list is called by getting the current context, then the current site and all the lists in the current site. objQuery will hold the CAML (Collaborative Application Markup Language) query XML to execute against the list to retrieve the list content. In the example, the following CAML is used:

```
<View>
    <Query>
        <Where>
            <Eq><FieldRef Name="ID"/><Value Type="Number">'+ strID+'</Value></Eq>
        </Where>
    </Query>
<ViewFields>
    <FieldRef Name="Title"/><FieldRef Name="Price"/>
</ViewFields>
</View>
```

This CAML query tells the API to get the items where the ID column value is provided by the strID variable. In <ViewFields/> tag, two columns have been mentioned that need to be returned for the selected items.

If the execution of the executeQueryAsync() method succeeds, then LoadItemSuccess() will iterate through all the returned items and will populate the text boxes for the user to update the values.

---

■ **Note** In this example, the loop will run once as there will be only one item with the provided ID.

---

The Update button will call the UpdateItem() method, which will get the list item by ID by calling the getItemById(intID) method of the list object. It will set the new values for the columns and update the item by calling the update() method of the item object and then calling the executeQueryAsync() method.

## Delete Functionality in the Edit Form

The Edit form (EditItemForm.aspx) can be upgraded with the delete functionality easily. The process is similar to updating a list item but you call a delete method instead of an update method.

1.  Edit the EditItemForm.aspx in SharePoint Designer.

2.  Update the HTML by adding a new HTML button, btnDelete, which will call the JavaScript function DeleteItem(), as shown in Figure 7-17.

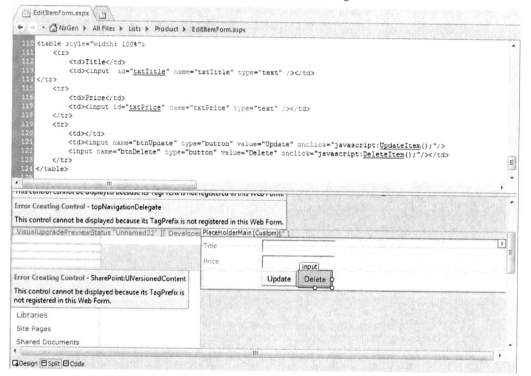

*Figure 7-17. The delete functionality*

3.  Add the code in Listing 7-3 to the <script> tag.

*Listing 7-3. Code for <script> Tag*

```
function DeleteItem()
{
        if(window.confirm('Are you sure you want to delete this item?'))
        {
                objContext = new SP.ClientContext.get_current();
                objWeb = objContext.get_web();
                objList = objWeb.get_lists().getByTitle("Product");

                objItem = objList.getItemById(strID);
                objItem.deleteObject();

            objContext.executeQueryAsync(Function.createDelegate(this,↵
 this.DeleteItemSuccess), Function.createDelegate(this, this.DeleteItemFail));
        }
}

function DeleteItemSuccess(sender, args)
{
        window.location = "AllItems.aspx";
}

function DeleteItemFail(sender, args)
{
    alert('Item is not updated.');
}
```

■ **Note** If you plan to use this code separately, don't forget to add the following line in the <script> tag:

```
ExecuteOrDelayUntilScriptLoaded(MainFunction, "sp.js");
```

4. Browse the EditItemForm.aspx page via browser and pass the ID of an existing
   item. (e.g.
   http://sps2k10dev01:5000/NxGen/Lists/Product/EditItemForm.aspx?ID=7)
   and press the Delete button, as shown in Figure 7-18.

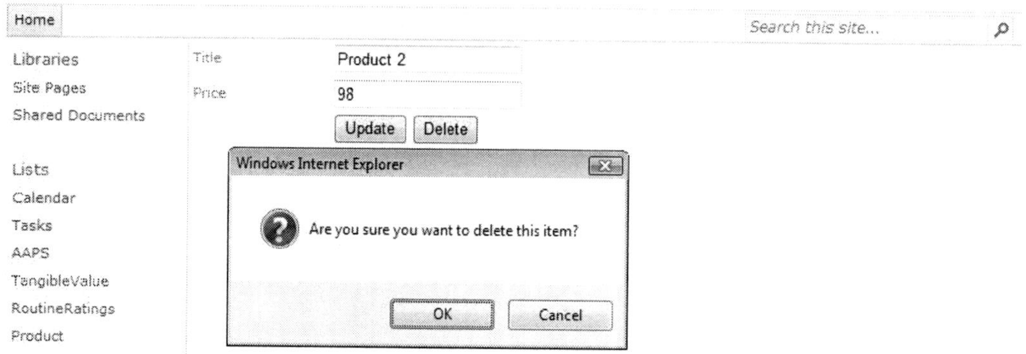

**Figure 7-18.** *Deleting an item*

The item will be deleted and user will be redirected to the `AllItems.aspx` page where the deleted item does not exist, as shown in Figure 7-19.

**Figure 7-19.** *The item no longer exists.*

## Explanation of the Delete Code

Once the Delete button is clicked, the item is loaded by calling the `getItemById(intID)` method of the `list` object and is deleted by calling the `deleteObject()` method of the `item` object. Once again, the actual execution will be taken placed when `executeQueryAsync()` is called.

## Why executeQueryAsync()?

While using SharePoint Client OM in .NET or Silverlight application, both `ExecuteQuery()` and `ExecuteQueryAsync()` are available to developers. `ExecuteQuery()` is a synchronous call, which means the client application will wait for the server's response before jumping onto next line of code. `ExecuteQueryAsync()` is an asynchronous call, so code continues to execute; the client application doesn't wait for server's response and will execute the next line of code. Each function has its advantages and disadvantages. For example, if the next piece of code needs input from server, it's okay to use `ExecuteQuery()`; however, if the server's response gets delayed, the application will simply hang there. This problem is solved by `ExecuteQueryAsync()` where the client application(especially when using the

Client OM API in the browser) doesn't wait for the server response so the application won't hang if there's a delay in the response from server. Server response delay can be caused by multiple things such as network traffic, huge calculation, slow servers, etc.

---

■ **Note** While executing the code, developers should massage the code to use `ExecuteQueryAsync()` to avoid hanging the browser due to server response delay. If `ExecuteQuery()` has been used in the application and browser hangs while waiting for server response, there is a good chance that the whole browser instance will crash; that means any applications running in other tabs could lose data. In ECMAScript, only the `executeQueryAsync()` method available and that is being used in this chapter.

---

# Summary

ECMAScript is a JavaScript-based client-side scripting language that is now supported in SharePoint 2010 and can be used to access Client Object Model. Users can write ECMAScript in an ASPX page for SharePoint 2010 sites and can manipulate the SharePoint content without the code compilation, Server Object model, or getting involved in the complexities of web services.

# CHAPTER 8

# Extending SharePoint Using Event Receivers

This chapter covers techniques to extend SharePoint 2010 functionality using event receivers. It starts with a discussion of common business scenarios for event receivers. It also describes situations where you may want to avoid using event receivers. You will then learn the core architecture of event receivers, their types, and categories. Various approaches to develop, deploy and register event receivers are covered with hands-on exercises. Later parts of chapter covers areas like common issues with event receivers and how to avoid them. Throughout the chapter best practices are highlighted while working with custom event receivers.

This chapter assumes that you are already familiar with SharePoint 2010 development using Visual Studio 2010 Tools for SharePoint 2010. Event receivers have been a part of SharePoint since the earlier versions; they have gone through many changes and enhancements to reach SharePoint 2010, and they will definitely be part of v.Next of SharePoint.

This chapter includes

- Common business scenarios for event receivers

- Event receivers architecture

- Developing event receivers

- Various approaches to registering event receiver

- Common issues and fixes for event receivers

- Cancelling events and redirecting users to error pages

- Event receivers best practices

Event receivers provide developers an ability to execute custom code against various events that occur during the life cycle of various SharePoint objects including SPSite, SPWeb, SPList, SPListItem, and SPContentType. For example, when you add a new List to a SharePoint site, ListAdding and ListAdded events are triggered. Similarly, when you create a new item in a list or upload a new document to a document library, ItemAdding and ItemAdded event are fired by SharePoint.

To better understand the usage of event receivers you need to look into various business scenarios where they provide great help to developers and help them meet business requirements. Of course, it's not possible to cover every possible scenario in which you can utilize event receivers but you will get an idea where event receivers can be good fit.

# Common Business Scenarios for Event Receivers

The following are a few of the business scenarios where event receivers are helpful.

## Auditing

The need to provide granular control for auditing is considered mandatory for many organizations. This is particularly important for organizations that follow standards like SAS 70, CMMI, etc. Consider a financial institute running their corporate portal on SharePoint 2010 with a need to ensure that they can keep track of who made what changes to their Global Financial Forecast List and when those changes took place. This includes but is not limited to tracking the adding, updating, and deleting of columns to the Global Financial Forecast List. These same requirements may also extend to individual list items. Event receivers provide a convenient way to track a broad range of changes including add, edit, and delete operations to a SharePoint list or items to the list. Better yet, you can log all these changes and then compile them into reports to present to auditors for compliance reviews as required.

## Validations

Often you need to perform custom validations against business requirements/rules before data can be saved to SharePoint. For example, consider implementing an organizational policy that restricts users from uploading documents to certain document libraries after the regular business hours of 9 a.m. to 5 p.m. EST. Similarly, you may want to limit deletion of items during certain time intervals even if user has the permissions to do so. In both cases, you can use event receivers to perform these validations; if validation fails, you can cancel the operation that user is performing and display custom message(s) to the user or even redirect them to custom error pages.

## Notifications

Organizations usually generates different kind of notifications (e.g. e-mail, SMS, entry to an Announcements List in SharePoint, etc.) to inform their users for various events and activities. When the source of these notifications is an object in SharePoint, event receivers can be used to easily send these notifications. Consider a SharePoint Tasks List named "Volunteer Tasks" within organization's corporate SharePoint portal that provides a place for managers to post tasks related to volunteer opportunities that exist throughout the organization. As items are added to the Tasks List and they go through various status changes throughout the life cycle of the task, notifications need to be sent to managers and designated employees in the form of e-mails.

Upon successful completion of a task within the Volunteer Tasks List, a new announcement is added to the Announcements List explaining the nature of the task. All of this can be easily achieved by implementing item-level event receivers for Tasks List and then using custom code within the event receivers to send e-mail notifications and add the items to Announcements list.

# When Not to Use Event Receivers

Event receivers execute code on the server side. This makes them ideal candidates for many scenarios, as you learned in previous section. However, there are occasions when they might add an unnecessary burden to the server by consuming its resources in an inefficient manner. The following are some of the scenarios when event receivers may not be an ideal fit and it would be better to look for an alternative solution:

1. Using event receivers to perform long-running and processor-intensive tasks that will consume extensive resources on the server. For example, using ItemAdded event on a document library to execute code that converts an uploaded file from a MS Word document to a PDF. Activites like these are better suited for custom batch jobs, Windows services, or SharePoint timer jobs bcause you need to control when to start/stop them and as a result, you can minimize the possibility of degrading server performance.

2. Executing validation logic inside event receivers, which can easily be done on the client side. For example, checking for valid date formats or e-mail addresses are good tasks for client-side validation. With SharePoint 2010 you now have the ability to use column-level validations to perform various client-side validations. This feature is available out of box (OOB), so it's easy to explore the possibilities of client-side validations.

3. Implementing workflow-like process logic inside event receivers instead of using SharePoint Workflows. **Simply put, event receivers are not meant for long-running processes especially when they require interaction with multiple users or machines.** For these scenarios you should use SharePoint workflows or start them using event receivers. SharePoint 2010 provides excellent support in developing both no-code to full-code workflow solutions by using SharePoint Designer 2010 and Microsoft Visual Studio 2010, respectively.

## Event Receivers Architecture

The architecture of event receivers is comprised of two major pieces—the first being the event receiver base class with virtual methods that SharePoint provides. You inherit your custom event receiver from one of these base classes, then override virtual methods in your custom event receivers. The second piece is the deployment and registration of custom event receivers. The following sections discuss both of them.

*Event receiver base class*: SharePoint provides various base classes for implementing custom event recievers. These base clases contains virtual methods that you override to implement your custom event recievers. These base classes include SPWebEventReceiver, SPListEventReiver, SPItemEventReceiver, SPWorkflowEventReceiver, SPFeatureReceiver, and SPEmailEventReceiver. The root of all of the SharePoint base event classes is SPEventReceiverBase with the exception of SPFeatureReceiver and SPEmailEventReceiver. Figure 8-1 shows this relationship.

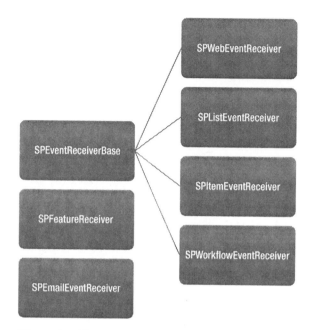

**Figure 8-1.** *SharePoint event receivers base class structure*

Table 8-1 lists the event receivers that are avialable for various SharePoint objects along with their base class.

**Table 8-1.** *List of SharePoint 2010 Events with Target SharePoint Objects*

| Event | SP Object | Base Class |
| --- | --- | --- |
| SiteDeleting(SPWebEventProperties)<br>SiteDeleted(SPWebEventProperties) | SPSite | SPWebEventReceiver |
| WebAdding(SPWebEventProperties)<br>WebProvisioned(SPWebEventProperties)<br>WebDeleting(SPWebEventProperties)<br>WebDeleted(SPWebEventProperties)<br>WebMoving(SPWebEventProperties)<br>WebMoved(SPWebEventProperties) | SPSite,SPWeb | SPWebEventReceiver |
| ListAdding(SPListEventProperties)<br>ListAdded(SPListEventProperties)<br>ListDeleting(SPListEventProperties) | SPSite,SPWeb | SPListEventReceiver |

| Event | SP Object | Base Class |
|---|---|---|
| ListDeleted(SPListEventProperties | | |
| FieldAdding(SPListEventProperties) | | |
| FieldAdded(SPListEventProperties) | SPSite, | SPListEventReceiver |
| | SPWeb, | |
| FieldDeleting(SPListEventProperties) | SPList, | |
| | SPContent | |
| FieldDeleted(SPListEventProperties) | Type | |
| FieldUpdating(SPListEventProperties) | | |
| FieldUpdated(SPListEventProperties) | | |
| | | |
| ItemAdding(SPItemEventProperties) | SPSite, | SPItemEventReceiver |
| ItemAdded(SPItemEventProperties) | SPWeb, | |
| ItemDeleting(SPItemEventProperties) | SPList, | |
| | SPContent | |
| ItemDeleted(SPItemEventProperties) | Type | |
| ItemUpdating(SPItemEventProperties) | | |
| ItemUpdated(SPItemEventProperties) | | |
| ItemFileConverted(SPItemEventProperties) | | |
| ItemFileMoving(SPItemEventProperties) | | |
| ItemFileMoved(SPItemEventProperties) | | |
| ItemCheckingIn(SPItemEventProperties) | | |
| ItemCheckedIn(SPItemEventProperties) | | |
| ItemCheckingOut(SPItemEventProperties) | | |
| ItemCheckedOut(SPItemEventProperties) | | |
| ItemAttachmentAdding | | |
| (SPItemEventProperties) | | |
| ItemAttachmentAdded(SPItemEventProperties) | | |
| ItemAttachmentDeleting(SPItemEventProperties) | | |
| ItemAttachmentDeleted(SPItemEventProperties) | | |

*Event receiver deployment and registration:* Custom event receivers first need to be deployed and registered into the SharePoint environment before they can be executed by SharePoint. This can be done either declaratively by using SharePoint Features or programmatically using SharePoint 2010 Server Side Object Model (OM). It is recommended that you should use a declarative approach to register event receivers as it provides ease of management and more flexibility to perform updates. However, as declarative approach provides only the subset of registration options, it's not always possible to use it; in those cases, you should revert to code-based registration. The deployment process essentially deploys artifacts like the event receiver assembly and other related artifacts into the SharePoint environment. Deployment should always be done using SharePoint Solutions in the form of a WSP file because that is the only way to ensure that it is done uniformly throughout the SharePoint farm. It also provides a consistent way to remove artifacts from the SharePoint farm.

## Synchronous and Asynchronous Events

SharePoint 2010 divides event receivers into two broad categories: synchronous and asynchronous events. Synchronous events provide developers an opportunity to act on the event and ability change the outcome of it (such as canceling the event). On the other hand, asynchronous events help developers react to an event that just happened and lets them send notifications or perform any post processing related to the event. The next sections cover synchronous and asynchronous events in detail.

### Synchronous

Synchronous events (also known as *before* events) are triggered as a result of actions that are performed against SharePoint objects like SPSite, SPWeb, SPList, SPContentType, etc. These events get executed before data is committed to the SharePoint content database. This very nature of synchronous events presents developers with an opportunity to perform various preprocessing tasks inside these events (e.g. ensure that a newly created list follows certain naming conventions). It also provides them with the ability to cancel these events if required, which in turns terminates the action and nothing will be committed to content database. SharePoint traditionally follows a naming scheme to represent these events by ending them with *ing*, like the ItemAdding event which represents addition of new item to the list or a library.

Synchronous events run in the same process and thread that triggers the event; usually it's same thread in which the SharePoint UI is running (e.g. when the user creates new item in the Tasks list using SharePoint UI) but this can easily be a different process (e.g. when you programmatically create new item in the Task list using Windows console application or through Windows service). You must avoid using complex time-consuming processing logic inside synchronous events as they block the execution of the current request thread until the event receiver completes its execution. This essentially means that your UI will be help up in rendering.

### Asynchronous Events

Asynchronous events (also known as *after* events) are triggered for SharePoint objects like SPSite, SPWeb, SPList, SPContentType, etc. after the action (e.g. creation of new list or deletion of a file from document library) has been committed to the SharePoint content database. As SharePoint already has updated the content database, you can't cancel these events but you can use them for post-processing tasks, such as sending notifications to users informing them about a new task list that just got created. SharePoint traditionally follows a naming scheme to represent these events by ending them with *ed*, like the ListAdded event that represents the addition of a new list/library to the site.

All asynchronous events by default run on a background thread, which means that they never block the UI thread and the user always retains control. Sometimes you will want to change this behavior, mainly because you want to update the UI with pieces of information that you processed during the execution of an asynchronous event receiver; for that the user should wait until the event receiver finishes its execution. To address this scenario SharePoint 2010 allows you to alter the default behavior of asynchronous events and make them run as if they are synchronous events by updating the *synchronization* property of event receiver to *synchronous*.

## Developing Custom Event Receivers

In this section you will address a business scenario by developing, deploying, and testing a custom event receiver using Microsoft Visual Studio 2010, which provides specific project templates for SharePoint 2010. One such template is specifically for creating SharePoint 2010 event receivers.

In order to perform steps in this section and others you will need to have SharePoint 2010 locally install on your machine. This is because Visual Studio 2010 only makes SharePoint 2010 project templates available if you have SharePoint 2010 locally installed on the same machine. Discussing the details of how to setup up SharePoint 2010 for development is out of scope for this chapter, but you can download a SharePoint 2010 Information Worker Demo and Evaluation Virtual Machine from `www.microsoft.com/download/en/details.aspx?id=21099`. This virtual machine contains SharePoint 2010 along with Visual Studio 2010. Also you can download and use the SharePoint 2010 Easy Setup Script from `www.microsoft.com/download/en/details.aspx?id=23415` to quickly create a SharePoint 2010 development environment.

Consider a business scenario where your company has SharePoint contacts list named "Employees" that contains contact details of all employees. As a new employee joins the company, a new contact item is created for that employee. This item contains details like employee full name, e-mail, and home and business phone numbers. When an employee joins the company there is a need to automatically post a welcome greeting on a SharePoint Announcements list to let all other employees know about their new colleague. You have decided to meet this requirement by implementing a custom event receiver. You will capture the ItemAdded event for the employees list and execute custom code inside it to create the new announcement with a greeting message. The following is the walkthrough for this scenario:

1. Start Microsoft Visual Studio 2010 with administrative privileges.

2. Create a new project in Visual Studio by clicking File ➤ New Project.

3. In the New Project dialog box, expand Visual C# in the Installed Templates box, expand SharePoint, and select 2010. From the list of templates, select Event Receiver.

4. Type ContactListEventReceiver for the Name, as shown in Figure 8-2. Click OK.

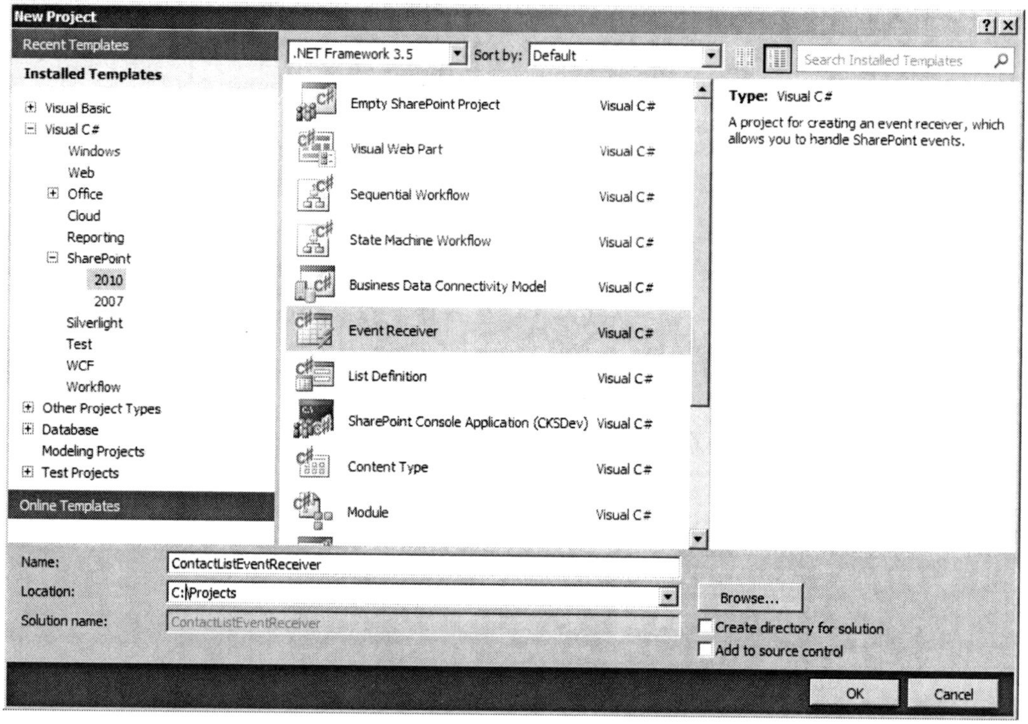

*Figure 8-2. Creating a new event receiver project*

5.  Type http[s]://<<SiteCollectionUrl>> for the local site combo box. Click
    Validate. Wait for Connection Successful message box to appear. Make sure
    you replace the http[s]<<SiteCollectionUrl>> with the actual URL of your site
    collection, such as `http://spdev01` or `http://contoso` (see Figure 8-3).

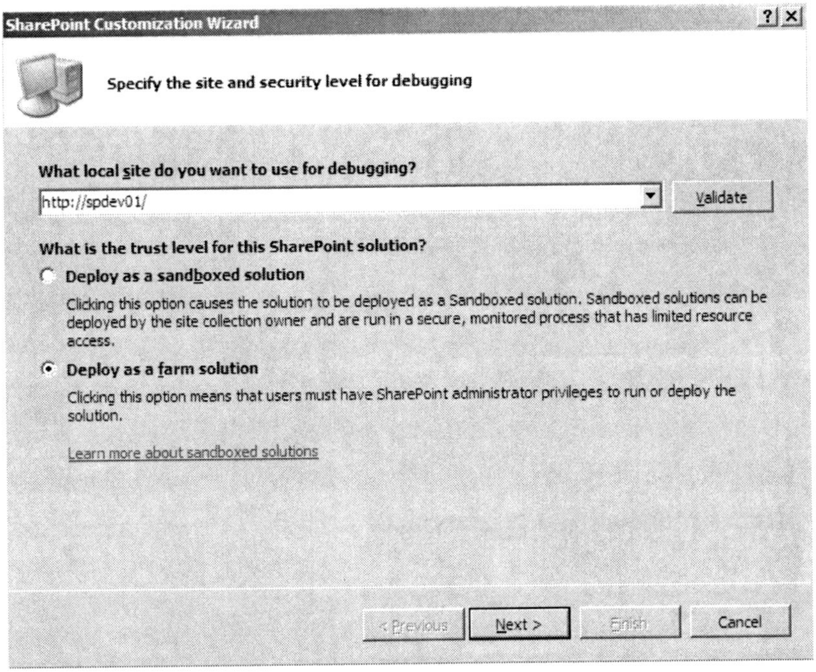

*Figure 8-3. SharePoint site URL and Solution settings*

6. Choose Deploy as a farm solution. Click Next.

---

▪ **Note** With SharePoint 2010 you can write code that can be deployed as a sandbox solution rather than farm solution. The major difference between farm and sandbox solutions is that of scope. Sandbox solutions put a number of constrains on your code but provide better manageability and security. For example, with sandbox solutions you are limited to accessing objects below the site collection level (e.g. lists, sub sites, etc.). Also, your code can't run under FullTrust, and certain SharePoint Server Side Object Model classes are not available, such as Microsoft.SharePoint.SPSecurity. Microsoft Visual Studio 2010 will disable the sandbox solution choice if that option isn't available for the particular event receiver. However, it's recommended that you choose between Sandbox and Farm solutions based on your actual business requirements rather than simply because of ease of deployment or management.

---

7. For the type of event, select List Item Events.

8. Select Contacts from the event source drop-down.

9. Select the check box "An item was added" from the events list box. Click Finish, as shown in Figure 8-4).

**SharePoint Customization Wizard**  ? ×

**Choose Event Receiver Settings**

**What type of event receiver do you want?**

List Item Events ▼

**What item should be the event source?**

Contacts ▼

**Handle the following events:**

☐ An item is being added
☐ An item is being updated
☐ An item is being deleted
☐ An item is being checked in
☐ An item is being checked out
☐ An item is being unchecked out
☐ An attachment is being added to the item
☐ An attachment is being removed from the item
☐ A file is being moved
☑ An item was added

< Previous | Next > | Finish | Cancel

*Figure 8-4. Select events to implement*

10. Your should now see the Event Receiver Solution along with the
ContactListEventReceiver Project, as shown in Figure 8-5.

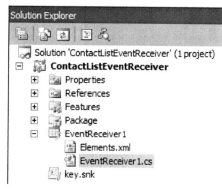

Solution Explorer

Solution 'ContactListEventReceiver' (1 project)
▧ **ContactListEventReceiver**
  ⊞ Properties
  ⊞ References
  ⊞ Features
  ⊞ Package
  ⊟ EventReceiver1
      Elements.xml
      EventReceiver1.cs
  key.snk

*Figure 8-5. ContactListEventReceiver Solution Explorer view*

11. Locate EventReciever1 folder and rename it as ContactEvents.

12. Locate `EventReceiver1.cs` inside ContactEvents folder and rename it to
`CustomEvents.cs`, as shown in Figure 8-6.

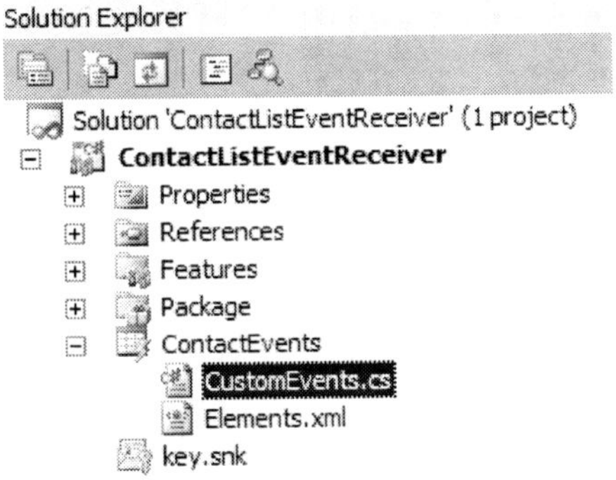

Solution Explorer

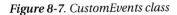

Solution 'ContactListEventReceiver' (1 project)
- **ContactListEventReceiver**
  - Properties
  - References
  - Features
  - Package
  - ContactEvents
    - CustomEvents.cs
    - Elements.xml
  - key.snk

*Figure 8-6. CustomEvent.cs file after rename*

13. Open the `CustomEvents.cs` file from ContactEvents folder. Notice that a stub for an ItemAdding method is already implemented for you.

14. Rename the namespace to ContactListEventReceiver (see Figure 8-7).

15. Rename the class name to `CustomEvents`.

```
using System;
using System.Security.Permissions;
using Microsoft.SharePoint;
using Microsoft.SharePoint.Security;
using Microsoft.SharePoint.Utilities;
using Microsoft.SharePoint.Workflow;

namespace ContactListEventReceiver
{
    /// <summary>
    /// List Item Events
    /// </summary>
    public class CustomEvents : SPItemEventReceiver
    {
        /// <summary>
        /// An item was added.
        /// </summary>
        public override void ItemAdded(SPItemEventProperties properties)
        {
            base.ItemAdded(properties);
        }


    }
}
```

*Figure 8-7. CustomEvents class*

16. Inside the CustomEvents class, replace the existing code with Listing 8-1.

*Listing 8-1. The ItemAdded Event*

```
public override void ItemAdded(SPItemEventProperties properties)
        {
            SPList announcementsList = properties.Web.GetList("/Lists/Announcements") as
SPList;
            if (null != announcementsList)
            {
                SPListItem contactItem = properties.ListItem;
                SPListItem newItem = announcementsList.Items.Add();
                newItem[SPBuiltInFieldId.Title] = string.Format("Please welcome {0} on board,
you can reach {1} at {2}", contactItem["FullName"],

contactItem["FirstName"],contactItem["Email"]);
                newItem.Update();
            }
        }
```

The code first gets the Announcements list using the GetList method of SPList class, and then it adds a new item to it by calling the Add method on the Items collection. Next, it sets the Title column to the welcome message using column values from newly added Contact item. Notice that as the Contact item is already added to the SharePoint you can easily access all of its columns along with the values. Finally, the Update method is called on the announcement item so all the changes get committed to the content database.

17. Open Elements.xml located inside ContactLists folder.

18. Inside the Elements.xml file, replace the markup with code in Listing 8-2.

*Listing 8-2. Elements.xml File for ContactListItemAdded Event*

```
<?xml version="1.0" encoding="utf-8"?>
<Elements xmlns="http://schemas.microsoft.com/sharepoint/">
  <Receivers ListUrl="/Lists/Employees">
      <Receiver>
        <Name>ContactListItemAddedEvent</Name>
        <Type>ItemAdded</Type>
        <Assembly>$SharePoint.Project.AssemblyFullName$</Assembly>
        <Class>ContactListEventReceiver.CustomEvents</Class>
        <SequenceNumber>10000</SequenceNumber>
      </Receiver>
  </Receivers>
</Elements>
```

The Elements.xml file contains the information that will be used to deploy and register the event receiver. You will learn more about deployment and registration of event receivers in a later section. For now, Visual Studio will take care of deployment; you don't have to worry about it.

> ▪ **Tip** Visual Studio 2010 provides replaceable parameters (also known as tokens) that are used to provide values for SharePoint solution items whose actual values are not known at design time. In the Listing 8-2, rather than hard-coding the assembly name inside the `Elements.xml` file, the `$SharePoint.Project.AssemblyFullName$` token is used. It will be replaced by the actual name of your fully qualified assembly as Visual Studio creates the SharePoint Solution file (WSP) as part of deployment process. You can learn more about replaceable parameters from `http://msdn.microsoft.com/en-us/library/ee231545.aspx`.

19. Expand the Features folder and rename Feature1 to ContactEventFeature.

20. Double click ContactEventFeature and enter the following information (see Figure 8-8):

    Title:  Contact List Custom Event Receiver Activation

    Description: This feature deploy ContactListItemAddedEvent Event Receiver

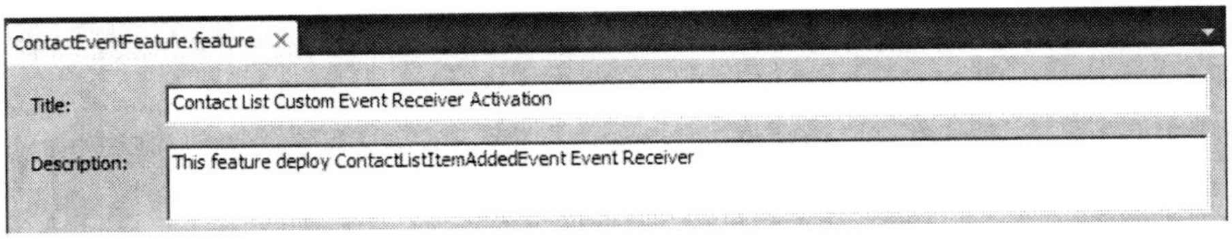

*Figure 8-8. ContactEventFeature title and description*

21. Right click the Project and select Properties. In the Build tab, set the Platform target to x64 (see Figure 8-9).

22. Press F5 inside Visual Studio, which will deploy the event receiver and enable debugging.

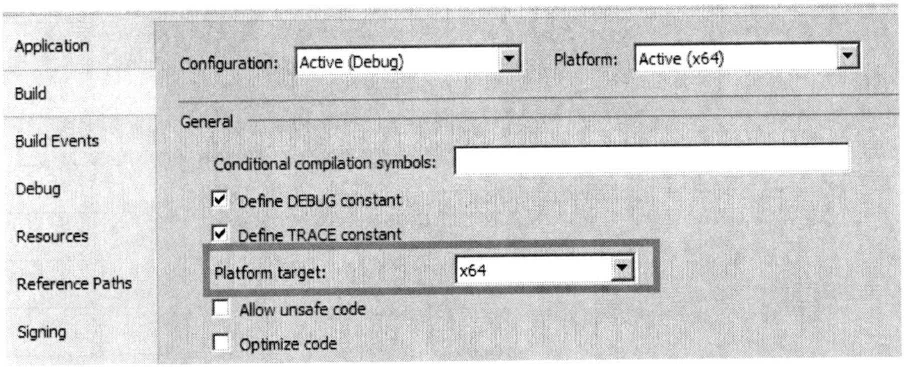

*Figure 8-9. Changing project target platform to x64*

23. Visual Studio will automatically open the SharePoint Portal default page.

24. To test your event receiver, you will first create a new contact list and then add a new item to it.

25. From the Site Actions menu, select View All Site Content.

26. Click Create. This will open up a dialog box. Select contact list from the list of installed items.

27. Type Employees for the name of the contacts list, as shown in Figure 8-10. Click Create.

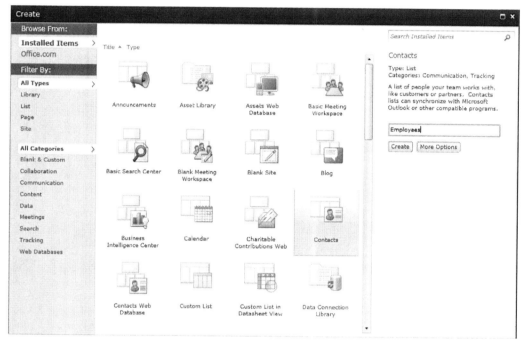

***Figure 8-10.*** *Creating the employees list*

28. In the Quick Launch menu on the left, click Employees.

29. To add a new item, click on the Add new item link.

30. On New Item dialog, enter values for Last Name, First Name, Full Name and E-mail Address, Business Phone and Home Phone columns (see Figure 8-11). Click Save.

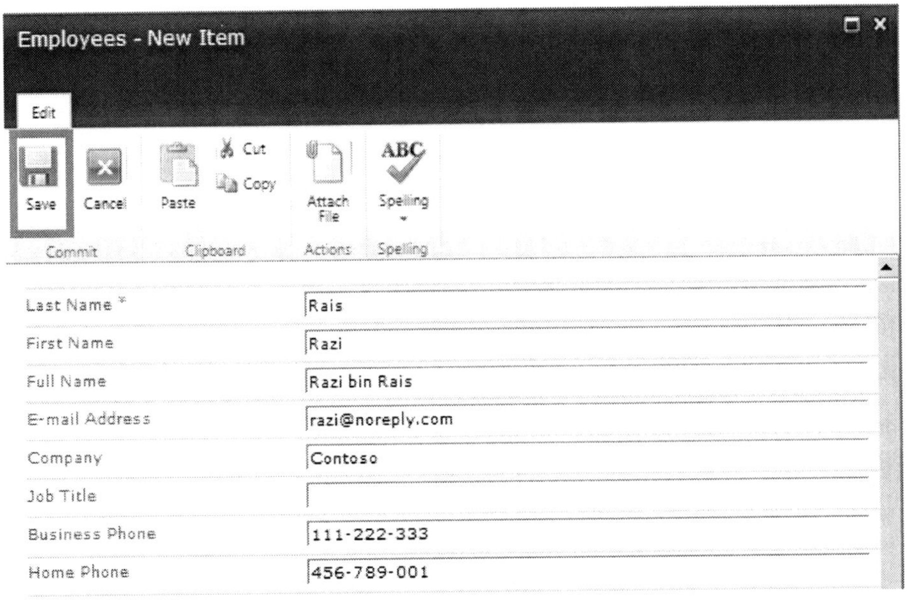

*Figure 8-11. Adding new item to Employees list*

31. You should see new contact being added to the Employees list, as shown in Figure 8-12.

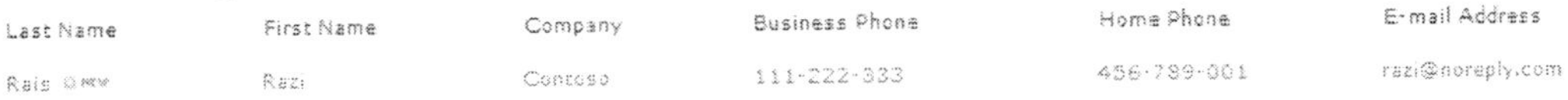

*Figure 8-12. New contact item in Employee list*

32. In the Quick Launch menu on the left, click All Site Content.

33. On the All Site Content page, locate and click on the Announcements list.

34. You should see a new announcement item already added to the list, displaying the welcome message, as shown in Figure 8-13.

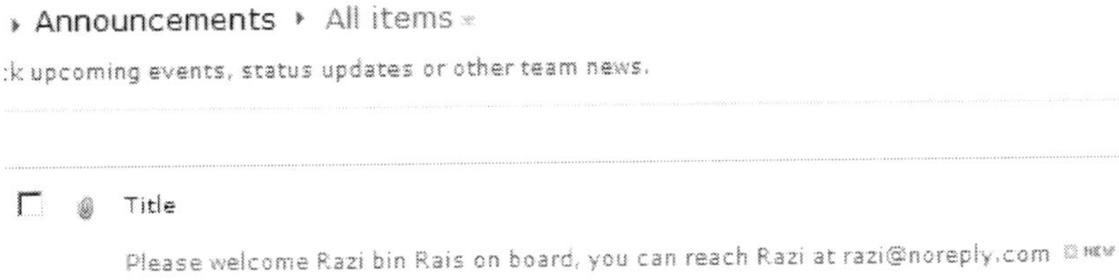

*Figure 8-13. New announcement created through an event receiver*

## Feature Receivers

Feature receivers provide developers with an opportunity to execute code as a feature goes through different stages. The following is the list of feature event receivers:

1. *FeatureActivated*

2. *FeatureDeactivating*

3. *FeatureInstalled*

4. *FeatureUninstalling*

5. *FeatureUpgrading*

As features are the cornerstone of SharePoint application architecture, by using feature receivers you can easily address a broad set of requirements without introducing unnecessary complexity. The following are some of the common scenarios for feature receivers:

- SharePoint delegate control functionality uses feature receivers to enable or disable the usage of a particular delegate control.

- Feature receivers enjoy the benefits of feature versioning and upgrades, making them easier to maintain and providing administrators a consistent mechanism to manage them throughout a SharePoint farm.

- Feature receivers provide an elegant way to register event receivers using code. As features can easily be activated and deactivated using the user interface, well-trained site admins can simply activate and deactivate them as needed. There is a step-by-step walkthrough later in this chapter that shows how to activate an event receiver using feature receivers.

- As features can be scoped at SharePoint farm, Web Application, site, and web level, you can use feature receivers to react and perform customizations on all four levels in a consistent manner.

## Using the ReceiverData Property

The `SPEventPropertiesBase` class provides the ReceiverData property, which allows you to populate it with a string value with a maximum size of 256 characters and to later read it inside your event receiver. Despite the character limit, this approach provides an easy way to store the data that you need to access within event receivers.

The `Elements.xml` file in Listing 8-3 shows how to declaratively set the ReceiverData property. Notice that the name of actual element is *Data* rather than *ReceiverData*.

*Listing 8-3. Elements.xml File with <Data> Element*

```xml
<?xml version="1.0" encoding="utf-8"?>
<Elements xmlns="http://schemas.microsoft.com/sharepoint/">
  <Receivers ListTemplateId="100">
    <Receiver>
      <Name>ItemAddingEventReceiver</Name>
      <Type>ItemAdding</Type>
      <Assembly>$SharePoint.Project.AssemblyFullName$</Assembly>
```

```
        <Class>EventReceivers.Examples</Class>
        <Data>Your custom values goes here</Data>
        <SequenceNumber>10000</SequenceNumber>
      </Receiver>
   </Receivers>
</Elements>
```

The code in Listing 8-4 shows how to access the Data property within the event receiver.

*Listing 8-4. Accessing Data Element Inside the Event Receiver*

```
    public override void ItemUpdating(SPItemEventProperties properties)
    {
        string data = properties.ReceiverData;

    }
```

Although the default limit of the Data property in `Elements.xml` is 256 characters, there is an easy workaround to go beyond that limit. Rather than putting your actual data inside the Data property, you put it inside an external file (e.g. within an XML file) and then put the file path inside Data property. For example, you can create a new XML file called `Security.xml` and place it inside the feature folder that will be used to register the event receiver (registration of event receivers is covered in later section). Now, update the Data element within the `Elements.xml` file (see Listing 8-3) with following value:

```
<Data>{YourFeatureName}\Security.xml</Data>
```

```
Please replace {YourFeatureName} with the name of the folder that contains the feature.
```

---

■ **Tip** Visual Studio 2010 provides replaceable parameters (also known as tokens). These are used to provide values for SharePoint solution items whose actual values are not known at design time. For example, rather than hard coding your feature name inside the `Elements.xml` file you can use `$SharePoint.Feature.DeploymentPath$` token, which will be replaced by the actual name of the folder that contains the feature within SharePoint solution package (WSP file). The Data element will contain following value:

```
<Data>$SharePoint.Feature.DeploymentPath$\Security.xml</Data>
```

You can learn more about replaceable parameters from `http://msdn.microsoft.com/en-us/library/ee231545.aspx`.

---

Finally you can access the `Security.xml` file inside the event receiver as shown in Listing 8-5.

*Listing 8-5. Accessing Security.xml File Inside the Event Receiver*

```
public override void ItemUpdating(SPItemEventProperties properties)
    {
        string filePath = string.Format(@"{0}\{1}",
SPUtility.GetGenericSetupPath(@"TEMPLATE\FEATURES"), properties.ReceiverData);

        System.Xml.Linq.XDocument xmlDoc = System.Xml.Linq.XDocument.Load(filePath);

    }
```

## Avoiding Event Recursion

When working with event receivers, there is always a chance that your code will trigger the same event again. If you don't address this issue properly you will end up with an event recursion or infinite looping of same event, which will eventually exhaust the application pool memory that SharePoint allocates for a SharePoint Web Application. As a result, the application pool will be recycled, which from an end user perspective looks like poor performance from SharePoint.

A simple way to avoid this is by using a Boolean property called EventFiringEnabled which is exposed by the **SPEventProperties** base class and is available within event receivers.

You should approach this issue as follows:

1. Set EventFiringEnabled property to false before you update the current item inside the event receiver.

2. Perform the desired updates, for example calling `properties.Item.Update()` on current item.

3. Set EventFiringEnabled property to true again after you perform all the updates on the current item (see Listing 8-6).

*Listing 8-6. How to Avoid Event Recursion*

```
public override void ItemUpdating(SPItemEventProperties properties)
    {
        try
        {
            EventFiringEnabled = false;
            //Perform required updates
            properties.ListItem.Update(); //Call Update method
        }
        catch
        {
          //Implement exception handling logic
        }
        finally
        {
```

```
            EventFiringEnabled = true;
        }

    }
```

## Using the UpdateOverwriteVersion() Method

When you update a list item inside a synchronous event using the Update method of SPListItem class, it creates a new version of the same item as part of updates rather than simply updating the current item. To avoid this behavior, you should always use the UpdateOverwriteVersion method of the SPListItem class instead—this way you will always get the expected results.

## Event Receivers and the Document Library

When you upload or create a new document within a document library, you end up getting more event receivers fired by SharePoint than expected. The events and the sequence in which they get triggered are as follows:

1. *ItemAdding*

2. *ItemAdded*

3. *ItemUpdating*

4. *ItemUpdated*

5. *ItemCheckingIn*

6. *ItemCheckedIn*

It is important to understand the logic behind this behavior. Actually it's rather simple: as you upload a document to a document library using the SharePoint user interface, you are presented with a dialog box that lets you choose the document(s) to be uploaded to the document library. After you select a document and click on the OK button, SharePoint triggers the ItemAdding event followed by the ItemAdded event. At this point, the document is already added to the document library (or to the content database, to be exact). However, additional data associated with the column(s) has yet to be filled in. Next, SharePoint automatically makes the document checked out to the current user and display the Edit Properties dialog box so you can fill in the column(s) with data as required. As you click on the OK button, the ItemUpdating event gets fired, followed by ItemUpdated event. Finally the ItemCheckingIn and ItemCheckedIn events are triggered. SharePoint doesn't give developers the option to capture ItemCheckingOut and ItemCheckedOut events because any changes to document within these events are not allowed.

If you try to upload multiple documents using the SharePoint upload dialog box, SharePoint will only trigger the ItemAdding and ItemAdded events and the entire set of documents will be checked out to the current user. Also SharePoint will not display the Edit Properties dialog box and you will miss an opportunity to fill in the values for the columns (even mandatory columns). You can, however, check in the uploaded document inside ItemAdded event. Listing 8-7 shows how to check in a document inside the ItemAdded event.

*Listing 8-7. Check-in a Document inside the ItemAdded Event*

```
public override void ItemAdded(SPItemEventProperties properties)

{

    try {

        EventFiringEnabled = false;

        if (properties.ListItem.File.CheckOutType != SPFile.SPCheckOutType.None) {

            properties.ListItem.File.CheckIn(string.Empty);

        }

    } catch (Exception ex) {

        //Handle exception here

    } finally {

        EventFiringEnabled = true;

    }

}
```

# Deploying/Registering Event Receivers

Once you complete the development of a custom event receiver, there are various ways to deploy it to the SharePoint environment. Regardless of the method you choose, the underlying .NET assembly containing the code of your custom event receiver needs to be deployed into the Global Assembly Cache (GAC). Once the underlying assembly is deployed to the GAC, you need to register the event receiver. You can register your event receiver either declaratively or programmatically/using code. Table 8-2 shows various approaches.

*Table 8-2. Event Receiver Registration Approches*

| Registration Approach | Method |
| --- | --- |
| Declarative (XML) | SharePoint Features |
| Code(SharePoint Server Side Object Model) | |
| | Feature Receivers |
| | .NET Applications |
| | PowerShell |

■ **Tip** You should never deploy event receivers to SharePoint Web Application's _app_bin directory (<<Drive>>:\inetpub\...\_app_bin) as this may lead to situations where your event receiver may never get executed. This happens because of the way the .NET assembly loader performs the probing to locate an assembly; it will first perform a lookup in Global Assembly Cache (GAC), and then look in the *Bin* folder under the current working directory. But SharePoint uses services like OWSTIMER.EXE, which is a Windows Service and doesn't reside in SharePoint Web Application _app_bin directory, so the .NET assembly loader will fail to load the event receiver assembly. As a result, your custom event receiver will never be executed. Even though you may able to put the event receiver assembly into the path which does get probed by the .NET Assembly Loader, it's not a best practice and GAC is the only place to deploy your event receivers.

## Registering Event Receivers: Declarative Approach

SharePoint Features provides easy to register event receivers. The Feature contains an `Elements.xml` file that stores information related to the event receiver including, but not limited to, underlying event receiver name, assembly details, the List/Library Template ID (e.g. Document Library has ID of 101), or server relative URL to List/Library.

■ **Note** The SharePoint 2010 user interface doesn't provide any means to view registered event receivers. In real world projects, you will need this information to troubleshoot issues with event receivers, especially for those that are registered to SharePoint lists/library. You can download the SPEventReceiverListing solution from `http://speventreceiverslist.codeplex.com`. It provides you with a complete list of registered event receivers for any SharePoint list or library using the SharePoint UI. Alternatively, you can use the PowerShell script file `DisplayListRegisteredEvents.ps1`, which is available as part of this chapter's download, to display the complete list of event receivers associated with the SharePoint list. You can easily tweak the script to make it work against a SharePoint site.

## Registering Event Receivers to Specific List

This approach allows you to register event receiver to a specific list/library using a SharePoint Feature. Listing 8-8 shows the `Elements.xml` file, which is used for registration of an ItemUpdated event to a SharePoint list called SalesEvents. Pay special attention to the ListUrl attribute, which contains a server-relative URL to SalesEvents List. Also note that the Class and Assembly elements must match the name of the `SalesEvents` class and its fully qualified assembly name. The SequenceNumber element is used by SharePoint to queue the event receivers for execution in case there are multiple event receivers of same type (i.e. ItemUpdated) registered for same SharePoint object (i.e. SalesEvents List). SharePoint will execute the event receiver with lowest sequence number first and so on. You will learn more about how to use the sequence number later in this chapter.

*Listing 8-8. Event Receiver Registration to SalesEvents List*

```
<Elements xmlns="http://schemas.microsoft.com/sharepoint/">
        <Receivers ListUrl="Lists/SalesEvents">
                <Receiver>
                        <Name>SalesEvents</Name>
                        <Type>ItemUpdated</Type>
                        <SequenceNumber>10001</SequenceNumber>
                        <Assembly>SalesEventReceivers, Version=1.0.0.0, Culture=neutral,
PublicKeyToken=3e1c9874674bk912m</Assembly>
        <Class>SalesEventReceivers.CustomEvents </Class>
            </Receiver>
        </Receivers>
</Elements>
```

## Registering Event Receivers Based on List Type

You used this approach to register an event receiver to all SharePoint Lists or Libraries based on their type (e.g. all document libraries or all contacts lists). The feature in Listing 8-9 registers the event receiver named DocumentUploadPolicy for the ItemAdding event on every document library. The ListTemplateId attribute takes the ID of List Template (for example, ListTemplateId of 101 denotes a document library).

*Listing 8-9. Event Receiver Registration to All Document Libraries*

```
<Elements xmlns="http://schemas.microsoft.com/sharepoint/">
        <Receivers  ListTemplateId ="101">
            <Receiver>
                    <Name>DocumentUploadPolicy</Name>
                    <Type>ItemAdding</Type>
                    <SequenceNumber>10001</SequenceNumber>
                    <Assembly>DocumentUpload Policies, Version=1.0.0.0, Culture=neutral,
PublicKeyToken=1k1c9424674b99lo</Assembly>
        <Class>DocumentUpload Policies.CustomEvents</Class>
            </Receiver>
        </Receivers>
</Elements>
```

■ **Note** The ListTemplateId and ListUrl attributes are mutually exclusive, so you can't use both of them at the same time to register your event receiver.

## Scope

By default when you deploy an event receiver declaratively using a Feature that is scoped at site collection level, the event receiver will be available to all sub sites too. If you want to override this behavior and limit the scope of the event receiver to only the top-level root site within the site collection, then you must use the Scope attribute within the Receivers element and set it to Web as shown below

```
<Receivers  Scope="Web">
```

Event receivers that do not work at site collection level cannot be scoped to that level. For example SPEmailEventReceiver cannot be scoped at site collection level, and cannot be scoped to that level.

## Sequence Number

You can register multiple event receiver assemblies against same type of event (such as ItemAdded) for a same SharePoint object (such as Employees List). In this situation, the SequenceNumber property enables you to control the execution order among multiple event receivers. SharePoint will first execute the event receiver with lowest sequence number and so on. As a best practice, use sequence number above 10,000 to avoid conflict with SharePoint OOB event receivers, which usually have sequence number below 10,000.

## Registering Event Receivers: The Code-Based Approach

You can register custom event receivers programmatically using SharePoint Server Side Object Model (OM). The SPEventReceiverDefinitionCollection provides access to a collection of all the event receivers registered for particular SharePoint object. You can use the EventReceivers property to access this collection. You then call the Add method on this collection to add new event receiver to it. The Add method of the SPEventReceiverDefinitionCollection class has four overloads. You will use different overloads throughout this section. For more information on the Add method, please visit http://msdn.microsoft.com/en-us/library/microsoft.sharepoint.speventreceiverdefinitioncollection.add.aspx.

The Listing 8-10 shows how to register event receiver using a minimal set of information. Notice that the assembly name and the class name for the event receiver are passed as parameters. In this case, the Add method is used with the overload that takes a type of event (ItemDeleted), assembly name, and class name to register the event receiver.

The details like class name and assembly name are passed to the RegisterItemDeletedEvent method as parameters; you can easily use the same method to register different event receivers for other lists. It's not difficult to create a more generic method that can do the event registration for you, but as you will learn later in this section, there are better approaches for doing this.

*Listing 8-10. Using Add Method of SPEventReceiverDefinitionCollection*

```
private void RegisterItemDeletedEvent(SPList eventList, string className , assemblyName)
{

SPEventReceiverDefinitionCollection receivers = eventList.EventReceivers;
receivers.Add(SPEventReceiverType.ItemDeleted, assemblyName, className);

}
```

A better way to address event registration is to use feature receivers; this way you can register/de-register the event receiver based on the feature activation/deactivation. You can still use the SharePoint Server Object Model to perform the actual registration or de-registration, but this approach is much more flexible compared to developing a custom application because features are much easier to deploy, manage, and upgrade. Also, site admins can activate/deactivate features using the SharePoint UI so there is no learning curve involve for them; you can simply provide the name of the feature to activate/deactivate to register/de-register an event receiver.

The following exercise demonstrates how to create a feature receiver to perform event receiver registration. You will use the event receiver that you created earlier in the "Developing Custom Event Receivers" section.

1. Start Visual Studio 2010 with administrative privileges.

2. Create a new project in Visual Studio by clicking File ➤ New Project.

3. In the New Project dialog box, expand Visual C# in the Installed templates box, expand SharePoint, and select 2010. From the list of templates, select Empty SharePoint Project.

4. Type ContactsEventFeatureReceiver for the name, as shown in Figure 8-14, and click OK.

5. Type http[s]://<<SiteCollectionUrl>> for the local site combo box. Make sure you replace the http[s]<<SiteCollectionUrl>> with the actual URL of your site collection (for example http://spdev01 or http://contoso).

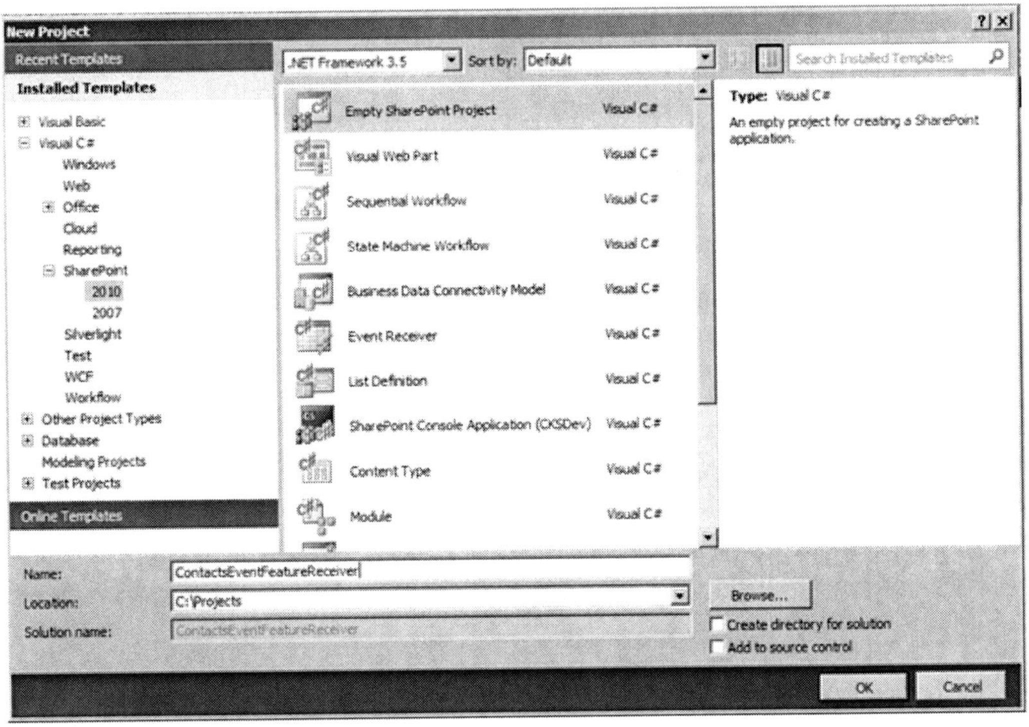

*Figure 8-14. Creating the ContactsEventFeatureReceiver project*

6. Click Validate. Wait for Connection Successful message box shown in Figure 8-15 to appear.

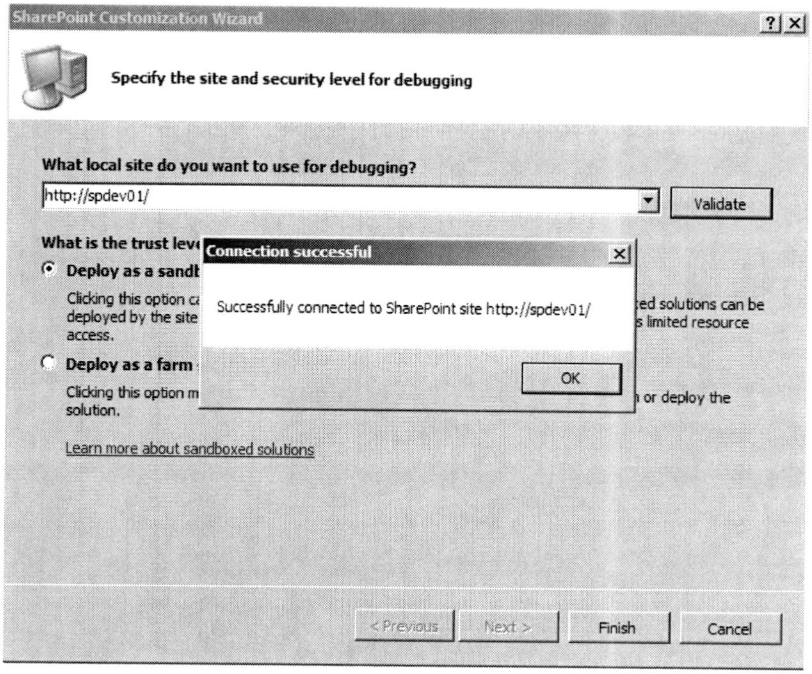

*Figure 8-15. Connection successful message*

7. Choose Deploy as a farm solution and then click Finish.

8. Right-click on Features folder and select Add Feature

9. Locate Feature1 folder and rename it to ContactsListRegFeature.

10. Double-click ContactsListRegFeature and enter the following information (see Figure 8-16):

   Title: Contacts List Registration Feature

   Description: This feature has associated feature receiver, which performs event receiver registration.

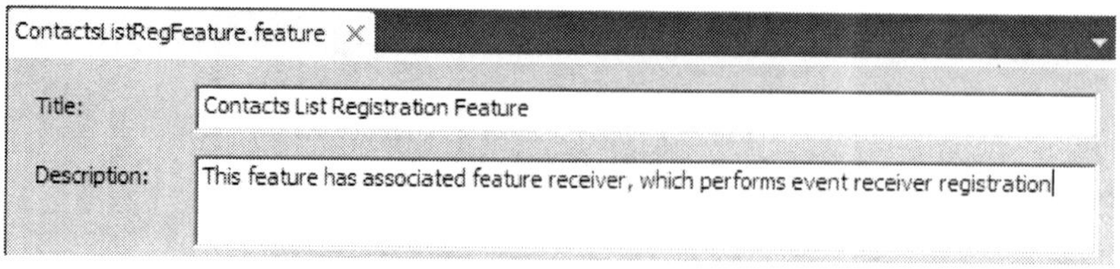

*Figure 8-16. Setting the title and description*

11. Right-click the BulkListOperationsFeature folder and select Add Feature Receiver, as shown in Figure 8-17.

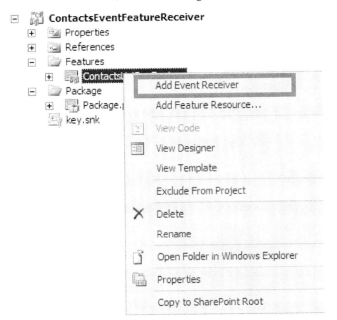

*Figure 8-17. Adding a feature receiver*

12. Open the `ContactsListRegFeature.EventReceiver.cs` file from ContactsListRegFeature.feature folder. Notice that a number of common Feature Receiver events have been written for you but all of these events are commented out. You can keep or delete them.

13. Replace the `ContactsListRegFeatureEventReceiver` class with the code in Listing 8-11.

*Listing 8-11. Register and De-Register an Event Receiver*

```
public class ContactsListRegFeatureEventReceiver : SPFeatureReceiver
    {
        Guid receiverId = new Guid("539BC7C2-9637-4233-B664-DC0C1DE12095");
        public override void FeatureActivated(SPFeatureReceiverProperties properties)
        {
            SPWeb web = properties.Feature.Parent as SPWeb;
            SPList empContactsList = web.GetList("/Lists/Employees") as SPList;

            if (null != empContactsList)
            {
```

```
                    if (!empContactsList.EventReceivers.EventReceiverDefinitionExist(receiverId))
                    {
                        SPEventReceiverDefinition def =
empContactsList.EventReceivers.Add(receiverId);
                        def.Type = SPEventReceiverType.ItemAdded;
                        def.Name = "ContactListItemAddedEvent";
                        def.Assembly = "ContactListEventReceiver, Version=1.0.0.0,
Culture=neutral, PublicKeyToken=c8b8250ecc14bbae";
                        def.Class = "ContactListEventReceiver.CustomEvents";
                        def.SequenceNumber = 10000;
                        def.Update();
                        empContactsList.Update();
                    }
                }
            }

        public override void FeatureDeactivating(SPFeatureReceiverProperties properties)
            {
                SPWeb web = properties.Feature.Parent as SPWeb;

                SPList empContactsList = web.GetList("/Lists/Employees") as SPList;

                if (null != empContactsList)
                {
                    if ( empContactsList.EventReceivers.Count>0 &&
                        empContactsList.EventReceivers.EventReceiverDefinitionExist(receiverId)
)
                    {
                        empContactsList.EventReceivers[receiverId].Delete();
                        empContactsList.Update();
                    }
                }
            }
        }
```

14. Expand the Package folder and double click Package.package.

15. In the Package.package window, click Advanced (see Figure 8-18).

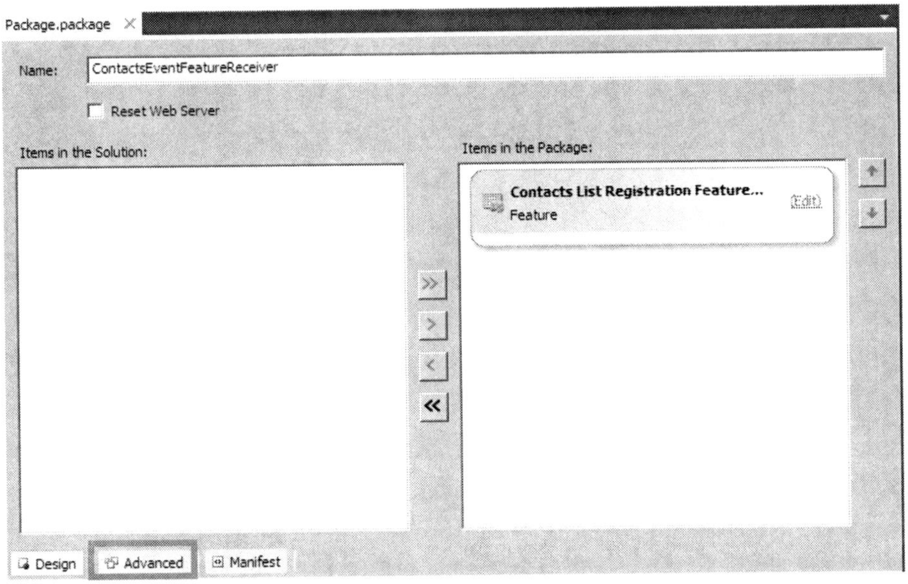

*Figure 8-18. Package advanced properties*

16. Click Add and select Add Existing Assembly, as shown in Figure 8-19.

*Figure 8-19. Adding an existing assembly*

17. In the Add Existing Assembly window, set the Source Path to the file location of ContactListEventReceiver.dll (see Figure 8-20). Click OK.

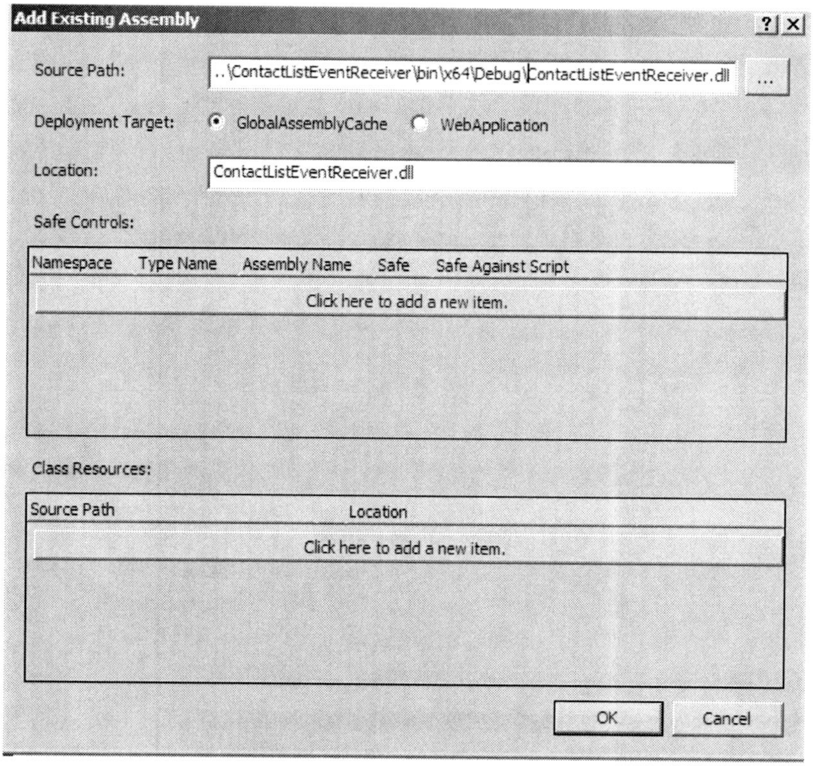

*Figure 8-20. Existing assembly path and location*

18. In Solution Explorer, click the ContactsEventFeatureReceiver project and press F4. This will open up the Properties window.

19. Change the Active Deployment Config property to No Activation, as shown in Figure 8-21.

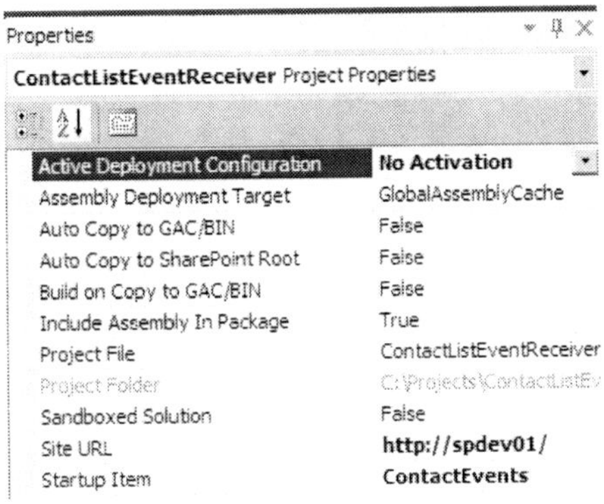

**Figure 8-21.** *Changing the Active Deployment Configuration*

20. Press F5 inside Visual Studio. This will deploy the feature event receiver and enable debugging.

21. Visual Studio will automatically open the SharePoint Portal default page.

22. From the Site Actions menu, select Site Actions ➤ Site Settings.

23. Click the Manage site feature located under Site Actions section (this is different from the Site Action menu). This will open the Manage Features page.

24. Locate the Contacts List Registration feature shown in Figure 8-22 and click Activate.

**Figure 8-22.** *Activate Contacts List Registration feature*

25. In the Quick Launch menu on the left, click Employees. Delete all existing contacts.

26. To add a new item, click on Add new item link.

27. In the New Item dialog, enter values for Last Name, First Name, Full Name and E-mail Address, Business Phone and Home Phone columns (see Figure 8-23). Click Save.

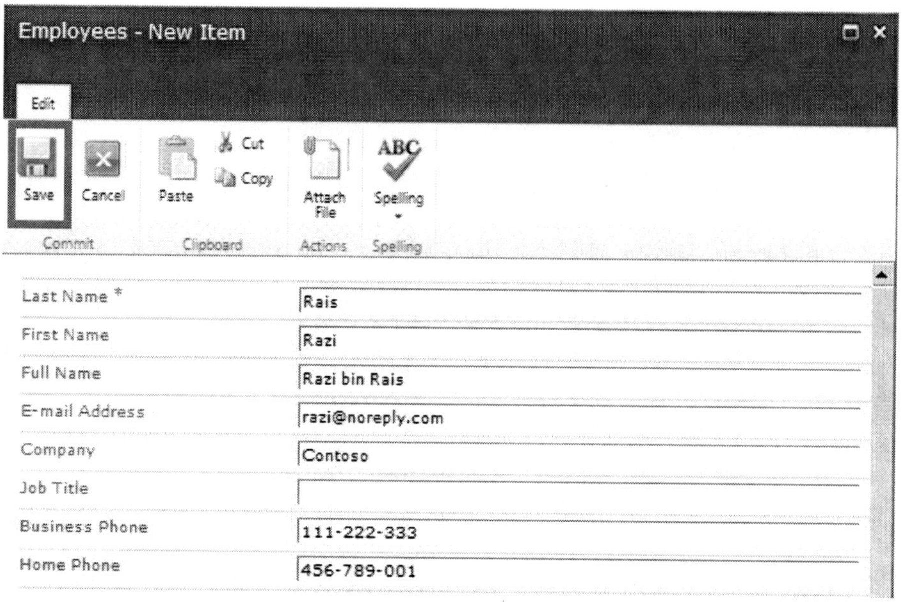

*Figure 8-23. Adding a new employee*

28. You should see new contact in the Employees list (see Figure 8-24).

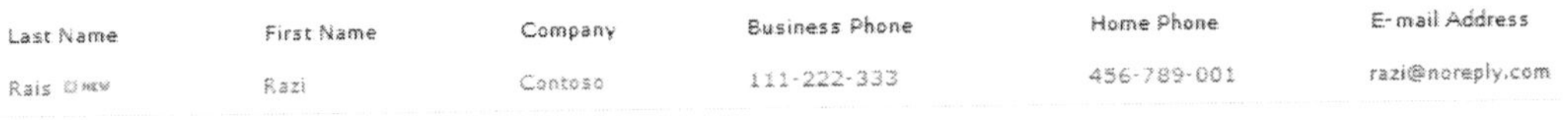

| Last Name | First Name | Company | Business Phone | Home Phone | E-mail Address |
|-----------|-----------|---------|----------------|------------|----------------|
| Rais □ NEW | Razi | Contoso | 111-222-333 | 456-789-001 | razi@noreply.com |

*Figure 8-24. A new employee*

29. In the Quick Launch menu on the left, click All Site Content.

30. On All Site Content page, locate and click on the Announcements list.

31. You should see new announcement item already added to the list, displaying the welcome message (see Figure 8-25).

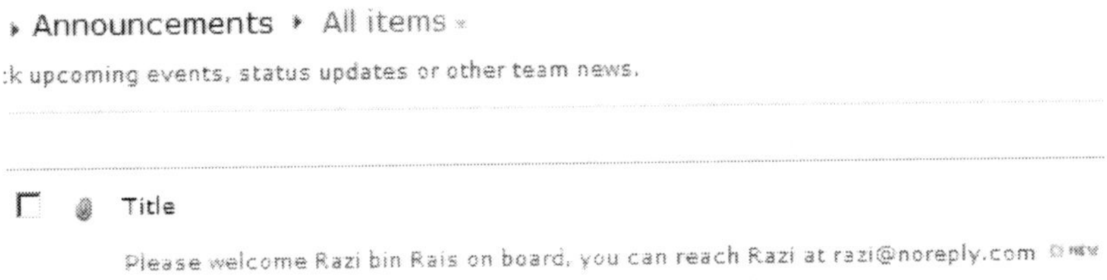

▸ **Announcements** ▸ All items ▾

:k upcoming events, status updates or other team news.

☐ ◉ Title

Please welcome Razi bin Rais on board, you can reach Razi at razi@noreply.com ▷ NEW

*Figure 8-25. New announcement*

32. To un-register the event receiver, browse to Manage Site Features page using steps 22 and 23.

33. Locate the Contacts List Registration Feature and click Deactivate, as shown in Figure 8-26.

**Contacts List Registration Feature**
This feature has associated feature receiver, which performs event receiver registration
| Deactivate | **Active** |

*Figure 8-26. Deactivate Contacts List Registration Feature*

34. If you perform steps 25 through 31 to create a new item inside Employees contact list, you will notice that no new greeting message is posted to the announcement list this time. This is because the event receiver isn't registered to the Employees contact list any more. You can re-register it by following steps 22 through 24.

## Using the PowerShell Approach

You can use a PowerShell script to register event receivers. PowerShell scripts still use the SharePoint Server Side Object Model, but you will end up with a script file you can easily edit using Notepad or the PowerShell ISE (Integrated Scripting Environment) and execute again without the need to compile it.

---

■ **Note** With SharePoint 2010 you can use PowerShell remotely. This provides great flexibility to execute script remotely. For more details on this topic, visit

```
http://blogs.msdn.com/b/opal/archive/2010/03/07/sharepoint-2010-with-windows-powershell-
remoting-step-by-step.aspx.
```

---

The following exercise shows you how to use a PowerShell script to register ContactListEventReceiver to Employees Contact List. You created this event receiver in the "Developing Custom Event Receivers" section. Make sure that you have ContactListEventReceiver assembly already deployed in GAC as PowerShell.

1.  Open the notepad by clicking Start ➤ All Programs ➤ Accessories ➤ Notepad.

2.  Inside Notepad, copy the script as shown in Listing 8-12.

*Listing 8-12. Registering an Event Reciever to a SharePoint List using PowerShell*

```
##############################################################################
# RegisterEventReceiverToList.ps1
##############################################################################
# Objective:- To register an event receiver to SharePoint List through PowerShell #script
#
# Usage:- RegisterEventReceiverToList.ps1 http://siteUrl  webUrl Listname
#
# Example:- RegisterEventReceiverToList.ps1 "http://spdev01/" "/" "Employees"
#
# This script should always run on the SharePoint WFE server with Site #Administrator rights
with proper #rights

# Begin script
```

1.      *param([string] $siteName , [string]$webName, [string]$listName)*

2.      $assemblyName = "ContactListEventReceiver, Version=1.0.0.0, Culture=neutral, PublicKeyToken=[KeyToken]"

3.      $className = "ContactListEventReceiver.CustomEvents"

4.      $eventName="ContactListItemAddedEvent"

5.      $sequenceNumber = 10000

6.      $exists = "false"

7.      $deleteIfExist = "true"

8.      [void] [System.Reflection.Assembly]::LoadWithPartialName('Microsoft.SharePoint' ) | Out-Null

9.      $site = New-Object -TypeName Microsoft.SharePoint.SPSite $siteName

10.     if ($site -ne $null)

11.     {

```
12.        [Microsoft.SharePoint.SPWeb] $web = $site.OpenWeb($webName)
13.        if ($web -ne $null)
14.        {
15.            [Microsoft.SharePoint.SPList] $spList = $web.Lists[$listName]
16.
17.                if ($spList -ne $null)
18.                    {
19.
20.            [Microsoft.SharePoint.SPEventReceiverDefinitionCollection] $eventReceivers =
$spList.EventReceivers
21.
22.                    if ($eventReceivers -ne $null)
23.                        {
24.
25.                [i              nt] $counter = 0
26.                        [int] $eventsCount = $eventReceivers.Count
27.
28.                        if ( $eventsCount -gt 0)
29.                            {
30.
31.
32.                for($counter = 0; $counter -lt $eventsCount; $counter++)
33.                            {
34.
35.                        if ( [Microsoft.SharePoint.SPEventReceiverType]::ItemAdded -eq
$eventReceivers[$counter].Type -and
36.                        $eventReceivers[$counter].Assembly -eq $assemblyName -and
37.                                    $eventReceivers[$counter].Class -eq $className -and
38.                                        $eventReceivers[$counter].Name -eq
$eventName )
39.                                {
40.
41.                    $exists= "true"
42.                    Write-Host "Event receiver """ $eventName """ is already registered for {" $spList
"} List"
43.
44.                        if ($deleteIfExist -eq "true")
```

```
45.                     {
46.                       $eventReceivers[$counter].Delete()
47.                       $spList.Update()
48.                       $exists= "false"
49.
50.                       Write-Host "Event receiver """ $eventName """ has been de-registered for {"
$spList "} List"
51.
52.                     }
53.
54.                           }
55.
56.                         }
57.
58.                     }
59.
60.                       }
61.           if( $exists -eq "false")
62.             {
63.                 #Register the event by providing information like name, type, class and assembly of an
event receiver
64.                             $eventDef = $eventReceivers.Add()
65.                             $eventDef.Assembly = $assemblyName
66.                             $eventDef.Class = $className
67.                             $eventDef.Name = $eventName
68.                             $eventDef.Type =
[Microsoft.SharePoint.SPEventReceiverType]::ItemAdded
69.               $eventDef.SequenceNumber = $sequenceNumber
70.                             $eventDef.update()
71.                             $spList.update()
72.                             Write-Host "Event receiver '" $eventName "' has been
registered successfully for {" $spList "} List"
73.             }
74.               }
75.       $web.Dispose()
76.     }
77.
```

78.     $site.Dispose()

79.     }

80.     #end of script

This Script takes three command line arguments to gather the site collection URL, the sub-site URL (relative to site collection), and the name of the SharePoint list to which you will register the event receiver.

Lines 2 through 5 declare variables to store key pieces of information related to ContactListEventReceiver event receiver, including a fully qualified assembly name, class name, event name, and sequence number. Your PublicKeyToken for the assembly will be different (unless you are using same assembly which is part of code downloads for this chapter), so change [KeyToken] accordingly. Line 6 and 7 define variables that are used later in the script to perform conditional deletion and registration of event receiver.

Lines 9 through 20 declare and initialize SharePoint objects SPSite, SPWeb, and SPList. SPEventReceiverDefinitionCollection is used to hold all event receivers that are registered for SPList; the variable $eventReceivers is used to hold this collection.

Lines 22 through 60 perform two major tasks. First, the script loops through all event receivers in the $eventReceivers collection and checks whether ContactListEventReceiver is already registered. If it is, then it sets value of $exists to "true," meaning that you will skip the event receiver registration later to avoid duplicate registration for the same event receiver. As $deleteIfExist is set to "true" by default, the script will delete the existing ContactListEventReceiver for the collection and then call the Update method on the $spList object to commit this change to SharePoint. At this point it sets $exists to "false" because it has already deleted the existing ContactListEventReceiver event receiver and new registration can be done.

Lines 61 through 73 essentially register the ContactListEventReceiver to the list. First you check the current value of $exists, which needs to be "false," meaning that the ContactListEventReceiver is not already registered to the list. The registration process itself is rather simple. It starts by calling the Add method on $eventReceivers collection which returns fresh event receiver definition of type SPEventReceiverDefinition which is stored in $eventDef. Next, set the $eventDef properties Assembly, Class, Name, and SequenceNumber with the values stored in $assemblyName, $className, $eventName and $sequenceNumber. Also notice how the Type property of $eventDef is set to [Microsoft.SharePoint.SPEventReceiverType]::ItemAdded.

Finally, a call is made to update methods of both $eventDef and $spList objects. This ensures that all the changes are committed to SharePoint.

As a best practice, the script disposes of both SPWeb and SPSite objects at the end of script once they are no longer required.

1.  Save the file by clicking File ➤ Save inside the Notepad.

2.  In the Save dialog, type RegisterEvent.ps1 for file name and select All Files(*.*) from Save as type drop-down.

3.  Note the location of the RegisterEventReceiverForList.ps1 file.

4.  Close Notepad.

5.  To execute the script, open the SharePoint 2010 Management Shell by clicking Start ➤ All Programs ➤ Microsoft SharePoint 2010 Products ➤ SharePoint 2010 Management Shell.

6. Inside the SharePoint 2010 Management Shell, type the following command, replacing the [Path] with the actual path of `RegisterEventReceiverForList.ps1` file which you created in step 5:

*[Path]\ RegisterEventReceiverForList.ps1 "http://spdev01" "/" "Employees"*

7. Press Enter.

8. The script should run and the console should display the output of "Event receiver ContactListItemAddedEvent has been registered successfully for Employees List".

## Cancelling Asynchronous Events

You can cancel asynchronous event and display relevant error message(s) to the users. When event processing is cancelled, nothing is committed to the content database. You cancel the event by setting Cancel property of event receiver properties parameter to true. It's a good practice to set the ErrorMessage property of the same parameter with an informative message that provides the user better understanding behind event cancellation. Listing 8-13 shows how to cancel ListAdding event for the SharePoint Tasks List; it also set the error message for the user (see Figure 8-27).

*Listing 8-13.* Cancelling ListAdding Event

```
public override void ListAdding(SPListEventProperties properties)
    {
        //Tasks List Template Id is 107
        if (properties.TemplateId == 107)
        {
            properties.Cancel = true;
            properties.ErrorMessage = "Adding new Tasks list is not allowed";
        }
    }
```

If you try to create a new Tasks list you get the error message as shown in Figure 8-27.

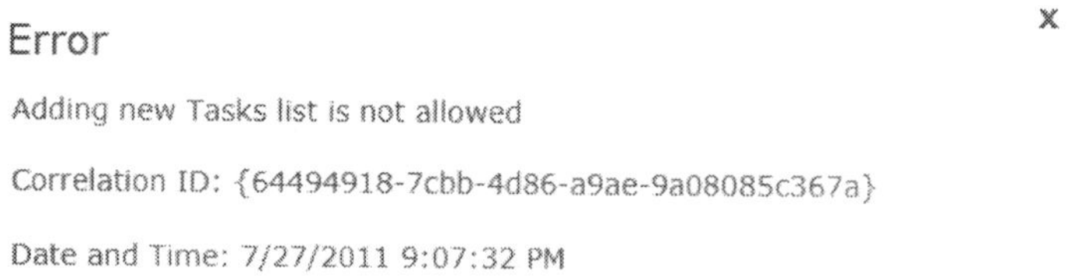

Error                                          ✗

Adding new Tasks list is not allowed

Correlation ID: {64494918-7cbb-4d86-a9ae-9a08085c367a}

Date and Time: 7/27/2011 9:07:32 PM

*Figure 8-27. Event Cancellation with Error Message*

Although this approach works for cancelling events and displaying error message(s) to the user, there will be times when you need to display custom error page rather than just a plain error message. The next section covers how to do that.

## Redirection to Custom Pages

With SharePoint 2010, as part of event cancellation you can now redirect users to a custom page; this can be a SharePoint site page within the same site collection that raises the event or you can use a SharePoint application page. This cancellation approach has various benefits: first, it allows you to provide users with a consistent UI rather than simply displaying a text message with correlation ID, which some users may even find annoying. Second, this approach helps you cater advance scenarios where you need to redirect the user to an existing page based on your business requirements. For example, consider a scenario where you have a requirement to ensure that users can't create new task in the Tasks list that starts on designated public holiday(s). Your business already has entry for public holidays within the Announcements list and you are required to redirect the user to the Announcements list when you cancel the event. Listing 8-14 shows the code that implements the ItemAdding event for the Task list to address this requirement.

*Listing 8-14.* Cancelling ItemAdding Event with Redirection

```
public override void ItemAdding(SPItemEventProperties properties)
        {

            if ( null != properties.AfterProperties["StartDate"])
            {
                DateTime taskStartDate =
DateTime.Parse(properties.AfterProperties["StartDate"] as string).ToUniversalTime();

                if ( IsPublicHoliday(taskStartDate) )
                {
                    properties.Status = SPEventReceiverStatus.CancelWithRedirectUrl;
                    string url = string.Format("{0}/Lists/{1}/AllItems.aspx",
                                                        properties.Web.Url,
"Announcements");
                    properties.RedirectUrl = url;
                }
            }

        }


        private bool IsPublicHoliday(DateTime taskStartDate)
        {
          //To keep this example short only single public holiday date is used
          //but you can also store dates externally in SharePoint Calendar
            List<DateTime> publicHolidayDates = new List<DateTime> {new DateTime(2012, 1, 1)};


return publicHolidayDates.Any(d => d.Day == taskStartDate.Day &&
d.Month == taskStartDate.Month && d.Year == taskStartDate.Year);

        }
```

Inside the ItemAdding event receiver you can use AfterProperties collection to access the value of StartDate column which contains the Task start date. SharePoint stores dates in UTC format so you parse the Date to DateTime and use the ToUniversalTime method to keep the UTC format. The IsPublicHoliday is just a handy utility method that takes the DateTime object and compares it with the list of holiday dates that are defined in the publicHolidayDates collection. It contains only a single date (i.e. 1/1/2012) to keep this sample easy to read but you can extend this method to get dates from sources like SharePoint List (e.g. Calender List) or some other external source like a web service. Finally, it compares the dates using LINQ and returns a Boolean value as a result. If the task start date turns out to be a public holiday, you cancel the event by setting Status property of the properties parameter to SPEventReceiverStatus.CancelWithRedirectUrl. Setting the status property will cancel the event and the user will be redirected to an error page which you set next using the RedirectUrl property of properties parameter. You also construct the redirect URL by using properties.Web.Url which gives the server a relative URL and then appends it with the URL to the AllItems.aspx page of the Announcements list. The redirection needs to be done using a server-relative URL, meaning that you can't redirect user to a non-server-relative URL like www.msn.com .

After you register this event using any of the registration methods described in the previous sections, you can test it by out creating a new Task item and using a start date of "1/1/2012," which is used as a designated public holiday inside the event receiver.

SharePoint executes the ItemAdding event receiver for the Task List; it will cancel the event and you will be redirected to the AllItems.aspx page of the Announcements list, which contains an entry for Public Holidays, as shown in Figure 8-28. If you don't have an entry in the default Announcements list, you should create one and test the event receiver again.

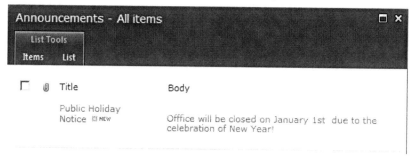

*Figure 8-28. Redirection to Announcements List*

In this example, you redirected the user to the AllItems.aspx page but you can easily use the same technique with the SharePoint application pages that reside under _layouts folder within the SharePoint 14 Hive (C:\Program Files\Common Files\Microsoft Shared\Web Server Extensions\14\TEMPLATE\LAYOUTS).

Generally it's a good practice to use site pages rather than application pages for displaying error messages mainly because of extra work involve in creating and deploying application pages. Also, as site pages can be deployed as part of a sandbox solution, they give you more flexibility in terms of their deployment. A good example where you should use custom site pages not custom SharePoint application pages is when you are targeting deployment for SharePoint Online (which is part of Office 365), which only supports sandbox solutions.

But consider a situation where you have to implement an organizational policy to block uploading of files to all SharePoint libraries throughout the SharePoint farm after regular office hours. You also want to use a standard error page throughout your SharePoint farm which displays the details of organizational policies. In this particular case, you can use a SharePoint application page as error page because it will minimize the deployment workload and can be updated and maintained from a single location.

In the previous example you used the SPEventReceiverStatus enumeration to cancel the event and redirect user to custom error page. The complete set of SPEventReceiverStatus enumeration values are described next.

## CancelWithError

The event is cancelled and the error page is displayed but no redirection to a custom error custom page will take place.

## CancelWithNoError

The event is cancelled silently and no error message is displayed.

## CancelWithRedirectUrl

The event is cancelled but redirection to custom error page can be done by setting RedirectUrl property of the event receiver parameter to a server-relative URL.

## Continue

The event is allowed to continue and is not cancelled.

# Summary

As SharePoint 2010 grows rapidly, developers need to leverage event receivers more than ever before to tackle wide range of business scenarios. In this chapter you gained understanding of business scenarios where event receivers are the right fit and where they may be burden to your SharePoint environment.

You also learned about event receiver architecture and categories to help you grasp the core working model of an event receiver, along with their behavior patterns. Tools like Microsoft Visual Studio 2010 provide great flexibility to develop and quickly deploy and test your event receivers locally. However various approaches are available as you register your event receivers into production environment. Microsoft PowerShell can be used intrinsically to register and perform other administrative operations on event receivers.

Event receivers are important but only one part of the big SharePoint 2010 product and that's why maintaining best practices throughout development, deployment, and registration is absolute essential. Poor performance from a single event receiver can severely impact the whole SharePoint Farm. Also, knowledge about common mistakes and known issues related to event receivers helps you identify potential bugs earlier in your development lifecycle—before they become part of final release and then you have to fix them though software patches.

With this knowledge of event receivers under your belt, you can now sit through team meetings more confidently. You now have important arsenal to battle complex business requirements as they come your way.

# CHAPTER 9

# Touch Points–Integrating SharePoint 2010 and ASP.NET

*"Ignorance is like a delicate fruit; touch it and the bloom is gone."*

Oscar Wilde

In this section of the book, we will delve into strategies and approaches for integrating ASP.NET applications and SharePoint 2010 solutions. In our previous chapters, we have built some of the core fundamentals of understanding for the SharePoint 2010 product from a development standpoint. We will build upon these concepts and fundamentals in the final three chapters to put together a solid fundamental approach to using SharePoint 2010 as a development platform and planning out and executing on approaches to SharePoint 2010 living and functioning in a full suite of ASP.NET-focused web sites and products.

As we have seen in previous chapters, SharePoint 2010 is a relatively complex product. We have barely scratched the surface with what we have covered in the feature set and makeup of SharePoint 2010. We have seen that SharePoint is an ASP.NET-based product in itself, and makes use of many of the advances in the ASP.NET platform over the years in its makeup and construct. In this chapter, we will explain the thinking behind *touch points* and their help in organizing your approach to blended SharePoint 2010 and ASP.NET development. We will define integration factors behind these, present example business scenarios, and talk about impact upon your organization depending upon the touch-point approach that you select. Then we will cover low touch-point solutions, which include concepts of branding and customization of SharePoint 2010 and ASP.NET sites, talk about Publishing Layouts in SharePoint 2010, and discuss modifications to navigation in blended solutions.

## Integration Factors

When we start to get into the process of integrating ASP.NET and SharePoint 2010, there are many factors to consider, and some of the top factors among them are really not software-related, but more related to the company doing the integrating and the makeup of the individuals, departments, and interactions among those companies. This may sound like a radical concept at this point in the book after spending so much time building up the technical aspects of the SharePoint 2010 product, but it is a good time to come up for air, get in our mental hot-air balloons, and take a ride back up to the 10,000-foot level where we can take a look at the countryside.

From a sheer business effectiveness standpoint, technical solutions are really of no more value than the value they provide end users to do their jobs. IT in general is a service industry. What this means is that in designing software, architecting solutions, and putting together plans for ongoing solutions, this concept must be in the forefront of our minds. How does my solution help the particular end user of my product? How does my solution help the business perspective of my end users' corporations? If we have a clear answer, then this is great. However, if the answer remains somewhat murky, then it is time to go back and examine what we are trying to accomplish with our solution.

The timeframe in which we are doing our architecture planning is absolutely the appropriate time to do this. Once we have decided upon an approach, set up servers and operating systems, installed SharePoint 2010, set up our development and test environments, and have our teams working on our projects appropriately blended, we have too large of a vested interest in traveling back to this level and re-examining things. And if our approach is flawed, then that flaw will typically carry through all the way to the end of the solution being delivered. Teams and organizations, once they set upon a path typically have a high level of difficulty backing up and going at a problem from a different approach. The best time to set the approach is right at the beginning. This is the time during which the approach and the methods we are most vital to the outcome of the solution and project. This is the time during which the top-level architects, strategists, and corporate sponsors should be involved. A lot of the beginning of this message is addressed to these individuals in an organization.

So, because I am taking the time to address this group of people, let me try to endeavor to help you clarify your business needs and approach to blended SharePoint 2010 and ASP.NET solutions. What is a good reason for doing this? What types of problems can I solve? How can I help my end users? Perhaps you already have a good idea about this, perhaps not.

With some of my work in developing this book, I have presented these concepts at a number of different .NET user groups, SharePoint user groups, and SharePoint conferences. I have carried out numerous discussions with members of the SharePoint community and the .NET development community, have talked over aspects of this with top-level individuals in both of these areas, including SharePoint product team members, Microsoft field consultants, MVPs, and MCMs in SharePoint and ASP.NET. Also, in giving presentations on this topic, I have been involved in numerous discussions with concerned IT professionals talking over their specific business environments and what they are hoping to accomplish with their approach and solutions. I have also coached teams of people working on these types of projects.

What I will present emerging from all of this and these sessions are some examples of business scenarios where both ASP.NET and SharePoint present a clear business solution that provides good end-user value. After that, I will discuss some aspects of IT organizations and cultures and how approaches may differ depending on these factors and variables.

The end goal we are trying to get to with this approach is a little bit like a popular advertising commercial for a tasty product that mixes peanut butter and chocolate. The advertisement in a number of its forms has two people walking around, one eating a chocolate bar, and another eating from a jar of peanut butter. They collide into each other and fall down, and in the ensuing conversation, one person says to the other, "You've got peanut butter on my chocolate". The other responds, "No, you've got your chocolate in my peanut butter". Then both of them taste the resulting mix and come up with smiles on their face.

This is the experience that I envision for all of you. You may be coming from different backgrounds in ASP.NET development, SharePoint development, and administration. You may be the leader of a team of developers looking for some help in navigating unfamiliar waters. You may be a corporate CIO with a technical background looking for the right resource and approach to point your smart and capable team at. From all aspects, my vision for you is to have your peanut butter and chocolate and the same smile on your faces that those individuals in the commercial had. The smile originating from coming up with a unique and wonderful solution that is a mixture of SharePoint and ASP.NET and brings to our world software that brings us more mastery over our world and business environment.

# Example Business Scenarios

In discussions with various individuals, there are a number of example cases and types of cases of business problems to solve and scenarios that in my estimation are solution categories. These categories all present markings of solutions that are absolutely going to require a combined SharePoint 2010 and ASP.NET approach to organization, planning, and implementation.

## Corporate Internet and Service Portals

This type of scenario is one that is a more generic solution for a corporate presence. SharePoint 2010, with its publishing feature set, offers a great option for a corporate Internet presence. There are many features there such as publishing workflows, great templates and designs, and other aspects of SharePoint 2010 that make it fantastic for corporate Internets.

Yet the reality remains that there are many times it may not represent the best solution to use SharePoint 2010 for the main corporate Internet site. These reasons could be as simple as there is a great deal of effort already invested into the current corporate web site, and replacing it is not the primary goal. The web site has an established brand, sections, and functionality. Other reasons could include some such as the corporate Internet site that exists is not an ASP.NET site, but built with one of the other available web technologies out there, such as Java or PHP.

In this solution, SharePoint 2010 is coming to the table on the services side. With rich content-management features, and excellent document management features, SharePoint is an excellent candidate for a services portal. You can offer users all of the rich access to features of SharePoint 2010 as part of the services your company offers. And you can retain the investment in your current Internet presence and web site. Both of these elements need to exist in your current environment, perhaps using the same hardware and IT personnel to maintain and enhance them.

## Existing ASP.NET Product

This scenario is one in which either your company or your division has an existing investment in a relatively complex ASP.NET product. The product has a fairly large number of pages, can do complex calculations, ties to many different external systems, and has a complex database involved.

New requirements for the product, or just a general realization, lead you to the fact that document management is a feature that would add a tremendous amount of value to the product. Technical documents, diagrams, pictures, Microsoft Office documents such as contracts, blueprints, contractual reporting, and other similar things are vital parts of the overall business process that your product is involved with. Perhaps your product could offer the generation of and storage of reports in a document library. Perhaps the offering of a lifecycle of documents that involve built-in versioning and workflow approvals routing is vital to your product.

Perhaps your product could benefit from some of the portal capabilities of SharePoint 2010, in that the product could offer the ability to expand using SharePoint 2010 team sites to spin out multiple department-level implementations of your product and solution.

Perhaps your product could benefit from some of the social networking capabilities of SharePoint 2010, incorporating rich internal networking and content capabilities. You might want to incorporate internal blogging as part of your blended solution.

## New Blended Solution

This scenario is one where there is no existing investment in either SharePoint 2010 or ASP.NET. However, in evaluating the options for developing the solution, it is seen that SharePoint 2010 offers a rich development platform to build upon that could reduce your time to market for the solution.

## Expanding Your Corporate Portal

In this scenario, you have an existing investment in SharePoint, perhaps are just upgrading to SharePoint 2010, and your portal has a large number of departmental users involved. You want to roll out new ASP.NET features and solutions to all of your existing users quickly and in an environment with which they are already familiar. You plan to leverage SharePoint 2010 as your solution delivery platform, and want to deploy your solution in a fashion that will present low impact to your existing environment, but rich features for your solutions.

## Talking to SharePoint

In this scenario, you have a new or existing product. The large majority of your customer install base uses SharePoint. You want to develop features on your product or present a solution that allows your existing software to talk to SharePoint and interact with SharePoint data.

___

■ **Note** These example business scenarios just represent a few of the possible types of use cases or scenarios that could arise. There are many more scenarios that are not represented here—you may find that your scenario is close to one of these, a combination of a couple of these, or a completely different one altogether. The purpose of the examples is to point out a few major categories of scenarios where blended SharePoint 2010 and ASP.NET solutions could make sense or provide business advantages.

___

# Organizational Factors

In addition to constraints in presenting solutions to end users, the reality of developing solutions, staffing projects, and working toward common goals is that you can only develop solutions with what you have, not with what you do not have.

How this comes into play in selecting approaches with blended SharePoint 2010 and ASP.NET solutions is that you need to take into account the makeup of the organization that you currently have to do this with. You can also do this by taking into account the organization that you will see after staffing it with where you want to go.

Where does this matter? In what way, shape, or form does this have anything to do with software development?

## Organizational Examples

Take a couple of the business scenarios explained previously as examples. Perhaps your company has an existing ASP.NET product. Your company may not have SharePoint currently, or may currently have a limited SharePoint portal for internal use. What does that organization look like? You probably will have a development team that can range in size from one individual to a few hundred that is involved with the development of your product. You may have another team that manages your SharePoint site. Here, the largest amount of current investment will impact and contribute toward the approach you want to take. The choices you make will most likely be easier to implement if they have a lesser amount of impact on your existing ASP.NET development team, as opposed to ramping up SharePoint expertise in-house or through outside engagements.

In another example, perhaps you have a large investment in a corporate SharePoint portal, including an architect and a team of SharePoint administrators and developers. In this scenario, you have a completely different makeup of organizational interaction, corporate culture, and politics. The choices you make will be easier to implement if you do not do things that will jeopardize your current SharePoint environment and farm. (Of course, the choice to not jeopardize your SharePoint farm is never a bad one.)

## SharePoint-Centric Organizations

In evaluating your organization for potential solution approaches, it is important to be cognizant of the current blend of your organization's personnel and culture. If your organization already uses SharePoint to a large extent—if SharePoint team sites are widely used across all organizations, if your corporate Internet presence consists completely of a SharePoint publishing site, or the number of personnel dedicated to the SharePoint side of your IT outnumbers the .NET development side of your company— then your organization can be looked at from a SharePoint-centric viewpoint. It is highly likely in this type of organization that the solutions you will be developing will be SharePoint-centric, and with that comes a particular approach. Some of the questions that you can ask yourself and your leadership to identify a SharePoint-centric organization are as follows:

- What is the ratio of dedicated SharePoint personnel to dedicated .NET development personnel in my company? >1, = 1, <1 ?

- What is the ratio of the dedicated SharePoint hardware to dedicated .NET production hardware? >1, =1, <1?

- Is the scope of the SharePoint farm that we will be dealing with in our solution much greater than the solution itself?

- What is the makeup of the current or envisioned user base of your proposed solution?

## Touch Points

In my presentations, discussions, and reflection upon many of the different concepts that we have introduced in the beginning of this chapter, the concept of *touch points* was one that emerged in my thinking. This concept is not a new or unique one in general, but may be when it is applied to the SharePoint 2010 and ASP.NET world. A touch point is simply a way to describe the interaction between two systems. Where two systems touch, there is a "touch point".

In thinking through blending ASP.NET and SharePoint solutions, this term is not meant to be literal or quantitative in that we go and count up the numerous individual points where the solution touches and report them. I am simply using them in more of an adjective format, where the level of interaction and integration is described. *Low* touch point describes a lower level of interaction and integration, *Moderate* Touch point" a higher level, and *high* touch point describes solutions that represent about the highest level of integration possible without going to an exclusive one-way-or-the-other solution.

There is nothing magical about touch points or nothing special about describing them in the fashion that I am doing so. They have simply become of use to me in helping to organize people's thoughts and approaches to SharePoint 2010 and ASP.NET solution development. So in that, they are of use in helping to describe your architectural approach and solution philosophy.

If you are striving toward a *low touch-point solution*, this means that your guiding thoughts and philosophies are going to steer toward your ASP.NET solution and your SharePoint 2010 farm being largely separate entities, running on their own processes (not necessarily hardware), being self-contained, and having a relatively lower amount of areas that they integrate. The rest of Chapter 8, after our introduction to touch points will cover this scenario.

If you choose a *medium touch-point'* approach, this means that there is a medium or moderate amount of integration between your ASP.NET solution and your SharePoint solution. Here, you may have portions of your SharePoint side mixed in with ASP.NET, and portions of your ASP.NET solution mixed in with your SharePoint. Our chapters on the Client Object Model and Business Connectivity Services represented ways that you can accomplish some of that. Chapter 9 will also highlight ways to blend solutions with the medium touch-point approach, as well as introduce some cutting-edge blended approaches with the use of Azure and advanced JavaScript techniques.

---

■ **Tip** Choosing an approach with respect to touch points does not make an invisible wall come up in your architecture approach or meetings that will force you into doing one specific thing only, or to never include any element of another solution type in your approach. It is simply a guiding principle overall. As a guiding principle, it is designed to help you navigate producing your solution with an organized approach as well as help you navigate your organization and business makeup. It will help in communications across the team and to stakeholders.

---

Choosing a *high touch-point solution* means that there is a high level of integration that SharePoint 2010 and ASP.NET have, and that the decisions you make ongoing will most likely have to include evaluating the impact on most environments. We will introduce specific examples and considerations in Chapter 10 for this approach.

Over the course of these last three chapters, we will highlight what makes up the particular touch point and examples of what selecting that approach and philosophy entails and how to do it.

## Low Touch Point

What is a low touch-point solution approach and philosophy? In explaining this, one key concept to consider is the relative level of complexity of your two different environments. SharePoint 2010 is a very deep and complex product, and it runs in an environment that is tuned for SharePoint. There is performance optimization that comes into play in the interaction between the SharePoint 2010 product, IIS, and the databases. Many ASP.NET applications also have complex elements to them.

So what is the easiest way to integrate the two? Don't.

That, of course, is the simple answer. The more complex answer is contained in all of the content throughout the rest of this chapter. In this philosophy and approach, each of your environments runs on its own. SharePoint 2010 runs self-contained in its own little world and farm, and your ASP.NET application does as well.

**Tip** This does not mean necessarily that you need to duplicate or use different hardware to implement a low touch-point solution. There are many options here—SharePoint Web Front-End (WFE) servers can support having other IIS web sites on them. Defining different users that run your IIS Application Pools is a great way to contain impact across systems. SharePoint database servers can have other databases on them; however, it violates a best-practice rule to place other SQL Server databases on the same instance of SQL Server that SharePoint 2010 resides on. So, in this case, if you are using the same SQL Server, define separate instances to house your SharePoint 2010 and other SQL Server databases. Another option that is becoming more and more viable every year is to utilize virtualization for your environments. Microsoft server operating systems such as Windows 2008 Server R2 offer the Hyper-V role for virtualization, and there are other vendors such as VMWare that offer capable virtualization offerings. Virtualization offers many benefits in managing server environments that are worth examining, but a little beyond the scope of this book.

Housing or wrapping ASP.NET solutions within the SharePoint environment can offer increased risk to a SharePoint farm. This is not to say that it is wrong or not recommended, it is just as we move up the scale on integration methods, the higher the touch point, the more it exposes potential risk.

## Pros

The pros to implementing a low touch-point solution are as follows:

- Performance maintained in SharePoint farms and ASP.NET applications with no cross-application implications.

- No constraints to ASP.NET application development.

- No additional development training necessary for ASP.NET team.

- Least amount of customization development work.

- SharePoint 2010 farm remains largely intact.

## Cons

The cons to implementing a low touch-point solution are as follows:

- Branding is more complex and performed for both the SharePoint 2010 farm as well as the ASP.NET application.

- Authentication and Authorization (AuthN/AuthZ) must be customized to duplicate across platforms.

- Navigation is not seamless—need to plan out user experience navigating through the areas of the two sites.

- Navigation may need customization work.

These are a few of the high-level pros and cons of choosing a low touch-point solution. Now, besides the reasons for choosing to implement low touch-point solutions, we will highlight ways to make them work in your environment.

A blended solution is a solution that presents the front of two applications functioning together. One of the primary ways to accomplish this is through branding. Branding is creating a unified look and user interface for both your SharePoint 2010 and ASP.NET applications. Branding specifically in low touch-point solutions can present to the end user a unified interface that provides common functionality throughout the solutions.

# Branding SharePoint Solutions

In this chapter, we will present examples of how to brand a SharePoint 2010 application in a few different ways. We will also cover high-level basics of branding an ASP.NET application. The way in which we will present this is by taking a common HTML template with images, colors, and fonts, such as one that you can purchase commercially on the Internet and utilize in your designs. We will take this design and apply it both to an ASP.NET master page for use in your ASP.NET application, as well as applying it to your SharePoint 2010 environment.

Prior to this example, we'll discuss some of the different options for modifying the user interface in SharePoint 2010, including some of the new functionality built into SharePoint 2010 for branding. Some of what is built in to SharePoint 2010 will depend on which version of the product that you are utilizing. All SharePoint 2010 products, including the free SharePoint Foundation 2010, offer the ability to customize or brand SharePoint. However, there are features within the Standard and Enterprise versions of SharePoint 2010 that offer enhanced abilities in the branding area. The SharePoint Server Publishing Features offers enhanced abilities for branding in SharePoint 2010.

## Branding Possibilities, Features, and Tools

There are a number of possibilities when we start to discuss branding a SharePoint site. From an initial perspective, SharePoint has built-in capabilities for changing certain things with respect to the brand, such as colors or font sizes.

Much as we are organizing our overall approach to SharePoint 2010 and ASP.NET blended architecture, we will also present branding options in a similar fashion, using low, medium, and high levels of branding effort.

### Low-Effort Branding

The lowest effort to brand your SharePoint 2010 is to utilize some of the built-in themes that come with SharePoint 2010. From any site, you can navigate to Site Settings from the Quick Launch menu, and select Site Themes. You will be presented with the ability to select color themes and palettes from the available installed themes in SharePoint 2010. The window to select these is shown in Figure 9–1.

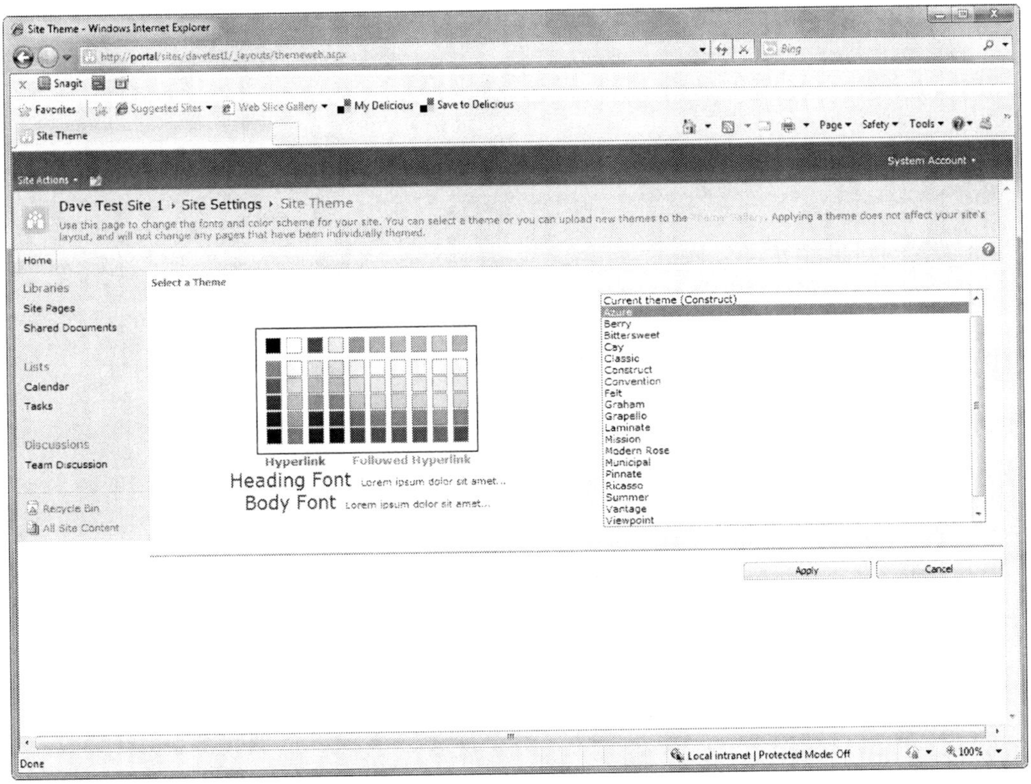

***Figure 9–1.*** *Branding with Site Themes*

Figure 9–1 shows what is available from SharePoint Foundation 2010. If you are using either the Standard or Enterprise products, the built-in themes also allow you to customize colors and fonts in a particular installed theme, as shown in Figure 9–2.

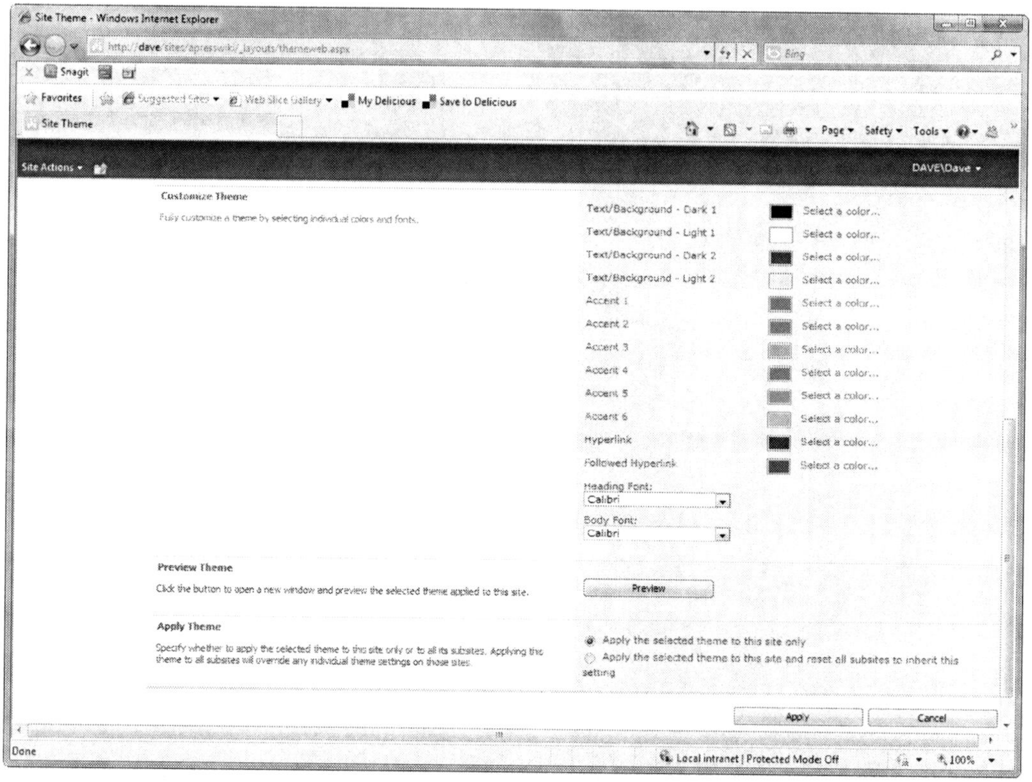

*Figure 9–2. Customizable themes—SharePoint Server 2010—Standard and Enterprise*

## Medium-Effort Branding

Traveling up the scale of effort, the next level of branding control you could take over a SharePoint 2010 site would be to design and import your own theme file. SharePoint supports themes that are created in PowerPoint 2010 for use in SharePoint.

---

**Tip** For detailed instructions on how to create a PowerPoint theme and save it, please refer to the Microsoft Office 2010 documentation article here:

---

http://office.microsoft.com/en-us/powerpoint-help/customize-and-save-a-theme-in-powerpoint-2010-HA010338409.aspx

Themes are a new feature in SharePoint 2010 and they are created after the OpenXML format specification. They consist of a packaged zipped file with a .thmx extension. When you create your theme in PowerPoint 2010 and save it, it will be a .thmx file extension. From here, you may import it into

SharePoint 2010 to the Theme Gallery, which should make it available to select along with the default built-in themes that ship with SharePoint 2010. The built-in themes in the Theme Gallery are physically stored on the SharePoint server in the following directory:

```
C:\Program Files\Common Files\Microsoft Shared\Web Server
Extensions\14\TEMPLATE\GLOBAL\Lists\themes
```

To add a new theme to the default ones on your site, navigate to the Site Settings page as shown in Figure 9–1. You will see a link to the Theme Gallery Library. You can scroll down to the bottom of the installed themes and select Add New Item to upload your created theme to your site. After this, you are able to select your customized theme to apply to your SharePoint 2010 site.

Another option for a medium level of effort in branding your SharePoint 2010 solution would be to make changes to the existing CSS in SharePoint. For a publishing site, you are able to specify an alternate CSS file to use in place of the built-in CSS that SharePoint 2010 installs by default. You can select this file along with the Master Pages setting in Site Settings in your SharePoint 2010 site. It is near the bottom of the screen, as shown in Figure 9–3.

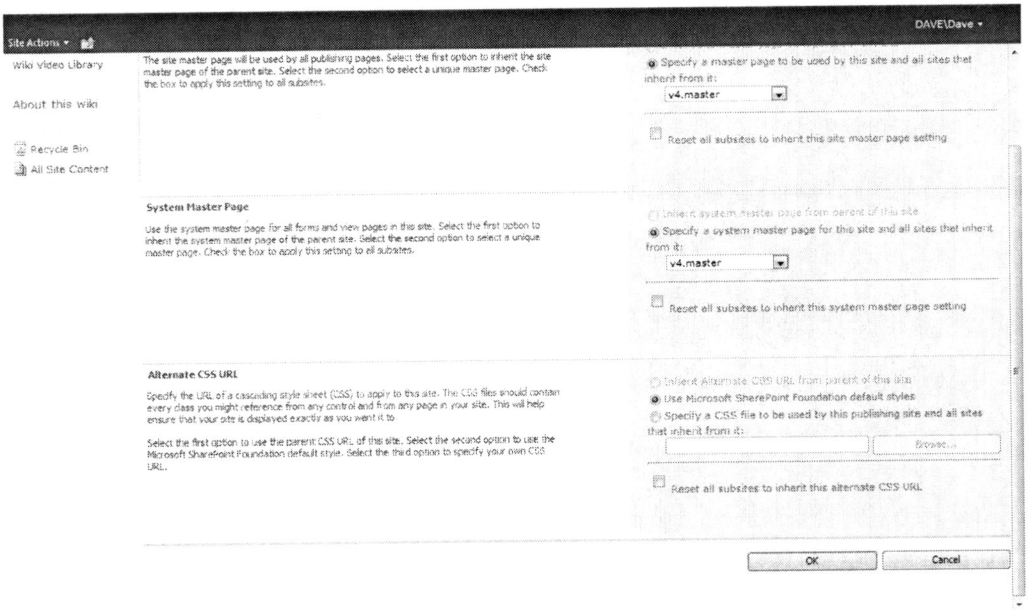

*Figure 9–3. Alternate CSS selection in Site Settings ➤ Master Pages*

# High-Effort Branding

If modifying the look and feel of your standard SharePoint 2010 chrome is not enough, then we will need to get in to a high-effort custom branding solution, with defining the brand for a custom master Page, and possible page layouts and content types.

If your SharePoint solution is of the type that will be published to the Internet, or that is public-facing, you may want to take advantage of SharePoint 2010 Publishing Features. If not, you will still customize a SharePoint 2010 Master Page.

# SharePoint Server 2010 Publishing Features

Publishing as a term in SharePoint means the authoring and deployment of branded items such as CSS and images, content, custom assemblies, and configuration files across a Microsoft SharePoint Server 2010 farm. SharePoint Server 2010 Publishing consists of two separate features—the SharePoint Server Publishing Infrastructure feature and the SharePoint Server Publishing feature. The SharePoint Server Publishing Infrastructure feature provides publishing functionality at the site collection level, and the SharePoint Server Publishing feature provides publishing functionality at the site level. The subset of features and functionality of each feature supports the goal of publishing as part of a Web content management solution.

Publishing features come into play in SharePoint 2010 as a design for web content management. Adding or turning on the publishing features in SharePoint 2010 automatically provisions a number of internal components for use in web content management. These components include specific site columns, content types, page layouts, master pages, and lists. Publishing features also changes the way in which the site operates in a number of ways. It applies work flows for publishing content, limits provisioning of subsites to conform to a publishing context, and creates several publishing-specific permissions groups to deal with content management.

One key thing that happens on a site is that a Pages library is created for web content, and this is set up as a document library with versioning and permissions set up. There are two types of publishing sites—the Publishing Portal, and the Enterprise Wiki.

- The Publishing Portal is set up basically ready to be exposed as an external Internet web site. It contains by default a Press Releases site, and a custom brand out-of-the-box. The intent is a head start to help define areas of web content that are specific for exposing to the Internet.

- The Enterprise Wiki, on the other hand, is geared more toward a corporate intranet application with the capability for end users to rapidly modify content in place and create more pages, areas, and links to pages with little restriction.

Publishing sites use customizable page layouts that help to organize the content and how it is displayed in the site. Page layouts can include default layouts such as an image on the left-hand side of the content area and text on the right, or can include columns for content. Page layouts are based upon a content type, which include specific site columns for content. We will discuss publishing layouts later on in the chapter after we define a branded master page to house the layout.

# Working With a Brand

We will start out our branding example from what typically would be a real-world example of implementing a template across an ASP.NET application and a SharePoint 2010 site. The first thing that is typically shown to a customer from a web design company is a representative mockup image that represents the interaction between the web designer and the customer. After the customer approves of the direction of the initial mockup, then the designers take the mockup and cut it up into images, CSS, HTML, and possibly JavaScript files. We have an example of this in Chapter 8's downloadable source code. The example consists of an HTML page, CSS scripts, images, and a JavaScript file. The mockup page.html looks like Figure 9–4 in a browser, and the files that make up the web designer deliverable are shown in Figure 9–5.

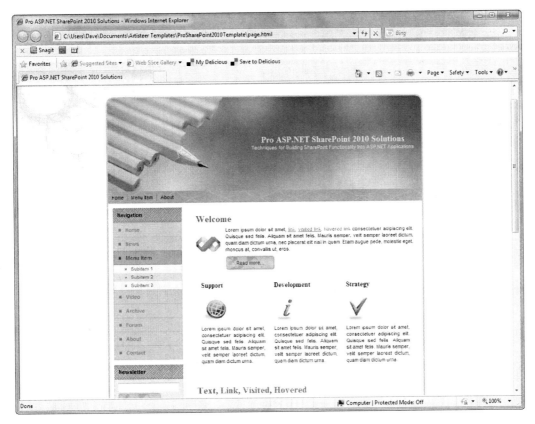

*Figure 9–4. Initial mockup of branding web design*

The design has a pencil yellow and blue theme, and a navigation menu at the left as well as the top of the header. There is a main content area in the center. We are mainly concerned with the look and feel of the UI, as opposed to implementing the exact menu items or working in the design.

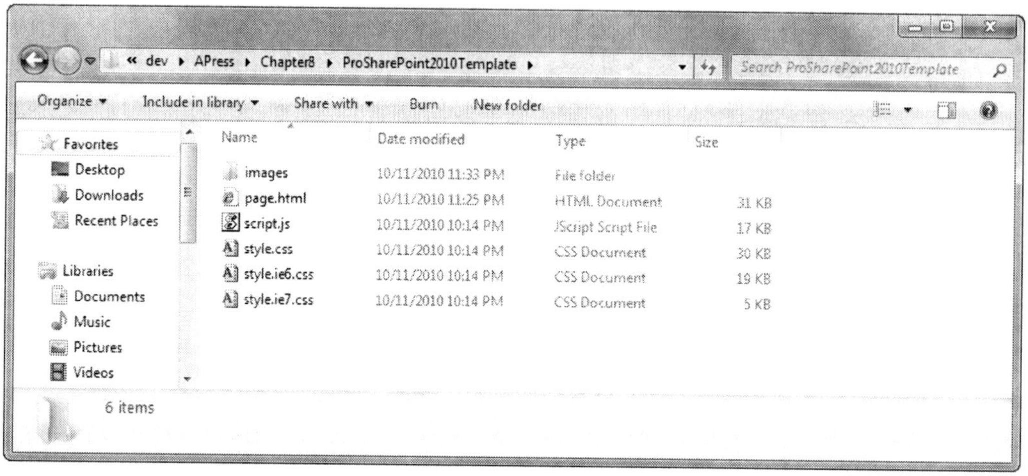

*Figure 9–5. Branding files included in initial web design*

Now that we have received our branding files from our web design company, we are ready to get started. All of the design is contained in one HTML file.

## Branding the ASP.NET Application

To apply our brand that is created in one page.html file and controlled by the CSS files style.css and browser-specific versions, we will transfer this brand over to ASP.NET. To do this, we will utilize master pages in ASP.NET, and we will build the sections of the header, the menus, and the sidebar in .ascx controls to place in content placeholders on the Master page. The articles and blocks we will add a little more code to so that they can be reused more than once on the page. The resulting files in our project appear as in Figure 9–6.

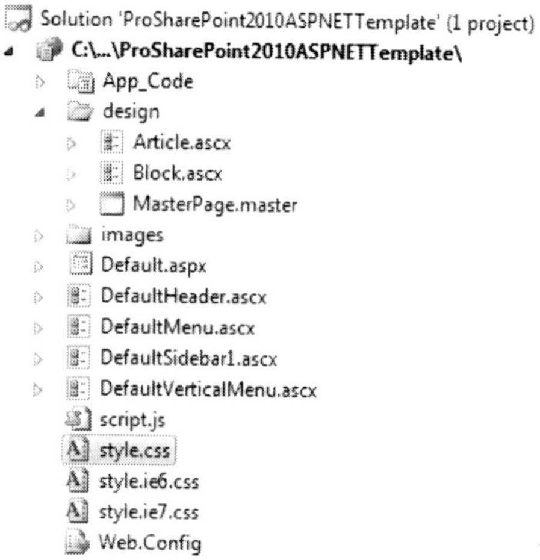

*Figure 9–6. ASP.NET branded application*

As you can see, we have preserved the images folder just as it was presented to us by the designer, as well as the CSS style sheets. The other components we have broken out so as to best use the built-in feature of master pages in ASP.NET. We are taking the external surrounding elements of our page.html file supplied by the designers and incorporating it into an ASP.NET master page.

The bulk of the approach that I took to brand the ASP.NET application was to take sections that represent certain areas of the layout, and wrap their inner <div> tags with a ContentPlaceHolder.

For example, following is the CSS and HTML surrounding the menu content:

```
<div class="art-nav">
                    <div class="l"></div>
                    <div class="r"></div>
                    <ul class="art-menu">
                        <li>
                            <a href="#" class="active"><span
class="l"></span><span class="r"></span><span class="t">Home</span></a>
                        </li>
                        <li>
                            <a href="#"><span class="l"></span><span
class="r"></span><span class="t">Menu Item</span></a>
                            <ul>
                                <li><a href="#">Menu Subitem 1</a>
                                    <ul>
                                        <li><a href="#">Menu Subitem
1.1</a></li>
                                        <li><a href="#">Menu Subitem
1.2</a></li>
                                        <li><a href="#">Menu Subitem
1.3</a></li>
                                    </ul>
                                </li>
                                <li><a href="#">Menu Subitem 2</a></li>
                                <li><a href="#">Menu Subitem 3</a></li>
                            </ul>
                        </li>
                        <li>
                            <a href="#"><span class="l"></span><span
class="r"></span><span class="t">About</span></a>
                        </li>
                    </ul>
                </div>
```

Here in Visual Studio 2010 we add a ContentPlaceHolder that will be populated by the DefaultMenu user control.

```
<div class="art-nav">
        <div class="l"></div>
        <div class="r"></div>
        <asp:contentplaceholder id="MenuContentPlaceHolder"
runat="server"></asp:contentplaceholder>
</div>
```

---

■ **Note** We will not cover in-depth each aspect of how we migrated the brand from the HTML file to the ASP.NET template solution. However, the complete source for both solutions—the HTML page as well as the ASP.NET application are available for download in the code that is associated with this book.

---

## Branding in SharePoint Designer Example

Next, we will highlight the steps to go through to create a brand in SharePoint Designer 2010.

1. Open up Designer, and connect to the Site Collection where we will modify the master page. In this example, we will want to take advantage of the publishing features to get the most use out of our master page. We will also want to define a page layout that will allow us to lay out sections of the page similar to the design delivered to us.

2. Select the Master Pages left-hand link and you will see a window similar to Figure 9–7.

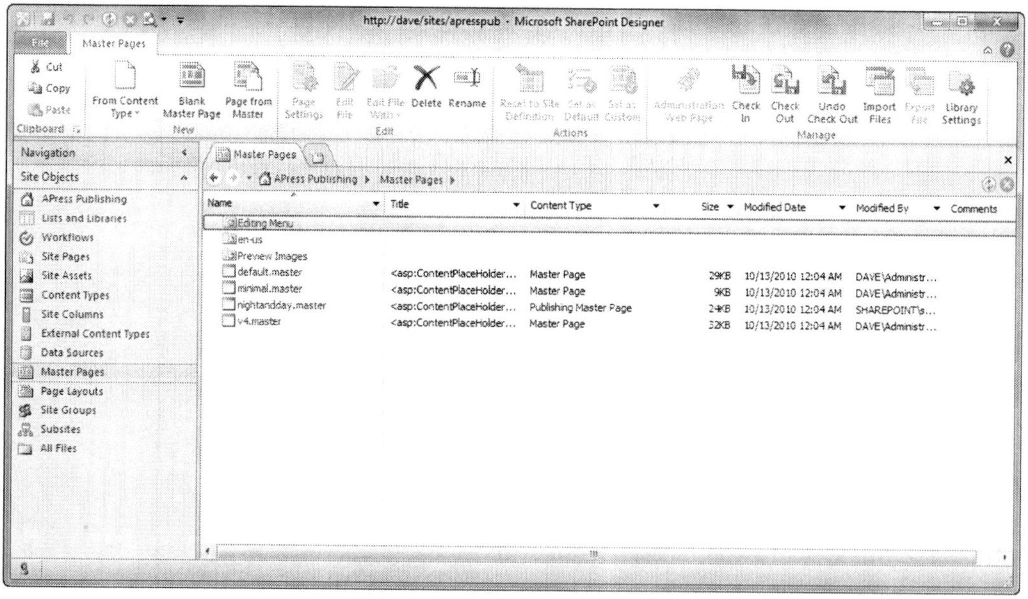

*Figure 9–7. SharePoint Designer and Publishing Site Master Pages*

3. We will select the nightandday.master Publishing Master Page to modify and apply to the site.

■ **Tip** You can brand a site by using either a publishing master page to affect the publishing content and creating page layouts, or you can brand a site by using the main overall master page, which is v4.master.

4. Right -lick nightandday.master, copy it, and paste it in the same library. We will call the corresponding master page pencilblue.master.

5. Once you have renamed the master page, right-click, check it out, and edit it in Advanced mode. You will be in a page editor that looks like Figure 9–8.

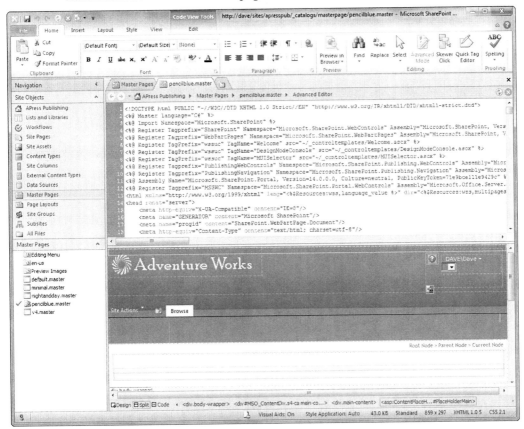

*Figure 9–8. Editing a publishing master page*

6. To proceed from this point, we will need to choose an approach to our modifications. There are basically two schools of thought as to how to tackle modifying master pages. One school approaches this from the perspective of taking the existing master page provided by Microsoft and modifying it until it meets your needs. The other school of thought is to use a bare-bones type of

master page that has the minimal elements in it to allow SharePoint 2010 to remain functional. We will do the latter and use the master pages developed by Randy Drisgill found on Codeplex at `http://startermasterpages.codeplex.com`. Download them and extract them to somewhere convenient.

---

■ **Tip** In SharePoint 2007, these pages were called minimal master pages. However, since then, Microsoft has included in the master page lineup in the main SharePoint 2010 product a master page named minimal.master, which has very little chrome on it and is used in scenarios requiring almost no external wrapper functionality.

---

7. The page we will be using from this project is _starter_publishing.master. If you are modifying a team site, you would instead use the _starter_foundation.master. When you download this file, you can right-click it and edit it directly in SharePoint Designer. To get to the start point, delete all the content in pencilblue.master, and cut and paste the content from _starter_publishing.master into it. You will then get a pop-up window seen in Figure 9–9.

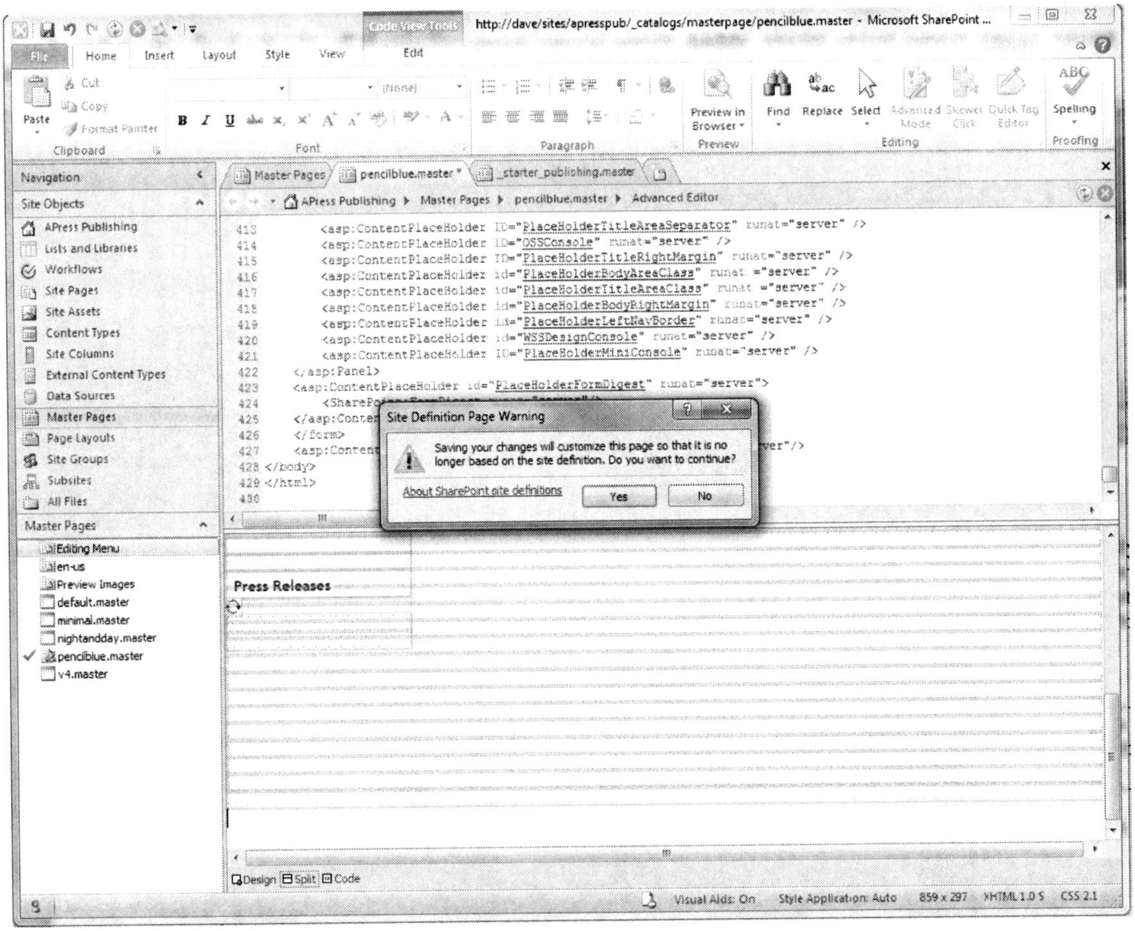

*Figure 9–9. SharePoint Designer starter master page and page warning*

This warning illustrates the difference between the design work we are doing now with SharePoint Designer, and the finished work that we can deploy to our web site. Customizing the page will make it depart from the page that is stored on the file system, and the page modifications will be stored in the database, as opposed to directly on the file system. It is not recommended to keep your master pages in this state, as it adds overhead to performance on every page. Instead, in a later section of the chapter, we will see how to take the work we have completed here and package a solution up for deployment to your production environment. Packaging a master page up as a solution will ensure that a non-customized page and all the artifacts it references, such as images, CSS files, and JavaScript, are deployed to the file system on your server, as opposed to remaining customized in a database.

---

■ **Tip** If all the talk about production environments is causing you to ask yourself "*what does he mean by production environment?*", please take a few steps backward, log off of your production environment, and start to see what you need to do to ensure that you are not editing live sites directly in your production environment with SharePoint Designer. At the very least, you can create a new Site Collection for you to hack up with designer change experiments to spare your end users the agony.

---

At the time of this writing, there are a few corrections to be made to the _starter_publishing.master page to get it to work correctly.

Lines 6 through 8 in the page appear as follows:

```
<%@ Register TagPrefix="wssuc" TagName="Welcome" src="_controltemplates/Welcome.ascx" %>
<%@ Register TagPrefix="wssuc" TagName="DesignModeConsole"
src="_controltemplates/DesignModeConsole.ascx" %>
<%@ Register TagPrefix="wssuc" TagName="MUISelector" src="_controltemplates/MUISelector.ascx"
%>
```

On my publishing site, this was throwing an error when applied. I needed to add a ~/ before the _controltemplates statement in each of these lines to correct this. The corrected lines appear as follows:

```
<%@ Register TagPrefix="wssuc" TagName="Welcome" src="~/_controltemplates/Welcome.ascx" %>
<%@ Register TagPrefix="wssuc" TagName="DesignModeConsole"
src="~/_controltemplates/DesignModeConsole.ascx" %>
<%@ Register TagPrefix="wssuc" TagName="MUISelector"
src="~/_controltemplates/MUISelector.ascx" %>
```

Also, on line 383, the SiteLogo currently does not exist in a freshly installed publishing site:

```
<SharePoint:SiteLogoImage  LogoImageUrl="/Style Library/sitename/logo.png" runat="server"/>
```

You can either correct that by uploading a graphic to the Style Library that does exist, or just change it back to the original Night and Day logo to start by making it the following:

```
<SharePoint:SiteLogoImage  LogoImageUrl="<% $SPUrl:~sitecollection/Style
Library/Images/nd_logo.png %>" runat="server"/>
```

Without the nightandday.css file, this will just show up blank for now, but without an image error.

Next, we will go ahead and check in, publish, approve our changes, and apply the starter master page to our publishing site. This will show the iterative steps necessary to continue to develop your branding solution for low touch-point solutions.

1. Navigate back to your Master Page list view, right-click pencilblue.master, and select Check-in. You will see the pop-up screen shown in Figure 9–10.

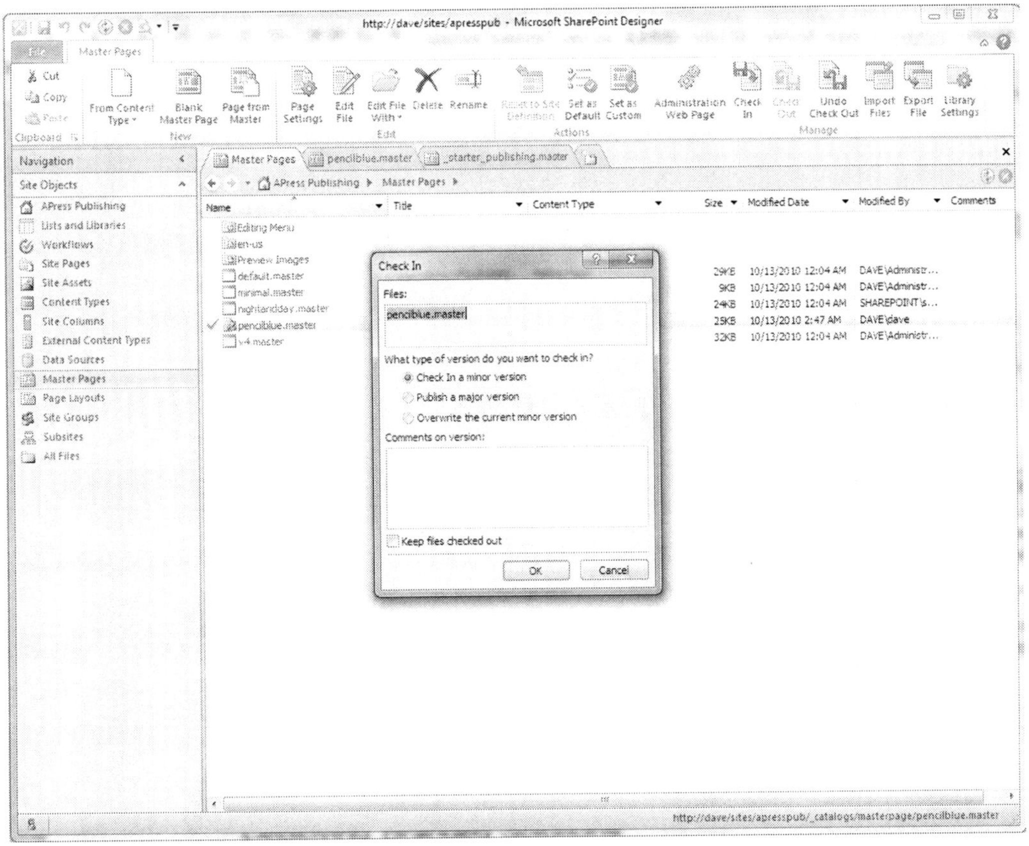

*Figure 9–10. Check In master page*

2. The options available are either "Check in a minor version," which will save your work in the content database but now allow you to apply it to a site or "Publish a major version." Publishing a major version also brings up the screen in Figure 9–11 to allow you to approve the changes. This will allow you to apply the master page to your site collection.

3. TIP Versioning in document libraries in SharePoint, such as the Pages library, is set by default to use major and minor versions. For an extranet publishing site, you need to select "Publish a major version" to get the approval workflows going and get your page published out so it is visible to the public.

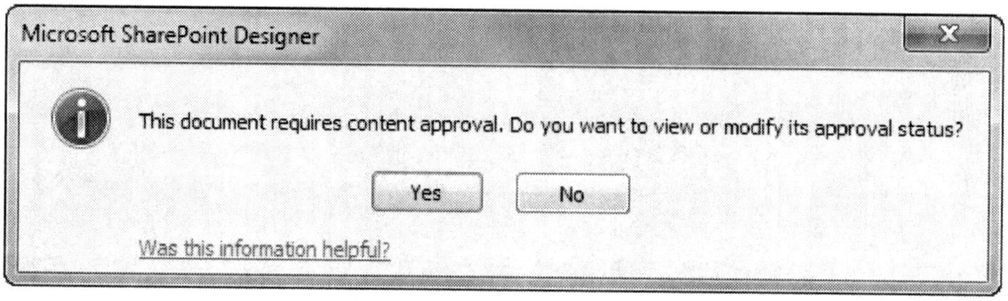

*Figure 9–11. Document approval status window*

4.  Clicking Yes will take you out of SharePoint Designer and directly to your SharePoint 2010 site's master page gallery, where you can select the page approval status and approve it, as in Figure 9–12.

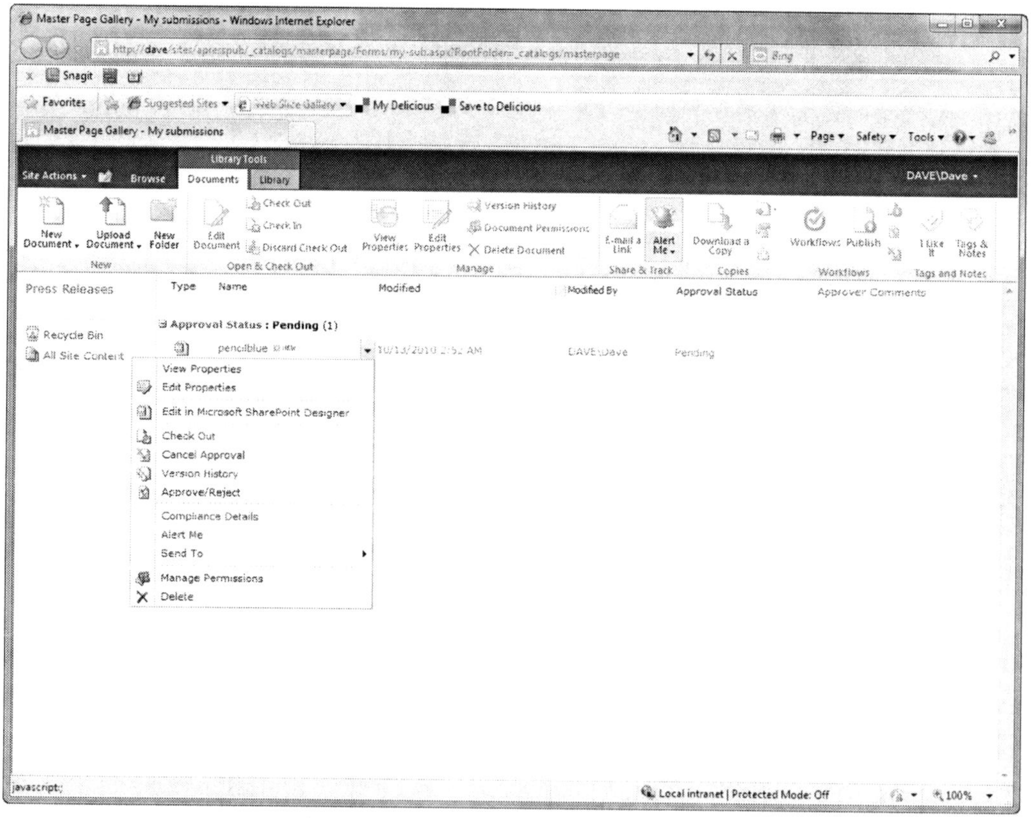

*Figure 9–12. Approving a publishing page change*

5.  There is one more screen after selecting Approve/Reject that will allow you to select the Approve radio button and apply it.

6. After this, you can select Site Settings from the top-left navigation menu, and from there select Master page as shown in Figures 9–13 and 9–14.

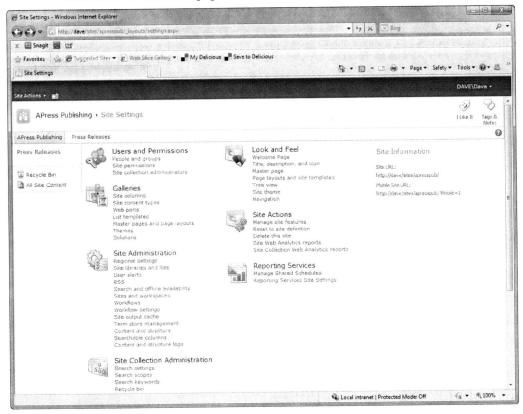

*Figure 9–13. Site Settings*

7. From here, select the Master Page link under the Look and Feel topic.

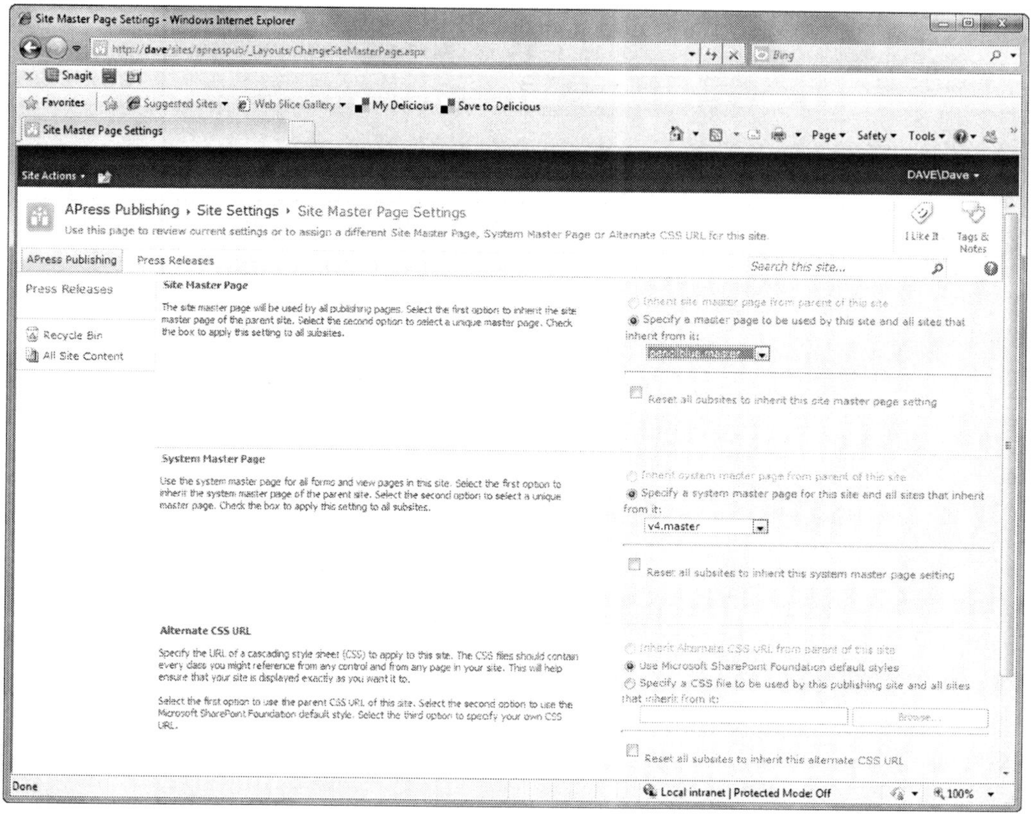

***Figure 9–14.*** *Master page selection*

Now we have a working starter master page in our publishing site that looks like Figure 9–15.

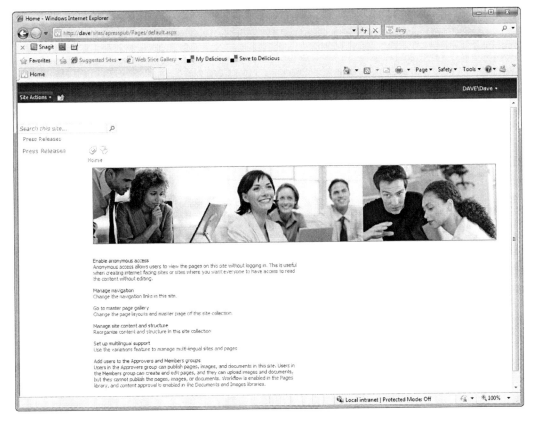

*Figure 9–15. Publishing site with starter master page applied*

---

■ **Tip** In addition to using Central Administration, you can use PowerShell to set your Master Page. A sample script is included in the downloads for this chapter and is called UpdateMaster.ps1.

---

From here, we will start to work with the master page in SharePoint Designer to apply the brand. We won't go through every step of branding the page, but just get started to get an idea about some of the process and the tools necessary. The final master page is available as part of the code downloads for the book.

Most of the work of branding will be to take the elements on the HTML page that we obtained from the designer and work them into the SharePoint master page. There are a few tricks to certain elements of SharePoint, but branding and design is an iterative process that changes the page a few small steps at a time, then we will publish the page and look at it on the SharePoint site.

---

■ **Tip** Because SharePoint master pages can be complex, it really is not recommended to do all your work at once and then deploy it. Doing that will typically result in a page error, which takes time to track down, and you probably will end up taking out at least portions of your changes to ensure that it will display. The best way to approach branding a master page is to start out with the starter master page as we have here, then change the file a little bit at a time, publishing it at every step and examining the results. When we finish this iterative process, we will package it up for deployment in a solution package with Visual Studio 2010. The final solution package is included in the code downloads for the book.

---

Actually, the first step in branding a master page is we will need to upload the images, scripts, and CSS files provided by our design company to SharePoint.

Cut all of the images from the Images folder, and paste them into the Images folder under the Style Library in SharePoint 2010. You will see the result as in Figure 9–16.

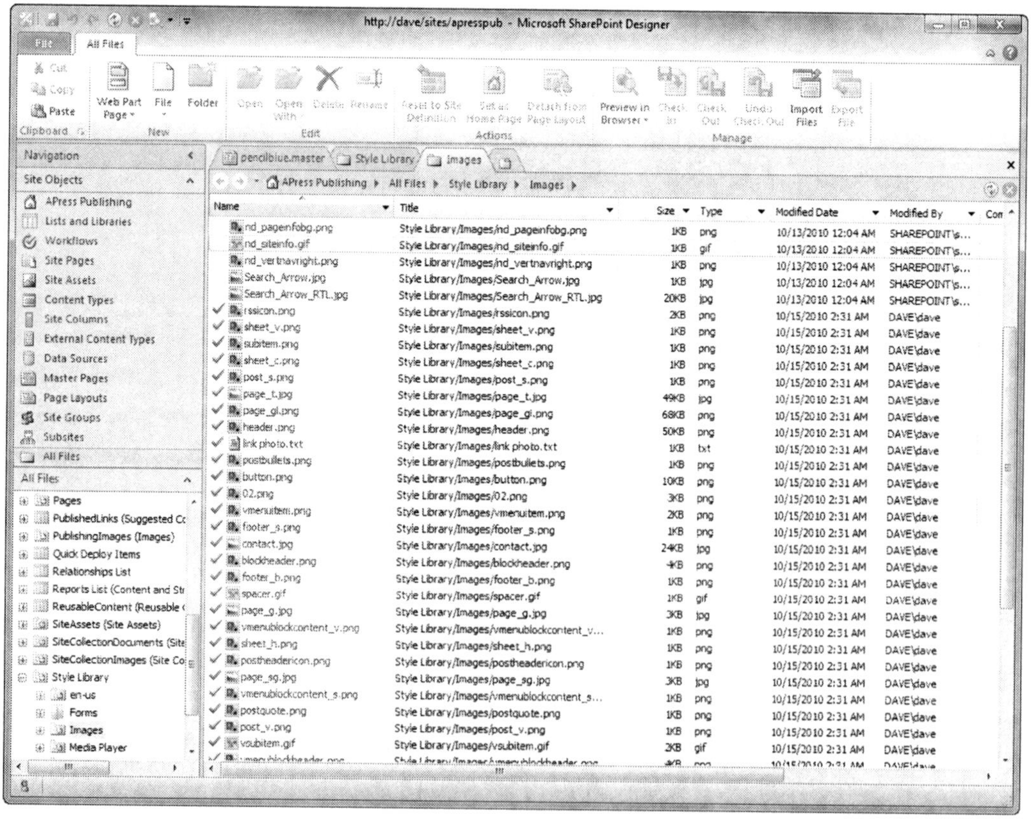

*Figure 9–16. Loading images into the Style Library*

We will do this similarly with the CSS files and JavaScript. Load the CSS files into the Style Library Core Styles. We are also renaming the files to have pencilblue as the first part, as shown in Figure 9–17.

| Name | Title | Size | Type | Modified Date | Modified By | C |
|------|-------|------|------|---------------|-------------|---|
| A] edit-mode-21.css | Style Library/en-us/Core Styles/edit-mode-... | 4KB | css | 10/13/2010 12:04 AM | SHAREPOINT\s... | |
| A] page-layouts-21.css | Style Library/en-us/Core Styles/page-layou... | 2KB | css | 10/13/2010 12:04 AM | SHAREPOINT\s... | |
| ✓ A] pencilblue.css | Style Library/en-us/Core Styles/pencilblue.css | 33KB | css | 10/15/2010 2:43 AM | DAVE\dave | |
| ✓ A] pencilblue.ie6.css | Style Library/en-us/Core Styles/pencilblue.i... | 20KB | css | 10/15/2010 2:43 AM | DAVE\dave | |
| ✓ A] pencilblue.ie7.css | Style Library/en-us/Core Styles/pencilblue.i... | 5KB | css | 10/15/2010 2:42 AM | DAVE\dave | |
| A] rca.css | Style Library/en-us/Core Styles/rca.css | 6KB | css | 10/13/2010 12:04 AM | SHAREPOINT\s... | |

***Figure 9–17.*** *Style Library folder for CSS files*

The final version of the PencilBlue.master master page from SharePoint Designer 2010 will be in the downloads section and will be called PenciBlueSPD.master to distinguish it from the one that is included in the Visual Studio Project.

After the brand is applied to SharePoint 2010, the site will look somewhat like Figure 9–18.

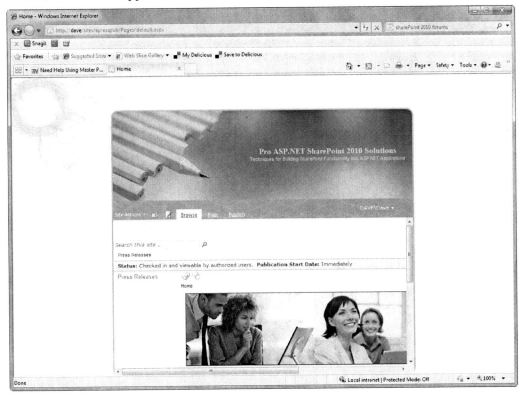

***Figure 9–18.*** *Branded SharePoint site*

> **Note** With a fixed-width design like this, you will need to adjust your content so that it fits into the space that is available.

Next, we will delve into packaging and deploying your branding solution.

## Deploying Branded Solutions

While we are working with SharePoint Designer 2010 in developing our master page, we will not want to be editing master pages directly on our production SharePoint sites. To handle the packaging and deployment of our SharePoint 2010 brand, we will utilize Visual Studio 2010.

1.  First, start up Visual Studio 2010 and select the Empty SharePoint Project, as shown in Fig 9–19.

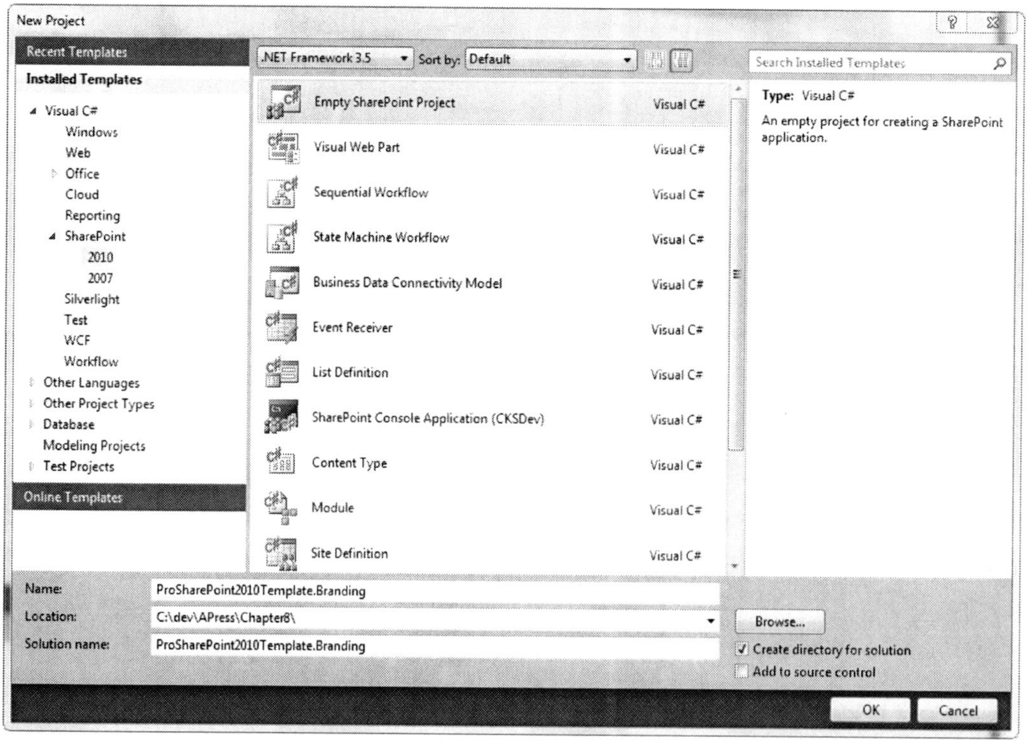

*Figure 9–19. SharePoint branding solution—Empty SharePoint Project.*

2.  Next, we will add a starter master page. I like to use the template that goes along with the CKSDev Toolkit. This is the Community Kit for SharePoint Development, which you can find on CodePlex here:

http://cksdev.codeplex.com/documentation

---

■ **Tip** The CKSDev Toolkit provides a number of additional project and item templates besides the ones that come out-of-the-box with SharePoint 2010, including a SharePoint 2010 Console application that is great for doing management types of tasks and testing out the SharePoint 2010 objects and libraries. Also included are a number of different helpful item templates, like a Basic Site Page, a Fluent UI Visual Web Part, the Starter Master Page we will be using, a Blank Site Template, a number of items around Custom Actions and Groups, a Delegate Control, a Full Trust Proxy, and a SPMetal Definition that will help you wire up your LINQ to SharePoint 2010 in an automated fashion.

---

3. Add a New Item using the Starter Master Page, as shown in Figure 9–20.

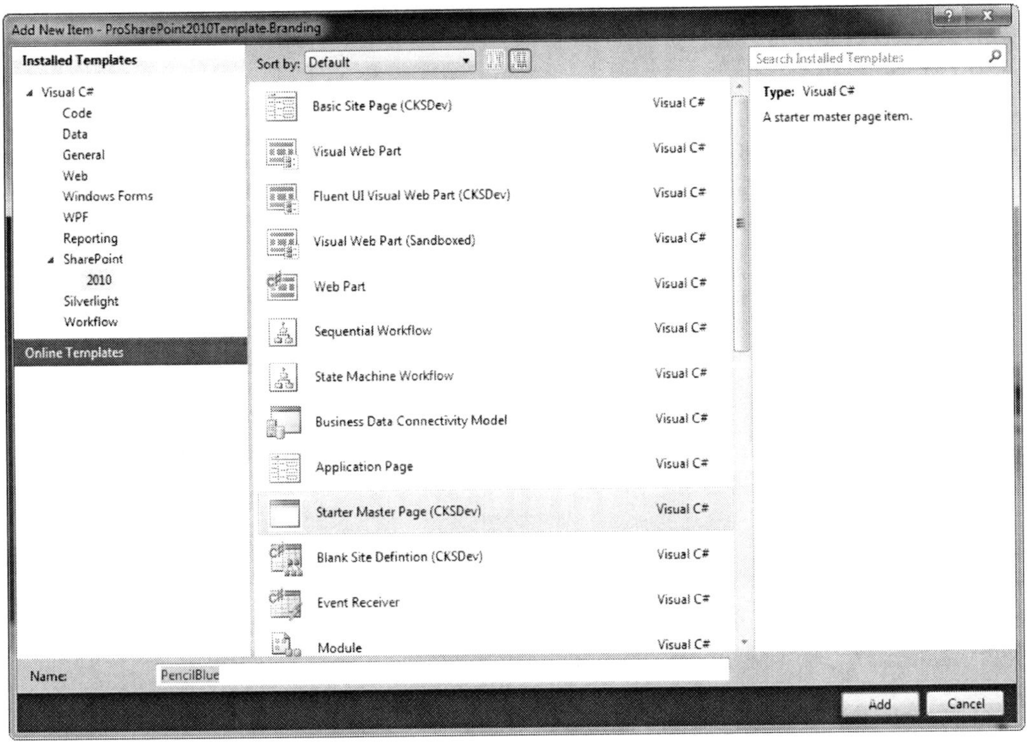

*Figure 9–20. Add a Starter Master Page*

4. The Project Item template for the Starter Master Page is very helpful in that it not only adds the page, but a Module for deploying it. All of this is automatically added to your Feature setup. Rename your Feature something

that you will be able to recognize if you are looking at it in a Site Administration or Central Administration web site, like ProSPBranding. Your entire project will look like Figure 9–21 after you are done with this.

Solution 'ProSharePoint2010Template.Branding' (1 project)
- ▲ ProSharePoint2010Template.Branding
  - ▷ Properties
  - ▷ References
  - ▲ Features
    - ▲ ProSPBranding
      - ▲ ProSPBranding.feature
        - ProSPBranding.Template.xml
  - ▷ Package
  - ▲ PencilBlue
    - Elements.xml
    - PencilBlue.master
  - key.snk

*Figure 9–21. SharePoint 2010 branding project*

5.  There is one thing that we will have to change in the Elements.xml file so that our master page will be seen by SharePoint 2010 as a master page, show up in the SharePoint 2010 library, and work correctly with the version 4 UI of SharePoint 2010. Add the following line to the File XML node in Elements.xml:

```
<Property Name="UIVersion" Value="4" />
```

6.  Next, we will need to change a little where we will deploy our images, CSS files, and JavaScript files. While storing these items in the Style Library for a site is fine for working with developing brands, and is indeed much easier than storing the items on the file system, for our SharePoint farm, we do want our files to be out there on the file system in a non-customized page. We will utilize the Layouts and Images directories on our SharePoint farm to store these artifacts. Right-click your project, select the Add menu, then select Add, as shown in Figure 9–22.

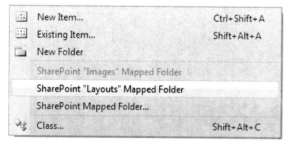

*Figure 9–22. Add SharePoint Images and Layouts Mapped Folders*

■ **Tip** Since your master page and related artifacts such as images, CSS, and JavaScript files are typically utilized throughout Site Collections, they are accessed very frequently. As such, storing these artifacts in the content database by way of using the Styles Library is not recommended as a best practice. Artifacts in the content database, and a master page stored there especially, are stored as a customization and will affect performance negatively for highly trafficked artifacts such as a master page. Storing these pages on the file system will help all of your pages using the brand be rendered uncustomized, which is the best practice for performance purposes.

7. After you have completed this, your project appears as shown in Figure 9–23. Note that Visual Studio automatically adds a folder under the main layouts and images directories for your project, so that any artifacts that you add there are kept separate from the SharePoint 2010 product artifacts. Note in Figure 9–23 the Images and Layouts directories added to your project. Copy all of the image files you are using to the Images directory under your project folder, and copy the CSS and JavaScript files you are using to the Layouts directory under your project folder.

- Solution 'ProSharePoint2010Template.Branding' (1 project)
  - **ProSharePoint2010Template.Branding**
    - Properties
    - References
    - Features
      - ProSPBranding
        - ProSPBranding.feature
          - ProSPBranding.Template.xml
    - Package
    - Images
      - ProSharePoint2010Template.Branding
    - Layouts
      - ProSharePoint2010Template.Branding
    - PencilBlue
      - Elements.xml
      - PencilBlue.master
    - key.snk

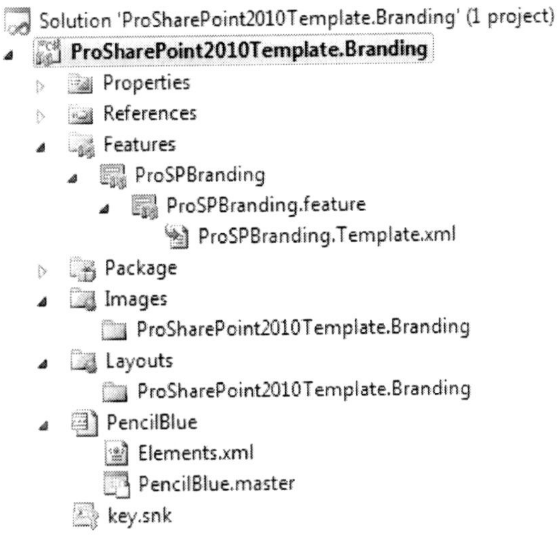

*Figure 9–23. SharePoint Branding Project with Mapped Layouts and Images*

■ **Tip** Sometimes questions related to internationalization come up when discussing branding. While it is important to utilize resources in our SharePoint 2010 development that support internationalization, when we are discussing branding, for the most part we will either be utilizing one global branding solution for multiple international language sites, including SharePoint 2010 Variations, or we will be developing a custom brand for different languages that may contain images in different languages or to impact different cultures. For this reason, we do not need to be as concerned with aligning our solutions under the language and regional settings in SharePoint 2010 (such as artificially creating en-us folders or 1033 folders underneath the layouts or images folders). It will be sufficient to name our project so that when it is deployed as a .wsp solution, we will know what it is.

8. Now cut and paste your Master Page from your SharePoint Designer 2010 editor directly into the page in your Visual Studio project. You will need to edit your CSS file and do a global Find and Replace to change the references to all of your images from where you have them stored in the Style Library on your development branding site to where they will be located on your production server. This will look something like Figure 9–24.

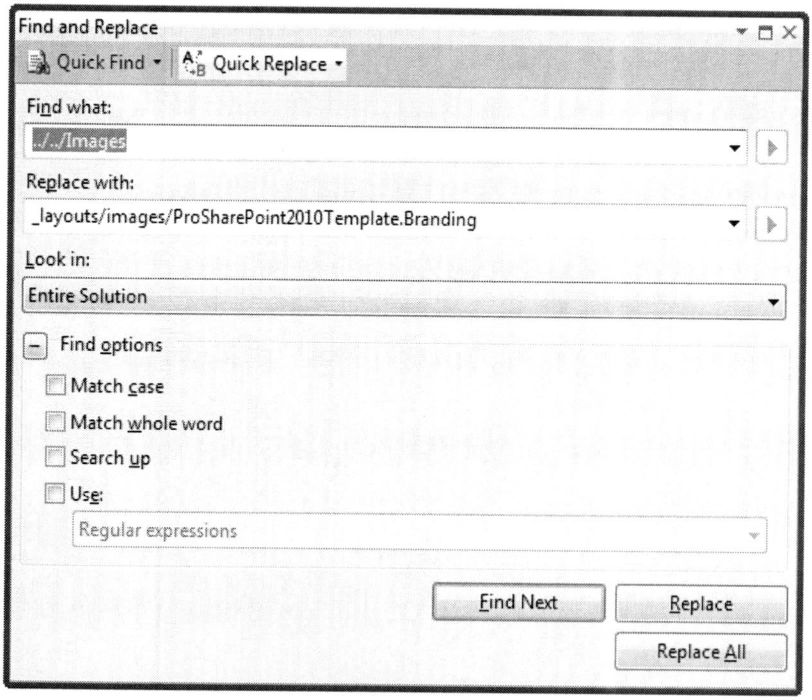

*Figure 9–24. Replacing image references in your CSS files*

9. After this, you are ready to deploy your solution to a Site Collection and use your new master page. You can deploy directly to your local environment, but to deploy to your production environment, change the Solution Configuration of your Visual Studio 2010 project to Release, then build your product. Select Package from the Build menu in Visual Studio 2010, as shown in Figure 9–25.

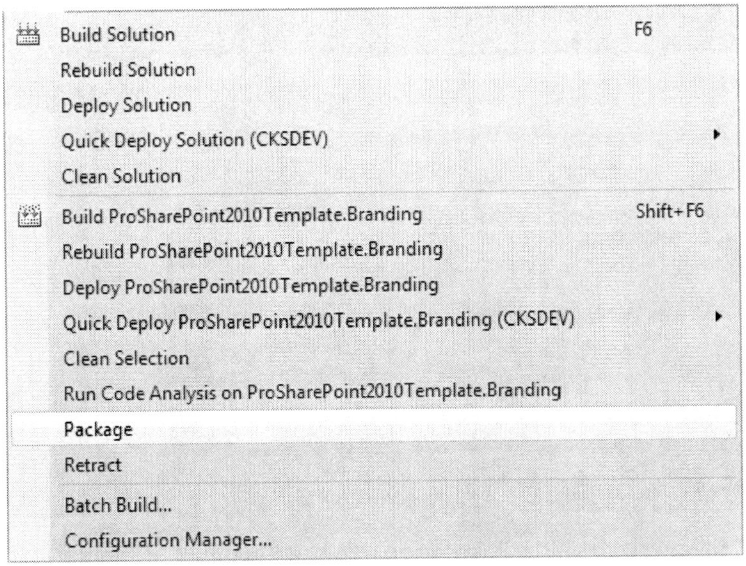

| | | |
|---|---|---|
| Build Solution | | F6 |
| Rebuild Solution | | |
| Deploy Solution | | |
| Quick Deploy Solution (CKSDEV) | | ▶ |
| Clean Solution | | |
| Build ProSharePoint2010Template.Branding | | Shift+F6 |
| Rebuild ProSharePoint2010Template.Branding | | |
| Deploy ProSharePoint2010Template.Branding | | |
| Quick Deploy ProSharePoint2010Template.Branding (CKSDEV) | | ▶ |
| Clean Selection | | |
| Run Code Analysis on ProSharePoint2010Template.Branding | | |
| Package | | |
| Retract | | |
| Batch Build... | | |
| Configuration Manager... | | |

*Figure 9–25. Package build in VS2010*

10. When your feature is deployed to your production environment, you will be able to see it in Site Settings ➤ Features. It will look similar to Figure 9–26.

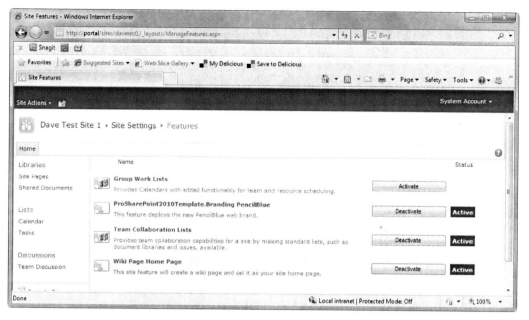

*Figure 9–26. Branding feature deployed*

Now that we have looked into branding with master pages and packaging a branding solution for deployment to production web sites, the next step is to discuss publishing page layouts, which are utilized in conjunction with SharePoint 2010 Publishing Features.

# Publishing Layouts

In beginning to highlight what publishing page layouts are, we will start with the reminder that everything in SharePoint is a list. How does this matter? Well, page layouts sit on master pages. Page layouts are based upon content types. Content types in SharePoint are implemented in lists. So the basic way to define a page layout is by constructing content types from site columns that are either currently in SharePoint or need to be added.

A page layout will have areas that you can place content from a particular content type. Page layouts can contain web-part zones add web parts into, as well as field controls.

All of this information about publishing page layouts contains a few different layers, so it may be helpful to walk through a simple example.

One default page layout is Article Left, which is based upon the Article page layout. Article Left contains an area for an image layout on the left-hand side, and an area for content on the right-hand side. There are many built-in publishing layouts contained in the SharePoint 2010 product that may be fine for you to use directly out-of-the-box. If they are not, you can modify publishing layouts in SharePoint Designer 2010, as shown in Figure 9–27. The built-in publishing layout ArticleLeft.aspx is shown in Figure 9–27.

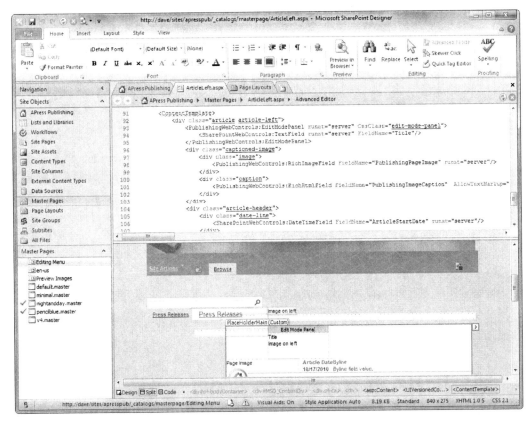

*Figure 9–27. Page layout ArticleLeft.aspx*

---

■ **Tip** Don't let all the SharePoint terms confuse you. Publishing page layouts simply will define different areas of display for information. When you edit the page, you are able to modify elements in each particular area. You as a solution provider will provide either the standard publishing layouts to use along with your master pages, or you will also define publishing layouts. End users can edit the published pages on your external facing web site and add content to them.

---

For example, the main page in our branded publishing page layout, when you edit the page content, appears as shown in Figure 9–28.

*Figure 9–28. Home page showing page layout*

As you can see, with all the content types and site columns in back of it, the page layout just presents simple areas to fill content in to the user, such as the title, a selectable image, an image caption, an article date and byline, and page content that is available to edit and includes quite a lot of options.

So when you define your master pages, if you have specific content layout needs on different pages, you may need to define a custom page layout for each page that will use the specifics. If the built-in page layouts will suffice, such as including an image and some content, you can use them.

You can customize page layouts in SharePoint Designer 2010 and packages similar to how we did the master pages in Visual Studio 2010.

# Customizing SharePoint 2010 Navigation

SharePoint 2010 offers a number of ways that the user, an administrator, or you as an architect and developer, can customize navigation. SharePoint primarily works with navigation through two main sources:

- Customizing the Quick Launch—this is the left-hand side navigation that is present in most SharePoint sites.

- Customizing the Top Navigation Bar—this is the top navigation menu structure that is shown near the header in most SharePoint sites.

We will highlight how to customize the navigation in SharePoint 2010 so that it will be the most compatible with ASP.NET

# Customizing Navigation Through the User Interface

You can update the Quick Launch by adding links and items through the user interface. You can select the Look and Feel section under Site Settings, then select the Quick Launch button. You will see the administrative interface built in to SharePoint 2010 for updating the Quick Launch, as shown in Figure 9–29.

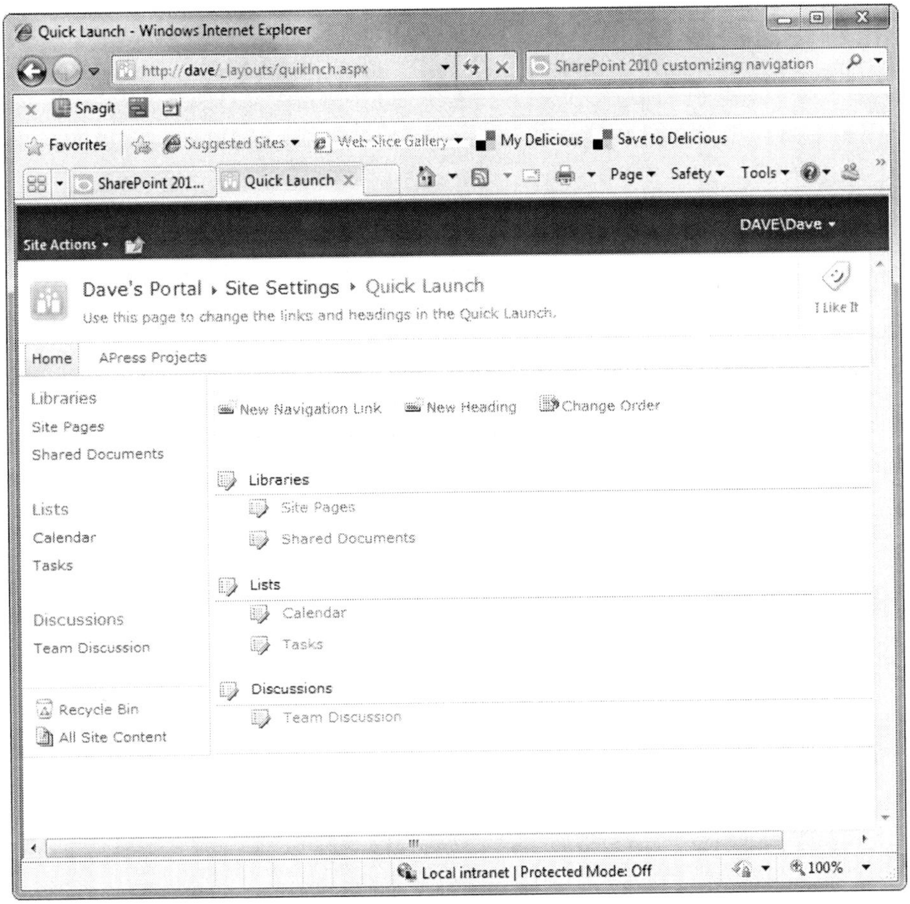

*Figure 9–29. Modifying the Quick Launch*

You can add new sections and new links to other areas into SharePoint 2010 directly through this interface—Figure 9–30 shows an example of adding a new group heading and two navigation links to a

SharePoint Foundation 2010 site. You potentially could duplicate any external links to ASP.NET applications using this method. Figure 9–30 shows the updated links.

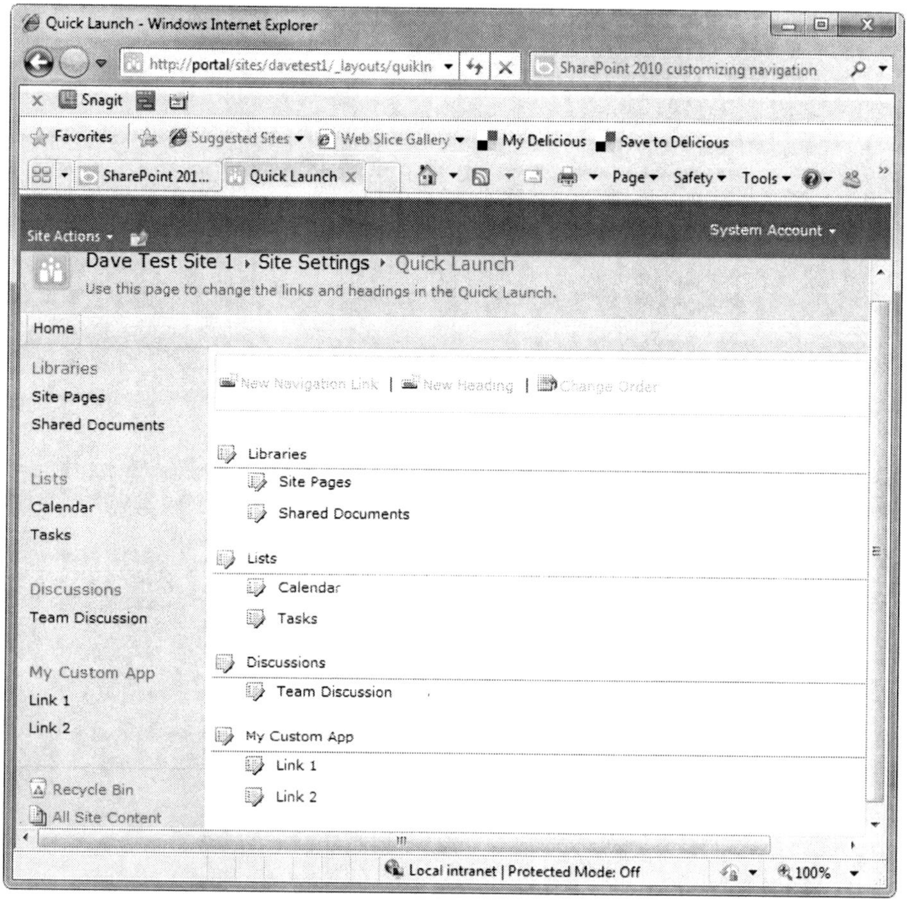

*Figure 9–30. Custom headings and links added*

Similarly, you can update the top navigation area using the user interface. you can add links as top navigation links, as shown in Figure 9–31.

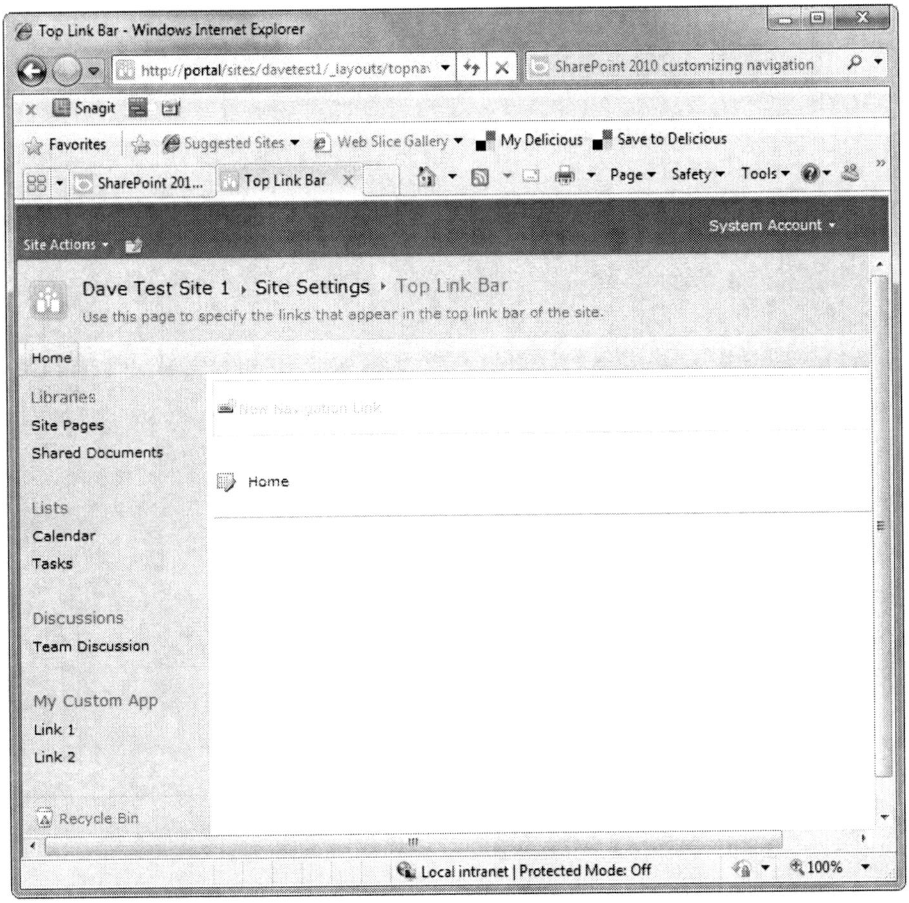

*Figure 9–31. Adding links to the top link bar*

As you can see, simply adding in navigation elements in addition to SharePoint's built-in navigation model can help to blend or integrate ASP.NET applications and SharePoint 2010. This, in addition to branding sites the same, can present a solid front-end experience to the users.

## Adding Links Through the Object Model

Navigation in SharePoint 2010 is done through standard ASP.NET controls—the standard Menu control in System.Web.UI.Webcontrols (System.Web.dll) is used for the Quick Launch and the top navigation menus. As such, it is relatively easy to modify the menu selections through the SharePoint Object Model. Following is an example of code that will add a link to the left-hand Quick Nav menu:

```
SPSite siteCollection = SPControl.GetContextSite(Context);
SPWeb site = siteCollection.AllWebs["DavePub"];
SPWeb subSite = site.Webs["DavePubSub"];
```

```
SPNavigationNodeCollection nodes = subSite.Navigation.QuickLaunch;
SPNavigationNode navNode = new SPNavigationNode("Dave's Blog", "http://www.davemilner.com",
true);
nodes.AddAsFirst(navNode);
```

## Navigation Custom Data Sources

It is also possible to completely override the custom SharePoint 2010 menu system by replacing navigation with a custom data source. The scope of going through this example is a little beyond what we will cover in this chapter, but for more information please see the following MSDN article:

http://msdn.microsoft.com/en-us/library/ms432695.aspx

This will step you through what it would take to completely replace the Quick Launch area with a menu provider.

# Summary

In this chapter, we have highlighted the approach to implementing professional SharePoint 2010 and ASP.NET applications in a blended environment using the low touch-point method. We have covered specifics by example of branding SharePoint 2010 and ASP.NET environments, have implemented a brand of the type delivered to us from a design company, and have covered many other features related to making the SharePoint UI as compatible to our ASP.NET application as we can. We have also highlighted organizational considerations for low touch-point solutions, and provided several examples of potential candidate solutions that could utilize the low touch-point approach.

# CHAPTER 10

# Client-Side Programming

At this point, you are going to take a slight detour from building the visual components of your sites into the magical realm of code writing. As you have seen throughout this book, some amazing things can be accomplished with SharePoint Server 2010 and SharePoint Designer 2010 without ever writing a line of code. However, in order to build the richest of user experiences, it is sometimes necessary to crack open the toolbox and pull out the power tools.

In this chapter, you will take a brief look at some of the tools that are available for writing high-performance client-side behaviors in SharePoint. This is not intended to be a comprehensive discussion of client-side programming in SharePoint. The purpose of this chapter is simply to make you aware of the tools that are available. Many excellent resources are available online, including on MSDN, and more are appearing all the time. The SharePoint client object models described here are catching on very rapidly, and a great deal of interest has been generated among developers who write blogs.

---

■ **Note** This chapter assumes that the reader has a certain familiarity with writing code that runs in a web browser. This includes technologies such as JavaScript, HTML, DOM, AJAX, and WCF. If these terms are foreign to you, don't feel too bad. You are in good company (with most of the human race) and should feel free to skip this chapter.

---

You will learn about the following topics in this chapter:

- How SharePoint 2010 exposes server functionality by using client-side object models (CSOMs).

- Why Microsoft felt this was an important feature to provide

- Why writing code that runs in the client browser is sometimes preferable to code that runs on the server

- How to make the browser interact with the server more efficiently

- Why we all love writing code so much!

# Understanding Client- vs. Server-Side Programming

In previous versions of SharePoint, we had two interfaces for accessing the objects and content stored within SharePoint: API calls or web services.

If our code was destined to run on the SharePoint server—for example, in a web part or event receiver—we could use the SharePoint API (a.k.a. the SharePoint server object model). This allowed us to create, read, update, and delete (CRUD) objects such as SPSite, SPWeb, SPList, and SPListItem. We could set permissions, configure features, and manipulate just about anything in the SharePoint environment as long as we had the necessary credentials. We could also write code against the API that would run as an add-on to the SharePoint Administration tool (STSADM) or in a .NET application. The only restriction was that it had to run *on the SharePoint server*. This interface still exists in SharePoint 2010, along with a new set of PowerShell commands that can be used for many of the same purposes.

If our SharePoint 2007 code needed to run on a computer other than the SharePoint server, we had to use SharePoint's web services interface. This interface was not as rich as the full server API, but it suited many scenarios well enough. The problem with the web services interface was that it worked well for the situations Microsoft designed it for, but not at all in most other cases. The web service method you needed either existed, or it didn't—and you were out of luck.

Many developers, me included, began routinely deploying custom web services within our SharePoint sites to allow client applications to perform actions not supported by the web services interface. Using AJAX-style code in the web browser, these services could be used to provide a richer user experience that did not require as many time-consuming page posts to the web server. JavaScript code running in the web browser would call the custom web service to carry out a server-side function, returning data objects to the browser. The script would then update the currently displayed page without posting the entire page to the server. Unfortunately, these services often performed poorly and affected scalability by transferring logic that could be done on the client side to the server.

Another approach to the problem was to redefine the *client* application as a *server* application. For example, integrating SQL Server Reporting Services (SSRS) with SharePoint 2007 required the SQL server to have SharePoint installed locally so that SQL could use the SharePoint API to communicate with SharePoint. This was true even if there was no plan to render pages or run any other SharePoint server processes on the SSRS server. Although this did not have a large impact when using the free Windows SharePoint Services (WSS) package, this could get very expensive once you started deploying Microsoft Office SharePoint Server (MOSS).

As Microsoft began developing the next version of SharePoint, they were flooded with requests for additional web services to be added to the interface. More and more web sites have the need for a flexible client-side programming interface to support rich browser interfaces and mobile web applications. At some point, Microsoft came up with a more elegant solution than continuing to add new SharePoint web services ad infinitum.

# Working with the SharePoint Client Object Model

SharePoint 2010 contains a new set of features called the *SharePoint Foundation 2010 client-side object model* (CSOM) or just the *client object model*. Note that I am using the abbreviation *CSOM* instead of *COM* to avoid confusing it with the old component object model. The purpose of the CSOM is to provide a client-side subset of the SharePoint API that can be used from a variety of platforms. The object model is available for .NET Framework applications, Silverlight applications, and web sites using ECMAScript-compatible scripting languages such as JScript and JavaScript.

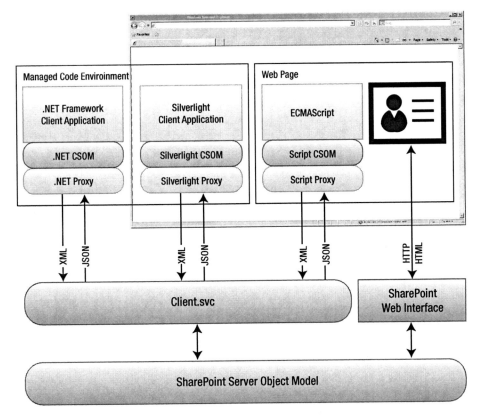

*Figure 10-1. Client-side object model components*

Each version of the client object model has a similar component structure. The specifics of each environment are presented in a later section. For now, you will look at the architecture that is common to them all (see Figure 10-1).

On the SharePoint server, there is a new component called Client.svc. As the name suggests, this is a Windows Communication Foundation (WCF) service. This service acts as a façade for the SharePoint Server object model running on the server. The client service receives client requests in XML form, executes the request against the server API, and returns objects to the caller in JavaScript Object Notation (JSON) format.

Each client object model implementation consists of two layers. The first layer is the client-side object model classes. These classes map directly in most cases to a corresponding SharePoint Server object model class. For example, the SPSite server object is represented by the Site object in each client object model.

The second layer of the implementation consists of a proxy layer, or *runtime*. The purpose of the proxy component is to streamline the passing of requests and responses to and from the server. A key difference between the server and client object models is the effect of the proxy layer. When a call is made to the client object model, that request is not immediately processed on the server. The proxy batches the requests until the client application explicitly tells it to contact the server. At that point, all of the outstanding requests are processed in order, and the results are returned to the client. This makes writing good client-side SharePoint code very different from writing server-side code. In the "Using Best

Practices" section, you will learn some of the ways to leverage this batching behavior to dramatically improve performance and scalability.

## .NET Framework Client Object Model

The .NET Framework client object model is used when writing client applications by using the .NET Framework version 3.5. This allows SharePoint calls to be made from console applications, Windows applications, and Windows services.

---

■ **Note** The .NET client object model assemblies for SharePoint 2010 are version 3.5 assemblies, not version 4.0. Be sure to select the correct .NET Framework version when writing code against the object model.

---

There are two assemblies to be referenced when building SharePoint client applications in .NET, as shown in Table 10-1. Both assemblies can be found in the 14 hive's ISAPI directory. By default, the full path is `C:\Program Files\Common Files\Microsoft Shared\Web Server Extensions\14\ISAPI`.

*Table 10-1. .NET Framework CSOM Files*

| Filename | Purpose |
| --- | --- |
| `Microsoft.SharePoint.Client.dll` | Object model classes |
| `Microsoft.SharePoint.Client.Runtime.dll` | Runtime classes |

## Silverlight Client Object Model

The Silverlight client object model is used when writing Silverlight applications. These applications may be hosted in a variety of environments, from mobile phones to SharePoint sites, using the Silverlight web part.

Again, two assemblies need to be referenced when building SharePoint client applications. Both assemblies can be found in the 14 hive's `TEMPLATE\LAYOUTS\ClientBin` directory. SharePoint's 14 hive is the location to which SharePoint installs the content files and executables that are deployed as part of a SharePoint site. The full default path to these files is `C:\Program Files\Common Files\Microsoft Shared\Web Server Extensions\14\TEMPLATE\LAYOUTS\ClientBin`. There is also an Extensible AJAX Platform (XAP) file containing both dynamic-link libraries (DLLs). Table 10-2 lists the files.

*Table 10-2. Silverlight CSOM Files*

| Filename | Purpose |
|---|---|
| `Microsoft.SharePoint.Client.Silverlight.dll` | Object model classes |
| `Microsoft.SharePoint.Client.Runtime.Silverlight.dll` | Runtime classes |
| `Microsoft.SharePoint.Client.xap` | Precompiled Silverlight package containing both DLLs |

# ECMAScript Client Object Model

The ECMAScript client object model is used when writing JavaScript code within web pages. The method of delivering the script to the web page may vary. It could be included in a Content Editor web part or other standard control, as you will see in our example. It could also be emitted by a custom web control or embedded in a .js script file.

In this case, only one file is needed for the client object model. All of the object and proxy logic is included in a single JavaScript file called sp.js. This file is commonly loaded at runtime by using a script statement like the one shown in Listing 10-1.

*Listing 10-1. JavaScript Reference for the sp.js File*

```
<script type="text/javascript">
    ExecuteOrDelayUntilScriptLoaded(MyFunction, "sp.js");
</script>
```

This causes the sp.js file to load before running the MyFunction routine, which can then use the client object model. This file is compacted and difficult to read. For debugging purposes, you may want to use the sp.debug.js file. It is easier to work with but is 40 percent larger than the production file. Table 10-3 lists the ECMAScript CSOM files.

*Table 10-3. ECMAScript CSOM Files*

| Filename | Purpose |
|---|---|
| sp.js | Production script file |
| sp.debug.js | Debug version of the script file |

The ECMAScript object model has some limitations because of the environment in which it executes. Objects created with the model can access only the local site collection. In the server API or the other client object models, you can create a Site (or SPSite) object that points to any SharePoint site collection anywhere on the network. Because script objects exist within a certain web page, any attempt to access another site collection would be considered a cross-site scripting attack and is therefore prevented.

The proxy layer in any of the client object models can batch multiple requests destined for the server. When the client application wants to send the batch, it calls either ExecuteQuery or

ExecuteQueryAsync. The former call blocks the current thread until the results are returned. The latter registers callback routines that are called asynchronously after the request is completed. Because blocking the browser's user interface thread can cause the browser to freeze, only asynchronous requests are permitted. The ExecuteQuery method is not even included in the script object model.

The ECMAScript version of the client object model is the one that we can use from within SharePoint Designer 2010, so we will limit our discussion to it for the rest of this chapter.

## SharePoint Object Model Comparison

All of the client object models are a subset of the server object model. Some of the objects, properties, and methods available within the server API are not available on the client side. That being said, most of the objects commonly used by SharePoint developers are available in a very similar form. Table 10-4 lists some of the most common objects and their client equivalents.

*Table 10-4. Comparing Objects in the Object Models*

| Server API | .NET CSOM | Silverlight CSOM | ECMAScript CSOM |
|---|---|---|---|
| SPContext | ClientContext | ClientContext | ClientContext |
| SPSite | Site | Site | Site |
| SPWeb | Web | Web | Web |
| SPList | List | List | List |
| SPListItem | ListItem | ListItem | ListItem |
| SPField | Field | Field | Field |

# Using Best Practices

This section covers some best practices around using client-side script with SharePoint solutions. You will examine the most common use cases for which client-side programming is useful or preferable. Then you will look at some of the architectural considerations that affect performance and scalability of a SharePoint farm when using server-side vs. client-side logic. For those familiar with AJAX-style programming, many of these points will seem obvious.

The two main reasons for moving logic to the client are to improve site performance and create a richer user experience. The key is to remember that moving logic to the client side improves the scalability of the SharePoint farm by removing that processing from the server. Eliminating unneeded full-page post-backs is good for both the user experience and reducing load on the server.

## User Experience

The new client object model is a powerful new tool for building SharePoint solutions, but when should it be used, and when is it best to avoid client-side scripting? It is important to understand what types of things can be done effectively from the client side. SharePoint server provides web parts and pages that handle most routine tasks by presenting a form to the user and receiving the data posted back from the form. Client-side forms allow more-complex behaviors to be created that make the user interface respond more quickly and interactively.

For example, in SharePoint 2007, when the user clicked the *+Add Document* link in a document library, the entire page was replaced by an upload form. Starting in SharePoint 2010, the same link will open a modal dialog box form to upload the document, as shown in Figure 10-2. Forms like this one are loaded without posting the entire page back to the server. When the form is submitted, the page behind it is redisplayed and updated only as necessary. This creates a much smoother interface.

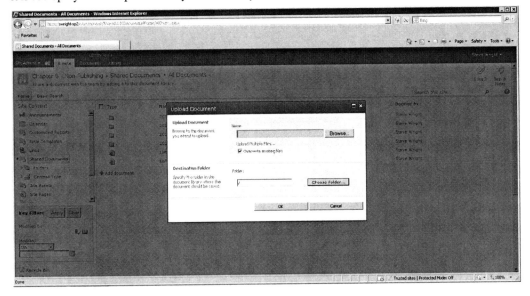

*Figure 10-2. Modal dialog box form*

The client object model contains a set of classes for displaying this type of modal dialog box easily from within client-side script. The dialog box can accept input, perform actions such as posting data back to the server, and return status and data elements to the calling client script.

Client-side scripts can also be used to update the elements on the current web page. A common scenario is to execute a Collaborative Application Markup Language (CAML) query against SharePoint server by using the client object model and then to render the results to controls already present on the web page. As you will see in the example later in this chapter, it is also simple to retrieve and update information about individual content objects that exist within the site. These objects can include web sites, lists, libraries, list items, and documents.

Using SharePoint Designer, it is also possible to create *custom actions* within the SharePoint site, as you can see in Figure 10-3. These are menu items that can launch a form, start a workflow, or navigate to a specific URL. By adding a JavaScript call to the custom action's URL, this feature can be used to run arbitrary client-side script when the menu item is selected.

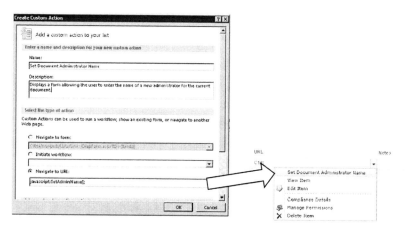

**Figure 10-3.** *Client-side custom actions*

Because the client object model is a subset of the server object model, many of the tasks traditionally performed within a site's web parts and forms can now be done on the client side.

# Performance and Scalability

Performance and scalability are two sides of the same coin. What the user experiences as performance from your web site is dependent on how quickly actions taken in the browser are communicated to the server and then reflected back in the browser. As additional users place additional load on the server, it naturally responds more slowly. SharePoint server farms are intended to provide scalability by providing additional servers to handle the load. However, the design of your application will determine how effectively those server resources can be used.

Getting the best performance possible requires balancing the functionality of the application against the capabilities of the hardware supporting it. The SharePoint client object models are designed to allow some of the processing that might have occurred on the servers to be performed on the client side of the network connection. This frees up server capacity and improves scalability.

Consider all of the logic that goes into a SharePoint application. This might include querying, reading, formatting, and updating data. It might also include time-consuming calculations or repetitive tasks. Some of these have to be done, at least in part, on the server side because they involve accessing SharePoint's databases. When designing functionality for the SharePoint environment, consider which pieces of logic can be done on the client and which cannot. Of those that can be moved to the client side, consider the savings in terms of server resources that could be gained by doing so.

Your goal is to reduce the physical load on the servers in terms of CPU time, memory usage, disk I/O, and network traffic. Because SharePoint is an IIS-based application, you also need to consider the worker threads allocated within IIS as a limited resource to be managed and conserved. Performing calculations and formatting tasks on the client side can help reduce CPU and thread usage. Carefully managing the volume of data being sent to and received from the server can make a big difference when network capacity is at a premium. Of course, having pages load faster is a boost to the user experience even when the servers are lightly loaded.

The following are some concrete suggestions for improving performance and scalability when using the client object model.

## Update Only a Small Portion of the Page

Using client-side script, you can retrieve information from the server and display it in the controls and display elements within the current web page instead of posting back and re-rendering the entire page. This eliminates the need to re-render those parts of the page that are not changing. For example, if you are adding an item to a list, there is no need to regenerate the page's navigation controls including all of the security checks and HTML creation that goes with them. Additionally, the network bandwidth consumed will be greatly reduced because there will be less redundant data to transmit.

## Carefully Design Request Batches Submitted to the Proxy Layer

When using the client object model, the proxy layer records the requests made to the objects in the `ClientContext` object. It sends those requests to the server only when explicitly instructed to do so via the `ExecuteQueryAsnyc()` method. At that time, it packages the requests into an XML document, establishes a connection to the server, and transfers the data. The server then transmits the response data back to the proxy layer as JSON objects. The amount of time and network bandwidth used sending and receiving data is proportional to the amount of data being sent. The overhead associated with the call (connecting, error correcting, and so forth) is fairly consistent for all calls made, no matter how big or small.

To maximize the efficiency of the interaction between the client and server, try to reduce the number of calls by planning the request batches that will be sent to the proxy layer. Each batch should contain as many requests as possible. In some cases, the results of one operation are needed as inputs to the next one. Those operations will have to be in separate batches, but the client object model was designed to minimize this type of dependency. It is possible to open a webpage, find a list, and create list items, all before sending anything to the server.

In short, remember to keep your interactions *chunky*, not *chatty*. A few large data transfers are more efficient than many small ones.

## Minimize Data Volume by Limiting the Items and Fields Returned

Wait a minute! Didn't we just say to make your request and response batches *bigger*? Yes—but only as big as they need to be.

When you retrieve an object by using the server-side SharePoint API, you generally expect the object to be populated with all of the properties for the object. In the client object models, you can specify which properties you are interested in so that none of the others need to be retrieved. If you are generating a list of documents in a library, you may be interested in its name and URL, but not its status, creation, and modification information. The size of the response sent from the server to the client can be greatly reduced by carefully selecting only those properties that you are actually going to use after the object is loaded. The concept is similar to writing SQL statements that avoid using `SELECT * FROM` to retrieve all of the fields in a table. If you cannot list all of the fields in the object, you probably do not need all of their values in the response.

It is also worth mentioning that you should limit the number of items being returned as well. Querying the properties of objects is one operation that is much better done on the server side. Imagine looking for a particular document in a library of a million items by pulling the entire list into the client web browser and then looping through it. The CAML query object is ideal for retrieving only those items and fields that are actually needed.

## Use Modal Dialogs Instead of Launching Forms on a New Page

As described earlier in the subsection "User Experience" and shown in Figure 10-2, the client object model contains utility classes, such as `SP.UI.ModalDialog`, for creating modal dialog boxes within the current page. Although this may seem quite trivial at first, just consider how that same interface would probably have appeared in SharePoint 2007. A full-page post-back would be executed to load a form into the web browser. Then, the form data would be posted to the server. The form data would be processed, and then the user's browser would be redirected to a new page that would have to be completely generated from scratch. By presenting the form in a dialog box, we have turned two complete round-trips to the server into a couple of small requests for HTML and posting data. The rest of the current page remains in the browser, ready for use.

# Client-Side Anti-Patterns

Just as it is important to know when to use the client object model, you also need to consider cases in which using it might not be desirable. The dangers introduced by using the client object model are similar to the risks that have always been associated with browser-based scripting.

The most obvious reason *not* to use client-side scripting is that it might not be available. All modern browsers support ECMAScript, but older browsers may not. Also, some organizations limit or disable scripts when they come from the Internet. Consider the network environment and required browser support when moving to client-side scripts. When creating a public-facing Internet site, your site needs to degrade gracefully when faced with old, or intentionally crippled, browsers.

When you write a client-side script and place it on a web page, you are essentially releasing your source code to the public. Anyone can view and copy the scripts associated with a web page. Never put proprietary logic into the scripts on a web page. Most client-side logic is fairly straightforward, so exposing it isn't really an issue. If your company's secret sauce is algorithms, such as a search technique or financial analysis process, keep it inside the firewall by keeping it on the server.

Remember too that there is nothing to keep hackers from writing their own client object model code or altering the code you include in your web page. Always make sure that the objects within your sites are properly secured against access and modification. Just because you don't provide an interface to access or modify something, doesn't mean that an intruder using a well-known interface, such as the client object model, couldn't do so.

# Creating a Client-Side Script

Now you will walk through a few examples using the client object model. You will start with simply reading an object. Then you will write to that object and verify that the change has taken effect. Finally, you will perform a CAML query against a list and display the results.

---

■ **Note** The source files for these exercises can be downloaded from the book's web site at www.apress.com.

---

# Creating a Test Environment

The first step in your exploration of the client object model will be to create a test page in which you can run your scripts. For simplicity's sake, you will your scripts within a Content Editor web part. The script files will be stored in a library on the site. Here are the steps:

1. Create a new site by using the Blank Site template.

2. Open the site in SharePoint Designer 2010.

3. From the Navigation pane, select Lists and Libraries.

4. From the New group on the menu, click the Document Library drop-down and select Document Library.

5. Name the new library **Scripts** and then click OK.

6. In the Navigation pane, click All Files.

7. Click the Scripts link in the file listing.

8. From the All Files tab on the menu, click the File drop-down in the New group and select HTML.

9. For the filename, type **ListWebTitle.html** and then press Enter.

10. Open the ListWebTitle.html file in the Page Editor.

11. Replace the default HTML with the code in Listing 10-2. The contents of the script are detailed in the next section.

*Listing 10-2. List Web Title Script*

```
<script type="text/javascript">
    ExecuteOrDelayUntilScriptLoaded(GetProperties, "sp.js");
    var web;

    function GetProperties() {
        var ctx = new SP.ClientContext.get_current();
        web = ctx.get_web();
        ctx.load(web);

        ctx.executeQueryAsync(
            Function.createDelegate(this, this.onLoadSuccess),
            Function.createDelegate(this, this.onLoadFail));
    }
    function onLoadSuccess(sender, args) {
        document.getElementById('output').innerText =
            'Current Web Title: ' + web.get_title();
    }
    function onLoadFail(sender, args){
        document.getElementById('output').innerText =
            'Failed to get the web. Error:' + args.get_message();
    }
</script>
```

```
<h1 id="output"></h1>
```

1. Save the file in SharePoint Designer.

2. Open the site's defa he Web-Part drop-down and select Content Editor.

3. Right-click the new web part and select ult.aspx file in the Page Editor.

4. Select the web part zone labeled Left.

5. From the Insert tab of the menu, click t

6. Web Part Properties.

7. In the Content Link text box, type scripts/ListWebTitle.html and then click OK, as shown in Figure 10-4.

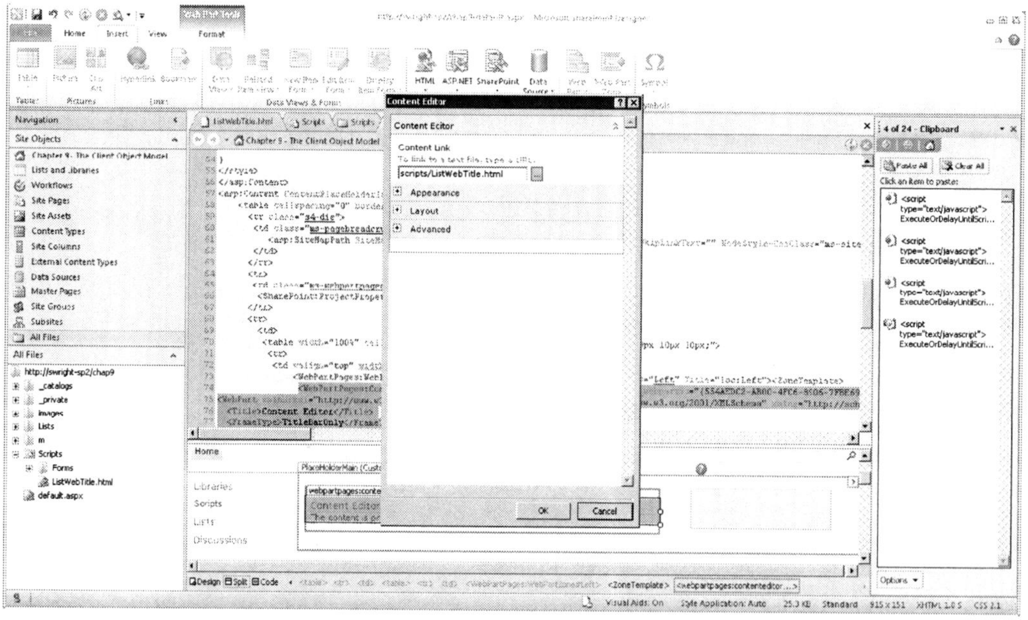

*Figure 10-4. Linking a script to a Content Editor web part*

8. Save the default.aspx page.

9. Press F12 to launch the page in a web browser.

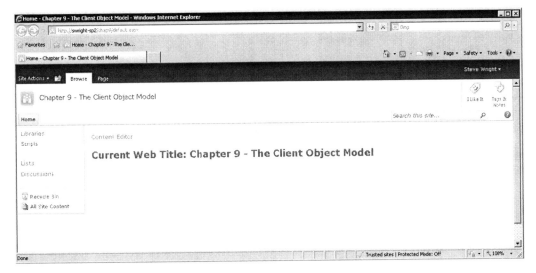

*Figure 10-5. Home page with client script*

At this point, you have a web part on the home page of your site that reads its contents from a file in the Scripts library. The script currently linked to the web part reads the current site's title property and displays it on the page, as shown in Figure 10-5.

# Reading and Writing Object Properties

Loading and manipulating SharePoint objects are probably the most common operations performed when using the SharePoint server object model. It is reasonable to assume that the same will be true for the client-side models. Let's take a closer look at the code in Listing 10-2.

At the highest level, you have a `<script>` tag followed by an `<h1>` header tag. The `<h1>` tag has an ID of `output` so that you can write into it by using JavaScript. Starting at the top, you can see that the script starts out by loading the `sp.js` file containing the ECMAScript client object model components:

```
ExecuteOrDelayUntilScriptLoaded(GetProperties, "sp.js");
var web;
```

You use `ExecuteOrDelayUntilScriptLoaded` to ensure that your CSOM code doesn't begin running before the library is loaded. Once loading is complete, you will run the `GetProperties` method. Next, you declare a global variable that will contain a reference to the site's web object. Remember that site collections are called `SPSite` or `Site` in the object models, and sites are `SPWeb` or `Web`.

The `GetProperties` method begins by retrieving a reference to the current client context object. Because this is ECMAScript, the current context is the only one available. You cannot connect to other site collections. Next, you get a reference to the local web object and tell the context to load the properties for it. Looking at the code, you might expect the web object to be ready to use, but you would be wrong. Remember, the proxy layer batches all requests until you explicitly tell it to send them. Up to this point, you have not sent any requests or data to the server whatsoever.

```
function GetProperties() {
    var ctx = new SP.ClientContext.get_current();
    web = ctx.get_web();
    ctx.load(web);

    ctx.executeQueryAsync(
        Function.createDelegate(this, this.onLoadSuccess),
        Function.createDelegate(this, this.onLoadFail));
}
```

The last statement in this routine calls the executeQueryAsync method. This causes a request to be sent to the server containing all outstanding requests. In this case, that consists of a request to load the current web site's property values into the object referenced by the web global variable. When the response is received, the proxy layer will populate the objects received and then call either onLoadSuccess, if the call succeeded, or onLoadFail, if it failed.

Both of the onLoad routines perform similar actions. They write a message into the <h1> tag for display on the web page. In the case of success, the object reference saved in the global web variable is used to retrieve the web site's title:

```
function onLoadSuccess(sender, args) {
    document.getElementById('output').innerText =
        'Current Web Title: ' + web.get_title();
}
function onLoadFail(sender, args){
    document.getElementById('output').innerText =
        'Failed to get the web. Error:' + args.get_message();
}
```

---

■ **Note** If this is the only thing you are going to do with the web object, this code is wasteful. The web object contains many properties that will also be returned by this code, which wastes bandwidth. This example would work just as well if you used the following statement to load the web object:

ctx.Load(web, 'Title'); // Load only the "Title" property

---

Now that you have seen how to read an object, let's look at updating one. In this example, you will add code to the script that will read the web's title, allow you to update it, and then reread it to ensure that it worked:.

1. Create a second HTML file in the Scripts library called **UpdateWebTitle.html**.

2. Replace the file's contents with Listing 10-3.

3. Edit the default.aspx page and replace the ListWebTitle.html reference with UpdateWebTitle.html.

4. Save both files.

*Listing 10-3. Update Web Title Script*

```
<script type="text/javascript">
    ExecuteOrDelayUntilScriptLoaded(GetProperties, "sp.js");
    var web;

    function GetProperties() {
        var ctx = new SP.ClientContext.get_current();
        web = ctx.get_web();
        ctx.load(web, 'Title');

        ctx.executeQueryAsync(
            Function.createDelegate(this, this.onLoadSuccess),
            Function.createDelegate(this, this.onLoadFail));
    }
    function onLoadSuccess(sender, args) {
        document.getElementById('output').innerText =
            'Current Web Title: ' + web.get_title();
        document.getElementById('txtTitle').value = web.get_title();
    }
    function onLoadFail(sender, args) {
        document.getElementById('output').innerText =

            'Failed to get the web. Error:' + args.get_message();
    }

    function UpdateTitle() {
        var ctx = new SP.ClientContext.get_current();
        web = ctx.get_web();
        web.set_title(document.getElementById('txtTitle').value);
        web.update();

        ctx.executeQueryAsync(
            Function.createDelegate(this, this.onUpdateSucceed),
            Function.createDelegate(this, this.onUpdateFail));
    }
    function onUpdateSucceed(sender, args) {
        alert('The title was updated, but you have to refresh the page to see it in the site
header.');
        GetProperties();
    }
    function onUpdateFail(sender, args) {
        alert('Unable to update the title. Error: ' + args.get_message());
    }
</script>
<h1 id="output"></h1>
<p>
New Site Title:
<input type="text" id="txtTitle" value="" size="50" />
</p>
<p>
<input name="btnUpdate" type="button" value="Update Title"
```

```
        onclick="javascript:UpdateTitle();" />
</p>
```

5.　Press F12 to launch the default.aspx page in your web browser.

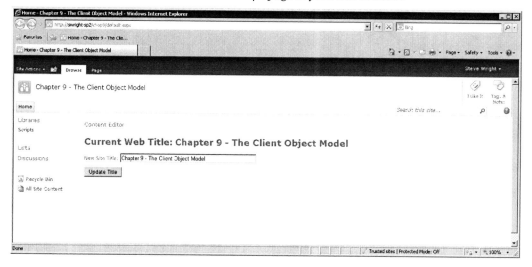

***Figure 10-6.*** *Home page with title*

6.　Type a new title for the web site into the text box, as shown in Figure 10-6.

7.　Click the Update Title button. An alert dialog box displays, as shown in Figure 10-7.

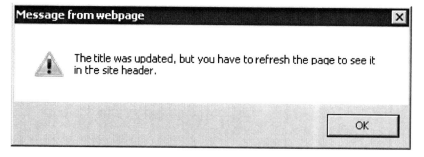

***Figure 10-7.*** *Alert dialog box*

8.　Click OK.

9.　Note that the site title at the top of the page no longer matches the one in the `<h1>` tag. This is because the title at the top of the page is updated only when the full page is retrieved from the server.

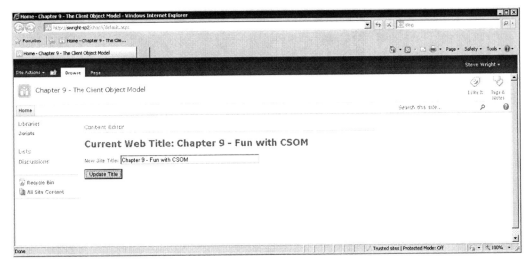

*Figure 10-8. home page with new title (not refreshed)*

10. Click the Refresh button on your web browser.

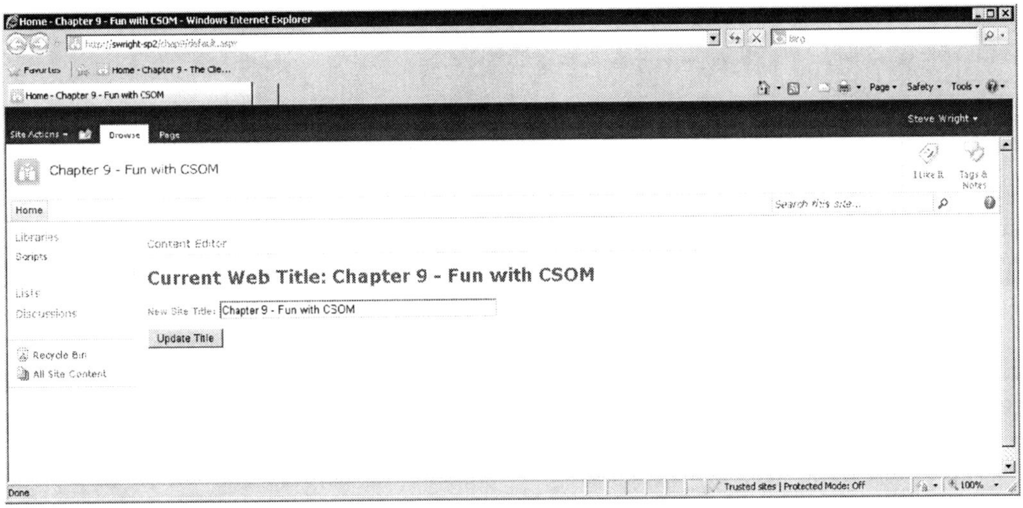

*Figure 10-9. Home page with title (refreshed)*

The new elements in this page are a text box, an input button, and some additional script. When the page loads, the title is loaded into the text box. The user can then update the title and click the Update Title button. This executes the UpdateTitle method:

```
function UpdateTitle() {
    var ctx = new SP.ClientContext.get_current();

    web = ctx.get_web();
    web.set_title(document.getElementById('txtTitle').value);
    web.update();

    ctx.executeQueryAsync(
        Function.createDelegate(this, this.onUpdateSucceed),
        Function.createDelegate(this, this.onUpdateFail));
}
```

At first glance, this method looks similar to the GetProperties method you looked at before. The difference is that you are setting the title instead of loading it. Take a close look at the code. You get the context and web objects and then you set the title *without loading the web object from the server first.* This is an important difference between loading and updating objects. Because of the way the CSOM handles the identity of objects, it is not always necessary to load an object before updating it. In this case, the web object represents the current web site, so there is no need to load it. The object to be updated has already been identified. The call to web.Update() instructs the proxy layer to send the changes to the web object to the server. Again, the request batch is sent only when you call executeQueryAsync.

If you needed to, you could create, update, and delete several objects before sending anything to the server. This makes the passing of requests and responses very efficient because the overhead of the call is shared among multiple requests.

## Querying Lists and Libraries with CAML

In our final example, you will see how to query the SharePoint content database efficiently. This includes limiting the number of items you retrieve and the number of properties for those items. Here are the steps:

1.    Create another HTML file in the Scripts library called **QueryFiles.html**.

2.    Replace the file's contents with Listing 10-4.

3.    Edit the default.aspx page and replace the UpdateWebTitle.html reference with QueryFiles.html.

4.    Save both files.

*Listing 10-4. Query Files Script*

```
<script type="text/javascript">

ExecuteOrDelayUntilScriptLoaded(LoadPages, "sp.js");

var ctx;
var web;
var list;
var itemCollection;

function LoadPages()
{
    ctx = new SP.ClientContext.get_current();

    web = ctx.get_web();
    ctx.load(web);

    list = web.get_lists().getByTitle("Scripts");
    ctx.load(list);

    var qry = new SP.CamlQuery();

    qry .set_viewXml(
        "<View>"
        + "<ViewFields><FieldRef Name='ID' /><FieldRef Name='FileLeafRef' /><FieldRef
Name='Modified' /></ViewFields>"
        + "<RowLimit>50</RowLimit>"
        + "</View>");
    itemCollection = list.getItems(qry);
    ctx.load(itemCollection);

    ctx.executeQueryAsync(
        Function.createDelegate(this, this.onQuerySuccess),
        Function.createDelegate(this, this.onQueryFailed));
}

function onQuerySuccess(sender, args)
{
    var s = '';

    var itemEnumerator = itemCollection .getEnumerator();
    while (itemEnumerator .moveNext())
    {
        var item = itemEnumerator .get_current();

        s = s + item.get_item('FileLeafRef')
                + ' modified on ' + item.get_item('Modified') + "<br />";
    }
```

```
    document.getElementById('output').innerHTML = s;
}

function onQueryFailed(sender, args)
{
    alert('Query failed.');
}
</script>
<div id="output"></div>
<p>
<input name="cmdRefresh" type="button" value="Refresh" onclick="javascript:LoadPages();"/>

</p>
```

5. Press F12 to launch the default.aspx page in your web browser (see Figure 10-10).

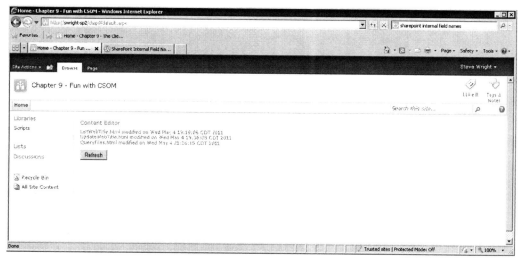

*Figure 10-10. Home page with query results*

When this script runs, the LoadPages method creates a CamlQuery object that defines the data that you want to retrieve. This is represented by a CAML view definition. In this case, you specify that you want only the ID, FileLeafRef, and Modified fields for up to 50 items. You then use the query to retrieve items from the Scripts document library.

```
    var qry = new SP.CamlQuery();
    qry .set_viewXml(
        "<View>"
        + "<ViewFields><FieldRef Name='ID' /><FieldRef Name='FileLeafRef' /><FieldRef
Name='Modified' /></ViewFields>"
        + "<RowLimit>50</RowLimit>"
        + "</View>");
```

```
itemCollection = list.getItems(qry);

ctx.load(itemCollection);
```

---

■ **Warning** You may have noticed that one of the fields listed in this query is called `FileLeafRef`. Unfortunately, SharePoint fields have two different names: display names and internal names. The display name for a field is the one you see on your web site. The internal field name is used…well…internally. CAML uses internal field names in its queries. `FileLeafRef` is the internal name for the Name column in a document library. There is no rhyme or reason to the internal names in many cases. For example, the `Modified` field is called Editor. The Web provides several lists of mappings from display to internal names. Here is one that I use:

```
http://sharepointmalarkey.wordpress.com/2008/08/21/sharepoint-internal-field-names
```

---

When the query completes, the data returned is placed into a collection of objects that can be enumerated and used to access the data returned, as shown here:

```
var itemEnumerator = itemCollection.getEnumerator();
while (itemEnumerator.moveNext())
{
    var item = itemEnumerator.get_current();

    s = s + item.get_item('FileLeafRef')
          + ' modified on ' + item.get_item('Modified') + "<br />";
}
```

CAML queries in SharePoint can do more than just return a certain number of items. They can include a <query> tag that allows the criteria for filtering items to be extensive. A CAML query can also be used to sort the returned items. This gives CAML a level of flexibility similar to that seen in SQL.

## Summary

In this chapter, you have

- Explored the various client-side object models exposed by the SharePoint `Client.svc` service

- Discussed the best practices for writing ECMAScript client-side code that leverages the client object model

- Considered why running code on the client may be preferable to running it on the server in some cases

- Examined the client object model code for loading, updating, and querying SharePoint objects

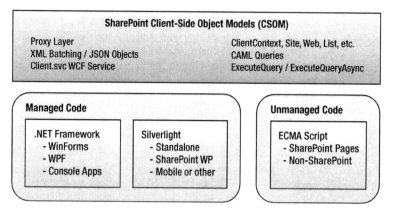

*Figure 10-11. SharePoint client object model concepts*

# CHAPTER 11

# SharePoint and Windows Phone 7 Development

The introduction of the Windows Phone 7 mobile platform is a significant step forward from the more business-focused Windows Mobile 6.5 platform. Windows Phone 7 is a consumer-focused, marketplace-driven environment where the specifications, design, and capabilities are tightly controlled by Microsoft. Microsoft's goal for Windows Phone 7 is to enable developers to create applications using tools common to the rest of the .NET platform like Visual Studio 2010, Silverlight, and XNA.

This chapter will explore how to create Windows Phone 7 applications that can access SharePoint list data and web services. You'll learn how to create a SharePoint Web application that can be accessed with a Windows Phone and then you'll explore how to authenticate your application. Finally, you'll explore the various SharePoint web services available and look at techniques for working with SharePoint data.

---

**Note** The information and coding practices presented in this chapter are based on the "NoDo" version of Windows Phone 7 OS (7.0.7390661.0). The code has been compiled and verified on the beta version code name "Mango." Microsoft is dedicated to continuous improvement of the platform so it is likely that the specific code samples may require minor changes in subsequent versions. The concepts and practices will remain valid for SharePoint 2010.

---

This chapter will cover the following:

- An introduction to Windows Phone 7

- Setting up the development environment

- SharePoint and Windows Phone 7 security

- SharePoint data access concepts

- Code examples for accessing SharePoint from Windows Phone 7

# Introduction

The demand for mobile applications has grown year after year. Mobile applications provide a broad range of functionality from games to sophisticated remote sensing and augmented reality applications. This chapter covers the uses of Windows Phone apps to access business information in a SharePoint farm. The goals of business applications range widely depending on the needs of the business. Recent statistics show that over 60% of smart phone purchases are being made by individuals in order to access corporate information. As the number of mobile devices grows, so too will the demand for mobile applications to facilitate the access to corporate information. The benefit of the portability of mobile devices is that they are readily available, connected, and don't have to "boot up". This means that the user can gain immediate access and respond to requests in a timely manner, rather than waiting "until they get back to work." Even in the absence of a connection, it is possible to craft applications that store data locally on mobile devices. This provides a better model for network bandwidth consumption as the network is only required if the cached information becomes stale or needs to be updated for other reasons. Lastly, rather than providing extensive access to a corporate portal, and requiring the user to browse for their information, a mobile app can be crafted to pull only the data required by the user (for example, assigned tasks), thereby decreasing the network bandwidth required to service the user's request.

Windows Phone 7 is Microsoft's latest mobile operating system. The minimum development environment required for creating applications for Windows Phone 7 is Visual Studio Express with the Windows Phone Developer Tools. Professional developers who want to create robust applications, test the applications, and work in a team environment like that provided by Microsoft Team Foundation Server will want to use Microsoft Visual Studio 2010 (Professional, Premium, or Ultimate) and install the Windows Phone Developer Tools. While Visual Studio can be used to develop the application user interface in XAML, Microsoft Expression Blend is the best tool to design and edit the user interface of a Windows Phone 7 application. It is worth noting that although this chapter will focus on Silverlight, you can also choose to create applications using the XNA Framework.

One of the most significant changes to the mobile offering from Microsoft is the Windows Phone 7 Marketplace. The Marketplace is a single location for all phone-related content for prospective try-ers and buyers. The Marketplace offers a robust search and shopping interface for developers to sell their apps and buyers to find the apps they seek. The platform offers a Trial API that enables developers to offer free trials of apps that can be unlocked upon purchase to reveal their full functionality.

Although developers can deploy applications (and games) directly to their personal registered phones, the general public will only be able to install your published application from the Windows Phone Marketplace. In order for developers to publish their applications to the marketplace, the application has to be submitted for approval. The application is submitted along with all of the required data that accompanies the application, such as the title, description, and screen shots. The application is then tested and validated against the criteria for the marketplace by Microsoft. Finally, the application is signed and made available for download.

## Windows Phone and SharePoint

The goal of this chapter is to prepare you with real world examples that demonstrate how to connect to and consume information stored in SharePoint with custom mobile applications that you write with Visual Studio 2010. You can use a Windows Phone browser to access SharePoint sites. It's important to note that Windows Phone is delivered with a native application that can perform some of these functions. Called the "Office Hub" (Figure 11-1), this application can connect to SharePoint and navigate sites and libraries and open Microsoft Office Documents like Word and PowerPoint.

*Figure 11-1. The Windows Phone 7 Office Hub*

When you decide to create a custom application you have to decide how you are going to securely access the information. Windows Phone does not currently support NTLM authentication in custom applications, so alternate authentication approaches may be required on the SharePoint server to provide secure access to your application. In this chapter we will use Forms Based Authentication in our samples. The next step is to determine what data you want to get from SharePoint. If you are accessing lists and libraries you may choose to use ODATA or REST. The current version of the SharePoint Silverlight Client Object Model assembly is not compatible with Windows Phone Development. For SharePoint content that can't be accessed through those means you may need to use one of the many SharePoint web services. At the extreme end of the spectrum where you are consolidating information from many sources or accessing resources and data provided by Azure, you may choose to write custom services to run in parallel with your SharePoint environment and connect to those services with your phone.

This is an exciting time to be a developer. With the introduction of Windows Phone 7, .NET developers have the tools and resources available to create, test, deploy, and sell stunning applications using the same familiar tools that you have been using for years. You don't need to learn a new language, you just need to learn how the platform works in order to start building applications in Silverlight or the XNA Framework. We have a lot to teach you in this chapter: you will learn to access lists and then dive into connecting to SharePoint Web Services. We hope this will help get you started building applications that can improve your business. The first step in building Windows Phone 7 and SharePoint 2010 applications is to set up a development environment.

# Development Environment

To develop Windows Phone 7 applications for SharePoint you will need a development environment that includes Windows 7, the Windows Phone Developer Tools, and access to a SharePoint 2010 server instance. The Windows Phone Developer Tools add support to Visual Studio 2010 to create Windows Phone Applications (see Figure 11-2). The current version of Windows Phone Developer Tools is only supported in a Windows 7 environment. If you normally develop SharePoint applications on a Windows Server 2008 machine you will need to have access to a Windows 7 machine to use the Windows Phone 7 Developer tools. You can't add the Windows Phone Developer Tools to a server operating system.

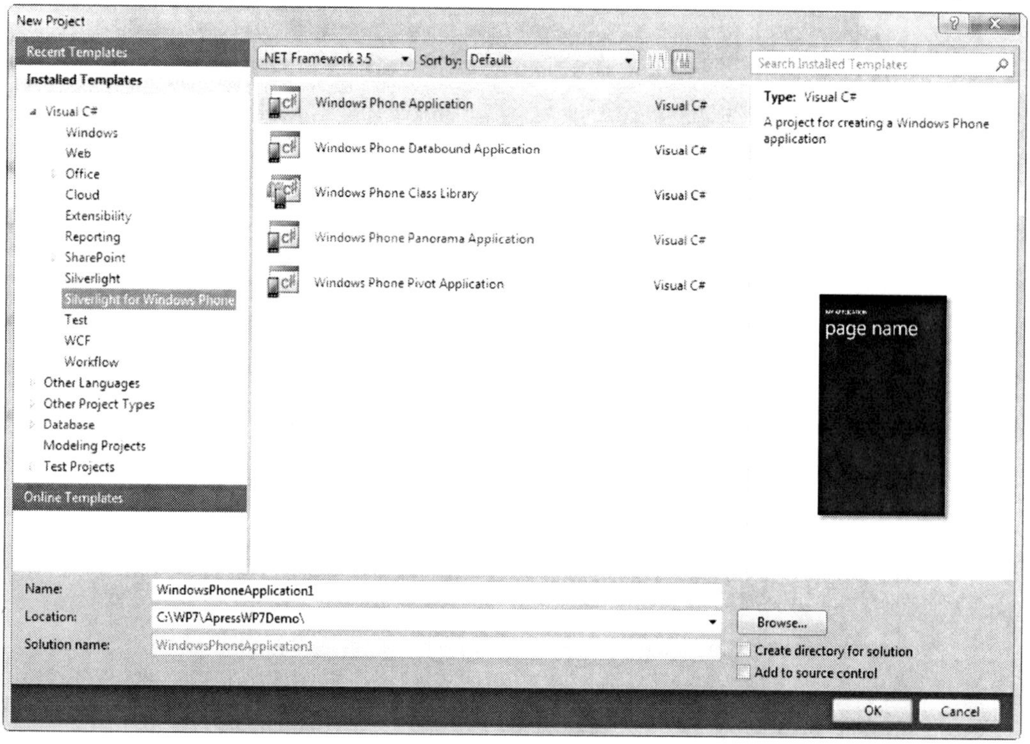

*Figure 11-2. Windows Phone 7 projects in Visual Studio 2010*

## Developing on Windows 7 with SharePoint

The simplest way to start developing Windows Phone 7 applications using SharePoint 2010 is to setup a 64-bit Windows 7 development environment that includes both SharePoint 2010 and Windows Phone Developer Tools. SharePoint 2010 can be installed onto the 64-bit version of Windows 7 in a development-only scenario.

A development environment can be created from a clean Windows 7 x64 client machine. Windows 7 can be either installed as the main operating system on "bare metal" or it can be installed using boot to VHD. Either method is supported.

With a clean and fully service-packed Windows 7 machine, the next step is to install SharePoint 2010. SharePoint Foundation or SharePoint Server (any version) can be installed on 64-bit Windows 7 as a development machine. SharePoint 2010 running on a Windows 7 client is not supported in a production environment. Installing SharePoint 2010 on a Windows 7 client is outside the scope of this chapter. Refer to "Setting Up the Development Environment for SharePoint 2010 on Windows Vista, Windows 7, and Windows Server 2008" currently located at http://msdn.microsoft.com/en-us/library/ee554869(office.14).aspx for installation guidelines. You can also review the SharePoint 2010 and Windows Phone 7 Training Course available from Microsoft. This training course includes a lab to set up a Windows 7 development environment with SharePoint 2010 and the Windows Phone development tools (http://msdn.microsoft.com/en-us/SharePointAndWindowsPhone7TrainingCourse). After SharePoint 2010 has been installed and configured on the Windows 7 client, install Visual Studio 2010. Any version of Visual Studio 2010 should work for these examples.

Next, download and install the Windows Phone 7 Developer Tools. The current version of the developer tools are located in the App Hub, a center focused around Xbox 360 and Windows Phone 7 development. The App Hub is currently located at http://create.msdn.com, as shown in Figure 11-3.

*Figure 11-3. Developer tools located in the App Hub*

The Windows Phone 7 Developer Tools include an update and a fix. First, download and install the January 2011 update located at: http://download.microsoft.com/download/1/7/7/177D6AF8-17FA-40E7-AB53-00B7CED31729/vm_web.exe. Then, the single fix required should be downloaded and installed. The fix is located at http://download.microsoft.com/download/6/D/6/6D66958D-891B-4C0E-BC32-2DFC41917B11/WindowsPhoneDeveloperResources_en-US_Patch1.msp.

There are many tools and toolkits available for Windows Phone 7 development. The code in this chapter does not require any other tools or toolkits. You should look at the Windows Phone 7 developer landscape and find tools that will help you be more efficient with your Windows Phone 7 application development.

# Developing on Microsoft Hyper-V

Many developers are creating virtual environments with Microsoft Windows Server 2008 R2 Hyper-V. If you are considering Hyper-V and want to test the waters with SharePoint Development, you can save yourself a lot of time by downloading the 2010 Information Worker Demonstration and Evaluation Virtual Machine from Microsoft (http://go.microsoft.com/?linkid=9728417). Once you download the virtual machine, install the server into an existing Hyper-V environment and test the networking configuration.

The Windows Phone 7 emulator is a virtual environment and it's not compatible with Windows Server 2008 R2 running the Hyper-V role. There is a trick to getting around this problem, though. Don't install the tools on the server (or any 64-bit server); instead, create a new virtual machine using Windows 7 32-bit. It's important to use the 32-bit version of the Windows 7 for this installation. Once you have installed and updated Windows 7, you can proceed by installing Visual Studio 2010 and the Windows Phone 7 Tools as usual. The advantage to this configuration is that your Windows Phone 7 emulator will use the local test network for all connections and have no issues connecting to the SharePoint Farm.

Regardless of the development environment you create, you will need to understand the available authentication options to access SharePoint 2010 data or services from your phone application. The next section briefly reviews the authentication options.

# Security

Security is a broad topic covering authentication, authorization, cross site access, and even the sandbox that prevents applications from accessing other application data. In this section, we will briefly discuss authentication. Windows Phone 7 is a new development platform. Accessing remote data as a known user can be challenging in the first version of Windows Phone 7. Authentication strategies can also decide your choice for SharePoint remote API access. Not all of the SharePoint remote APIs support the authentication methods supported by the platform.

## Windows Authentication

Developers and end users alike love Windows authentication. The ability to pass user credentials seamlessly in the background provides a great user experience. In fact, .NET developers, including SharePoint developers, love the simplicity of authentication where the client and the server can pass credentials using Windows authentication. Many SharePoint Web applications, particularly intranets, use Windows authentication.

While Windows authentication is what you expect as a SharePoint developer, it is not what you get as a Windows Phone developer. The current version of Windows Phone 7 at the time of this writing doesn't support Windows Authentication. This means that a Windows Phone 7 application can't authenticate to any SharePoint Web application that is using Classic mode authentication (NTLM or Basic). Unified Access Gateway can provide some relief in this area by acting as a gatekeeper who can request users' credentials via a form and subsequently creating and presenting a Windows user to SharePoint.

## Forms Based Authentication

Forms Based Authentication (FBA) is a common authentication scenario. SharePoint 2010 web applications can be set to Claims mode, which allows users and applications to authenticate using FBA. Currently FBA is one of the most common means to access secured data from a SharePoint server using a mobile client. Windows Phone 7 can easily use most SharePoint 2010 remote APIs using FBA authentication.

SharePoint 2010 provides the authentication web service that can be used to authenticate a user using the user's account and password. The authentication web service returns a FEDAUTH cookie in the response header when a user's credentials are successfully validated. The FEDAUTH cookie is used by SharePoint on subsequent calls to verify the user has been authenticated. An interesting point about the cookie: it is an HTTPOnly cookie and can't be viewed or worked with using code in the Windows Phone 7 framework. Effectively, it is a cookie that you need but can't easily access.

---

■ **Note** The beta Windows Phone 7 "Mango" version will allow access to HTTP-only cookies.

---

Fortunately there is a way to work around the limitation of the HTTPOnly FEDAUTH cookie. This involves retrieving the container that includes the HTTPOnly FEDAUTH cookie and attaching the container to subsequent calls to SharePoint. The container for the cookie is a CookieContainer.

After the initial call to the Authentication Web service, the CookieContainer containing the HTTPOnly FEDAUTH cookie is stored for later use. In each subsequent call to SharePoint (for example, to query a list), the CookieContainer is attached to the web request, and the user can query the list (assuming the user has permissions to the specific list). This pattern works great for most SharePoint remote APIs. For example, a web service proxy created by Visual Studio exposes the CookieContainer attached to the web request. It is simple to attach your CookieContainer to the web request via the FEDAUTH cookie. This authentication pattern will work as long as you can attach the CookieContainer to the request. Listing 11-1 shows an example of attaching a CookieContainer to the CookieContainer property of a web service proxy object created by Visual Studio.

*Listing 11-1. Attaching a CookieContainer to a Web Service Proxy Object*

```
ListsSoapClient svc = new ListsSoapClient();
svc.CookieContainer = App.Cookies;
svc.GetListItemsCompleted += new
                EventHandler<GetListItemsCompletedEventArgs>
                            (svc_GetListItemsCompleted);
svc.GetListItemsAsync("MyLinks", string.Empty, null,
                            viewFields, null, null, null);
```

Not every web request exposes a CookieContainer property. Two common examples where you will not be able to attach a CookieContainer is when using a WebClient object or a Visual Studio proxy generated for a Rest API. Neither of these examples exposes a CookieContainer property when working with the phone framework. This simply means that you should replace the WebClient object with an HttpWebRequest object and manually create REST calls using an HttpWebRequest object and an XML payload. This creates more code and injects more possible errors but does allow you to use FBA in these scenarios.

## Anonymous Access

We have covered the two common authentication scenarios—NTLM and FBA. Now we must discuss anonymous access. SharePoint can support anonymous access to a SharePoint site and list data. Anonymous access must be enabled and configured on the SharePoint Web application and site collection. It is not hard to think of many scenarios where a phone application accessing anonymous data would make sense. For example, consider an application retrieving events or consuming images from a public-facing SharePoint site where the events or images are available to the general public.

Unfortunately, there is little in the way of support for anonymous access to SharePoint using a mobile device. Currently, there are no SharePoint APIs supported on the current Windows Phone 7 platform that can access SharePoint anonymously—with the exception of RSS feeds. If an RSS feed does not fit the data integration requirements (for example, you need to read and write list data), then you must consider a custom application. SharePoint provides RSS feeds out of the box. A creative developer could use an RSS feed to access list data. The "Data Access" section later in this chapter discusses the use of RSS feeds and custom applications

## Unified Access Gateway

Microsoft Forefront Unified Access Gateway (UAG) is a product that provides remote client endpoints to access enterprise applications like SharePoint 2010. UAG "publishes" applications via a web portal, enabling users access to corporate applications through a secure endpoint that can validate the security of the client and network connection. If you are planning to use UAG to publish your SharePoint site for mobile applications, you have to consider how UAG performs authentication and request redirection.

---

**Note** Installing and configuring UAG is beyond the scope of this chapter. You can refer to the whitepaper "Building Windows Phone 7 applications with SharePoint 2010 Products and Unified Access Gateway" (http://go.microsoft.com/fwlink/?LinkId=216118) This paper describes how to set up networking and install and configure a UAG server to publish a SharePoint web site for Windows Phone 7 development.

---

When a SharePoint site is published through UAG, requests for SharePoint resources that don't contain an authorization header are redirected based on the endpoint configuration in UAG. This redirection can cause issues when your application is expecting a specific response from SharePoint and must be accounted for in your code. In general, your application should prompt for, encrypt, and store user's credentials prior to making any requests that require authorization. With UAG, the web request should be made over HTTPS and passed, as in Listing 11-2. The important points in this technique are the construction of the authorization header as a Base64 encoded string and the use of the User Agent string "Microsoft Office Mobile". Construction of the request in this way will notify UAG who the user is and prevent default mobile redirection from interfering with your application. For example, in Listing 11-2 a request to the SharePoint User Profile Web service "ups" is modified by setting the Request Authorization header to work with UAG.

*Listing 11-2. Passing Authorization Header to UAG*

```
using (OperationContextScope scope = new ↵
       OperationContextScope(ups.InnerChannel))
{
  //Create the Request Message Property
  HttpRequestMessageProperty request = new HttpRequestMessageProperty();
  //Set the Authorization Header
  request.Headers[System.Net.HttpRequestHeader.Authorization] =  "Basic " + ↵
    Convert.ToBase64String(Encoding.UTF8.GetBytes(AppSettings.Username + ↵
    ":" + AppSettings.Password)) + System.Environment.NewLine;

  //Set the User Agent header
  request.Headers[System.Net.HttpRequestHeader.UserAgent] = ↵
    "Microsoft Office Mobile";
```

```
//Add the headers to the request
OperationContext.Current.OutgoingMessageProperties.Add(↵
  HttpRequestMessageProperty.Name, request);

//Call the method
ups.GetUserColleaguesAsync(account);
}
```

Now that you have an understanding that authentication in the current phone framework is limited to FBA and Anonymous access unless UAG is included in the solution, you should now consider the various data access methods. The next section will provide a basic understanding of the avaiable data access methods that can be used by a Windows Phone 7 application to work with SharePoint 2010 data and services.

# Data Access

SharePoint 2010 provides many APIs to query SharePoint data. Most of the SharePoint remote APIs such as web services and Rest APIs can be used from a Windows Phone 7 application to integrate with SharePoint data and services. It is not just the remote API that you need to consider when selecting a method to access SharePoint data but the authentication scenario that will be used with the data access. Not all data access methods are available or easy to use with all authentication scenarios. As discussed in the previous section, none of the data access options work with Windows authentication because the current phone platform doesn't support Windows authentication.

## Web Services

Web services are one of the most common methods you will use with the Windows Phone 7 platform to work with SharePoint data. Web services have the most coverage of SharePoint data and services available to the phone platform and can be used with the most authentication scenarios, including FBA. Web services cover data access from lists and libraries with the Lists.asmx web service to working with key services including the User Profile Service using the UserProfileService web service. Table 11-1 lists the web services available in SharePoint 2010.

*Table 11-1. SharePoint Web Services*

| Service Name | Description |
| --- | --- |
| Admin.asmx | Management of deployment including creating sites. |
| Alerts.asmx | Works with alerts including listing and deleting subscriptions. |
| Authentication.asmx | Authenticating to a FBA SharePoint site |
| BDCAdminService.svc | Management of BCD models in BCS. |
| Copy.asmx | Supports copying files within or between sites. |
| Diagnostics.asmx | Logging of diagnostic information. |

| Service Name | Description |
| --- | --- |
| Forms.asmx | Returns forms used when working with list content. |
| Imaging.asmx | Creates and manages pictures in a picture library. |
| Lists.asmx | Work with lists and list data. |
| Meetings.asmx | Creates and manages Meeting Workspace sites. |
| People.asmx | Service to find a person's SharePoint identification. |
| Permissions.asmx | Works with permissions for a site or list. |
| SiteData.asmx | Returns site metadata and list data. |
| Sites.asmx | Returns information about site collections. |
| SPSearch.asmx | Searches access to a SharePoint site. |
| UserGroup.asmx | Management of users, role definitions, and groups. |
| Versions.asmx | Management of file versions. |
| Views.asmx | Management of list views. |
| Webs.asmx | Methods for working with sites and subwebs. |

Table 11-1 does not include every service available in SharePoint but those listed are the most common web services. The SharePoint web services cover most, but not all, of the SharePoint API.

Calling a SharePoint Web Service from the phone platform is similar to calling the same service from a Silverlight client. All communication is asynchronous. Visual Studio will create asynchronous method calls in the proxy classes to call the service methods. Listing 11-3 shows an example of retrieving items from a list using the Lists.asmx web service. Notice in Listing 11-3 that we attach the CookieContainer to the proxy object. This allows for FBA authentication.

*Listing 11-3. Retrieving List Items from a List Using the Lists.asmx Web Service*

```
public void LoadMyLinks()
{
  XElement viewFields = new XElement("ViewFields",
                          new XElement("FieldRef",
                              new XAttribute("Name", "ows_URL")));

  ListsSoapClient svc = new ListsSoapClient();
  svc.CookieContainer = App.Cookies;
  svc.GetListItemsCompleted += new
                      EventHandler<GetListItemsCompletedEventArgs>
```

```
                  (svc_GetListItemsCompleted);
    svc.GetListItemsAsync("MyLinks", string.Empty, null,
                                viewFields, null, null, null);
}

void svc_GetListItemsCompleted(object sender, GetListItemsCompletedEventArgs e)
{

    IEnumerable<XElement> rows = e.Result.Descendants
                                (XName.Get("row", "#RowsetSchema"));
    var myLinks = from element in rows
                  select new Link(
                               (int)element.Attribute("ows_ID"),
                                (string)element.Attribute("ows_URL")
                                );

}
```

# Client Side Object Model (CSOM)

CSOM is rapidly becoming popular with SharePoint developers as a remote API of choice. CSOM provides coverage of the core server functionality when compared to other remote APIs and it is packaged into three different implementations (.NET, JavaScript and Silverlight). Unfortunately, the current version of SharePoint Client Site Object Model is not supported on the Windows 7 Phone platform.

# REST/ODATA

That leads us to REST and ODATA. When used with a service proxy created by Visual Studio, REST data access is simple. SharePoint 2010 provides REST-based data access using the ListData.svc service. This is a Windows Communication Foundation service. REST is an HTTP-based protocol where data access is accomplished using standard HTTP with an XML payload.

The SharePoint REST interface exposes list data from a URL address as XML making it easy to consume for read operations. To view all lists in a site you simply call the ListData.svc directly. For example, to display all the lists in the DemoFBA site, use the following URL:

```
http://demofba/_vti_bin/Listdata.svc.
```
To display a single list in the site, the list title is added to the URL, like so:

```
http://demofba/_vti_bin/Listdata.svc/contacts.
```
The ListData service can do inserts, updates, and deletes, as well as reads. To perform these operations, a complex XML payload must be sent with the correct HTTP verb. This XML can be generated by hand or through code. Code generation is generally left to the DataSvcUtil application to generate the proxy classes. When used with UAG the proxy classes can easily manage the inserts, updates, and deletes. When used with FBA, the proxy can't be used as it doesn't expose the CookieContainer property. The only other option is to create the HTTPWebRequest object and the XML payload manually. Manually creating the code and XML payload for inserts, updates, and deletes is not a simple task. For this current version of the phone platform you might consider avoiding REST-based access when using inserts, updates, and deletes unless your solution includes UAG. Generating a query using the URL syntax and an HTTPWebRequest object is simple enough to do without a proxy object but inserts, updates, and deletes are complex.

## RSS

The last out-of-the-box SharePoint remote API we will discuss is RSS feeds. RSS is the one data access method that everyone seems to forget about. One thinks of RSS feeds as being consumed by end-user RSS feed readers, forgetting that RSS is structured data that can be parsed and processed. SharePoint RSS feeds are the only out-of-the-box method for accessing data anonymously.

RSS is probably not the best solution for working with SharePoint data when presented with other remote API options. First, RSS feeds are read-only. You can't insert, update, or delete items using an RSS feed. Next, there are no proxy objects that can be created to simplify development. The .NET Framework does have a Syndication library that can be used to parse ATOM and RSS feeds but it doesn't equal a rich proxy object created by Visual Studio when working with a web service. The Syndication library doesn't produce strongly typed objects like a service proxy object. The final reason why RSS is not the best solution for data access is that outside of the common fields in RSS (title and link), any other list fields you make available in the feed are formatted HTML and not XML, which is difficult to parse at best. Even though RSS feeds look like they should be avoided when accessing data from SharePoint, RSS feeds could fill a need when anonymous access is required.

## Custom SharePoint Applications

We covered all the major Remote APIs for SharePoint. The last data access method to consider is a custom SharePoint application. A custom SharePoint application has the least amount of limitations but potentially requires the most amount of work. Custom SharePoint applications also require a server-side component. A mobile solution that requires a server-side component means that a user can't simply add the application from the marketplace to their phone. Before the application can work, the server-side solution must be installed and configured. There is no support in the marketplace to download or install a server-side component of a phone application. The server-side component must be obtained outside of the Marketplace.

In some scenarios, a custom SharePoint application does make sense or is the only solution that solves the authentication and data needs. Consider a scenario for a corporation that creates a phone application to retrieve data from a list located on a public-facing SharePoint site. The list allows for anonymous access to the data. The only out-of-the-box method to anonymously access this data from a phone application is the list's RSS feed. Unfortunately, the RSS feed is difficult to parse when it contains columns other than common RSS feed elements such as title and author. Additional columns are formatted not as XML but as HTML.

## Accessing your SharePoint Data

Now you should have a basic understanding of all the main points to start creating a Windows Phone 7 and SharePoint 2010 application. In this section, you will put it all together and create two Windows Phone 7 and SharePoint 2010 applications.

The first application will demonstrate how to access SharePoint list data—one of the most common integrations between a Windows Phone 7 application and SharePoint 2010. This application will demonstrate how to work with a SharePoint links list.

The second application will demonstrate how to access non-list data using the User Profile Service. This application will demonstrate how to view the current user's profile and colleagues in a Windows Phone 7 application. Working with users profiles are another common integration point for Windows Phone 7 and SharePoint. Note that these examples use FBA security and assume that you have created a SharePoint Web application that uses FBA.

# Working with List Data

Accessing list data is one of the most common tasks a SharePoint developer will do. Lists are the main data source for almost any SharePoint implementation. As a developer, you can create Windows Phone 7 applications that read and write data to a list. Beyond reading and writing to a list, your application can also create and delete lists as well as change list schemas.

In this section, you will learn how to read and write data to an existing SharePoint list. In order to access data in a SharePoint list, you will need to learn how to authenticate to SharePoint using the Authentication Web Service and query a list using the Lists.asmx Web Service. You will also learn how to use Lists.asmx Web Service to add data to a SharePoint list.

This example creates a Windows Phone 7 application that reads and writes links from an existing SharePoint links list. The patterns presented in this application can be used for any SharePoint list template. This example demonstrates how to use the Authentication.asmx Web service to authenticate to SharePoint and how to use theLists.asmx Web service to read and write list data in a Windows Phone 7.

The steps are as follows:

1. Create a Link model class. This class will contain the data retrieved from the SharePoint links list.

2. Add a service reference to the Lists Web Service. The service reference will create a proxy class that contains all the necessary code for working with the methods and objects defined by the Lists Web Service.

3. Create a ViewModel for the links and populate a collection of links. The ViewModel contains the collection of Link model objects that will be bound to the user interface controls.

4. Create a ViewModel to add new links to the SharePoint list. This ViewModel is bound to the user interface that will add a new link to the SharePoint list.

5. Databind a list to the collection of links. This will display the links retrieved from the SharePoint list.

---

■ **Note** In order to complete this demo you will need to have access to a FBA-enabled SharePoint web application. You will also need to have access to a SharePoint links list located in a site in the web application.

---

## Open the Apress.SharePoint.WP7.MyLinks Solution

The full source code for the MyLinks application is included with the book's source code. The application is too large to expect you to type each line of code to recreate it. This example covers the main SharePoint and Windows Phone 7 interaction points.

1. Locate the Apress.SharePoint.WP7.MyLinks solution from the start folder.

2. Open the Apress.SharePoint.WP7.MyLinks solution.

## Modify the Application Constants

The Constants.cs file contains a list of values used in this application. You will need to provide the correct values for your environment.

1. In Visual Studio, expand the Utilities folder in the project. Open the Constants.cs file.

2. Modify the AUTHENTICATION_SERVICE_URL value to include the site that contains the links list.

3. Example:

```
public const string AUTHENTICATION_SERVICE_URL =
"http://fbaDemo/_vti_bin/authentication.asmx";
```

4. Modify the MYLINKS_LIST_TITLE value to include the title of the links list that will contain your links.

## Complete the Link Class

The Link model is a model class that contains the basic properties and methods for a link object. This is a representation of the SharePoint link in the link list.

1. In Visual Studio, right click the Models folder and open the Link.cs file.

2. Copy the code in Listing 11-4 into the *Link* class definition.

*Listing 11-4. The Link Model Class*

```
private int id;
public int Id
{
  get
  { return id; }
  set
  {
    id = value;
    NotifyPropertyChanged("Id");
  }
}

private string hyperLink;
public string HyperLink
{
  get { return hyperLink; }
  set
  {
    hyperLink = value;
    NotifyPropertyChanged("HyperLink");
  }
}
```

```
private string title;
public string Title
{
  get { return title; }
  set
  {
    title = value;
    NotifyPropertyChanged("Title");
  }
}

public Link() { }

public Link(int id, string SPLinkValue)
{
  Id = id;
  string[] split = SPLinkValue.Split(',');

  HyperLink = split[0];
  Title = split[1];
}

public static string BuildSPLink(string title, string url)
{
  return string.Format("{0}, {1}", url, title);
}
```

This model is a data container for the application. Each link retrieved from a SharePoint list will result in one instance of the link model class. The link model class implements the INotifyPropertyChanged interface. The INotifyPropertyChanged interface works with the user interface data binding. It, along with the calls to the NotifiedPropertyChanged method, notifies any bound objects of a change to the data, allowing the data bound object to rebind and display the new data. This call also implements a simple static method BuildSPLInk that will create the correct format for the link before saving to the SharePoint list.

## Add a service reference For the Lists.Asmx Web Service

In this example you will use SharePoint's Lists.asmx Web Service to retrieve the list data. You will also configure the service to enable CookieContainers. CookieContainers are used to attach the authentication cookie for FBA.

1. In Visual Studio, right click on the Service References folder and choose Add Service Reference.

2. In the Add Service Reference dialog, enter the address of the Lists.asmx web service, such as http://fbaDemo/_vti_bin/lists.asmx.

3. Click Go and wait for Visual Studio to populate the list of services.

4. Once the Lists service appears in the Services section, enter ListSvc for the Namespace value. The complete dialog should look like Figure 11-4.

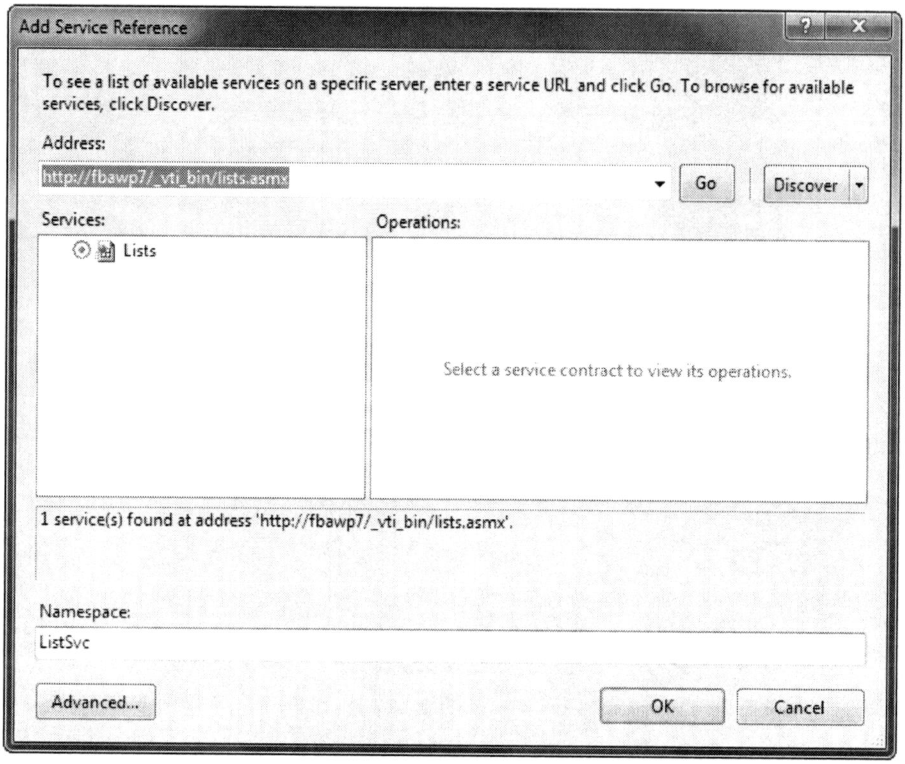

*Figure 11-4. The Add Service Reference dialog*

5. Click OK to create the proxy for the Lists Web Service.

6. You will see the new ListSvc reference added to your project, as shown in Figure 11-5.

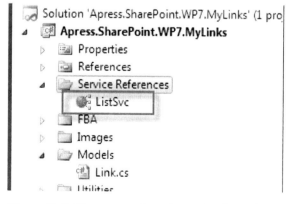

*Figure 11-5. The new service reference in the project*

7. Open the `ServiceReferences.ClientConfig` file and locate the binding ListSoap and add the enableHttpCookieContainer="true" attribute to support FBA, as shown in Figure 11-6.

```
<configuration>
    <system.serviceModel>
        <bindings>
            <basicHttpBinding>
                <binding name="ListsSoap" enableHttpCookieContainer ="true" maxBufferSize="21474
                    <security mode="None" />
                </binding>
```

*Figure 11-6. Setting enableHttpCookieContainer value*

The enableHttpCookieContainer attribute is required to use FBA for SharePoint authentication in a Windows Phone 7 application. Enabling this attribute allows the code to access the CookieContainer, which will have the FEDAUTH cookie you need to access to SharePoint data and services. After the attribute is added to the binding element you will not be able to edit or remove the service reference until you manually remove the enableHttpCookieContainer attribute.

## Add a Static Property to Store the FBA CookieContainer

1. In Visual Studio, right click the `App.xaml` class and select View Code.

2. Scroll to the end of the file and add the definition for the Cookies property:

```
public static CookieContainer Cookies { get; set; }
```

The Cookies property is a static property available anywhere in the application. This property stores the CookieContainer that is returned from the SharePoint Authentication Web service. The CookieContainer is passed into SharePoint on subsequent remote method calls.

## Review and Finalize Authentication code

This example uses the Authentication SharePoint Web Service to authorize remote users. The authentication code calls the Authentication Web Service, passing in the user's login name and password. The result is a success or failure response from the web service. If the authentication call is successful then the CookieContainer that includes the authentication cookie is stored in the `App.xaml`'s Cookies property.

In this example, the code used to authenticate a user with SharePoint using FBA is located in the FBA class. The authentication code is responsible for submitting the user's credentials to the SharePoint Authentication web service and providing the caller with the CookieContainer containing the FEDAUTH cookie. The authentication code defines two events to notify the client of success or failure. Listing 11-5 displays the methods used to authenticate a user with SharePoint. Notice that the web service call is asynchronous. Silverlight only supports asynchronous communication with external services.

*Listing 11-5. Authentication Code*

```
public void Authenticate(string userId, string pwd, string authServiceURL)
{
    System.Uri authServiceUri = new Uri(authServiceURL);
    AuthHTTPWebRequest authRequest = new AuthHTTPWebRequest();
```

```
    HttpWebRequest spAuthReq = HttpWebRequest.Create(authServiceURL) as HttpWebRequest;
    authRequest.req = spAuthReq;
    authRequest.req.CookieContainer = cookieJar;
    authRequest.req.Headers["SOAPAction"] =
"http://schemas.microsoft.com/sharepoint/soap/Login";
    authRequest.req.ContentType = "text/xml; charset=utf-8";
    authRequest.req.Method = "POST";
    authRequest.userId = userId;
    authRequest.pwd = pwd;

    authRequest.req.BeginGetRequestStream(new AsyncCallback(AuthReqCallBack), authRequest);
}

private void AuthReqCallBack(IAsyncResult asyncResult)
{
    string envelope =
    @"<?xml version=""1.0"" encoding=""utf-8""?>
        <soap:Envelope xmlns:xsi=""http://www.w3.org/2001/XMLSchema-instance""
                xmlns:xsd=""http://www.w3.org/2001/XMLSchema""
                xmlns:soap=""http://schemas.xmlsoap.org/soap/envelope/"">
            <soap:Body>
                <Login xmlns=""http://schemas.microsoft.com/sharepoint/soap/"">
                    <username>{0}</username>
                    <password>{1}</password>
                </Login>
            </soap:Body>
        </soap:Envelope>";

    UTF8Encoding encoding = new UTF8Encoding();
    AuthHTTPWebRequest request = (AuthHTTPWebRequest)asyncResult.AsyncState;
    Stream _body = request.req.EndGetRequestStream(asyncResult);
    envelope = string.Format(envelope, request.userId, request.pwd);
    byte[] formBytes = encoding.GetBytes(envelope);

    _body.Write(formBytes, 0, formBytes.Length);
    _body.Close();

    request.req.BeginGetResponse(new AsyncCallback(AuthCallback), request);
}
```

To finalize the code to authenticate the user via FBA, the AuthCallback method must be completed. This method looks at the authentication call result and raises the appropriate success or failure event to the caller.

1. In Visual Studio, right click the FBA folder, and open the FBA.cs file.

2. Copy the code in Listing 11-6 into the AuthCallback method located in the FBA class.

*Listing 11-6. The AuthCallback Event Code*

```
string authResult = "";
```

```
AuthHTTPWebRequest request = (AuthHTTPWebRequest)asyncResult.AsyncState;
HttpWebResponse response =
                       (HttpWebResponse)request.req.EndGetResponse(asyncResult);
Stream responseStream = response.GetResponseStream();

if (request != null && response != null)
{
  if (response.StatusCode == HttpStatusCode.OK)
  {
    XElement results = XElement.Load(responseStream);
    XNamespace n = "http://schemas.microsoft.com/sharepoint/soap/";

    var r = from result in results.Descendants(n + "ErrorCode")
            select result.Value;

    authResult = r.ToList().FirstOrDefault<String>();
  }
}

if (authResult == "NoError")
{
  EventHandler<FBAAuthenticatedEventArgs> authenticated = OnAuthenticated;
  if (authenticated != null)
  { authenticated(this, new FBAAuthenticatedEventArgs(cookieJar)); }
}
else
{
  EventHandler failedAuth = OnFailedAuthentication;
  if (failedAuth != null)
  { failedAuth(this, null); }
}
```

The AuthCallback event is called when the Authentication Web Service call returns. This method parses the results and raises either the OnAuthenticated or OnFailedAuthentication event. The OnAuthenticated event will pass back the CookieContainer, which includes the authentication cookie. Clients can hook into these events to determine if the user has access to the site. Listing 11-7 displays the Login.xaml.cs code, which includes the registration of the authentication events. The Login.xaml.cs file includes the code to save the CookieContainer to the App.Cookies property.

3. In Visual Studio, right click the Views folder, right-click Login.xaml, and select View Code.

4. Copy the code in Listing 11-7 into the LogIn class below the class constructors.

*Listing 11-7. The Login.Xaml.cs Login Code*

```
private void Login_Click(object sender, RoutedEventArgs e)
{
  if ((!String.IsNullOrEmpty(UserNameValue.Text)) &&
      (!String.IsNullOrEmpty(PasswordValue.Password)))
  {
```

```
        FBA fba = new FBA();
        fba.OnAuthenticated += new
                EventHandler<FBAAuthenticatedEventArgs>(fba_OnAuthenticated);
        fba.OnFailedAuthentication += new
                EventHandler(fba_OnFailedAuthentication);
        fba.Authenticate(UserNameValue.Text,
                         PasswordValue.Password,
                         Constants.AUTHENTICATION_SERVICE_URL);
    }
    else
    {
        MessageBox.Show("Please enter a user name and password.");
    }
}

void fba_OnFailedAuthentication(object sender, EventArgs e)
{
    this.Dispatcher.BeginInvoke(() =>
    {
        MessageBox.Show("Failed Login");
    });
}

void fba_OnAuthenticated(object sender, FBAAuthenticatedEventArgs e)
{
    App.Cookies = e.CookieJar;
    this.Dispatcher.BeginInvoke(() =>
    {
        NavigationService.Navigate(new Uri("/Views/MainPage.xaml",
                                           UriKind.Relative));
    });
}
```

The Login_Click method creates a new FBA class and registers the OnAuthenticated and OnFailedAuthenticated events. The method then calls FBA class's Authenticate method to attempt to authenticate the user. Depending on the result, either the OnAuthenticated or OnFailedAuthentication events are raised. When a user is authenticated, the CookieJar with the authentication cookie is sent back in the FBAAuthentication parameters and is stored in the App.Cookies parameter. The event then navigates the user to the MainPage.

## Retrieve Links from a Links List

You have the FBA authentication in place, so let's now look at calling remote SharePoint APIs to work with list data. This example will retrieve list data from SharePoint using the Lists.asmx Web Service. The data access is accomplished in the MyLinksViewModel class. The ViewModel classes contain the methods used to interact between the view (user interface) and the model (in this case, the Link class). I will only review the SharePoint-specific code in this section. Remember that Silverlight only allows asynchronous communications. Therefore, the example has two methods to manage retrieving links from a links list: one to start the request and a method to handle the completed event. There is also a public ObservableCollection property that is used to store the individual links. It is this property that will be data-bound to the UI.

To begin the request to retrieve links from a links list, follow these steps:

1. In Visual Studio, right click the ViewModel folder, and open the MyLinksViewModel.cs file.

2. Copy the code in Listing 11-8 into the MyLinksViewModel class. This property should be placed between the class declaration and the first defined method.

*Listing 11-8. The MyLinks ObservableCollection*

```
private ObservableCollection<Link> myLinks;
public ObservableCollection<Link> MyLinks
{
  get { return myLinks; }
  set
  {
    myLinks = value;
    NotifyPropertyChanged("MyLinks");
  }
}
```

3. Copy the code in Listing 11-9 into the LoadMyLinks method in the MyLinksViewModel class.

*Listing 11-9. The LoadMyLinks Method*

```
XElement viewFields = new XElement("ViewFields",
                            new XElement("FieldRef",
                             new XAttribute("Name", "ows_URL")));
ListsSoapClient svc = new ListsSoapClient();
svc.CookieContainer = App.Cookies;
svc.GetListItemsCompleted += new
            EventHandler<GetListItemsCompletedEventArgs>
(svc_GetListItemsCompleted);
            svc.GetListItemsAsync("MyLinks", string.Empty, null,
                            viewFields, null, null, null);
```

The LoadMyLinks method defines the fields needed in the results. In this example you only need the ows_URL field. This field contains the URL and the text associated with the URL in a comma-separated string.

The method will use the proxy generated when the service reference was added to define a new callback handler (svc_GetListItemsCompleted) and calls the GetListItemsAsync method. This will start the asynchronous get from the list.

4. Copy the code in Listing 11-10 into the svc_GetListItemsCompleted method in the MyLinksViewModel class.

*Listing 11-10. The svc_ GetListItemsCompleted Method*

```
IEnumerable<XElement> rows = e.Result.Descendants
                            (XName.Get("row", "#RowsetSchema"));
var myLinks = from element in rows
            select new Link(
                        (int)element.Attribute("ows_ID"),
```

```
                                    (string)element.Attribute("ows_URL")
                            );

Deployment.Current.Dispatcher.BeginInvoke(() =>
{
  if (MyLinks == null)
  {
    MyLinks = new ObservableCollection<Link>();
  }
  MyLinks.Clear();
  myLinks.ToList().ForEach(a => MyLinks.Add(a));
});
```

The svc_GetListItemCompleted method handles the return from the asynchronous call. Linq to XML is used to parse the results. Linq is also used to create a project Link model object for each row. The method clears and updates the MyLinks collection. The collection is data-bound to the UI controls. The Dispatcher object is used to run this code on the UI thread and therefore avoids a cross-thread error.

## Add a Link to a Links List

Finally, the example will allow a user to add a new link to a link list. Adding a link to the link list is accomplished using the Lists.asmx Web Service. The NewLinkViewModel file includes the code required to add a new link to the link list.

1. In Visual Studio, right click the ViewModel folder and open the NewLinkViewModel.cs file.

2. Copy the code in Listing 11-11 into the AddLink method in the NewLinkViewModel class.

*Listing 11-11. The AddLink Method*

```
XElement updateQuery =
    new XElement("Batch",
            new XAttribute("OnError", "Continue"),
            new XAttribute("ListVersion", "1"),
            new XElement("Method", new XAttribute("ID", "1"),
                new XAttribute("Cmd", "New"),
                new XElement("Field", new XAttribute("Name", "ID"), "New"),
                new XElement("Field", new XAttribute("Name", "URL"),
                                    Link.BuildSPLink(link.Title, link.HyperLink))
            ));

ListsSoapClient svc = new ListsSoapClient();
svc.CookieContainer = App.Cookies;
svc.UpdateListItemsCompleted += new
        EventHandler<UpdateListItemsCompletedEventArgs>
                                    (svc_UpdateListItemsCompleted);

svc.UpdateListItemsAsync(Constants.MYLINKS_LIST_TITLE, updateQuery);
```

The AddLink method includes batch instructions to add a new item. These instructions are created as XML and passed into the UpdateListItemsAsynch method of the Lists.asmx Web Service. This will update the list and call the defined callback, svc_UpdateListItemsCompleted. Notice the code uses the static BuildSPLink method to create a link with the text title as a comma-separated string.

3. Copy the code in Listing 11-12 into the svc_UpdateListItemsCompleted method in the NewLinkViewModel class.

*Listing 11-12. The svc_UpdateListItemsCompleted Method*

```
Deployment.Current.Dispatcher.BeginInvoke(SaveCompleteAction);
```

The svc_UpdateListItemsCompleted method is simple. Once the update is complete, the SaveCompleteAction delegate is called on the UI thread. The delegate is passed in from the Save button's click event in the user interface. This action will set a flag to alert the user interface to refresh the list and navigate the phone back one page.

## Save and Run the Application

The application should now compile and run.

1. In Internet Explorer, open the link list to view the links in the list. If there are no links in the list, create links to use in this example. Figure 11-7 shows the links in the link list used in this example.

*Figure 11-7. Links in the example's list*

2. Select Windows Phone 7 Emulator as the deployment location (see Figure 11-8).

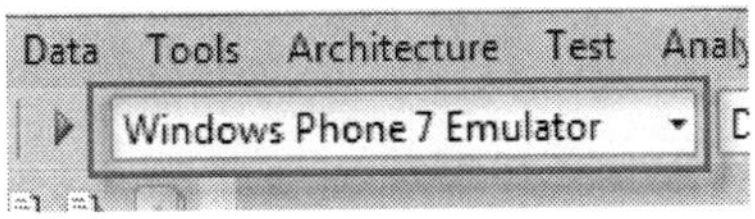

*Figure 11-8. Windows Phone 7 Emulator selected*

3. Press F5 to run the program.

4. Enter the user name and password in the login screen, as shown in Figure 11-9. The user must be a FBA user with access to the link list used in this example.

5. Click Login.

*Figure 11-9. The Login screen*

6. After you log in you will see the links in the links list, as shown in Figure 11-10.

*Figure 11-10. The main screen displaying links*

7. Click a link to view the associated web page (see Figure 11-11).

**Figure 11-11.** *Apress web site displayed in the browser*

8. Click the back button on the phone to return to the list of links.

9. Click the plus icon to add a new link.

10. Enter the link title and URL. The URL field must start with http:// (see Figure 11-12).

*Figure 11-12. Adding a new link*

11. Click Save to add the link. You can see the result in Figure 11-13.

My Links
Apress SharePoint
Aptillon
Apress Home

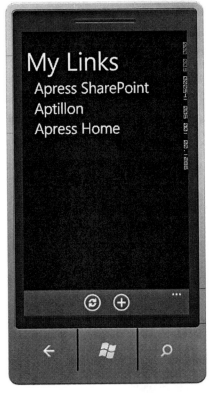

*Figure 11-13. The new link displayed in the phone application*

12. Return to Internet Explorer displaying the list and press F5 to refresh. Figure 11-14 displays the new link in the example's list.

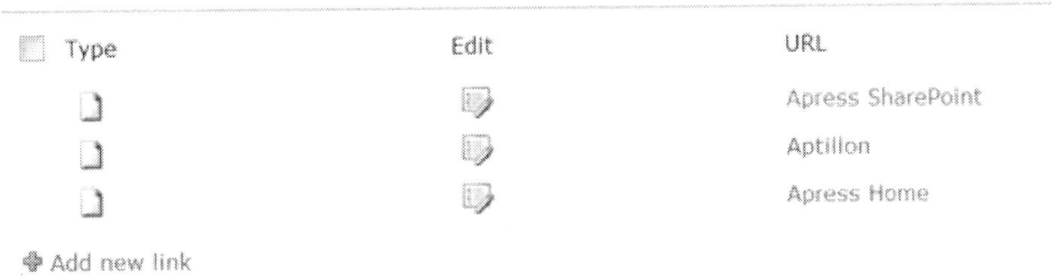
Type
Edit
URL
Apress SharePoint
Aptillon
Apress Home
Add new link

*Figure 11-14. The new link displayed in the list*

This exercise demonstrates how easy it is to create an application that can read and write SharePoint list data. The patterns shown in this example can be used for any SharePoint list template. In the next section you will see how to create a Windows Phone 7 application that works with non-list data.

## Call User Profile Web Service

The SharePoint Server 2010 User Profile service application provides a means to import user profile information from Active Directory and other LDAP stores. Once imported, this user information store can be enhanced and made available to the SharePoint Search and Social services to greatly improve employee social interaction through SharePoint. As an application developer, you can enhance your SharePoint-connected applications with "people information" by leveraging the data stored in the User Profile service through the User Profile web service. The SharePoint User Profile web service provides the ability to view, create, edit, and manage user profile information in SharePoint 2010. The web service is the primary entry point for the application to retrieve information about user colleagues and user profiles.

---

■ **Note** The User Profile service application and User Profile web service are features of SharePoint Server 2010. The code presented here uses the User Profile web service to retrieve a user's profile and colleagues. To make this code work, you must connect to the site using an account that has a user profile and colleagues.

---

In this section, you will learn how to connect your application to the SharePoint User Profile web service to retrieve the user profile for the current user and the colleagues for the test user. The process is very similar to working with SharePoint lists and libraries. There are specific considerations for working with the returned data, like the profile photo, when the URLs returned are not part of the FBA site you are authenticated against. Creating a My Site host that is accessible through FBA is required if you want to serve the images from the profile. Additionally, FBA does not require the user to provide the full account name for authentication. Calls to the User Profile web service do require the full account name. The code sample uses the People.asmx service to determine the full account name for the user after authentication is successful. The details of this procedure are in the LogIn.xaml.cs file. This sample will detail how to call the User Profile web service from the phone and work with the text data that is returned.

The steps are as follows:

1. Add a service reference to the User Profile Service. The service reference will create a proxy class that contains all of the necessary code for working with the methods and objects used by the User Profile Service.

2. Create a ViewModel for the Colleagues and populate the collection. The ViewModel will define the properties of the Colleague object that will be bound to the user interface controls.

3. Data bind a list to the Colleagues collection and add text boxes to display the results. In order for the application to update the UI, you will data bind the controls to the selected item in the Colleagues list.

## Open the Apress.SharePoint.WP7.Personal Project

The complete project source code and starting source code for the Personal application is included with the book's source code. The application includes all of the FBA authentication code configured so you can focus on the parts of the project that pertain to the User Profile Service. This example details the specifics of the interaction between SharePoint and Windows Phone 7.

1. Locate the Apress.SharePoint.WP7.Personal solution from the start folder.

2. Open the Apress.SharePoint.WP7.Personal solution.

## Modify the Application Constants

The Constants.cs file contains the values used in this application. You will need to provide the correct values for your environment.

1. In Visual Studio, expand the Utilities folder in the project. Open the Constants.cs file.

2. Modify the AUTHENTICATION_SERVICE_URL value to reference the site that is configured for FBA.

3. Example:

```
public const string AUTHENTICATION_SERVICE_URL =
"http://fbaDemo/_vti_bin/authentication.asmx";
```

4. Modify the USERPROFILE_SERVICE_URL value to include the site configured for FBA.

5. Example:

```
public const string USERPROFILE_SERVICE _URL =
"http://fbaDemo/_vti_bin/userprofileservice.asmx";
```

6. Modify the PEOPLE_SERVICE_URL value to reference the site configured for FBA.

7. Example:

```
public const string PEOPLE_SERVICE _URL = "http://fbaDemo/_vti_bin/people.asmx";
```

## Add a service reference

1. In Visual Studio, right click the Service References folder and choose Add Service Reference.

2. In the Add Service Reference dialog, enter the address of the User Profile Service.

3. Example: http://fbademo/_vti_bin/userprofileservice.asmx

4. Click Go and wait for Visual Studio to populate the list of services.

5. Once the UserProfileService appears in the Services section, in the Namespace textbox, enter UserProfileSvc. The complete dialog should look like Figure 11-15.

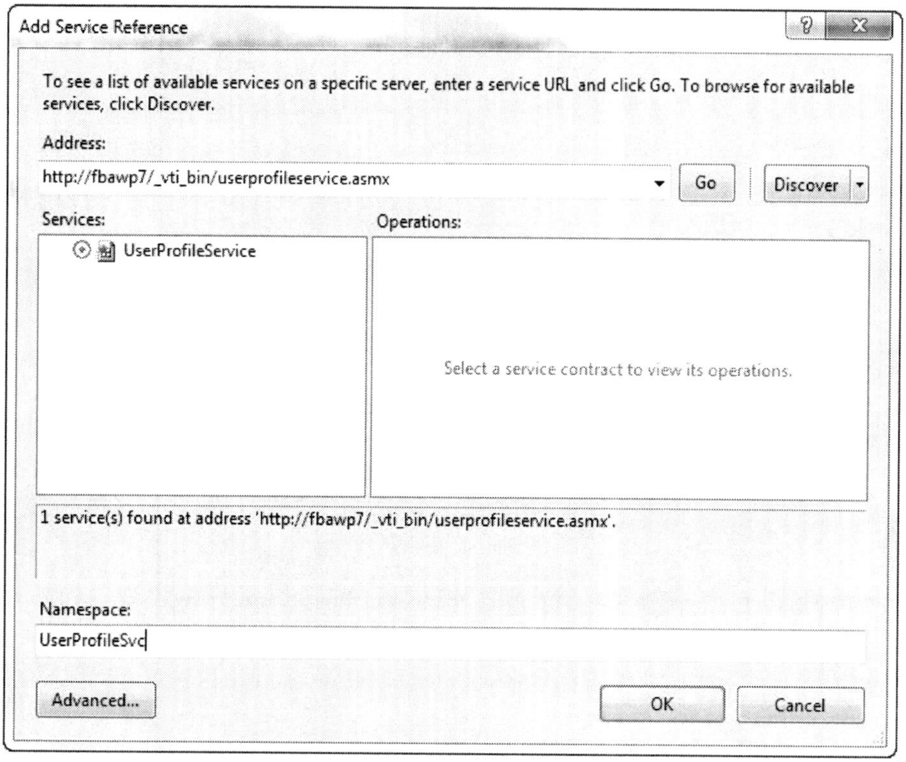

*Figure 11-15. The Add Service Reference dialog*

6. Click OK to create the proxy class for the User Profile Service.

7. You will see the new UserProfileSvc service reference added to your project, as shown in Figure 11-16.

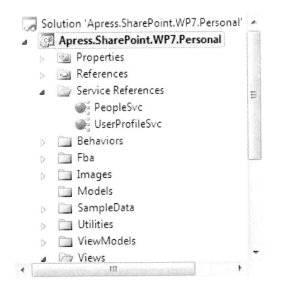

*Figure 11-16. The new service reference in the project*

8.  Open the ServiceReferences.ClientConfig file and locate the binding
    UserProfileServiceSoap element. Add the enableHttpCookieContainer="true"
    attribute to the binding element to support FBA. Locate the binding
    PeopleSoap element. Add the enableHttpCookieContainer="true" attribute to
    the binding element.

## Complete the Colleagues ViewModel Class

1.  In Visual Studio, open the ViewModels folder and right click on
    ColleaguesViewModel and select open.

2.  In the ColleaguesViewModel class, add the code in Listing 11-13. This code
    defines the properties of the Colleague that you will display in the application.

*Listing 11-13. The ColleagueViewModel Class*

```
private string _fullName;
/// <summary>
/// Colleague ViewModel FullName property;
/// this property is the Full Name of the colleague.
/// </summary>
/// <returns></returns>
public string FullName
{
  get
  {
    return _fullName;
  }
```

```
    set
    {
      if (value != _fullName)
      {
        _fullName = value;
        NotifyPropertyChanged("FullName");
      }
    }
  }

  private string _accountName;
  /// <summary>
  /// Colleague ViewModel AccountName property;
  /// this property is the Colleagues Account Name.
  /// </summary>
  /// <returns></returns>
  public string AccountName
  {
    get
    {
      return _accountName;
    }
    set
    {
      if (value != _accountName)
      {
        _accountName = value;
        NotifyPropertyChanged("AccountName");
      }
    }
  }

  private string _personalUrl;
  /// <summary>
  /// Colleague ViewModel PersonalUrl property;
  /// this property is the URL to the Colleagues Personal Site.
  /// </summary>
  /// <returns></returns>
  public string PersonalUrl
  {
    get
    {
      return _personalUrl;
    }
    set
    {
      if (value != _personalUrl)
      {
        _personalUrl = value;
        NotifyPropertyChanged("PersonalUrl");
      }
    }
```

```
}
private string _title;
/// <summary>
/// Colleague ViewModel PersonalUrl property;
/// this property is the Title from the User Profile.
/// </summary>
/// <returns></returns>

public string Title
{
  get
  {
    return _title;
  }
  set
  {
    if (value != _title)
    {
      _title = value;
      NotifyPropertyChanged("Title");
    }
  }
}

private string _email;
/// <summary>
/// Colleague ViewModel PersonalUrl property;
/// this property is the E-mail from the User Profile.
/// </summary>
/// <returns></returns>
public string EMail
{
  get
  {
    return _email;
  }
  set
  {
    if (value != _email)
    {
      _email = value;
      NotifyPropertyChanged("EMail");
    }
  }
}
```

## Create the ColleaguesViewModel Collection

1.  In the project ViewModels folder open the `MainViewModel.cs` file.

2.  Create a new public property in the MainViewModel class for the
    ObservableCollection of ColleagueViewModels. To do this, add the code in
    Listing 11-14 to the MainViewModel class. This collection will be bound to the
    user interface for display of the data in the collection.

*Listing 11-14. The ColleagueViewModel Observable Collection*

```
/// <summary>
/// A collection for ColleagueViewModel objects.
/// </summary>
public ObservableCollection<ColleagueViewModel> Colleagues { get; private set; }
```

3.  In the constructor of the MainViewModel add the code to create the Colleagues
    ObservableCollection. For clarity, the code in Listing 11-15 shows the entire
    constructor.

*Listing 11-15. The New ColleagueViewModel Collection*

```
public MainViewModel()
{
  this.Colleagues = new ObservableCollection<ColleagueViewModel>();
}
```

4.  In the LoadMyColleagues method in the MainViewModel class, add the code in
    Listing 11-16. This method sets the authentication header for FBA and then
    calls the web method GetUserColleaguesAsync to return the colleagues for the
    user.

*Listing 11-16. The LoadMyColleagues Method*

```
UserProfileSvc.UserProfileServiceSoapClient svc = new ↵
        UserProfileServiceSoapClient();
svc.CookieContainer = App.Cookies;
svc.GetUserColleaguesCompleted += ↵
        new EventHandler<GetUserColleaguesCompletedEventArgs>(↵
        svc_GetUserColleaguesCompleted);
svc.GetUserColleaguesAsync(App.UserName);
```

5.  In the svc_GetUserColleaguesCompleted method in the MainViewModel class,
    add the code shown in Listing 11-17. This code takes the return result of the
    GetUserColleaguesAsync method and extracts the ContactData to create
    Colleague objects and load them into the Colleagues ObservableCollection.

*Listing 11-17. The svc_GetUserColleaguesCompleted Method*

```
  if (e.Error == null)
  {
    Deployment.Current.Dispatcher.BeginInvoke(() =>
    {
      Colleagues.Clear();

      foreach (ContactData contactData in e.Result.ToList())
```

```
    {
      Colleagues.Add(new ColleagueViewModel()
      {
        AccountName = contactData.AccountName,
        FullName = contactData.Name,
        Title = contactData.Title,
        EMail = contactData.Email,
        PersonalUrl = contactData.Url
      });
    }
  });

}
else
{
  Debug.WriteLine("Error: {0}", e.Error.Message);
}
```

## Databind The Colleagues Collection to a ListBox

The last step is to add a ListBox to the UI and data bind the list to the Colleagues ObservableCollection.
This step is performed in the XAML for the Pivot Item.

1. Expand the Views folder and open MainPage.xaml and locate the Pivot control.
   Locate the Pivot Item with the header "my colleagues".

2. Inside the PivotItem markup, add the code in Listing 11-18. This XAML creates
   a ListBox with a template that is composed of StackPanel and TextBlock
   controls to present the data from the Colleagues ObservableCollection. The
   controls are bound to the collection using element binding.

*Listing 11-18. The ColleaguesListBox XAML*

```
<ListBox x:Name="ColleaguesListBox" Margin="0,0,-12,0"
  ItemsSource="{Binding Colleagues}">
  <ListBox.ItemTemplate>
    <DataTemplate>
      <StackPanel Margin="0,0,0,-2" Height="134">
      <TextBlock Text="{Binding FullName}"
                 TextWrapping="NoWrap"
                 Margin="12,0,0,0"
                 Style="{StaticResource PhoneTextExtraLargeStyle}"
                 Height="50"/>
      <TextBlock TextWrapping="Wrap"
                 Text="{Binding Title}" Margin="12,0,0,0"/>
      <TextBlock TextWrapping="Wrap"
                 Text="{Binding EMail}" Margin="12,0,0,0"/>
      <TextBlock Text="{Binding PersonalUrl}"
                 TextWrapping="NoWrap"
                 Margin="12,-6,0,0"
                 Style="{StaticResource PhoneTextSubtleStyle}"/>
```

```
          </StackPanel>
        </DataTemplate>
      </ListBox.ItemTemplate>
</ListBox>
```

3. Save and run the project. You should see results similar to Figure 11-17 after logging in with an account with associated colleagues.

---

▪ **Note** This example is based on users in the "Contoso Demo" available from Microsoft. The profile data rendered in your demo will be based on the names and titles you entered in your demo environment. The FBA user that is used to log in must have colleagues in order for this code to display results.

---

*Figure 11-17. The colleagues list*

4.  End the debugging session and return to Visual Studio.

# Retrieve the User Profile Properties for a Specific User

The SharePoint User Profile contains over 50 properties out of the box. The User Profile is configurable and more properties can be added to define user attributes that are specific to your enterprise. If you want to use the properties of the User Profile in your custom applications, you need to request the User Profile from the User Profile Web Service and then parse the resulting PropertyData object to get the property names and values. In this exercise, you will retrieve the User Profile for the current user and then display the resulting properties in the Windows Phone 7 application.

The steps are similar to retrieving Colleagues. Since you already created a reference to the SharePoint User Profile web service, you will reuse that service reference. The steps are as follows:

1.  Create a ViewModel for the User Profile. Since you are only retrieving a single user profile, you only need a single ViewModel instance for the profile.

2.  Call the User Profile Service GetUsetProfileByName method and store the result in the User Profile ViewModel.

3.  Data bind the text boxes to the User Profile object to display the values.

---

■ **Note** In the current version of Silverlight for Windows Phone there is a known issue with calling certain methods of the User Profile Service. What you will encounter is an error indicating that the application is unable to deserialize known types like GUIDs when using web methods that return the PropertyData type. The details of the issue are beyond the scope of this chapter, but the solution is included with the source code download in the project Behaviors folder.

---

## Complete the MyProfileViewModel Class

1.  Open the MyProfileViewModel class located in the ViewModels folder.

2.  Complete the MyProfileViewModel class definition by inserting the code in Listing 11-19. This code defines the properties for the User Profile.

*Listing 11-19. MyProfileViewModel Class*

```
private string _fullName;
/// <summary>
/// Sample ViewModel property; this property is used
///  in the view to display its value using a Binding.
/// </summary>
/// <returns></returns>
public string FullName
{
  get
  {
```

```
      return _fullName;
    }
    set
    {
      if (value != _fullName)
      {
        _fullName = value;
        NotifyPropertyChanged("FullName");
      }
    }
  }

  private string _title;
  /// <summary>
  /// Sample ViewModel property; this property
  ///  is used in the view to display its value using a Binding.
  /// </summary>
  /// <returns></returns>
  public string Title
  {
    get
    {
      return _title;
    }
    set
    {
      if (value != _title)
      {
        _title = value;
        NotifyPropertyChanged("Title");
      }
    }
  }

  private string _pictureUrl;
  /// <summary>
  /// Sample ViewModel property; this property
  ///  is used in the view to display its value using a Binding.
  /// </summary>
  /// <returns></returns>
  public string PictureUrl
  {
    get
    {
      return _pictureUrl;
    }
    set
    {
      if (value != _pictureUrl)
      {
        _pictureUrl = value;
```

```
                NotifyPropertyChanged("PictureUrl");
            }
        }
    }

    private string _aboutMe;
    /// <summary>
    /// Sample ViewModel property; this property
    ///  is used in the view to display its value using a Binding.
    /// </summary>
    /// <returns></returns>
    public string AboutMe
    {
      get
      {
        return _aboutMe;
      }
      set
      {
        if (value != _aboutMe)
        {
          _aboutMe = value;
          NotifyPropertyChanged("AboutMe");
        }
      }
    }
```

# Add the MyProfileViewModel Property to the MainViewModel

1. Open the `MainViewModel.cs` file and add a new property for MyProfile to the class, as shown in Listing 11-20. This code creates the property that stores the User Profile and is data bound to the UI.

*Listing 11-20. The MyProfileViewModel Property*

```
private MyProfileViewModel _myProfile;
/// <summary>
/// MyProfileViewModel property; this property is used in
///   the view to display the current user profile
/// </summary>
/// <returns></returns>
public MyProfileViewModel MyProfile
{
  get
  {
    return _myProfile;
  }
  set
  {
```

```
    if (value != _myProfile)
    {
      _myProfile = value;
      NotifyPropertyChanged("MyProfile");
    }
  }
}
```

2.  In the MainViewModel constructor, create the instance of the
    MyProfileViewModel. The complete constructor is shown in Listing 11-21.

*Listing 11-21. The MainViewModel Constructor*

```
public MainViewModel()
{
    this.Colleagues = new ObservableCollection<ColleagueViewModel>();
    this.MyProfile = new MyProfileViewModel();
}
```

# Load Data from the User Profile Service

1.  Complete the LoadMyProfile method located in the MainViewModel class by
    inserting the code in Listing 11-22 This code adds a message inspector to the
    request to resolve a known issue in Silverlight described previously in this
    section. Then it calls the GetUserProfileByNameAsync method to request the
    user profile data.

*Listing 11-22. The Complete LoadMyProfile Method*

```
//Create the Message Inspector
//ToDo : You MUST have the Behaviors folder from the sample for this to work
SPAsmxMessageInspector messageInspector = new SPAsmxMessageInspector();
//Apply the Message Inspector to the Binding
BasicHttpMessageInspectorBinding binding = new ↵
  BasicHttpMessageInspectorBinding(messageInspector);

EndpointAddress endpoint = new ↵
  EndpointAddress(Constants.USERPROFILE_SERVICE_URL);

UserProfileSvc.UserProfileServiceSoapClient svc = new ↵
  UserProfileServiceSoapClient(binding, endpoint);
svc.CookieContainer = App.Cookies;
svc.GetUserProfileByNameCompleted += new ↵
  EventHandler<GetUserProfileByNameCompletedEventArgs>( ↵
  svc_GetUserProfileByNameCompleted);
svc.GetUserProfileByNameAsync(App.UserName);
```

2.  Complete the svc_GetUserProfileByNameCompleted method in the
    MainViewModel class by inserting the code from Listing 11-23. This code parses

the returned PropertyData object and populates the MyProfile object with the
data.

*Listing 11-23. The GetUserProfileByNameCompleted Event Handler*

```
if (e.Error == null)
{
  foreach (UserProfileSvc.PropertyData propertyData in e.Result)
  {
    switch (propertyData.Name)
    {
      case "PreferredName":
        MyProfile.FullName = propertyData.Values.Count > 0
          ? (propertyData.Values[0].Value as string)
          : String.Empty;
        break;
      case "Title":
        MyProfile.Title = propertyData.Values.Count > 0
          ? (propertyData.Values[0].Value as string)
          : String.Empty;
        break;
      case "AboutMe":
        MyProfile.AboutMe = propertyData.Values.Count > 0
          ? (propertyData.Values[0].Value as string)

          : String.Empty;
        break;
      case "PictureURL":
        MyProfile.PictureUrl = propertyData.Values.Count > 0
          ? (propertyData.Values[0].Value as string)
          : String.Empty;
        break;
    }
  }
}
else
{
  Debug.WriteLine("Error: {0}", e.Error.Message);
}
```

## Add a PivotItem for the Profile

1.  Open MainPage.xaml and locate the second PivotItem with the header that
    reads "my profile".

2.  Add the code in Listing 11-24 between the start and end PivotItem elements.
    This code creates the UI to display the profile property information in the
    MyProfile object. This XAML creates a grid with TextBlock controls to present
    the data from the MyProfile property. The controls are bound to the collection
    using element binding.

*Listing 11-24. The Profile PivotItem XAML*

```
<Grid>
  <TextBlock TextWrapping="NoWrap" Text="{Binding MyProfile.FullName}"
    VerticalAlignment="Top" Margin="123,4,7,0" d:LayoutOverrides="Width"
    Style="{StaticResource PhoneTextLargeStyle}"/>
  <TextBlock TextWrapping="NoWrap" Text="{Binding MyProfile.Title}"
    VerticalAlignment="Top" Margin="127,45,0,0" HorizontalAlignment="Left"
    Style="{StaticResource PhoneTextSmallStyle}"/>
  <TextBlock TextWrapping="Wrap" Text="{Binding MyProfile.AboutMe}"
    Margin="8,124,12,16" Style="{StaticResource PhoneTextSmallStyle}"/>
</Grid>
```

3.  Save and run your project. After you log in, flick the pivot to the second pivot item. You should see the user's profile, as shown in Figure 11-18.

*Figure 11-18. The current user's profile*

# Summary

This latest incarnation of Microsoft's mobile vision makes it easy for .NET developers to create rich mobile applications with familiar tools. Advances in the platform are under development and new features will make your job as a developer easier. Two things are certain: the mobile market will continue to grow as will Microsoft's market share, so investing time now in learning how to develop for Windows Phone 7 is a good choice.

At this time, Windows Phone 7 does not support Windows authentication in custom applications. Authentication must use either FBA or UAG. Depending on how your farm is configured, FBA may already be available or you may have to extend a web application to include FBA. UAG can provide alternatives to FBA and includes secure portal access to your SharePoint farms.

The SharePoint remote APIs work with little or no limitations, while the SharePoint Client Side Object Model is not supported on the current phone platform. Web services provide the most coverage because CSOM is not available. REST\ODATA can be used but it can be complex to do anything more than read operations when using FBA. Again, UAG provides some relief when configured correctly.

Even though authentication and remote APIs can be challenging, with a little time and imagination you will find that there is always a way to get access to the data you require. As the Windows Phone 7 platform matures and business cases are made for mobile support, SharePoint developers will be well positioned to take advantage of the platform with this fundamental knowledge of SharePoint and Windows Phone 7.

# SharePoint Solution Deployment

This chapter will focus on best practices for deploying your SharePoint 2010 customizations developed with Visual Studio 2010 SharePoint 2010 tools. This chapter does not provide an introduction to the Visual Studio 2010 SharePoint 2010 tools that automate much of the work to create features and solutions (WSP files). It is assumed you already know what SharePoint features and solutions are, and that you have a good hands-on working knowledge of how to create these in Visual Studio 2010. Rather, this chapter will demonstrate some best practices that will encourage you to carefully plan out the structure of your Visual Studio solutions, SharePoint features, and SharePoint solutions. Here are some of the best practices that will be covered in this chapter:

1. Think deployment first! Plan your Visual Studio Solution, SharePoint solution, and SharePoint feature strategy carefully.

2. Plan to maintain your application with feature versioning and feature upgrading.

3. Define your feature and solution activation dependencies.

4. Automate the provisioning of your solutions and features with PowerShell.

5. Defined lists should be backed with schema defined in content types.

6. Sign all of your Visual Studio projects with the same Strong Name Key (SNK) file

7. Feature Stapling is a great way to enhance out of the box site definitions.

## Observations from the Field

In my experience of reviewing probably hundreds of developed customizations for SharePoint (both the 2007 and 2010 versions), the packaging and then deployment of SharePoint solutions consistently seems to be an afterthought. That is, something that had to be done at the end of the project in order to move the customizations out of development and on to Testing and/or Production environments. Not Surprisingly, planning out the strategy and structure for features and solutions is almost never done.

Please see if some of the following deployment experiences and observations apply to you:

- *The "big bang" deployment:* All of the features are packaged into a single WSP file and deployed to the farm. This will definitely work for an initial deployment, but have you felt the pain of deploying updates, patches, and enhancements?

- *Visual Studio and SharePoint Designer mix:* While some features such as Web Parts are deployed as solutions, many others were created "in browser" or with SharePoint Designer. How do you deploy site columns, content types, list creations, data population, and workflows that were not done via Visual Studio (and therefore not packaged as features/solutions)?

- *Manual deployment:* Many steps to get an application running on a "clean server" are manual. Manual changes to the web configuration, and a variety of required content migrations using an export/import tool or PowerShell extensions.

- *Lack of deployment automation:* You have a 100-page deployment guide because of the number of manual and tedious steps to get an application running on a clean server. There is little scripting in evidence to help automate the steps and reduce the effort to deploy an application.

- *Actually, there is no real deployment:* This is a new application anyway, and you are just planning on backing up and restoring the content database from development to production. But how are you going to maintain the customizations moving forward?

## Example Overview

In order to demonstrate typical considerations for designing SharePoint features and solutions, a simple but useful example has been created. The example, when fully deployed, will provide a "footer links" Web Part that can be placed at the bottom of your master page. Footer links are the links you might typically see at the bottom of your web site page such as Contact Us, Privacy Statement, and Site Map. The Web Part will read entries from a footer links list so that it will be easy for the web master to maintain the footer links on the site. The "schema" for the footer links is defined as a content type with corresponding site columns. The content type is then attached to the list where the footer links are created. There is a feature stapler to ensure the Footer Links feature and Web Part are available automatically when a team site is provisioned.

This example contains a typical core pattern of customization to formulate the best practice recommendations, all managed in Visual Studio 2010 SharePoint 2010 tools.

- Defined schema (site columns and content types).

- Lists provisioned with attached content types.

- A Web Part that performs a content query against the content type.

I am presuming you have available a local development environment or access to a SharePoint environment. Go to Central Administration and create a site collection. In my case, I have created a site collection at http://intranet.theopenhighway.net/sites/Apress.

Open the Visual Studio solution provided for this chapter, FooterLinks.sln. Figure 12-1 shows what the solution looks like when open.

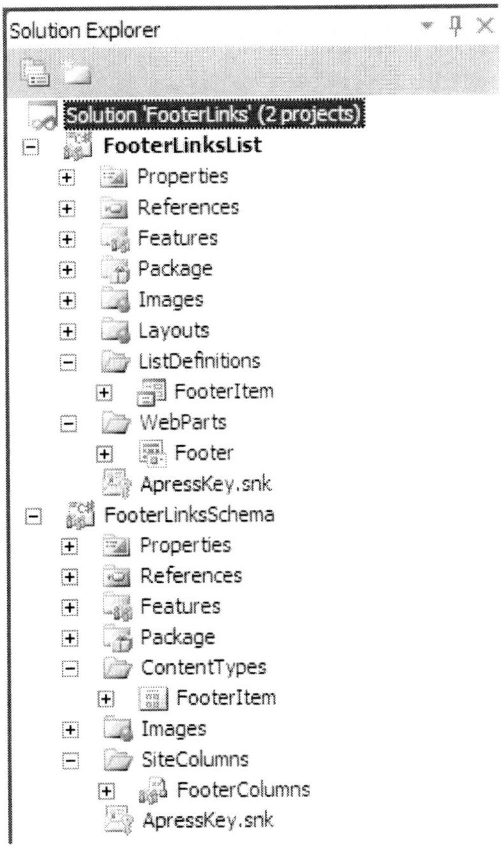

*Figure 12-1.* *The Footer Links Visual Studio solution*

Click on each of the projects in the solution—FooterLinksList and FooterLinksSchema—and change the site URL property (in the Properties window) so it matches the site collection you just created. Save the changes. Right click on the FooterLinksSchema project and choose Deploy. Once the deployment succeeds (view the Output window to verify), right click on the FooterLinksList project and select Deploy. Once the deployment succeeds, view the Output window to verify.

---

■ **Tip** Generate a key file unique for your application and use the key file in all of your Visual Studio projects. Note the APressKey.snk file in the above projects. This will ensure the public key token for all of your DLLs will be the same.

---

Figure 12-2 shows a view of the Footer Link site collection features activated.

*Figure 12-2. Site collection features for Footer Links*

Figure 12-3 shows a view of the Footer Link site feature activated.

**Footer Item List**
This feature will define and create a list for footer items.

Deactivate   **Active**

*Figure 12-3. Site feature for Footer Links*

---

■ **Tip** (Well, this is more of a pet peeve than a tip.) Notice that I have set the ImageURL property for my feature and included an image as the icon for the feature. This is a professional touch that makes your features stand out, and I suggest you take the time to mark your features with your company logo or whatever else might be appropriate for the project.

---

Figure 12-4 shows a view of the defined site columns in the Site Column Gallery.

| Site Column | Type | Source |
| --- | --- | --- |
| **Apress Columns** | | |
| Sort Order | Number | Solution Deployment Best Practices |

*Figure 12-4. Site Column gallery*

Figure 12-5 shows a view of the defined content type in the Content Type Gallery.

| Site Content Type | Parent | Source |
| --- | --- | --- |
| **Apress Content Types** | | |
| Footer Link | Item | Solution Deployment Best Practices |

*Figure 12-5. Content Type gallery*

Figure 12-6 shows a view of the Footer links list settings; note the content type.

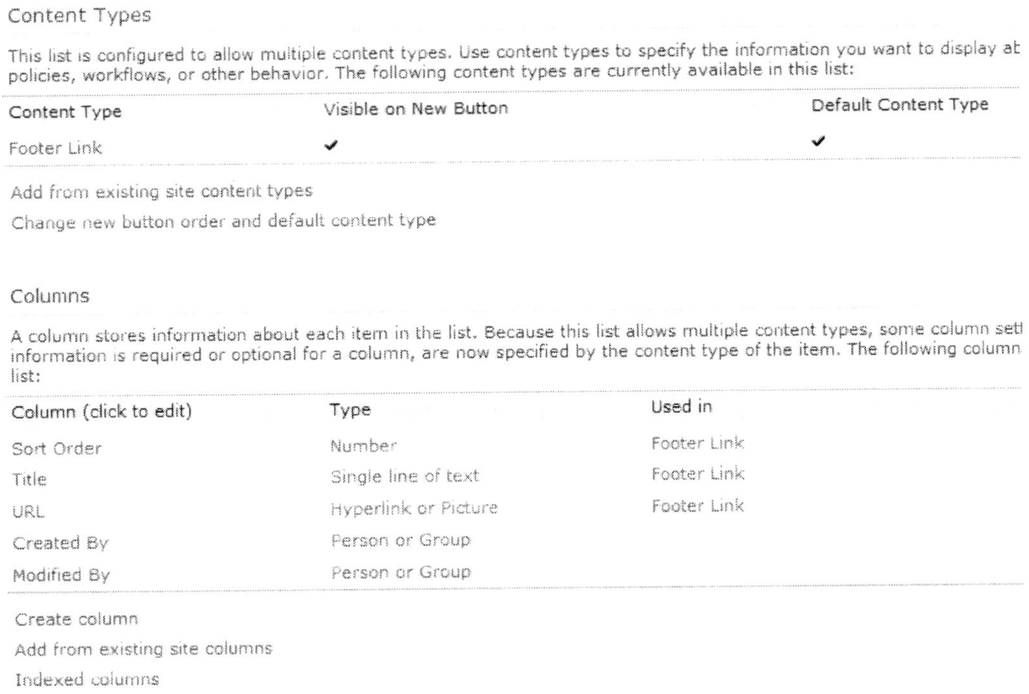

## Content Types

This list is configured to allow multiple content types. Use content types to specify the information you want to display at policies, workflows, or other behavior. The following content types are currently available in this list:

| Content Type | Visible on New Button | Default Content Type |
|---|---|---|
| Footer Link | ✔ | ✔ |

Add from existing site content types

Change new button order and default content type

## Columns

A column stores information about each item in the list. Because this list allows multiple content types, some column setti information is required or optional for a column, are now specified by the content type of the item. The following column list:

| Column (click to edit) | Type | Used in |
|---|---|---|
| Sort Order | Number | Footer Link |
| Title | Single line of text | Footer Link |
| URL | Hyperlink or Picture | Footer Link |
| Created By | Person or Group | |
| Modified By | Person or Group | |

Create column

Add from existing site columns

Indexed columns

*Figure 12-6. Footer Links list settings*

Figure 12-7 shows an example of some footer link list entries.

| ☐ | 🔗 | Title | URL | Sort Order |
|---|---|---|---|---|
| | | Privacy Statement 🆕 | Privacy Statement | 1 |
| | | Contact Us 🆕 | Contact Us | 2 |
| | | Site Map 🆕 | Site Map | 3 |

✛ Add new item

*Figure 12-7. Sample Footer Link list entries*

Figure 12-8 shows an example of the footer links Web Part in use on a master page. Note that the red box was a deliberate image highlight to point out the footer links near the bottom of the page.

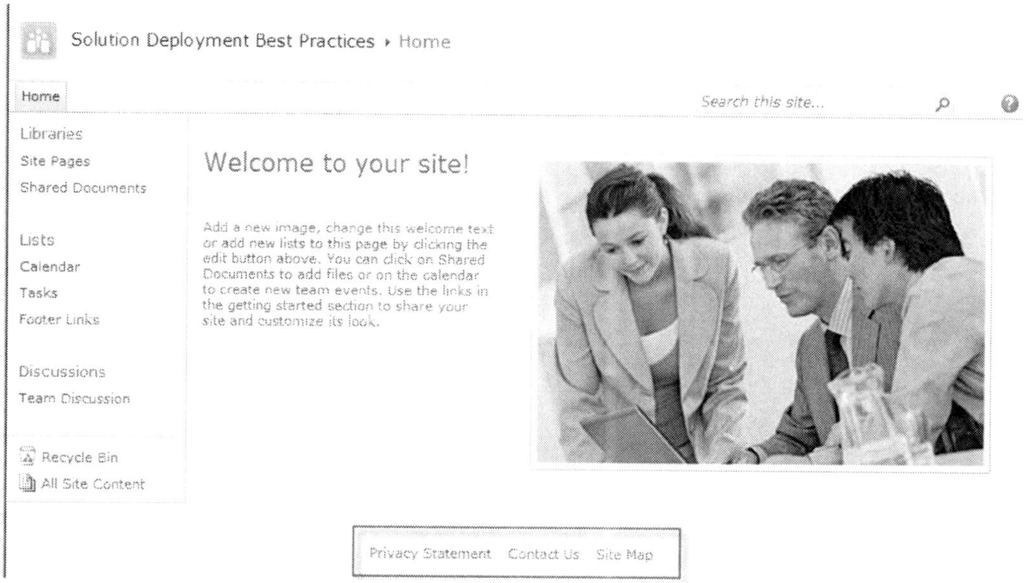

**Figure 12-8.** *Footer Links control on the master page*

# Feature Best Practices

## Using Features

It should be an assumption at this point in time that one, would, of course deploy their SharePoint items (content types, Web Parts, list schemas, or whatever) through the use of features. These features would be appropriately scoped at the farm, web application, site collection (site) or site (web) level according to the type of SharePoint item. The SharePoint 2010 tools for managing features and associated properties are absolutely fantastic. Figure 12-9 offers a quick look at the Feature Designer for the Footer Links Web Part.

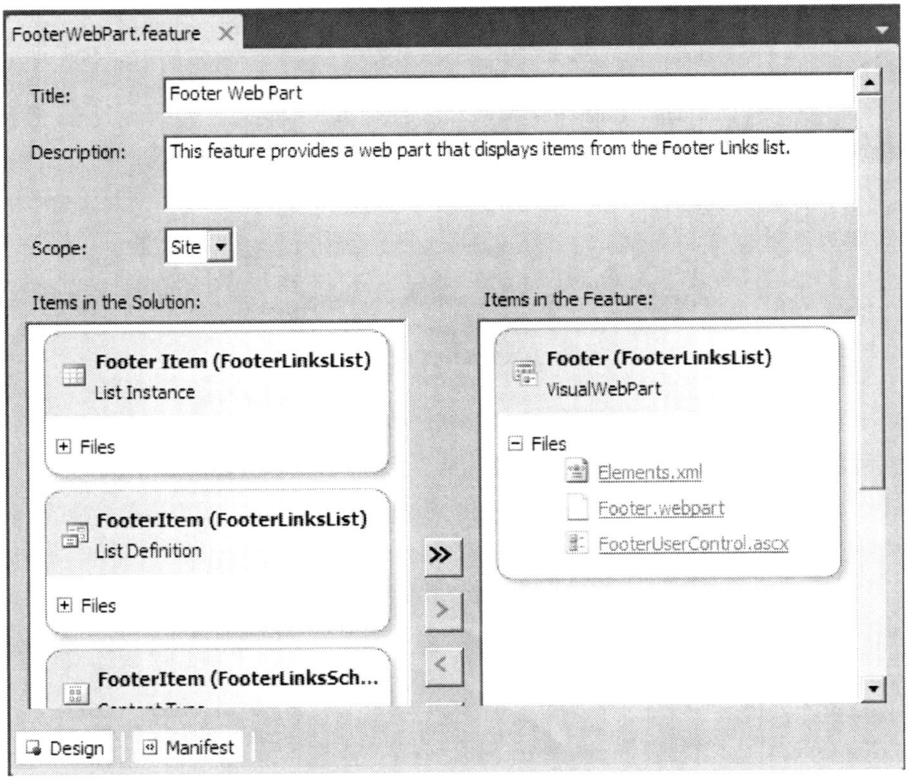

*Figure 12-9.* *The Feature Designer for the Footer Web Part feature*

Figure 12-10 shows the Properties window for the feature. I have set the image URL (as mentioned in my pet peeve/tip earlier) and set the feature version to 1.0.0.0. I will also discuss other important properties, such as the Receiver Assembly/Class and the Upgrade Actions Receiver Assembly/Class.

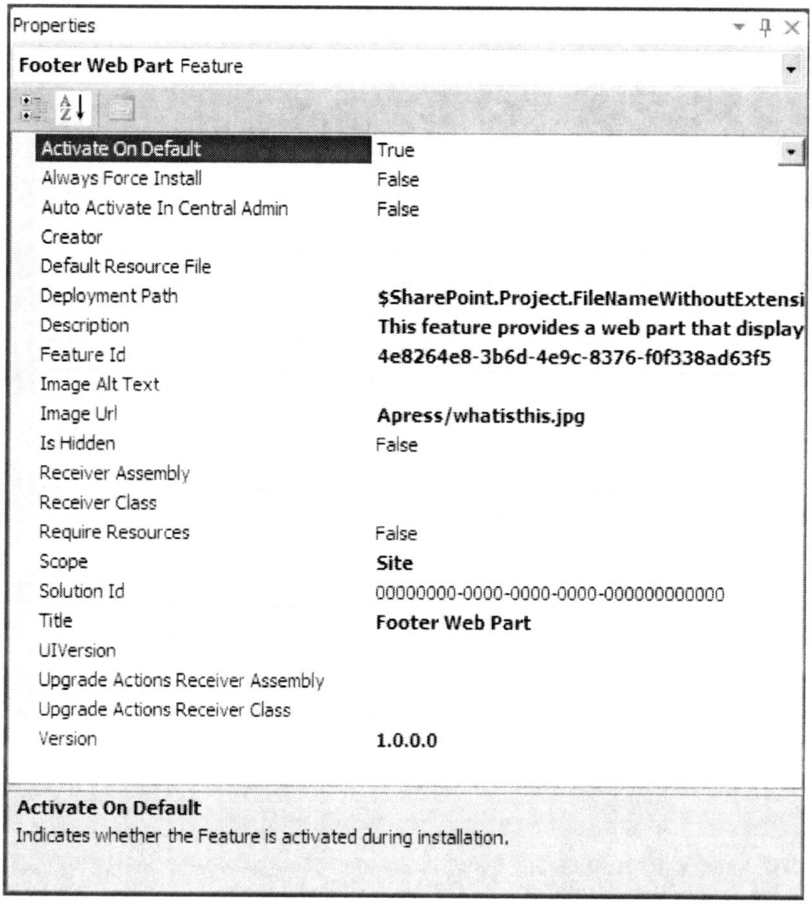

*Figure 12-10. The Properties window for the Footer Web Part feature*

---

░ **Tip** Most importantly, set the initial version of your feature to 1.0.0.0. The usefulness of feature versions will be discussed later in this chapter.

---

The property that is Deployment Path is exactly as follows:

```
$SharePoint.Project.FileNameWithoutExtension$_$SharePoint.Feature.FileNameWithoutExtension$
```

I tend not to like the project_feature naming format, but this is just a preference. I have left it as the default in this chapter example but normally would change it to the last half, namely:

```
$SharePoint.Feature.FileNameWithoutExtension$
```

# Feature Receivers

Feature receivers are code that (typically) runs as you press the Activate and Deactivate buttons on a feature. Well, the code will run regardless of how the feature is activated or deactivated (such as PowerShell), but it is easier if you can visualize it that way. Feature receivers can handle any initialization or clean up task. In this example, for the Footer Links list feature, you must (in code) set the Allow Management of Content Types setting on the Footer Links list. Now the footer content type will display properly in the Footer Links list settings, and when you create a new item, you get new Footer item. Upon deactivate, you have made the choice to completely remove the footer links list form the site (i.e. delete it). Listing 12-1 shows the feature receiver code you have in place.

*Listing 12-1. The Feature Receiver Code*

```
public class FooterItemListEventReceiver : SPFeatureReceiver
{
    public override void FeatureActivated(SPFeatureReceiverProperties properties)
    {
        SPWeb site = properties.Feature.Parent as SPWeb;

        // Enable Management of Content Types for Footer Links list
        SPList listFooterLinks = site.Lists["Footer Links"];
        listFooterLinks.ContentTypesEnabled = true;
        listFooterLinks.Update();
    }

    public override void FeatureDeactivating(SPFeatureReceiverProperties properties)
    {
        SPWeb site = properties.Feature.Parent as SPWeb;
        if (site != null)
        {
            SPList list = site.Lists.TryGetList("Footer Links");
            if (list != null)
            {
                list.Delete();
            }
        }
    }
}
```

■ **Tip** If you provision lists with attached content types, always include a feature receiver that sets "Allow Management of Content Types." If you examine the feature properties after adding a feature receiver, you will note the Receiver Assembly and Receiver Class properties have been automatically set.

## Feature Activation Dependencies

Feature activation dependencies prevent, as the name implies, activation of a given feature if the dependent feature has not been activated on the site/site collection. In your example, bad things would happen if the Footer Links list were provisioned while the underlying content types and site columns were not there. Since the schema is in one feature and the list provisioning in another feature, this requires that the schema feature be present and activated before you can activate the list provisioning feature. Without activation dependencies, nothing at all would prevent you from doing these bad things. Open up the Feature Designer for the Footer Item List feature. Scroll to the bottom if necessary. Expand the Feature Activation Dependencies section. Click the Add button, and select the Footer Links Schema feature. The result will look as shown in Figure 12-11.

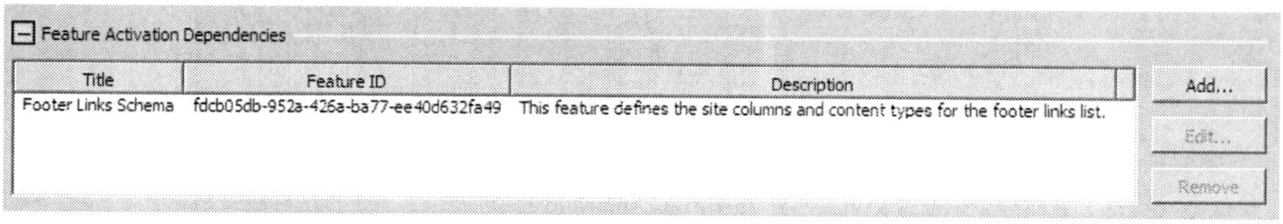

*Figure 12-11. A defined feature activation dependency*

To see feature activation in action, redeploy all of the SharePoint solutions, but don't activate any of the features (or, simply deactivate all of the features if they already are deployed). Now, go the example site and go to Site Actions ➤ Site Settings ➤ Site features. You should see the text shown in Figure 12-12, where the Footer Item List feature is not currently activated.

*Figure 12-12. The Footer Item list feature is ready to be activated.*

The following feature activation dependency is in place: Footer Item List site features depends on Footer Links Schema site collection feature. Attempting to activate the Footer Item List feature results in the message shown in Figure 12-13.

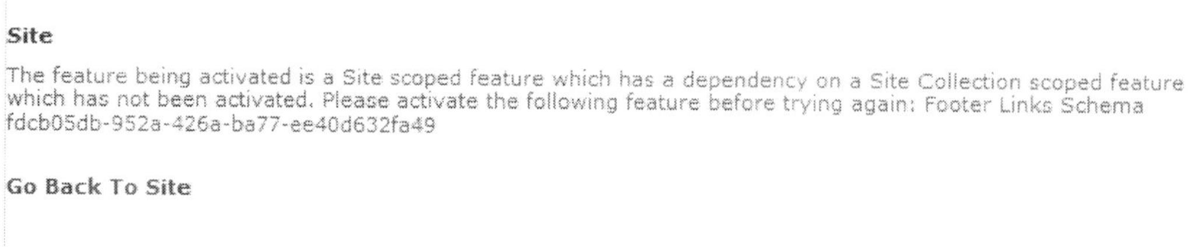

**Site**

The feature being activated is a Site scoped feature which has a dependency on a Site Collection scoped feature which has not been activated. Please activate the following feature before trying again: Footer Links Schema fdcb05db-952a-426a-ba77-ee40d632fa49

**Go Back To Site**

*Figure 12-13. The feature activation dependency has not been met.*

## Limitations

Unfortunately, you can't define all the dependencies that you would like. For example, say you would like to have the following activation dependency: "Footer Web Part site collection feature depends on

Footer Item List site feature." However, you can't define an activation dependency on a feature of a lower scope (i.e., the site collection feature depends on the site feature). It makes sense, because you don't want your Web Part to be available if the Footer Item List is not available. You can actually go into Visual Studio and declare the activation dependency in the Footer Web Part feature, as shown in Figure 12-14.

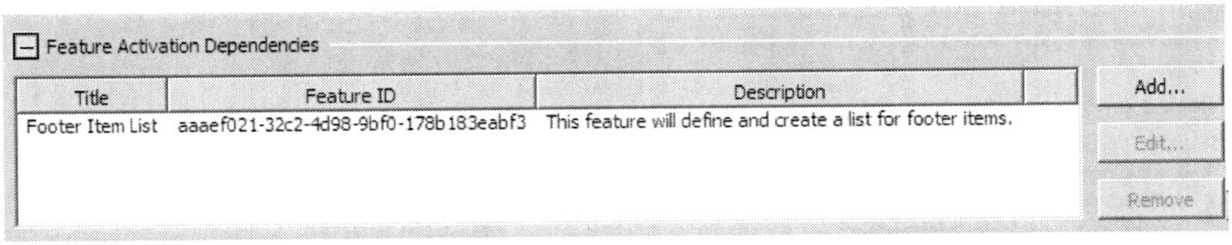

*Figure 12-14. Attempting to define footer Web Part dependency*

You can package and deploy the solution and then attempt to activate Footer Web Part, as shown in Figure 12-15.

**Footer Links Schema**
This feature defines the site columns and content types for the footer links list.    [ Activate ]

**Footer Web Part**
This feature provides a web part that displays items from the Footer Links list.    [ Activate ]

*Figure 12-15. The Footer Web Part feature wating to be activated.*

But you will receive the error message shown in Figure 12-16.

**Web**

The feature you are trying to activate is from the scope Site. It is dependent on another feature with lower scope Web . It is not valid for a feature to depend on a feature at a lower scope.

**Go Back To Site**

*Figure 12-16. Error message for invalid feature activation dependency*

Also, nothing will prevent the deactivation of dependent features. If all of the Footer features are currently activated, you can deactivate the Footer Links Schema feature without complaint from SharePoint. Finally, if you decide to have some of your features be hidden, then you can't define activation dependencies on them.

Ok, it is not perfect. But as a best practice, you should declare as many valid activation dependencies as possible!

# Feature Stapling

Feature stapling allows you to attach (or, I guess, "staple") a feature to a site definition. Put another way, it lets you add your own feature to an *existing* site definition without having to alter the site definition in any way. That is especially good news when it is an out-of-the-box site definition such as team site. In your case, any time a team site is created, the footer links Web Part (and associated footer links list and content type) are automatically available for use.

For this example, a separate Visual Studio solution was created with a separate feature, so as not to interfere with the coming upgrade example. You can open the sample solution, build it, and deploy it. The structure of the solution is quite simple—just a web application scoped feature and one Elements.xml file, as shown in Figure 12-17.

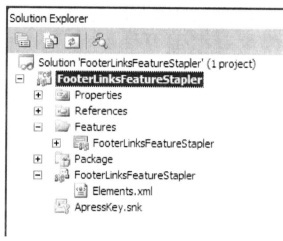

*Figure 12-17. Structure of Feature Staple solution*

The Elements XML file is also quite simple. It contains the ID of the feature you want to staple, and you must give the ID of the site template you want to attach the feature to. As an example, STS#0 is the team site definition and STS#1 is the blank site definition. You have chosen to staple the footer links features to the team site definition consisting of three features: Schema, List, and Web Part, as shown in Figure 12-18.

*Figure 12-18. Elements.xml showing Feature staple to Team Site definition.*

To see this feature deployed, go to Central Administration ➤ Application Management ➤ Manage Web Applications. Click on the web application you are using for this chapter (in my case, The Open

Highway), and click on the Manage Features button in the ribbon. You will see the Footer Links Feature Staple activated in the list, as shown in Figure 12-19.

**Footer Links
Feature Stapler**

This will staple the
footer links features
to the team site
definition.

Deactivate    **Active**

*Figure 12-19. Elements.xml showing Feature staple to Team Site definition.*

So when does the magic happen?!? Use Central Administration to create a new site collection of whatever name you wish and choose the Team Site template. When the site is created, follow the link note that the footer links list has been defined. Note that in Figure 12-20 I took the additional step to add a sample value and the Footer Web Part, quite inappropriately, near the top of the page. ☺

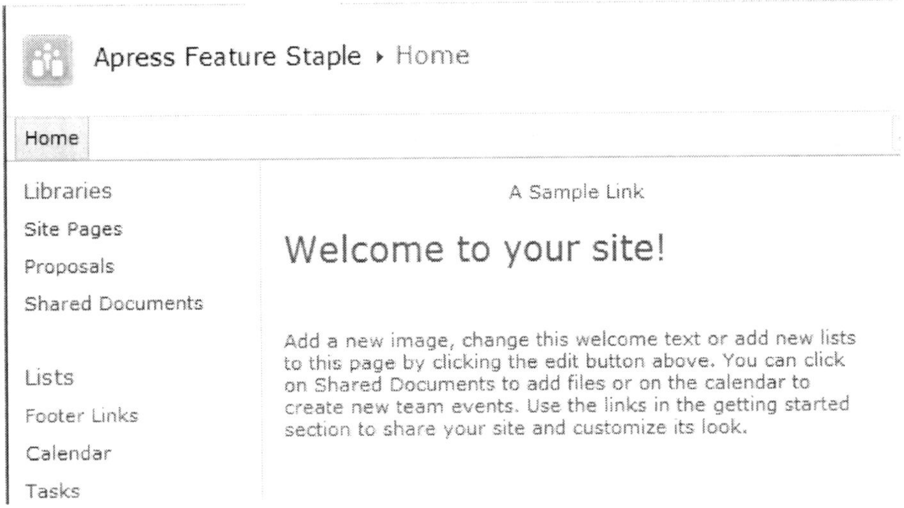

Apress Feature Staple ▸ Home

Home

Libraries                    A Sample Link

Site Pages                   Welcome to your site!

Proposals

Shared Documents
                             Add a new image, change this welcome text or add new lists
                             to this page by clicking the edit button above. You can click
Lists                        on Shared Documents to add files or on the calendar to
                             create new team events. Use the links in the getting started
Footer Links                 section to share your site and customize its look.

Calendar

Tasks

*Figure 12-20. Team Site with Footer Link Features activated upon site creation*

■ **Tip** A feature staple is a fast and easy way of customizing out-of-the-box site definitions within a given web application so that it is provisioned and even branded exactly as you want it to be.

# SharePoint Solution Best Practices

## Provisioning with PowerShell

In order to fully understand the provisioning of SharePoint solutions, you must understand the solution lifecycle from the perspective of the PowerShell commands that operate on it. Let's first assume that the SharePoint solution has never been deployed to the farm. Starting with the FooterLinksSchema solution, the first PowerShell command to execute is Add-SPSolution. This simply adds the WSP file to the solution store of the Central Administration configuration database, and nothing more. The next command to execute is Install-SPSolution. This physically pushes the files within the WSP to the SharePoint root folder of all the servers in the farm and takes other specified actions (add entries to web.config, deploy DLLs to global assembly cache, etc.). The features you have deployed will now be available according to the specified feature scope.

Now let's assume you have made some significant changes to the SharePoint solution or otherwise need to fully re-deploy the contents. You would have created an updated WSP file. With the PowerShell command Uninstall-SPSolution, you are physically retracting (deleting) all of the files from all the SharePoint servers in the Farm as well as reversing other specified actions (such as removing deployed DLLs). The features previously deployed are now no longer available. Next, with the PowerShell command Remove-SPSolution, delete the WSP file from the solution store in the Central Administration database. Now you repeat the Add-SPSolution and Install-SPSolution but with the updated WSP file.

So now any full solution deployment can be done via the script in Listing 12-2 (included along with sample code for this chapter).

***Listing 12-2.*** *Script for Full Solution Deployment*

```
Add-PSSnapin Microsoft.SharePoint.Powershell -ErrorAction SilentlyContinue

$WebApp = "http://intranet.theopenhighway.net"
$Path = "C:\Projects\Apress\Deployment\FooterLinksList.wsp"
$SolutionPackage  = "FooterLinksList.wsp"

$solution = Get-SPSolution | where-object {$_.Name -eq $SolutionPackage}
if ($Solution -ne $null) {
  if($Solution.Deployed -eq $true) {
    Write-Host "Retracting Solution from the Farm..."
    Uninstall-SPSolution -Identity $SolutionPackage -Local -Confirm:$false
-WebApplication $WebApp
    Write-Host "Solution retracted."
    Write-Host
  }
  Write-Host "Deleting Solution from solution store..."
  Remove-SPSolution -Identity $SolutionPackage -Confirm:$false
  Write-Host "Solution deleted."
  Write-Host
}

Write-Host "Adding Solution to solution store..."
Add-SPSolution -LiteralPath $Path
Write-Host "Solution added."
Write-Host
```

```
Write-Host "Deploying Solution to the Farm..."
Install-SPSolution -Identity $SolutionPackage -Local -GACDeployment
-WebApplication $WebApp
Write-Host "Deployment complete."

Write-Host
Write-Host "Script has completed. Press Enter to continue."
Read-Host
```

■ **Note** If the solution file contains any web application dependent items, such as Web Parts, you must add a "-WebApplication" parameter to both Install-SPSolution and Uninstall-SPSolution along with the URL of the web application. This will deploy the solution to a specified web application. You can optionally deploy to all defined web applications with the parameter "-AllWebApplications".

■ **Tip** If you run your SharePoint PowerShell scripts via the SharePoint 2010 Management Shell (available via Program Files ➤ Microsoft SharePoint 2010 Products), then you don't require the Add-PSSnapIn command, as the cmdlets for SharePoint will already have been automatically loaded.

## Activation Dependencies

SharePoint solution activation dependencies work in a similar fashion to feature activation dependencies. However, they are just slightly misleadingly named when deployed to the farm (the terminology is geared towards sandboxed solutions in the Solutions gallery). It acts like more of a deployment dependency in this scenario. That is, say you have Solution B that has its activation dependency set on Solution A. Solution A is *not* deployed to the farm. The attempt to deploy Solution B will result in an error.

In your example, the FooterLinksList solution is dependent upon the FooterLinksSchema solution. This makes sense, because you won't be able to provision a footer links list instance if the corresponding site columns and content types have not been deployed. So your first check point will be to ensure the FooterLinksSchema solution has been deployed to the Farm.

To add the activation dependency, expand the Package node in the FooterLinksList project and double-click on package.package to bring up the package designer. Click on the Manifest tab. Unlike adding feature activation dependencies, there is no convenient way of adding the solution activation dependency. You must edit the Manifest.xml file manually. Expand the Edit Options section and click Open in XML Editor, and you will see the code shown in Figure 12-21.

```
Package.package    Package.Template.xml  X

    <?xml version="1.0" encoding="utf-8"?>
    <Solution xmlns="http://schemas.microsoft.com/sharepoint/">
      <ActivationDependencies>
        <ActivationDependency SolutionId="25621bc8-13bc-46e4-9715-4c361724b244" />
      </ActivationDependencies>
    </Solution>
```

*Figure 12-21. Solution activation dependency manually defined*

---

■ **Tip** Always set solution activation dependencies for your SharePoint solution packages (WSP files) to avoid potential deployment errors.

---

To trigger the solution activation dependency, uninstall and remove both solutions (FooterLinksList and FooterLinksSchema) using PowerShell. Add the FooterLinksList solution using PowerShell. Go to Central Administration ➤ System Settings ➤ Manage Farm Solutions. Click on `footerlinkslist.wsp`. You should see the information shown in Figure 12-22.

Deploy Solution    Remove Solution    Back to Solutions

| | |
|---|---|
| Name: | footerlinkslist.wsp |
| Type: | Core Solution |
| Contains Web Application Resource: | Yes |
| Contains Global Assembly: | Yes |
| Contains Code Access Security Policy: | No |
| Deployment Server Type: | Front-end Web server |
| Deployment Status: | Not Deployed |
| Deployed To: | None |
| Last Operation Result: | No operation has been performed on the solution. |

*Figure 12-22. Footer Link List solution details in Central Administraiton*

Click Deploy Solution and accept the deployment option defaults on the following screen and click OK. You will see the error screen shown in Figure 12-23 stating that the dependent solution (FooterLinksSchema) has not been activated (i.e. deployed).

*Figure 12-23. Error statement*

As an exercise, recreate this situation, deploy the FooterLinksSchema solution, and then come back and verify you can also deploy the FooterLinksList solution.

# The Right Number of SharePoint Solutions

In this context, I am referring to SharePoint Solution (WSP) files, not a Visual Studio 2010 solution (SLN) file. In fact, please go right ahead and have one Visual Studio 2010 SLN file for your project if that makes sense for you. However, the current limitation with the SharePoint 2010 Visual Studio 2010 tools is that a Visual Studio project equals exactly one "Package" definition, which in turn means one WSP file. Each Visual Studio Project/SharePoint Package can contain one or more SharePoint Features, and each feature can consist of one or more items.

So what is the right number of SharePoint solutions? I can state with certainty that for your set of planned customizations the wrong answer is "one." It seems temptingly simple to go for one big package of features—after all, this is all brand new functionality, right? Or maybe you have otherwise not had to think about the deployment, so one big package does the job of getting the customizations "out there" at the end of the project.

I would prefer, if you are in doubt, that you define a new Visual Studio Project/SharePoint solution file rather than adding to your existing one. It is certainly more feasible to consider consolidating features into WSP files rather than to break apart a monolith. Here are some considerations for when to split out SharePoint features into new SharePoint solution files:

- *Partition your solutions with feature scope in mind*: For example, farm- and web application-scoped features have a tendency to be isolated, although mixing feature scopes in a SharePoint solution may still make packaging sense (if they have more in common with Site and Site Collection scoped features).

- *Partition your solutions with reusability in mind*: What features may other sites and site collections take advantage of independent of others?

- *Partition your solutions with maintainability in mind*: Consider now that features will require bug fixes and enhancements in isolation of one another. How can you minimize the impact of a solution upgrade or redeployment on other deployed features/solutions?

- *Partition your solutions along activation dependency lines, both solution and feature*: Draw out a map of the full feature and solution activation dependencies, both logical and those you can physically define. You will find this may drive your solution structure.

- *Always put the definition of "schema" (site columns and content types) into its own solution at minimum*: Consider reusability of sub-groups of the schema for further solution splitting.

- *Always provision list instances in a separate solution from the schema*: You may consider put related items with the list instance, such as a Web Part that specifically queries the list.

- *Particular types of SharePoint items have a tendency to be grouped together*: You may consider grouping specific types of SharePoint items together in a solution, such as workflow templates. A previous example was site columns and content types. Again, if this makes sense for you!

Figure 12-24 shows the structure and content of this chapter's example code, with the two solutions and three features defined. The arrow between the two solution files depicts the activation dependency between them, and the arrows between the features depict the feature activation dependencies that are *logically* in place.

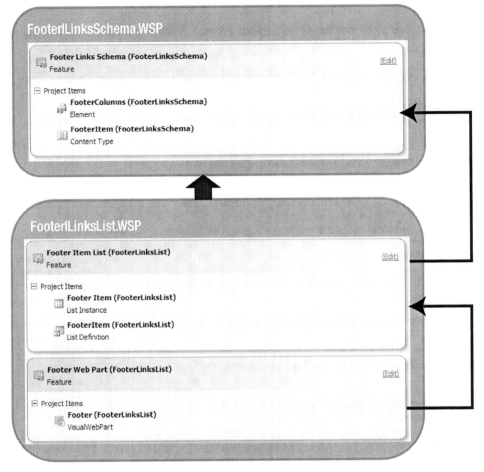

*Figure 12-24. Solution and feature dependencies depicted*

Note that the only activation dependency you can't *physically* define is the one between the footer Web Part and the footer item list. See the previous section on feature activation dependencies on why this is not possible.

---

▪ **Note** I don't mean to imply that in this scenario you couldn't have *one* Visual Studio solution file containing all three of these projects. Two of the projects could each have a package with the contents outlined above. So, yes, I have taken some liberties with this very simple example for the purposes of highlighting the possible best practices that more likely would be applied to a much larger customization project.

---

---

■ **Tip** Draw out and think carefully about your SharePoint solutions and what features they will contain. Also define as many physical solution activation dependencies and feature activation dependencies as possible.

---

# Upgrading Features and Solutions

As a developer, you will be providing updates to your SharePoint solution (WSP) files. Perhaps you are deploying enhancements or bug fixes to the Testing or Production environments. Different versions of your solution are likely currently running in each of those environments. The latest version will be in Development, a lower version in Testing, and current release (oldest) version in Production. Historically, this has been difficult to manage!

One choice would be to rip and replace the WSP using the full deployment lifecycle cmdlets for SPSolution: Remove and Uninstall the old WSP, then Add and Install the new WSP. This is often too drastic, quite unnecessary, and can lead to unpredictable results as you may not know exactly what might happen in your feature receiver code. Also, you may have a chain of dependent features. Obviously, things can get complicated quickly.

SharePoint 2010 has the cmdlet Update-SPSolution, which is the preferred and recommended way to push out an updated WSP to the farm. Caveat: I will add "when it is valid to do so." "Update" means you have some new elements or updated code for the GAC—not completely different or additional features! You will know when you have crossed the boundary because the update solution will fail. If you have a WSP that is already deployed to several environments and not easy to rip and replace, then I recommend that you put your new features into a new and separate WSP as they will be easier to deploy and manage.

We have had this ability to update a solution even in SharePoint 2007 (via an STSADM command), so this has been around for a while. There is a common misconception that it performs the same set of commands as rip and replace. It does *not*; key, for example, is the fact that feature receiver activate/deactivate code will not be fired.

What does the Update Solution do? It simply pushes out new and updated files from the WSP (primarily) into the SharePoint root folder (i.e. out to the SharePoint web front ends). It's perfectly fine on its own if you are simply updating files, such as newly compiled DLLs (to GAC), ASCX files (to control templates directory), new element files, updated feature.xml, images, application pages (to layouts directory), etc.

Update Solution is categorically *not* useless, as prevailing wisdom might indicate. In fact it is, and has been, extraordinarily useful and many time painless for deploying updated WSPs. However, I will certainly agree that it is often times *not* sufficient to only deploy new/updated files. Let's imagine there was no feature receiver nor Activate and Deactivate methods for us to insert custom code on our initial (and full) deployment. We could push the files out to the web server, but would have no means of custom initialization or clean up. Those were precisely the limitation we had in SharePoint 2007 with update solution, where we had to follow up the WSP update with custom script or C# (console app) code, and maybe run through a list and update some data related to the changes.

You probably have already heard many times by now about the new upgrade capability for features. This can either be in the form of a new declarative UpgradeActions section for the Feature.xml file or the new imperative FeatureUpgrading method in the feature receiver. In the remainder of this section, you will learn that Update Solution and Upgrade Solutions are separate steps. You will explore the mechanics of each and the process for accomplishing the upgrades.

## Getting Ready for the Walkthrough

Please define a second site collection. In my case I have called it
`http://intranet.theopenhighway.net/sites/Apress2`. If you are following along with the changes, please
do *not* activate any of this chapter's sample features or even deploy the updated solutions (which will
happen if you press F5 in Visual Studio, for example).

---

■ **Tip** Create a snapshot of your virtual machine before running the actual upgrade commands. This way, you can
easily go back to the machine state before the upgrade in case you wish to explore the upgrade in more detail or
try the upgrade scenario again.

---

You will be able to compare the first site collection against the second, where I will demonstrate that
the feature version running in a particular site collection can in fact be *different* from the installed
version!

## Version 1.1 Changes

Open up the Version 1.1 of the Visual Studio solution for this Chapter, `FooterLinksV2.sln`. You can
follow along as I detail the changes made to version 1 of the solution.

You have created Version 1.1 at the request of the client, who has stated that there are too many
Footer Link entries in the list. They don't want to delete any entries, but they want a means of managing
which ones are displayed. You have decided to add an Is Active flag (a Boolean) to the schema to indicate
which items are displayed. This requires numerous small changes through your projects and features.

1. First, start by updating the version number property of all of your features to
   1.1.0.0 (as all will be affected by changes in the scenario). Version 1.1 is the
   "right" upgrade, given the nature of the changes. Expand the feature folder of
   each project. Double-click on each feature to expose the properties. Figure 12-
   25 shows a sample of changing FooterLinksSchema feature to Version 1.1.

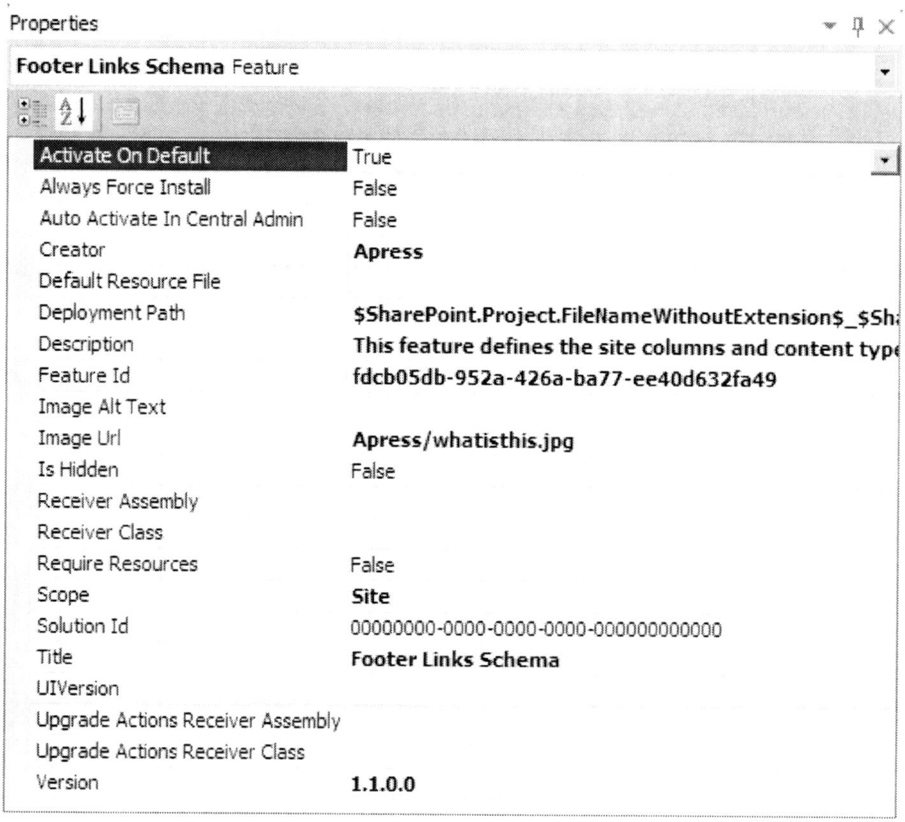

**Figure 12-25.** *Changing Feature Version to 1.1*

■ **Tip** Only increment the feature version if there has been a change. Always increment the feature version number if there is a change! Remember to make the *appropriate* change increment. The four-part build number is Major.Minor.Build.Revision. The Major.Minor version is typically the product version. For instance, SharePoint 2010 is version 14.0 (at time of release).

■ **Tip** Only publish a major feature version if there have been very significant changes to the software. Use of this number is ultimately up to the author. Sometimes it's used to designate the release number of the software. You might typically increment the build of software (such as 1.0.1, 1.0.2, etc) until you have a patch or point release, at which point it becomes 1.1.

2. Why the sideline discussions on versioning and the importance of the four-part number? You will see shortly that you have further control over your upgrades. You are able to trigger a v2v (the default), which upgrades from one product version to another (deals with Major.Minor version number changes), or trigger a b2b upgrade, which upgrades from one build to another (deals with Build.Revision version changes). In the real world, I have never seen anyone get this serious and detailed about their versioning and upgrade strategy for Features. This is an advanced note you will likely never use, but nevertheless keep in mind that this possibility is there if you need it!

3. In the FooterLinksSchema project, under Footer Columns (in SiteColumns folder) add an additional XML file, Elements2.xml. Ensure the Deployment Type property is set to ElementManifest, as shown in Figure 12-26.

*Figure 12-26. Footer Columns SharePoint item*

4. In the Elements2.xml file, define a new site column that will be named Is Active. You will see shortly why you are putting this site column in a separate XML file versus adding to the Elements.xml file containing the Sort Order column. Ensure the GUID is unique!

```xml
<?xml version="1.0" encoding="utf-8"?>
<Elements xmlns="http://schemas.microsoft.com/sharepoint/">
  <Field ID="{BB8EB2D5-3A68-4607-88F4-8338DACBD8E4}"
         Group="Apress Columns"
         Type="Boolean"
         Name="IsActive"
         DisplayName="Is Active"
         ShowInDisplayForm="TRUE"
         ShowInNewForm="TRUE"
         ShowInEditForm="TRUE" />
</Elements>
```

5. In the FooterLinksSchema project, edit the Elements.xml file that is under the FooterItem content type (under the content types folder), as shown in Figure 12-27.

*Figure 12-27. Edit the Elements.xml file*

6. In the Elements.xml file, using the GUID from the previous step, add the FieldRef to the content type, immediately below SortOrder.

```xml
<FieldRef ID="{BB8EB2D5-3A68-4607-88F4-8338DACBD8E4}" Name="IsActive" />
```

7.  In the FooterLinksList project, edit the Schema.xml for the FooterItem list definition (under the ListDefinitions folder). Add the FieldRef to the ContentTypes section (created in step 3). Add the Field to the Fields section (created in step 2).

8.  In the FooterLinksList project, edit the codebehind for the user control for the footer Web Part (under the Web Parts folder). Modify the footer links list query to include checking for the active flag:

```
<Where>
    <Eq>
        <FieldRef Name=""IsActive"" />
        <Value Type=""Integer"">1</Value>
    </Eq>
</Where>
<OrderBy>
    <FieldRef Name=""SortOrder"" Ascending=""True"" />
</OrderBy>
```

■ **Tip** Alright! Yes, this is a CAML (Collaborative Application Markup Language) query. Clearly this should be a new and shiny SP LINQ query, but for sake of this example, I didn't want to introduce the dependency to run `spmetal.exe` to generate the `datacontext` class (or to download and use the Visual Studio 2010 Power Toys).

So that takes care of the coding changes required to implement the new Is Active flag. Now you need to put in some changes that will drive an upgrade process from Version 1.0 to 1.1.

9.  Double-click on the FooterLinksSchema feature in the FooterLinksSchema project to bring up the feature designer. Click on the Manifest tab. Expand the Edit Options section. Add the UpgradeActions section shown in Figure 12-28— but you will want to do so using the Open in XML Editor option!

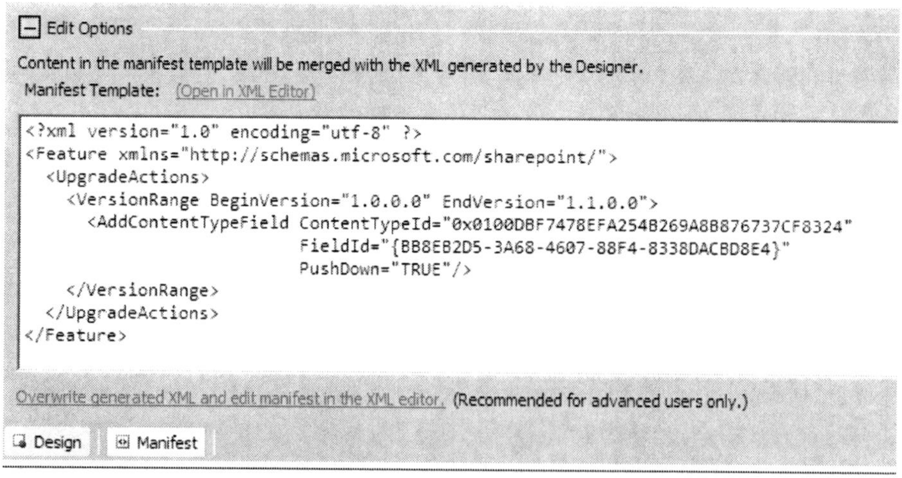

*Figure 12-28. Manually adding Upgrade Actions to FooterLinksSchema feature*

10. The UpgradeActions section in the `Feature.xml` file is new to SharePoint 2010. It allows you to specify actions to take as you upgrade from one specific version to another. Note the BeginVersion and EndVersion are actually optional; if not specified, the UpgradeActions would apply to any upgrade. Best practice? Be explicit about your upgrade actions by using version number ranges.

11. The first upgrade action is to add a field to an existing content type. The field ID specified is for the IsActive flag. Put another way, the IsActive flag field is the difference between the schema for the Version 1.0 of the Footer Item content type and Version 1.1. The PushDown attribute updates all instances of the content type in the site. Remember, there is the definition of the Content Type at the site collection level—but the Footer Links list has a literal copy of the content type and this copy must also be updated.

12. The existing list will now have the IsActive flag, but all current values will be false. According to the logic in your revised Web Part query, all the footer links will disappear! The solution is to make sure you run through all the entries on the current footer links list and update the IsActive value to true. Double-click on the FooterItemList feature in the FooterLinksList project to bring up the feature designer. Click on the Manifest tab. Expand the Edit Options section. Add the following UpgradeActions section, but do so using the Open in XML Editor option, as shown in Figure 12-29.

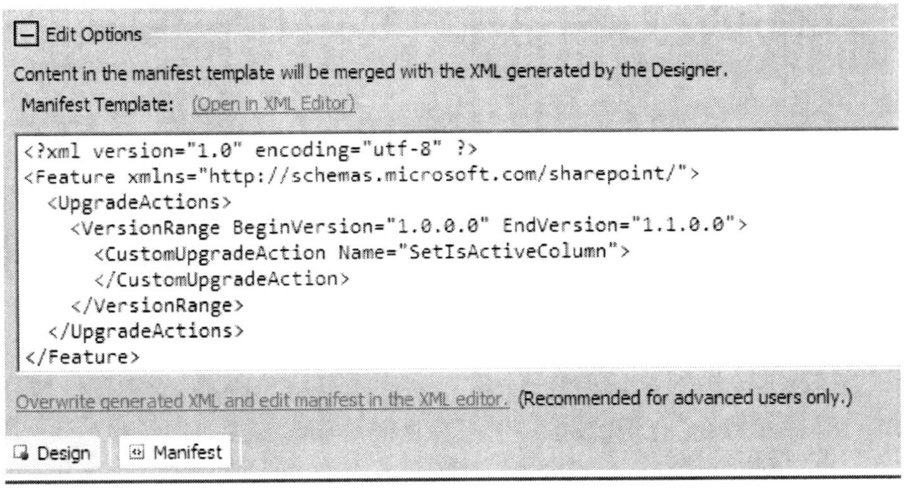

```xml
<?xml version="1.0" encoding="utf-8" ?>
<Feature xmlns="http://schemas.microsoft.com/sharepoint/">
  <UpgradeActions>
    <VersionRange BeginVersion="1.0.0.0" EndVersion="1.1.0.0">
      <CustomUpgradeAction Name="SetIsActiveColumn">
      </CustomUpgradeAction>
    </VersionRange>
  </UpgradeActions>
</Feature>
```

*Figure 12-29. Manually adding Upgrade Actions to FooterLinksList feature*

13. One other example that Upgrade Actions provides is the ability to trigger a FeatureUpgrading method in a Feature Receiver (this, too, is new to SharePoint 2010), by specifying a Custom Upgrade Action. There is only one specified here, but note I can have multiple nodes of Custom Upgrade Action. The FeatureUpgrading method would be called for each node, passing in the name and an optional subset of parameters (there are no parameters in this

example). Let's first view the FeatureUpgrading method and then I will describe
how this works.

14. Open up the FooterItemList.FeatureEventReceiver.cs file. Add the following
    code. You can see that the guts of this goes through the Footer Links list and
    update each item IsActive column to true.

```
public override void FeatureUpgrading(SPFeatureReceiverProperties
props, string upgradeActionName,
System.Collections.Generic.IDictionary<string, string> parameters)
{
    SPWeb site = props.Feature.Parent as SPWeb;
    if (site != null)
    {
        // determine which custom upgrade action is executing
        switch (upgradeActionName)
        {
            case "SetIsActiveColumn":
                // See if the Footer Links List exists
                SPList list = site.Lists.TryGetList("Footer Links");
                if (list != null)
                {
                    // Set the new IsActive Flag for each item on
// the current list
                    SPListItemCollection items = list.Items;
                    foreach (SPListItem listItem in items)
                    {
                        listItem["IsActive"] = true;
                        listItem.Update();
                    }
                }

                break;
            default:
                // exit if unknown feature action
                break;
        }
    }
}
```

15. So each call made to FeatureUpgrading from each CustomUpgradeAction in
    the Feature.xml will pass in the string "upgradeActionName". In your case, the
    value will be SetIsActiveColumn. The best practice is demonstrated here where
    you use a switch statement to process values for the action name, and a default
    break in case an unknown value makes its way in so it will exit cleanly.

16. You can also see that you will be passed a dictionary collection of parameters,
    if they were specified in the CustomUpgradeAction. Again, I'm not requiring
    parameters for this upgrade example.

17. There's just one last *very important* setting to make! This setting is easy to
    overlook. Double-click on FooterItemList.Feature to expose the properties.
    Note that the Upgrade Actions Receiver assembly and the Upgrade Actions

Receiver class will initially be blank. You can copy them exactly from the respective properties , Receiver Assembly and Receiver Class. Don't forget to double check that the version is set to 1.1.0.0, as shown in Figure 12-30.

| Properties | ▾ ₊ |
|---|---|
| **Footer Item List** Feature | |

| | |
|---|---|
| Activate On Default | True |
| Always Force Install | False |
| Auto Activate In Central Admin | False |
| Creator | **Apress** |
| Default Resource File | |
| Deployment Path | **$SharePoint.Project.FileNameWithoutExtension$_$SharePoint.Feature.FileNa** |
| Description | **This feature will define and create a list for footer items.** |
| Feature Id | **aaaef021-32c2-4d98-9bf0-178b183eabf3** |
| Image Alt Text | |
| Image Url | **Apress/whatisthis.jpg** |
| Is Hidden | False |
| Receiver Assembly | **$SharePoint.Project.AssemblyFullName$** |
| Receiver Class | **$SharePoint.Type.89d43549-8b5b-43a0-b266-b15bb31615ee.FullName$** |
| Require Resources | False |
| Scope | Web |
| Solution Id | 00000000-0000-0000-0000-000000000000 |
| Title | **Footer Item List** |
| UIVersion | |
| Upgrade Actions Receiver Assembly | **$SharePoint.Project.AssemblyFullName$** |
| Upgrade Actions Receiver Class | **$SharePoint.Type.89d43549-8b5b-43a0-b266-b15bb31615ee.FullName$** |
| Version | **1.1.0.0** |

*Figure 12-30. Setting Upgrade Actions properties*

18. Wow! That was as much work as the actual upgrades you made to your code. Now you can build and package the new SharePoint solution (WSP) files for Footer Links schema and Footer Links list (but, again, don't deploy them at this time).

## Solution Updating

I have provided a Query Features PowerShell script that does a Get-SPFeature versus QueryFeature. This script compares the installed version versus the version currently running in the various sites. For now (before the upgrade), we still have version 1.0.0.0 installed and running for our three features in the Apress site, as shown here:

```
Feature: FooterLinksSchema_FooterLinksSchema
======================================================================
The following version is the INSTALLED Version:  1.0.0.0
Version  1.0.0.0  is currently RUNNING in site at↵
  http://intranet.theopenhighway.net/sites/apress

Feature: FooterLinksList_FooterItemList
```

```
===========================================================================
The following version is the INSTALLED Version:  1.0.0.0
Version  1.0.0.0  is currently RUNNING in site at↵
  http://intranet.theopenhighway.net/sites/apress

Feature: FooterLinksList_FooterWebPart
===========================================================================
The following version is the INSTALLED Version:  1.0.0.0
Version  1.0.0.0  is currently RUNNING in site at
http://intranet.theopenhighway.net/sites/apress
```

There is another script provided that will take the new solution files and perform the PowerShell command Update-SPSolution; this will physically push the new files out to the SharePoint Root folder.

With these commands executed, let's verify that the files were in fact pushed out. Go to the SharePoint Root folder in your virtual machine (located at `C:\Program Files\Common Files\Microsoft Shared\Web Server Extensions\14`). Go to the `Template/Features` folder and find the feature beginning with the name FooterListSchema (either by name or sort directory descending by date). In the FooterItem sub directory, you can verify the newly created `Elements2.xml` is there (as shown in Figure 12-31).

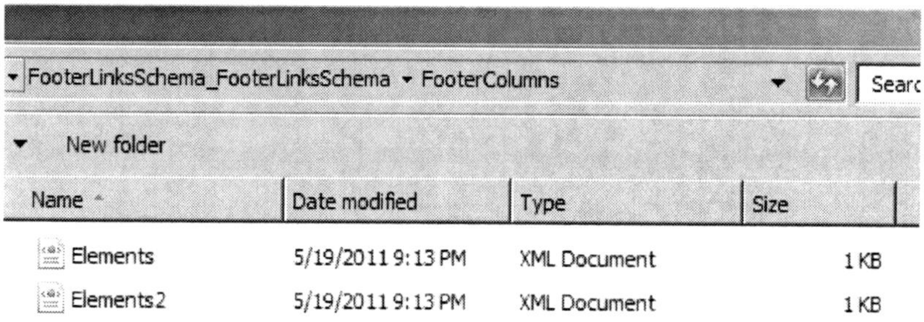
FooterLinksSchema_FooterLinksSchema ▸ FooterColumns
Searc
New folder
Name
Date modified
Type
Size
Elements
5/19/2011 9:13 PM
XML Document
1 KB
Elements2
5/19/2011 9:13 PM
XML Document
1 KB

***Figure 12-31.** Examining the deployed Feature files*

Open up the Feature.xml file. Note that the version number is now 1.1.0.0, as shown in Figure 12-32.

```xml
<?xml version="1.0" encoding="utf-8" ?>
<Feature xmlns="http://schemas.microsoft.com/sharepoint/" Title="Footer Links Schema"
    Creator="Apress" Description="This feature defines the site columns and content types for the
    footer links list." Id="fdcb05db-952a-426a-ba77-ee40d632fa49"
    ImageUrl="Apress/whatisthis.jpg" Scope="Site" Version="1.1.0.0">
  <UpgradeActions>
    <VersionRange BeginVersion="1.0.0.0" EndVersion="1.1.0.0">
      <AddContentTypeField
        ContentTypeId="0x0100DBF7478EFA254B269A8B876737CF8324"
        FieldId="{BB8EB2D5-3A68-4607-88F4-8338DACBD8E4}" PushDown="TRUE" />
    </VersionRange>
  </UpgradeActions>
  <ElementManifests>
    <ElementManifest Location="FooterColumns\Elements.xml" />
    <ElementManifest Location="FooterColumns\Elements2.xml" />
    <ElementManifest Location="FooterItem\Elements.xml" />
  </ElementManifests>
</Feature>
```

*Figure 12-32. Confirming deployed Feature.xml is at Version 1.1.0.0*

Go to the Apress2 site created in the Getting Ready section (in my case
`http://intranet.theopenhighway.net/sites/Apress2`). Manually activate the Footer Links Schema
feature at the site collection level. Then activate the Footer Item List feature at the site level and finally
come back to activate the Footer Web Part feature at the site collection level.

If you re-run the Query Features PowerShell script again, you now see the following:

```
Feature: FooterLinksSchema_FooterLinksSchema
=======================================================================
The following version is the INSTALLED Version:  1.1.0.0
Version  1.0.0.0  is currently RUNNING in site at↵
  http://intranet.theopenhighway.net/sites/apress
Version  1.1.0.0  is currently RUNNING in site at↵
  http://intranet.theopenhighway.net/sites/apress2


Feature: FooterLinksList_FooterItemList
=======================================================================
The following version is the INSTALLED Version:  1.1.0.0
Version  1.0.0.0  is currently RUNNING in site at↵
  http://intranet.theopenhighway.net/sites/apress
Version  1.1.0.0  is currently RUNNING in site at↵
  http://intranet.theopenhighway.net/sites/apress2


Feature: FooterLinksList_FooterWebPart
=======================================================================
The following version is the INSTALLED Version:  1.1.0.0
Version  1.0.0.0  is currently RUNNING in site at↵
```

```
   http://intranet.theopenhighway.net/sites/apress
Version 1.1.0.0 is currently RUNNING in site at↵
   http://intranet.theopenhighway.net/sites/apress2
```

I think that is pretty amazing—that you can actually have multiple versions of a feature running simultaneously in different site collections of the same web application.

# Feature Upgrading

According to the Query Features PowerShell script, you are at the point where you have Version 1.1 of your features deployed, the Apress site has version 1.0 of the features running, and the Apress2 site has version 1.1 of the features running. What remains to be done is to upgrade the sites running the older version of the features. With the upgrade code, I hope that you can see you are targeting the differences in functionality between version 1.0 and version 1.1. These differences are as follows:

- Define an additional site column called Is Active.

- Update the content type to include this new site column, and push down this change (which means update all references to the content type to include the new site column definition). In your case, the Footer Link content type attached to your Footer Link List will be updated.

- Update the list schema.

- Update the query in the Web Part to include the Is Active flag.

- Run an update on existing items in the Footer Link list to set the Is Active flag to true.

I have provided a full script to upgrade each of the features to Version 1.1. Here are the key lines of the script:

```
features = $webApp.QueryFeatures($FeatureId, $true)
foreach($feature in $features){
  $feature.Upgrade($true)
}
```

QueryFeatures with the true parameter will retrieve all features in the current web application that are scoped to site or web and have a specific needsUpgrade state. And then, in an anti-climactic fashion, the $feature.Uprade will perform all of the upgrade actions as listed.

If you re-run the Query Features PowerShell script again, you now see the following:

```
Feature: FooterLinksSchema_FooterLinksSchema
=====================================================================
The following version is the INSTALLED Version: 1.1.0.0
Version 1.1.0.0 is currently RUNNING in site at↵
  http://intranet.theopenhighway.net/sites/apress
Version 1.1.0.0 is currently RUNNING in site at↵
  http://intranet.theopenhighway.net/sites/apress2

Feature: FooterLinksList_FooterItemList
=====================================================================
The following version is the INSTALLED Version: 1.1.0.0
Version 1.1.0.0 is currently RUNNING in site at↵
```

```
http://intranet.theopenhighway.net/sites/apress
Version  1.1.0.0  is currently RUNNING in site at↵
  http://intranet.theopenhighway.net/sites/apress2

Feature: FooterLinksList_FooterWebPart
==========================================================================
The following version is the INSTALLED Version:  1.1.0.0
Version  1.1.0.0  is currently RUNNING in site at↵
  http://intranet.theopenhighway.net/sites/apress
Version  1.1.0.0  is currently RUNNING in site at↵
  http://intranet.theopenhighway.net/sites/apress2
```

Now everything is running at version 1.1. Success! As a quick verification, in the original Apress site, look at the list settings for Footer Links, as shown in Figure 12-33. Note the IsActive field appears; it has been pushed down from the content type update.

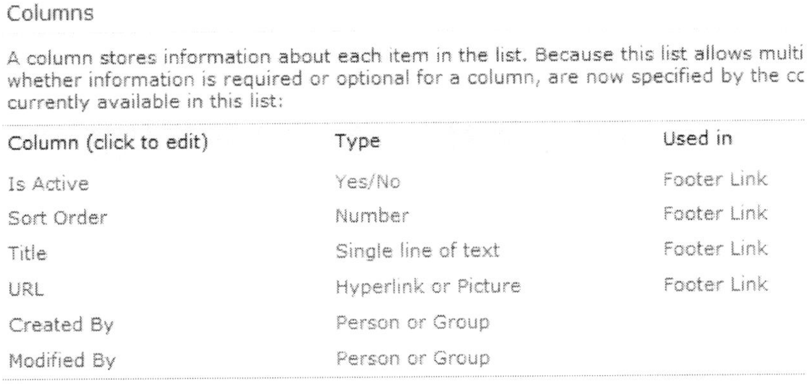

Columns

A column stores information about each item in the list. Because this list allows multi whether information is required or optional for a column, are now specified by the cc currently available in this list:

| Column (click to edit) | Type | Used in |
| --- | --- | --- |
| Is Active | Yes/No | Footer Link |
| Sort Order | Number | Footer Link |
| Title | Single line of text | Footer Link |
| URL | Hyperlink or Picture | Footer Link |
| Created By | Person or Group | |
| Modified By | Person or Group | |

*Figure 12-33. Footer Links list settings*

Edit any of the items in the list and note that the IsActive flag is set, verifying that your FeatureUpgrading code ran (see Figure 12-34).

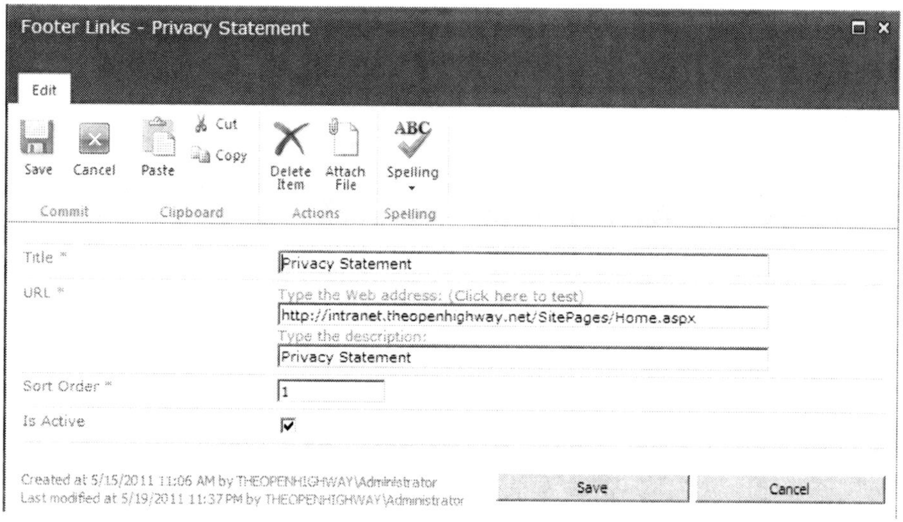

*Figure 12-34. Confirming that the Feature Upgrading code has run*

## Upgrading with PSCONFIG.EXE

The command line upgrade for SharePoint (`psconfig.exe`) offers one advantage over upgrading with PowerShell Feature.Upgrade and that is the ability to control which upgrades are performed. If, after Update-SPSolution, you run the following command line:

```
psconfig -cmd upgrade -inplace b2b
```

It will trigger the upgrade for version 1.0.0.1 to 1.0.0.2, but *not* 1.1.0.0. That is, it will make any change in the last two places of the x.x.x.x format version number. If you run the following command line:

```
psconfig -cmd upgrade -inplace v2v
```

It will trigger the version upgrade from 1.0.0.0 to 1.1.0.0, as in our example. That is, it will make any change in the first two places of the x.x.x.x format version number.

Again, I haven't run across this requirement in practice, but it's there if you need it!

## Summary

Have you "been there" regarding my scenarios of observations from the field? If you haven't, I am clearly recommending that you don't "go there." Perhaps you now see why this is the case in so many situations. SharePoint solutions, features, packaging, versions, and dependencies require much thought and advance planning. I hope I have shown that taking the time to do so is a great investment. I hope, too, that you have a solid understanding of the mechanics involved—invaluable for the troubleshooting days ahead. If you keep one main thought in mind—and that is the maintenance and upgrading of features *in the future*—then you will create a great structure with which to work. I encourage you to think beyond simply the first deployment.

# CHAPTER 13

# Business Intelligence

This chapter will look into how Business Intelligence is integrated into the SharePoint 2010 platform, starting with an overview of the basics of Business Intelligence, introducing the new additions made available to Business Intelligence in SharePoint 2010, exploring how to optimize your Business Intelligence Resources to get the most out of them, followed by Web Parts and the enhancements that are readily available for your use. This chapter will also review the new features in Excel Services, talk about planning PerformancePoint Services, and culminate with assessing which Reporting Services type of mode is suitable for your needs.

If you are already familiar with the basics of Business Intelligence, feel free to move directly into the topic of your choice or interest.

## Overview

The term Business Intelligence has been a buzz word for some time. Buzz words lose their true meaning with the passing of time and thus cause confusion, so let's start by defining the meaning of Business Intelligence.

*Business Intelligence is understood as a variety of methodologies and techniques used in identifying, gathering, extracting, analyzing and providing data to empower users in the decision making process.*

Why has Business Intelligence become such an important focus for businesses? It has steadily attracted the attention of management executives. To cite a few reasons, it can

- Identify problem areas in a company.

- Reduce and accelerate the decision making process.

- Save money.

- Reduce costs.

When the amount of time required for decision making has been reduced, the possibility of impacting the bottom line increases as the company's efficiency and processing times are boosted by enhancing and providing a competitive advantage against their competitors. As a result, businesses have realized that it is no longer a luxury but a worthwhile and essential investment.

# New Additions to Business Intelligence in SharePoint 2010

Business Intelligence within SharePoint has grown since the previous version. In fact, there has been a considerable investment and expansion to what is known as the self-service Business Intelligence arena.

The self-service Business Intelligence area has consolidated a previously known product named ProClarity with PerformancePoint; the result is called PerformancePoint Services within SharePoint 2010. Likewise, Excel Services has grown more robust since its previous implementation in Microsoft Office SharePoint 2007; it is no longer confined to data within Excel thanks to the integration of PowerPivot with Excel. Excel Services can now gather data from multiple sources and perform calculations on large amounts of data very quickly. Moreover, it includes a new and improved Excel Web Access Web Part that Reporting Services has made available; as a result, elegant and visually appealing charts that were not available before in SQL Server 2008 are now possible.

The Business Intelligence Center has been revamped and includes dashboards and template options; you're no longer confined to a predetermined template. A new Chart Web Part allows charts to be generated from data in SharePoint Lists, plus new and improved Reporting Services Web Parts are AJAX-enabled.

There are even two new additions to the Business Intelligence area: Access Services and Visio Services. The biggest advantage of these new additions is that they don't require Microsoft Access or Microsoft Visio on the client computer; also, both are available through the SharePoint 2010 User Interface (UI).

Access Services provides the ability to publish Access databases into SharePoint 2010; while this might not seem important, it does have a distinct advantage of accessing a central location for tables within an Access published database, and one that is updated through the browser. It does have its limitations, such as no support for VBA, but there is the ability to recreate the Microsoft Access Database from the site. This last feature is helpful because you can publish the Access database as a SharePoint Site and whenever you are ready to re-consolidate it as an MDB, you can do so. Reporting is also available without the need for SQL Server Reporting Services.

Visio Services provides the ability to share Visio diagrams and Visio data-driven diagrams without requiring Microsoft Visio to be installed on the client computer. Depending on who you talk to, these two new features are not always considered part of the Business Intelligence area—most likely because they are neither as powerful nor as tightly integrated as the other features. Because these are the first versions of Access and Visio Services, given enough time, they will improve and become more powerful and versatile just as Excel Services and other previous new kids on the block have.

# Optimizing Your Business Intelligence Resources

Before even creating a dashboard, report, or Excel workbook, it's of the utmost importance to assess how many end users will be using the Business Intelligence area(s) of SharePoint 2010; in other words, it's important to plan. As the saying goes, "If one does not plan, one plans to fail."

This is vital for a successful deployment of the services in the Business Intelligence area of SharePoint 2010. The Business Intelligence Application Services will be relying upon the hardware architecture that was planned and deployed for the delivery of dashboards, reports, and workbooks to the end user. Adding to the situation is the fact that it is highly likely that the users that belong to the Business Intelligence areas of the company are not your typical day-to-day users. Most Business Intelligence users are high profile individuals that make important decisions based on the tools they use on a daily basis. If these are not fast or robust enough, the end result of the Business Intelligence project will not be considered successful; instead it might be seen as a waste of resources.

A Business Intelligence project must provide data immediately, so it is extremely important to plan the processes to deliver the data for analysis while simultaneously supplying on-the-fly analysis for all end users. The system must be able to respond in a timely fashion and accommodate multiple requests at the same time.

# Architecture Planning

Architecture planning is more than just the assessment of the number of servers, memory, and storage required for the project to be deployed. In this scenario, you are targeting resources that will support PerformancePoint, PowerPivot, Excel, and Reporting Services at a minimum.While there are many factors and variables to consider, the following list can serve as a guideline:

- Number of simultaneous end users.

- Estimated workload of end users.

- Data amounts related to the end user's workloads.

- Business Intelligence Services that will be up and running.

Once you have a good estimate of these items, you can establish a preliminary budget. Then you can shop around and determine what you can purchase within your budget—or determine if your budget is large enough to make any of it happen. Sometimes budgets are predetermined and you don't have much choice regarding what hardware resources can be purchased. If this is the case, it's important to make the target users aware of these limitations and coordinate how everyone can coexist without affecting performance for the entire group of Business Intelligence end users. Microsoft has published the following links to assist in this process:

- Capacity management and sizing overview for SharePoint Server 2010

    http://technet.microsoft.com/en-us/library/ff758647.aspx

- Capacity management for SharePoint Server 2010

    http://technet.microsoft.com/en-us/sharepoint/ff601870

- SharePoint 2010 performance and capacity technical case studies

    www.microsoft.com/download/en/details.aspx?displayLang=en&id=7480

- SharePoint Server 2010 performance and capacity test results and recommendations—This contains the planning for

    - Business connectivity services

    - Large Scale Document Repositories

    - Social computing

    - Office web apps

    - SharePoint server caches

    - Visio services

    - Word automation services

    www.microsoft.com/download/en/details.aspx?displayLang=en&id=12768

Additionally, a great tool for capacity planning is an Excel workbook made available by Tihomir Ignatov (Microsoft ). It contains three tabs.

- General Sites Sizing: Collects current database size and file count, and projects based on entered estimates the growth for a year

- Capacity: Content, search index and LUN sizes

- About: Author and more details

- Available at `http://tihomirignatov.blogspot.com/2010/12/sharepoint-2010-capacity-planning-and.html`

Most of the time, existing hardware for the initial rollout of SharePoint 2010 is used and serves as a starting point for the Business Intelligence initiative. While this is a valid way to start, it is not a recommended situation for the Business Intelligence initiative because it is a very different system when it comes to resource consumption. Keep in mind that every project varies, so the architecture that worked well for a specific project may not work well for a different project. That said, it's recommended as a starting point for a pilot hardware infrastructure to begin with a separate server for each layer. So in this case, the layers would be Web Front Ends, Applications, and Database. You should also do the following:

- Involve all users for the pilot and final rollout to use the setup infrastructure.

- Gather and collect usage and performance data.

- Review the collected data to assess what the next steps might be. These could include

  - The fine tuning or increase of

    - Memory
    - Storage
    - Hardware
    - Etc.

Last but not least, it's necessary to pinpoint where the majority, if not all, of the data will be coming from. Why do you need to know the data source(s)? Because of storage, as listed previously. It's recommended to have a structured and performant source for your Business Intelligence inquiries.

---

■ **Note** While there can be many different data sources, I recommend using Microsoft SQL Server Databases and Data Warehouses instead of Lists or Workbooks, particularly since they provide a variety of tools that are useful in the optimization processes.

---

## Data Storage Optimizations

Data can be stored in SharePoint lists and/or databases. Part of the planning process is to decide which provides the most options. Often SharePoint lists are chosen as the main storage source, but it is by no means the only or the most versatile choice. What follows is a review of the details of SharePoint lists and databases.

# Lists

Lists are a key component in any version of SharePoint; improvements have been made since their introduction. A list is very similar to a database table—the keyword being "similar." The small differences can matter when making use of lists in SharePoint. These small differences include the following:

- A key is automatically created and selected on every list (usually the column named Title).

- Lists exist within a site and are not generally available to all sites.

- Lists can be throttled to manage large amounts of data and improve response times.

---

≋ **Note** Throttling can be thought of being very much like caching, in which you are indicating how many list items will be retrieved when a request is made.

---

Even though lists are an excellent way of sharing and collaborating and have improved greatly with SharePoint 2010, it is important to remember the following key aspect:

---

≋ **Note** Lists are not database tables, nor should they be used as such.

---

What is often forgotten is: Where are SharePoint Lists stored? Well, guess where? In the SharePoint content databases. That said, it doesn't hurt to question if there is the need to have an extra step involved in the process for the retrieval of data, particularly if you can go directly to the source and that source can be optimized in more ways than a SharePoint list.

## List Planning Guidelines

Below are the top items to reference when planning your Lists (a comprehensive list is available at: http://technet.microsoft.com/en-us/library/cc262787.aspx#ListLibrary):

- A maximum items are 30 million per list.

- A maximum of 100 selected items per bulk operation through the UI.

- A maximum of 48 calculated columns.

- A maximum of 94 managed metadata columns.

- A list view threshold of 5,000.

  - This can be modified; when increased, it will directly impact performance.

  - It's also known as list throttling.

- A 2GB file size limit for attachments.

  - This can be increased if needed; performance will be directly impacted.

- A maximum of 8 join operations in a query.

  - When exceeded, operations are blocked on the list.

- Mobile views availability: Out of the box, the limits are constrained to the real estate available for the mobile devices.

- Data availability:If the data will grow and will need to be available to multiple applications enterprise wide, a database is the best choice, particularly because it has the potential to be accessed by a large range of applications ( Microsoft Office, Microsoft SharePoint 2010, Business Connectivity Services, Custom Developed Applications, etc. ).

---

■ **Note** `http://technet.microsoft.com/en-us/library/cc262787.aspx#ListLibrary` is updated with the latest updates made available with the SharePoint 2010 Service Pack 1 Update.

---

## SharePoint Content Databases

The content database aspect is often forgotten and thus not always planned well; most of the time this happens because of budget limitations. But once the performance starts affecting the usage of SharePoint and Business Intelligence within SharePoint, questions will be asked; many times there are no straight answers to those questions.

Because most applications, if not a large majority nowadays, depend and store the data used directly in databases, it's of the utmost importance to take into account the following considerations when it comes to the SharePoint content databases:

- Regularly monitor the available free space in your database drives and files. This includes

  - Dedicating your drives to your database files, preferably for exclusive use. This concept should be applied throughout the different types of storage in use.

  - Placing your log and database files in separate drives and LUNs.

- Plan and/or leverage quota management to keep track of the maximum sizes for your site collections.More details are available at `http://technet.microsoft.com/en-us/library/cc891489.aspx`.

- Plan the location for your content database files.

- Plan for High Availability.

- Prepare and regularly test a disaster recovery plan. Make sure to include

  - Mirroring, which is available natively in SharePoint 2010. I recommend mirroring for setting up an offsite backup infrastructure. Post SPI I would strongly recommend considering SQL Server 2012 and AlwaysOn.

  - Backup Tools include

    - SharePoint Central Administration

    - SQL Server

    - PowerShell

    - Explore and review third party products that could align with your needs; each one varies in their offerings and features provided.

    - I recommend using a mix of SQL Server and PowerShell, mostly due to the cost benefits and flexibility that both provide.

  - Backup storage locations: Use both onsite and offsite options.

  - Security

    - Plan for the security of the data in the backups. If necessary, decide if data in certain sites or site collections should be covered in a different plan or perhaps a completely separate software/hardware infrastructure.

    - Breaches

      - Lost backups.

      - Unauthorized access to data: Adhere to company policies or create one if it doesn't exist.

  - Frequency: Options include full, incremental, and a mix of both.

  - Test the backups to ensure that they are not corrupt and can be used for a recovery when disaster occurs.

  - Database maintenance.

  - Scheduled drills for disaster recovery preparation.

  - If a Disaster Recovery Plan is not available, a starting point is available at http://technet.microsoft.com/en-us/library/cc261687.aspx.

  - Drill executions

    - Executed as often as the Disaster Recovery Plan stipulates.

    - The drills should be executed as often as the amount of data loss that is acceptable.

  - The drills can be separated into

- External Facing
- Internal Facing
  - Full: Allows for operations to continue without any change.
  - Limited: Allows for the internal operations to continue operating at a reduced capacity.
- Full recovery on a similar environment
- Off site on an alternate environment
- Content Only
  - Site Collection
  - Sites
  - Lists
  - Document Libraries
- Never recover backups directly into the current failed environment. Test in a separate and identical environment prior to making the restore to the target environment. This allows for finding out if there any problem has affected the data in the backup.

While this list is not necessarily all inclusive, it has been my experience that many companies forget to implement one or more items from this list. The worst chase is when a company doesn't even bother to address them at any point in time after the implementations have been set to "live."

When everything is working, things are fine. That's when this list is easily dismissed and ignored. But when disaster strikes—which it always does; it's just a matter of time—then it becomes a high priority to recover the data. Stress and pressure become a constant until the data is recovered and the failed systems are working as they should.

## Best Practices

- Assess which storage is best suited for your data
  - SharePoint
  - Database: Keep in mind that when data is stored in a database, it's easier to export or share.
- How much data will be stored in the list(s)
  - The maximum limit is 30 million items in a list.
  - Consider throttling; this can, in certain cases, enhance performance.
- If the data stored in SharePoint lists will be shared, consider the following:
  - Site columns and/or content types

- Usingcontent types instead of folders when possible; folders can affect performance.

- Organize the data to be presented from lists in views.

    - Create multiple views if needed; most of the time, it is related to how the data will be organized. Some users or departments might only need certain columns, specific sorting, and/or grouping; this will vary depending on end user requests and needs.

- Plan the steps involved with the SharePoint lists.

    - Data entry and/or manipulation

    - Charting

    - Reporting

    - Creation of multiple Web Part pages. The Web Part pages should be created from the standpoint of the following:

    - Performance

    - Organization

    - Ease of use

- Disable the following settings if they won't be used:

    - Versioning: They can grow out of control if not monitored.

    - The limit for major versions is 400,000.

    - This should be reviewed if versioning has reached double digits.

    - Attachments: Most of the time they aren't used.

    - Folders: Help organize content through a SharePoint list or document library; while they are useful, content types should always supersede the usage of folders particularly due to the searchability features that content types provide.

- Enable inline editing. It simplifies data editing for the end user.

- Determine the items to limit or display, taking into account the following criteria:

    - Performance

    - Boundaries and limits

    - List throttling

    - Mobile devices

- Total the columns that contain relevant amounts or numbers.

- Index columns that will be used frequently for better performance (remember that the maximum is 20).

- Limit your lookups to a maximum of 8.

- Ensure that the target end users have the proper permissions setup on the list(s).

If you would like to learn more about managing large lists and throttling, the following links will interest you:

```
http://office.microsoft.com/en-us/sharepoint-server-help/sharepoint-lists-v-techniques-for-
managing-large-lists-RZ101874361.aspx
```

```
http://msdn.microsoft.com/en-us/library/ee557257.aspx
```

# Web Parts

Web Parts are everywhere within SharePoint 2010. For instance, they are used to display, create, update, and delete data inside SharePoint lists. Web Parts have a variety of uses and they can be used for just about for anything within sites. Within every SharePoint site, a SharePoint Web Part is most likely being used.

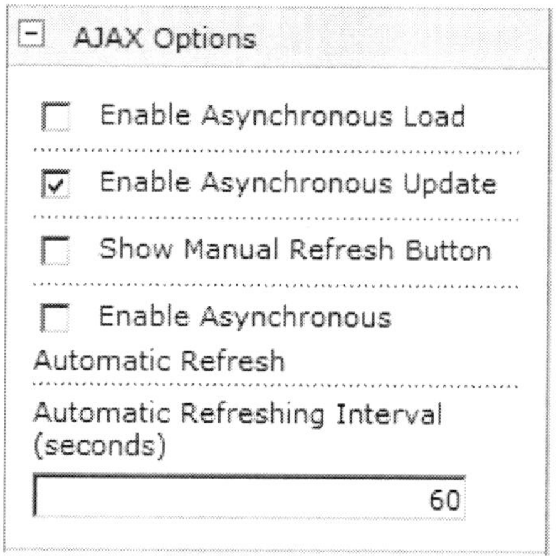

*Figure 13-1. Enhanced List View Web Part*

Figure 13-1details the enhanced List View Web Part, which is the ability to configure the AJAX options of the Web Part. The AJAX Options enhancement is a welcome enhancement that does make a difference when used with other Web Parts that support AJAX. A quick example would be by connecting with other List Web Parts to filter them.

## Filtering Lists

In order to illustrate the use of filters in SharePoint lists, an example site called "BI Lists" has been provided. The BI Listssite contains the following SharePoint lists:

- Sales People

- Month And Year

- Yearly Sales

Additionally, it contains the following site pages:

- Sales

- FilterBySalesPerson

The sample is not all-inclusive or extensive but it does serve the purpose of illustrating how filtering can be used to your advantage. The Sales site page contains a Chart Web Part, which serves to demonstrate the Chart Web Part by creating a bar chart report based on the data from the Yearly Sales SharePoint list. The FilterBySalesPerson site page contains Text Filter, SharePoint List Filter, Sales People, and Yearly Sales Web Parts. If you're not familiar with the Filter Web Parts, they did exist in Microsoft Office SharePoint Server 2007, but they are seldom discussed. They are very useful and powerful, particularly when filtering data from List View Web Parts.

The difference between the Text Filter and the SharePoint List Filter Web Parts is that the Text Filter Web Part the filter values are typed in while the SharePoint List Filter Web Part displays the choices as radio buttons.

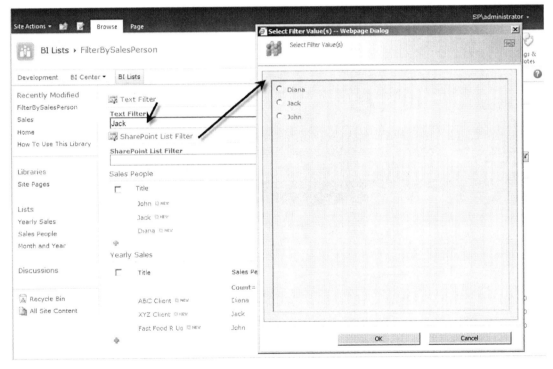

*Figure 13-2. Filter Web Parts*

Figure 13-2illustrates the values for the Text Filter and SharePoint List Filter Web Parts.Once the values have been selected, it's noticeable that the Sales People and Yearly Sales Web Parts have been filtered based on the typed-in value of "Jack" from the Text Filter Web Part.

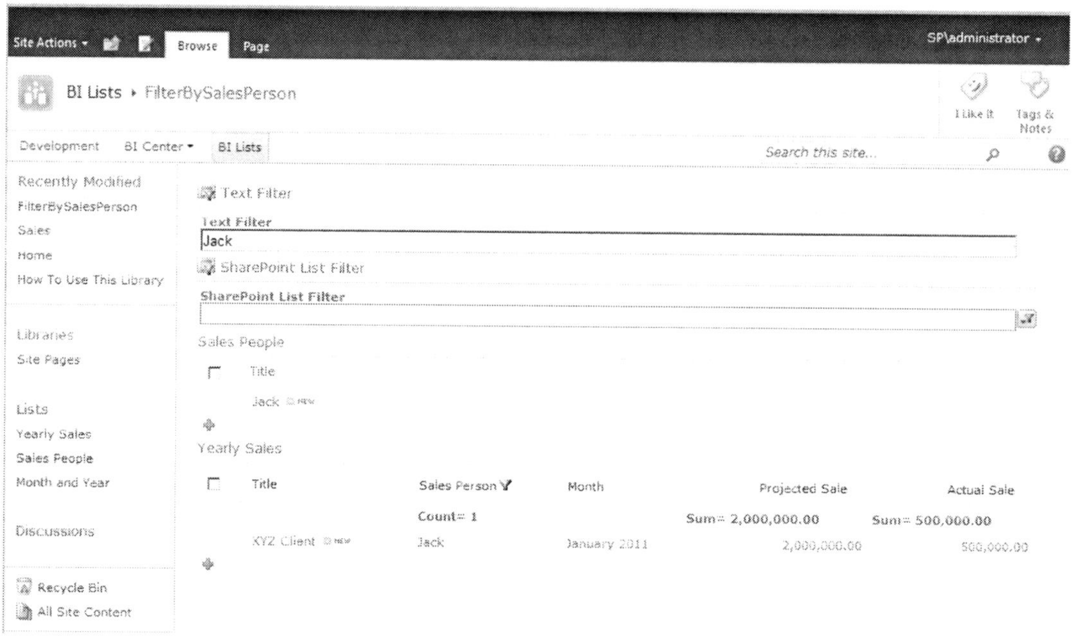

**Figure 13-3.** *Filtered List View Web Parts*

Figure 13-3 depicts the filtered List View Web Parts based on the typed in value into the Text Filter Web Part.The filtering occurred by creating a connection that goes from the Text Filter Web Part towards the Sales People and Yearly Sales Web Part.

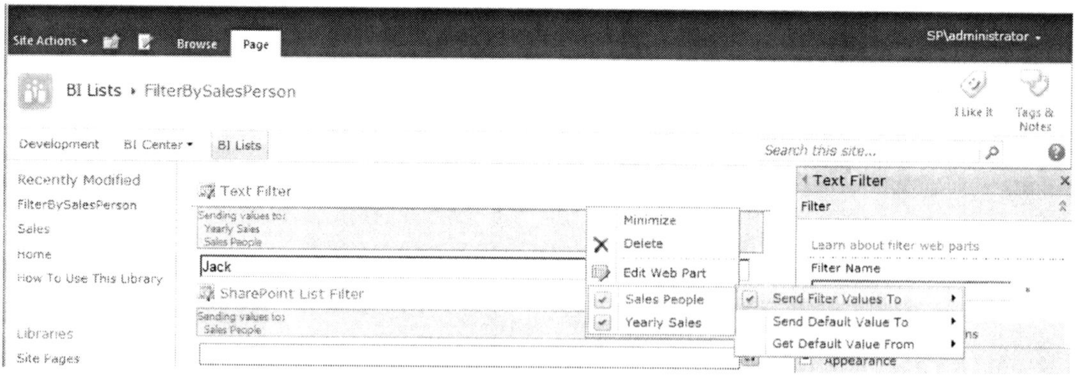

**Figure 13-4.** *Filtered List View Web Parts with a Text Filter*

Figure 13-4 illustrates the connection between the Text Filter and List View Web Parts. Why would you want to filter the values within SharePoint lists? Because it's easier to view the data when it's displayed and filtered with specific values. In the provided SharePoint lists, there are not many list items, but can you imagine when you have thousands or list items? It can be difficult to distinguish, let alone get a grasp and digest all that data.

## Chart Types

- The Chart Web Part is new in SharePoint 2010. If you had a chance to use or work with the Dundas Web Parts, you will notice a very similar look and configuration. The Chart Web Part can produce a variety of charts, such asBar

- Line

- Financial

- Polar

- Range

- BoxPlot

- Pyramid

- Area

- Point/Bubble

- Pie

- Gantt/Range Column

- ErrorBar

- Funnel

## Charting from Different Data Sources

The Chart Web Part provides the ability to chart from different data sources. The easiest to configure is a SharePoint list. That's not the only option available; it is very easy to configure the data into a chart because of the intuitive interface that it offers out of the box.

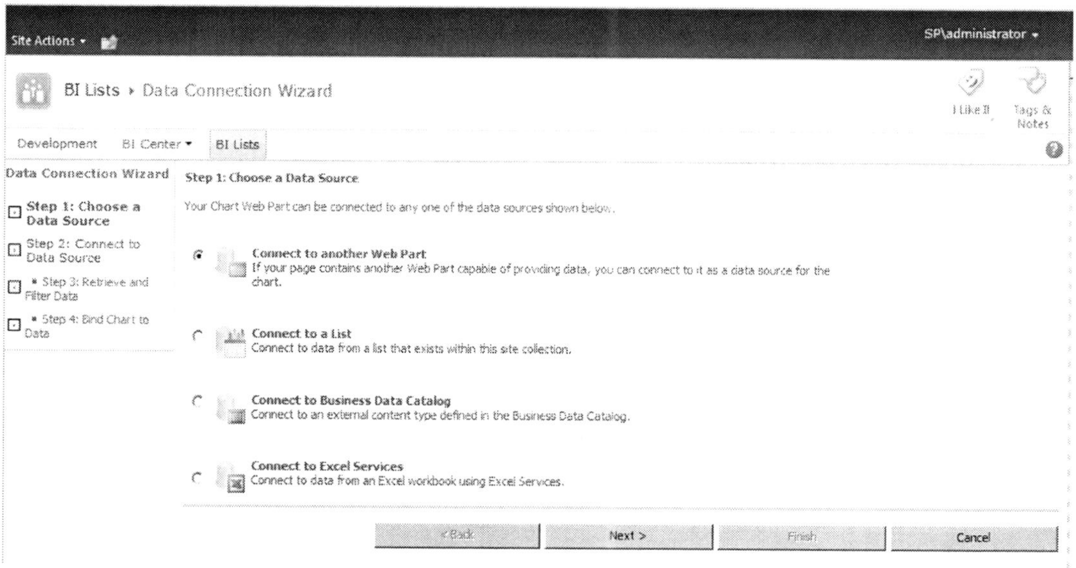

**Figure 13-5.** *Chart Web Part Available Data Sources*

Figure 13-5 shows the data connection wizard. The configuration process is divided among the following steps:

- Clicking the "Data & Appearance" toolbar link.

- Connecting the chart to the data.

- Selecting the data source.

- Providing a filter for the data to chart.

- Binding the data by selecting the series and X and Y fields.

Once the Web Part has been provided with information, the data is charted and displayed by the Chart Web Part. Figure 13-6 illustrates what a chart could look like.

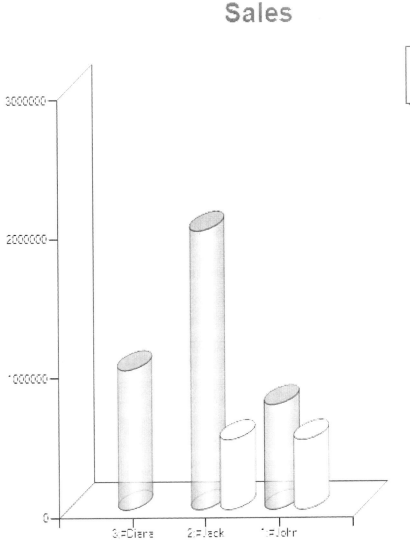

**Figure 13-6.** *Sales Chart*

## Benefits of Filtering Lists

By now, you have probably figured out that this looks like a very light Business Intelligence site within the SharePoint 2010, which is the point I was trying to convey. You can create a very simple, small, and lightweight site that allows you to drillthrough data in your SharePoint lists. The out-of-the-box functionality within SharePoint lists offers the pros and cons outlined in Table 13-1.

*Table 13-1.Pros and Cons of SharePoint Lists*

| Pros | Cons |
|------|------|
| No need to retrain end users to learn additional out of the box browser SharePoint skills. | Not as powerful as PerformancePoint. |
| Out-of-the-box collaboration. | Lightweight. |
| Easy to update data. | This design is constricted by the limitations of SharePoint Lists. |

## External Data Sources

List View Web Parts can also display data from external data sources such as databases. This is achieved by using external content types. By combining data within SharePoint Lists and from external data sources, you can truly increase the value of the sites you have created.

The data that will be made available from an external data source will be presented within SharePoint with the List View Web Part. This means you can filter and manipulate it as if it were a SharePoint list.

## Suggested Best Practices

- Review and ensure that the data within the SharePoint lists is accurate. Whatever decisions are made upon this data will be as reliable as the data.

- Plan how many Web Parts you will have on a page. The more Web Parts exist on a page, the slower the response time.

- When large amounts of data exist within a list, you should do the following:

  - Index columns

  - Leverage the Filter Web Parts or simply enable the filtering capabilities available within the List View Web Parts.

- Plan how to incorporate and combine data from SharePoint lists and external data sources.

## Excel Services

Excel Services 2010 has improved greatly since what was made available in Microsoft Office SharePoint Server 2007. Because Excel Web Applications are new to SharePoint 2010, it's easy to get confused with Excel Services. However, both serve different purposes. Excel Web Applications are a limited subset rich client of Excel 2010 and are used to present Workbooks; Excel Services is more of a server-side Excel.

Since Excel Web Applications provide the ability to display workbooks just like an Excel Web Access Web Part, which one should you use? Well, does the workbook need interaction with data from or to Web Parts?If the answer is yes, then the task is most likely suited to use the Excel Web Access Web Part.

## New Features

Many enhancements and improvements have been made to Excel Services, including the following:

- Trusted locations are now defaults.

- Slicers: New filtering functionality for Excel 2010 workbooks is available in combination with PivotTables and PivotCharts.

- Sparklines: Mini charts that appear in designated column and row of a worksheet.

- Show Value As: Simplifies how data will be shown as through a context menu.

- Excel Web Access Web Part

    - Changes are now saved into the workbook being edited.

    - Includes AJAX support.

    - Has the ability to send and receive data from other Web Parts.

## Reducing the Workload from the SharePoint Server and Document Libraries

As mentioned, Excel Services can be thought as a server-side Excel installed within SharePoint 2010. With this analogy, add to the thought that when a workbook is being worked upon through the browser, every time it is saved or a calculation needs to be performed, it is being done on the server(s) used by the SharePoint 2010 farm.

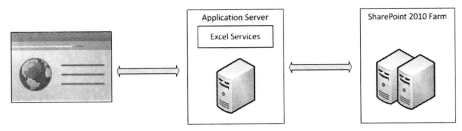

*Figure 13-7. Depiction of workloads generated by workbooks*

All these thoughts are represented with Figure 13-7. As illustrated, a lot of traffic can be generated back and forth just by working on workbooks. This increases exponentially based on the number of users, amount of data, calculations, and the number of times a workbook is saved.

> For this reason, it is recommended to work and save the workbooks locally; the effect of this simple procedure can be dramatic.

## Suggested Best Practices

- Plan for the following:

  - Trusted locations: Is a feature that allows to configure which files are allowed to be loaded safely. Trusted Locations extends to: Access 2010, Excel 2010, PowerPoint 2010, Word 2010 and folders. By taking control of what files are trusted it simplifies their management, otherwise they can out of control.

  - Manage Excel Services trusted locations (SharePoint 2010)

  - `http://technet.microsoft.com/en-us/library/ff191194.aspx`

  - How Excel Services will be setup; in particular the following settings:

    - File access method

    - Connection encryption

    - Allow cross domain access

    - Load balancing scheme

    - Maximum session per user: If you want to manage your resources tightly, set a specific number; otherwise, set it as -1.

- Have users use their local drafts folder when checking out workbooks.

- Publish only the worksheets that need to exist in the workbook.

- Leverage the following:

  - Named Sets to facilitate referencing a commonly used set of items. Named sets can be thought of dimension members; once created, they ease the ability to filter data.

  - PowerPivot is a useful add-on that increases the functionality of Excel 2010.

- When in doubt whether a user has Excel 2010 available on their desktop, consider using the Excel Web Access Web Part for displaying the workbook(s).

# PerformancePoint Services

PerformancePoint Services is a new and welcome addition to SharePoint 2010. It once existed as a separate product and is now tightly integrated within SharePoint 2010. Because it is integrated into SharePoint 2010, the dashboards are now deployed into a folder within a document library. This allows for securing the content of the dashboards.

Creating dashboards is done through the Dashboard Designer, which is usually installed and started through the Run Dashboard Designer button of the deployed BI Center.

# Planning

Before creating the BI Center site, consider the following: a BI Center site is a site not a site collection. While this might not seem that important initially, when managing, maintaining, and backing up one or more BI Centers, it will become quickly important for the planning and configuration of these BI Center sites.

## Questions to Ask When Planning

- Client Deployments
    - Do the target BI end users have the permissions (Administrator on the local box) to install the Dashboard Designer?
- BI Centers
    - Will a single BI Center be deployed?
    - Will there be a need to create more BI Centers?

The answers to the previous questions will clearly indicate a structure that will be used to create BI Center(s). It's recommended to create a top BI Center(s) and create BI Centers under it; this will provide a centralized BI Center Site structure. Other questions include:

- Dashboards
    - How many dashboards will be developed?
    - Do these dashboards need to be organized in a certain fashion?
    - Will dashboards require customization to their look and feel?

This is just a quick list of questions that can give you a sense of what needs to happen before BI Center sites are created plus how and where the dashboards will be developed and published.

# Suggested Best Practices

- Determine the following:
    - Exact or estimated number of BI Centers.
    - Structure for the BI Centers to be provisioned.
- Establish a naming convention for the following:
    - Folders: Helps organize dashboards.
    - Dashboards
    - I recommend the following format (expand or improve it according to your needs):

        [Dashboard]_[Author]_[Date]_[Revision] – Without the brackets
- Plan the following:

- Location: A centralized location is recommended. A network share would work well once the permissions are set to full so that the end users could create folders as well as organize and manage the folder structure.

- Dashboard definition files: The dashboard definition files end with ddwx.

- Published dashboards

- Dashboard deployment steps or procedures.

- How to handle customizations:

  - Perform them on the dashboard definition file, not on the ASPX file.

  - Create separate master pages and select the modified master page when publishing.

# Reporting Services

Reporting Services has improved with each version of SharePoint. This latest version has better integration and better charts. When developing the reports, take into account these new and improved charting controls that provide a very attractive and easy way to represent data in reports. A major consideration point is the integration mode to use between SharePoint 2010 and Report Services. The local mode is not integrated with a report server; it's also known as native mode. The connected model integrates the Reporting Services Report Server into the SharePoint Farm, allowing its management through SharePoint Central Administration; it's also known as integrated mode.

## Assessing Which Type of Installation is Best for You

Before deciding which type of mode you should use, it's a good idea to dedicate enough time to research which type of installation fits your needs. They both have pros and cons. Note that switching back and forth between either installation modes is not recommended nor should it be undertaken lightly.

Table 13-2 contains links that may help you decide which type of installation is best for you.

*Table 13-2. Installtion Information*

| Topic | Link |
| --- | --- |
| Planning a deployment mode | http://msdn.microsoft.com/en-us/library/bb326345.aspx |
| Planning for SharePoint integration | http://msdn.microsoft.com/en-us/library/bb326405.aspx |
| Overview of reporting services and SharePoint technology integration | http://msdn.microsoft.com/en-us/library/bb326358.aspx |
| Features supported by reporting services in SharePoint integrated mode | http://msdn.microsoft.com/en-us/library/bb326290.aspx |
| Security overview for reporting services in SharePoint integrated mode | http://msdn.microsoft.com/en-us/library/bb283324.aspx |

---

⬚ **Note** I recommend local mode over connected mode because it provides you with a clear separation between SharePoint 2010 and Microsoft SQL Server Reporting Services. The advantage of that separation is the ability for easier management and recovery in case of an upgrade, service pack installation, disaster, etc.

---

## Report Building Tools

When developing SQL Server reporting services reports it is usual to use BIDS (Business Intelligence Developer Studio) which ends up being added into Visual Studio 2008 at the moment of installation. Yes, that was Visual Studio 2008; not a typo. Visual Studio 2010 is still not supported for report building.

The other tool is Report Builder 3.0, which is a free client side download available at: http://www.microsoft.com/downloads/en/details.aspx?FamilyID=d3173a87-7c0d-40cc-a408-3d1a43ae4e33&displaylang=en.

### Which Tool Should You Use?

Sometimes the tool is determined by the budget and/or the target developing users, mostly because if Microsoft Visual Studio 2008 is necessary, so is a license, which requires a purchase. Microsoft Visual Studio Express is an option, but unfortunately the Express version is limited in its functionality; at this point in time, it doesn't support the ability to develop reports. If the purchase of Microsoft Visual Studio 2008 isn't possible, Report Builder 3.0 is a free option. In my experience, both developers and non-developers find it very comfortable to build, test, and deploy reports within the Visual Studio 2008 environment and Report Builder 3.0.

## Suggested Best Practices

- Decide which type of installation best fits your needs.

- Be sure to use Report Builder 3.0 exclusively with SQL Server 2008 and SQL Server 2008 R2.

- Leverage the following:

  - Shared Datasets: Offers improved reusability and sharing.

  - Report Parts: For reusability with other reports.

  - Snapshots: For displaying reports at a specific point in time.

  - Caching reports: Improves response time with Reports.

  - Report Viewer Web Part: For displaying reports within SharePoint.

# Summary

In this chapter, you have explored the basics of Microsoft Business Intelligence;reviewed the new additions to Business Intelligence in Microsoft SharePoint 2010; learned about the optimization of the Business Intelligence Resources; got some ideas for utilizing Web Parts for filtering and charting data;

learned about some of the enhancements to Excel Services and how to reduce the workload from the SharePoint 2010 Server(s);examined which reporting services mode would best suityour needs; and learned about the available tools for developing reports.

## Next Steps

Hopefully this chapter has encouraged you to consider leaping into organizing a pilot BI Center site(s); developing PerformancePoint dashboards,  Excel Services workbooks, and SQL Server reporting services reports; charting data with Web Parts; integrating two or more of the developed items in Web Part pages; and deploying the pilot and impressing the executives.

## Bibliography and Links

- Access Services Planning

  http://technet.microsoft.com/en-us/library/ee683869.aspx

- Visio Services overview

  http://technet.microsoft.com/en-us/library/ee663485.aspx

- Techniques for managing large lists

  http://office.microsoft.com/en-us/sharepoint-server-help/sharepoint-lists-v-techniques-for-managing-large-lists-RZ101874361.aspx?CTT=1

- Report Builder 3.0 download

  http://www.microsoft.com/downloads/en/details.aspx?FamilyID=d3173a87-7c0d-40cc-a408-3d1a43ae4e33&displaylang=en

- Plan for backup and recovery

  http://technet.microsoft.com/en-us/library/cc261687.aspx

- SharePoint Server 2010 Capacity Management: Software Boundaries and Limits

  http://technet.microsoft.com/en-us/library/cc262787.aspx#ListLibrary

- Capacity management and sizing overview for SharePoint Server 2010

  http://technet.microsoft.com/en-us/library/ff758647.aspx

- Capacity management for SharePoint Server 2010

  http://technet.microsoft.com/en-us/sharepoint/ff601870

- SharePoint 2010 performance and capacity technical case studies

  www.microsoft.com/download/en/details.aspx?displayLang=en&id=7480

- SharePoint Server 2010 performance and capacity test results and recommendations

  www.microsoft.com/download/en/details.aspx?displayLang=en&id=12768

- SharePoint 2010 Capacity Planning Tool

> http://dougortiz.blogspot.com/2011/07/sharepoint-2010-capacity-planning-tool.html

- SharePoint Server 2010 capacity management: software boundaries and limits

  http://technet.microsoft.com/en-us/library/cc262787.aspx#ListLibrary

- Plan quota management (SharePoint Server 2010)

  http://technet.microsoft.com/en-us/library/cc891489.aspx

- Manage Excel Services trusted locations (SharePoint Server 2010)

  http://technet.microsoft.com/en-us/library/ff191194.aspx

# Business Connectivity Services

After completing this chapter, you will be able to

- Understand the Business Connectivity Services architecture

- Understand how BCS integrates both inside and outside SharePoint 2010

- Create BCS solutions of simple and medium complexities

- Create custom .NET connectors using Visual Studio 2010

- Configure the Secure Store Service for use by Business Connectivity Services

- Add basic security trimming using Visual Studio 2010

- Understand the potential that BCS exposes for your organization

Business Connectivity Services (BCS) makes it possible to integrate external data sources—typically line-of-business data—with SharePoint 2010. The most exciting features in BCS for SharePoint 2010 are the SharePoint Designer 2010 (SPD 2010) integration, its search capabilities, and Microsoft Office 2010 integration.

The new BCS offers similar functionality to the Business Data Catalog (BDC) in SharePoint 2007. In contrast to the BDC, the BCS is accessible to a much wider audience due to its integration with SharePoint Designer 2010. This was not the case with the BDC in SPD 2007. Also, accessing and manipulating LOB data is now easy. With BDC it was relatively easy to read external data, but manipulating external data presented a number of complexities. The new BCS interface in SPD 2010 makes it easy to both define CRUD operations and even aggregate data between different content types across multiple data sources.

Now BCS is available in SharePoint Foundation 2010, which means it is free. This allows for creating complex business-driven solutions at a low cost.

This chapter describes the high-level architecture, capabilities, and components of BCS, with a special focus on search-related topics. Examples will be given of how to use SPD 2010 to create declarative solutions and Visual Studio 2010 to create custom content types using C# and enable searching of these content types.

## BCS Architecture

The architecture of BCS is comprehensive but still makes it easy to use. Considering that BCS can be used for both SharePoint and the MS Office clients, it offers an excellent framework that enables administrators to easily understand and set up BCS solutions that integrate content types from most typical content sources all the way through the pipeline of BCS, finally presenting a data interface in an intuitive way to the end user. Furthermore it allows developers to create new, reusable components as either .NET connectors or custom connectors. BCS can be divided into three layers: presentation, core components, and content sources, as shown in Figure 14-1.

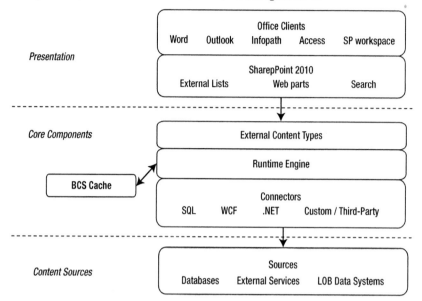

**Figure 14-1.** *BCS architecture*

# Presentation

BCS presents data that can be consumed or manipulated by SharePoint 2010 and MS Office clients. SharePoint 2010 contains three primary consumers of data exposed through BCS.

- External lists
- Out-of-the-box Web Parts
- Search

## External Lists

SharePoint contains a new list type named external lists. This list acts as any other list, with the exception that an external content type must be defined for the list. It does not support version info and alerts, however, as its data is stored externally.

## Web Parts

BCS Web Parts are similar to those found in BDC for SharePoint 2007. Although BCS is included for free in SharePoint Foundation 2010, BCS Web Parts are included only in the SharePoint 2010 Enterprise edition. Included Web Parts are

- Business Data Actions
- Business Data Connectivity Filter
- Business Data Item
- Business Data Item Builder
- Business Data List
- Business Data Related List

## Business Data Actions

Actions are executed on single results from BCS. The concept is also known from search centers with result actions, which are context-specific actions, such as opening documents in their native application or opening a web page in a new window—in short, actions that differ based on the specific result. Actions are configured by specifying a target URL of an HTTP handler, .aspx page, or similar. By adding parameters to the URL, an action can be constructed such that the URL can invoke a translation using the Bing translation service, looking up addresses on Bing Maps, or even invoke special purpose functionality if a custom HTTP handler or .aspx page is implemented and deployed. The configured actions for a BCS result are displayed in the Business Data Actions Web Part.

## Business Data Connectivity Filter

The Business Data Connectivity Filter Web Part is used to perform data filtering of SharePoint Web Parts based on values passed from the Business Data Connectivity (BDC) Filter Web Part. A number of filters are included, allowing manual input such as text or date and time, values picked from a list of choices, or fixed values either defined for the site or passed by URL. If a filter exists on a page, the Connections option becomes available on the Edit page. This allows for creating an association or connection between a filter and, for instance, a list view or data view Web Part. This way selected data columns will be filtered based on the defined filter values to show a custom view for a department, user, KPI event, etc.

## Business Data Item

The Business Data Item Web Part shows a single result in a vertical view. A typical use is to show detailed or expanded data of a particular result row from a summarized Business Data List Web Part. The Business Data Item Web Part can be connected to the Business Data List Web Part and respond to selected rows.

## Business Data Item Builder

This Web Part is used to pass a unique identifier from the URL parameter to the Web Parts on the page. Using this Web Part, it is possible to pass the unique identifier across pages containing Business Data Item Web Parts.

### Business Data List

This is a grid view Web Part and the core display method for BCS data, allowing an overview of the LOB data obtained from a BCS source. The key feature is the connection option that allows this Web Part to be connected to detailed view Web Parts and otherwise used for filtering and/or custom actions by clicking a result row.

### Business Data Related List

Sometimes a particular result from one external content type has associations to data in another external content type. The Business Data Related List Web Part is used to show the "many" part of the relationship by using values from other BCS Web Parts or URL-based identifiers to look up associated data for the external content type defined for the Business Data Related List Web Part.

## Search

Search results originating from BCS are displayed in a page called the profile page, when the BCS result item gets clicked or opened. The profile page is an .aspx page built with BCS Web Parts. The Web Parts display the relevant BCS entity based on the entity's ID, which is passed to the profile page as URL parameters. Multiple profile pages can be created to accommodate different external content types.

Profile pages are not created automatically for an external content type. Per default, clicking a search result from a BCS source yields the well-known 404 error (page not found). The profile page must be created and configured from the Search service application.

■ **Note** Searching for external content using BCS is available only in SharePoint 2010 Standard and Enterprise versions.

## Core Components

The core of BCS is the ability to connect to a large set of data sources using its connector framework. By defining content types from the data sources, the runtime engine is able to execute CRUD operations on these content types. The core components are

- Runtime engine
- BCS Rich Client Cache
- Connectors
- External content types

The runtime engine is responsible for executing BCS operations on the content sources. The runtime engine is integrated into the supported office applications, SharePoint workspace, InfoPath, and, of course, SharePoint 2010. The integration into these applications makes them independent of SharePoint 2010 as a middle layer for using BCS to connect to content sources.

## BCS Rich Client Cache

Business Connectivity Services offers cache and offline features that also support cache-based operations. For users that work with solutions deployed to supported Office 2010 applications (Word, Outlook, SharePoint 2010 Workspace, etc.), they can manipulate external data, even when they are working offline or if the server connectivity is slow or unavailable. The operations performed against cached external entities are synchronized when connection to the server becomes available. It also provides a flexible external data caching mechanism that is as transparent as possible while still enabling the user or application to have explicit control over the content of the cache when required via automatic and manual cleanup.

## Connectors

The BCS connector framework in SharePoint 2010 comes with built-in support for creating external connections to SQL, WCF, and .NET assemblies. In general this covers the majority of connection requirements. It would have been nice, however, if a flat file or .xml connector was built in as well. Fortunately the BCS connector framework is designed to be extendable with either custom connectors or custom-made .NET connectors. Later in this chapter, an example will be presented of how to create a .NET flat file connector using Visual Studio 2010.

## External Content Types

External content types are the glue of BCS. They describe the metadata definitions of the external content data, connectivity information, and data access capabilities. This way an ECT provides a reusable schema to be used in SharePoint lists and Web Parts.

The external content type is what the IT professional creates in SharePoint Designer 2010. A typical business requirement for an IT professional is to create an ECT for a customer database. This database might contain names, addresses, payment info, and a unique customer ID. When the IT professional creates an ECT for this data source, the ECT will contain both the column definitions for the required fields as well as names and optionally credentials for the customer database. It will also contain information on which CRUD operations can be executed on the customer database. From the IT professional's point of view, an ECT is a mapping between the external data source and SharePoint 2010. The key difference from BDC in SharePoint 2007 is that the ECT now also contains the full CRUD behavior, whereas in BDC it had to be programmed.

Behind the scenes, an ECT is an .xml grammar file containing metadata that describes the ECT. For the ECT to be available, it has to be deployed to the metadata store in SharePoint (or through a click-once package, e.g., Outlook 2010).

Depending on the capabilities of the data sources and connectors, it is possible to create an ECT that provides easy data access with complex logic, such as aggregating data across multiple sources, providing complex transformations, evaluating complex business logic or custom security requirements, or calling systems multiple times in order to provide a single view of data.

---

■ **Note** This chapter uses the term external content type. Sometimes it is also referred to as an entity. This generally is the term used by developers, as it is the name given to the ECT in Visual Studio 2010. They do, however, mean the same thing.

---

## Content Sources

Content sources are the external part of BCS. They are used by the search engine to index external data. As mentioned, BCS comes with built-in support for connecting to content sources of the types SQL, WCF, and .NET assemblies. Often the content source is made available through installation of Microsoft SQL Server or a data server program that can be accessed and controlled through WCF. In more advanced cases, the content source might provide a .NET API for performing these operations.

On some occasions, the content source does not provide any of the foregoing options for interfacing with the data. In these cases, a developer has to develop either a .NET Assembly Connector or create a custom connector for BCS. Both options have their own benefits and weak points that the developer should be aware of.

# Business Connectivity Services Deployment Types

Understanding how and where a BCS solution can be deployed is fundamental when planning how to leverage this new functionality in SP 2010. With the new tool support and wide range of client program support, BCS is a strong candidate to consider when analyzing opportunities to meet business requirements. This section gives an overview of where BCS can be deployed and the general complex levels of deployment.

## Functionality for Normal Users "Out-of-the-Box"

SharePoint 2010 now has out-of-the-box support for users to display external data using BCS in a seamless way. Similarly BCS integrates MS Word 2010, MS Outlook 2010, and SharePoint Workspace with SharePoint 2010 to allow users to use it in a well-known manner. Especially the support for Outlook 2010 was a much sought-after functionality in SharePoint 2007. Little or no administrator intervention is required for users to leverage list data in these applications. In most cases, the permissions setup is the most important step to be conscious about when preparing the SharePoint lists, etc. for use by these applications.

Using the external list, Business Data Web Parts, or the new Chart Web Part in SP 2010, it is easy for users to display external data. It is also possible to extend existing standard lists or document libraries by adding an external data column.

External columns can also be used in MS Word 2010 by creating a Quick Part for content control. This is useful, for instance, when a document template is to reflect the latest available data from the SharePoint-based intranet.

MS Outlook 2010 and SharePoint Workspace provide special integration with SharePoint. External lists can be taken offline from the SharePoint server. This way, users can interact with the data in the external list without leaving the client program. The major benefit is that the integration becomes transparent to the user, since the look and behavior are the same as in Outlook and Workspace. The required add-in for Outlook is installed as part of Microsoft Office 2010.

One thing to be aware of is that offline lists in MS Outlook 2010 and SharePoint Workspace require synchronization. This can be done either automatically or on user request. If automatic synchronization is activated, the default interval is three hours. As the structure of the offline list can change or new views can be added or modified, it is even possible to update the structure or view automatically without any user intervention.

The external content types and external lists/columns for these types of solutions are usually created by an administrator using SPD 2010. The SharePoint ribbon has buttons to make a connection between Outlook 2010 or SP Workspace 2010 and the external list/column.

# Functionality for Advanced Users and Administrators

Some uses of BCS require the administrator or IT professional to perform certain tasks, such as publishing, to make it available to users. It also allows the IT professional to use custom code-based solutions as reusable components. This is particularly beneficial for the way many companies operate, as a consultant company can make components that the internal IT professionals can use and configure to meet changing demands, without having to go back to the vendor or consultant that provided the custom code-based solution for every tiny change to how the component is used. It makes the BCS installation easier, faster, and cheaper to maintain.

InfoPath forms presenting external data can be customized in terms of look and feel. This can be done by adding declarative rules and business logic. It is also possible to add code-behind to the forms. The form is published to the server by the administrator.

SharePoint workflows can be extended with new capabilities through SPD 2010 by adding read and write capabilities to external lists or using custom workflow activities from VS 2010. These must be published in SharePoint.

Site administrators can create Web Part pages based on multiple Business Data Web Parts and Chart Web Parts. By creating connections between the Web Parts, it is possible to create highly customized and information-rich pages with data from most common data sources.

When working with external lists in Outlook 2010, it is possible for users of the Outlook client to create new customized views to show this external data. The custom view can then be saved back to SharePoint. This makes it available as a public view for other Outlook users who use the same external list in Outlook.

Microsoft has a number of applications for creating these solutions. The most common tools are the InfoPath Designer, which is used to create forms, and the SharePoint Designer, which is used to create Web Part pages and workflows. Web Part pages can also be created through the browser. Finally MS Outlook 2010 can be used for creating customized views specifically for Outlook.

# Code-Based Solutions

Code-based solutions are solutions created in Visual Studio 2010 by a developer. These solutions enable the creation of reusable components as either a .NET Assembly Connector to aggregate or transform data from external systems, custom Web Parts, custom workflow activities, code-behind for InfoPath forms, and code-based actions or external data parts for use in Outlook declarative solutions. Code-based solutions are now made easy for developers with built-in support in Visual Studio 2010. In SharePoint 2007, it required advanced coding skills to do anything more complex than data reading. Now the developer can focus on issues such as reusability instead.

A code-based Microsoft .NET Framework solution created in a tool such as Visual Studio can use any element of the public Business Connectivity Services object model and can enable users to interact with external data. It can register with the Business Data Connectivity service by using the BDC object model to present data in SharePoint, an Office 2010 application such as Microsoft Excel, or a custom application. This object model and BCS runtime is installed with SharePoint 2010 and Office 2010. External data can be retrieved directly from the external system while connected, or it can be retrieved locally from the BCS Rich Client Cache, provided it is already available, for instance, from an offline external list in SharePoint Workspace or Outlook. This type of solution can also be used to extend BCS to MS Office applications that are not integrated with BCS. Typically this will be Excel but also PowerPoint.

Alternatively an entire end-to-end solution that leverages the public Business Connectivity Services object model can be created. The deployment process is, however, more difficult, and there is no tool support for this custom connector solution.

In a code-based end-to-end solution, commonly referred to as a custom connector, the developer controls all of the user interface, packaging, and deployment. This type of solution cannot make use of the Business Connectivity Services rich client runtime, which is used by integrated and declarative solutions to integrate data.

---

■ **Note** For most purposes, a .NET Assembly Connector is sufficient to meet business needs, and it is by far the easiest way to go.

---

By using "click once" packages, it is possible to create and deploy new task panes or present external data in external data parts in MS Outlook 2010. This requires a number of XML files to be created and use of the BCS Software Developer Kit to create the package.

A BCS project type is available to facilitate the creation of .NET Assembly Connectors. An example of a flat file .NET connector is described later in this chapter.

When working with BCS, creating the external content types is the key task to perform by IT professionals. With the new support for creating ECTs in SPD 2010, it is surprisingly easy to do. This is definitely one of the most powerful new additions to SharePoint 2010. It is also possible to create an ECT from the SharePoint site, but SPD 2010 is the better choice when available.

To give an example of creating an ECT, assume a database with customer information (Figure 14-2) that is to be made accessible through an external SharePoint list. The Contact office type is chosen to make it integrate nicely into Outlook as an offline external list.

| | CustomerKey | CompanyName | PhoneNumber | EmailAddress | ContactPerson |
|---|---|---|---|---|---|
| 1 | 1 | Microsoft | 555-xxxxxx1 | mail@microsoft.com | John Doe |
| 2 | 2 | SurfRay | 555-xxxxxx2 | mail@surfray.com | John Doe |
| 3 | 3 | Apple | 555-xxxxxx3 | mail@apple.com | John Doe |
| 4 | 4 | IBM | 555-xxxxxx4 | mail@ibm.com | John Doe |

*Figure 14-2. Sample customer data*

In SPD 2010, connect to a site and open External Content Types from the Navigation menu, as in Figure 14-3. On this page, all current ECTs for the site are displayed. The ribbon has quick access buttons for the typical tasks to be performed.

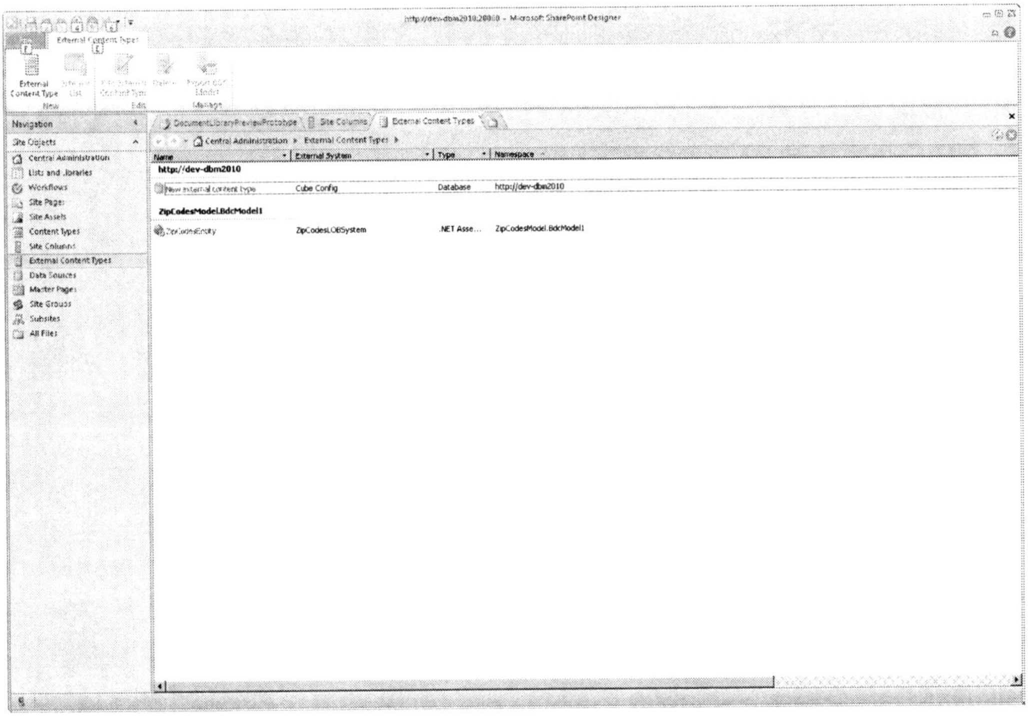

*Figure 14-3. External Content Types window*

The first step is to create a new external content type

1.  Click the New External Content Type button. The External Content Type dialog (Figure 14-4) will be displayed.

2.  Enter a Name and Display Name for the external content type. As this example contains contact info, select Contact as Office Item Type in the External Content Type Information section.

3.  Click the link named "Click here to discover external data sources and define operations." This opens the Operation Designer dialog.

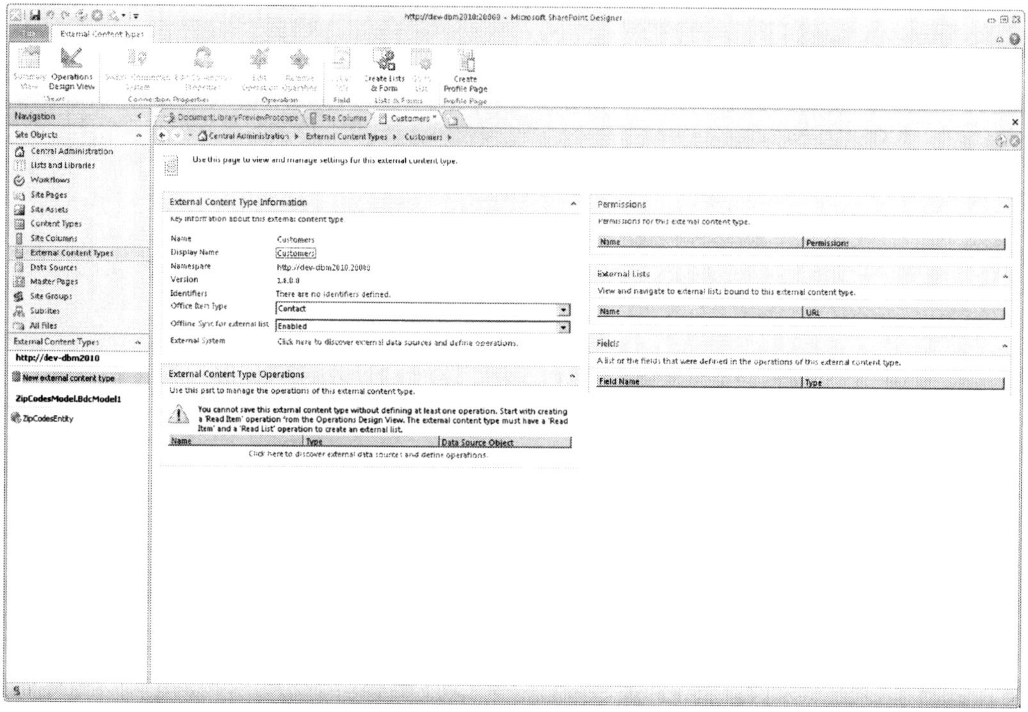

**Figure 14-4.** *Create External Content Type window*

On the Operation Designer dialog, click Add a Connection to connect to the database. In this example, it is called CustomersDatabase. This will establish a connection, and the database tables will be displayed. In this example, it has only one table, named CustomersTable.

To specify the types of operations that can be performed, right-click CustomersTable and select the option Create All Operations, as in Figure 14-5. This will enable all CRUD operations on the database table and open the operations wizard.

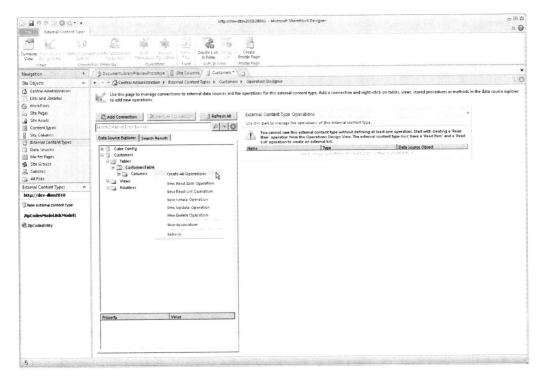

**Figure 14-5.** *Operation Designer*

Use the operations wizard (Figure 14-6) to map columns to the respective office properties. To do this, select the appropriate data source elements such as company name, phone number, etc. in the Properties window and specify the corresponding office property. Optionally a display friendly name can be specified. This name is what is showed later on the profile page for the ECT. Finally choose the column containing the values to be used as unique identifiers.

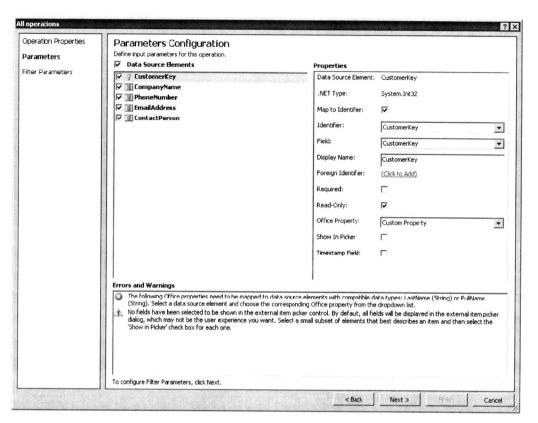

*Figure 14-6. Operations wizard*

Close the wizard when done, which returns to the Operation Designer window, shown in Figure 14-7.

---

**Note** The wizard gives real-time information on suggested and missing tasks in the Errors and Warnings window. The errors must be resolved before the wizard is completed.

---

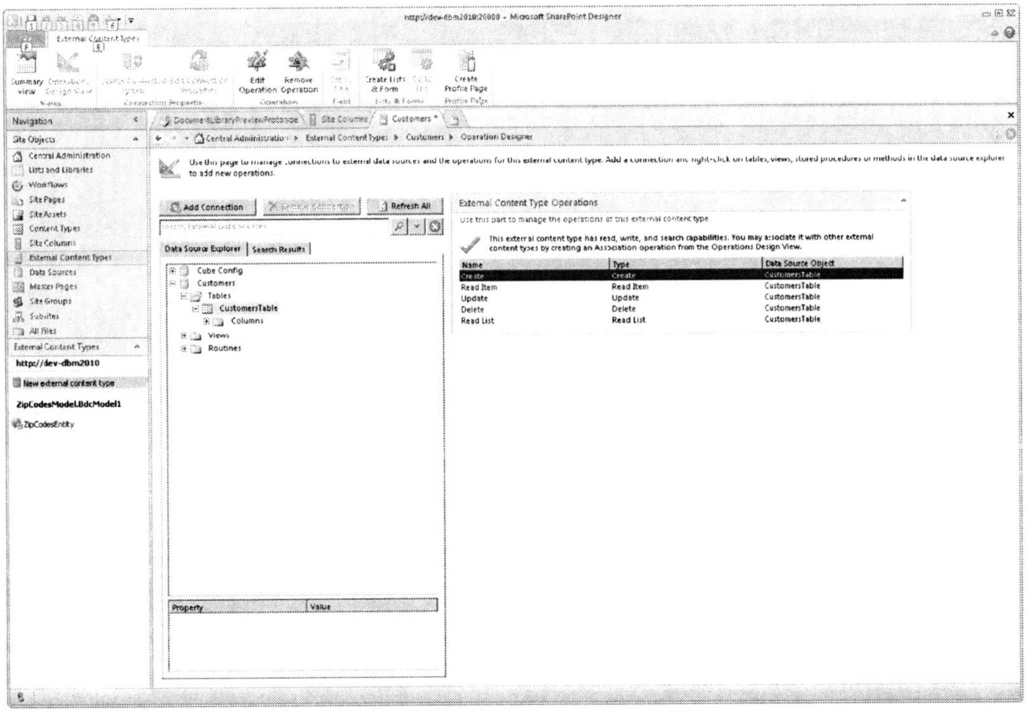

*Figure 14-7. Operation Designer*

After completing the wizard, save the ECT by clicking File and Save on the ribbon. The new external data type is saved to the metadata store and can be used for creating new external lists in SharePoint 2010.

Navigate to Site Actions, and view all site content. Select External List, and then click Create. This opens the New External List page, shown in Figure 14-8. Enter the name of the new list, select the External Content Type, and finally click Create.

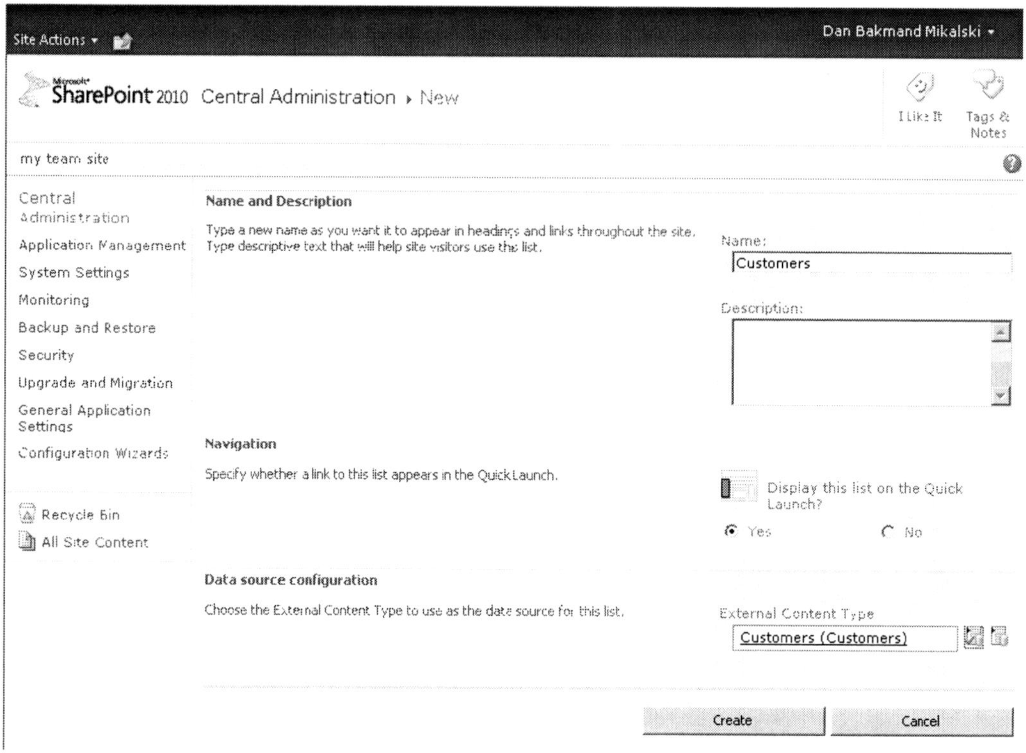

**Figure 14-8.** *Creating an external list*

Before users can access the list, the proper permissions must be configured. Go to the service application for the Business Data Connectivity service. Select the newly created external content type and click Set Metadata Store Permissions, as shown in Figure 14-9.

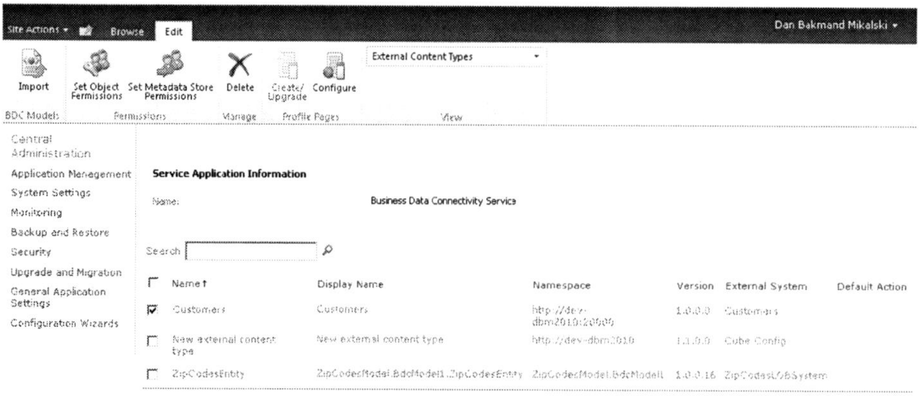

**Figure 14-9.** *Business Data Connectivity service main page*

On the Set Metadata Store Permissions page (Figure 14-10), enter the appropriate user permissions, and click OK. Typically at least one administrative user should have all permissions. As administration here is time-consuming in the case of many users, consider using groups instead for easier maintenance.

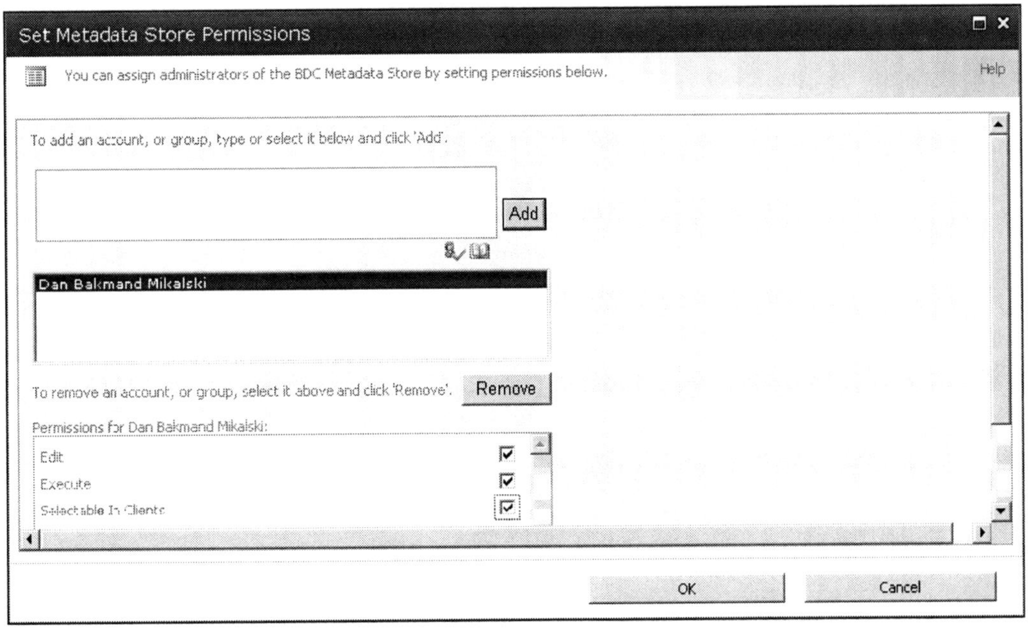

*Figure 14-10. Setting metadata store permissions*

> ■ **Note** If the ECT is to be used in search, make sure to grant the content access account appropriate permissions. In this example, the content access account is set as the author's account.

The new external list looks and behaves as any other ordinary list (Figure 14-11), with the exception of not supporting version history or setting up alerts. Items can be displayed, added, changed, and deleted—for example, changing the PhoneNumber in the list updates the value in the CustomersDatabase database.

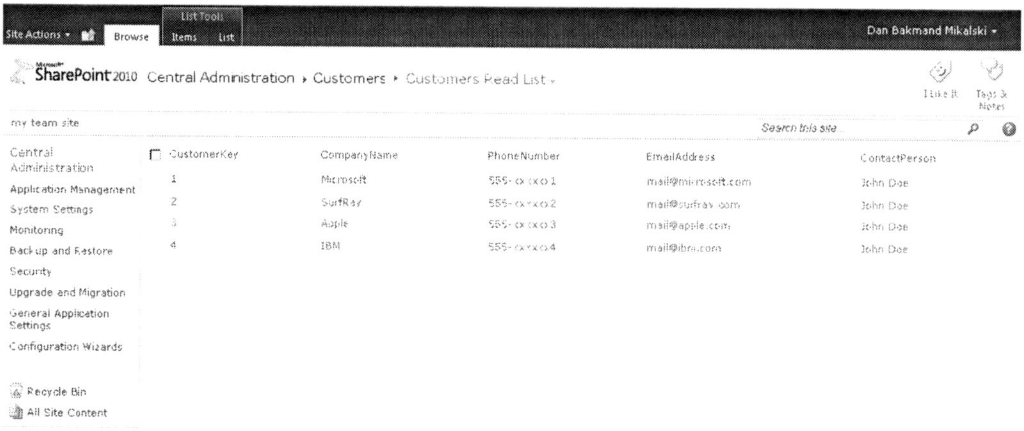

*Figure 14-11. The external list displaying external data*

A key feature of BCS is the option to index the external data and present it nicely as search results. There are some required configuration steps for this to be available. The following sections focus on making the Customers ECT, created in the previous section, searchable.

## Set the Title Field in the External Content Type

It is not required that a title property is configured for the external content types, but this is essential for achieving meaningful search results. It can be configured in SPD 2010.

In SPD 2010, connect to the site containing the external content type. In the Fields section (shown in the bottom right corner on the summary page in Figure 14-12), highlight the Name field of the most meaningful field to use as the title. Click the Set as Title button on the ribbon, and save the external content type by clicking File and then Save on the ribbon.

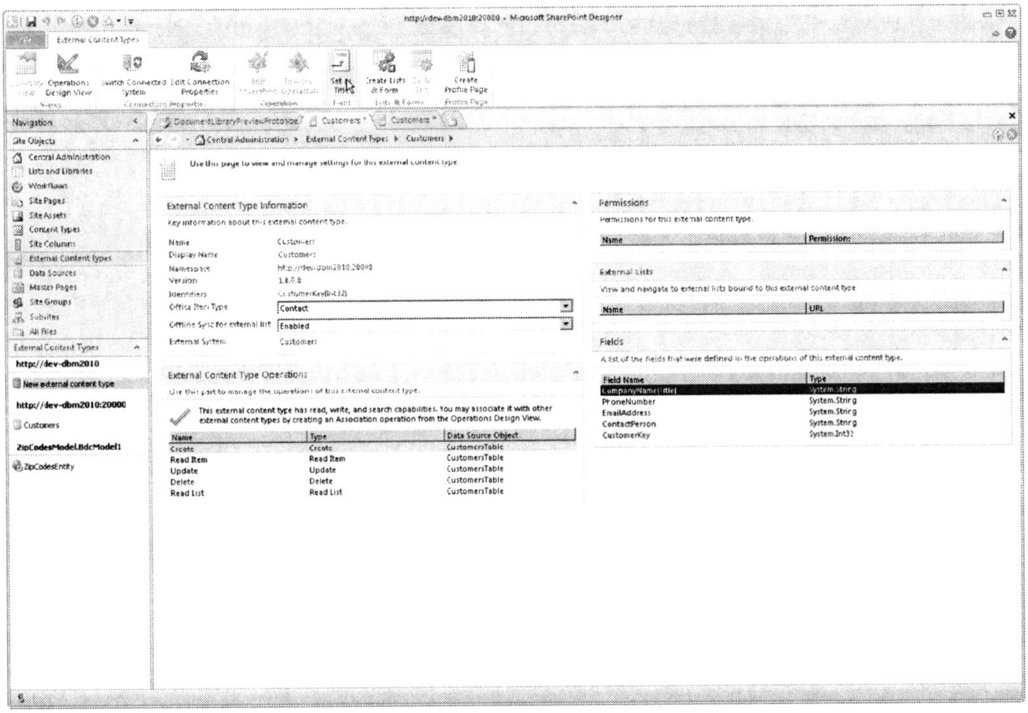

*Figure 14-12. Setting the external content type title*

# Creating a Profile Page to Display BCS Results

The profile page is used to display search result items from external content types. Open Central Administration and navigate to Create Site Collections. Create a new blank site to host the profile page, as shown in Figure 14-13. Give it a meaningful name according to the external source it gets paired with. It is important to write down the URL, as it has to be entered manually later.

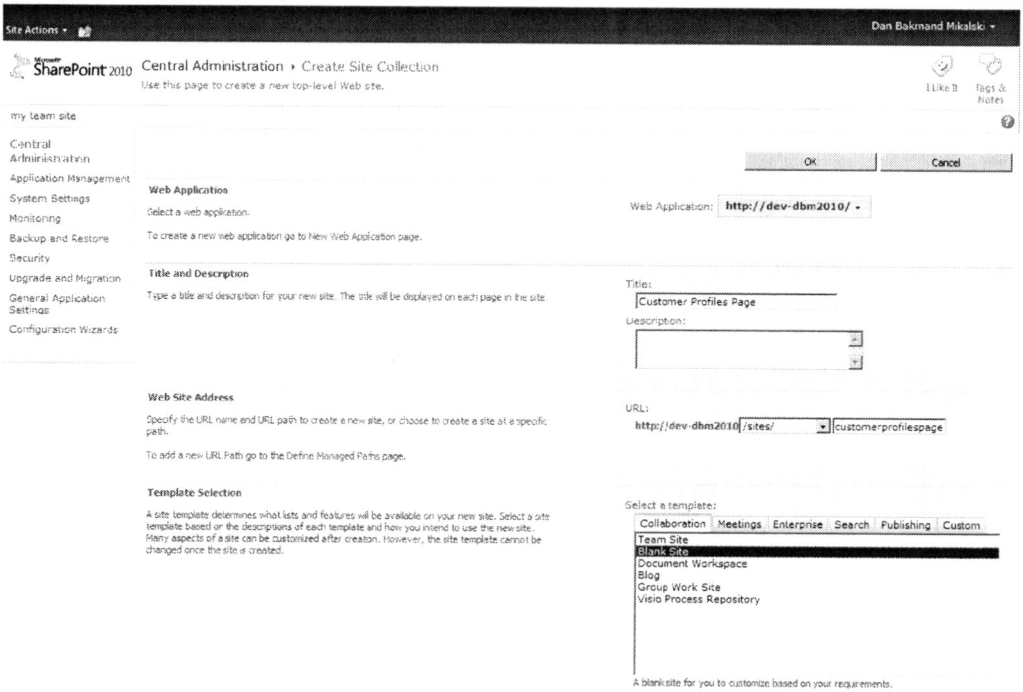

*Figure 14-13. Creating a profile page*

Navigate to the Manage Service Applications page in Central Administration, and click the Business Data Connectivity service application. On the Edit tab of the ribbon at the top of the page, click Configure. This opens the dialog shown in Figure 14-14.

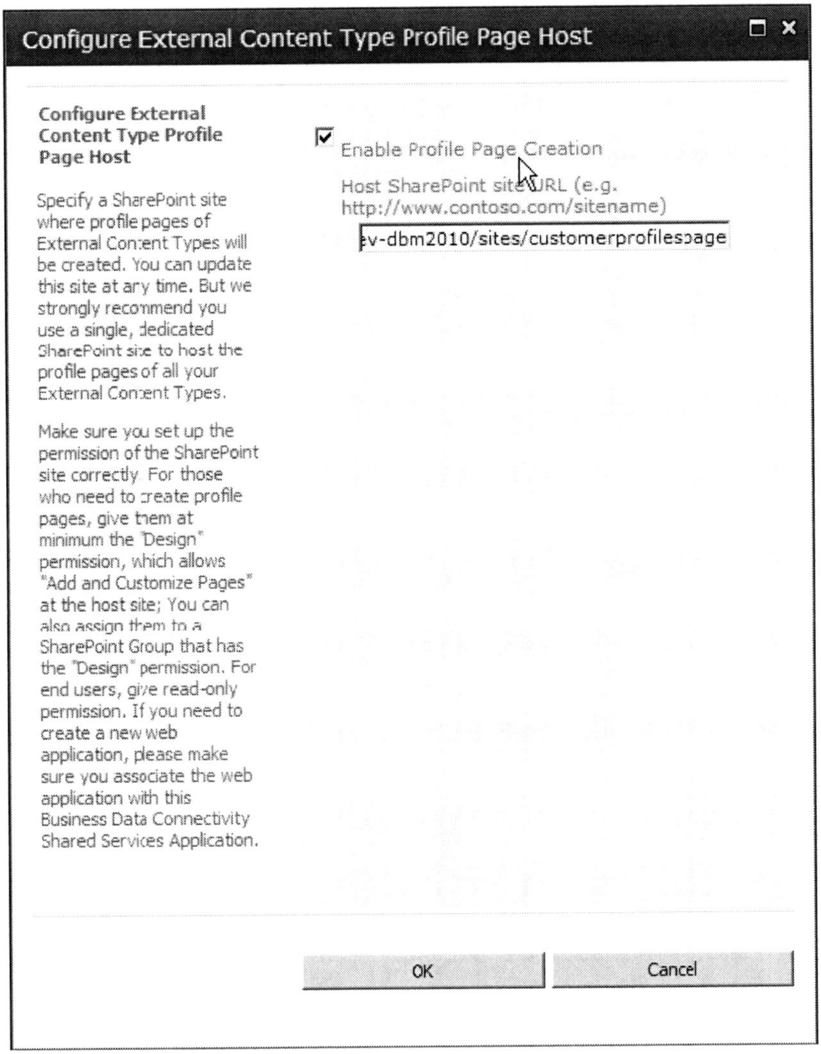

*Figure 14-14. Associating the external content type with a profile page*

Enter the URL of the profile page into the Host SharePoint site URL field, and click OK. Select the Customers external content type (or your own ECT) using the check box, and click Create/Upgrade. This will create a new profile page and View action for the external content type. Click OK for the warning in Figure 14-15.

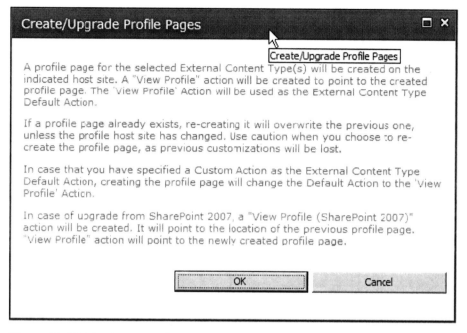

*Figure 14-15. Warning page when creating a profile page*

Clicking OK to the warning will create a new default action pointing to the profile page, with the ID passed as a URL parameter on the query string. A notification that the operation has succeeded (Figure 14-16) will be displayed.

*Figure 14-16. Confirming the profile page has been created*

## Configure Indexing

Now the external content type is fully configured and ready to get indexed. BCS indexing is easy in SharePoint 2010 compared to BDC in SharePoint 2007. Just add the BCS data source as a new search content source in the Search service application by navigating to the Manage Service Applications page in Central Administration. Click the Content Sources link in the navigation pane, which opens the Manage Content Sources page, shown in Figure 14-17. This page shows a list of all content sources.

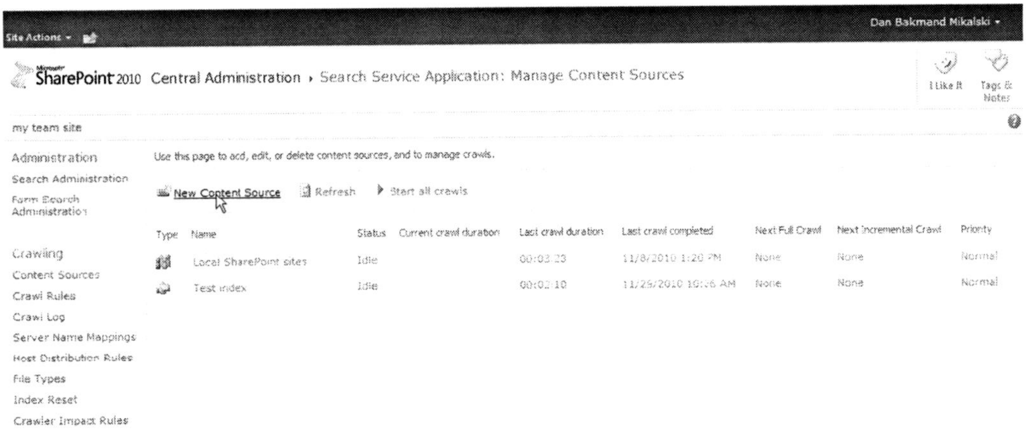

*Figure 14-17. Content sources page*

Click New Content Source, and enter an appropriate name for the content source. Choose Line of Business Data as the content source type, and choose the relevant BCS application and external data source, as in Figure 14-18.

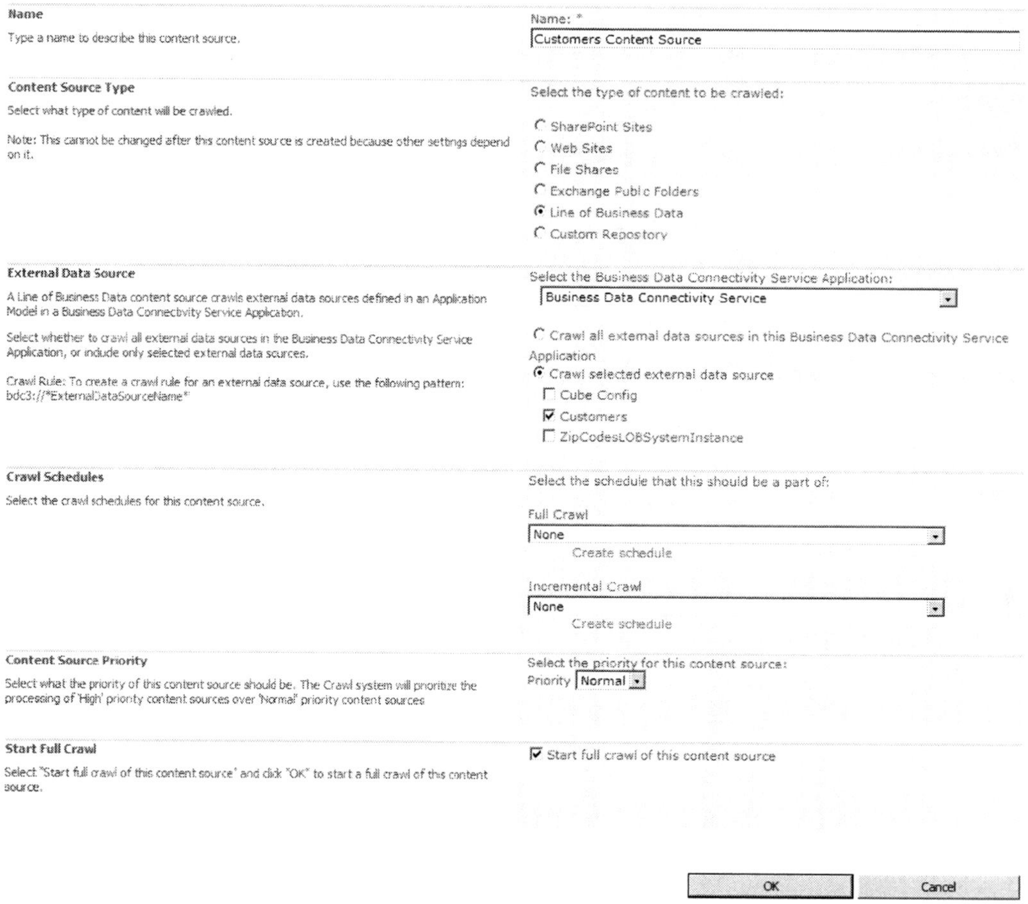

**Figure 14-18.** *Creating a new content source for the LOB data ECT*

Now select "Start full crawl", and click OK. It usually takes a few minutes for the indexer to update and start. When it goes back to idle, the external content source has been crawled.

## Performing a Search

In order to test the search, a site that is configured to perform enterprise searches is required (see Chapter 4). Go to the Enterprise Search Center site, and search for a customer name or other contact detail (if you followed the Customers example). The search should now return results from the BCS, as shown in Figure 14-19.

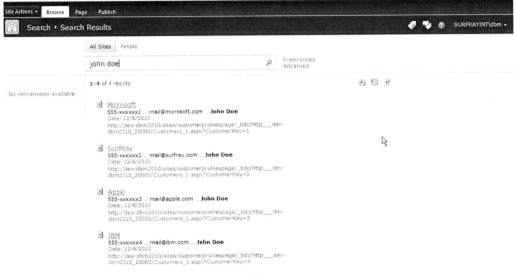

*Figure 14-19. Search results displaying external data*

Clicking a search result from the BCS source opens it in the newly created profile page, as shown in Figure 14-20. The profile page automatically shows the metadata properties from the external content type.

*Figure 14-20. Search results item displayed on the profile page for the ECT*

After following this walkthrough, it should be easy to create and configure searching for other external content types as well.

# Creating a .NET Connector in Visual Studio 2010

One of the major strengths of BCS is how easy it is to integrate with almost any external data source. This section introduces the API and how to use Visual Studio 2010 to create a simple .NET connector. This connector example connects just to a data file but can be extended to connect to more complex data sources. .NET connectors can be discovered through the Discover function in SPD 2010.

## Creating a Sample Flat File Data Source

First of all, we need a flat file with some data in it. Start by adding a .txt file on this path on the SharePoint server:

C:\Shared\zipcodes.txt

In real-life scenarios, it is likely to be on a file share, but for this example we keep it simple. In this example, the file contains city names and zip codes, separated with a comma and each name/zip pair on a new line. For this example, Danish zip codes are used. The file should look like this:

```
2750,Ballerup
1810,Frederiksberg
1720,Copenhagen West
...
```

## Creating a .NET Assembly Connector Project in Visual Studio 2010

A .NET Assembly Connector is created as the project type Business Data Connectivity Model (BDC Model) in Visual Studio 2010. Open Visual Studio 2010, click File, select New, and then select Project. Choose the Business Data Connectivity Model project type, and name the project ZipCodesModel, as shown in Figure 14-21. Then click OK.

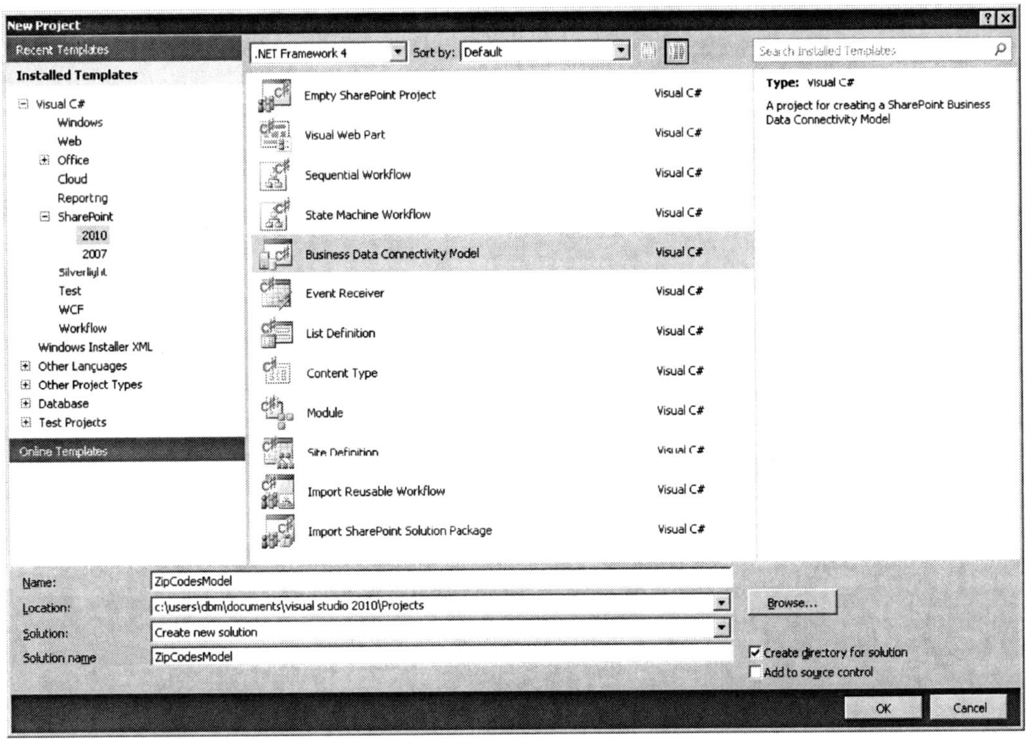

*Figure 14-21. Selecting the Business Data Connectivity Model from the Projects window*

Specify the SharePoint site where the model should be deployed (Figure 14-22), and click Finish.

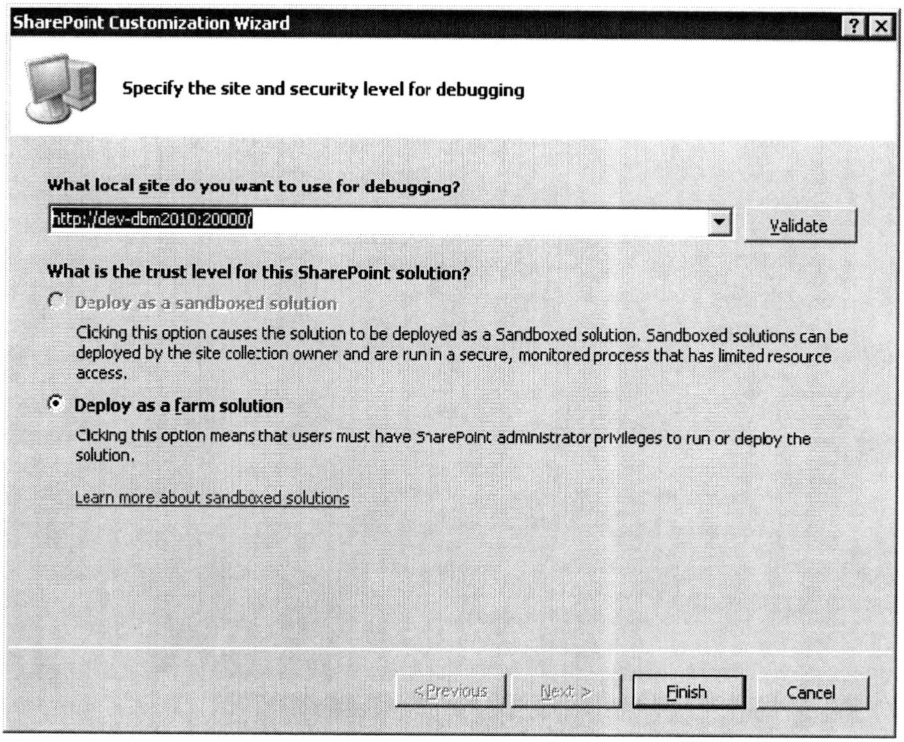

*Figure 14-22. Setting deployment site*

Note that BDCM projects can be deployed only as a farm solution. This is because the model has to be deployed to the metadata store.

The BDCM project type creates a number of files automatically. These files shown in Solution Explorer (Figure 14-23) are the minimum required to make a new model and deploy it. If the BDCM is part of a third-party solution, it is likely that an alternative deployment method is used and the feature files and WSP package files can be removed.

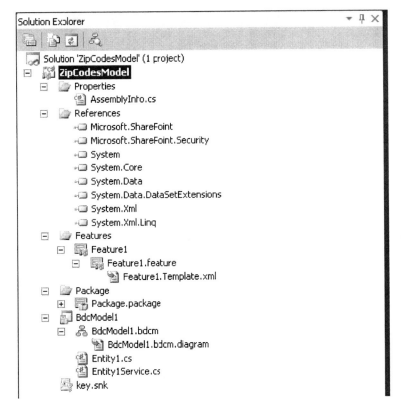

**Figure 14-23.** *Solution Explorer showing the BDC model*

The required references to the SharePoint assemblies are automatically added. A feature for enabling and disabling the BDCM is included, and a WSP package containing the feature and model is added.

The BDC model itself contains a definition of the data source, connection information, and access layer information (query and return type information). The BDC model contains two classes: a class that defines the entity or external content type that this BDC model returns, and a class containing the code used to connect to the data source, query it, and return the entities it contains.

## Creating an Entity (External Content Type)

The first real development task is to create the entity to be returned. It is very important to make sure that the entity contains the appropriate data to fulfill the business requirement for this .NET connector. To do this, the Entity1.cs file will be renamed ZipCodesEntity.cs and modified to map to the zip codes file.

To rename the file called Entity1.cs, right-click it in Solution Explorer and select Rename from the context menu. Type in ZipCodesEntity.cs, and click Yes when asked if all references should be renamed.

To modify the mapping, open the entity file by double-clicking ZipCodesEntity.cs. Delete the existing properties, and add two new properties called ZipCode and City. The class should now look as follows:

```
using System;
using System.Collections.Generic;
using System.Linq;
using System.Text;

namespace ZipCodesModel.BdcModel1
{
    public partial class ZipCodesEntity
    {
        public string ZipCode { get; set; }
        public string City { get; set; }
    }
}
```

# Creating an Entity Service Class

The entity service class is this example is used to query the data source—in this example, the zipcodes text file. The output of the entity service class will be one or all objects of the `ZipCodesEntity` class, depending on the operation performed.

Rename the `Entity1Service.cs` file to `ZipCodesEntityService.cs` as with the entity file, and click Yes when asked to update all references.

In Solution Explorer, double-click `ZipCodesEntityService.cs` to open it in code view.

As the data source is a text file, add the `System.IO` namespace, which contains the required classes for reading from the zipcodes text file.

```
using System.IO;
```

Some methods are required for the entity service class to function. The entity service class defines the Finder and Specific Finder methods used to return entities from the data source (zipcodes text file).

`ReadList()` is the Finder method of the BDC model. In this example, it should return all zipcode/city pairs from the data source. The method returns an IEnumerable generic collection of entities, which, in this case, is a collection of `ZipCodesEntity` objects. In this example, the objects are just created in memory, but advanced streaming schemes might be applied if the data source contains larger data sets. The `ReadList()` method can be implemented as shown in Listing 14-1.

*Listing 14-1. Implementation of the ReadList Method*

```
public static IEnumerable<ZipCodesEntity> ReadList()
{
    List<ZipCodesEntity> zipCodesEntityList = new List<ZipCodesEntity>();
    TextReader textReader = new StreamReader(@"C:\Shared\ZipCodes.txt");
    string zipCodeEntry;

    while ((zipCodeEntry = textReader.ReadLine()) != null)
    {
        ZipCodesEntity zipCodesEntity = new ZipCodesEntity();

        string[] entityData = zipCodeEntry.Split(',');
        zipCodesEntity.ZipCode = entityData[0];
        zipCodesEntity.City = entityData[1];
        zipCodesEntityList.Add(zipCodesEntity);
    }
```

```
        textReader.Close();

        return zipCodesEntityList;
    }
```

The ReadItem(string zipCode) method defines the Specific Finder method for the BDC model. In this example, it returns a ZipCodesEntity object with the zipcode/city pair matching the zipcode argument. The ReadItem() method can be implemented as shown in Listing 14-2.

*Listing 14-2. Implementation of the ReadItem Method*

```
public static ZipCodesEntity ReadItem(string zipCode)
    {
        foreach (ZipCodesEntity zipCodesEntity in ReadList())
        {
            if (zipCodesEntity.ZipCode == zipCode)
                return zipCodesEntity;
        }
        return null;

    }
```

It should now be possible to compile the assembly, which can be considered a .NET Assembly Connector at this point. Now the BDC model will be created, and the connection to the relevant data source, query capabilities, and return value type are defined.

# BDC Modeling Tools

After defining the entity and service, the BDC model can be created. The BDC model defines how to connect to the data source and how it can be queried. It also defines the type of information it returns. The BDC Explorer and the BDC Designer are used to define the BDC model. Both of these new VS 2010 components are described ahead.

## BDC Explorer

VS 2010 extends the windows list with the BDC Explorer, shown in Figure 14-24. This window is used to create or edit the BDC model.

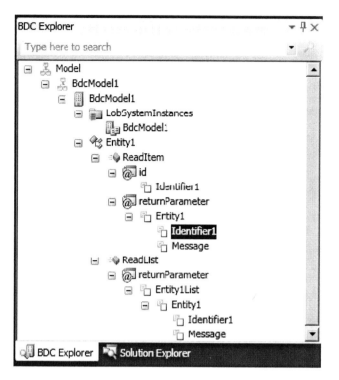

**Figure 14-24.** *BDC Explorer showing the BDC model*

Just like with Solution Explorer and class view windows, the BDC Explorer is linked to the Properties window. It shows the relevant properties allowing the developer to view and edit the BDC model. Figure 14-25 demonstrates this. When Identifier 1 is selected in the BDC Explorer, the corresponding properties are displayed in the Properties window.

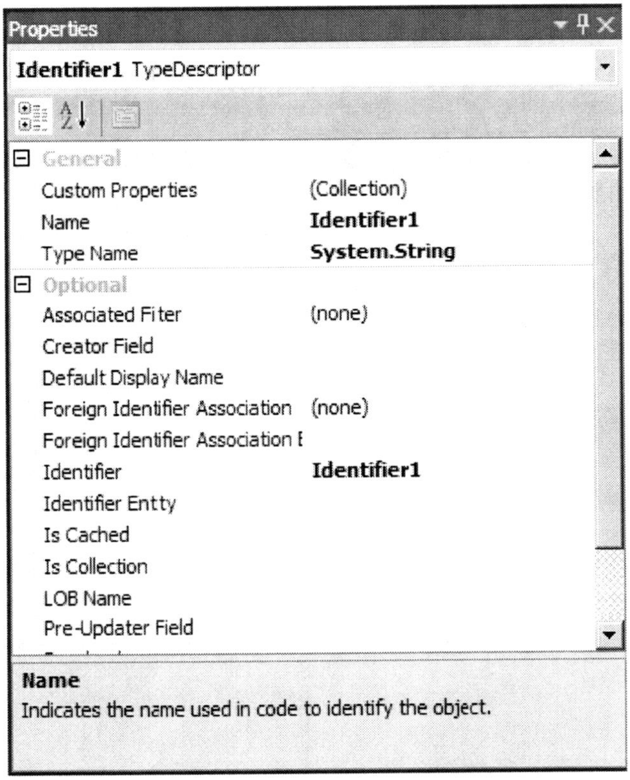

## Properties

**Identifier1** TypeDescriptor

▣ General

| | |
|---|---|
| Custom Properties | (Collection) |
| Name | **Identifier1** |
| Type Name | **System.String** |

▣ Optional

| | |
|---|---|
| Associated Filter | (none) |
| Creator Field | |
| Default Display Name | |
| Foreign Identifier Association | (none) |
| Foreign Identifier Association E | |
| Identifier | **Identifier1** |
| Identifier Entity | |
| Is Cached | |
| Is Collection | |
| LOB Name | |
| Pre-Updater Field | |

**Name**
Indicates the name used in code to identify the object.

*Figure 14-25. Entity properties displayed beneath the BDC Explorer*

## BDC Designer

VS 2010 includes the BDC Designer (Figure 14-26). This designer window allows the developer to create and edit a BDC model. The BDC Designer works the same way as the BDC Explorer regarding the Properties window.

*Figure 14-26. A BDC entity displayed in the BDC Designer*

# Defining the BDC Model

Defining a BDC model is essentially to define the mapping between your .NET Assembly Connector and the BDC. In this series of steps, the mappings between the .NET Assembly Connector and the BDC are defined. To create the mapping, double-click the BDC Explorer to open the BDCModel1.bdcm file in Solution Explorer. The BDC Designer will then open and be visible. From the View menu, select Other Windows. Then click BDC Explorer to open the window.

## Configuring the BDC Model and LOB System

Rename the BDC model to ZipCodesModel, as shown in Figure 14-27. Right-click the second node from the top, named BdcModel1, and click Properties. Change the Name property to ZipCodesModel in the Properties window.

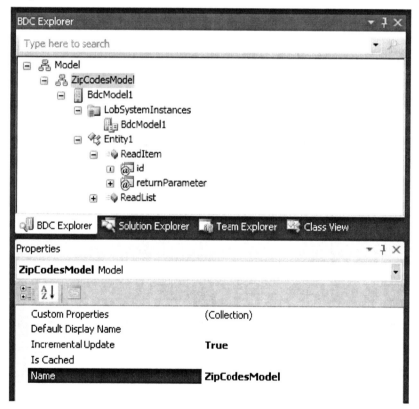

*Figure 14-27. Renaming the BDC model*

The third node from the top (the LOB system) should also be renamed. Change the Name property to ZipCodesLOBSystem using the Properties window, as shown in Figure 14-28.

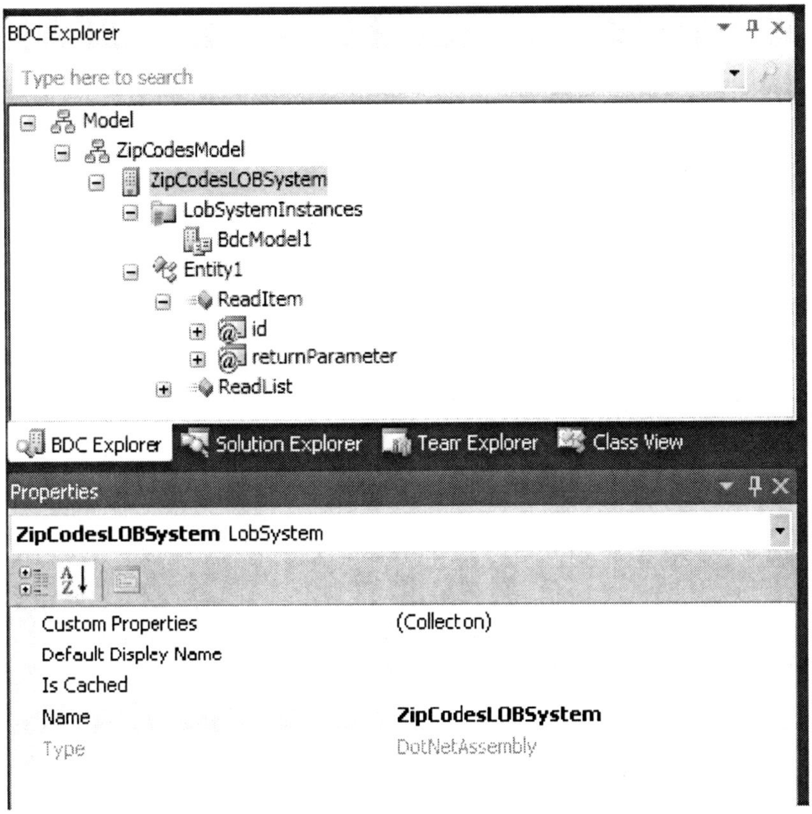

*Figure 14-28. Renaming the LOB system*

The fifth node from the top (the LOB system instance) should be renamed to ZipCodesLOBSystemInstance by using the Properties window to change its Name property, as shown in Figure 14-29.

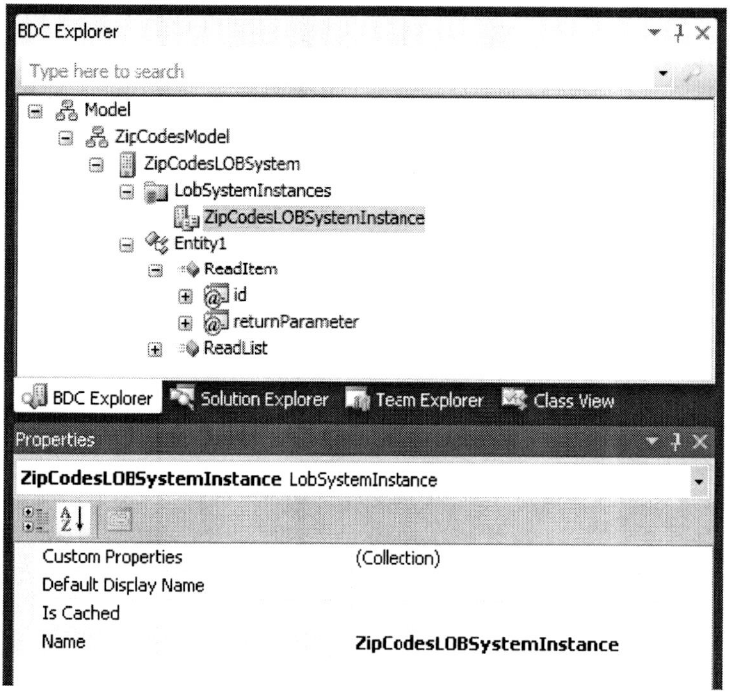

**Figure 14-29.** *Renaming the LOB system instance*

The ShowInSearchUI property on the ZipCodesLOBSystemInstance must be set to allow the ZipCodesLOBSystemInstance to be crawled and searched by the SharePoint search service. If the LOBSystemInstance should not be crawled or searched, this property does not need to be changed. To set the ShowInSearchUI property on the ZipCodesLOBSystemInstance, click the ZipCodesLOBSystemInstance node in the BDC Explorer. Then click the button in the Custom Properties row in the Properties window. Use the Properties Editor to set the ShowInSearchUI property. Give it the data type System.String and set the value to x, as shown in Figure 14-30. Click OK.

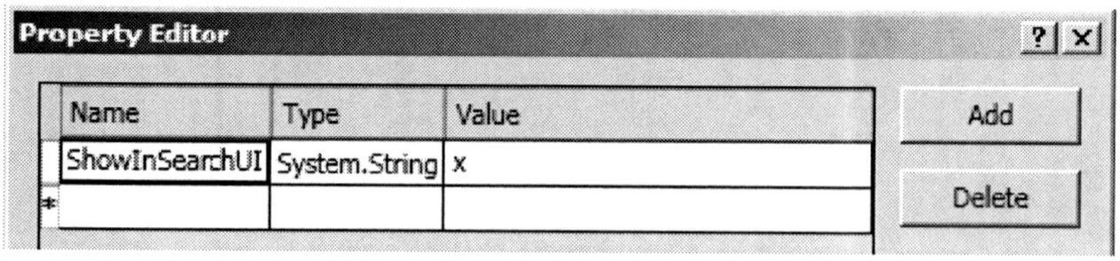

**Figure 14-30.** *Adding the ShowInSearchUI property to the LOB system instance*

## Configuring the Entity and Entity Methods

The BDC model entity should be renamed to match the entity defined in the .NET Assembly
Connector. This is done by selecting Entity1 from the BDC Explorer. Then change the Name property to
ZipCodesEntity in the Properties window, as shown in Figure 14-31.

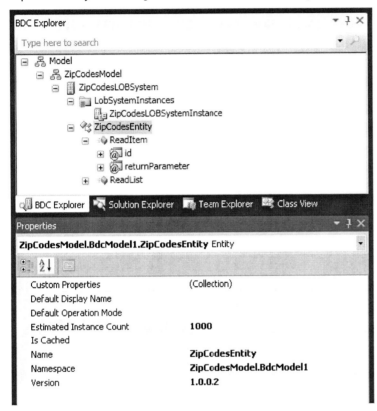

**Figure 14-31.** *Renaming the BDC model entity*

The RootFinder property on the Finder method must be set to specify the Finder method used to
enumerate the items to crawl. If the Finder method shouldn't be used for crawling, this property can be
ignored and left unset. The RootFinder property on the Finder method is set in the BDC Explorer by
clicking the ReadList node. After that, click the button in the Custom Properties row in the Properties
window. Add the RootFinder property, with a data type of System.String and a value of x in the
Properties Editor, as shown in Figure 14-32.

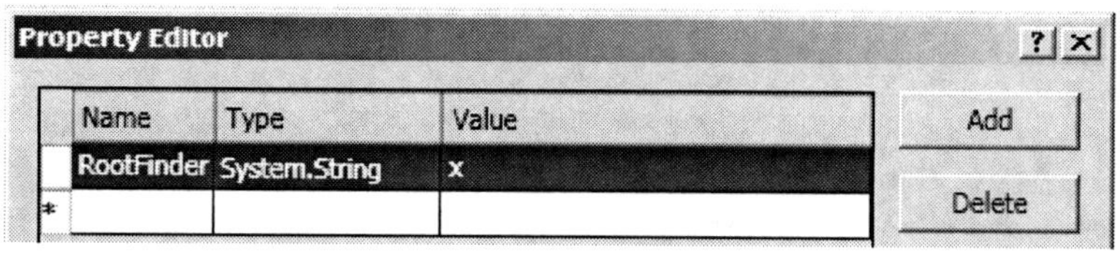

*Figure 14-32. Adding the RootFinder property to the Finder method*

Next, the identifier for the Finder method return parameter is set for the entity. This is done by selecting the Identifier1 node under the Finder method return parameter for the ZipCodesEntity. Then, in the Properties window, change the Name property to ZipCode, as shown in Figure 14-33.

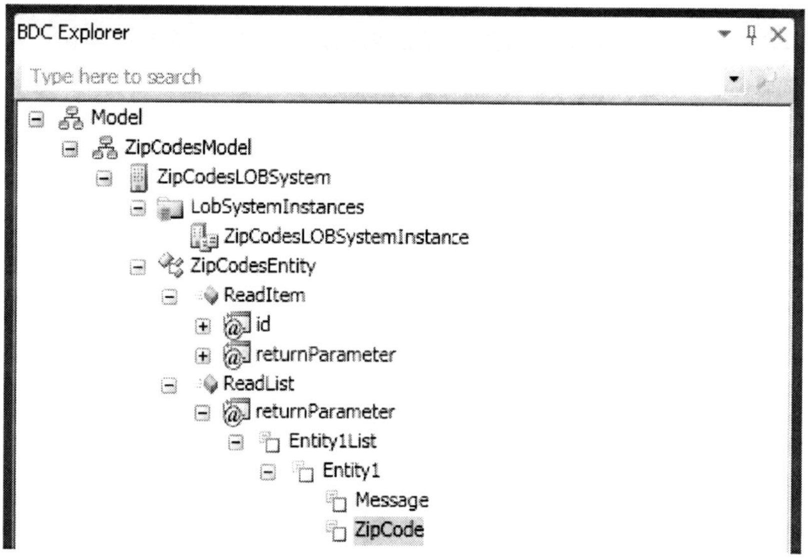

*Figure 14-33. Renaming the Finder method*

Next, set the identifier for the specific Finder method return parameter and the input parameter in the entity. To do so, first select the Identifier1 nodes under the specific Finder method return parameter for the ZipCodesEntity. Then, in the Properties window, change the Name property to ZipCode, as shown in Figure 14-34.

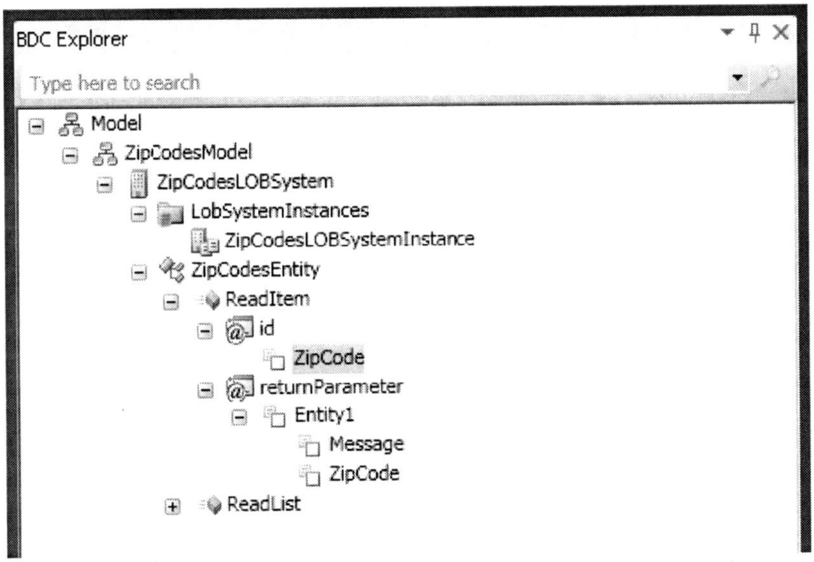

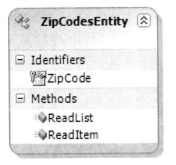

*Figure 14-34. Renaming the Finder method return parameter*

Right-click `Identifier1`, and select Rename in the BDC Designer (Figure 14-35). Change the identifier to ZipCode.

*Figure 14-35. Renaming the BDC model in Designer view*

The message parameters are not needed, so they should be removed. Right-click the message parameter on the Finder method, and select Delete. This removes the Message node from the BDC Explorer. Repeat this on the specific Finder method. Alternatively delete the entity, and recreate a new "empty" entity.

## Adding Parameters to Map the Data Source

Parameters must be added that map to the data in the zipcodes text file data source. In this example, the only parameter to map is the city name.

In the BDC Explorer, right-click Entity1 and select Add Type Descriptor. In the Properties window, change the Name property to City and the Type Name property to System.String, as shown in Figure 14-36. Repeat this for the Finder and the Specific Finder methods.

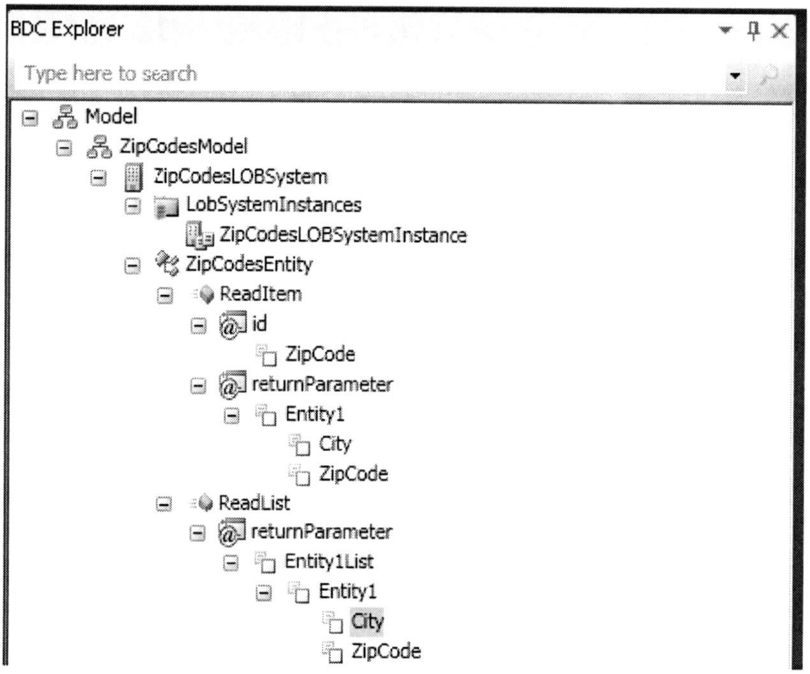

*Figure 14-36. Adding parameters to the Finder and Specific Finder methods*

## Configuring the Finder Method Instance

The method instance properties are configured from the BDC Method Details window. This window is also new in VS 2010. Selecting a method in the BDC Designer will display the corresponding method instances in the BDC Method Details window, as shown in Figure 14-37.

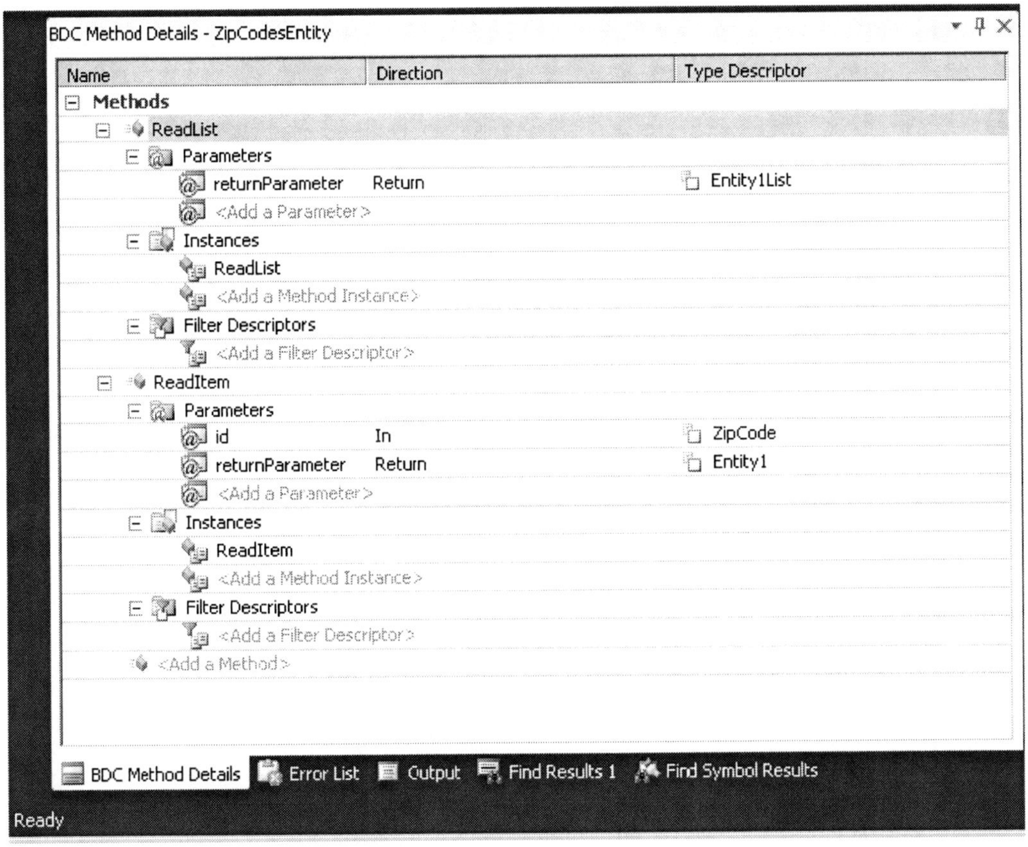

BDC Method Details - ZipCodesEntity

| Name | Direction | Type Descriptor |
|---|---|---|
| ☐ **Methods** | | |
|     ☐ ReadList | | |
|         ☐ Parameters | | |
|             returnParameter | Return | Entity1List |
|             <Add a Parameter> | | |
|         ☐ Instances | | |
|             ReadList | | |
|             <Add a Method Instance> | | |
|         ☐ Filter Descriptors | | |
|             <Add a Filter Descriptor> | | |
|     ☐ ReadItem | | |
|         ☐ Parameters | | |
|             id | In | ZipCode |
|             returnParameter | Return | Entity1 |
|             <Add a Parameter> | | |
|         ☐ Instances | | |
|             ReadItem | | |
|             <Add a Method Instance> | | |
|         ☐ Filter Descriptors | | |
|             <Add a Filter Descriptor> | | |
|     <Add a Method> | | |

BDC Method Details    Error List    Output    Find Results 1    Find Symbol Results

Ready

*Figure 14-37. Configuring the Finder method instance*

The Finder method is specified by setting the RootFinder property on the Finder method instance. It specifies that this instance is used to enumerate the items to crawl. If the Finder method instance is not to be used for crawling, this property can be ignored and left unset. Click the ReadList node in the BDC Method Details window. To set the RootFinder property on the Finder method instance, click the button in the Custom Properties row in the Properties window. Add the RootFinder property. Set the data type as System.String, and set the value to x, as shown in Figure 14-38.

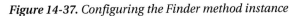

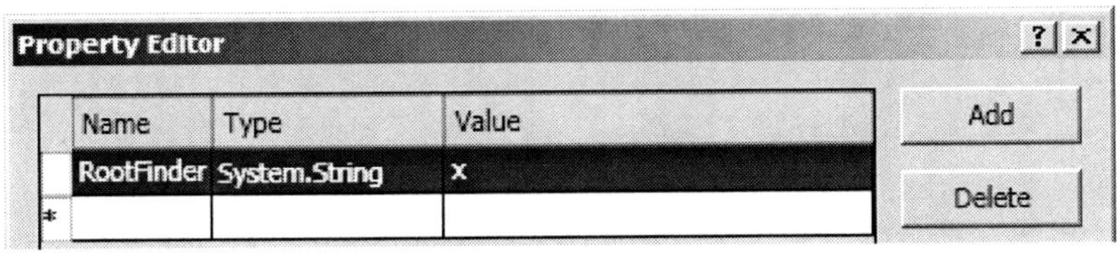

**Property Editor**    ?|×|

| Name | Type | Value | |
|---|---|---|---|
| RootFinder | System.String | x | Add |
| * | | | Delete |

*Figure 14-38. Adding the RootFinder property to the Finder method instance*

If the data source contained data suitable for incremental crawls, the `LastModifiedTimeStampField` property on the Finder method instance could also be set. This is not feasible in this example.

## Deployment

Deploying the .NET Assembly Connector is made easy in Visual Studio 2010. Open the Build menu on the top bar, and click Deploy Solution. Now VS 2010 begins to compile and packages the .NET Assembly Connector code, BDC model, and the feature. Finally it creates a WSP, which is the package type used for deploying solutions to SharePoint.

The WSP package is then deployed to the specified SharePoint site. The feature is activated, which registers the external content type associated with this .NET Assembly Connector.

# The Secure Store Service

The Secure Store Service is used to store accounts inside SharePoint to use when authorizing against databases that require authorization, etc. It typically stores credentials in the form of username and password, but it can also store tokens, pin numbers, etc.

The Secure Store Service application works by a scheme being defined providing authentication information. Then the user- or group-level permissions to pass to the database are mapped in the Secure Store application. The Secure Store Service allows connections using the federation, delegation, or impersonation level. In cases of Business Connectivity Services, the mapped credentials are passed from the Secure Store to the data source.[1]

## Configuring the Secure Store Service

In this section and the ones that follow, we will go through the procedure of configuring the Secure Store Service, while explaining the individual steps and configuration options. The first step is to ensure that the Secure Store Service is started:

1. Navigate to Central Administration  Manage Service on Server (Figure 14-39).

2. Locate the service called Secure Store Service.

3. If the Secure Store Service is not started, then start it.

---

[1] Loosely based on http://lightningtools.com/blog/archive/2010/01/20/bcs-secure-store-services.aspx.

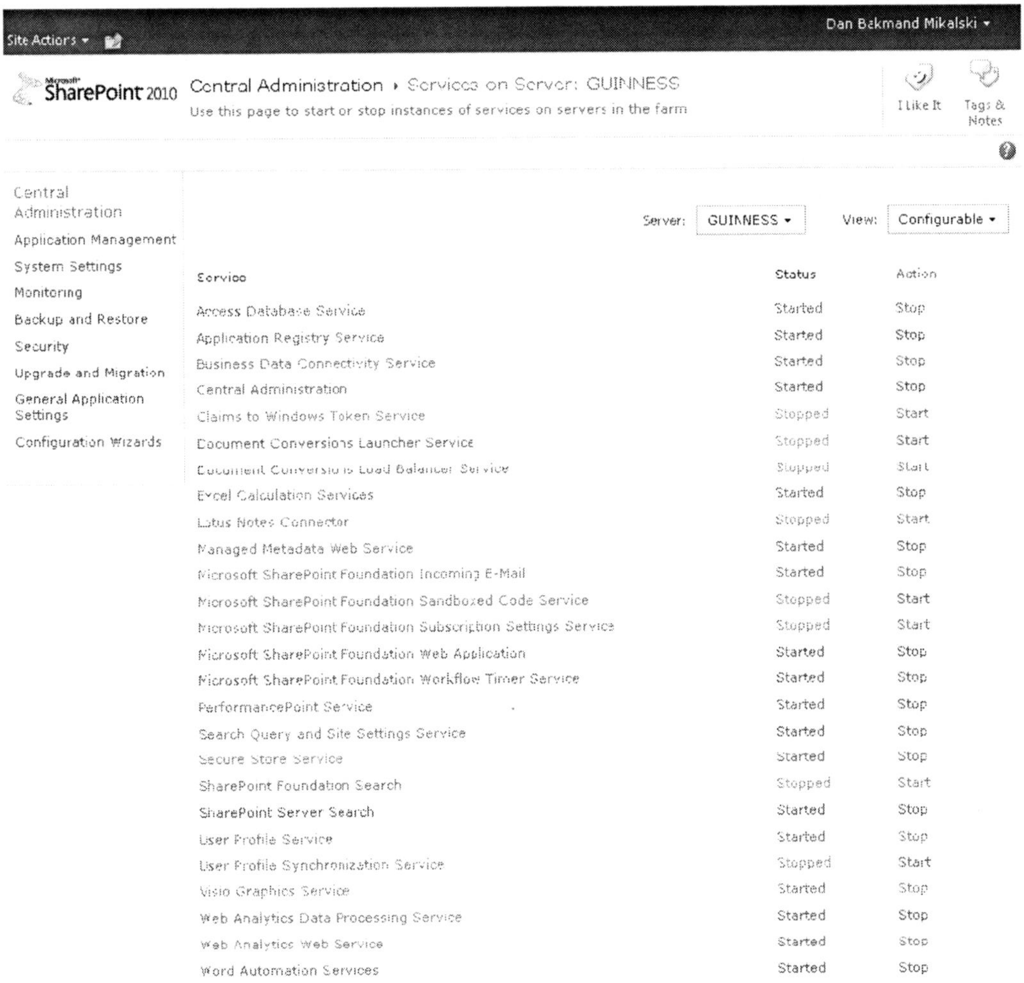
Site Actions
Dan Bækmand Mikalski
SharePoint 2010
Central Administration ▸ Services on Server: GUINNESS
Use this page to start or stop instances of services on servers in the farm
I Like It
Tags & Notes
Central Administration
Application Management
System Settings
Monitoring
Backup and Restore
Security
Upgrade and Migration
General Application Settings
Configuration Wizards
Server: GUINNESS
View: Configurable
Service
Status
Action
Access Database Service Started Stop
Application Registry Service Started Stop
Business Data Connectivity Service Started Stop
Central Administration Started Stop
Claims to Windows Token Service Stopped Start
Document Conversions Launcher Service Stopped Start
Document Conversions Load Balancer Service Stopped Start
Excel Calculation Services Started Stop
Lotus Notes Connector Stopped Start
Managed Metadata Web Service Started Stop
Microsoft SharePoint Foundation Incoming E-Mail Started Stop
Microsoft SharePoint Foundation Sandboxed Code Service Stopped Start
Microsoft SharePoint Foundation Subscription Settings Service Stopped Start
Microsoft SharePoint Foundation Web Application Started Stop
Microsoft SharePoint Foundation Workflow Timer Service Started Stop
PerformancePoint Service Started Stop
Search Query and Site Settings Service Started Stop
Secure Store Service Started Stop
SharePoint Foundation Search Stopped Start
SharePoint Server Search Started Stop
User Profile Service Started Stop
User Profile Synchronization Service Stopped Start
Visio Graphics Service Started Stop
Web Analytics Data Processing Service Started Stop
Web Analytics Web Service Started Stop
Word Automation Services Started Stop

***Figure 14-39.** Services overview*

With the Secure Store Service started, it is now possible to provision a Secure Store Service application as follows:

1. Navigate to Central Administration  Manage Service Application (Figure 14-40).
2. Click the New button on the ribbon.
3. Click Secure Store Service to open the dialog for creating the new service application.

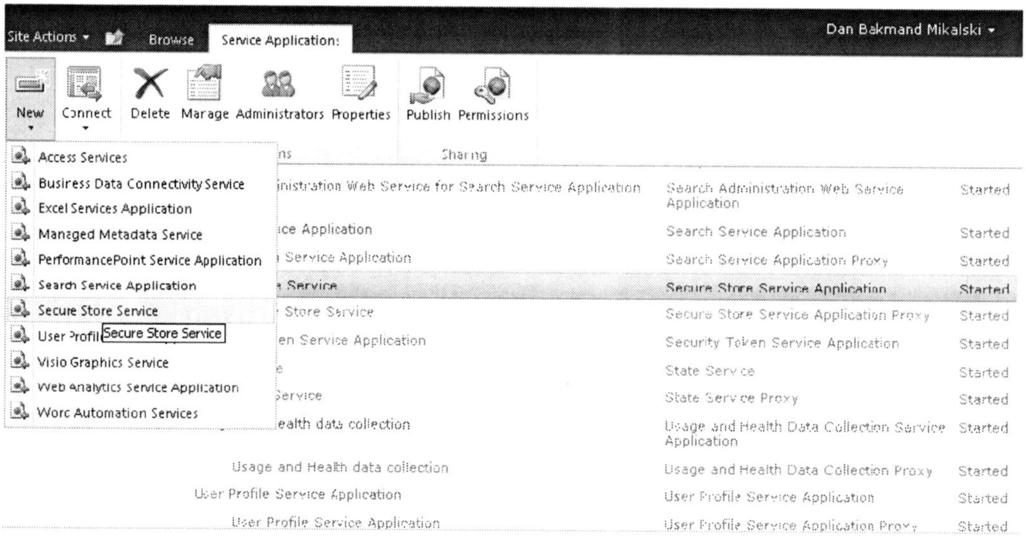

**Figure 14-40.** *Provisioning the Secure Store Service application*

The Create New Secure Store Service Application dialog (Figure 14-41) allows administrators to specify a database where the credentials are stored. The credentials are encrypted and accessible by the Secure Store Service application. To create the Secure Store Service, do the following:

1. Enter a unique service name.

2. Specify the database instance name where the Secure Store database will be created. Also specify a name for the Secure Store database.

3. Choose or create an application pool identity, which the Secure Store Service application will run under. It is suggested to use a unique account for this particular service application for security reasons.

4. Click OK. The Secure Store Service application and proxy should now be created.

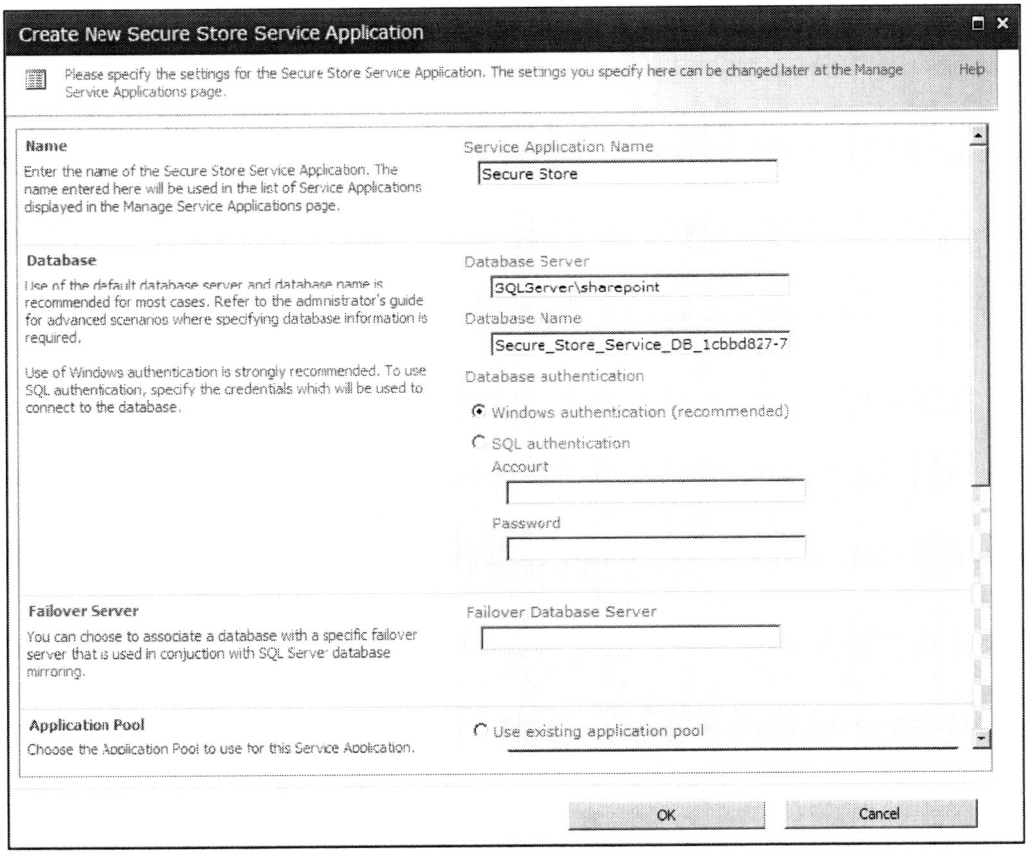

*Figure 14-41. Provisioning the Secure Store Service application*

With the new Secure Store Service application created, it must be configured with a pass phrase (Figure 14-42) that allows it to securely encrypt and decrypt the stored credentials from the database.

1.  Click the Secure Store Service application to begin configuring it.

2.  If it is the first time the Secure Store Service application is being configured, a prompt will appear, asking for a new key to be generated. Click Generate New Key on the ribbon.

3.  Enter a pass phrase, and click OK.

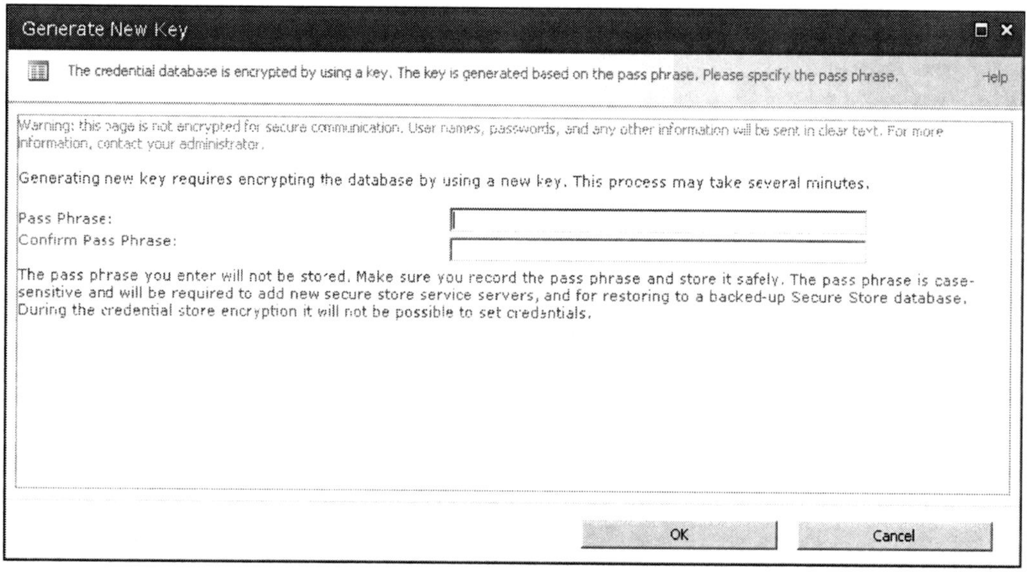

*Figure 14-42. Secure Store Service key generation*

## Creating a Secure Store Service Application for Impersonating

For the Secure Store Service to be able to apply the stored credentials, an application must be created that uses these credentials. In SharePoint, this is called a Secure Store Target Application. In essence the impersonation of the securely stored credentials is done through this application.

1. Go to the Secure Store Service application.

2. Click New on the ribbon, as shown in Figure 14-43. This opens the Create New Secure Store Target Application page.

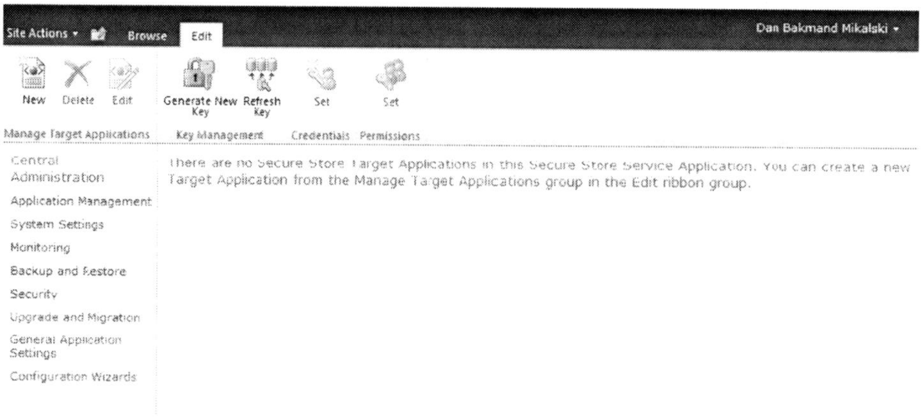

*Figure 14-43. Secure Store Service application overview*

On the Create New Secure Store Target Application page, the target application settings are specified. In the example in Figure 14-44, Group is chosen as the target application type. This allows members to be defined whose accounts can be impersonated by another account. This is the most often used scenario. Other options include tickets with a limited valid lifetime. On the target application page, do the following:

3.  Enter a unique name for the application. This is not changeable after the application is created.

4.  Enter a screen-friendly name and the e-mail address of the administrator, which typically is the creator.

5.  Choose the Target Application Type, as described before.

6.  Select a Target Application Page URL. A custom URL can be specified to allow mapping this application to a custom page for users to assign accounts, if there is an organizational need for doing so.

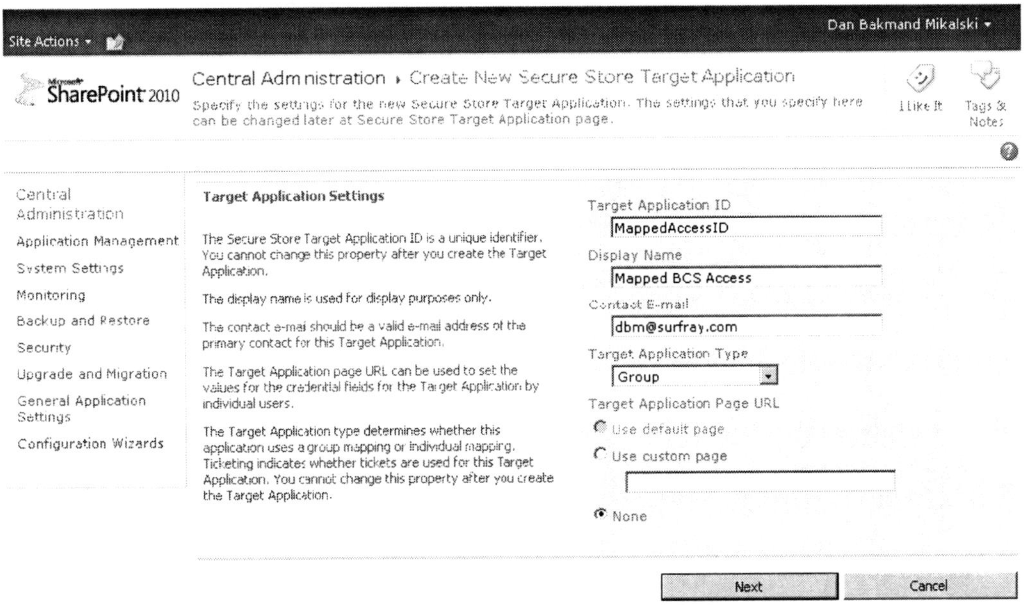

*Figure 14-44. Secure Store Service application creation*

To alter the fields and thereby information used by this application, add additional fields that the user will have to fill out to authenticate. The default fields are Windows username and password, as shown in Figure 14-45.

7.  Change fields as required.

8.  Click Next to go to the credentials mapping page.

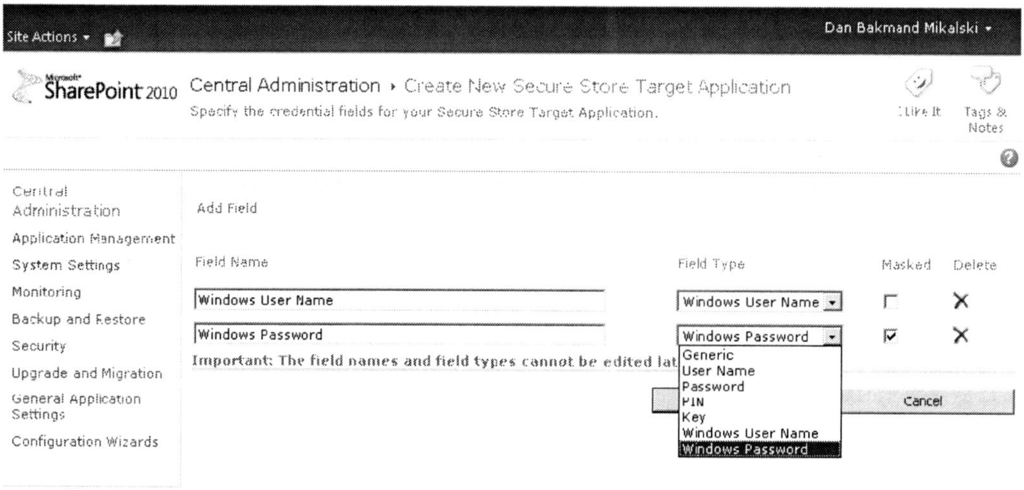

*Figure 14-45. Secure Store Service application field mapping*

On the user mappings page, the administrators and members are configured. These are then the members and administrators of the target application. In Figure 14-46, one administrator and two users are added: SP_TestUser1 and SP_TestUser2. It will be explained how to add specific permissions to individual users in the "Setting Permissions" section.

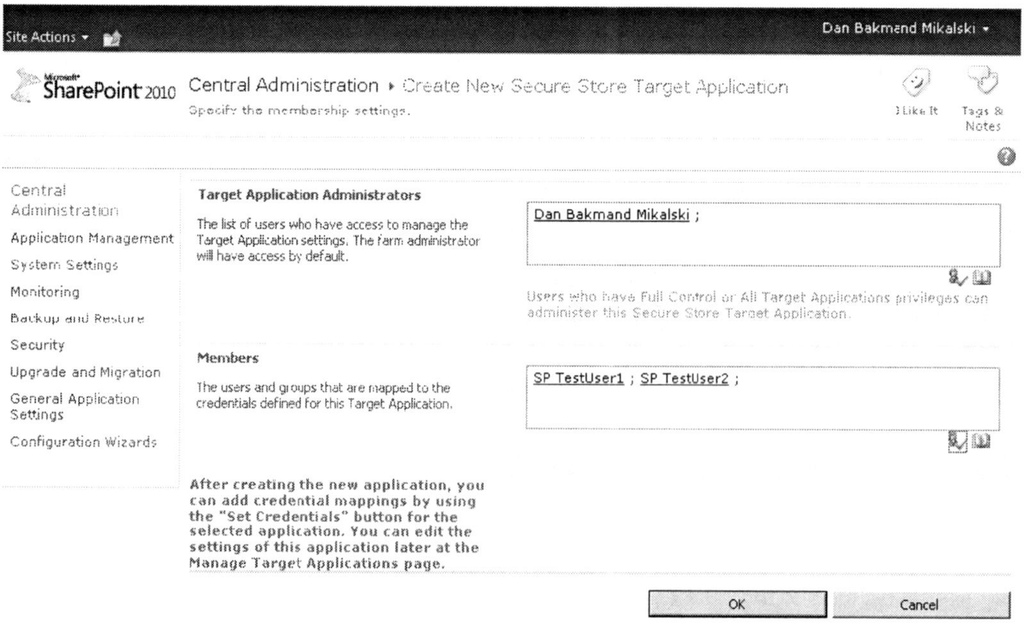

*Figure 14-46. Secure Store Service credentials mapping*

Finally click the OK button, and the target application will be created. SharePoint now automatically navigates to the Secure Store Service Application page where the target applications are shown, as in Figure 14-47. It lists the target applications by ID, their types, and display name.

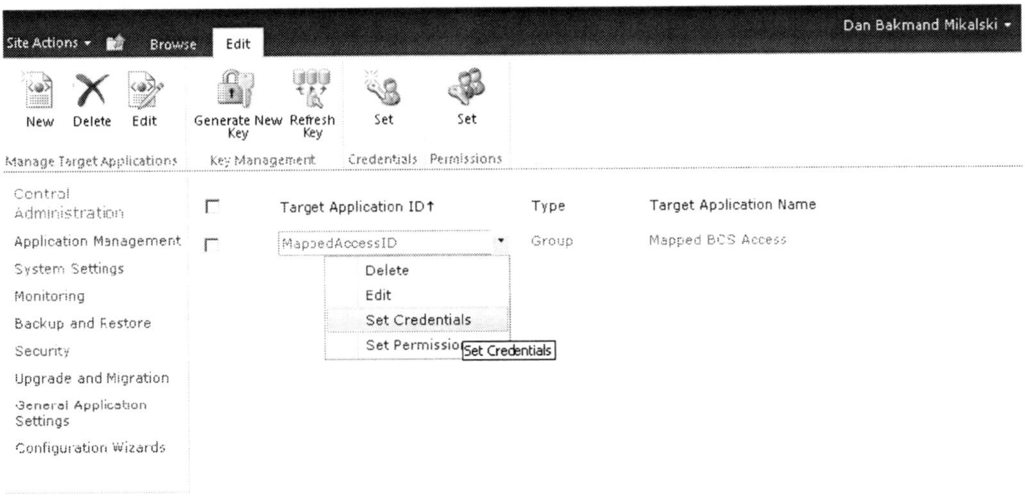

**Figure 14-47.** *Secure Store Service application overview*

## Setting the Application Impersonation Credentials

Now, the Secure Store Target Application is configured and administrators, members, and credentials type have been defined. At this point, the application impersonation credentials are configured for the members of the target application, as shown in Figure 14-48.

1.  Provide one or more credential owners, which are the credentials that map to the custom defined credentials.

2.  Enter the Windows username and password(s) to be used when impersonating in the Secure Store Target Application.

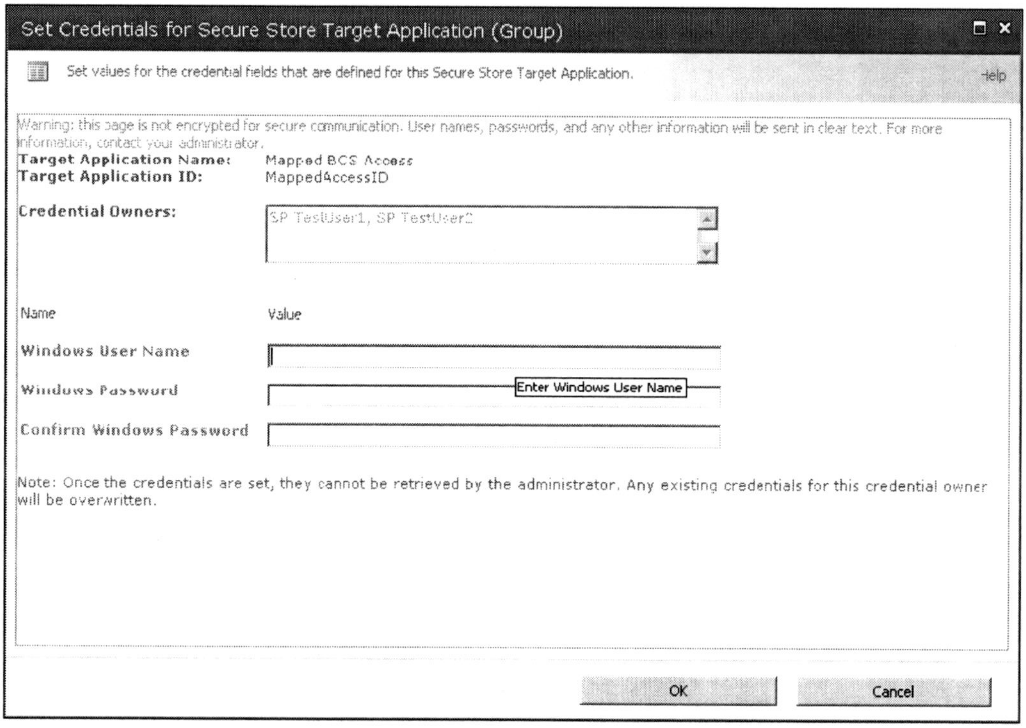

*Figure 14-48. Setting the Secure Store Target Application credentials*

With everything configured relating to credentials, the Secure Store Target Application can be used by BCS when creating connections to its data sources, as shown in Figure 14-49.

3. Select a connection type.

4. Enter proper connection details (here it is a SQL Server connection, as shown in Figure 14-49).

5. Enter the target application name at the time of creating a connection to the back end. Given the example data used in the section "Creating an External Content Type," now select the Secure Store Application ID option and enter the application name.

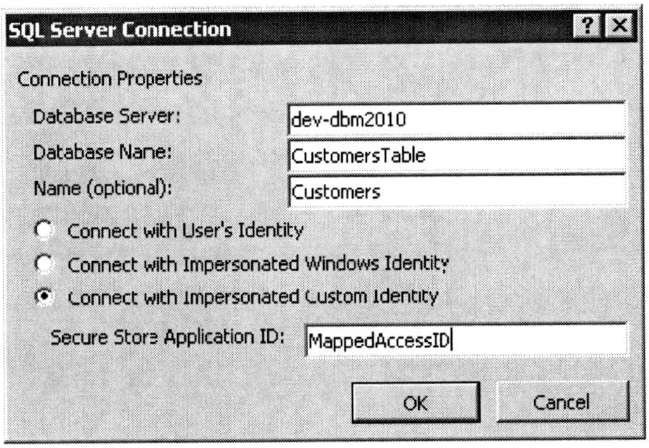

*Figure 14-49. Map BCS connection to Secure Store Application ID*

As mentioned earlier in this example, two users were added as members. These users can be delegated individual rights. When these users open an external list based on this external content type, they should be able to see the data pulled from the BDC using the impersonation. For this to work, the users must be members of the BCS application, as the BCS checks permissions using the incoming user account before doing the impersonation and getting the data from the back end. This means that the impersonation is not for communicating with the BCS application itself, but for allowing BCS to get data from its data source. Users still need permissions to access the external content type objects.

## Setting Permissions

Based on the data source created in the previous section, setting permissions on external content type objects is done by doing the following:

1. Going to Central Administration site   Manage service applications

2. Selecting the BCS service application just created

3. Setting permissions on the external content type, as shown in Figure 14-50

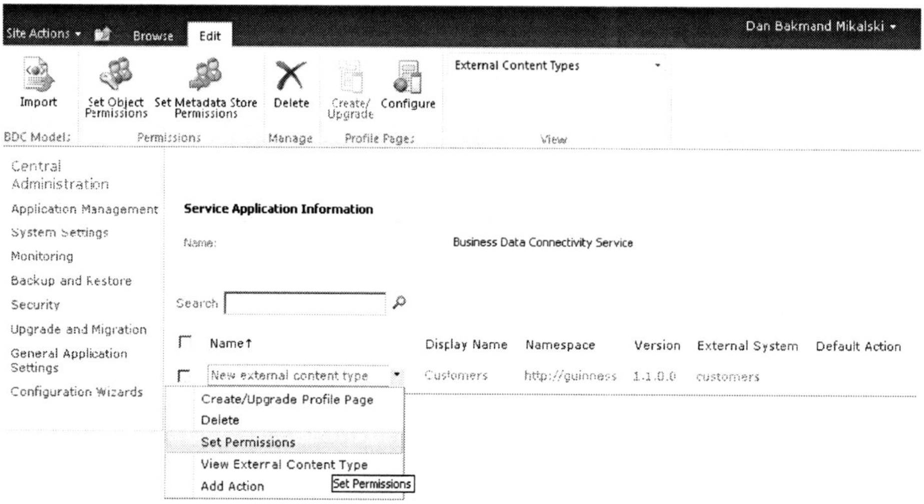

*Figure 14-50. Accessing external content type permissions settings*

In this case, the users are granted Edit and Execute permissions on the customers external content type object, as shown in Figure 14-51.

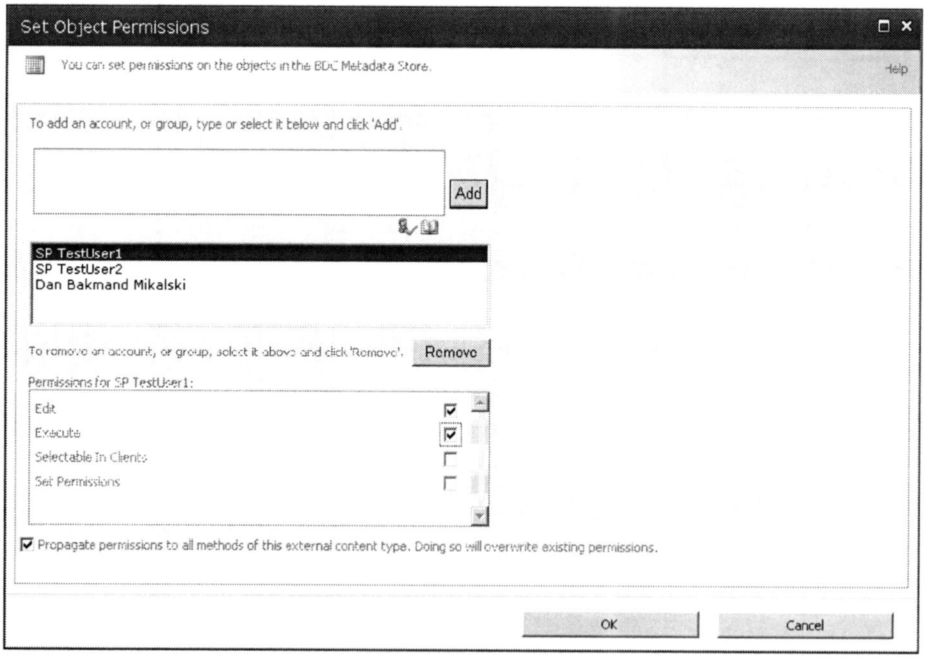

*Figure 14-51. Setting external content type permissions*

At this point, the external content type permissions are fully configured and can now be used in BCS Web Parts, external lists, etc. by persons with the appropriate credentials.

# Creating Security Trimmed CRUD Operations on a SQL Database Using Visual Studio 2010

Earlier it was shown how to create a flat file .NET connector using Business Data Connectivity Designer in Visual Studio 2010. Here we will show you how to pull data from an external database into an external list and enable Create, Read, Update, and Delete (CRUD) functions to the external list.[2] The example is based on the same customer data used earlier.

This list will implement security trimming by using a rights table that holds security identifiers for each row.

## Connecting Model to Data Source

To begin with, create a new BDC Model project and give it a proper name. Here it is named BdcCustomersModel. To make it easy to use the data obtained from the Customers database, the best way is to add a LINQ to SQL model. LINQ is not the fastest implementation method performance-wise, so if performance is critical, you might prefer to implement a dedicated data adaptor instead.

1. Select the project by left-clicking it.

2. Click Add New Item on the projects menu to open the Add New Item dialog.

3. Select Data templates from the Installed Templates panel.

4. Choose the LINQ to SQL Classes project type from the Templates panel.

5. Give the project a proper name—here it is called "Customer"—and then click Add.

6. Open the Server Explorer, and add a connection to the Customers database.

7. Drag Customers tableand drop it on the Customer.dbml design surface.

At this point, a designer class named CustomerDataContext is automatically added. To allow a connection to be created using a custom connection string, a new class should be added. Name the class CustomerDataContext.cs. Make this class a partial class. Then pass the connection string to the base class through the constructor, as in Listing 14-3.

*Listing 14-3. Data Context for Connecting to a Database with a Custom Connection String*

```
public partial class CustomerDataContext
{
    private const string ConnectionString = @"Data Source=localhost\SQLEXPRESS;Initial⏎
        Catalog=CustomersDatabase;Integrated Security=True;Pooling=False";
```

---

[2] Loosely based on http://www.facebook.com/note.php?note_id=338666619441.

```
        public CustomerDataContext() :
            base(ConnectionString, mappingSource)
        {
            OnCreated();
        }
}
```

---

■ **Note** We made the connection string a constant in the code for exemplifying it. In a production environment, it should be added to the Web.Config file in encrypted format. When using your own database, the connection string should be modified to match your database and credential requirements.

---

## Mapping BDC Model to Data Source

At this point, the BDC model should be mapped to the data source. This involves making a number of entities and specifying appropriate methods. The purpose is to create the interpretation layer between the database and the BDC model. First an entity with an identifier key needs to be created:

1. An entity named "Entity1" is automatically created. Delete it.

2. Create a new entity. This can be done using "Drag and Drop" on the Entity from Toolbox and dropping it on the design surface.

3. Change the default name of the entity to "Customer."

4. Create a new identifier named, CustomerKey, on the entity "Customer." This is most easily done by right-clicking the entity and selecting the Add Identifier option. This adds a new identifier to the entity.

5. Give the identifier the name "CustomerKey".

To add functionality, a number of method instances must be added to the entity. This is most easily done by selecting the entity and clicking the <Add a Method> button that appears in the Method Details panel. Create a Specific Finder method on the entity. This will add the ReadItem, as shown in Figure 14-52.

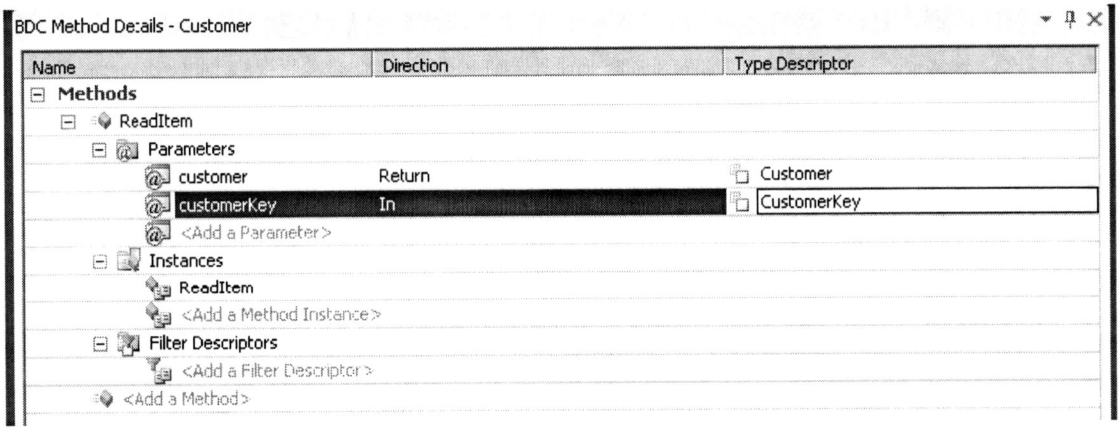

**Figure 14-52.** *Specific Finder method*

As shown in the Method Details panel, the ReadItem method has two parameters, namely an In parameter, which takes the identifier key, and a Return parameter, which is an object instance of the identity type. VS2010 offers some functionality for making it easy to create new methods by copying type descriptors automatically when possible. Therefore it is a good idea to configure those for the Specific Finder method before adding the other methods.

To complete the identifier key configuration, the type descriptor for the return parameter named CustomerKey should be added.

6. Open the Method Details panel.

7. Choose the <Edit> command from the type descriptor menu named CustomerKey.

8. In the BDC Explorer, add a type descriptor by right-clicking the CustomerKey, as shown in Figure 14-53, and choose the Add Type Descriptor option. This will create a new type descriptor.

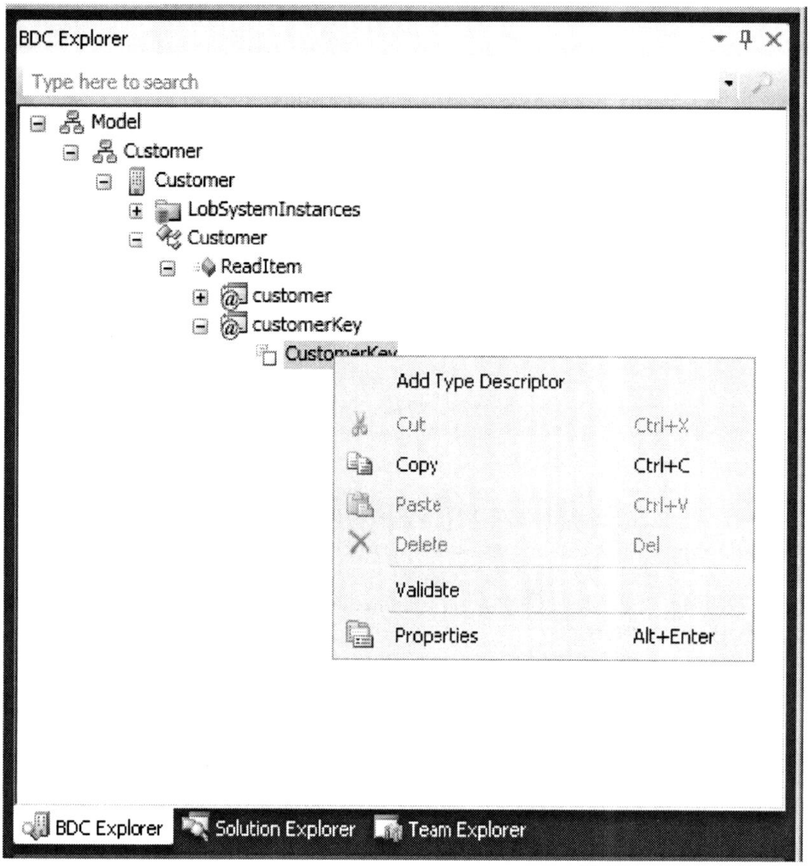

*Figure 14-53. Adding type descriptors*

9. Rename the just-created type descriptor to "CustomerKey", using the Properties panel.

10. Change the `Identifier` property to `CustomerKey`, as in Figure 14-54. This is how the BCS runtime knows that this type descriptor maps to the `CustomerKey` identifier.

11. Change the `Type  Name` property to match the type from the LINQ model. In this example, it is not required to change it.

12. Repeat steps 1–6 for all required type descriptors.

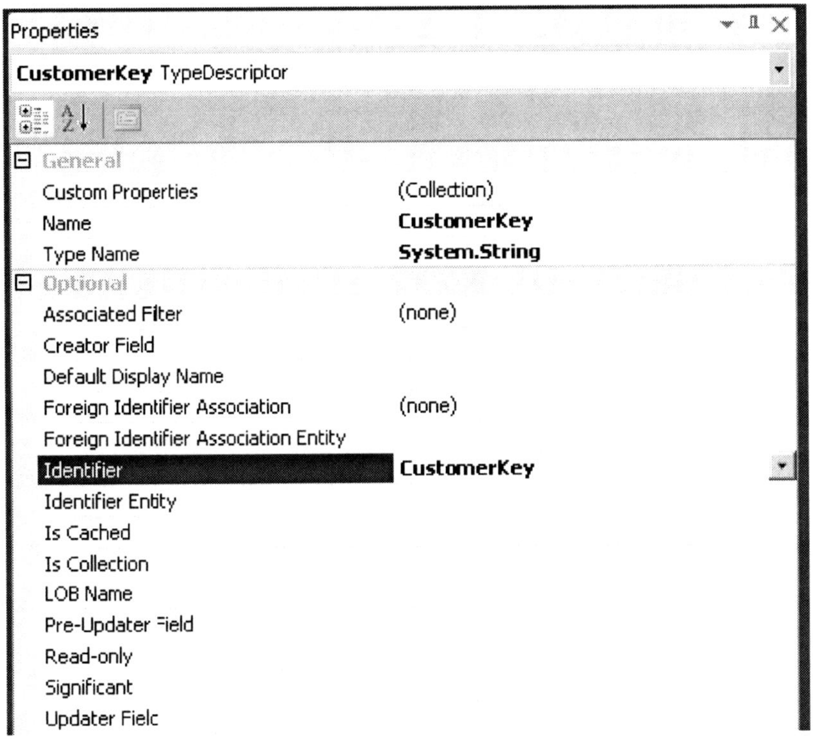

**Figure 14-54.** *Configuring type descriptors*

When all type descriptors are added as in steps 1 through 7, the type descriptors shown in Figure 14-55 should be visible. It is always a good idea to check the spelling and Type Name properties at this point, as updating them later on can be a pain. Refactoring does not currently support this.

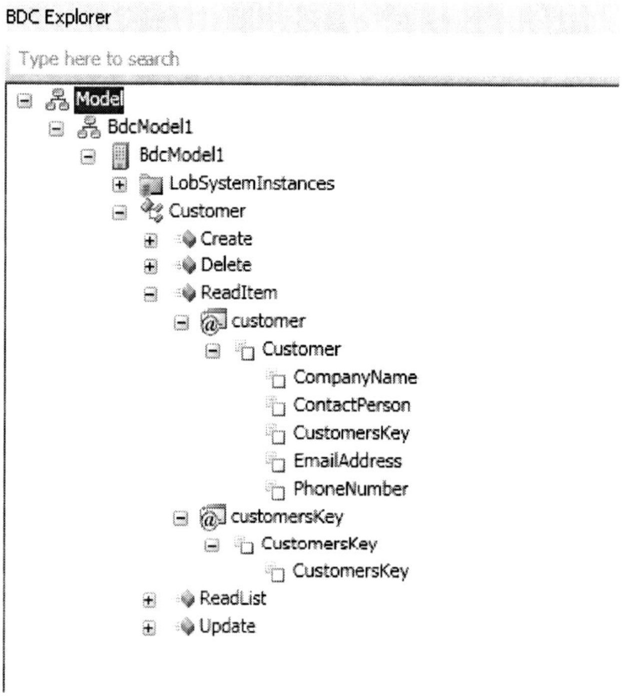

**Figure 14-55.** *All type descriptors configured*

At this point, the other methods available need to be created the same as the ReadItem (Specific Finder) method. These are the methods that support the BDC operations that are the CRUD operations. To do this, repeat the steps in this section for each of the following methods: ReadList, Create, Update, and Delete. Also counting the ReadItem method, a total of five methods should be defined for the entity named Customer. It is, however, much easier to create the last four methods, as the type descriptors of the return parameters are automatically defined the same way as with the ReadItem method. The BDC Designer automatically applies type descriptors defined in the other methods of an entity and copies them to the newly created methods.

With the required type descriptors in place for the methods, the LOB system–qualified type name of the type descriptor Customer should be defined. This is done by selecting the Customer type descriptor in the BDC Explorer panel. In the Properties panel, its value should be changed from System.String to BdcCustomer.Customer, BdcModel1. This is now the underlying data type of the data structure that the Customer type descriptor returns.

## Adding Code-Behind to Access External Data Source

To implement the logic required for performing the actual CRUD operations, the method body of the methods in the CustomerService.cs code file should be changed to match the code in Listing 14-4.

*Listing 14-4. Implementation of CRUD Operations in the BDC Method Instances*

```
public static Customer ReadItem(string customersKey)
{
    CustomerDataContext context = new CustomerDataContext();
    Customer cust = context.Customers.Single(c => c.CustomerKey == customersKey);
    return cust;
}

public static Customer Create(Customer newCustomer)
{
    CustomerDataContext context = new CustomerDataContext();
    context.Customers.InsertOnSubmit(newCustomer); context.SubmitChanges();
    Customer cust= context.Customers.Single(c => c.CustomerKey ==newCustomer.CustomerKey);
    return cust;
}

public static void Delete(string customersKey)
{
    CustomerDataContext context = new CustomerDataContext();
    Customer cust = context.Customers.Single(c => c.CustomerKey == customersKey);
    context.Customers.DeleteOnSubmit(cust);
    context.SubmitChanges();
}

public static IEnumerable<Customer> ReadList()
{
    CustomerDataContext context = new CustomerDataContext();
    IEnumerable<Customer> custList = context.Customers;
    return custList;
}

public static void Update(Customer customer)
{
    CustomerDataContext context = new CustomerDataContext();
    Customer cust = context.Customers.Single(c => c.CustomerKey == customer.CustomerKey);
    cust.CustomerKey = customer.CustomerKey;
    cust.CompanyName = customer.CompanyName;
    cust.ContactPerson = customer.ContactPerson;
    cust.EmailAddress = customer.EmailAddress;
    cust.PhoneNumber = customer.PhoneNumber;
    context.SubmitChanges();
}
```

# Adding Security Trimming to .NET Connectors

Being able to do security trimming is important in many corporations. This can be a challenge, especially if the LOB data system uses custom security descriptors. Extending the database .NET connector described in the previous section will show how this can be accomplished. Here we will assume one particular form of security descriptor, but in reality it could be in any format that supports mapping between the user context and the descriptor.

First a rights table must be added to the model to support security trimming. Here we have created a CustomerAccessRights table containing the SecurityDescriptor, Rights, and CustomerKey. The SecurityDescriptor is a binary unique value for a particular user. Rights will contain a simple numeric schema representing user rights to a particular row. It also contains creation rights.

- Read Allowed

- Read / Write / Update / Delete Allowed

No Entry means the user has no rights to this data row represented by the CustomerKey. In a production environment, a different and more fine-grained access rights mapping might be desired, but this should give a good idea about how to implement security trimming that allows multiple users with different access to the same data rows. Given the customer table contains this information, we can create a CustomerAccessRights table containing the security mappings. The SecurityDescriptor should be based on the same method used by the model to trim security. In this example, it is the GetSecurityDescriptor() method displayed in Tables 14-1 and 14-2.

*Table 14-1.* *Customers Table*

| CustomerKey | CompanyName | PhoneNumber | EmailAddress | ContactPerson |
|---|---|---|---|---|
| 2 | Microsoft | 555-xxxxxx1 | mail@microsoft.com | John Doe |
| 5 | SurfRay | 555-xxxxxx2 | mail@surfray.com | John Doe |
| 6 | Apple | 555-xxxxxx3 | mail@apple.com | John Doe |
| 7 | IBM | 555-xxxxxx4 | mail@ibm.com | John Doe |

*Table 14-2.* *Customer Access Rights Table*

| Rights | CustomerKey | SecurityDescriptor |
|---|---|---|
| 1 | 2 | <binary data> |
| 2 | 2 | <binary data> |
| 2 | 5 | <binary data> |
| 2 | 6 | <binary data> |
| 2 | 7 | <binary data> |

To add the CustomerAccessRights table to the model, add a new LINQ to SQL Classes item to the project and name it CustomerAccessRights. In the Server Explorer, add a connection to the Customers database if it does not already exist. Then drag the CustomerAccessRights table, and drop it on the CustomerAccessRights.dbml design surface.

Next the required method for computing the SecurityDescriptor is added as in Listing 14-5. This method can be added to the CustomerService.cs class that also contains the Customer methods. This method computes a security descriptor in the form of a byte array.

*Listing 14-5. Implementation of Method for Getting a Security Descriptor*

```
static Byte[] GetSecurityDescriptor(string domain, string username)
{
    NTAccount acc = new NTAccount(domain, username);
    SecurityIdentifier sid = (SecurityIdentifier)acc.Translate(typeof(SecurityIdentifier));
    CommonSecurityDescriptor sd = new CommonSecurityDescriptor(false, false,
        ControlFlags.None, sid, null, null, null);

    sd.SetDiscretionaryAclProtection(true, false);

    //Deny access to everyone
    SecurityIdentifier everyone = new SecurityIdentifier(WellKnownSidType.WorldSid, null);
    sd.DiscretionaryAcl.RemoveAccess( AccessControlType.Allow, everyone,
        unchecked((int)0xffffffffL), InheritanceFlags.None, PropagationFlags.None);

    //Grant full access to specified user
    sd.DiscretionaryAcl.AddAccess( AccessControlType.Allow, sid,
        unchecked((int)0xffffffffL), InheritanceFlags.None, PropagationFlags.None);

     byte[] secDes = new Byte[sd.BinaryLength];
     sd.GetBinaryForm(secDes, 0);

     return secDes;

}
```

Having the Rights table and the security descriptor method in place, the next step is to modify the Customers methods for updating, reading, etc., such that they are trimmed based on the security descriptor. Here (Listing 14-6) the Reader methods are updated to apply security trimming during search.

*Listing 14-6. Adding Security Trimming to the BDC Method Instances*

```
public static IEnumerable<Customer> ReadList()
{
    CustomerDataContext context = new CustomerDataContext();
    CustomerAccessRightsDataContext accessContext = new CustomerAccessRightsDataContext();

    List<Customer> tempCustList = new List<Customer>();
    foreach(Customer customer in context.Customers)
    {
       CustomerAccessRight custAccess = accessContext.CustomerAccessRights.SingleOrDefault(
            c => c.CustomerKey == customer.CustomerKey  && c.SecurityDescriptor.ToArray()
            == GetSecurityDescriptor(Environment.UserDomainName,Environment.UserName));

       if(custAccess.Rights > 0)
```

511

```
                    tempCustList.Add(customer);
        }

    IEnumerable<Customer> custList = tempCustList;
    return custList;
}

public static Customer ReadItem(string customersKey)
{
    CustomerDataContext context = new CustomerDataContext();
    Customer cust = context.Customers.Single(c => c.CustomerKey == customersKey);

    CustomerAccessRightsDataContext accessContext = new CustomerAccessRightsDataContext();

    CustomerAccessRight custAccess = accessContext.CustomerAccessRights.SingleOrDefault(
        c => c.CustomerKey == cust.CustomerKey && c.SecurityDescriptor.ToArray()
        == GetSecurityDescriptor(Environment.UserDomainName, Environment.UserName));

    if (custAccess.Rights > 0)
        return cust;
    else
        return null;
}
```

Using this methodology as a baseline, it is possible to create simple security trimming. When doing security trimming, performance of the trimming mechanism is relevant. Different caching mechanics can be applied with success to increase performance. Also other security descriptor implementations that better fit specific requirements can be implemented using this example as a template for how to approach the topic. Microsoft does provide some resources on this topic.[3]

# Summary

The goal of this chapter was to provide insight into the new Business Connectivity Services framework offered in SharePoint 2010. BCS is in itself an extensive framework out of the box, spanning not only SharePoint but also Outlook, InfoPath, and other Office applications.

One of the powerful capabilities of BCS is its relative ease in creating complex security configurations using the Secure Store Service or programming in Visual Studio 2010. This was much more difficult to accomplish with the Business Data Catalog in SharePoint 2007.

Hands-on examples of how to create and integrate BCS in the organization should encourage the reader to do further exploration of the capabilities. Finally an example of how easy it can be to code a .NET Assembly Connector for exposing an external content type from a data source not supported out of the box should also encourage IT professionals in the organization to view BCS as an opportunity as opposed to the much more difficult and expensive solutions of yesteryear's SharePoint 2007 BDC.

---

[3] http://msdn.microsoft.com/en-us/library/aa374815%28v=vs.85%29.aspx

# CHAPTER 15

# Designing Mashups with Excel and Visio

Business Intelligence and reporting have been two of the most important functions of data management systems over the last several decades, and as technology changes, the means for reporting and creating dashboards has evolved to meet the changing needs and capabilities in the market. In today's world, the availability of services such as geographic mapping and social networking on a global scale has led to the redefining of how information is organized and portrayed on the Web. In many cases, dashboards now need to provide a high level of relevance, far beyond a simple tabular report or even charts, and the information expressed should be cohesive and dynamic, allowing the user to incorporate the data they need with external systems that complete a picture for them. This new dashboard for the Web is known as a *mashup*, and in SharePoint 2010, Microsoft has provided a framework for completing their services that they refer to as Composites. With tools such as Visio, Excel, and PerformancePoint Services, SharePoint has a full feature set for reporting. This chapter will address some aspects of how to extend the out-of-the-box experience from Visio and Excel to quickly create a mashup.

## Visio Mashups

Microsoft Visio is a graphical modeling tool used for everything from designing software systems and databases to specifying network architecture and the layout of an office space. The ability to easily create and link shapes together makes Visio a very practical tool for custom dashboards, where the visual representation of information is more important than just seeing the data alone.

Using this capability makes sense when the information portrayed is process or goal driven and the end user of the dashboard needs less analytical information and more visual indication. A good example of process driven data is an air traffic controller, where reams of data is less vital than seeing flashing indicators or live radar. A goal-driven Visio drawing may use something simpler, like a thermometer for showing a company's annual growth or donation amounts at a fundraising drive.

Mashups for Visio include more than just plain old Visio drawings published and viewable on the Internet. End users are able to create data-driven Visio drawings that tie to one of many types of sources published in SharePoint; then they publish the drawing to their sites. Then a JavaScript developer may add code to interact with the Visio drawing on a given web page. Extending the Visio drawing with the Mashup API creates a powerful integration point between the drawing and other services that are available, such as an online mapping or social networking service. The possibilities are only limited by the imagination of those who are implementing the solution. In this section, you will learn how to create data Visio drawings and how to utilize the JavaScript API components.

■ **Note** I am very excited about the release of Visio Services for SharePoint 2010; it has opened up a completely new avenue of process-based dashboards that was traditionally difficult to represent without designing and building a custom application.

## Creating Data Driven Shapes

Creating a Visio mashup requires that you create data shapes and provide data for them to use. In order to complete the following examples, you will need a copy of Visio Premium 2010 and SharePoint 2010 Enterprise. You will also need to install the "Charity Drive" List Template from the Chapter 15 folder of the downloadable content to a site on your SharePoint portal, and then create an instance of the list on your site. The first step in creating your data-driven shape is to link to data sources. The next steps describe how to link the Visio drawing to a data source.

1. Open Visio 2010 Premium and select the option to create a blank drawing. You should have an empty canvas ready for your new Visio drawing, as shown in Figure 15-1.

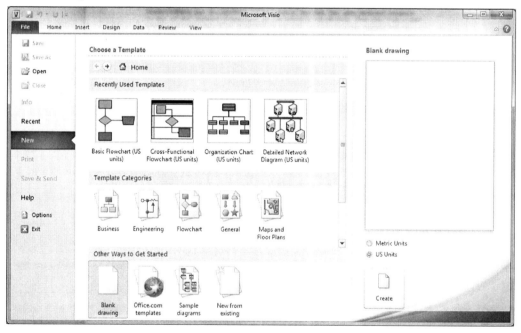

***Figure 15-1.*** *Create new Visio diagram.*

2. Next, open the Data tab on the ribbon and select Link Data to Shapes. In this example you will use a SharePoint list, so select the Microsoft SharePoint Foundation List option, and click Next.

3. In the next window, provide the URL to a valid SharePoint site, specifically one that contains the data that you intend to report on your Visio dashboard.

4. Click Next, and you will be provided with a listing of the Lists on the site provided. Select the Charitable Drive list, and click Finish.

After you have defined the data sources, you will need to draw the shape and link it to a row of the data source. For this example, you will utilize a Thermometer gradient control to represent progress on the Charity Drive charitable contributions.

1. Open the Basic Shapes group and select the 3-D box, dragging it onto the drawing surface.

2. Make sure the 3-D shape is selected on the canvas, then right click on the Friends of Chickens record in the External Data window, and click the Link to Selected Shapes option.

3. Now that the data and the shape are linked, you need to add the visual data components to the shape. Right-click on the shape and expand the Data sub-menu and select the Edit Data Graphic option.

4. Remove the ID field by selecting the row and clicking the Delete button. Select the Title row and click the Edit button to edit the appearance of the data element. On the Edit Item screen, uncheck the Default Position checkbox and then set the Horizontal option to Left and the Vertical option to Top, then select the Heading 1 option in the Style drop-down list.

5. Add a new item from the Edit Data Graphic screen, then select the Last Date Checked for the Data Field and Text for the "Displayed as" value. Uncheck the Default Position checkbox and then set the Horizontal option to Center and the Vertical option to Top. In the Details section, set the Border Type to None, and click OK.

6. Next, add a new item from the Edit Data Graphic screen, then select the Current Value for the Data Field and Text for the "Displayed as" value. Uncheck the Default Position checkbox; then set the Horizontal option to Center and the Vertical option to Top. In the Details section, set the Value Format to Currency, the Border Type to None, and click OK.

7. Finally, add a new item from the Edit Data Graphic screen. Then select the Current Value for the Data Field. This time, set the "Displayed as" value to Data Bar. In the Style list box, select Thermometer. Uncheck the Default Position checkbox; then set the Horizontal option to Center and the Vertical option to Top. Next, under Details, set the Maximum Value to $30,000,000 (without the formatting, so 30000000), then both the Value Position and Label Position to Not Shown, and then click OK.

8. The Edit Data Graphic screen should look like Figure 15-2.

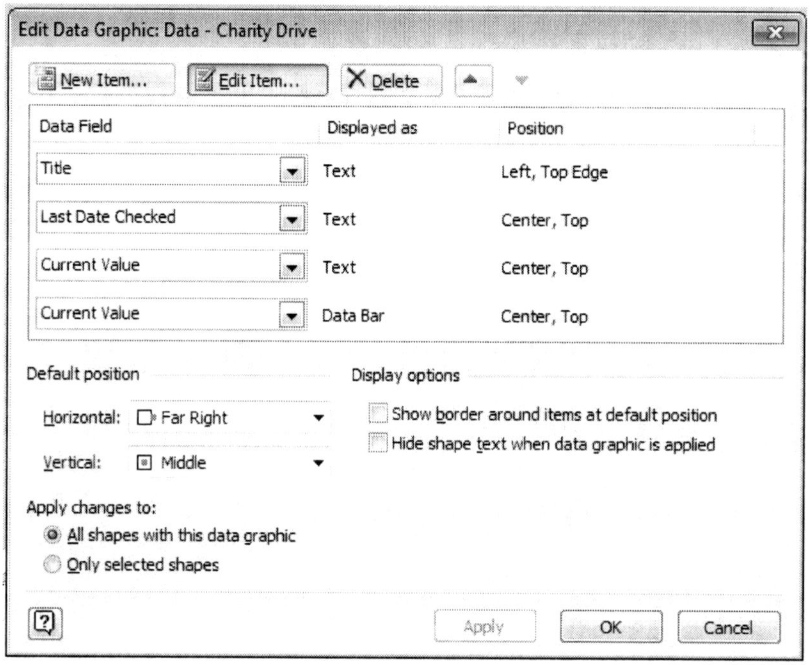

**Figure 15-2.** *Edit Data Graphic dialog*

9.  Click OK on the Edit Data Graphic screen and Visio will update the shape on the canvas with the new settings. The data shape should look something the one in Figure 15-3.

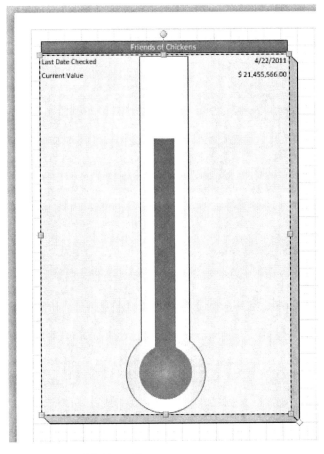

*Figure 15-3. Visio Data Shape*

This Visio drawing is now a bona fide data graphic and ready for a SharePoint Mashup. This particular example is very simplistic, but it gives the general idea of what is possible with Visio data shapes. The final step is to publish the drawing as a web drawing into SharePoint. The following steps describe how to publish a web drawing from Visio:

1.  In Visio, open the file panel and click the Save & Send option.

2.  Select the Save to SharePoint option, then click "Browse for a location" and select Web Drawing (*.vdw) under File Types. Finally, click the Save As button.

3.  Save the document to a Shared Documents Library on your SharePoint site.

Now you can open the Visio Drawing in the browser or view it in a Visio Web Access Web Part. So now that you have a published Visio data shape, in order to make it interactive with the user through the browser, you need to learn about the Visio Services JavaScript Mashup API.

# Visio Services JavaScript Mashup API

The Visio Services JavaScript Mashup API provides the means for web developers to write scripts that allow users to interact with the Visio diagram using a web browser. This interaction goes beyond just viewing the contents of the diagram; it actually allows for other components on a web page to have content driven by or drive the appearance of the drawing. JavaScript is easy to learn; however, the discussion of how to write and use it is beyond the scope of this book. I will assume that you, the reader, have a firm grasp on the fundamentals and are ready to plunge into the following sections that describe the objects and events that comprise the Visio JavaScript API.

The objects that make up the JavaScript API are logical representations of the underlying components in the Visio document. These objects are organized hierarchically to allow the user to interact with the drawing starting at the Web Part level, moving into the page, then a Shape collection, and finally an individual shape. The following tables describe each of the JavaScript objects.

## Control Object

The VwaControl represents the actual Web Part that is hosting the drawing—rather, it's the Visio Web Access Web Part encapsulated for the browsers scripting engine. This class provides the primary access point for interacting with the web drawing. The methods and events provide the functionality that allows the developer to tap into and respond to the user with actions that leverage the information in the Visio drawing. Table 15-1 describes several of the more common methods that a developer can use to interact with the Visio diagram.

*Table 15-1. VwaControl Methods*

| Name | Description |
| --- | --- |
| addHandler | Adds an event handler to the current Web Part, which is necessary to add custom handlers to the callstack on the control. Additionally there are clearHandler and removeHandler methods to remove one or all of the handlers. |
| displayCustomMessage | Shows an HTML message to the user and restricts usage of the current Web Part. The use is universal, but you should always use this in the DiagramError event. |
| hideCustomMessage | This hides the HTML message that is displayed using the displayCustomMessage method. It is always a good idea to put a button in the custom HTML message that displays and have it invoke this method to allow the user to close out the message. |
| getActivePage | This method returns an instance of the Vwa.Page that is currently visible for the drawing in the browser, which you need in order to start processing data from VwaShapes. |
| setActivePage | Change the page currently rendered in the browser, using the current Visio Web Drawing loaded. If you wanted to build a custom page-switching interface, this would be the method to use. |

| Name | Description |
|------|-------------|
| refreshDiagram | Requests a data refresh for data in a Visio drawing. If you built a form that updates data that is driving the Visio dashboard, it would make sense to add this method call to the operations performed in the submit action, so that the Visio diagram refreshes after the data changes. |

The events associated with the VwaControl are the most important component when dealing with the JSOM. These events provide the passages into the actions that occur in the lifecycle of the Web Part to permit the developer to interact with it. So when developing a mashup, you will need to tap into this lifeline of the Visio Web Part on the page in order to execute the functionality you desire; see Table 15-2.

*Table 15-2. VwaControl Events*

| Name | Description |
|------|-------------|
| diagramcomplete | Fires when the drawing has finished loading, refreshing, or changing. This is the end of the page load cycle for the drawing. |
| diagramerror | A request to the drawing failed for some reason. This is available because Visio uses Silverlight, and you need to catch that Silverlight rendering error in your JavaScript. |
| shapemouseenter | Fires when the mouse cursor has entered the boundaries of a shape. Use this event to update other dependent information on the page with data from the currently focused shape. |
| shapemouseleave | Fires when the mouse cursor has left the boundaries of a shape. You might use this method to counteract the results of the shapemouseenter, for instance, hiding display elements. |
| shapeselectionchanged | Fires when the user selects a new shape on the drawing. This is more of an onclick event and might mimic the shapemouseenter functionality in most cases. |

■ **Best Practice** Recognizing the order of the events on the page is important to understanding when to perform certain operations. It doesn't make sense to start performing operations that involve objects on the diagram before the diagram has completed loading in the browser. Analyze the operations you need to perform and map them into the lifecycle appropriately. This will also save on unnecessary asynchronous calls to the SharePoint server.

## Page Object

The Vwa.Page represents the current page that is loaded into the viewable space of the Visio Web Access Web Part. This object provides methods for interacting with the page, as well as gaining access to the shapes on the page (see Table 15-3). There are no events for the page object, since only the VwaControl object handles events.

*Table 15-3. Vwa.Page Methods*

| Name | Description |
|------|-------------|
| centerViewOnShape | Set the view of the diagram to center on the specified shape. You could use this in a shapeselectionchanged event to center the canvas on the new shape. |
| getSelectedShape | This will return an instance of Vwa.Shape that the user has selected on the page. Using this will allow you to avoid maintaining a variant for the selected shape. |
| getShapes | This method returns all shapes in the page as a ShapeCollection and allows you to iterate over them as Shape objects. |
| isShapeInView | If the shape is visible in the current view, it returns true; otherwise, it returns false. A good use for this is on the VwaControl.shapeselectionchanged event to check if the shape is visible, and if not, invoke the centerViewOnShape method. |
| setSelectedShape | Sets the currently selected shape to the specified value. This will fire the VwaControl.shapeselectionchanged event and is useful for setting up external navigation of the Visio diagram. |

## Shape Collection

The Vwa.ShapeCollection reveals a collection of Vwa.Shape objects to the Vwa.Page so that the developer can discover the shapes on a page. This class allows the developer to find and provide an instance of an existing shape on the page but won't allow the developer to add new shapes to the page. It's helpful if you need to list out the shapes for navigation or something similar; see Table 15-4.

*Table 15-4. Vwa.ShapeCollection*

| Name | Description |
|------|-------------|
| getCount | Returns the total number of Shape objects in the collection. |

| | |
|---|---|
| getItemById | This method will return the Shape object with the ID in the collection of shapes on the page. There are similar methods to find shapes by name, index, and GUID. |

## Shape Object

The Vwa.Shape class (Table 15-5) represents an individual Shape object on the Visio drawing. The methods in this class provide access to the underlying shape data and some that will allow visual cues to be created on the shapes.

*Table 15-5. Vwa.Shape*

| Name | Description |
|---|---|
| addHighlight | Adds a rectangular border around the shape and is usually found in the shapemouseentered event handler. |
| addOverlay | Defines and shows an overlay for the shape on the drawing surface and is usually found in the shapemouseentered event handler. |
| getId | Returns the ID of the shape in the web drawing. Used typically with the shapeselectionchanged event to capture the ID for reuse. |
| getShapeData | Returns an array of objects that represent the data row associated with the shape and is used to surface the underlying data. |
| removeHighlight | Removes the current highlight from the shape and is typically associated with a shapemouseleave event firing. |
| removeOverlay | Removes the current overlay from a shape and is typically associated with a shapemouseleave event firing. |

▪ **Note** It's important to recognize here that the addOverlay method has several parameters, as you will see in the following example. The second argument is a string variant that requires XAML formatted output if the Visio Display Mode is using Silverlight, which is the default mode in any browser with a Silverlight plug-in. Recognizing this will save you some debug time in trying to figure out why your perfectly formatted XHTML is causing a very strange error.

So let's look at some code in action. Please notice in Listing 15-1 that "{WebPartID}" needs to be replaced by the actual ID of the Visio Web Access Web Part on the rendered page. This is done by viewing the source of the SharePoint Web Part page on which the Web Part resides, and then searching for the Web Part title (the ID will be close by). The good news is that you should only have to figure out what this ID is the first time.

*Listing 15-1. SharePoint JSOM for Visio Web Parts*

```
<script type="text/javascript">
Sys.Application.add_load(App_Load);

var Exception;
var WebPart;
var Page;
var Shapes;
var CurrentShape;

function App_Load()
{
   try
   {
      WebPart = new Vwa.VwaControl ("{WebPartID}");
      WebPart.addHandler ("diagramcomplete", Diagram_Complete);
      WebPart.addHandler ("diagramException", Diagram_Exception);
   }
   catch (e)
   {
      Exception = e;
   }
}

function Diagram_Complete ()
{
   try
   {
      Page = WebPart.getActivePage ();
      Shapes = Page.getShapes ();
      CurrentShape = Page.getSelectedShape ();

      WebPart.addHandler ("Shapeselectionchanged", Shape_SelChanged);
      WebPart.addHandler ("shapemouseenter", Shape_MouseEnter);
      WebPart.addHandler ("shapemouseleave", Shape_MouseLeave);
   }
   catch (e)
   {
      Exception = e;
   }
}

function Diagram_Exception ()
{
   WebPart.displayCustomMessage ("Exception: " + Exception);
```

```
}

function Shape_SelChanged (id)
{
        if (CurrentShape != null)
      {
           CurrentShape.removeHighlight ();
        }

   CurrentShape = Page.getSelectedShape ();
   CurrentShape.addHighlight (5, "#FF0000");
}

function Shape_MouseEnter (source, id)
{
   try
   {
      Shapes = Page.getShapes ();
      var shape = Shapes.getItemById (id);
      var shapeData = shape.getShapeData ();

      var shapeInfo = '';

// iterate through all data fields and add them to the overlay


      for (var i = 0; i < shapeData.length; i++)
      {
         var field = shapeData[i].label;
         var value = shapeData[i].formattedValue;

         shapeInfo = shapeInfo + field + ' = ' + value + '<LineBreak/>';
      }


      shapeInfo = '<ContentControl Width="300"><TextBlock
TextWrapping="Wrap">'+shapeInfo+'</TextBlock></ContentControl>';

// Add the overlay to the shape, using the div element as content
      shape.addOverlay (
         'dataoverlay',                 // id of the overlay
         shapeInfo,                     // XAML content to display
         Vwa.HorizontalAlignment.right, // horizontal alignment
         Vwa.VerticalAlignment.middle,  // vertical alignment
         300,                           // 300 pixels wide
         300);                          // 300 pixels tall

   }
   catch (e)
   {
      Exception = e;
   }
```

```
}

function Shape_MouseLeave (source, id)
{
   try {
      var shape = Shapes.getItemById (id);
      shape.removeOverlay('dataoverlay');
   }
   catch (e)
   {
      Exception = e;
   }
}
</script>
```

---

■ **Best Practice** The first event fired for the Web Part is the `diagramcomplete` event, but in order to handle this event, you must be sure to add a handler before it fires. The best way of doing this is to add a handler to the AJAX `Sys.Application.Load` event.

---

In this example, you added a handler to the `ApplicationLoad` event from the AJAX event model and used that handler to instantiate the `visiowp` object with your Visio Web Access Web Part. After that, you can start adding handlers for the `diagramcomplete` and `diagramerror` handlers. Notice that you don't bother with Page or Shape objects at this point because they are not available until the `diagramcomplete` event has fired, which is the next stop in the page lifecycle. In the `diagramcomplete` handler, the Visio drawing has fully loaded into the browser, and the developer has access to all of the Visio API objects. This is where you will need to initialize the mashup functionality and start laying the groundwork for user interactions, such as adding handlers to the `shapeselectionchanged`, `shapemouseenter`, and `shapemouseleave` events.

In the `Shape_SelChanged` method, you provide functionality to execute when a new shape is selected. In this simple case, you are removing the highlight from the previous shape and adding it to the new shape. This method would also be a good place to interact with other elements on the page, such as a service call to gather updated information based on data for the new shape. In the final section of this chapter, you will use this event handler to provide filter data from a list using the Client Object Model.

The `Shape_MouseEnter` and `Shape_MouseLeave` methods provide functionality to add overlays based on the shape that has the mouse cursor over it. It's important to note with these two handlers that you wouldn't want to perform an action that requires much time to complete, because it may only be a few seconds from the time the `mouseenter` fires to when the `mouseleave` fires.

---

■ **Best Practice** With `shapemouseenter` and `shapemouseleave`, it's best to limit yourself to operations that are stateful. This would include showing or revealing information with the `mouseenter` and hiding information with the `mouseleave`. If you try to make the these events do anything else, such as a long running process (which on the

---

Web tends to be anything greater than 30 seconds), calculations, or callbacks, you run the risk that multiple objects on the page will fire simultaneous requests and cause unexpected visual consequences.

# Excel Driven Dashboards

Microsoft Office Excel, at its simplest, is a spreadsheet or simple database tool. Over the years, Microsoft has extended this tool to allow more powerful and dynamic data analysis using formulas, charts, and most recently, PowerPivot. Excel has a grand 30-year history of being one of the best spreadsheet applications on the market; with the introduction of Excel Services for SharePoint 2007, Microsoft took this tool to the Web.

As usual, the 2010 version of Excel provides the world with even more power and flexibility for data analysis, and right along with it, SharePoint 2010 has gone to a new level of support for the product through Excel Services 2010. For the business intelligence developer, these components are crucial to providing the rich interactive experience that you are looking to leverage through mashups and dashboards in SharePoint 2010. The JavaScript Object Model (JSOM) for Excel provides the same granular interaction to spreadsheets that the Visio Mashup API provides to diagrams, and the REST API provides read and update capabilities with documents through a web service. Since everyone pretty much knows how to create data in Excel and upload it into SharePoint 2010, I will skip ahead and just cover the JSOM. If you are curious about using Excel files in SharePoint 2010 or have not done it before, I recommend the following resource: `http://bit.ly/ivvde5`

> ⬛ **Note** I have often found that Excel is the first tool implemented in department-level solutions. For this reason, in many cases it's often enough to load Excel documents from a network file share into SharePoint 2010 and utilize Excel Services to get a BI project off the ground.

# JavaScript Object Model (JSOM) for Excel

The JSOM for Excel provides the web developer with a means to read and update information in an Excel spreadsheet displayed on a SharePoint Web Part page using the Excel Web Access Web Part. Using the JSOM, the developer will have access to sheets, ranges, tables, PivotTables, and charts found in the Excel document. Using these tools, you can extend the information in the Excel document to affect other portions of a web page, to make web service calls, or even to update or change the appearance of the contents in the document.

## Control Object

The `EwaControl` class represents an Excel Web Access Web Part on a page. This object instance is the entry point for working with Excel documents using the JavaScript Client Object Model. The methods and events provided by this class will permit interaction with one or more workbooks, sheets, and other components from Excel Services; see Table 15-6 and 15-7.

*Table 15-6. EwaControl Methods*

| Name | Description |
|---|---|
| getActiveWorkbook | This method returns an instance of a Workbook class for the currently selected workbook. |
| getDomElement | Returns the HTML element in which the EwaControl is contained. You could use this to change properties on the parent node of the Web Part, such as to change the display property from "block" to "none." |
| getInstances | This is a static method to return all instances of EwaControl running in the current page as an EwaControlCollection, in case you have multiple Excel Web Parts on the page. You might use this to refresh the view in another Web Part when you change the data in one or more cells. |

*Table 15-7. EwaControl Events*

| Name | Description |
|---|---|
| activeCellChanged | This fires when the active cell has changed and applies to a single cell. You could use this as an onblur type of event to perform an operation on the previous cell. |
| activeSelectionChanged | This fires when the current cell selection has changed, applying to a range of cells. |
| enteredCellEditing | The user has started editing the contents of a cell, which is a great time to capture the current value of the cell if you need it, or perhaps to create a visual cue that the document has been edited. |
| gridSynchronized | The grid is finished rendering, the workbook has loaded or reloaded, or the grid blocks have been updated. |
| workbookChanged | The workbook has either changed or finished reloading, so this is where you can update information in the rest of your mashup with current data. |
| applicationReady | This event fires when the Excel Web Part has finished loading the first time the page loads. |

# Workbook Object

The Workbook class represents an instance of an Excel Workbook on the server and provides access to all of the objects contained in the workbook. This is the primary object that will be used throughout a JSOM application using Excel; see Table 15-8.

*Table 15-8.* *Workbook Methods*

| Name | Description |
|---|---|
| getActiveCell | Returns the active cell as a range object or null if there is no active cell or the active object is not a cell. Always make sure to check the return value before continuing. |
| getActiveNamedItem | This will return the active named item or null if the workbook is not in Named Item view. Always make sure to check the return value before continuing. |
| getActiveSelection | Returns the current selection as a range object or null if there are no cells selected. Always make sure to check the return value before continuing. |
| getActiveSheet | Returns the Sheet object that represents the active sheet in the current workbook. |
| getNamedItems | This will provide you with a NamedItemCollection for the current workbook, which contains instances of the NamedItem class. |
| getRange | This method returns a Range object by providing a start row and column, and counters for how many rows and columns to return. |
| getRangeA1Async | As opposed to the getRange, this method returns the calculated values of a range of cells using Excel's A1 nomenclature in an asynchronous callback. It's best to use this method for potentially large ranges of cells. |
| getSheets | This returns a SheetCollection for the workbook, which contains instances of the Sheet class. |
| recalcAsync | Recalculates the workbook using an asynchronous callback, which is preferred overall, since you don't always know how long it might take to finish. |
| setParametersAsync | Sets workbook parameters, such as data filters using an asynchronous callback, after which you would want to invoke recalcAsync. |

## NamedItem Object

The NamedItem class represents a named item in an Excel document and may include cell ranges, tables, parameters, charts and PivotTables; see Table 15-9.

*Table 15-9. NamedItem Methods*

| Name | Description |
| --- | --- |
| activateAsync | This method makes an asynchronous callback to activate the named item on the sheet. |
| getName | Returns the name of the item as it appears in Excel. |
| getNamedItemType | Returns the object type of the named item as it appears in Excel. |

## Sheet Object

The Sheet class represents an instance of a worksheet or chart sheet object in an Excel workbook. Sheets that are hidden will not be available to Client JSOM in SharePoint; see Table 15-10.

*Table 15-10. Sheet Methods*

| Name | Description |
| --- | --- |
| activateAsync | This uses an asynchronous callback to activate the sheet for Excel. You would use this method if you were iterating through a SheetCollection and wanted to activate a different sheet than the current one. |
| getName | This returns the display name of the sheet from Excel. |
| getRange | This works just like the Workbook.getRange for the current sheet object. |
| getRangeA1Async | This works just like the Workbook.getRangeA1Async for the current sheet object. |

## Range Object

The Range class represents a range of cells in a Workbook object; see Table 15-11. The range uses the A1 nomenclature from Excel and can identify one or more cells. This class is useful for defining ranges and performing on-the-fly calculations out of the document and displaying the values in HTML DOM elements. Since the API doesn't have a `Cell` object, the `Range` object may actually represent only a single cell on the document.

*Table 15-11. Range Methods*

| Name | Description |
|------|-------------|
| activateAsync | This makes use of an asynchronous callback to select and activate a range of cells in a workbook. |
| getAddressA1 | This method returns the coordinates of the range using the A1 format, including the sheet name, so that it can be used in a `Workbook.getRangeA1Async` call if needed. |
| getColumn | This will return the left-most column position using a zero-based index from column A of the worksheet. |
| getColumnCount | This returns the number of columns in the range. |
| getRow | This will return the top-most row position using a zero-based index from row 1 of the worksheet. |
| getRowCount | This returns the number of rows in the range. |
| getSheet | Returns the instance of `Sheet` on which the range exists, or returns a null if in named item view mode. Always make sure to check the return value for null before continuing. |
| getValuesAsync | Returns the values from the range as a two-dimensional array where the cell ID is in the first dimension and the value in the second dimension. Returned values are either formatted using the specified cell formatting or the raw contents of the cell. |
| setValuesAsync | Sets the values for a range of cells using a two-dimensional array object where the first dimension of the array is the cell identifier and the second is the value to place in the range. |

# REST API

A discussion of the programming around Excel Services would not be complete if I didn't mention the REST API for Excel Services. Unfortunately, describing the REST API for Excel or SharePoint in general really deserves an entire book of its own, so I will only discuss this in light detail, and trust that you, the reader, will become inspired to read a book or the many MSDN articles on this topic.

Representational State Transfer (REST) is not a new concept on the World Wide Web, having been introduced in 2000. The purpose of REST is to leverage the strengths of the HTTP protocol to perform commanded operations, rather than building defined endpoints that you see in traditional SOAP-based web services. In a SOAP service, you would create an ASMX file, for instance, and then define several methods with the [WebMethod] attribute to allow external calls to that method. In REST-ful services, you have a single endpoint that receives a packet of information and performs operations based on the HTTP method: GET, PUT, POST and DELETE. Using this model, SharePoint 2010 can also return strongly typed results to the calling point. Thus, REST services in SharePoint 2010 are a very nice addition because it's very easy to make a call to a web service, drop some data in the request, and then send it off with the command you want to execute.

For Excel Services, the implications are almost mind-numbing. Applications can request specific ranges or objects like charts out of Excel documents, and you can use the PUT and POST commands to modify the information in that Excel document. As mentioned, entire volumes could be written on the REST API for SharePoint 2010; I hope you will find some time to sit down and read one of them.

# Putting it all Together—Help Desk Mashup

Now that we have discussed the various components that comprise the SharePoint 2010 Insights, you are going to build a composite, or mashup, using several of them. For the purposes of this book, you'll bring a few of these tools together, but in a real-world environment, you would need to assess the strengths of each and use them logically to meet your needs. For this example, you're going to leverage Visio on a page and throw in Bing Maps just for fun. You're going to build a Help Desk dashboard for a company that is currently viewing their Help Desk metrics with an Excel document. The company has 9 locations on the east coast of the United States and the Help Desk must provide support to all locations. You'll use the Visio Help Desk Flow Template available from http://visio.microsoft.com/en-us/Templates_And_Downloads/Sample_Diagram_Templates/Pages/Help_Desk_Flow.aspx

## Excel Data Source

The Excel document in this example is going to be the metrics data source. You will assume that your fictitious company has a robust SQL Server back end and that they exported the metrics to an Excel document for reporting purposes only. In order for the Visio to work as expected, the data will show only the desired data components, such as the number of calls, the average wait time at each tier, the percentage of calls that reach the tier that are resolved by the tier, and the percentage of all calls resolved by the tier for all calls. This data must be stored in SharePoint Document Library in order to act as a valid source for the Visio document. The following steps describe how to create the Excel Data Source:

1. Open Microsoft Office Excel (preferably 2010 version, but 2007 should work fine).

2. In cells A1 through G1, put the following values:

    - Step

    - Number of Calls

    - Average Wait Time

    - % Resolved

    - % Total Resolved

    - % Transferred

    - Average Time on Call

3. In cells A2 through A7, place the following values:

    a. Customer Contacts Help Desk

    b. Help Desk

    c. Tier 1 Tech Support

    d. Tier 2 Tech Support

    e. Tier 3 Tech Support

    f. Monthly Totals

4. For all of the other values, you can make numbers up. It should look something like Figure 15-4.

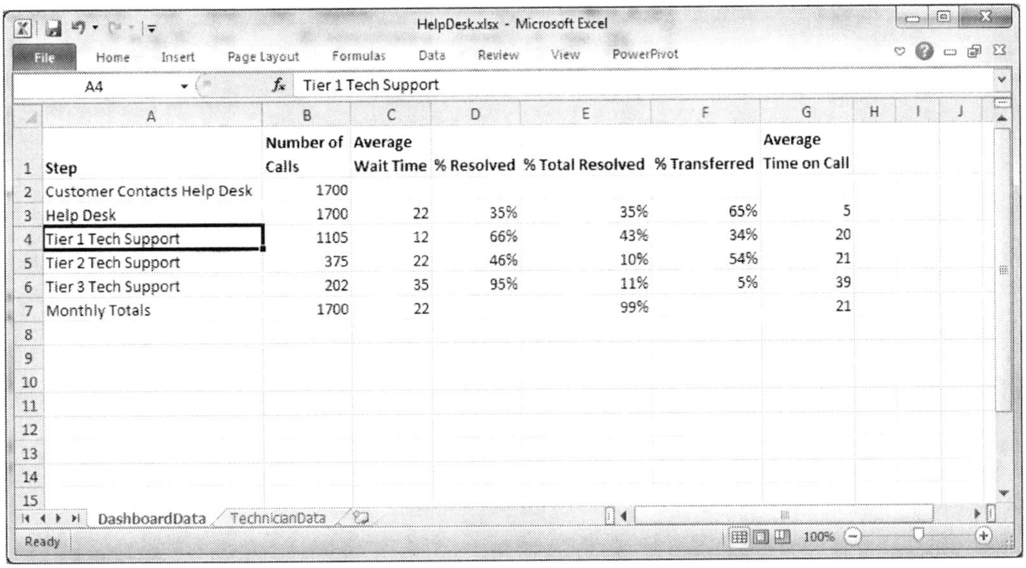

**Figure 15-4.** *The Help Desk metrics spreadsheet*

Once the data source is uploaded and published to the Document Library, you can continue.

# List Data Source

In order to highlight the ability to pull data from multiple sources and tying them together using the JavaScript Client Object Model and Services, I have set up a List of Technicians. When a user clicks on one of the support tiers in the Visio diagram, It will filter the list of technicians. Each technician operates at one of the 9 locations, with 14 technicians in total. Figure 15-5 shows how the data appears in the SharePoint List view.

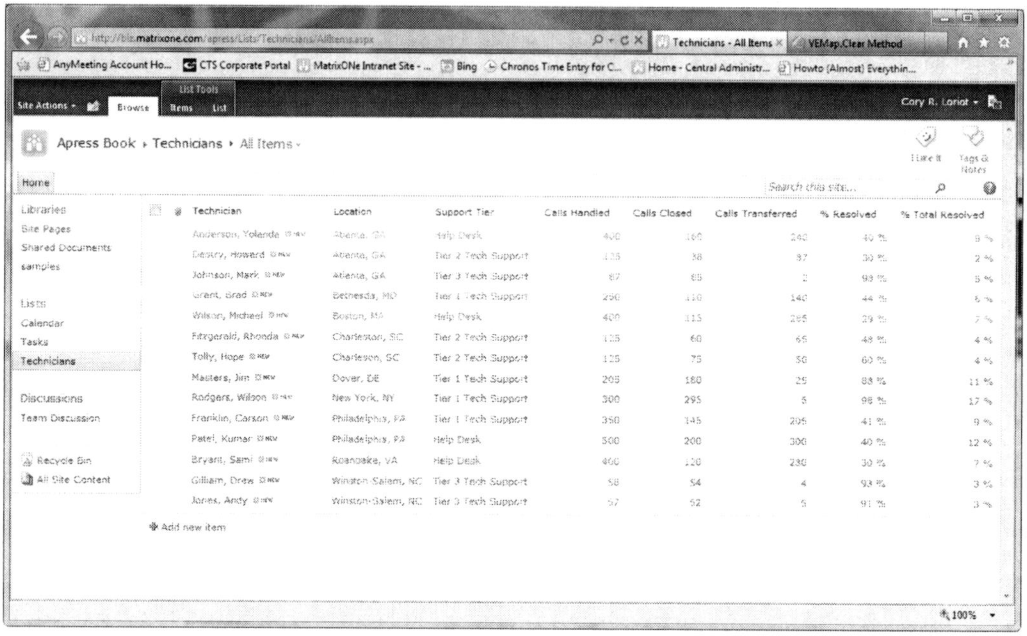

**Figure 15-5.** *Technicians and locations SharePoint List*

## Visio Dashboard

The Visio Dashboard will show the relevant information for your Help Desk metrics. The diagram will indicate the flow of help calls from the beginning of the process through to the end, and then provide totals for all of the numbers. Each shape will contain data relevant to that step of the process and will use status bars to indicate how well each level is doing. Since setting up a Visio data-driven dashboard was discussed in a previous section, I am not going to go into detail here. Figure 15-6 is an image of the Visio Diagram that will be uploaded to the SharePoint site. A copy of this Visio document has been provided in the downloadable content included as part of the book.

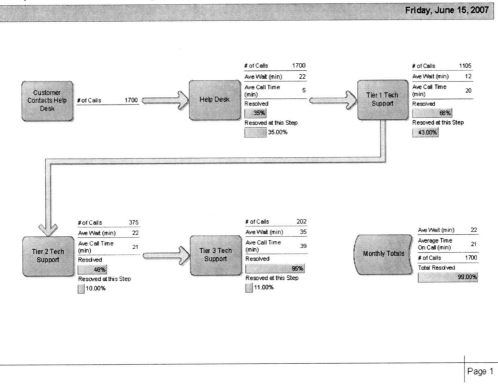

Help Desk Data Summary - May

Friday, June 15, 2007

Page 1

*Figure 15-6. Visio diagram*

Interestingly enough, by combining the Excel document data source with the Visio dashboard and uploading them both to SharePoint 2010, you have already met the minimum requirements for a composite or mashup in SharePoint 2010. However, in this chapter you are learning about going beyond the OOTB capabilities, so let's continue by writing some JavaScript to pull data out of the Visio document and light up the dashboard.

## The Glue: JavaScript

The JavaScript Object Model provides the necessary component to tie all of the pieces together, thus it is the glue. When the user clicks on one of the data objects, it will highlight the object and feed the information to read the list of technicians and display them in a div. You are also going to use JavaScript to interact with the Bing API and place overlays on the map for each location that the company has an office. When the user clicks on one of the technicians, the map will zoom to their office location. So let's look at the JavaScript code in Listing 15-2; it will be described it in more detail at the end.

*Listing 15-2. JavaScript Mashup Code using JSOM*

```
<script src="http://ecn.dev.virtualearth.net/mapcontrol/mapcontrol.ashx?v=6.2"
type="text/javascript"></script>

<script type="text/javascript">
Sys.Application.add_load(App_Load);

var Exception = null;
var WebPart = null;
var Page = null;
var Shapes = null;
var CurrentShape = null;

var ContentEditor = null;
var ContentEditorDisplayPanel = null;
var ContentEditorMapPanel = null;

var SelectedSupportTier = null;
var Context = null;
var Web = null
var List = null;
var Query = null;
var ListItem = null;
var ListItemCollection = null;

function App_Load()
{
    try
    {
        WebPart = new .Control ("WebPartQ2");
        WebPart.addHandler ("diagramcomplete", Diagram_Complete);
        WebPart.addHandler ("diagramException", Diagram_Error);

        ContentEditor = document.getElementById("WebPartQ3");
        ContentEditorDisplayPanel = document.createElement("div");
        ContentEditorDisplayPanel.setAttribute("id", "TechnicianResults");

        ContentEditorMapPanel = document.createElement("div");
        ContentEditorMapPanel.setAttribute("id", "MapResults");
        ContentEditorMapPanel.setAttribute("style", "position: relative; width: 400px; height:
400px;");

        ContentEditor.appendChild(ContentEditorDisplayPanel);
        ContentEditor.appendChild(document.createElement("br"));
        ContentEditor.appendChild(ContentEditorMapPanel);

        GetMap();
        FindLoc("Winston-Salem, NC", "Headquarters");
    }
    catch (e)
```

```
    {
        Exception = e;
    }
}

function Diagram_Complete ()
{
    try
    {
        Page = WebPart.getActivePage ();
        Shapes = Page.getShapes ();
        CurrentShape = Page.getSelectedShape ();

        WebPart.addHandler ("shapeselectionchanged ", Shape_SelectionChanged);
    }
    catch (e)
    {
        Exception = e;
    }
}

function Diagram_Error ()
{
    WebPart.DisplayCustomMessage ("Error: " + Exception);
}

function Shape_SelectionChanged (source, id)
{
    try
    {
        Shapes = Page.getShapes ();
        CurrentShape= Shapes.getItemById (id);
        var ShapeData = CurrentShape.getShapeData ();

        for (var i = 0; i < ShapeData .length; i++)
        {
            var fieldName = ShapeData [i].label;

            if (fieldName == 'Step')
            {
                SelectedSupportTier  = ShapeData [i].formattedValue;
            }
        }

        GetTechnician();
    }
    catch (e)
    {
        Exception = e;
        Diagram_Error();
    }
}
```

```
function GetTechnician ()
{
   Context = new SP.ClientContext.get_current();
   Web = Context.get_web();
   List = Web.get_lists().getByTitle("Technicians");

   Query = new .CamlQuery();
   Query.set_viewXml('<View><Query><Where><Eq><FieldRef Name="Support_x0020_Tier"/><Value
Type="Text">'+ SelectedSupportTier +'</Value></Eq></Where></Query>' +
                        '<ViewFields><FieldRef Name="Title"/><FieldRef
Name="Location"/><FieldRef Name="Calls_x0020_Handled"/><FieldRef Name="Calls_x0020_Closed"/>'
+
                        '<FieldRef Name="Calls_x0020_Transferred"/></ViewFields></View>');

   ListItemCollection = List.getItems(Query);

   Context.load(ListItemCollection);

   Context.executeQueryAsync(Function.createDelegate(this, this.LoadSucceeded),
Function.createDelegate(this, this.LoadFailed));
}

function LoadSucceeded(sender, args)
{
   var ListItemEnumerator = ListItemCollection.getEnumerator();

   ContentEditorDisplayPanel.innerHTML = '';

   var Table = document.createElement("table");
   Table.setAttribute ('border', '0px');
   Table.setAttribute ('cellacing', '0px');
   Table.setAttribute ('cellpadding', '3px');

   var HeaderRow = document.createElement('tr');
   HeaderRow.setAttribute ('class', 'ms-viewheadertr ms-vhltr');
   var TechnicianCell = document.createElement('th');
   var LocationCell = document.createElement('th');
   var CallsHandledCell = document.createElement('th');
   var CallsClosedCell = document.createElement('th');
   var CallsTransferredCell = document.createElement('th');

   TechnicianCell.innerHTML = 'Technician';
   LocationCell.innerHTML = 'Location';
   CallsHandledCell.innerHTML = 'Calls Handled';
   CallsClosedCell.innerHTML = 'Calls Closed';
   CallsTransferredCell.innerHTML = 'Calls Transferred';

   HeaderRow.appendChild(TechnicianCell);
   HeaderRow.appendChild(LocationCell);
   HeaderRow.appendChild(CallsHandledCell);
   HeaderRow.appendChild(CallsClosedCell);
```

```
    HeaderRow.appendChild(CallsTransferredCell);

    Table.appendChild(drHeaderRow);

     while (ListItemEnumerator.moveNext())
     {
        ListItem = ListItemEnumerator.get_current();

        var drTechnicianRow = document.createElement("tr");
        TechnicianRow.setAttribute ('class', 'ms-itmhover');
        TechnicianRow.setAttribute ('onclick', 'FindLoc ("' + ListItem.get_item("Location") +
'", "' + ListItem.get_item("Title") + '");');

        TechnicianCell = document.createElement("td");
        LocationCell = document.createElement("td");
        CallsHandledCell = document.createElement("td");
        CallsClosedCell = document.createElement("td");
        CallsTransferredCell = document.createElement("td");

        TechnicianCell.innerHTML = ListItem.get_item('Title');
        LocationCell.innerHTML = ListItem.get_item('Location');
        CallsHandledCell.innerHTML = ListItem.get_item('Calls_x0020_Handled');
        CallsClosedCell.innerHTML = ListItem.get_item('Calls_x0020_Closed');
        CallsTransferredCell.innerHTML = ListItem.get_item('Calls_x0020_Transferred');

        TechnicianRow.appendChild(TechnicianCell);
        TechnicianRow.appendChild(LocationCell);
        TechnicianRow.appendChild(CallsHandledCell);
        TechnicianRow.appendChild(CallsClosedCell);
        TechnicianRow.appendChild(CallsTransferredCell);

        Table.appendChild(TechnicianRow);
    }

    ContentEditorDisplayPanel.appendChild(Table);
}

function LoadFailed(sender, args)
{
    alert('Failed to load');
}

var BingMap = null;
var Coordinates = "";

function GetMap() {
    try {
        BingMap = new VEMap("MapResults");
        BingMap.LoadMap();
    } catch (e) {
        alert(e.message);
    }
```

```
}

function GetSearchResult(layer, resultsArray, places, hasMore, veErrorMessage) {
   Coordinates = places[0].LatLong;
}

function FindLoc(location, technician) {
   try {
      BingMap.Clear();
      BingMap.Find(null, location, null, null, 0, 1, true, true, false, true,
GetSearchResult);
      window.setTimeout(function() { AddPushpin(location, technician); }, 1000);
   } catch (e) {
      alert(e.message);
   }
}

function AddPushpin(location, description) {
   var shape = new VEShape(VEShapeType.Pushpin, Coordinates);

   BingMap.ClearInfoBoxStyles();
   shape.SetTitle('<h4>' + description + '</h4>');
   shape.SetDescription(description + ' - ' + location);
   BingMap.AddShape(shape);
}
</script>
```

There's a lot going on in this code. The first thing you do is create the App_Load method to set the stage for the rest of the operations. This will be used to wire up the events for the Visio Web Access Web Part (WebPartWPQ2) and then add some DOM elements to the Content Editor (WebPartWPQ3) that is hosting the script. The method closes out by initializing your map in the MapResults div that was created in your Content Editor Web Part.

The next event in the lifecycle of the page will be the Diagram_Complete handler, which wires up the last of the events, Shape_MouseEnter. When the user moves the cursor over one of the Visio Shapes, the Shape_MouseEnter will use the Client JavaScript Object Model to initialize a collection that roughly resembles an SPListItemCollection and then performs an executeQueryAsync callback to the SharePoint Services, passing the CAML query. The CAML query is designed to select all of the SPListItems from the Technicians list that have a Support Tier matching the Step of the current shape on the Visio page.

After the callback executes, either the LoadSucceeded or LoadFailed methods will be called. The purpose of each of these is pretty much self-explanatory, but suffice to say, I prefer it when the LoadSucceeded fires and execution continues normally. LoadSucceeded performs some JavaScript DOM work to add a table with headers, and then adds rows dynamically for each Technician returned in the ListItemCollection. For each row created, an OnClick attribute is added that will make the FindLoc method call.

FindLoc is the entry point for centering the map on a location and adding a pinpoint to the location. When this invokes, the map will center and provide the pinpoint with a tooltip showing the technician name and location. Ultimately, the finished product should look something like the Figure 15-7.

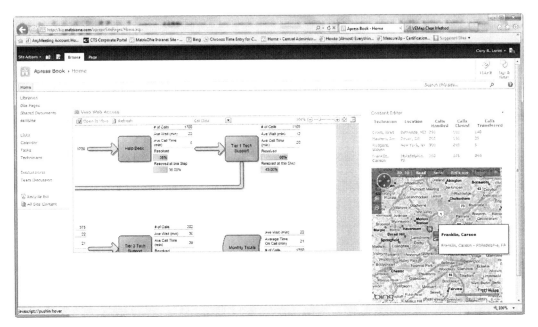

*Figure 15-7. The finished product*

## Conclusion

In this chapter you learned how to take the out-of-the-box Business Intelligence capabilities of SharePoint 2010 and extend them to make a rich and dynamic dashboard. Whether you're using Visio, Excel, or PerformancePoint, the possibilities for customization really rely on the imagination of those envisioning the project. Using an Excel file, a SharePoint List, and a Visio Web Drawing, you were able to combine previously unrelated data together, and then use an external service like Bing Maps to help make the data relevant. I sincerely hope that you have developed an appetite for the information in this chapter and are inspired to delve further into the deep world of SharePoint Insights and Composites more thoroughly.

# CHAPTER 16

# Tips, Tricks, and Traps

*Truth is what stands the test of experience.*

—Albert Einstein

The intent of this chapter is to organize a collection of experiences into a reference for some PowerPivot situations that don't necessarily apply to every solution developer. For example, you may have the occasional failure of the PowerPivot add-in for Excel. This chapter incorporates a set of tasks to troubleshoot the add-in so you can get the PowerPivot for Excel environment back to work.

Also included is information on dealing with the quirks, nuances, dare we say features of PowerPivot. Finally, there are some techniques for tuning your PowerPivot for Excel solutions. You'll learn how to use slicer overload to increase worksheet performance. You will also learn to trace the Multidimensional Expressions (MDX) query language by which PowerPivot makes requests to the in-memory database engine.

## PowerPivot Annoyances

Sometimes they are referred to as "features," sometimes as "bugs," and other times by the harsher term "defect." By whatever name, PowerPivot for Excel contains the sometimes curious behaviors common to any complex software product in the initial release.

### Disabled PowerPivot Add-In

Upon starting Microsoft Excel, you may find the PowerPivot ribbon item is missing, as illustrated in Figure 16-1. It is, of course, exceedingly difficult to do work in PowerPivot for Excel without the PowerPivot ribbon menu. The missing PowerPivot ribbon menu is the principal symptom of a disabled PowerPivot add-in.

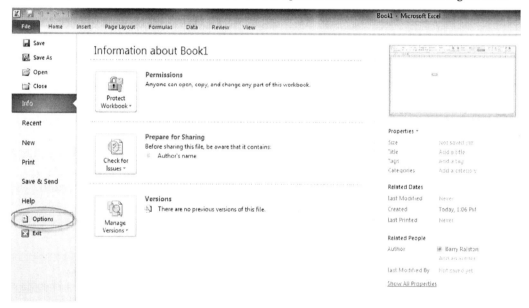

***Figure 16-1.*** *Missing PowerPivot add-in*

In order to get your PowerPivot for Excel environment back up and running, perform the following steps. First, select the File ribbon item and then the Options submenu, as circled in Figure 16-2.

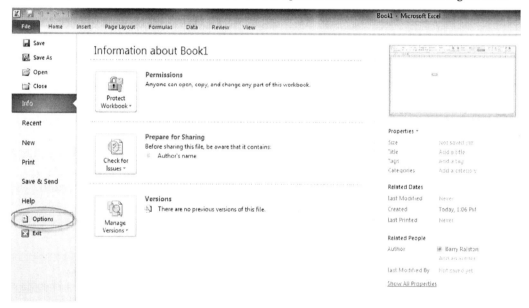

***Figure 16-2.*** *File Options submenu*

Selecting the Options submenu will display the Excel Options panel, illustrated in Figure 16-3. Select the Add-ins menu item, circled in Figure 16-3.

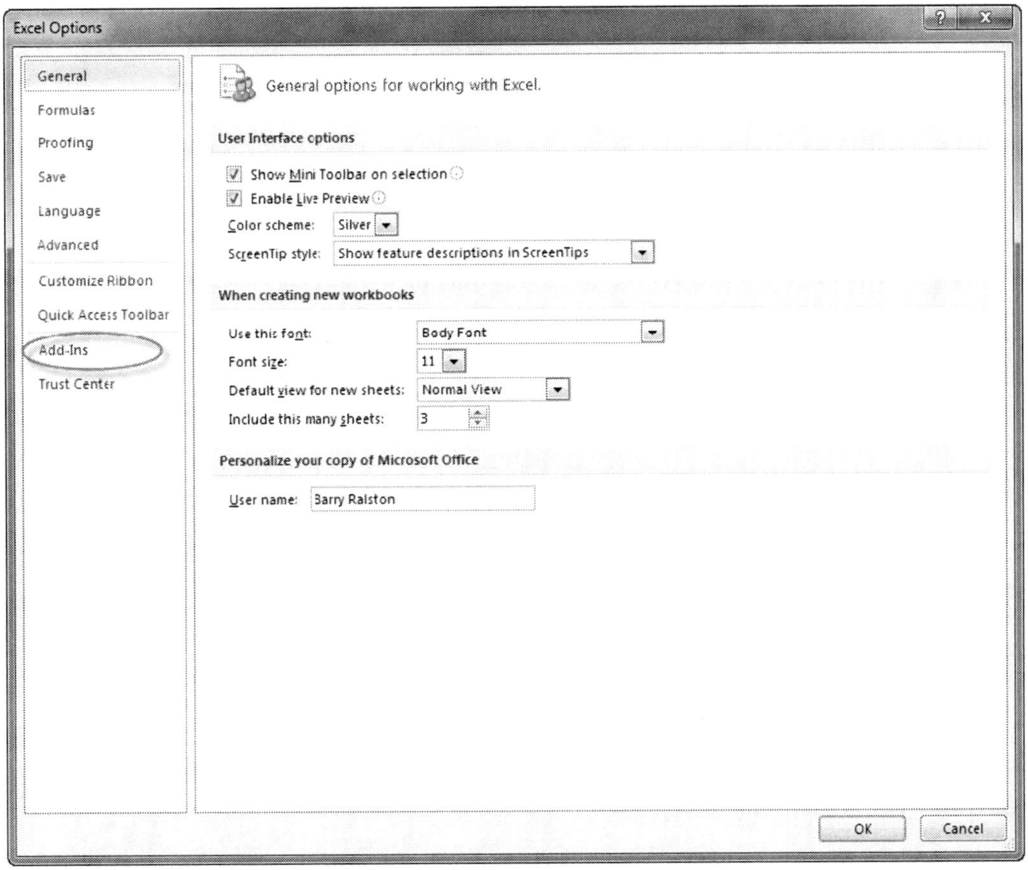

*Figure 16-3. Excel Options panel*

The Add-ins panel, illustrated in Figure 16-4, will display all of the currently installed Excel extensions. Note the PowerPivot for Excel add-in is a COM-based (Component Object Model) add-in.

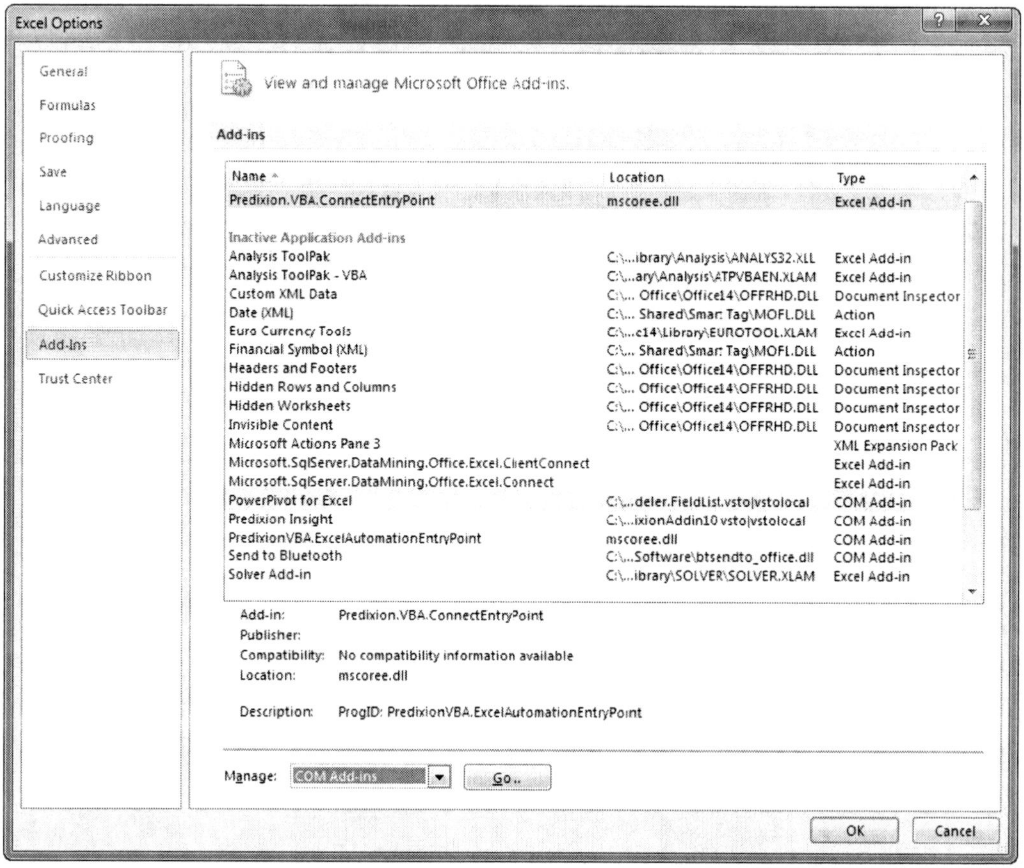

*Figure 16-4. Microsoft Office add-ins*

Also note the PowerPivot for Excel add-in is in the group of inactivated items. Following the next set of steps will re-enable the add-in, restoring the PowerPivot for Excel features. Using the Manage pull-down illustrated in Figure 16-5, select COM Add-Ins (recall PowerPivot for Excel is COM-based) and click the Go button.

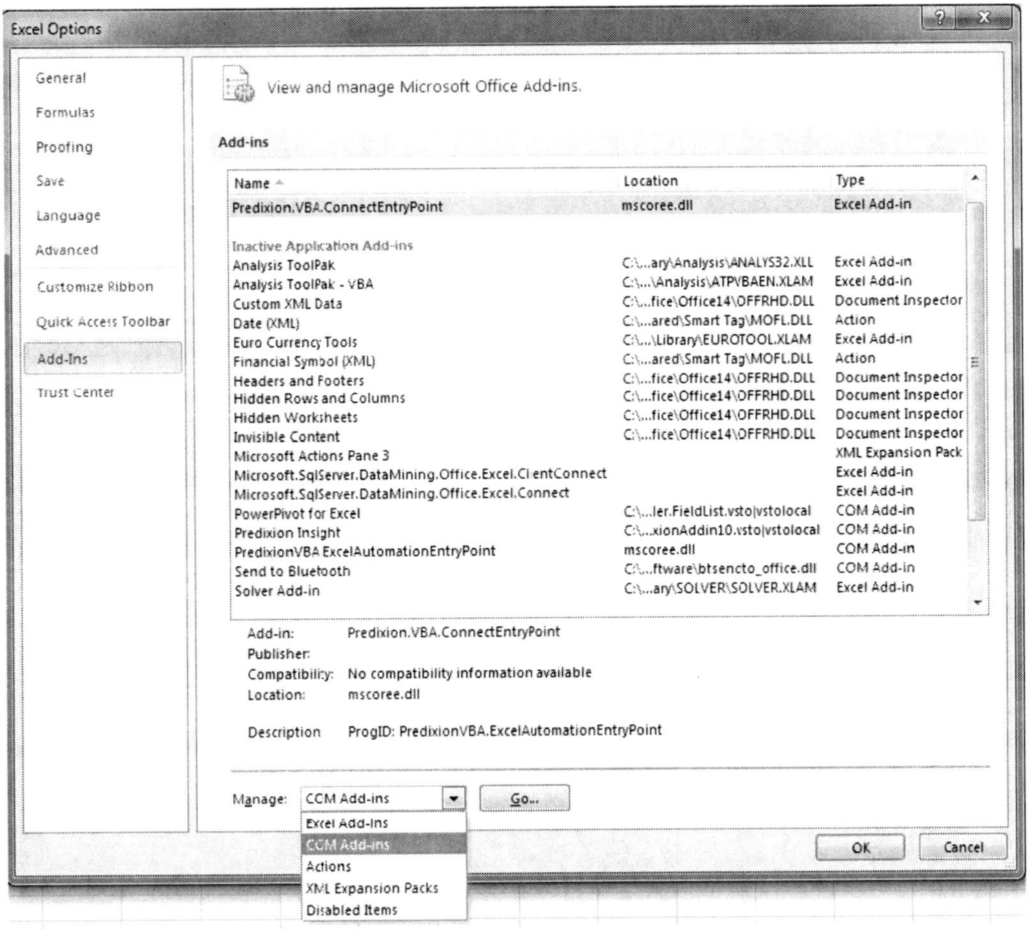

*Figure 16-5. Managing COM add-ins*

The dialog for managing available COM add-ins, illustrated in Figure 16-6, will be displayed. A disabled PowerPivot for Excel add-in will have an empty check box in the list of available add-ins. Click the check box corresponding to PowerPivot for Excel, ensuring it is in a "checked" state, and click the OK button. The PowerPivot for Excel add-in will be activated, and the PowerPivot menu will reappear on the ribbon.

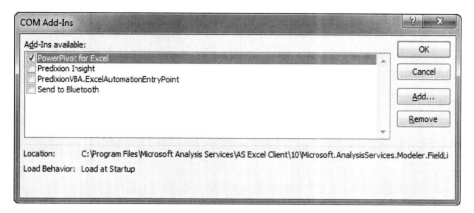

*Figure 16-6. Activating the PowerPivot for Excel add-in*

## Calculated Column Missing

As you use calculated columns in your PowerPivot data, it is important to remember the PowerPivot Field List is not immediately synchronized with the PowerPivot data metadata. For example, after adding a calculated column to a PowerPivot table, the PowerPivot Field List in Excel will display the "PowerPivot data was modified" warning, as circled in Figure 16-7.

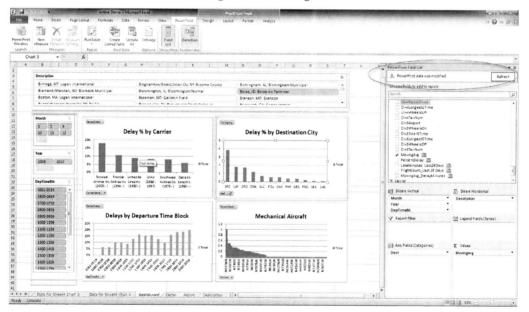

*Figure 16-7. "PowerPivot data was modified" warning*

However, it's important to remember that pressing the Refresh button doesn't refresh the PowerPivot Field List. In order for the new calculated column to appear in the field list, you must send a query to the underlying SQL Server Analysis Services (SSAS) database. Simply interact with any of the slicer selections, even changing the selection illustrated in Figure 16-7 from Boise to any other value and back. Changing the selection will result in the new calculation appearing in the PowerPivot Field List.

# User Experience for PowerPivot Solutions

PowerPivot for Excel provides an environment for rapid development of reports and dashboards from related yet potentially disparate data sources. However, the ease with which the data can be combined and reports created can cause the user experience to be overlooked.

---

■ **Note** I am at heart a database guy who geeks out over the data capabilities of PowerPivot. The intent of this section is to share a few tips on creating a pleasing user interface with PowerPivot. I am not a user experience professional but have found my way to creating workable user interfaces.

---

## Connect Slicers Visually

The ease with which PowerPivot slicers can be added can cause user confusion. This is especially the case in a PowerPivot report when all slicers don't relate to all charts/tables. For example, if a single slicer applies only to a subset of the PivotCharts or PivotTable elements of the report, there is no visual cue as to how a slicer is filtering each report element.

In this case, you can use Excel formatting to visually link the elements that relate to each other. To illustrate the example, consider the reports in Figure 16-8. The Origin State and Departure Airport are connected in that they filter data for the Weather PivotChart. Those two fields affect only the Weather chart, and not others that you see in the figure. To make the relationship plain to the user, you can color the background cells to match the bars in the chart, as I've done using the color blue. You may need to explain that approach once or twice to your users, but you'll find that they quickly catch on.

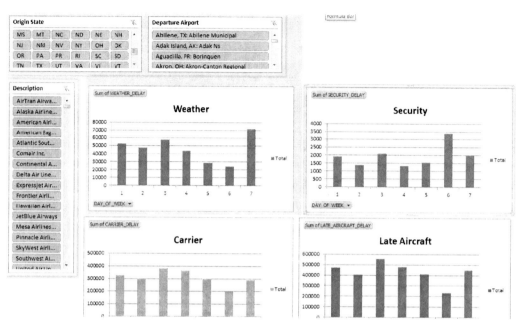

*Figure 16-8. Visual cue for slicer connection*

## Lose the Grid

To reduce the number of steps, many of the examples in this book don't adhere to this very powerful tip to create a more pleasing user interface. However, it is widely held that PowerPivot tables and charts simply look more appealing to users without Excel's gridlines. Combined with removing the row and column headers, a custom application look and feel can be quickly created.

To hide the gridlines, select Page Layout from the ribbon. Then uncheck the Gridlines View check box, as illustrated in Figure 16-9. Similarly, row and column headings can be removed by unchecking the adjacent Headings View check box.

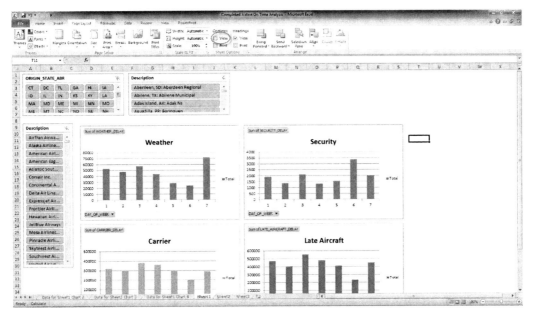

*Figure 16-9. Removing gridlines*

# Tuning PowerPivot Performance

PowerPivot for Excel's features for loading and combining data can be dazzling. In certain cases, these very data loading features can also lead to slow-performing PowerPivot for Excel solutions.

## Slicers: Less Is More

In my opinion, slicers are the most visually unique element of PowerPivot. However, they can greatly impact the performance of report (PivotTable and PivotChart) updates. If you incur this type of performance issue in your PowerPivot solutions, here are a couple of suggestions for decreasing update runtimes.

First, endeavor to source slicers from dimension tables as opposed to fact tables in your solution. For example, consider an organization that works with a product set that contains 200 distinct products, and therefore only 200 distinct product names. The fact table for the same solution contains 500 million orders. The PowerPivot engine will more quickly update a slicer based on the 200-row product table as opposed to determining the distinct products using the 500-million–row fact table.

Second, consider eliminating the relationship between slicers. Recall how, by default, multiple slicers on the same PivotTable or PivotChart structure interrelate to visually indicate slicer tiles for which no fact data exists. While removing this feature is not applicable for all solutions, the reduction in workload for the PowerPivot engine is significant. Disabling this feature is a matter of right-clicking the slicer, choosing Slicer Settings from the context menu, and then unchecking the items highlighted in the resulting Slicer Settings dialog, illustrated in Figure 16-10.

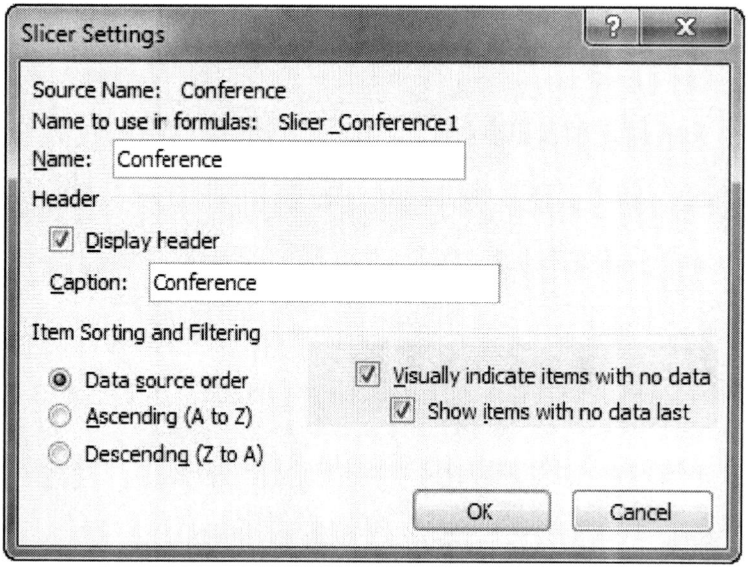

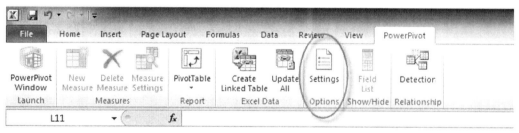

**Figure 16-10.** *Disabling slicer relationships*

## PowerPivot and SSAS Interaction

PowerPivot for Excel is an environment for developing solutions using the SSAS in-memory runtime. Because the language for querying SSAS databases is Multidimensional Expressions (MDX), you may find it useful in your PowerPivot tuning efforts to examine the queries being sent from PowerPivot for Excel to SSAS. This tactic requires SQL Server Profiler in order to use the trace files that are generated from PowerPivot for Excel. To begin generating trace files, follow these steps.

First, open a PowerPivot solution from Microsoft Excel. Next, select the PowerPivot ribbon menu and then the Settings selection, as illustrated in Figure 16-11.

**Figure 16-11.** *PowerPivot Settings menu*

The Settings dialog illustrated in Figure 16-12 will be displayed. Check the "Client tracing is enabled" check box, and select a location for the resulting trace file. The default location is fine for our purposes.

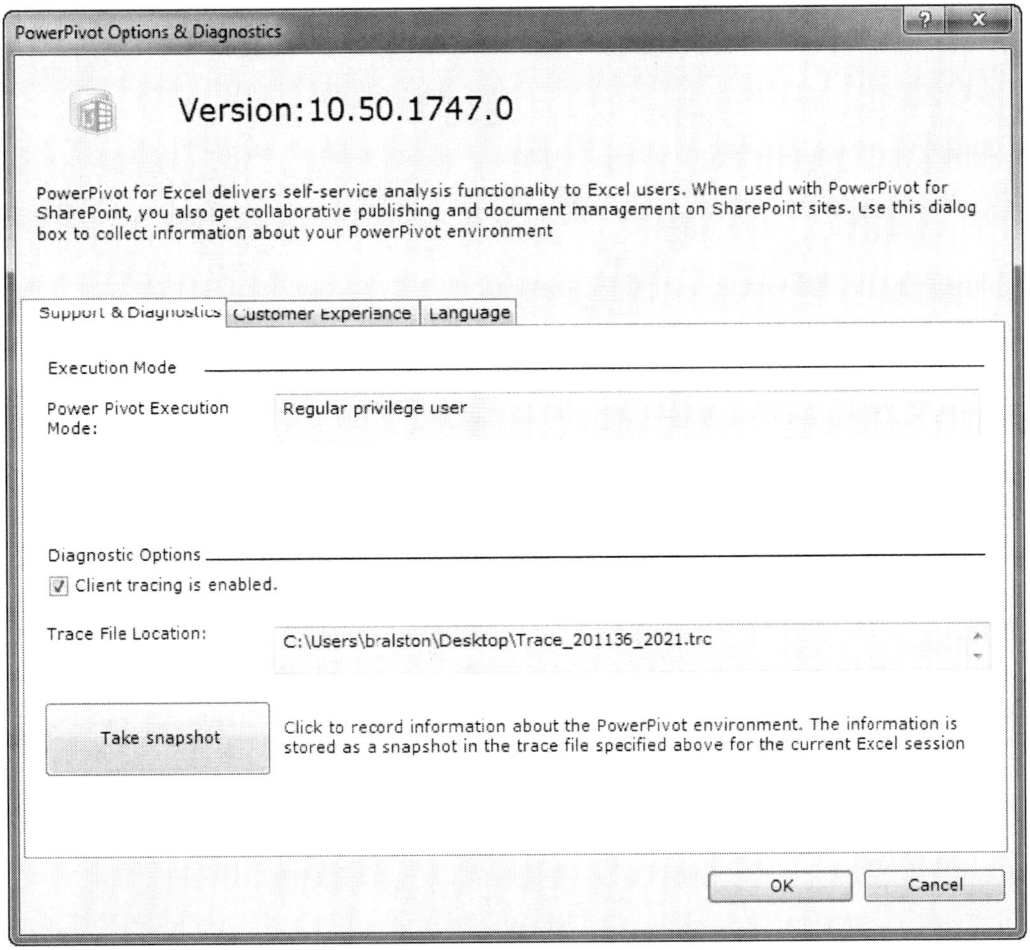

**Figure 16-12.** *PowerPivot settings*

Interact with the PowerPivot for Excel slicers or alter the composition of a PivotChart or PivotTable in your solution. By doing this, several queries are sent to the PowerPivot engine (SSAS). Return to the PowerPivot settings, and disable the client tracing feature by unchecking the check box illustrated in Figure 16-12. This is very important, as otherwise all PowerPivot activity will continue to be logged to the trace file.

The trace file created by PowerPivot requires SQL Server Profiler in order to actually open and view the contents. Figure 16-13 illustrates a portion of a trace file, highlighting the Query End event.

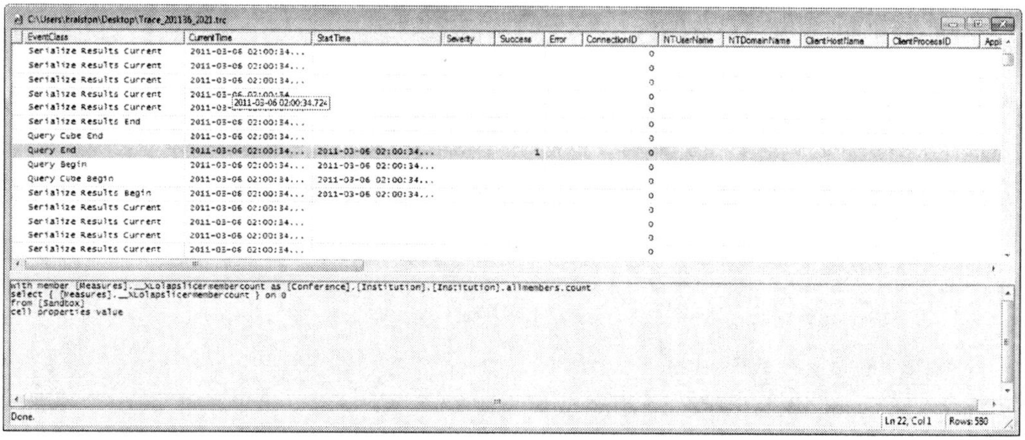

*Figure 16-13. Trace file in SQL Profiler*

Combined with SQL Profiler, the client trace files can be used to determine the actual query execution times and data volumes being utilized in the PowerPivot engine.

## Summary

All tools have their rough edges, and PowerPivot is no different. The tips in this chapter are part of my hard-won experience. Don't be put off by the rough edges. PowerPivot is a powerful tool for bringing data mining to the end user. Take advantage of PowerPivot in your business and apply the tips and techniques in this chapter to make your work easier.

# CHAPTER 17

# PerformancePoint Services

In this chapter, we will discover how PerformancePoint Services allows us to build integrated business intelligence solutions that bring these capabilities together into powerful interactive dashboards.

## What Will You Learn in This Chapter?

- Introduction to PerformancePoint Services
- The architecture of PerformancePoint Services
- Setting up PerformancePoint Services
- Authoring and publishing PerformancePoint solutions in SharePoint 2010
- Integrating PerformancePoint dashboards with Visio and Excel Services
- Managing PerformancePoint using PowerShell

## Software Prerequisites

- SharePoint Server 2010 Enterprise Edition
- Office Excel 2010
- Office Visio 2010
- SQL Server 2008 R2 / SQL Server 2008
- AdventureWorks Database (SQL Server 2008 R2) downloadable at http://msftdbprodsamples.codeplex.com/
- SQL Server 2008 R2 Client Tools – downloadable at http://technet.microsoft.com/en-us/library/ms143219.aspx

## Introduction

Though PerformancePoint Services is a new feature in SharePoint Server 2010, it is far from being a new product. Like many Microsoft products, including SharePoint itself, PerformancePoint has a long, and sometimes inglorious, history.

In the early years of this century, the "scorecard" became a popular business metaphor for bringing together related pieces of information from throughout the enterprise to provide decision makers with a high-level view of the business. Special-purpose scorecards like the "Balanced Scorecard" became popular but there were no good tools available to deliver them. After a few attempts at getting Excel and web-based templates deployed, Microsoft published the Office Business Scorecard Manager 2005.

In 2007, Microsoft purchased ProClarity Corporation, thereby acquiring one of the premiere business intelligence software companies. Microsoft immediately began integrating features of ProClarity's rich server- and client-based data analysis tools into its products.

When MS PerformancePoint Server was released in 2007, it contained two major modules: monitoring & analysis (M&A) and planning. The M&A component combined the features of the Business Scorecard Manager product with new capabilities brought in from ProClarity and saw good adoption. Use of the planning module, however, was sparse and in 2009, Microsoft dropped it due to lack of market interest. What remained of PerformancePoint was then rolled into the enterprise license of Microsoft Office SharePoint Server (MOSS) 2007. In fact, at that point, the MS PerformancePoint Server 2007 product could be loaded onto a MOSS server farm (with Enterprise Client Access Licenses, or CALs) without additional licensing.

Now, with the release of SharePoint Server 2010, PerformancePoint has become a fully integrated service within the SharePoint environment. You get all of SharePoint's administration and content management tools along with the analytic abilities of PerformancePoint.

# PerformancePoint Services Architecture

PerformancePoint Services is implemented using the new service application framework introduced in SharePoint Server 2010. In the same way that Excel Services and Visio Services run as separate service processes, so does PerformancePoint.

## Service Components and Interfaces

Figure 17–1 shows the primary components that cooperate to provide the business intelligence experience PerformancePoint Services makes possible.

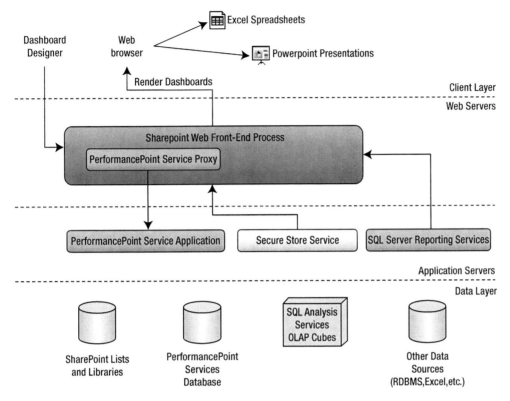

**Figure 17–1.** *PerformancePoint services and related components*

The PerformancePoint end-user experience is designed to be very simple. A PerformancePoint dashboard is deployed as nothing more than a folder containing one or more web pages within a SharePoint library. These pages contain all of the user interface elements necessary to perform complex business analysis on the underlying business data. This user interface is designed to require very little specialized training. With some experience, most users find the scorecards, charts, and reports very easy to interpret and manipulate. All of this content is delivered via a web browser, of course, but there are also many opportunities to take data offline into office applications such as Excel for deeper ad hoc analysis.

In order to deliver this sophisticated user interface, the KPIs, scorecards, dashboards, and other BI components must first be defined and deployed to SharePoint. The tool for accomplishing this is the Dashboard Designer, a Windows application for defining BI components and deploying them to SharePoint. This tool does not need to be separately downloaded and installed. It is automatically installed as a "one-click" application when needed. See "Authoring and Publishing PerformancePoint Solutions" later in this chapter for a tour of this tool. Note that this is a development tool and is not designed for use by most end users.

At the application layer, PerformancePoint conforms to the typical design of a SharePoint service. It is made up of a service process and a proxy component. The proxy component provides code running within the IIS application pool process with access to the functionality of the PerformancePoint service application. The service runs as an independent process in the operating system and is often deployed on a separate tier of application servers that sits between the web front-end server and the database servers, as shown in Figure 17–1.

Other application-level services commonly employed as part of a PerformancePoint solution include the Secure Store Service (SSS) and SQL Server Reporting Services (SSRS). SSS provides a location for logon credentials to be securely stored within the SharePoint environment. For more details on the purpose and configuration of the Secure Store Service, see Chapter 5. While not part of SharePoint Server, the SSRS component of SQL Server is frequently leveraged in conjunction with PerformancePoint solutions due to the ease with which it allows complex reports to be created and delivered.

On the database layer of the architecture, there are several data sources you'll have to become familiar with.

## SharePoint Content Lists and Libraries

As you are probably aware, SharePoint stores its web site contents in content databases. These databases contain the site collections, sites, lists, libraries, and pages that make up the sites served by SharePoint. In the context of PerformancePoint, most of the business intelligence objects, including the dashboards themselves, are also stored in lists and libraries within SharePoint's content databases.

## PerformancePoint Service Databases

Like the other service applications in SharePoint Server 2010, PerformancePoint Services needs to store data that does not fit well into the usual format of lists and libraries in SharePoint. This data is stored in a separate database that's created when a new instance of the PerformancePoint service application is created. The tables in this database, like all SharePoint databases, should never be manipulated directly but only through PerformancePoint Services. These tables contain various parameters used by PPS, as well as dashboard annotations and comments entered by users.

## SQL Server Analysis Services (SSAS) Cubes

Because of the types of analysis normally performed with PerformancePoint Services, perhaps the most common data source for Key Performance Indicators (KPIs), scorecards, and dashboards is SQL Server Analysis Services (SSAS). The cubes stored in SSAS contain the raw business information that PPS will "slice and dice" to perform the analysis required by the user. For a full description of using SSAS cubes to store and manipulate multidimensional data, see Chapter 1.

## Other Reporting Data Sources

While SQL Analysis Services is the most common source of information for PPS dashboards, it is far from the only option. Any data store from which you can read data is a potential data source for PerformancePoint. Additional data sources supported out of the box include SQL Server relational tables, Excel spreadsheets (either file-based or via Excel Services), and SharePoint lists.

With a little more effort, you can expand the available data sources to include any ODBC-compliant relational database and even data accessed via custom code written and deployed by the user's organization. For details on creating custom data source providers for PerformancePoint Services, see msdn.microsoft.com/en-us/library/bb8317514.aspx. To access other non-Microsoft databases, you can use either Business Connectivity Services (see Chapter 4) to expose the data as a SharePoint list or a SQL linked server to expose the data as a SQL Server table (msdn.microsoft.com/en-us/library/ms188279.aspx).

# Securing PerformancePoint Solutions

Much of the security for a PerformancePoint solution is handled by the SharePoint Foundation component. The dashboards exposed by PerformancePoint Services are stored as ASPX pages in a folder within a SharePoint document library. The permissions associated with the libraries, folders, and dashboard pages will control who is allowed to access which pages.

However, the page itself is not usually what is most important. It is the data that we want to protect. Security can become problematic when we have to access data sources outside of SharePoint. PerformancePoint Services provides three authentication methods for accessing backend data sources: per-user identity, an unattended service account (USA), and a custom connection string for SQL Server Analysis Services.

Per-user identity allows a PPS dashboard to impersonate the user's credentials when accessing backend data. This is a very secure way to access data because it provides a second check before allowing the user to access not just the dashboard, but the data underlying the dashboard. However, this form of authentication requires Kerberos delegation to be in place between the PerformancePoint server and the data source, so it's not always possible to use this type of authentication. See "Planning Considerations for Services that Access External Data Sources" at technet.microsoft.com/en-us/library/cc5170988.aspx#ConsiderationsForAccessingExternalData.

The most commonly used form of authentication with PerformancePoint services is the unattended service account. This is an account that is configured in the Secure Store Service and used to access a backend data source. The data source will see only the service account's credentials, so it will not be able to filter the data it returns based on the identity of the user accessing the dashboard. The service account must be given access to all necessary data within all data sources in order for PerformancePoint to function properly. It is a best practice to use a service account with the least permissions that will allow it to access the needed data.

The last option, called "Custom Data," uses the unattended account but also includes the user's login name on the connection string. This option works only with SQL Server Analysis Services 20017 or later. In SSAS, this is known as "Dynamic Security." The idea is to allow the SSAS server to filter the query results when full Kerberos delegation is not possible. The user's login can be used in MDX queries and SSAS role assignments to limit the data returned by the cube.

The most important thing to note when choosing among these authentication options is that the choice can now be made for each data source that is configured. In PerformancePoint Server 2007, it was necessary to configure a single authentication mode for the entire server application. It was not possible to configure one data source using per-user identity and another to use an unattended service account. In SharePoint 2010, if multiple types of authentication are required, you don't need to configure multiple PerformancePoint service application instances. Creating separate data sources is sufficient. However, the unattended account is configured for a PPS application instance so all data sources running against the USA in that instance will use the same account. See "Setting up PerformancePoint Services" and "Creating a Data Source" later in this chapter for details.

# Business Intelligence Solution Components

A PerformancePoint solution is built by creating a set of business intelligence components that work together to control how business data is aggregated and displayed. This section will introduce the concepts behind these components and how they are deployed to a PerformancePoint service environment. For a step-by-step guide to creating a real-world PPS solution, see "Authoring and Publishing PerformancePoint Solutions" later in this chapter.

# BI Component Types

The components that go into a PerformancePoint solution are described at a conceptual level in this section. Later we'll describe how these components are represented and stored in SharePoint.

## Dashboards

A *dashboard* is a set of web pages displayed by SharePoint to allow the user to view and analyze data. Figure 17–2 shows a sample dashboard.

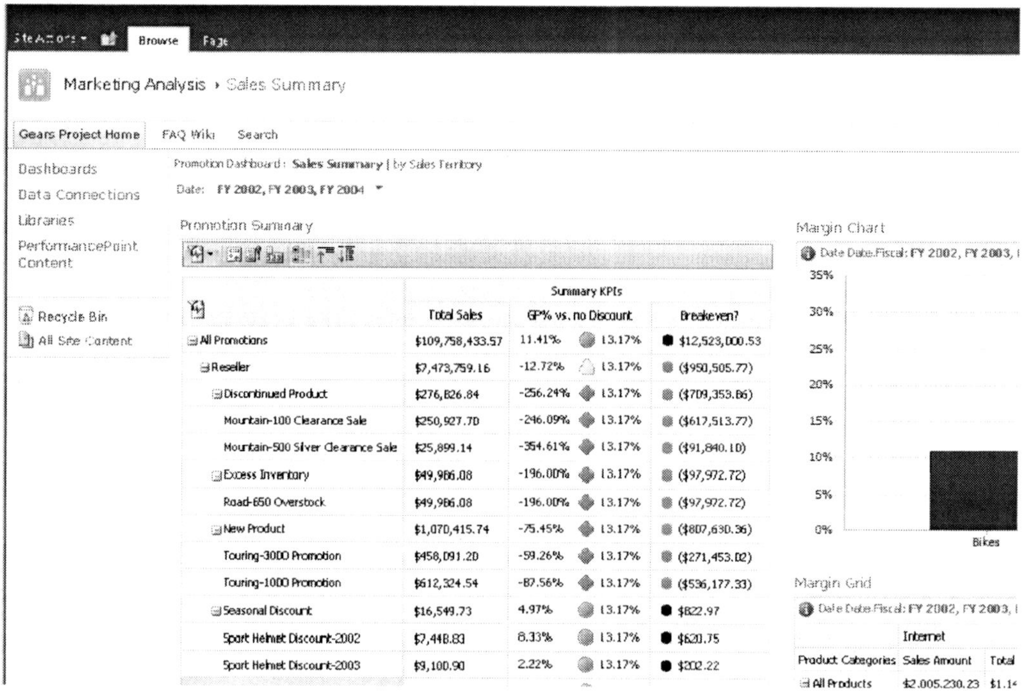

***Figure 17–2.*** *A typical PerformancePoint dashboard*

A dashboard page consists of several parts. Typically, a page contains a navigation area at the top of the page, as shown in Figure 17–3. In this case, the pages of the dashboard, "Sales Summary" and "by Sales Territory," are presented as links in the header of the page. Clicking on an active link takes the user to a new page in the dashboard while preserving the filters used on the current page. This allows multiple pages to act as a single dashboard.

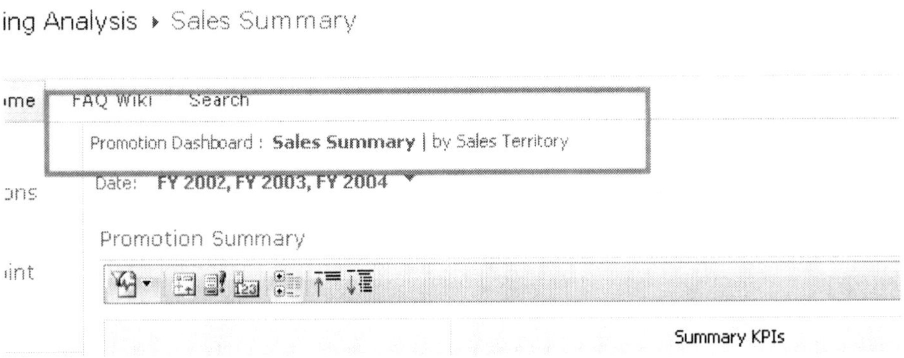

ing Analysis ▸ Sales Summary

*Figure 17–3. Dashboard navigation links*

The rest of the page is separated into *zones*, similar to the web part zones used in SharePoint pages. The difference is that dashboard zones can be added, modified, and removed from a dashboard page after it is created. These zones allow dashboard components, including filters, scorecards, and reports, to be stacked and connected in the same way web parts can be manipulated on a web part page. Figure 17–4 highlights the zones and direction (vertical vs. horizontal) of the default dashboard page layout.

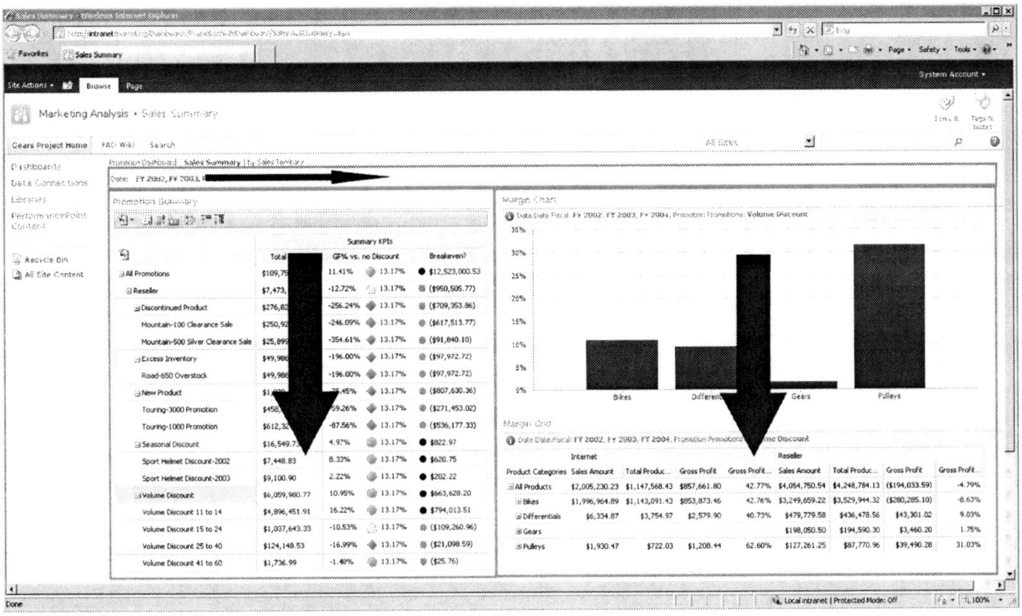

*Figure 17–4. Default dashboard zones*

The BI components that make up the page are assembled, arranged, and connected using the Dashboard Designer. When the dashboard is deployed to SharePoint, the various object definitions control the page's behavior. A common pattern, as shown in Figure 17–4, is to place visible filters in the header zone of the page and then to fill the other zones with scorecards and reports as needed.

The connections created between components allow them to act together. For example, when the user changes the Date filter on the sample dashboard, each of the scorecards and reports on the page are updated to reflect data only from those periods. When a row is selected in the scorecard shown on the left, the data on the reports in the right column are filtered to match. We will be creating this dashboard and its connections later in this chapter.

## Indicators and Key Performance Indicators

A *Key Performance Indicator* is a definition of business-relevant measurements (or "metrics") used to display easy-to-understand conditions as shown in Figure 17–5.

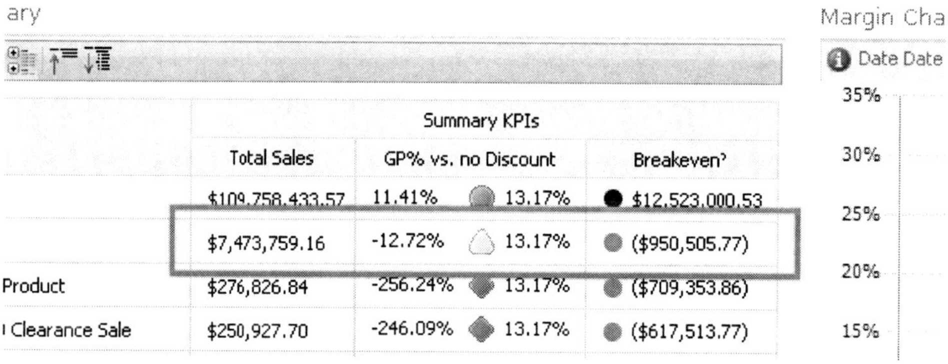

*Figure 17–5. A key performance indicator*

KPIs are defined in PerformancePoint as a set of metrics that are either "actual" or "Target" metrics. Actual metrics are the values that are calculated from the underlying business data. In the example in Figure 17–5, "Total Sales" is an actual metric. Target metrics, in contrast, define a desired goal for the actual metric, based on some condition or formula specified as part of the KPIs definition. The "GP% vs. no Discount" column is a target metric in this example. Target metrics can be displayed in several ways but include three basic components: the indicator and a value before and/or after the indicator. The meaning of these values can be defined wherever the KPI is displayed. In this case, the highlighted line shows an actual value of "-12.72%", a yellow triangle indicator, and a target value of "13.17%".

The definition of the KPI specifies where the actual and target values come from as well as what type of indicator to show. PerformancePoint comes with a large set of indicators to choose from, as Figure 17–6 shows. Through Dashboard Designer you can also create your own custom indicators using custom images.

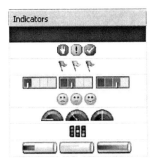

*Figure 17–6. Some common indicator types*

## Data Sources

The first components to be created in a PerformancePoint solution are data sources. These define the locations and parameters to use when accessing the data that will be used by the dashboard. PerformancePoint supports two major categories of data sources: tabular and multidimensional.

*Tabular* data sources are those that provide PPS with a relational table of data to work with. The most commonly used data sources of this type are SQL Server tables. Other options include cells retrieved from Excel spreadsheets, either through Excel Services or directly from a file, or the items in a SharePoint list. It is also possible to use SharePoint's Business Connectivity Services (BCS) or SQL linked servers to pass data from other RDBMS or line-of-business applications into a PerformancePoint dashboard.

*Multidimensional* data sources are the most common type used in PerformancePoint solutions. They use SQL Server Analysis Services (SSAS) cubes to furnish and process data. Analysis Services is the only currently supported OLAP data source.

## Filters

Filters are components that let users select parts of the data set to examine while excluding the rest. For example, you can use a filter to examine data only for certain time periods, as Figure 17–7 shows.

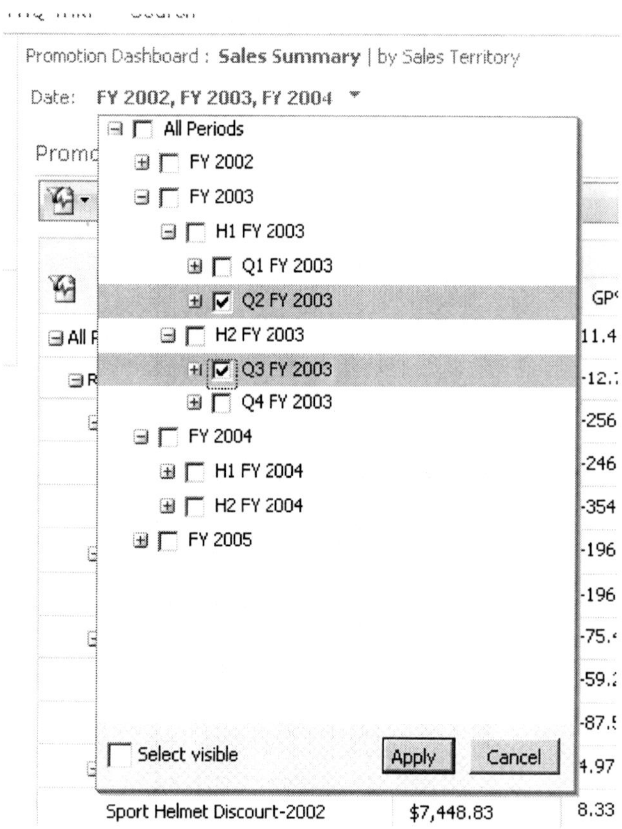

*Figure 17–7.* *A multi-selectable member-selection filter*

When creating a filter, there are two primary considerations: the type of filter and the display method to be used.

The types of filters available are:

- *Custom Table:* This filter connects to a tabular data source to retrieve a list of options from a table.

- *MDX Query:* This filter evaluates an MDX query against an OLAP data source to produce a set of members to serve as options in the filter control.

- *Member Selection:* This filter takes its options directly from a dimension in an OLAP data source, which can be either all members or a subset of the members in the dimension.

- *Named Set:* This filter uses an SSAS Named Set (i.e., an MDX expression) to evaluate which members to include. Note that SQL Server 2008 introduced the concept of "dynamic" named sets that are context-aware, which can make them very powerful in this context. For more information on SSAS Named Sets, see msdn.microsoft.com/en-us/library/ms11717594.aspx.

- *Time Intelligence:* This filter uses time dimensions in a way that lets users make time-based selections such as "year-to-date," "last six months," or "last year". The developer specifies formulas that select a subset of the time dimension's members to include in the calculation.

- *Time Intelligence (Connection Formula):* This variation on the Time Intelligence filter allows the user to select a single "current date." When connected to a dashboard, this date is evaluated against a date formula to create a dynamic time period based on that date. The user can therefore specify, for example, "5/11/2010" and generate a report on the six months of data prior to that date.

Once the type of filter has been selected, it can be displayed in three different ways.

- *List:* The filter options are presented in a drop-down list control as a flat list from which only one item can be selected.

- *Tree:* This form displays a hierarchical tree of members from which one option can be selected.

- *Multi-Select Tree:* This control, shown in Figure 17–7, also displays a tree but allows the user to select an arbitrary set of members from the tree.

When a filter is placed on a dashboard, it is not just a user interface control that controls the data displayed on that page. The selections made are written to PerformancePoint's database for later use. If the user returns to that page days later, that selection will still exist. The number of days the selection is retained can be configured in SharePoint Central Administration. See "Setting up PerformancePoint Services" later in this chapter. Because the filter is part of the dashboard, not just the page, that same filter selection will also be transferred to any other page that is part of the same dashboard. Therefore, if a selection is made on one page and then the user navigates to another page on the same dashboard, all of the filter selections made on the previous page apply to the new page as well.

## Scorecards

A PerformancePoint scorecard, shown in Figure 17–8, is used to display a set of key performance indicator metrics. You can configure the KPIs to display differently depending on what you need the scorecard to reflect. For example, the designer may choose to use a background color for a KPI cell instead of displaying the indicator image.

Promotion Summary

| | Summary KPIs | | |
|---|---|---|---|
| | Total Sales | GP% vs. no Discount | Breakeven? |
| ⊟ All Promotions | $109,750,400.57 | 11.41%  ⬤ 13.17% | ⬤ $12,523,000.53 |
| ⊟ Reseller | $7,473,759.16 | -12.72%  ⬡ 13.17% | ⬤ ($950,505.77) |
| ⊟ Discontinued Product | $276,826.84 | -256.24%  ◆ 13.17% | ⬤ ($709,353.86) |
| Mountain-100 Clearance Sale | $250,927.70 | -246.09%  ◆ 13.17% | ⬤ ($617,513.77) |
| Mountain-500 Silver Clearance Sale | $25,899.14 | -354.61%  ◆ 13.17% | ⬤ ($91,840.10) |
| ⊟ Excess Inventory | $49,986.08 | -196.00%  ◆ 13.17% | ⬤ ($97,972.72) |
| Road-650 Overstock | $49,986.08 | -196.00%  ◆ 13.17% | ⬤ ($97,972.72) |
| ⊟ New Product | $1,070,415.74 | -75.45%  ◆ 13.17% | ⬤ ($807,630.36) |
| Touring-3000 Promotion | $458,091.20 | -59.26%  ◆ 13.17% | ⬤ ($271,453.02) |
| Touring-1000 Promotion | $612,324.54 | -87.56%  ◆ 13.17% | ⬤ ($536,177.33) |
| ⊟ Seasonal Discount | $16,549.73 | 4.97%  ⬤ 13.17% | ⬤ $822.97 |
| Sport Helmet Discount-2002 | $7,448.83 | 8.33%  ⬤ 13.17% | ⬤ $620.75 |
| Sport Helmet Discount-2003 | $9,100.90 | 2.22%  ⬤ 13.17% | ⬤ $202.22 |
| ⊟ Volume Discount | $6,059,980.77 | 10.95%  ⬤ 13.17% | ⬤ $663,628.20 |
| Volume Discount 11 to 14 | $4,896,451.91 | 16.22%  ⬤ 13.17% | ⬤ $794,013.51 |
| Volume Discount 15 to 24 | $1,037,643.33 | -10.53%  ⬡ 13.17% | ⬤ ($109,260.96) |
| Volume Discount 25 to 40 | $124,148.53 | -16.99%  ◆ 13.17% | ⬤ ($21,098.59) |
| Volume Discount 41 to 60 | $1,736.99 | -1.48%  ⬤ 13.17% | ⬤ ($25.76) |

*Figure 17–8. A PerformancePoint scorecard*

In addition to the KPI metrics, scorecards generally also include one or more sets of dimension attributes that are used to drill down or roll up the KPIs.

## Reports

A report in PerformancePoint refers to a component that displays business data other than KPIs. Reports are authored separately and then connected to the filters and scorecards on a dashboard to filter the data returned in the report. Our sample dashboard contains two of the most common reports used in PerformancePoint server: the analytic chart and the analytic graph (Figure 17–9).

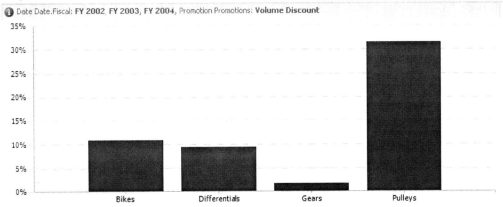

Margin Chart

Margin Grid

| Date Date.Fiscal: **FY 2002, FY 2003, FY 2004**, Promotion Promotions: **Volume Discount** | | | | | | | | |
|---|---|---|---|---|---|---|---|---|
| | Internet | | | | Reseller | | | |
| Product Categories | Sales Amount | Total Produc... | Gross Profit | Gross Profit... | Sales Amount | Total Produc... | Gross Profit | Gross Profit... |
| ⊟ All Products | $2,005,230.23 | $1,147,568.43 | $857,661.80 | 42.77% | $4,054,750.54 | $4,248,784.13 | ($194,033.59) | -4.79% |
| ⊞ Bikes | $1,996,964.89 | $1,143,091.43 | $853,873.46 | 42.76% | $3,249,659.22 | $3,529,944.32 | ($280,285.10) | -8.63% |
| ⊞ Differentials | $6,334.87 | $3,754.97 | $2,579.90 | 40.73% | $479,779.58 | $436,478.56 | $43,301.02 | 9.03% |
| ⊞ Gears | | | | | $198,050.50 | $194,590.30 | $3,460.20 | 1.75% |
| ⊞ Pulleys | $1,930.47 | $722.03 | $1,208.44 | 62.60% | $127,261.25 | $87,770.96 | $39,490.28 | 31.03% |

***Figure 17–9.*** *Analytic chart and graph reports*

PerformancePoint generates some reports entirely within itself but some reports are created in cooperation with other technologies. Here are the report templates supported:

- *Analytic Grid:* As shown in Figure 17–9, this type of report displays figures as a set of rows and columns. This control is very similar in look and feel to the PivotTable report used in previous versions of PerformancePoint.

- *Analytic Chart:* As shown in Figure 17–9, this report displays an interactive chart of the specified data. The user can drill into and roll up the data on this type of chart just as with an Analytic Grid.

- *Excel Services:* An Excel spreadsheet published using Excel Services can be referenced and used to display its data as an integrated part of a dashboard. See Chapter 5 for a full description Excel Services' capabilities.

- *KPI Details:* This simple report displays all of the properties of a selected KPI metric on a scorecard. This report must be connected to a scorecard in order to display any data.

- *ProClarity Analytics Server Page:* To support backward compatibility with ProClarity's installed server base, this report will bring in a page defined in that product running separately from the SharePoint server farm.

- *Reporting Services:* An SSRS report can be connected to a dashboard for rich report rendering.

- *Strategy Map:* This type of report uses a Visio diagram as a template for displaying KPIs in a graphical format. A typical use of a strategy map report is to display a map color-coded by a KPI's indicators. It is also possible to display numeric and text data on the map.

- *Web Page:* An ordinary web page can also be used to display data on a dashboard. While this may be as simple as displaying an Internet site within your dashboard, the real purpose of this report type is to act as a jack-of-all-trades for PerformancePoint reporting. When dashboard components, like reports, are connected to other components, like filters and scorecards, the parameters selected in those connections are passed to the connected component in the "Request.Params" collection. This allows a custom ASPX page to be deployed that accepts filter and selection values to display arbitrary data in HTML format.

Each of these reports is rendered on the dashboard page using a web part that manages the connection with other parts of the dashboard.

# PerformancePoint SharePoint Components

Now that we're familiar with the basic concepts of a business intelligence solution, let's take a look at how these pieces are put together in a SharePoint site.

## PPS Content Types

A content type in SharePoint defines all of the metadata about how a particular type of list item or library document will be handled by SharePoint. This includes a list of the fields associated with the object and any custom actions it may support. In the case of PerformancePoint, the following content types are defined to enable its functionality.

- PerformancePoint Dashboard

- PerformancePoint Data Source

- PerformancePoint Filter

- PerformancePoint Indicator

- PerformancePoint KPI

- PerformancePoint Report

- PerformancePoint Scorecard

With the exception of data sources, all of these content types define items in a SharePoint list. Data sources are stored as documents in a library because they are stored as Office or Universal Data Connection (UDC) files or as PerformancePoint data source files. Bear in mind that these items represent the definition of the object, not an end-user-viewable object. These items can be edited using the Dashboard Designer but don't display any content on their own. Only when a dashboard is "deployed" is it compiled into a set of ASPX pages that can be viewed by users.

A major advantage of PerformancePoint Services over PerformancePoint Server 2007 is the use of content types. With content types, all of the functionality of SharePoint is now available for use with PerformancePoint artifacts. This includes participating in workflows, using information rights management policies, and including PPS objects in any list or library where the PPS features and content types are active. You are no longer constrained to using a special site definition with a predefined structure for your PPS solutions.

## List and Library Templates

PerformancePoint defines list and library templates designed to store PerformancePoint artifacts.
  List Templates:

- PerformancePoint Content List – Lists based on this template are used to store all of the PPS components listed in "Content Types" above except for Data Sources.

  Library Templates:

- Data Connections Library for PerformancePoint – This template is used to store data sources defined by Dashboard Designer or as ODC or UDC files.

- Dashboards Library – This template is designed to store deployed PerformancePoint dashboards. Each dashboard is stored as a set of ASPX pages within a folder.

## Web Parts

Dashboard pages are created as ordinary web part pages. The various components of a page are created as connected web parts. The web parts used by PerformancePoint are:

- The Filter Web Part, which displays the list or tree control for a filter component.

- The Scorecard Web Part, which displays the grid associated with a scorecard component.

- The Report View Web Part, which displays a PPS report. Depending on the type of report, this web part may link to other sites or applications.

- The Stack Web Part, which is used as a container for the web parts associated with a zone on a dashboard page.

## Business Intelligence Center Site Template

PerformancePoint defines a sample site template to help designers begin using the service (Figure 17–10). This template is nothing more than an ordinary site with some prepopulated content to introduce the user to PerformancePoint features. The content is contained in a Content Editor Web Part and can be deleted when no longer needed. You can also add the PPS lists, libraries, and content types to any existing site instead of using the template. All that's required is for the PPS features to be activated.

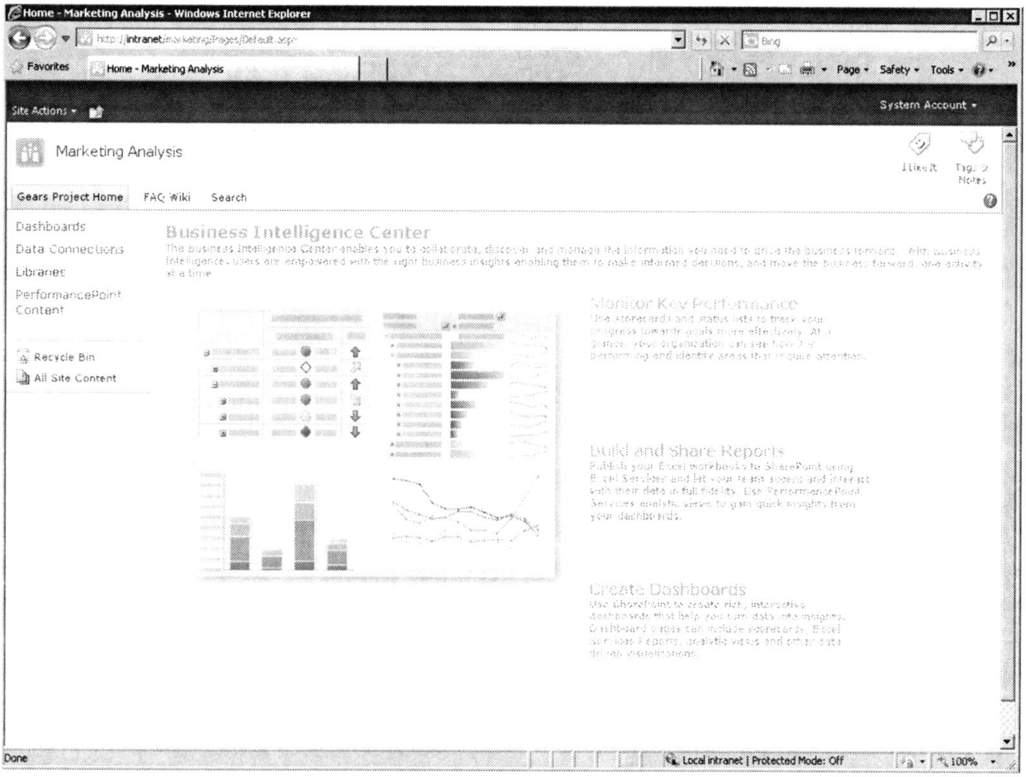

*Figure 17–10.* The Business Intelligence Center Home Page

In addition to this home page, the site template contains an instance of each of the lists and libraries described in "List and Library Templates" above. This makes the site a good location for one or more complete solutions to be stored. Additional content can be added to the site as needed.

## Features

PerformancePoint Services is part of the Enterprise Client Access License (ECAL) for SharePoint Server 2010. In order to use any such features, your SharePoint site collection must have the SharePoint Server Enterprise Site Collection Features feature activated under the Site Collection Features.

The PerformancePoint functionality is enabled using two additional features. The first is the PerformancePoint Services Site Collection Features feature. This feature can also be found under Site Collection Features. The second feature is activated at the site level and is named PerformancePoint Services Site Features. See "Deploy the Business Intelligence Center" later in this chapter for step-by-step instructions for enabling these features.

# Setting Up PerformancePoint Services

Like the other services we have examined in this book, PerformancePoint Services are configured using Central Administration or PowerShell commands (cmdlets). Let's take a look at the settings for PerformancePoint Services, along with the procedures for setting up a PPS instance.

The default, wizard-based installation of SharePoint Server 2010 includes an instance of the PerformancePoint Services application, so creating a new instance is not normally necessary. If you do need to create one, however, this can be easily accomplished through SharePoint Central Administration.

1.  Open the Central Administration web site using the SharePoint 2010 Central Administration link available in the server's Start menu.

2.  Navigate to the Central Administration ➤ Application Management ➤ Service Applications ➤ Manage Service Applications page. Note the default instance of PPS highlighted in Figure 17–11.

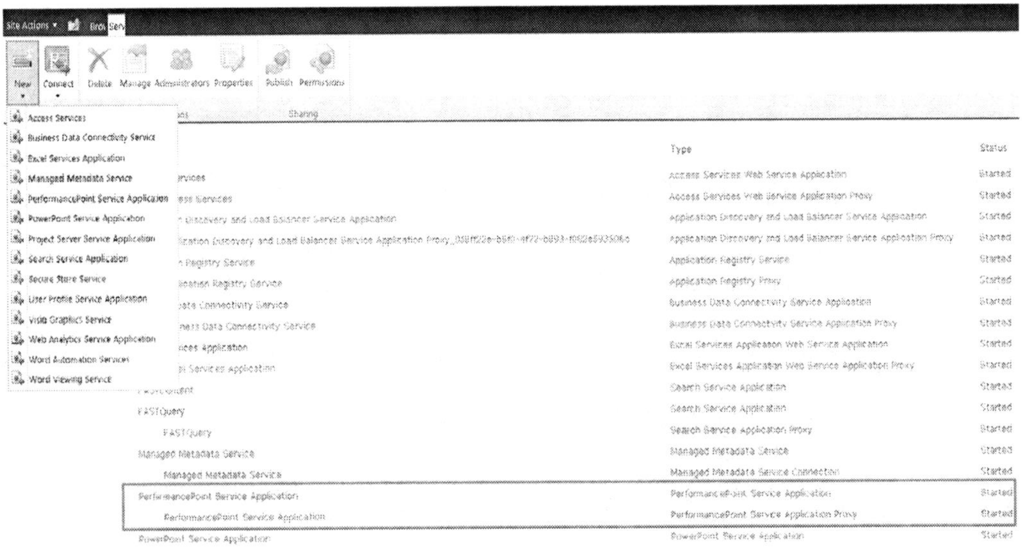

*Figure 17–11. The Manage Service Applications page*

3.  To create a new PPS instance, select PerformancePoint Service Application from the New section of the ribbon, as shown in Figure 7–11. This brings up the New PerformancePoint Service Application dialog (Figure 7–12).

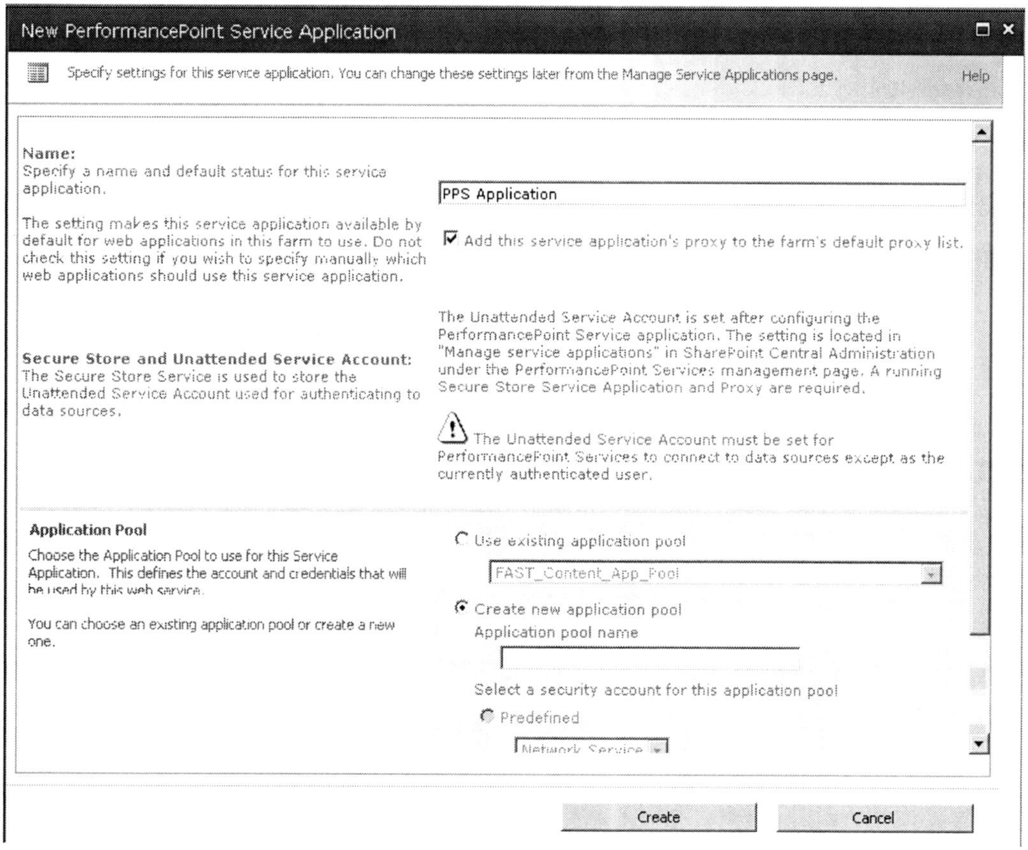

*Figure 17–12. New PerformancePoint Service Application dialog*

4. Set the name and application pool for the new PPS application instance or select an existing one. Use a new application pool when you wish to isolate PPS processing from other components within IIS.

5. Click Create.

After a few moments, the Manage Service Applications page will reappear with the new PPS application listed. It is now time to configure the application. If you are working with the default PPS instance, you should review the default settings, paying particular attention to the unattended service account, which should have the minimum privileges. See "Security PerformancePoint Solutions" earlier in this chapter to review why the USA is important.

To begin configuring the service application, click on the name of the service (PPS Application in our case) to be taken to the Manage PerformancePoint Services page as shown in Figure 17–13.

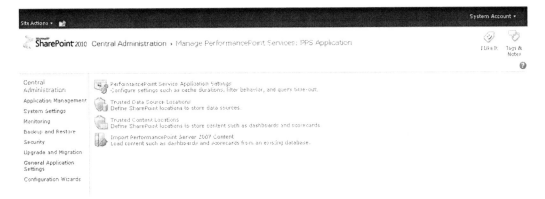

***Figure 17–13.*** *Manage PerformancePoint Services page*

On the Manage PerformancePoint Service page, there are various settings to configure, which we'll discuss now. While most of the settings can be left to their default values, some need to be configured in order to address specific requirements.

# Application Settings

The PerformancePoint Server Application Settings page (Figure 17–14) contains a variety of settings that control the performance and behavior of PPS. These settings apply only to sites associated with this instance of PerformancePoint Services.

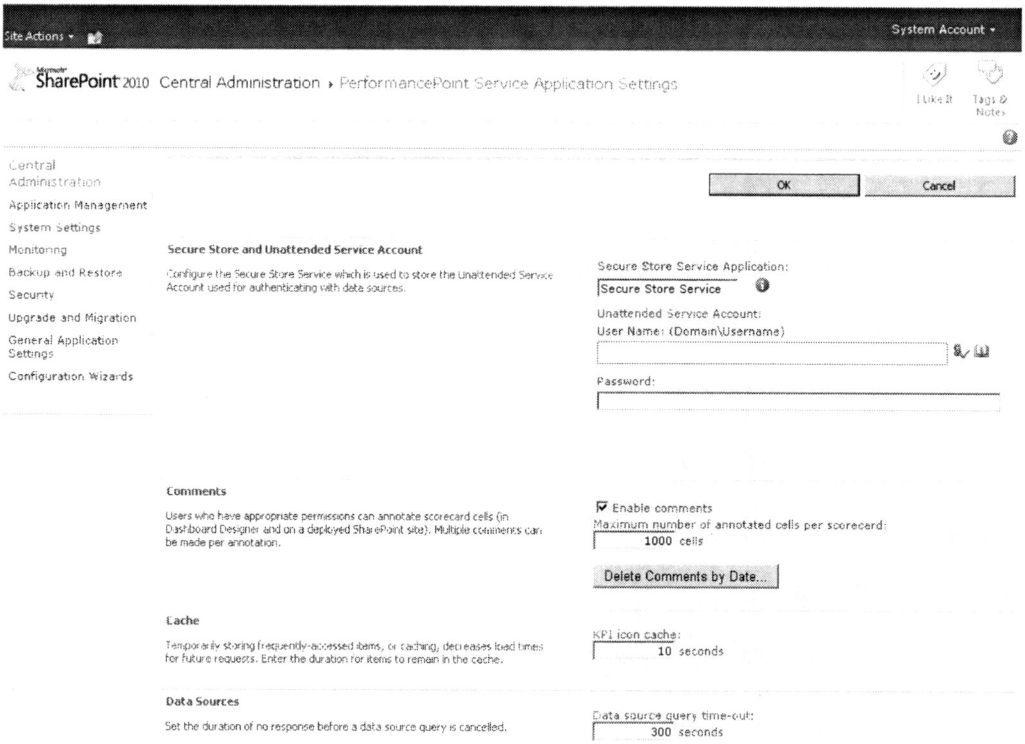

*Figure 17–14. PerformancePoint Services Application Settings page*

## Secure Store and Unattended Service Account

The purpose of this section is to configure the unattended service account. Recall that this is the Active Directory domain account that will be used when accessing data sources without using the user's own identity (Kerberos). The credentials for this account are stored in the Secure Store Service. See "Securing PerformancePoint Solutions" earlier in this chapter.

This section of the page has three entry boxes. The first textbox is used to identify the SSS application to be used for the account's credentials. The second and third boxes allow for the entry of the user name and password of the account, respectively. Remember that this account should have minimal permissions but provide access to all necessary data.

## Comments

Each dashboard user can be given permission to add comments to the cells in a PPS scorecard. These comments are then available to other users when they view that scorecard. The comment functionality also uses the term *annotation*. Technically, a scorecard cell can have one annotation and each annotation can have multiple comments.

This section of the page contains a checkbox that can be used to enable the annotation feature within the PPS instance. There is also a setting that limits the number of annotations that can exist on a single scorecard. The default is 1,000 annotations per scorecard.

There is also a Delete Comments by Date... button that displays the dialog shown in Figure 17–15. This dialog can be used to start a background job that will clean up comments older than a given date, which can use useful if it becomes necessary to reclaim space in the SQL database associated with this PPS instance. The name of this database is based on the name of the PPS application and a unique GUID, like "PPS Application_d17430dcfa17de40817a84dcb1b0c39f78e".

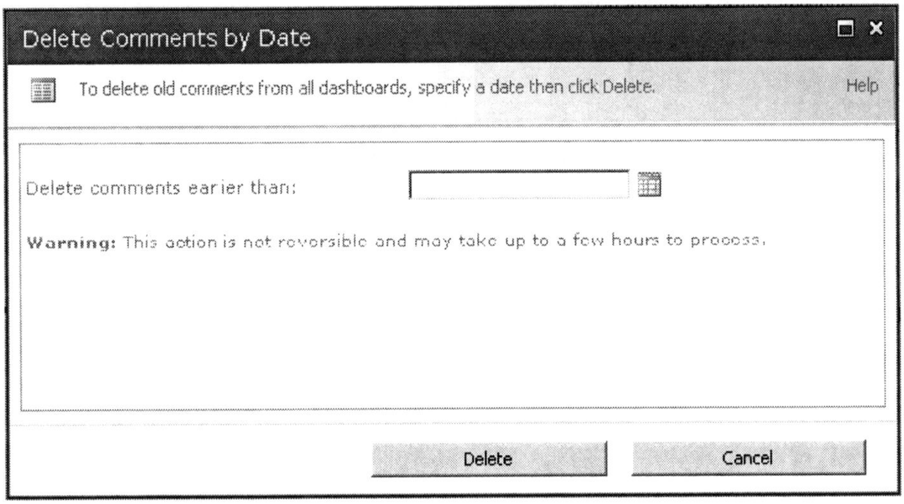

*Figure 17–15. The Delete Comments by Date dialog*

# Cache

The cache section of the page contains a single entry that sets how long (in seconds) the images associated with KPIs should remain in memory before the memory is reclaimed. The default is 10 seconds, which should allow the image to be reused several times during the rendering of a single page. If your site makes heavy use of only a few unique indicators, it may make sense to extend this value to keep from frequently reloading them from disk.

# Data Sources

This section allows the administrator to set a standard timeout on a data source, preventing pages from becoming unresponsive when a data source becomes slow or unavailable. The default is 300 seconds, which should be sufficient in most cases. If data access is consistently over 5 minutes, either the data source is not responding properly or the queries being used to access the data should be reconsidered. When data access for a dashboard page takes a very long time, two major problems result.

First, system resources are consumed processing and returning large amounts of data that will, most likely, never be used. The thread, table, memory, and I/O locking and contention created by executing very large queries can quickly drain system performance for all users.

Second, users are not going to wait for several minutes each time they interact with the dashboard. A user viewing a dashboard is trying to avoid information overload, so loading 1,000 or more records defeats this purpose. Long wait times degrade the user experience and lead to dashboards that aren't used.

## Filters

Filters are used on dashboards to set how the data is "sliced." PerformancePoint dashboards have the ability to remember the last filter values used by each user. This is valuable when moving from one dashboard page to another or when returning to a dashboard on a future visit.

To avoid storing this data forever, this configuration section allows the administrator to set a time out (in days) for how long to retain unused filter values.

The maximum number of members that can be loaded into a filter tree (see Figure 17–16) is configured here as well. Each time you use a filter, you are selecting a set of values to apply with the filter. For example, if you select the year 2010 at the Months level of the date hierarchy, you are selecting 12 values that must be stored for the filter. If you are selecting at the Day level, there are 365 values that must be stored. Each of these values is called a *member* of the filter. This setting prevents very large selection lists from slowing down the server for all users.

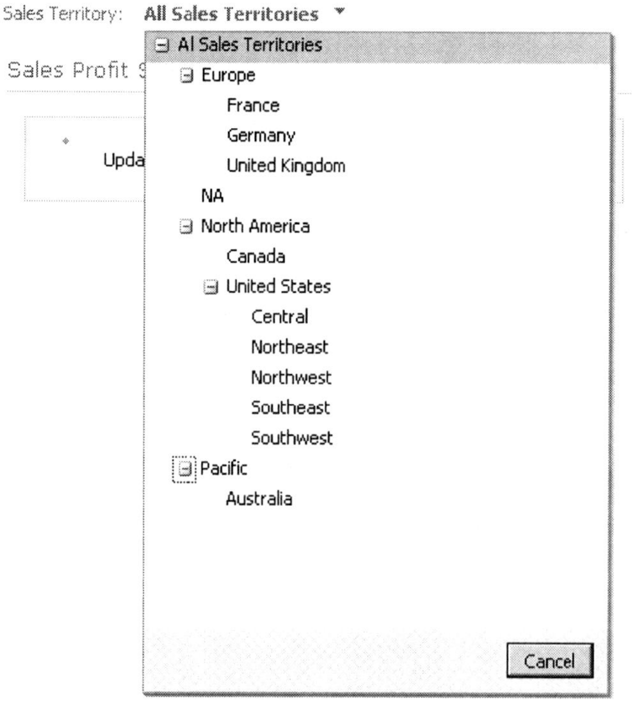

*Figure 17–16. Sample filter tree control*

## Select Measure Control

This setting is similar to the Filters section except that it applies to the selection of measures on a dashboard.

## Show Details

The Show Details feature allows an end-user to drill into a value that is derived from Analysis Services. The functionality of the drill-through is controlled by Analysis Services but it is rendered by PerformancePoint Services (see Figure 17–17). These settings limit the performance impact that this feature can have on the server hosting the PPS application.

| Reseller Sales Amount | Reseller Order Quantity | Reseller Extended Amount | Reseller Tax Amount | Reseller Freight Cost | Discount Amount | Reseller Unit Price | Unit Price Discount Percent | Res |
|---|---|---|---|---|---|---|---|---|
| 164.4279 | 1 | 234.897 | 13.1542 | 4.1107 | 70.4691 | 234.897 | 0.3 | |
| 1973.1348 | 12 | 2818.764 | 157.8508 | 49.3284 | 845.6292 | 234.897 | 0.3 | |
| 164.4279 | 1 | 234.897 | 13.1542 | 4.1107 | 70.4691 | 234.897 | 0.3 | |
| 780.8182 | 1 | 780.8182 | 62.4655 | 19.5205 | 0 | 780.8182 | 0 | |
| 28.8404 | 1 | 28.8404 | 2.3072 | 0.721 | 0 | 28.8404 | 0 | |
| 780.8182 | 1 | 780.8182 | 62.4655 | 19.5205 | 0 | 780.8182 | 0 | |
| 35.994 | 1 | 35.994 | 2.8795 | 0.8999 | 0 | 35.994 | 0 | |
| 40.373 | 2 | 40.373 | 3.2298 | 1.0093 | 0 | 20.1865 | 0 | |
| 1242.8518 | 1 | 1242.8518 | 99.4281 | 31.0713 | 0 | 1242.8518 | 0 | |
| 109.341 | 3 | 109.341 | 8.7473 | 2.7335 | 0 | 36.447 | 0 | |
| 283.23 | 2 | 283.23 | 22.6584 | 7.0808 | 0 | 141.615 | 0 | |
| 45.588 | 2 | 45.588 | 3.647 | 1.1397 | 0 | 22.794 | 0 | |
| 2485.7036 | 2 | 2485.7036 | 198.8563 | 62.1426 | 0 | 1242.8518 | 0 | |
| 182.352 | 8 | 182.352 | 14.5882 | 4.5588 | 0 | 22.794 | 0 | |
| 224.97 | 5 | 224.97 | 17.9976 | 5.6243 | 0 | 44.994 | 0 | |
| 20.1865 | 1 | 20.1865 | 1.6149 | 0.5047 | 0 | 20.1865 | 0 | |
| 33.7745 | 1 | 33.7745 | 2.702 | 0.8444 | 0 | 33.7745 | 0 | |
| 5.1865 | 1 | 5.1865 | 0.4149 | 0.1297 | 0 | 5.1865 | 0 | |
| 60.5595 | 3 | 60.5595 | 4.8448 | 1.514 | 0 | 20.1865 | 0 | |
| 22.794 | 1 | 22.794 | 1.8235 | 0.5699 | 0 | 22.794 | 0 | |
| 105.294 | 2 | 105.294 | 8.4235 | 2.6324 | 0 | 52.647 | 0 | |

*Figure 17–17. Sample Show Details report*

The "Initial retrieval limit" limits the number of rows that can be retrieved on the first page of the details report. The default of 1,000 is generally sufficient without creating too great a load on the server. The "Maximum retrieval limit" is used to prevent excessively large datasets from being returned on subsequent pages of the report. You can either choose a fixed number of rows or leave control of this setting with Analysis Services. To reduce page load times and unnecessary server traffic, consider reducing this value to one in line with the expected use of the report.

## Decomposition Tree

The Decomposition Tree feature is a very powerful analytical tool, with an interface designed to be simple and intuitive to an untrained user (see Figure 17–18). The Decomposition Tree leverages the dimensions already built into the solution to drive the analysis. It allows users to do complex analysis without involving a developer.

However, because of the large number of members that a dimension might contain, it can become a performance drain on the system.

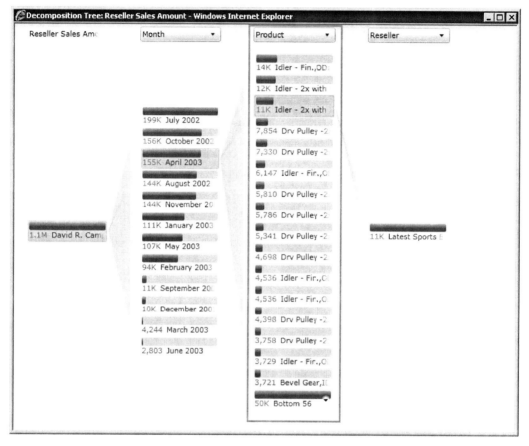

*Figure 17–18. Decomposition Tree*

Each item listed in a vertical column of the decomposition tree is counted against this limit. Note that this limit applies to only one column of items as highlighted in Figure 17–18. The total number of items in all columns may well exceed this value. This limit should not be set higher than is needed for the users to perform the analysis required.

## Trusted Data Source Locations

PerformancePoint Services stores its metadata in SharePoint lists and libraries. These locations must be listed as "trusted" before PPS will consider them valid locations from which to read its objects. By default, all locations within SharePoint are automatically considered trusted, as Figure 17–19 shows.

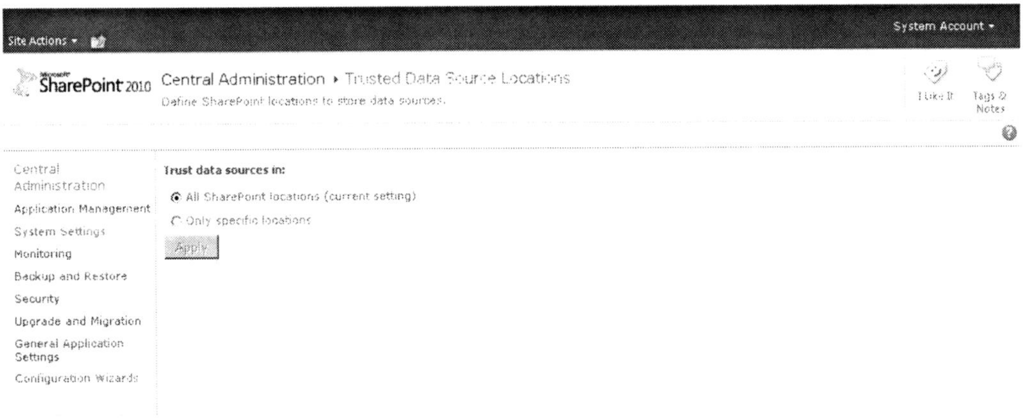

**Figure 17–19.** *Trusted data source locations (default setting)*

Note that just because the location is trusted by PerformancePoint, it is not necessarily accessible by any particular user. The SharePoint permissions on those items still control access to them. The fact that they are in a trusted location only allows PPS to use them if the user has access to them.

If there's a need to restrict the locations from which a PPS application can load data sources, switch this setting to "Only specific locations" and click Apply. This will enable a new set of options for adding specific locations, as shown in Figure 17–20.

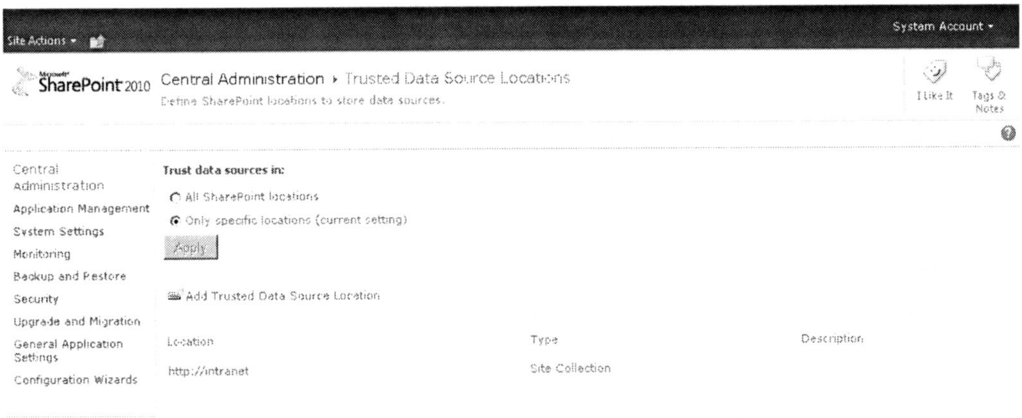

**Figure 17–20.** *Trusted data source locations (specific locations enabled)*

To add a location with this dialog box:

6. Click on Add Trusted Data Source Location. The dialog shown in Figure 17–21 will be displayed.

7. Enter the URL of a SharePoint-based site or document library. Only SharePoint locations can be used.

8. Click on the validation button to the right of the URL textbox. If the location is a valid one, the other controls will be enabled.

9. Select the Location Type option to use and enter a description for the trusted location.

10. Click OK to create the trusted location.

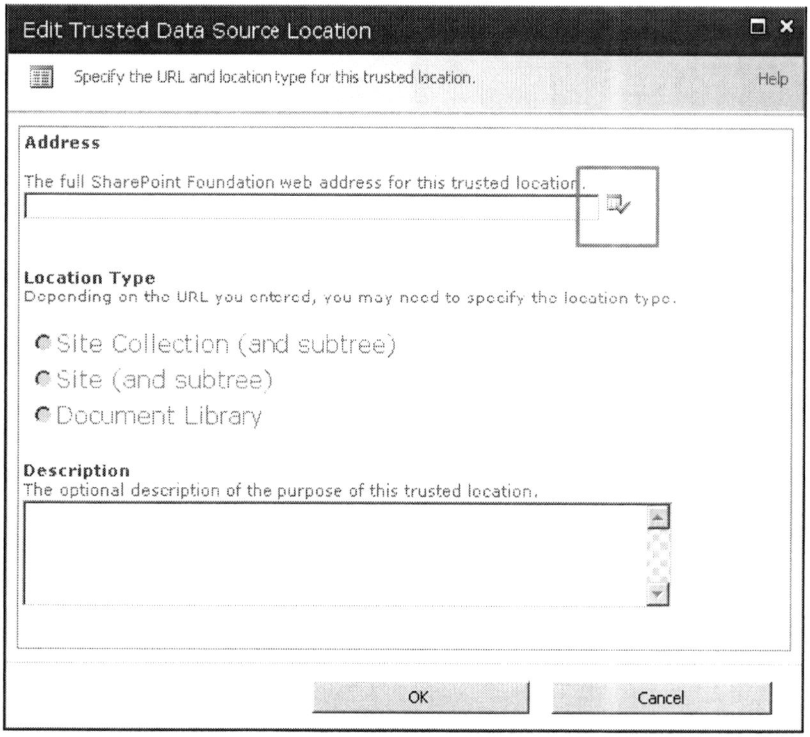

*Figure 17–21. Creating a specific trusted data source location*

# Trusted Content Locations

Trusted Content Locations are configured in the same way as trusted data source locations with the following exception. PPS content items created by the Dashboard Designer application, such as KPIs, Scorecard, Reports, and so on are stored in SharePoint lists instead of in document libraries. Therefore, when selecting trusted locations, the options are Site, Site Collection, or List.

# Import PerformancePoint Server 2007 Content

As mentioned in the introduction to this chapter, PerformancePoint was previously a stand-alone server product called Microsoft PerformancePoint Server 2007. The Monitoring module of that product supported many of the same types of objects (including scorecards and dashboards) that PerformancePoint Services now supports. The last option on the Manage PerformancePoint Services page is used to import objects from a PPS 2007 monitoring database into the SharePoint lists and libraries to be used with PerformancePoint Services. A wizard helps with the upgrade process.

The first page of the import wizard (Figure 17–22) contains general information about the import process. Before using the import wizard, you'll want to become familiar with both the PPS 2007 and SharePoint 2010 environments, including security and source and destination locations. Microsoft provides guidance specifically for planning this process, which you'll find at `http://technet.microsoft.com/en-us/library/ee74817117.aspx`.

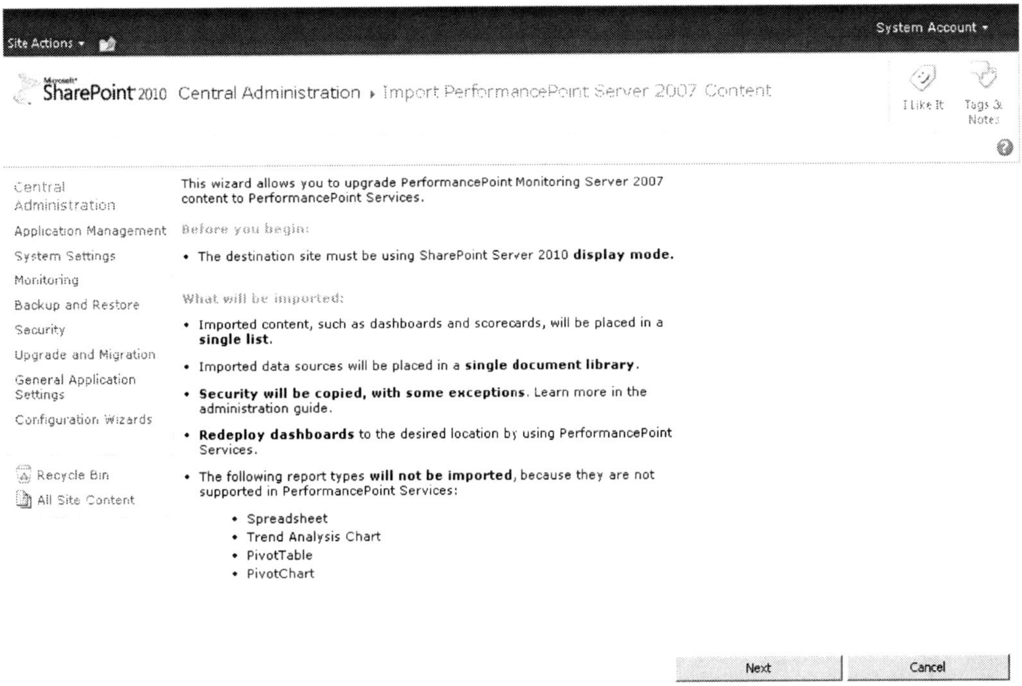

**Figure 17–22.** *The import wizard introduction page*

After you click Next on the introduction page, you'll see the page shown in Figure 17–23. This page lets you identify the security mode used by the original PerformancePoint Server 2007 installation. Select the correct mode and click Next.

**Figure 17–23.** *Step 1–Identifying the authentication mode*

In step 2 of the wizard (Figure 17–24), you enter the database credentials to be used to connect to the PPS 2007 content database. This is the database where the dashboards were stored in the previous installation.

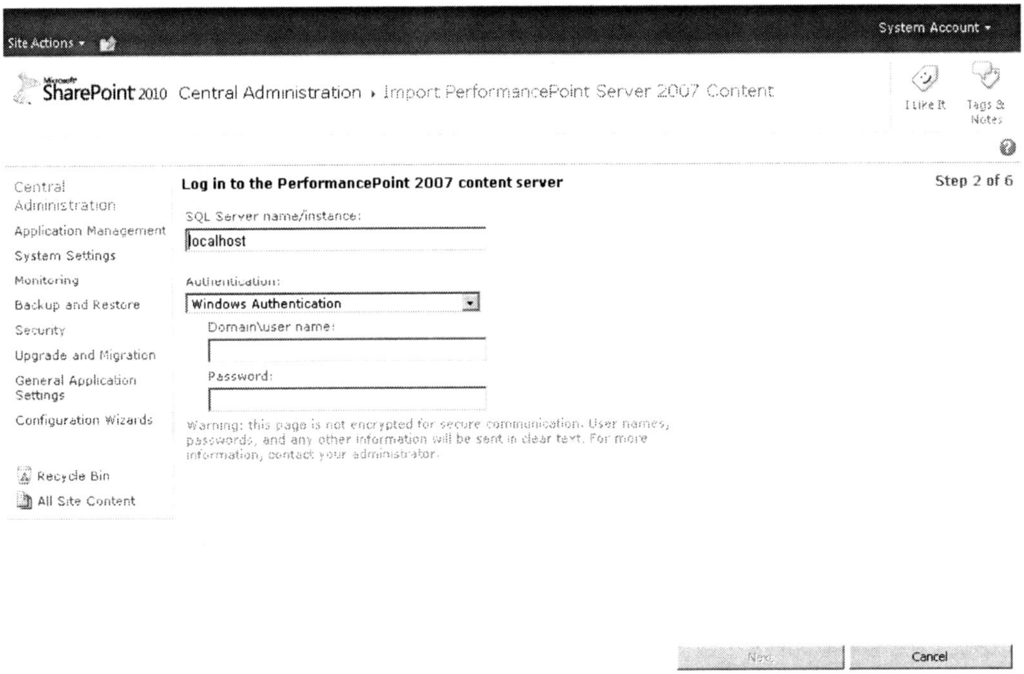

*Figure 17–24. Step 2–Entering credentials*

The credentials you enter can use either SQL or Windows authentication but they must have access to the PPS 2007 content to be migrated. Click Next when ready.

Step 3 (Figure 17–25) identifies the name of the content database to be accessed. Select the database and click Next.

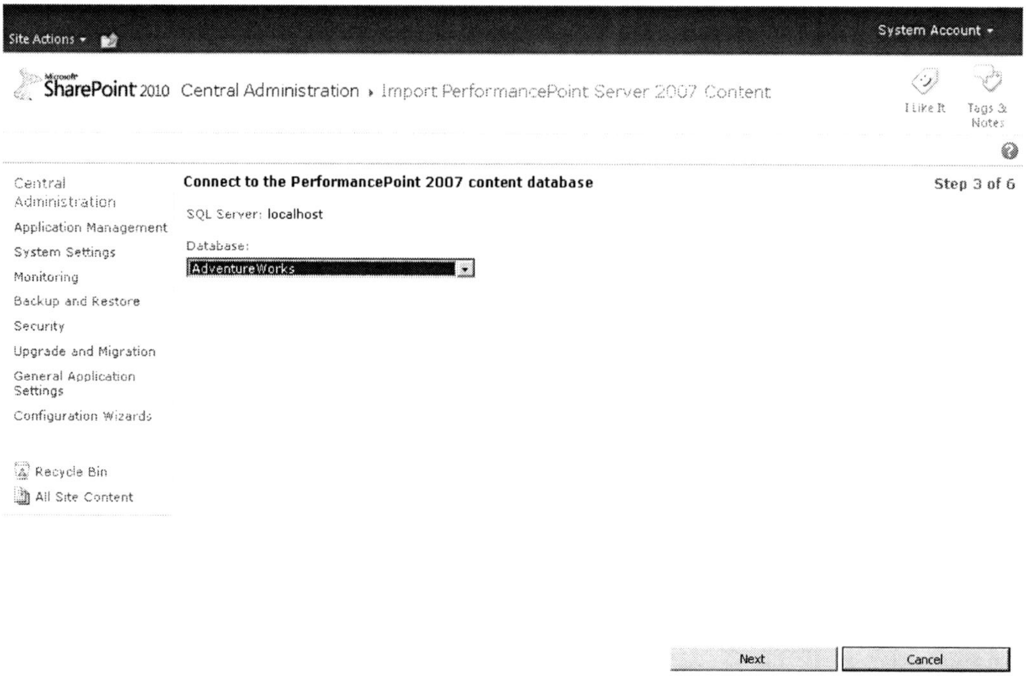

*Figure 17–25. Step 3 – Supplying the name of the content database*

In the remaining steps, you select the destination list and library that will receive the migrated content items. Once the migration starts, a bar will display showing its progress. When the migration is complete, be sure to review the objects and security permissions to resolve any inconsistencies between the old environment and the new. Remember, some PPS 2007 report types are not supported in SharePoint Server 2010, so it may be necessary to rework and redeploy some of your dashboards.

For a complete discussion of the options for upgrading PerformancePoint 2007 content to SharePoint 2010, take a look at the MSDN blog entry at
`blogs.msdn.com/b/performancepoint/archive/2010/02/25/upgrading-performancepoint-server-2007-to-pps-2010.aspx`.

# Managing PerformancePoint with PowerShell

The commands we'll discuss next are the same ones you used in "Setting up PerformancePoint Services," but now we'll use PowerShell commands. As you can see in Tables 17–1, 17–2, 17–3, and 17–4, there are four basic groups of commands: *New* operations, *Get* operations, *Set* operations and *Remove* (clear) operations.

■ **Tip** To obtain additional details and examples for each of these PowerShell commands, use the following commands from the PowerShell command line.

**Get-Help <PS Cmdlet>** for details and

**Get-Help <PS Cmdlet> -examples** for samples

*Table 17–1. New Operations*

| PowerShell Command | Description |
| --- | --- |
| New-SPPerformancePointSericeApplication | Creates a new PerformancePoint Service application.<br><br>Example:<br>New-SPPerformancePointServiceApplication<br> -Name "PPS Application"<br> -ApplicationPool PPSAppPool2 |
| New-SPPerformancePointSericeApplication Proxy | Creates a new proxy for an existing PPS application.<br><br>Example:<br>New-SPPerformancePointServiceApplicationProxy<br> -Name "PPS Application Proxy"<br> -ServiceApplication "PPS Application"<br> -Default |
| New-SPPerformancePointSericeApplication TrustedLocation | Creates a new trusted location for data sources and/or PPS content types.<br><br>Example:<br>New-SPPerformancePointServiceApplication TrustedLocation<br> -ServiceApplication "PPS Application"<br> -url "http://intranet/central/dslib"<br> -Type DocumentLibrary<br> -TrustedLocationType DataSource |

*Table 17–2. Get Operations*

| PowerShell Command | Description |
|---|---|
| Get-SPPerformancePointSecureDataValues | Shows the values of the configuration parameters for the unattended service account. |
| | Example:<br>Get-SPPerformancePointSecureDataValues<br>–ServiceApplication "PPS Application" |
| Get-SPPerformancePointSericeApplication | Retrieves an instance of a PerformancePoint Service application. |
| | Example:<br>Get-SPPerformancePointApplication<br>–ServiceApplication "PPS Application" |
| Get-SPPerformancePointSericeApplication<br><br>TrustedLocation | Retrieves one or more trusted data source and/or content locations for a PPS application. |
| | Example:<br>Get-SPPerformancePointApplication<br>TrustedLocation<br>–ServiceApplication "PPS Application" |

*Table 17–3. Set Operations*

| PowerShell Command | Description |
|---|---|
| Set-SPPerformancePointSecureDataValues | Sets the values of the configuration parameters for the unattended service account. |
| | Example:<br>Set-SPPerformancePointSecureDataValues<br>-ServiceApplication "PPS Application"<br>-DataSourceUnattendedServiceAccount<br>(New-Object<br>System.Management.Automation.<br>PSCredential "CONTOSO\PPSService",<br>(ConvertTo-SecureString<br>"pass@word1" -AsPlainText<br>-Force)) |

| PowerShell Command | Description |
|---|---|
| Set-SPPerformancePointSericeApplication | Sets top-level configuration parameters for an existing PPS instance.<br><br>Example:<br>Set-SPPerformancePointServiceApplication<br> -Identity "PPS Application"<br> -SelectMeasureMaximum 100 |

*Table 17–4. Remove / Clear Operations*

| PowerShell Command | Description |
|---|---|
| Clear-SPPerformancePointSericeApplication<br><br>TrustedLocation | Removes all of the configured trusted data source and/or content locations for a PPS instance.<br><br>Example:<br>Clear-SPPerformancePointServiceApplication<br>TrustedLocation<br> -ServiceApplication "PPS Application"<br> -TrustedLocationType Content |
| Remove-SPPerformancePointSericeApplication | Removes an instance of the PerformancePoint Service application.<br><br>Example:<br>Remove-SPPerformancePointService Application<br> -Identity "PPS Application" |
| Remove -SPPerformancePointSericeApplication<br><br>Proxy | Removes a PPS application proxy object.<br><br>Example:<br>Remove-SPPerformancePointService<br>ApplicationProxy<br> -Identity "PPS Application Proxy" |
| Remove -SPPerformancePointSericeApplication<br><br>TrustedLocation | Removes one trusted data source and/or content location.<br><br>Example:<br>Get-SPPerformancePointApplication<br>TrustedLocation<br> –ServiceApplication "PPS Application"<br> \| Remove-<br> SPPerformancePointServiceApplication<br> TrustedLocation |

# Authoring and Publishing PerformancePoint Solutions

In this section, we will create all of the PerformancePoint content objects necessary to implement a typical business intelligence dashboard using data from the AdventureWorks sample database. Our solution will include the KPIs, scorecards, filters, reports, and dashboards necessary to provide the user with a rich data analysis environment. We will deploy this solution to SharePoint and explore the resulting user experience.

In the following section, "Advanced Report Types," we will then expand on this solution by adding reports to the dashboard based on Excel Services and Strategy Map report types.

---

■ **Note** This tutorial will make extensive use of the AdventureWorks SSAS solution. You can download the Adventure Works database from `http://msftdbprodsamples.codeplex.com/`. Take a look at Chapter 1 for details about deploying the solution as an SSAS database.

---

## PROBLEM CASE

Author and publish a BI solution that allows a marketing manager at AdventureWorks to analyze the effectiveness of their marketing campaigns by product and sales channel.

### Solution:

The solution for this case will be created in the following sequence.

1. Enable all necessary features in SharePoint and create a site using the Business Intelligence Center site template.

2. Create a Dashboard Designer workspace in which to create the solution components.

3. Create a data source from which to retrieve the business data.

4. Create a set of key performance indicators (KPIs) representing the data.

5. Create a scorecard to display the KPIs.

6. Create a set of filters to control how the data is sliced by the user.

7. Create a set of reports allowing the user to perform analysis on the underlying data.

8. Create a dashboard that integrates all of these components into an interactive analysis engine designed to help the user make decisions.

9. Deploy the solution to SharePoint and examine the user experience exposed by the dashboard.

Before attempting to follow this tutorial, you should already be familiar with basic BI and PPS concepts such as dimensions, measures, KPIs, scorecards, etc. If not, please refer to "Business Intelligence Solution Components" earlier in this chapter for PPS components and Chapter 1 for dimensional modeling concepts.

# Deploying the Business Intelligence Center

We will create a work area for our solution by deploying the PerformancePoint Business Intelligence Center site template. First we must verify that the necessary features are activated at the site-collection level. You will need site collection administrator rights in order to enable features and create the site.

- Open the root web site in the site collection to host the solution.

- Select Site Settings from the Site Actions menu.

- Select Site Collection Administration ➤ Site Collection Features.

- Activate the SharePoint Server Enterprise Site Collection Features feature if it's not already active (Figure 17–26).

- Activate the PerformancePoint Services Site Collection Features feature if it is not already active(Figure 17–26).

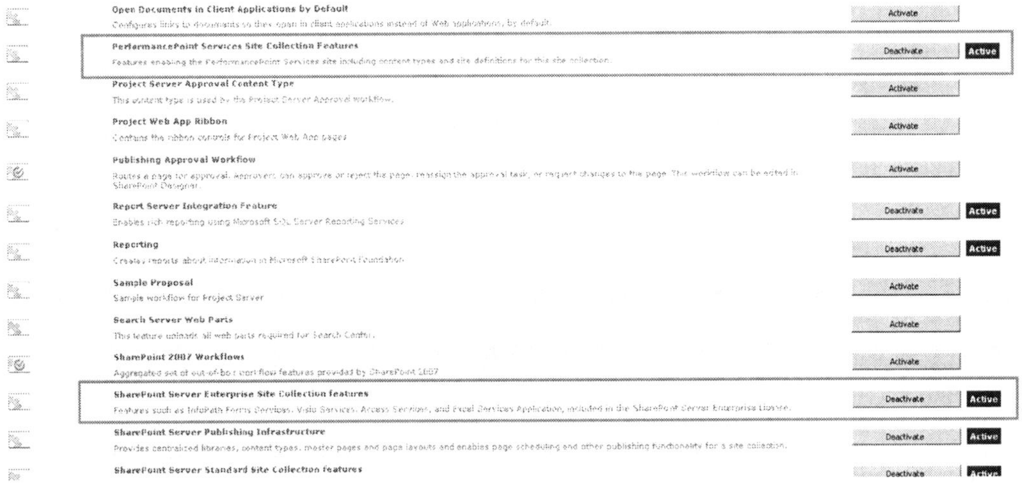

*Figure 17–26. Activating SharePoint and PerformancePoint site collection features*

- Navigate to the site under which you want to create the BI Center. In the parent site, create the site using the Business Intelligence Center site template (Figure 17–27).

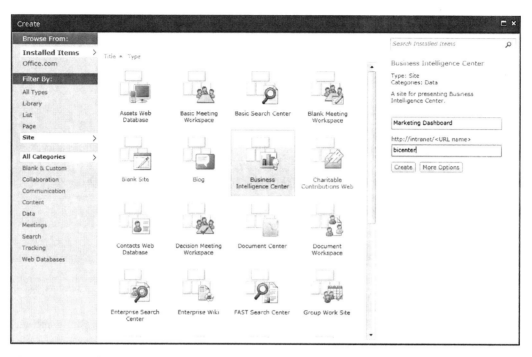

*Figure 17–27. Selecting the Business Intelligence Center site template*

The site created has all of the lists and libraries needed to deploy a complete PerformancePoint solution. It also contains informational content describing the site's purpose, which you can delete when you no longer need it.

## Creating a Dashboard Designer Workspace

All of the objects we create for our solution will be stored in a Dashboard Designer Workspace file, which is stored on your local desktop with a DDWX file extension. This file acts as an offline store for these objects until you are ready to publish them to SharePoint. The workspace file is similar to a Visual Studio solution file in that it allows you to organize, edit, and manage all of the components of your solution in one place.

Because the Dashboard Designer is a one-click Windows application, there is no executable to download and install on the desktop. The easiest way to install it is simply to use it and then save a file. We will do this as part of the next section.

## Creating a Data Source

Now let's create a data source from which to retrieve business data for our dashboard.

- Navigate to the BI Center site and click on the Data Connections library link in the Quick menu to the left. This will take you to the data source library for the solution.

- From the ribbon menu at the top of the page, select Library Tools ➤ Documents ➤ New Document ➤ PerformancePoint Data Source (Figure 17–28).

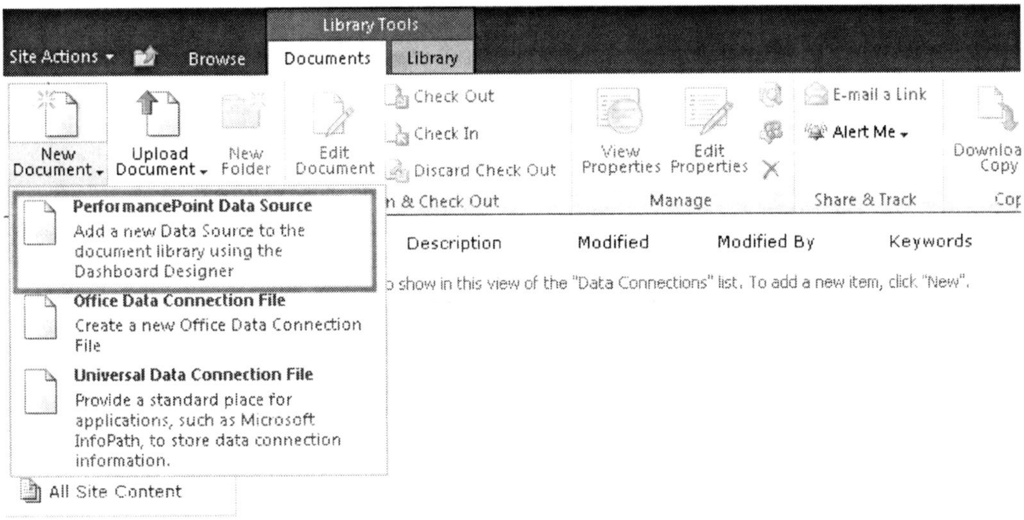

*Figure 17–28. Adding a PerformancePoint data source*

This will launch the Dashboard Designer. If this is the first time you've used it, you'll see messages and progress bars indicating that it's installing. The Web browser may ask you to authorize the installation. Finally, the designer will be shown with an empty workspace and the Select a Data Source Template dialog displayed, as shown in Figure 17–29.

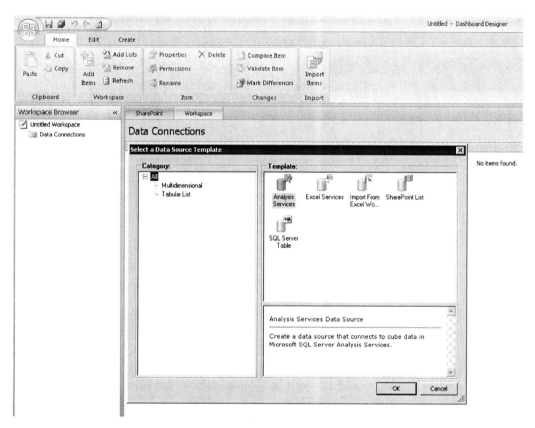

**Figure 17–29.** *Selecting a data source template*

- Our data will come from the Adventure Works OLAP database, so select the
  Analysis Services template and click OK, and you'll see the dialog shown in Figure
  17–30.

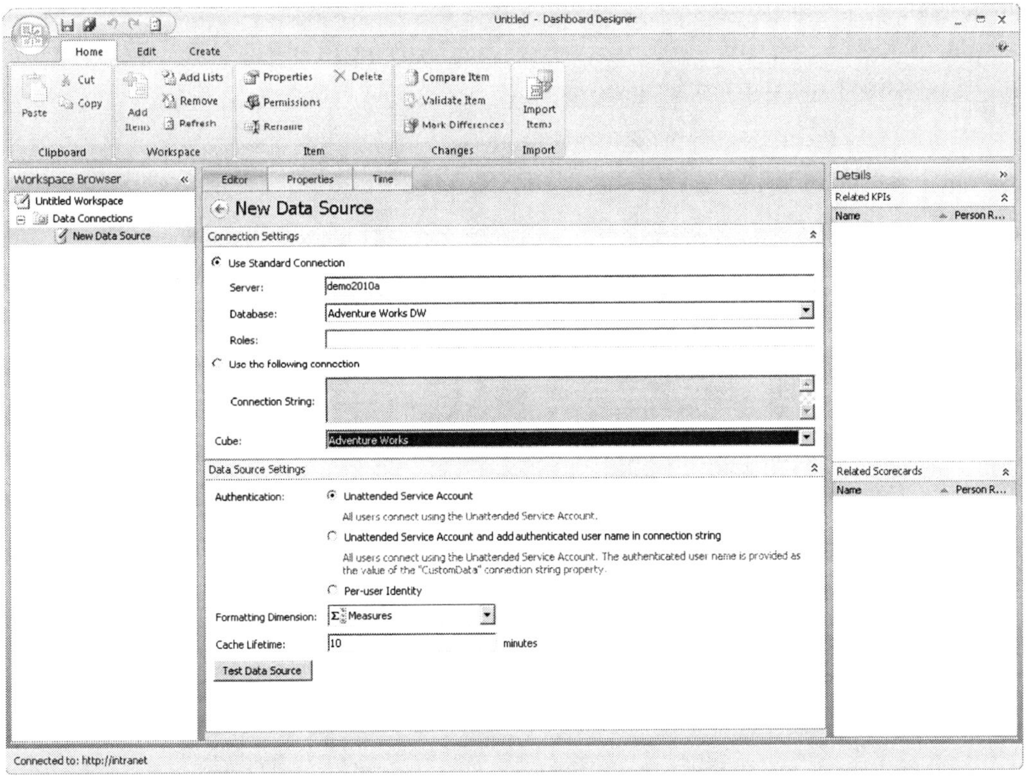

*Figure 17–30. The New Data Source screen*

Take a moment to find your way around the Dashboard Designer application—you'll spend a lot of time here! At the top is a ribbon menu system that works like any Office 2010 application. The options that appear in the ribbon will change as the context of the central window changes.

On the left side of the window is the Workspace Browser, which is a tree listing the contents of the workspace. Currently, this list shows one workspace file called Untitled Workspace, one SharePoint list called Data Connections, and one item within that list—a data source currently named New Data Source.

The editor for the item selected in the left-hand list is displayed in the center window where changes can be made. This window will have a set of tabs across the top based on the type of object being edited. The Properties tab is common to all objects and is used to name and organize objects within the workspace.

To the right of the center window are panels that list the objects within the workspace that are related to the current item.

- In the center window, under New Data Source ➤ Connection Settings ➤ Use Standard Connection, enter the name of the SSAS server instance containing the AdventureWorks OLAP cubes in the Server textbox.

- Select the "Adventure Works DW" SSAS database from the Database list.

- At the bottom of Connection Settings, select the Adventure Works cube from the Cube list.

- Note the defaults for the Data Source Settings panel but don't make any changes.

- Switch to the Properties tab in the center window.

- Enter "Adventure Works" for the name of the data source.

- Switch to the Time tab, where you can specify the cube's primary time dimension (Figure 17–31).

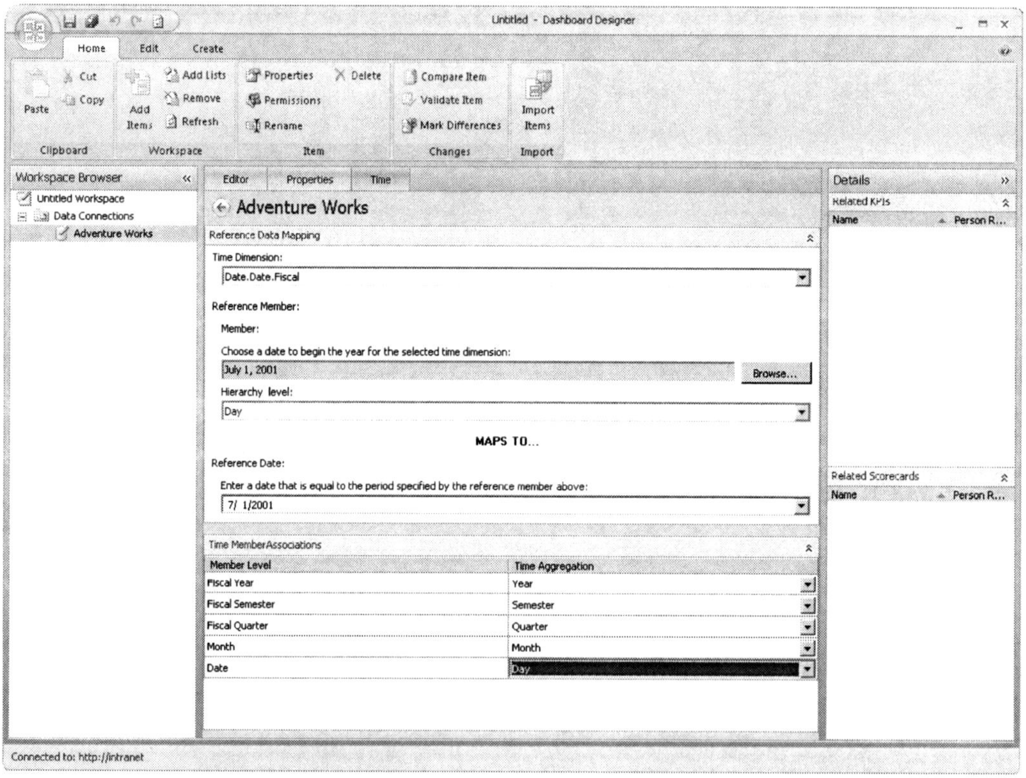

*Figure 17–31. Selecting a time dimension*

- The Time Dimension drop-down will list all of the hierarchies available in the cube. Select "Date.Date.Fiscal." This is a fiscal calendar that begins on the first of July of each year.

- Under Reference Member, select a member from the dimension that represents the first day of the fiscal year, such as July 1, 2001.

- For the Reference Date, enter the same date in your regional format. This allows PerformancePoint to understand how years are structured in the date dimension.

■ **Note** Depending on when you downloaded the AdventureWorks sample databases, the actual dates available in your cube may be different from those shown. The sample database used here has data from FY 2002 to FY 2005.

- Under Time Member Associations, select the time dimension hierarchy levels as shown in Figure 17–32.

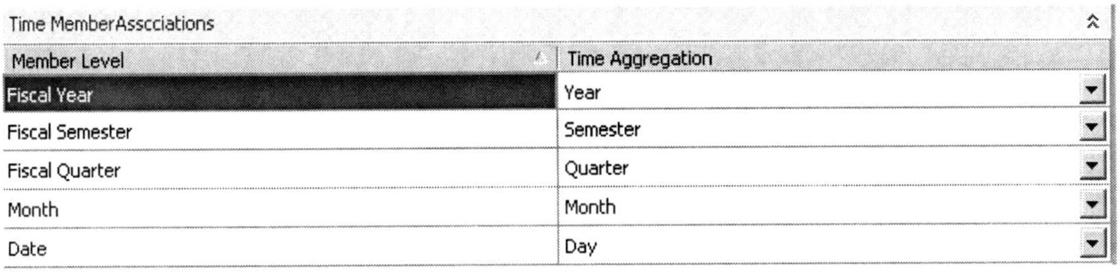

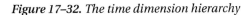

| Time Member Assosciations | | ≫ |
| --- | --- | --- |
| Member Level | Time Aggregation | |
| Fiscal Year | Year | ▾ |
| Fiscal Semester | Semester | ▾ |
| Fiscal Quarter | Quarter | ▾ |
| Month | Month | ▾ |
| Date | Day | ▾ |

*Figure 17–32. The time dimension hierarchy*

At first glance, it may seem strange to enter all of this information about the time dimension in the editor you're using to create a data source. The reason for doing this is that it allows the use of Time Intelligence filters. These very powerful tools will help when it comes time to present data to the user. See "Creating Filters" later in this chapter for details. Now that the data source is set up, let's go back and finish setting up the workspace itself.

- Select Untitled Workspace on the Workspace Browser.

- Click the Save icon at the top of the window. This will cause the file save dialog to be displayed (Figure 17–33).

***Figure 17–33.*** *Saving the workplace*

If you go back to the Data Connections library in your BI Center site, you'll see that there's one data source there. Why is it called New Data Source? The answer is that we haven't yet published the data source we created to SharePoint. We've only saved it to the workspace file.

---

■ **Hint:** You can tell that an item hasn't been published because there is a pencil superimposed on its icon in the Workspace Browser.

---

- Select the Adventure Works data source in the Workspace Browser.

- Click the Save icon again. The pencil icon will disappear from the item and the data source should appear correctly in the Data Connections Library (Figure 17–34).

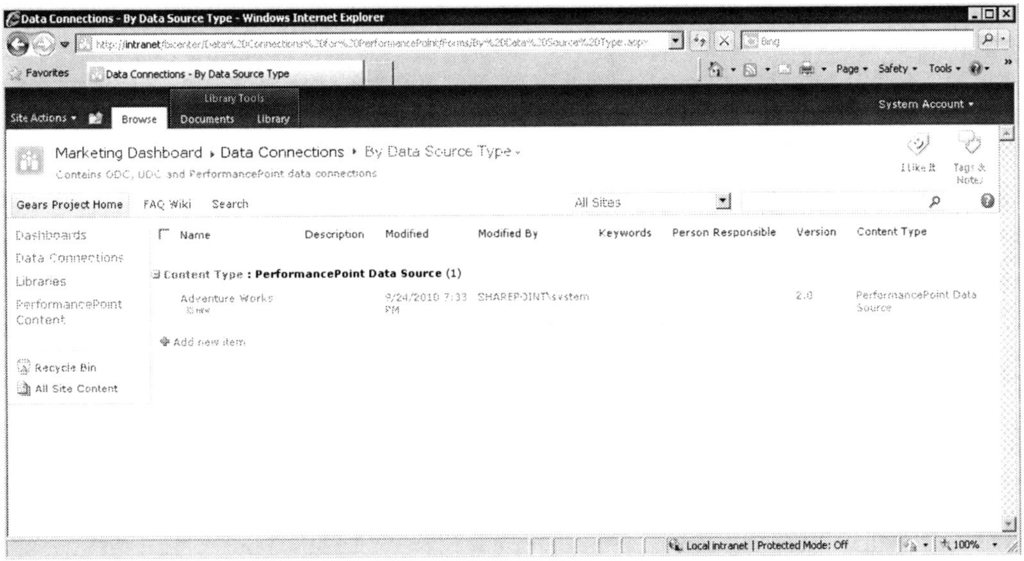

*Figure 17–34. Saving the PerformancePoint data source to the Data Connections library*

Now that we have set up our data source and started our workspace file, let's get ready to retrieve data for analysis.

# Creating Key Performance Indicators

Our dashboard will contain one set of KPIs. We will create a set of actual and target metrics that will allow the marketing department to track the effectiveness of their promotions in terms of their effect on Gross Profit Margin.

Our workspace is currently connected to the Data Connections library, but that area can only be used to store data sources. To create the KPI, we need to connect our workspace to the PerformancePoint Content list in the BI Center site.

- Open the workspace file Marketing.ddwx that you created in the previous section.

- In the Dashboard Designer's ribbon menu, select Home ➤ Workspace ➤ Add Lists.

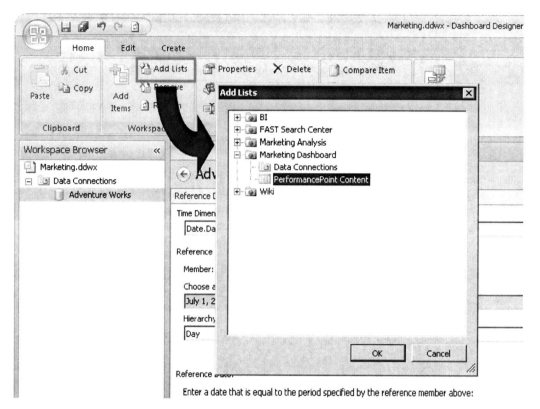

**Figure 17–35.** *Selecting the PerformancePoint content*

- Select PerformancePoint Content from the BI Center site you created earlier and click OK (see Figure 17–35). The PerformancePoint Content list now appears in the Workspace Browser.

- Right-click on the PerformancePoint Content list in the Workspace Browser and select New ➤ KPI (Figure 17–36).

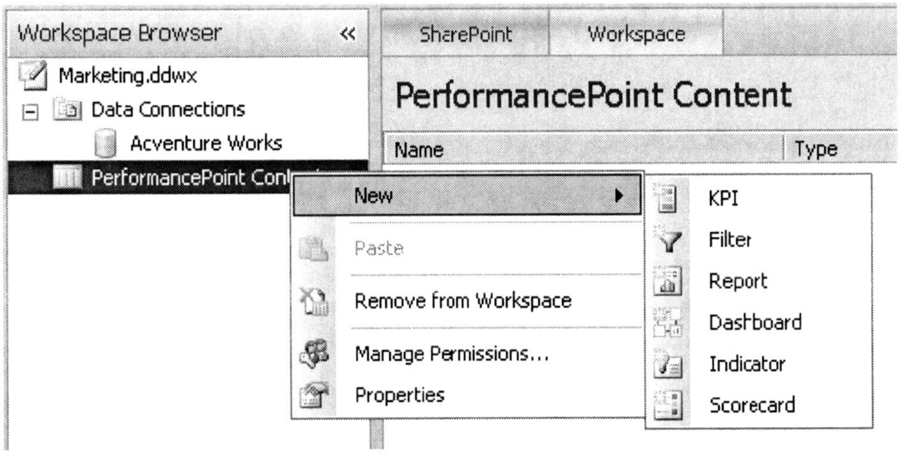

*Figure 17–36. Creating a new KPI*

- Select Blank KPI from the Select a KPI Template dialog (Figure 17–37)and click OK.

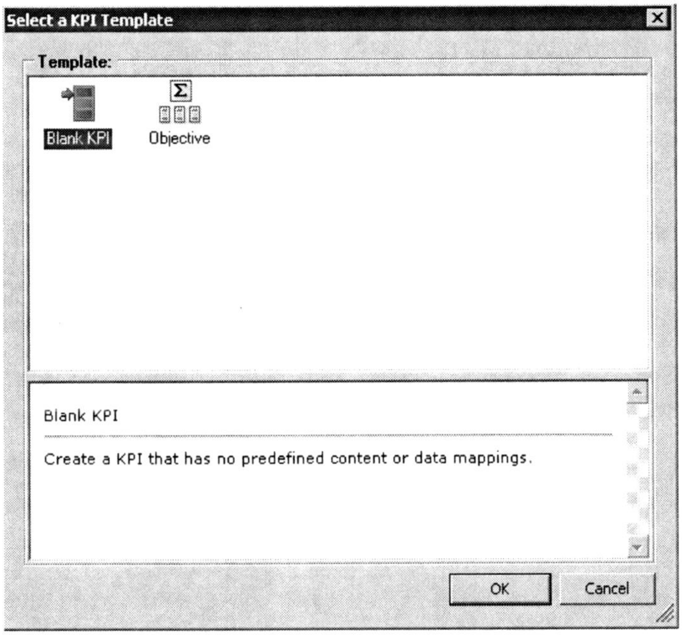

*Figure 17–37. Choosing a blank KPI template*

- The KPI will be created with the name selected in the Workspace Browser, so you can immediately type a name for the KPI. Enter "Profit Margin KPI" and press Enter.

• Select the Properties tab and set the Display Folder to "KPIs" (Figure 17–38).

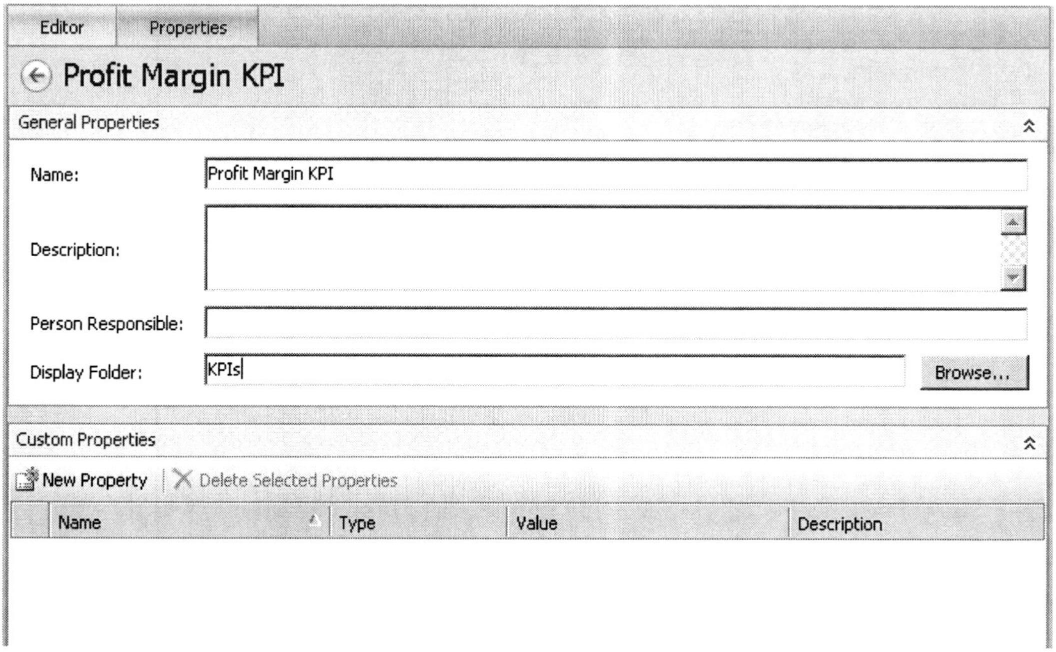

**Figure 17–38.** *Setting the Display Folder;*

• Note that the KPI now appears inside a folder in the Workspace Browser (Figure 17–39).

**Figure 17–39.** *The Profit Margin KPI in the Workspace Browser*

■ **Note** The use of display folders within the Dashboard Designer is entirely optional. Their purpose is only to help keep the solution organized. They have no effect on anything other than how items are displayed in the Workspace Browser. Workspace folders do not get reflected in the folder structure of the content list in PerformancePoint or anywhere else outside of Dashboard Designer. Typically, they are used to separate items by type (KPIs, Filters, Dashboards, etc.) or functionally by the part of the solution with which they are associated. Folders can be nested as needed by separating folder names with a backslash (\) character. For the rest of this chapter, items will be placed into such folders but the directions won't mention it each time from here on out.

- Switch to the Editor tab (Figure 17–40), which displays the actual and target metrics for the KPI along with their various settings. We will customize the two metrics that were created by default and then add some or our own.

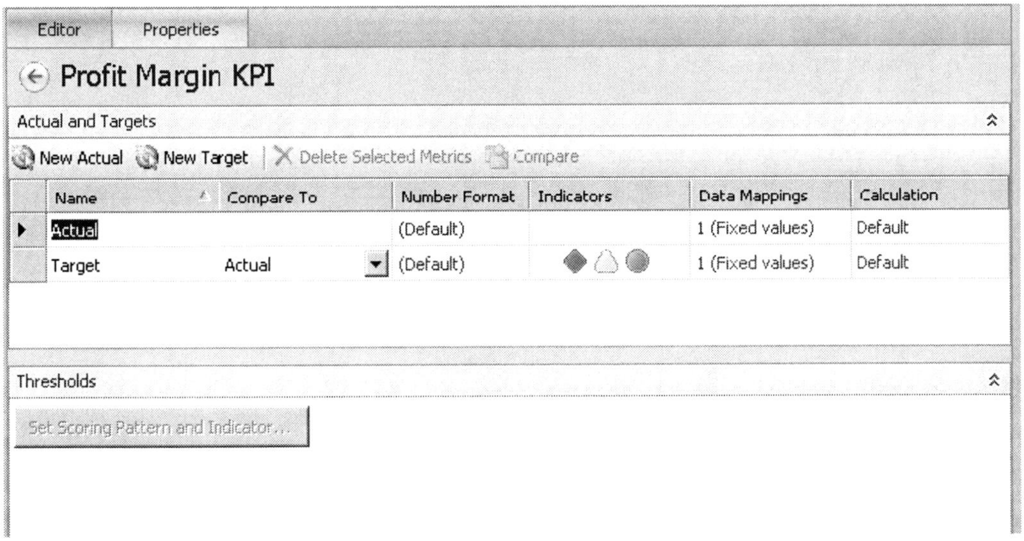

| Editor | Properties |  |  |  |  |  |
|---|---|---|---|---|---|---|

### ← Profit Margin KPI

**Actual and Targets** ⌃

New Actual | New Target | ✕ Delete Selected Metrics | 🔲 Compare

| Name | Compare To | Number Format | Indicators | Data Mappings | Calculation |
|---|---|---|---|---|---|
| ▶ Actual | | (Default) | | 1 (Fixed values) | Default |
| Target | Actual ▾ | (Default) | ◆ △ ● | 1 (Fixed values) | Default |

**Thresholds** ⌃

Set Scoring Pattern and Indicator...

*Figure 17–40. Editing the KPI*

- Select the Name cell, which currently contains "Actual," and change the name to "Gross Profit."

- Click on the cell for the same row under Data Mappings to launch the data mapping dialog. Currently, it is set to return a fixed value of 1. Click the Change Source button to bring up the Select a Data Source dialog (Figure 17–41).

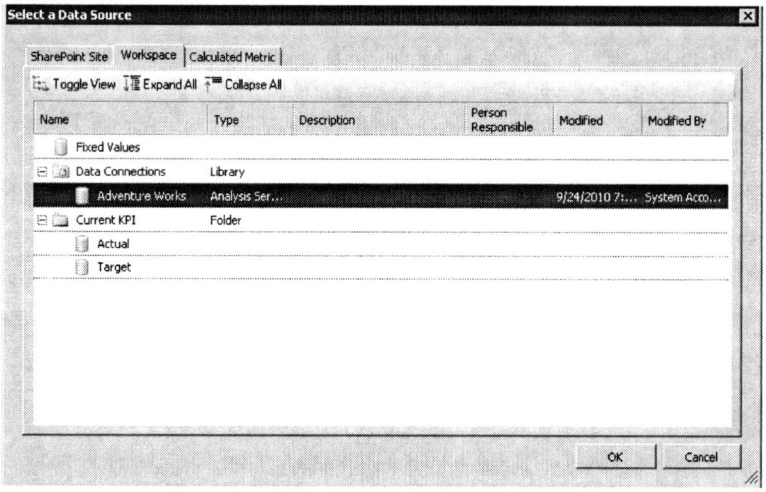

*Figure 17–41. Changing the data source*

- This dialog allows us to select the data source from which we will retrieve the value of the metric we are creating. In this case, the Gross Profit will come from the cube we've configured as a data source. Select "Adventure Works" and click OK. The Dimensional Data Source Mapping dialog is displayed (Figure 17–42).

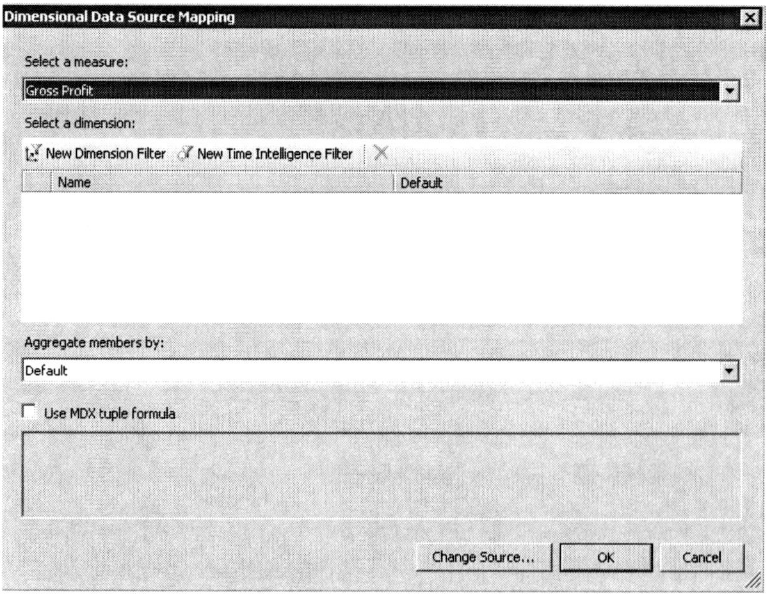

*Figure 17–42. Selecting a measure*

- This dialog allows the designer to select a measure from the cube and, optionally, perform filtering on it or enter an MDX query expression to retrieve the value. Select "Gross Profit" from the Select a measure drop-down and click OK. The result is shown in Figure 17–43.

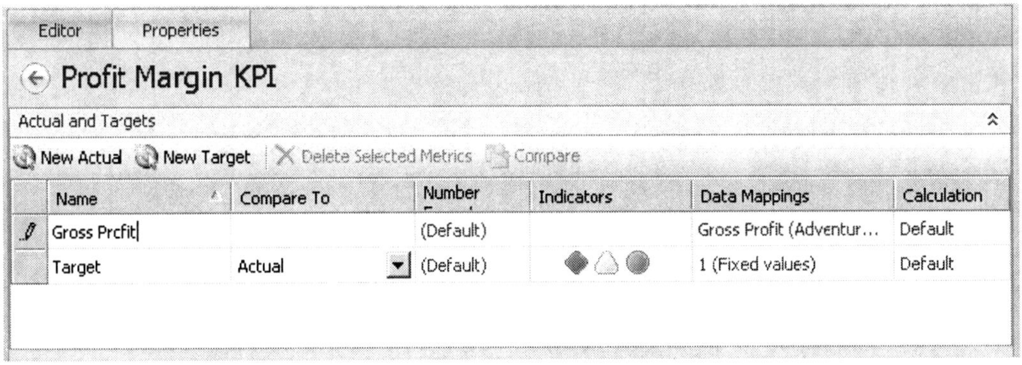

| | Name | Compare To | Number | Indicators | Data Mappings | Calculation |
|---|---|---|---|---|---|---|
| | Gross Prcfit| | | (Default) | | Gross Profit (Adventur... | Default |
| | Target | Actual | (Default) | | 1 (Fixed values) | Default |

*Figure 17–43. Mapping to the Gross Profit measure*

- Now we will create a target that indicates that we want to break even (GP >= $0) on each promotion. Set the name of the target metric to "Breakeven." Then, change the data mapping value to "0" instead of the default of "1". Notice that the Compare To field points to the Gross Profit actual metric. This indicates that the target value, 0, will be compared to the actual value, which is the Gross Profit measure returned from the cube (Figure 17–44).

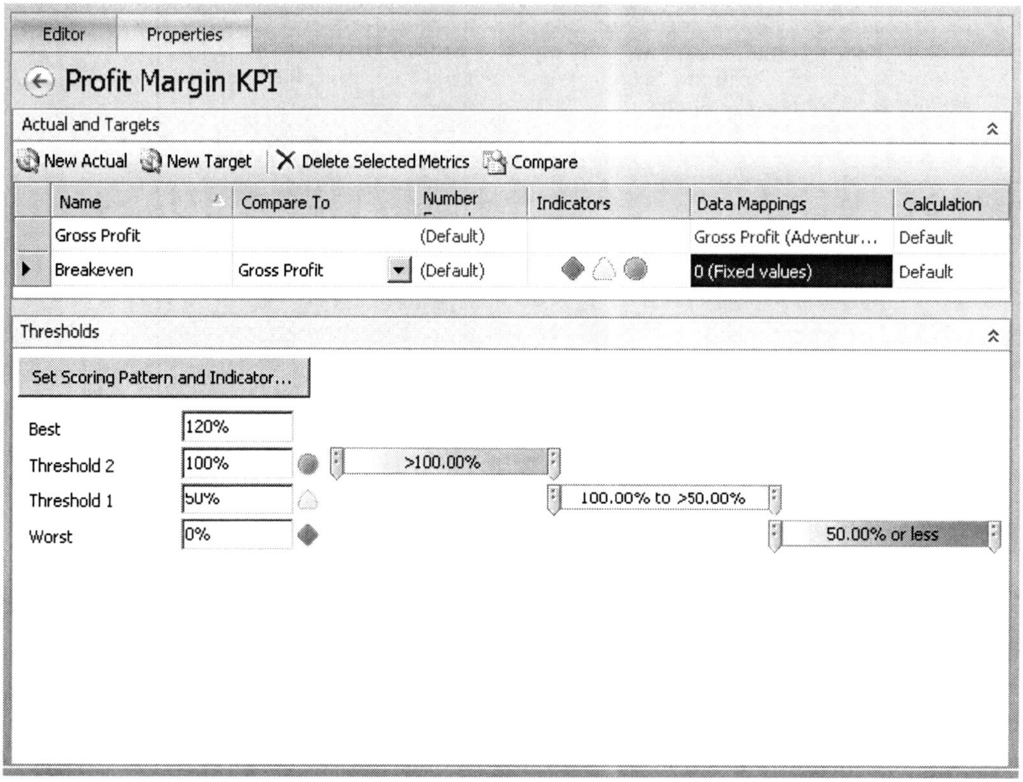

**Figure 17–44.** *Creating a breakeven metric for Gross Profit*

- Now that the actual and target values are set, the Thresholds area at the bottom of the window is activated. The indicator type shown by default is not really appropriate so we will customize it. Click on the Set Scoring Pattern and Indicator… button in the Thresholds panel. This displays a three-step wizard we'll use to configure the appearance of this target metric (Figure 17–45).

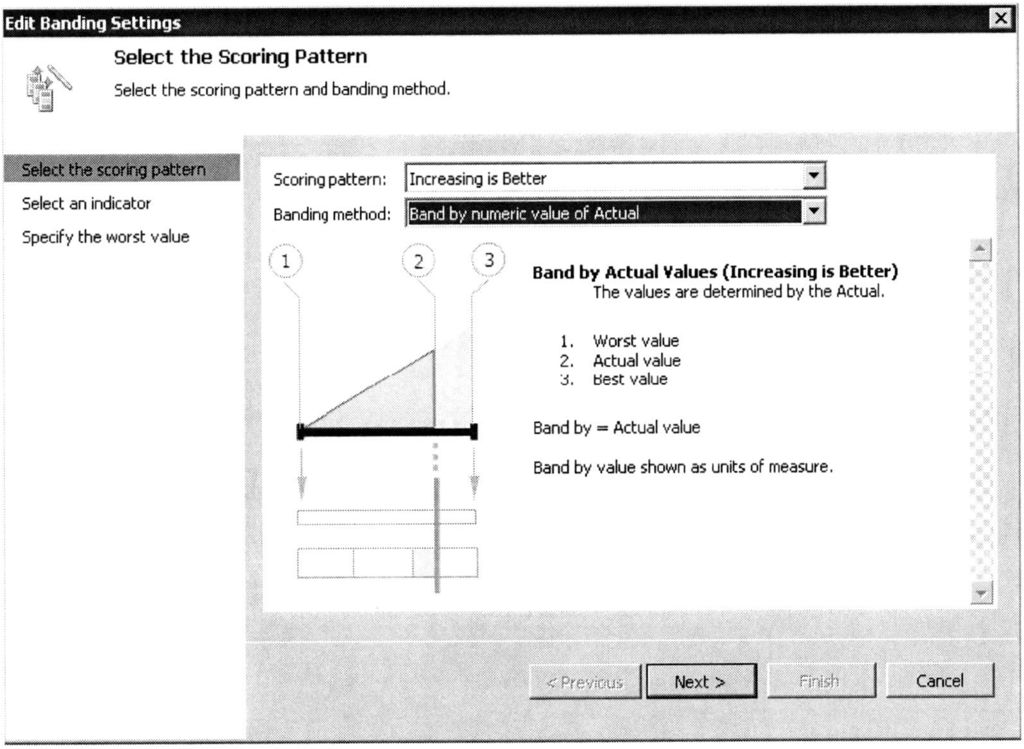

*Figure 17–45. Selecting the scoring pattern*

- Select "Increasing is Better" and "Band by numeric value of Actual". Click Next.

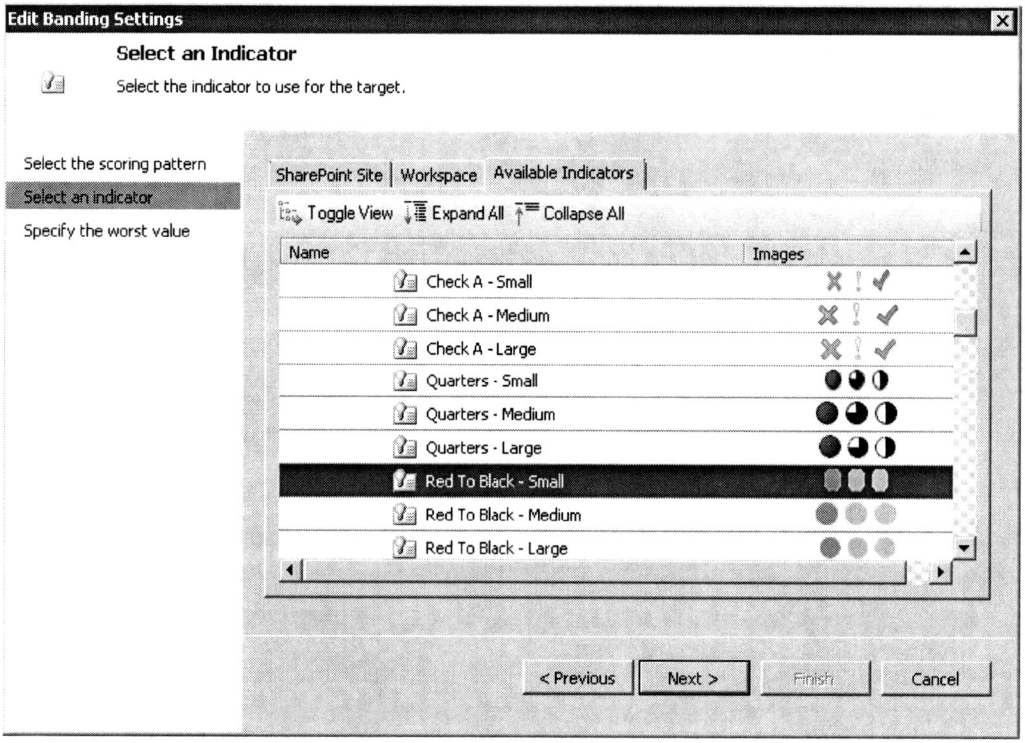

*Figure 17–46. Choosing the indicator*

- Select "Red to Black – Small" under the Miscellaneous category (Figure 17–46). Click Next.

- In this case, there is no selection to be made on the third step of the wizard, so click Finish.

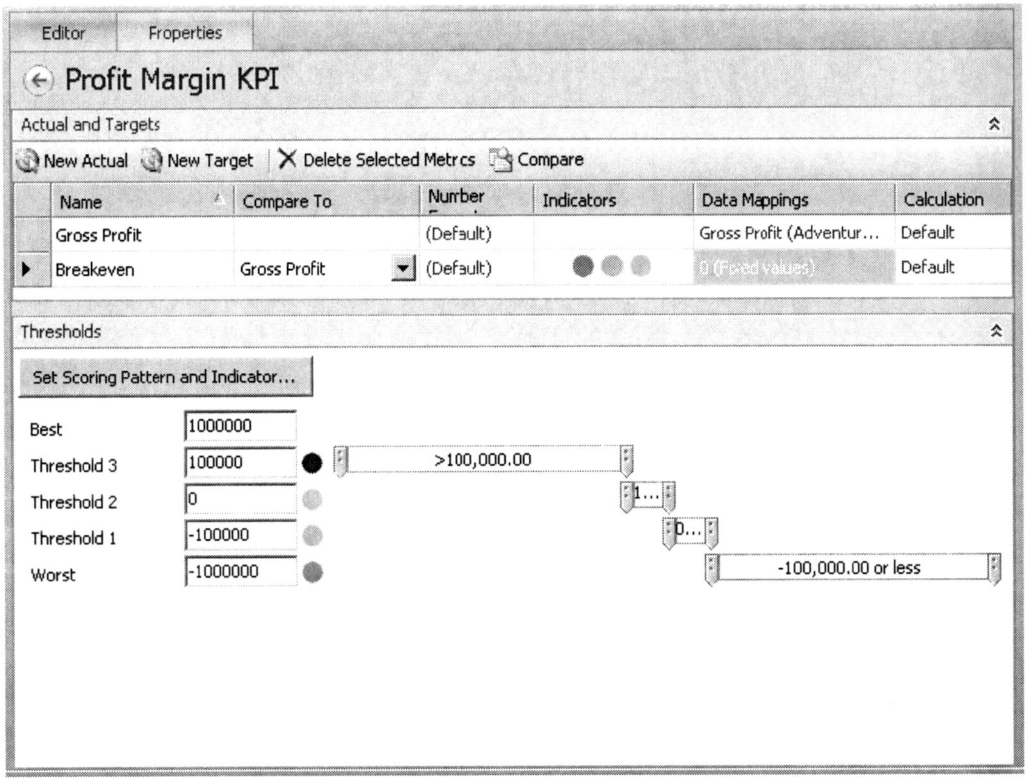

*Figure 17–47. Threshold values*

- The indicator we selected has four possible statuses: black, grey, light red, and red (Figure 17–47). Thresholds configure the points at which black becomes gray and so on. In this case, set the thresholds to the values shown above. These values will be compared with the Gross Profit amount to show whether or not we are "in the black" or "in the red" for a particular promotion.

- Use the New Actual button to create two more actual metrics named "Total Sales" and "Gross Profit Margin." Set the data mappings in the same way as for Gross Profit above. Map the new actual metrics to the "Sales Amount" and "Gross Profit Margin" measures, respectively.

- On the Gross Profit Margin row, click on (Default) in the Number Format column. Set the value to be displayed as a Percentage using parentheses for negative numbers and 1 decimal place (Figure 17–48).

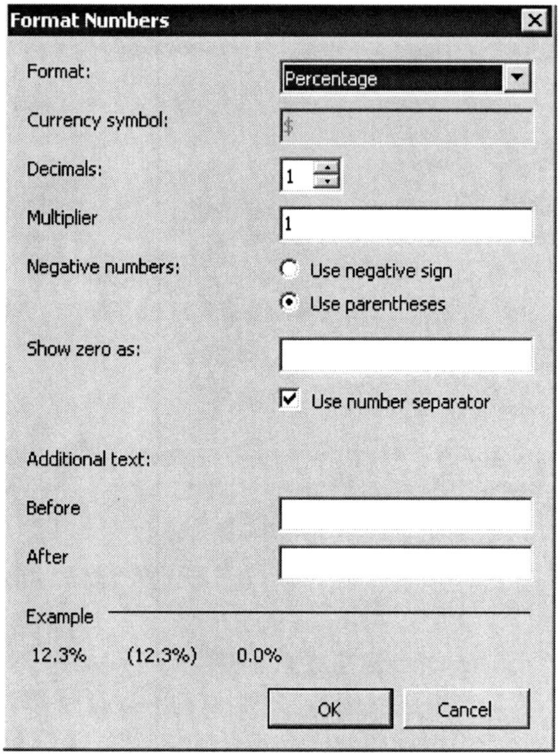

**Figure 17–48.** *Setting the number format*

- Click on New Target to create a second target metric. In this case, instead of breaking even, our goal is to do better with a promotion than without one. Therefore, we will compare the gross profit margin obtained with a promotion to the margin obtained when the promotion is "No Discount."

- Set the name of the new target to "GP% vs. no Discount."

- Set the Compare to field to "Gross Profit Margin."

- Click on the link to set the data mapping and select the Gross Profit Margin measure just as you did when setting the actual metric.

- Instead of finishing the dialog, we will add a filter to find the value of the gross profit margin in a specific case. Start by clicking on the New Dimension Filter button under Select a dimension (Figure 17–49).

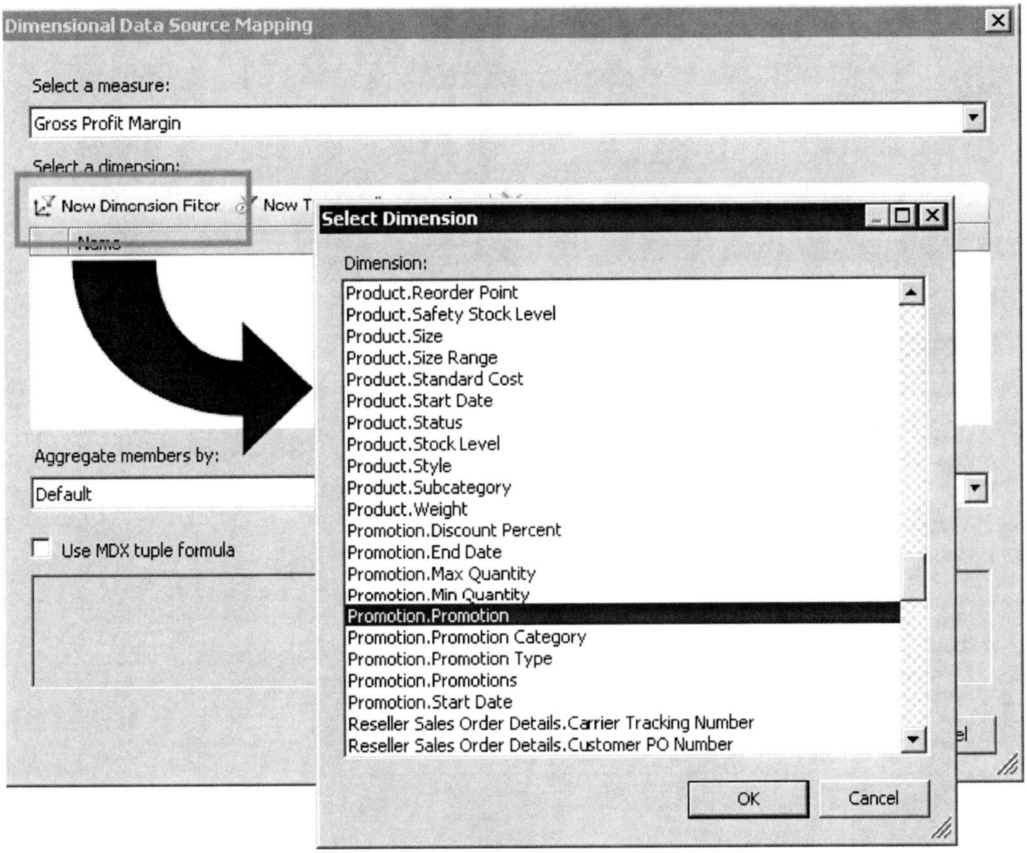

*Figure 17–49. Creating a filter*

- The Select Dimension dialog is somewhat misnamed. The list under Dimension isn't really a list of dimensions. It is a list of dimension hierarchies that can be used to filter the selected measure. Select "Promotion.Promotion" and click OK.

- Click on the "Default Member (All Promotions)" link (Figure 17–50).

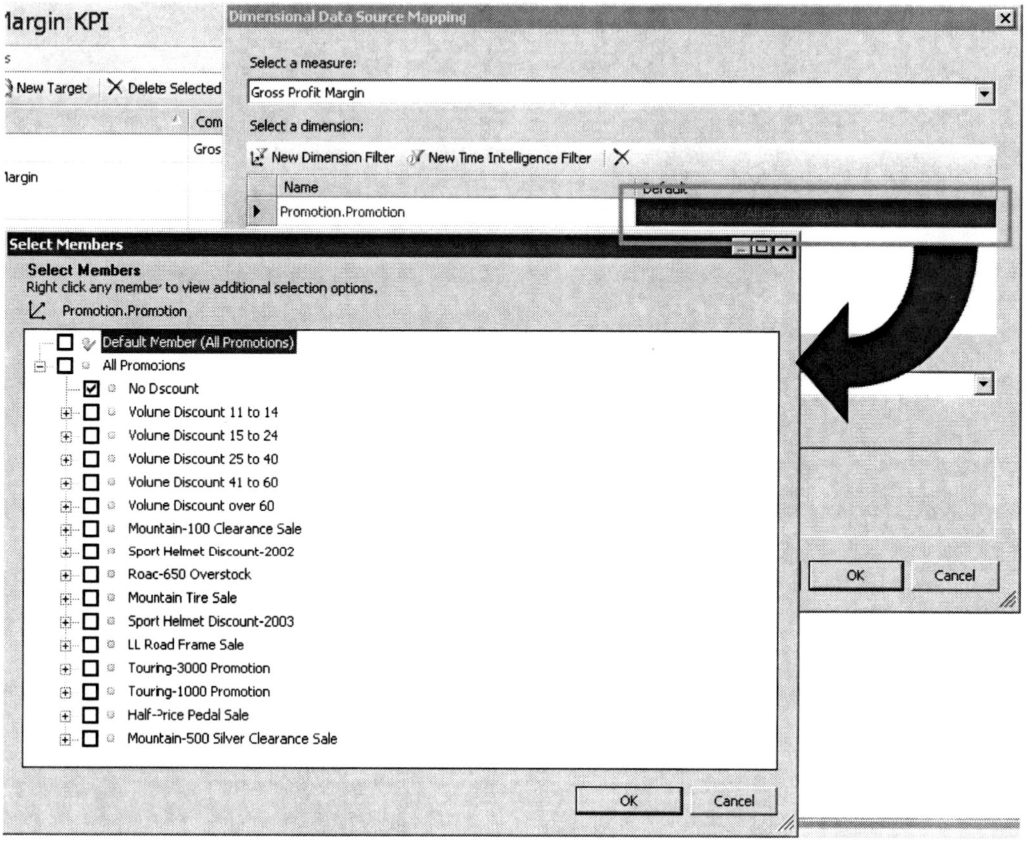

*Figure 17–50. Selecting the filter criteria*

- In the Select Members dialog, check only the No Discount member. This will cause the target value for this metric to include only data related to the No Discount promotion. Click OK.

- Click on the Set Scoring Pattern and Indicator… button. Review all of the default options but don't change anything. Click Cancel to close the wizard.

- Set the thresholds as shown in Figure 17–51.

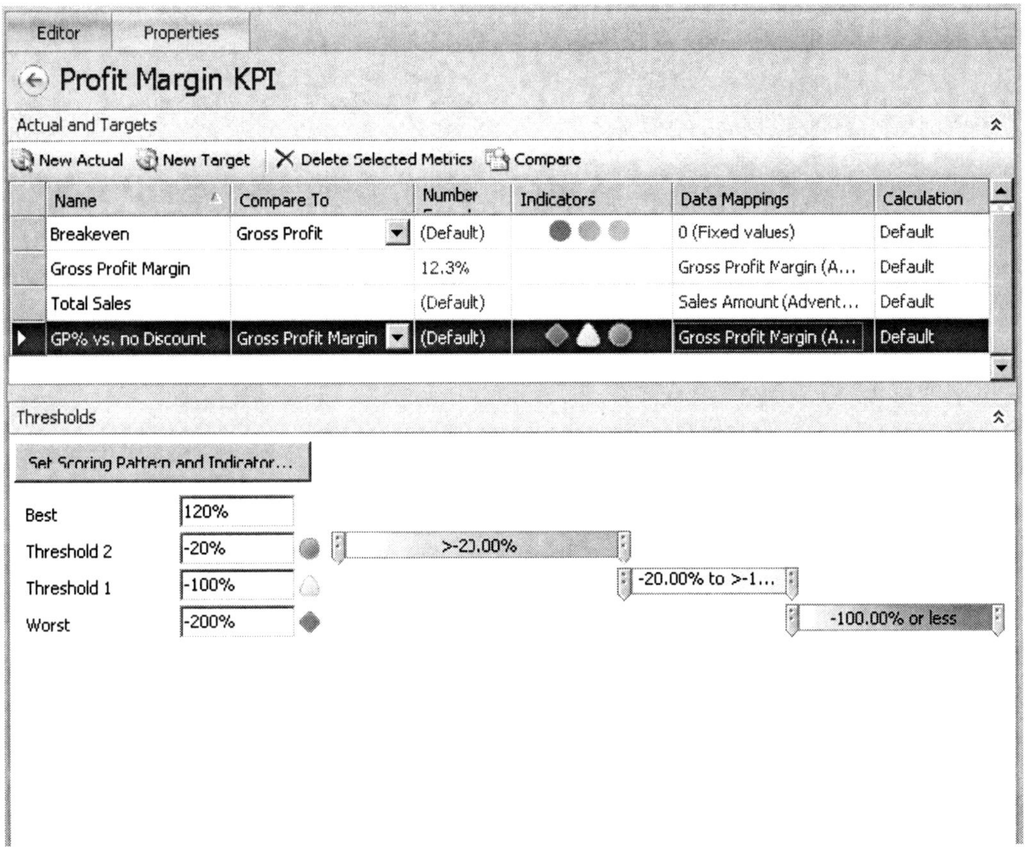

*Figure 17–51. Setting the thresholds*

- Save the KPI and workspace file.

The thresholds used in the last target created may not seem to make sense at first. The default banding pattern used by PerformancePoint is "Band by normalized value of Actual/Target". In this mode, a calculation is performed on each actual and target value for the KPI. A percentage is assigned based on the distance the actual and target are from the "worst value" set in step 3 of the scoring pattern wizard. By default, the "worst value" is set to 0. The worst value is somewhat arbitrary since it is quite possible for actual values to be below it. The percentages calculated in that case are simply negative.

In our case, 0% indicates that the gross profit margin for the selected promotion is exactly the same as for the No Discount promotion. If it's lower, the percentage value is negative. If it's better, the value is positive. Adventure Works management has decided that our profitability goal for these promotions is to be within 20 percent of the non-discounted value (green indicator). A value worse than 100 percent below the standard indicates a serious problem, so the indicator turns red. Anywhere between -20 percent and -100 percent, the indicator will show a slight problem or a yellow indicator.

# Creating a Scorecard

On our dashboard, we want to display a list of the promotions we've run and the values of our KPIs for each promotion. This is called a *scorecard* (see Figure 17–52), which we will create as a separate component in our workspace (inserted using text markup feature).

- Open the Marketing.ddwx workspace file.

- Right-click on the PerformancePoint Content list in the Workspace Browser and select New ➤ Scorecard.

- Name the scorecard "Promotion Scorecard" (and add it to a display folder if you wish).

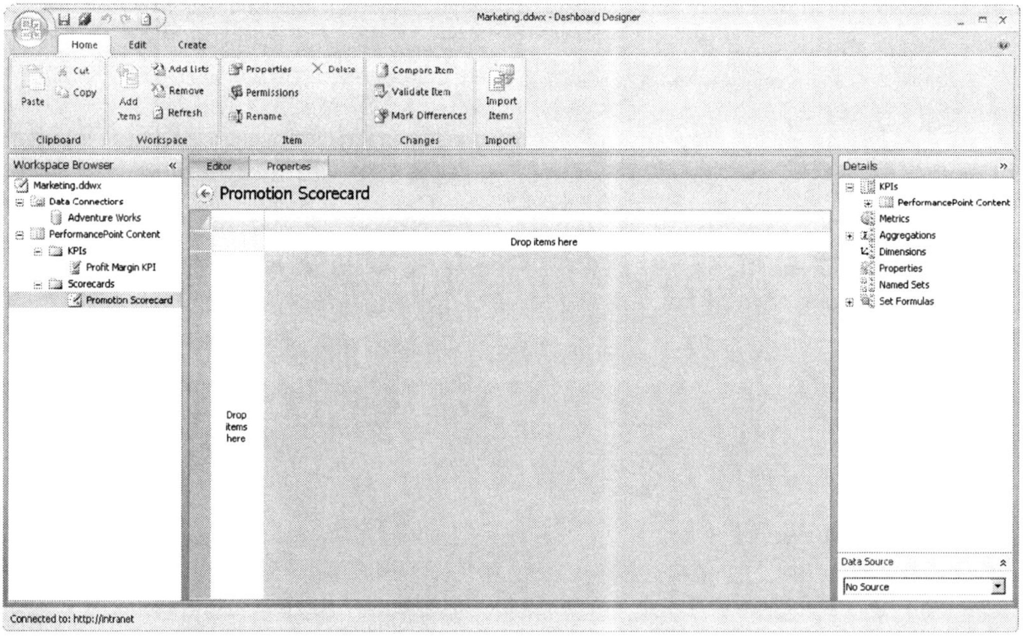

*Figure 17–52. An empty scorecard*

The empty scorecard shown in Figure 17–52 has two main areas. The center window is where you design the scorecard; you will be able to arrange and format items in this window. To the right are panels that provide the elements to go on the scorecard. First, we identify the KPIs to be shown, then we identify the rows and grouping to use in calculating the KPIs.

- In the Details panel, open the KPIs branch of the tree until you reach the Profit Margin KPI (Figure 17–53).

*Figure 17–53. The Profit Margin KPI*

- Drag the Profit Margin KPI from the Details panel to the header area of the scorecard (Figure 17–54).

*Figure 17–54. Adding the KPI to the scorecard*

- Select Adventure Works from the drop-down list under Data Source (Figure 17–55). Note that the Data Source panel is in the bottom right corner of the designer window, under the Details panel.

*Figure 17–55. Choosing Adventure Works as the data source*

- Under Details, select Dimensions ➤ Promotion ➤ Promotions. This is main hierarchy of promotions that will allow us to roll up or drill down into our KPIs.

- Drag the Promotions hierarchy onto the row area of the scorecard. This displays the Select Members dialog (Figure 17–56).

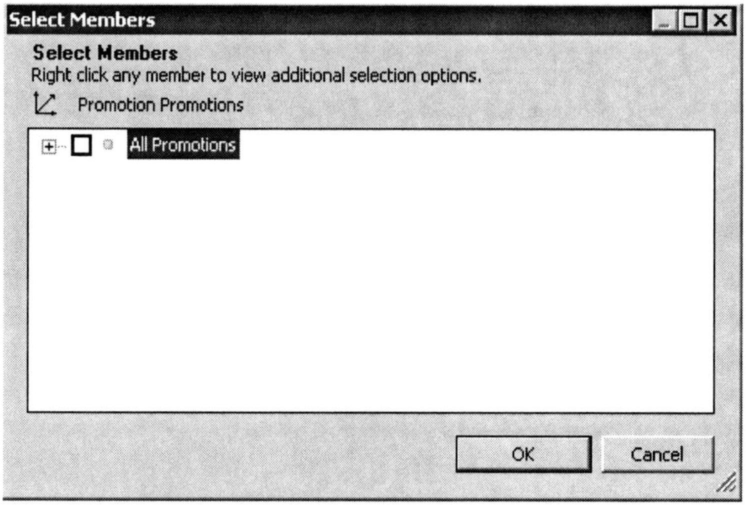

*Figure 17–56. The Promotions hierarchy*

- Open the All Promotions node.

- Right-click on the Customer node and select Autoselect Members ➤ Select All Descendants (Figure 17–57).

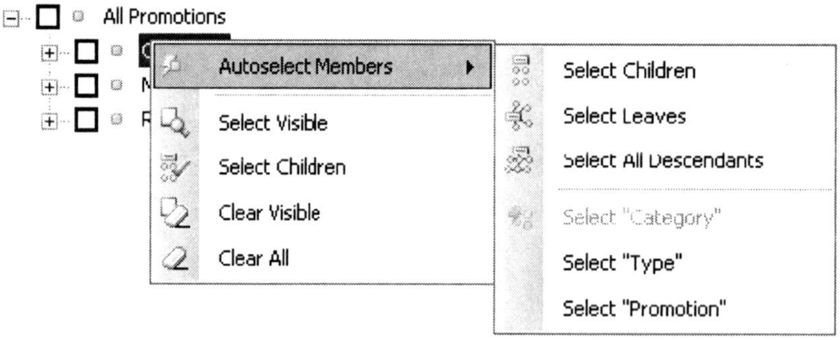

*Figure 17–57. Selecting members*

- Do the same for the Reseller node.

- Check the All Promotions, Customer, and Reseller nodes, as well as the two All descendants of nodes. Do not check No Discount (Figure 17–58).

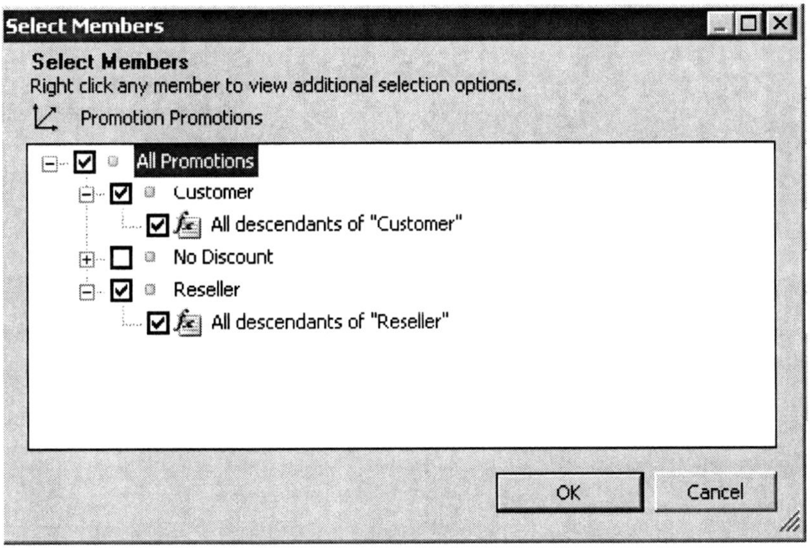

*Figure 17–58. Confirming member selection*

- Click OK. The scorecard should now look like what's shown in Figure 17–59.

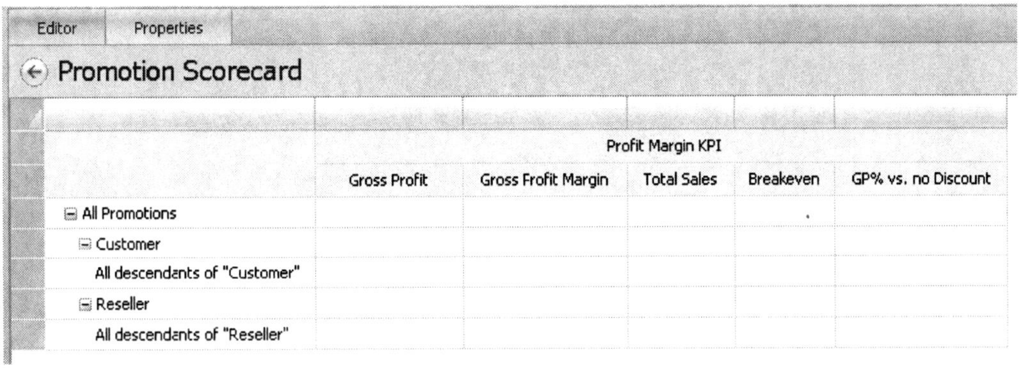

*Figure 17–59. The scorecard with added elements*

- Right-click on the Gross Profit column header and select Delete.
- Right-click on the Gross Profit Margin column header and select Delete.
- Right-click on the Breakeven column header and select Metric Settings....

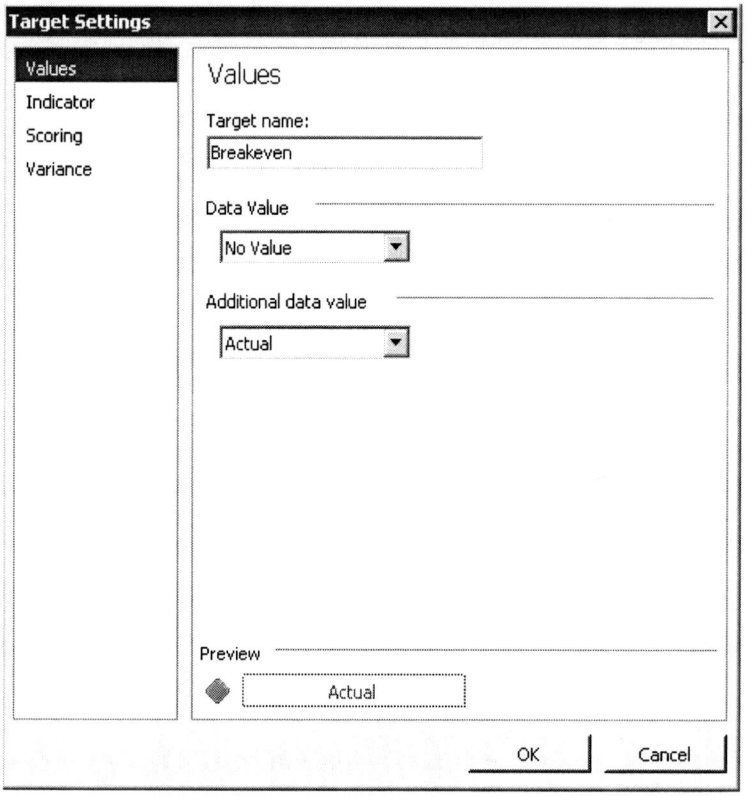

*Figure 17–60. Target settings for Breakeven*

- Select "No Value" for Data Value and "Actual" for Additional Data Value (Figure 17–60).

- Review the other settings but retain the defaults. Click OK.

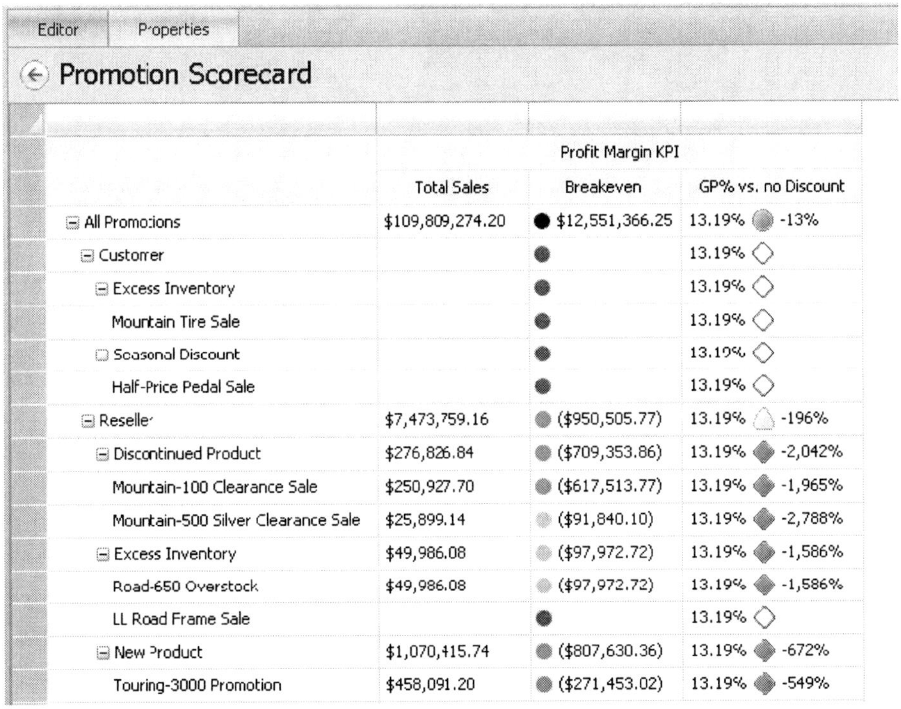

| | | Profit Margin KPI | |
|---|---|---|---|
| | Total Sales | Breakeven | GP% vs. no Discount |
| ⊟ All Promotions | $109,809,274.20 | ● $12,551,366.25 | 13.19% ◉ -13% |
| ⊟ Customer | | ● | 13.19% ◇ |
| ⊟ Excess Inventory | | ● | 13.19% ◇ |
| Mountain Tire Sale | | ● | 13.19% ◇ |
| ⊟ Seasonal Discount | | ● | 13.19% ◇ |
| Half-Price Pedal Sale | | ● | 13.19% ◇ |
| ⊟ Reseller | $7,473,759.16 | ● ($950,505.77) | 13.19% △ -196% |
| ⊟ Discontinued Product | $276,826.84 | ● ($709,353.86) | 13.19% ◆ -2,042% |
| Mountain-100 Clearance Sale | $250,927.70 | ● ($617,513.77) | 13.19% ◆ -1,965% |
| Mountain-500 Silver Clearance Sale | $25,899.14 | ◉ ($91,840.10) | 13.19% ◆ -2,788% |
| ⊟ Excess Inventory | $49,986.08 | ◉ ($97,972.72) | 13.19% ◆ -1,586% |
| Road-650 Overstock | $49,986.08 | ◉ ($97,972.72) | 13.19% ◆ -1,586% |
| LL Road Frame Sale | | ● | 13.19% ◇ |
| ⊟ New Product | $1,070,415.74 | ● ($807,630.36) | 13.19% ◉ -672% |
| Touring-3000 Promotion | $458,091.20 | ● ($271,453.02) | 13.19% ◉ -549% |

*Figure 17–61. The processed scorecard*

At this point, the scorecard will automatically be processed. It should look something like the one in Figure 17–61. The rows show the promotion hierarchy, including rolling up to parent levels. The columns show our KPIs as they are currently configured. Notice that rows are appearing for promotions even though there were no sales for those promotions.

- Right-click on the Total Sales column header and select Filter Empty Rows. Note that the rows that should be filtered are now shown with red labels (Figure 17–62). This indicates they will be filtered at runtime.

- Right-click on the GP% vs. no Discount column header and select Metric Settings….

- Select Actual for Data Value and Target for Additional Data Value.

- Click OK.

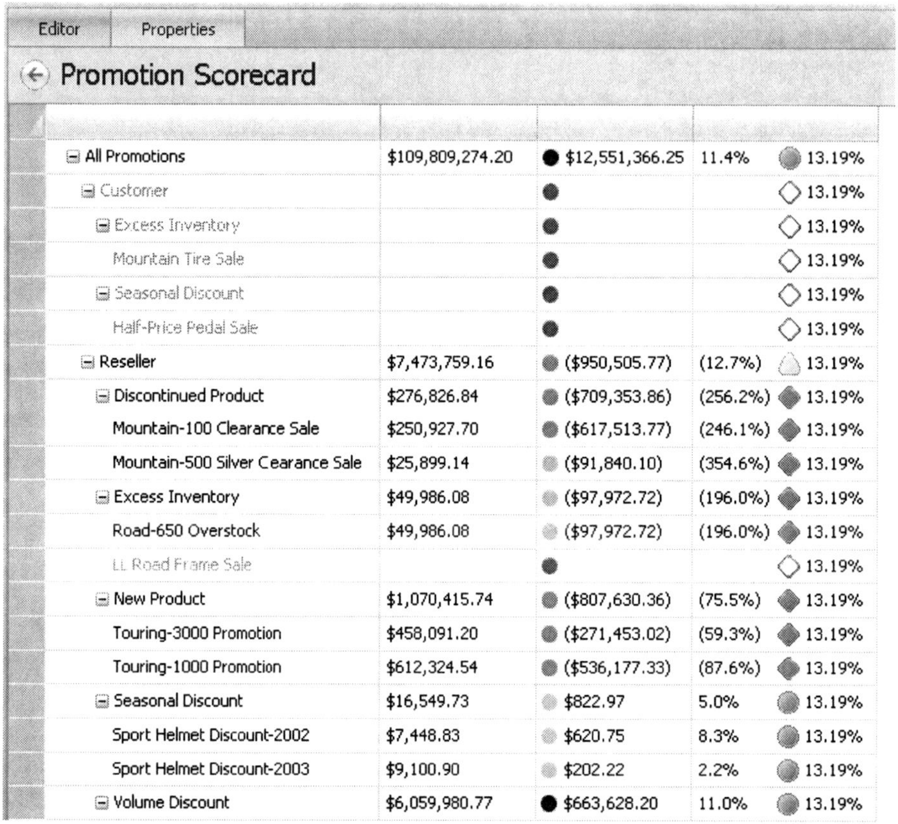

| | | | | | |
|---|---|---|---|---|---|
| **Editor** | **Properties** | | | | |
| ← **Promotion Scorecard** | | | | | |
| ⊟ All Promotions | $109,809,274.20 | ● $12,551,366.25 | 11.4% | ◉ 13.19% |
| ⊟ Customer | | ● | | ◇ 13.19% |
| ⊟ Excess Inventory | | ● | | ◇ 13.19% |
| Mountain Tire Sale | | ● | | ◇ 13.19% |
| ⊟ Seasonal Discount | | ● | | ◇ 13.19% |
| Half-Price Pedal Sale | | ● | | ◇ 13.19% |
| ⊟ Reseller | $7,473,759.16 | ◉ ($950,505.77) | (12.7%) | ◔ 13.19% |
| ⊟ Discontinued Product | $276,826.84 | ◉ ($709,353.86) | (256.2%) | ◕ 13.19% |
| Mountain-100 Clearance Sale | $250,927.70 | ◉ ($617,513.77) | (246.1%) | ◕ 13.19% |
| Mountain-500 Silver Cearance Sale | $25,899.14 | ◉ ($91,840.10) | (354.6%) | ◕ 13.19% |
| ⊟ Excess Inventory | $49,986.08 | ◉ ($97,972.72) | (196.0%) | ◕ 13.19% |
| Road-650 Overstock | $49,986.08 | ◉ ($97,972.72) | (196.0%) | ◕ 13.19% |
| LL Road Frame Sale | | ● | | ◇ 13.19% |
| ⊟ New Product | $1,070,415.74 | ◉ ($807,630.36) | (75.5%) | ◕ 13.19% |
| Touring-3000 Promotion | $458,091.20 | ◉ ($271,453.02) | (59.3%) | ◕ 13.19% |
| Touring-1000 Promotion | $612,324.54 | ◉ ($536,177.33) | (87.6%) | ◕ 13.19% |
| ⊟ Seasonal Discount | $16,549.73 | ◉ $822.97 | 5.0% | ◉ 13.19% |
| Sport Helmet Discount-2002 | $7,448.83 | ◉ $620.75 | 8.3% | ◉ 13.19% |
| Sport Helmet Discount-2003 | $9,100.90 | ◉ $202.22 | 2.2% | ◉ 13.19% |
| ⊟ Volume Discount | $6,059,980.77 | ● $663,628.20 | 11.0% | ◉ 13.19% |

*Figure 17–62. Empty rows are red, indicating they will be filtered at runtime.*

- Save the scorecard and workspace file.

## Creating Filters

Our dashboard will contain two filters. The first filter will control the date range for the figures displayed. The second will allow us to select from among our sales territories.

- Open the Marketing.ddwx file in Dashboard Designer.
- Right-click on the PerformancePoint Content list and select New ➤ Filter.

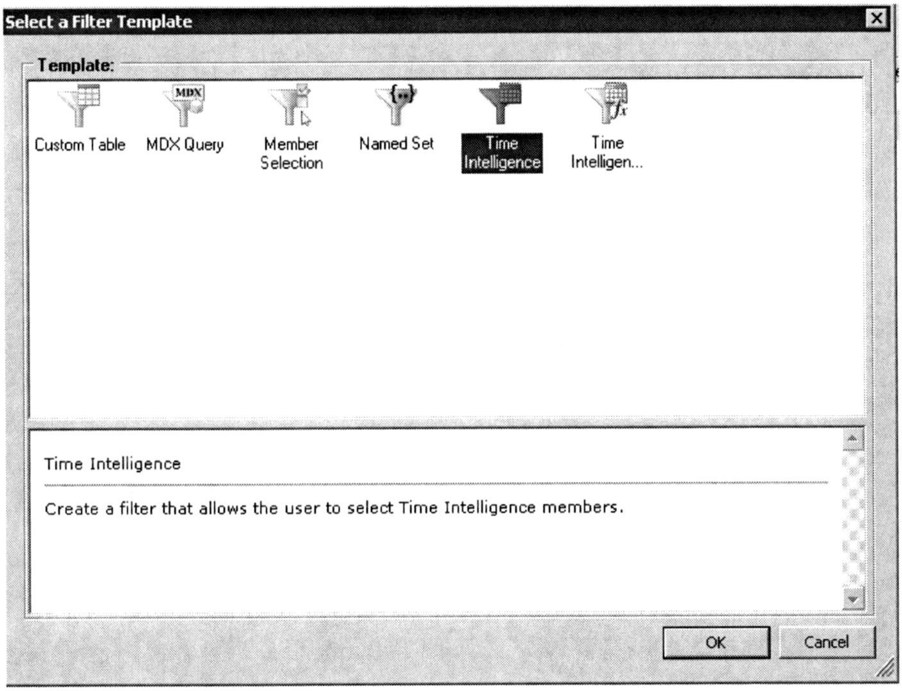

*Figure 17–63. Creating a date filter*

- Select Time Intelligence from the Select a Filter Template dialog as shown in Figure 17–63. Be careful not to select "Time Intelligence with Connection Filter" by mistake.

- Click OK.

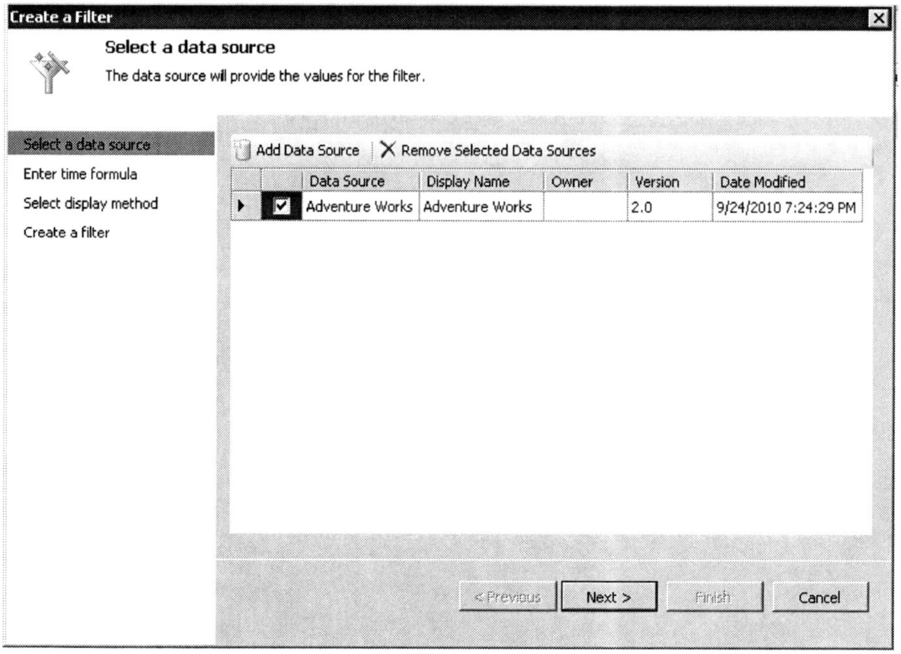

*Figure 17–64. Selecting a data source for the filter*

- Click Add Data Source and select the Adventure Works data source and click Next (Figure 17–64).

For the "Enter time formula" step, we will define the options the user will have for selecting time periods. The formulas are entered on the left and the name displayed to the user is on the right. The formulas are designed to output a list of members of the cube's time dimension as specified in the data source. For a good overview of these formulas, go to
blogs.msdn.com/b/performancepoint/archive/2010/01/21/time-intelligence-formula-quick-
reference.aspx.

- Enter the formulas and display names shown in Figure 17–65 and then click Next.

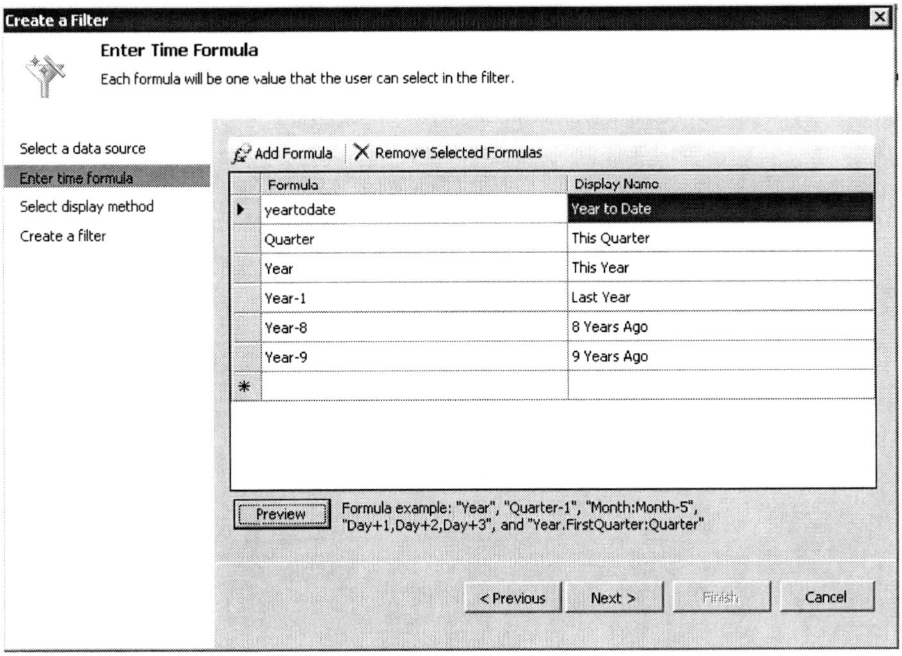

*Figure 17–65. Adding date formulas*

- Select List for the Display Method and click Finish (Figure 17–66).

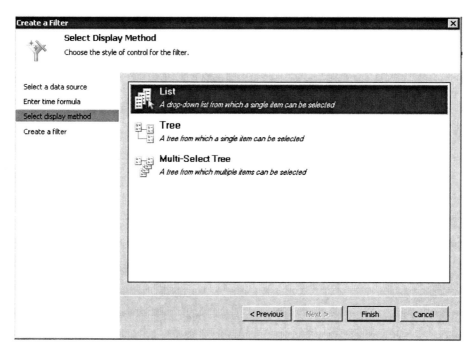

*Figure 17–66. Selecting a display method for the date filter*

- Set the name of the filter to "Date."

- Save the filter and workspace.

Now we'll create a filter for selecting from the Sales Territory dimension. This filter will display a tree for the territory hierarchy and allow us to select one territory or higher-level region.

- Right-click on the PerformancePoint Content list and select New ➤ Filter.

- Select the Member Selection filter template and click OK.

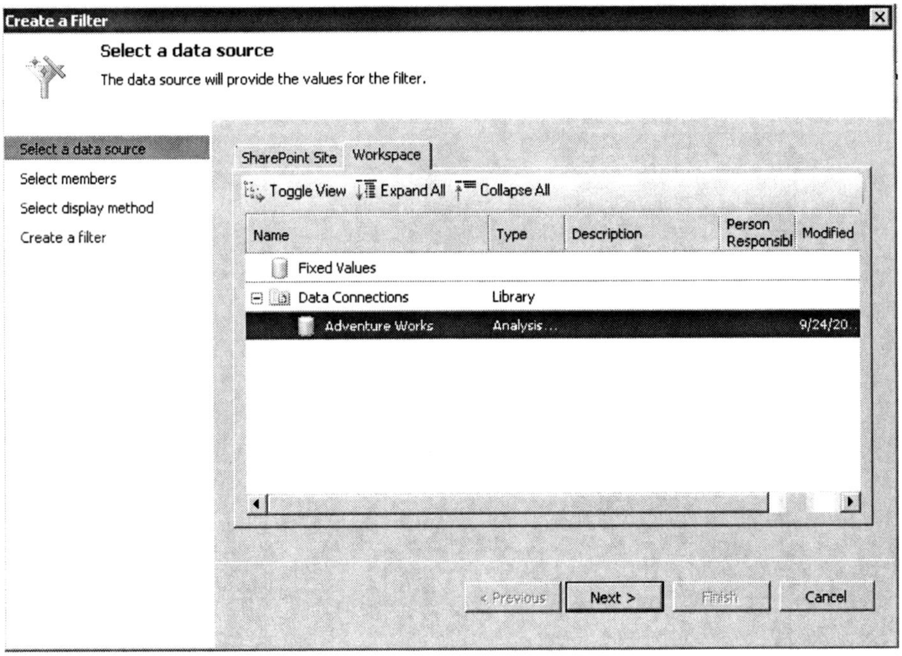

*Figure 17–67. Selecting the data source for the filter*

- Select the Adventure Works data source and click Next (Figure 17–67).

- This displays the Select Members page of the wizard where we will specify the members to show in the filter (Figure 17–68).

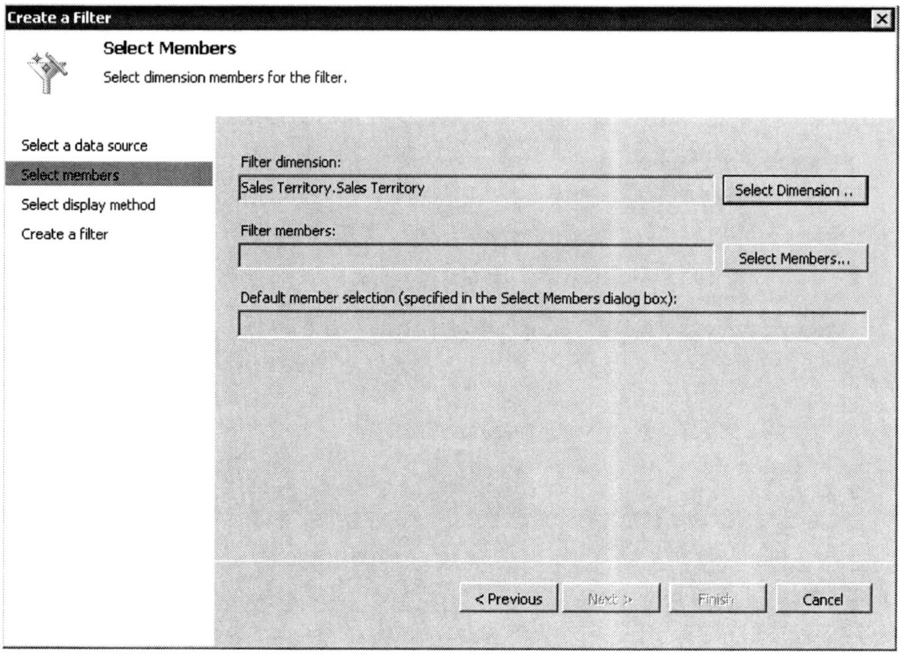

**Figure 17–68.** *Selecting members for the filter*

- Click the Select Dimension button.

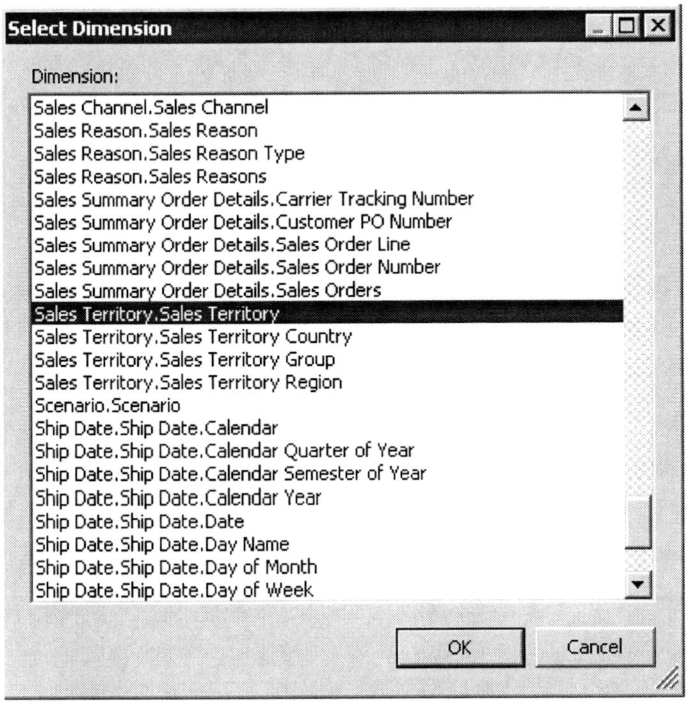

***Figure 17–69.*** *Choosing the dimension*

- Select Sales Territory.Sales Territory and click OK (Figure 17–69).

- Click the Select Members button.

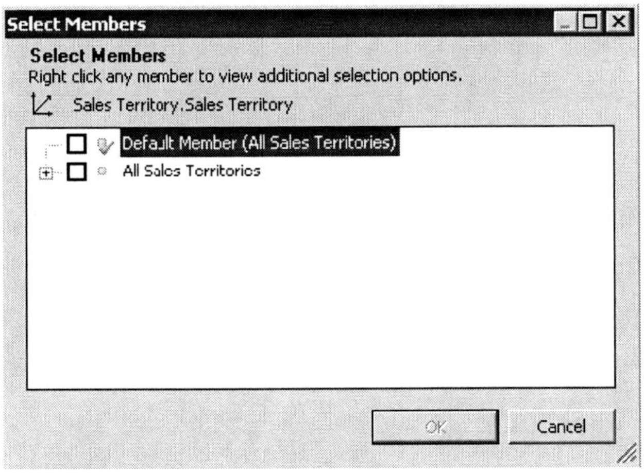

***Figure 17–70.*** *Selecting Sales Territory members*

- Right-click All Sales Territories (Figure 17–70) and select Autoselect Members ➤ Select All Descendants.

- Check both All Sales Territories and All descendants of All Sales Territories (Figure 17–71) .

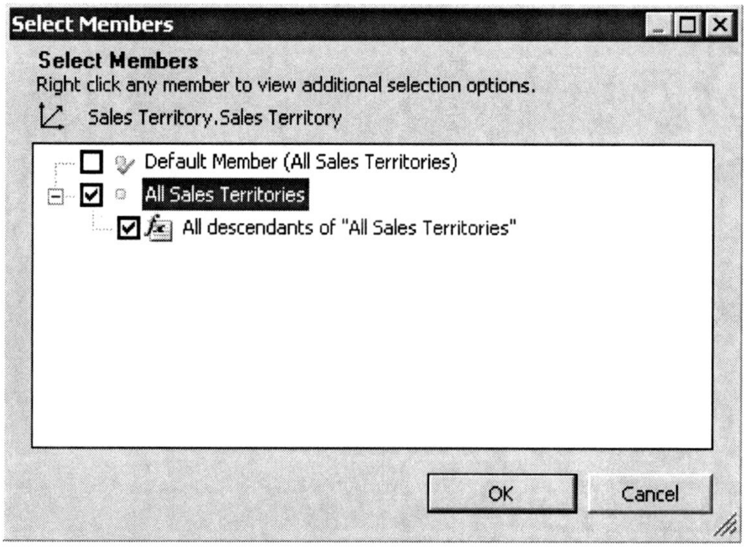

*Figure 17–71. Confirming the members*

- Click OK.

- Select Tree from the Select Display Method page and click Finish (Figure 17–72).

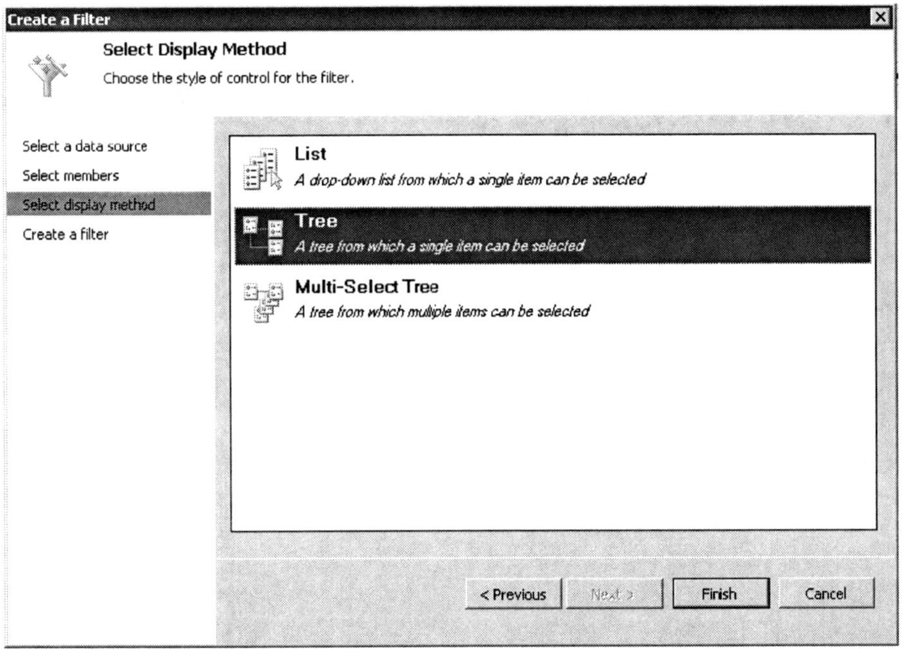

*Figure 17–72. Choosing a display method for the Sales Territory filter*

- Change the name of the filter to "Sales Territory".
- Save the filter and workspace file.

## Creating Reports

KPIs and scorecards allow us to compare business data against goals. Once we have identified the problem areas in the enterprise, we need to be able to understand the conditions that are causing problems. A "report" in PerformancePoint is a generic term referring to a window of information that has been sorted out based on the filters and scorecard selections made in the dashboard.

The two most common types of reports in PerformancePoint are Analytic Charts and Analytic Grids. We will create one of each for our dashboard.

- Open the Marketing.ddwx file in Dashboard Designer.
- Right-click on the PerformancePoint Content list and select New ➤ Report.

625

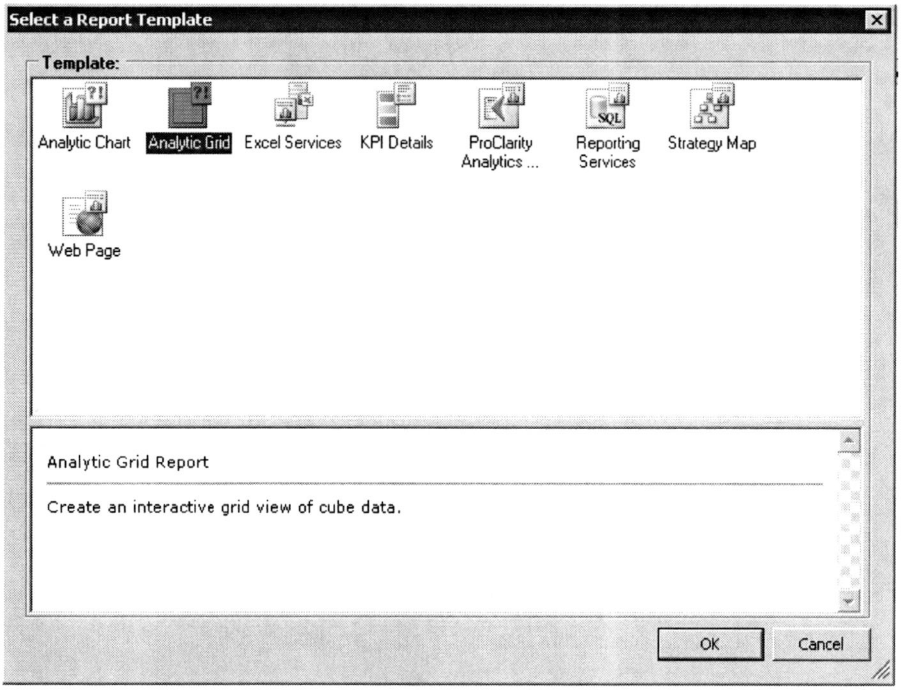

*Figure 17-73. Choosing a report template*

- Select the Analytic Grid template and click OK (Figure 17-73).
- Select the Adventure Works data source and click Finish (Figure 17-74).

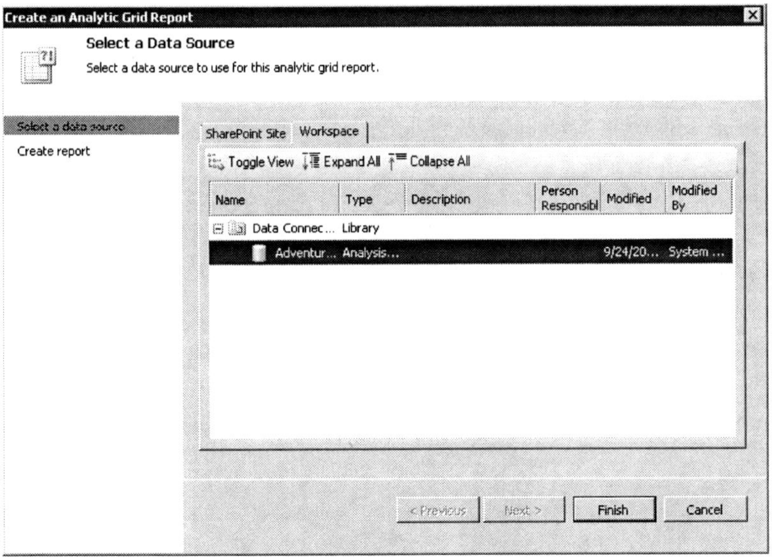

*Figure 17–74. Choosing Adventure Works as the data source*

- Set the name of the report to "Margin by Sales Channel" (Figure 17–75).

*Figure 17–75. The empty Margin by Sales Channel report*

The empty grid report window is divided into several areas. The draft view of the report appears in the center window. Beneath the center window are panels labeled Rows, Columns and Background that will be used to specify the contents of the report. In the report designer, "background" refers to the ways in which the data in the report can be filtered.

To the right is a Details tree from which we'll select items to add to the report by dragging them onto one of the panels at the bottom of the window.

- From the Details panel, drag Dimensions ➤ Sales Channel and drop it on the Columns panel.

- From the Details panel, drag Measures ➤ Sales Amount and drop it on the Columns panel.

- Drag and drop these measures to Columns as well: Total Product Cost, Gross Profit, and Gross Profit Margin.

- From the Details panel, drag Dimensions ➤ Product ➤ Categories and drop it on the Rows panel.

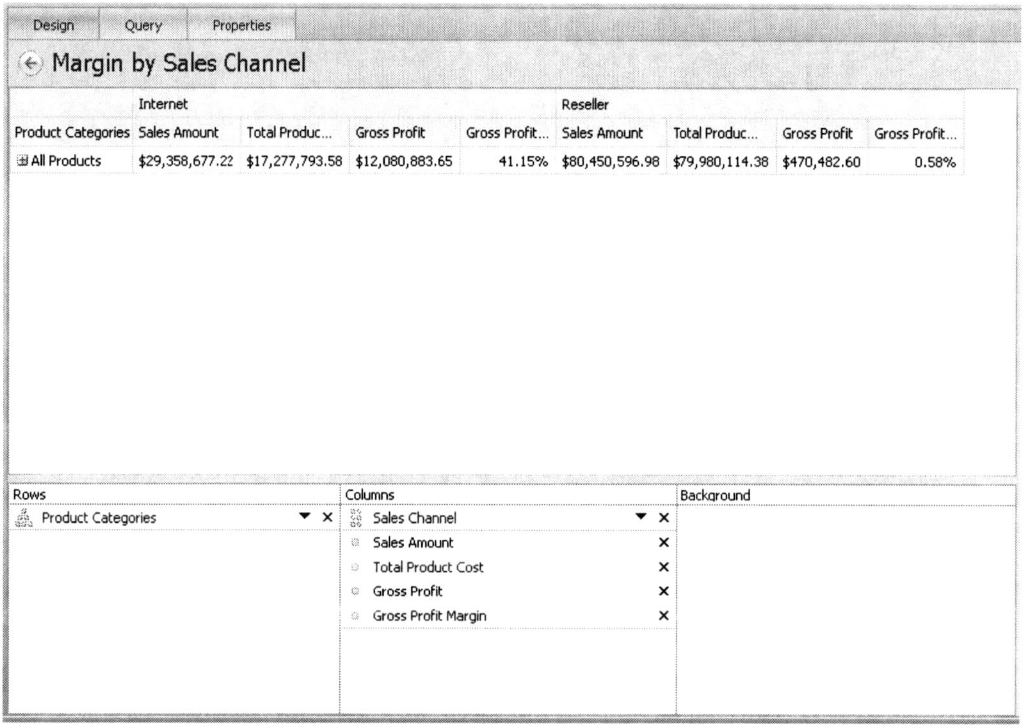

| | Design | Query | Properties |
| --- | --- | --- | --- |

### ◁ Margin by Sales Channel

| | Internet | | | | Reseller | | | |
| --- | --- | --- | --- | --- | --- | --- | --- | --- |
| Product Categories | Sales Amount | Total Produc... | Gross Profit | Gross Profit... | Sales Amount | Total Produc... | Gross Profit | Gross Profit... |
| ⊞ All Products | $29,358,677.22 | $17,277,793.58 | $12,080,883.65 | 41.15% | $80,450,596.98 | $79,980,114.38 | $470,482.60 | 0.58% |

| Rows | Columns | Background |
| --- | --- | --- |
| 🔀 Product Categories ▼ ✕ | ▦ Sales Channel ▼ ✕ | |
| | ▫ Sales Amount ✕ | |
| | ▫ Total Product Cost ✕ | |
| | ▫ Gross Profit ✕ | |
| | ▫ Gross Profit Margin ✕ | |

*Figure 17–76. Defining the report's rows and columns*

Now that we have defined the rows and columns for the report (Figure 17–76) it will automatically display a default view. In our dashboard, we want to see the product categories by default. We also want to be able to filter this report by date, territory, and promotion.

- Right-click on Product Categories in the Rows panel and choose Select Members.

- Right-click on All Products and select Autoselect Members ➤ Select Category.

- Ensure that All Products and Category descendants of All Products are checked and click OK (Figure 17–77).

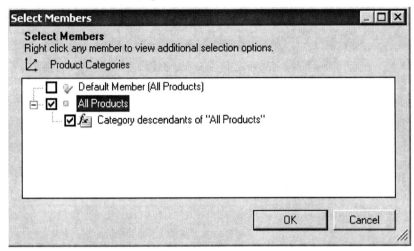

*Figure 17–77. Selecting members for the report's default view*

- From Details, drag Dimensions ➤ Date ➤ Fiscal ➤ Fiscal to the Background panel (Figure 17–78).

- From Details, drag Dimensions ➤ Promotion ➤ Promotion to the Background panel.

- From Details, drag Dimensions ➤ Sales Territory ➤ Sales Territory to the Background panel.

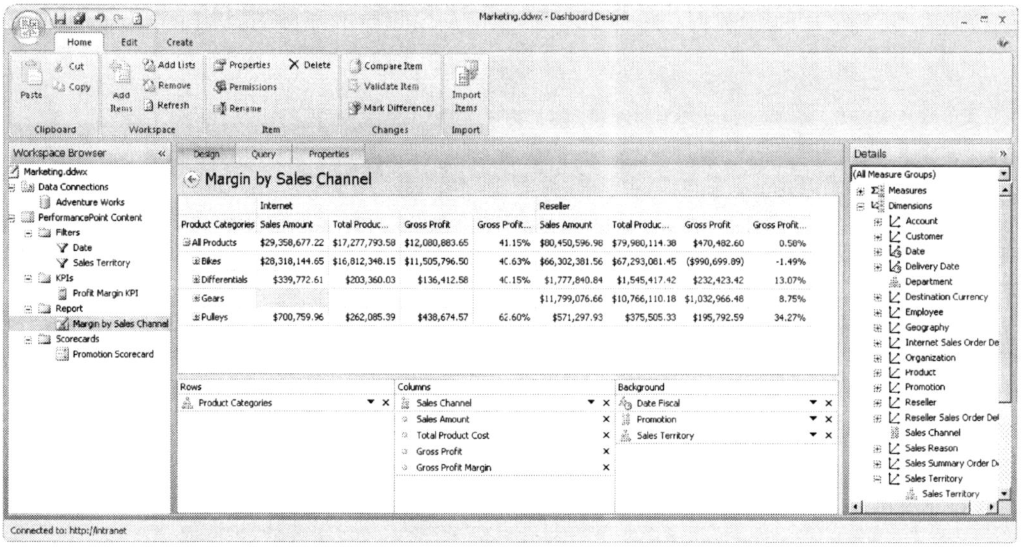

**Figure 17–78.** *Adding dimensions to the report's default view*

- Save the report and workspace

Now let's create an Analytic Chart report. This report will compare the gross profit margin across product categories.

- Right-click on the PerformancePoint Content list and select New ➤ Report.

- Select the Analytic Chart template and click OK.

- Select the Adventure Works data source and click Finish.

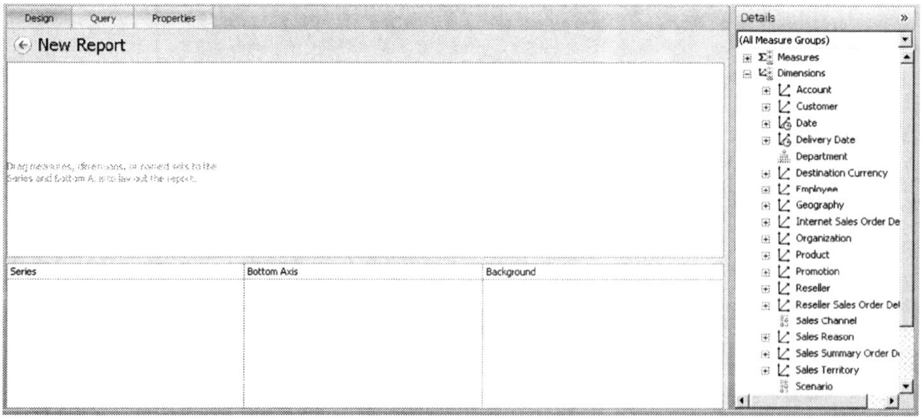

**Figure 17–79.** *The empty analytic chart report*

At this point, the chart report looks almost exactly like the grid report. The difference is that the panels across the bottom are Series, Bottom Axis, and Background (see Figure 17–79).

- From the Details panel, drag Measures ➤ Gross Profit Margin and drop it on the Series panel.

- From the Details panel, drag Dimensions ➤ Product ➤ Category and drop it on the Bottom Axis panel.

- From Details, drag Dimensions ➤ Date ➤ Fiscal ➤ Fiscal to the Background panel.

- From Details, drag Dimensions ➤ Promotion ➤ Promotion to the Background panel.

- From Details, drag Dimensions ➤ Sales Territory ➤ Sales Territory to the Background panel (Figure 17–80).

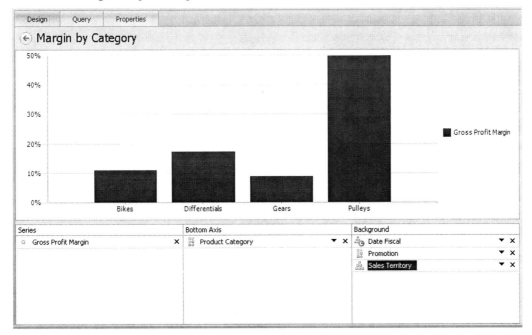

*Figure 17–80. Adding dimensions to the Background panel*

- Right-click anywhere in the center window and select Format Report ➤ Don't Show.

- Right-click anywhere in the center window and select Show Information Bar.

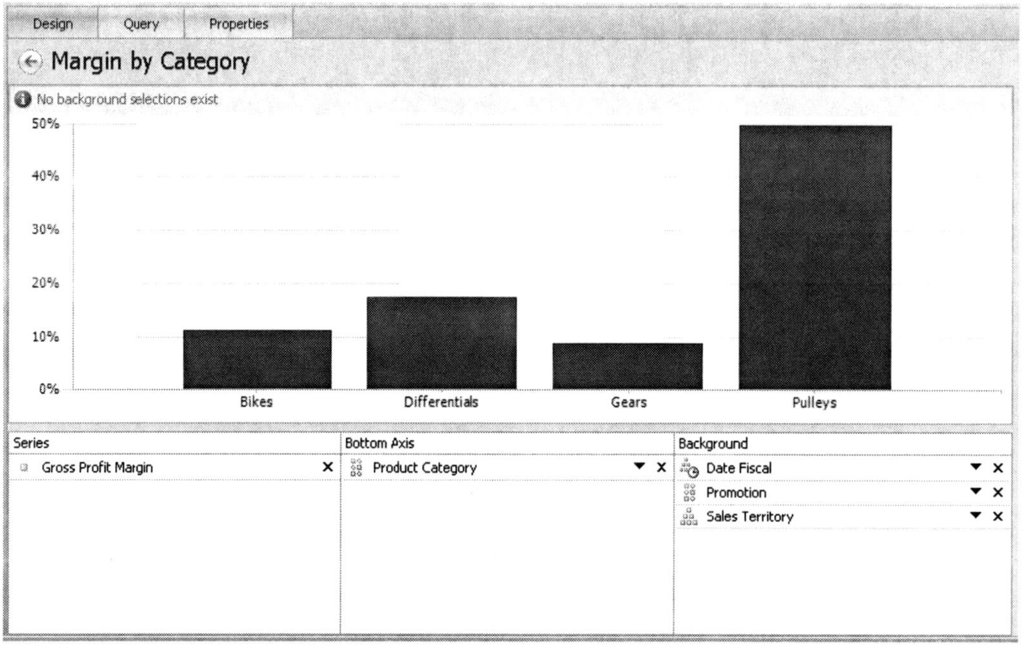

**Figure 17–81.** *The Information Bar turned on*

The Information Bar is a useful feature on reports. When this is turned on it shows the user exactly how the data in the report is being filtered. In the designer, the bar shows "No background selections exist" because there are no filters applied until the report is embedded into a dashboard (Figure 17–81).

- Set the name of the report to "Margin by Category".
- Save the report and workspace.

## Creating a Dashboard

We have created all of the components for our dashboard. Now we'll put it all together and make it work as an integrated package.

- Open the Marketing.ddwx file in Dashboard Designer.
- Right-click on the PerformancePoint Content list and select New ➤ Dashboard.

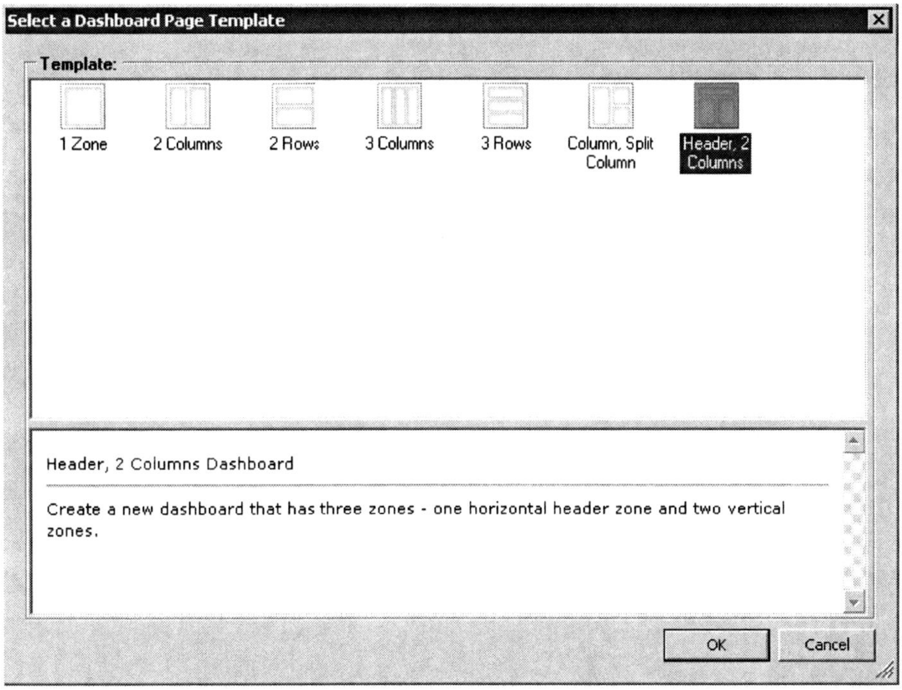

*Figure 17–82. The default page template*

- Select the default page template: Header, 2 Columns, as shown in Figure 17–82.
- Click OK.
- Set the name of the dashboard to "Marketing Dashboard".

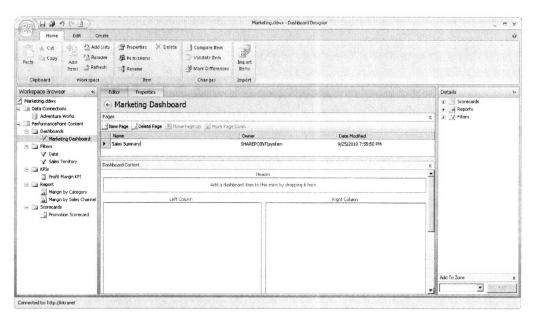

**Figure 17–83.** *The empty dashboard page*

This will create an empty dashboard page with three zones (Figure 17–83). At the top of the center window is a list of the pages in the dashboard. Beneath the pages is the Dashboard Content panel. This is where the selected dashboard page will be assembled from the components we've created. At the right, the Details panel contains the components that can be used.

- Set the name of the dashboard's initial page to "Sales Summary" in the Pages panel.

- On the Details panel, open the Filters node until you find Date and Sales Territory filters. Drag and drop both filters onto the Header zone of the page.

- On the Details panel, open the Scorecards node until you find the Promotion Scorecard. Drag and drop it onto the Left Column zone.

- On the Details panel, open the Reports node until you find the "Margin by Category" and "Margin by Sales Channel" reports. Drag and drop both reports onto the Right Column zone.

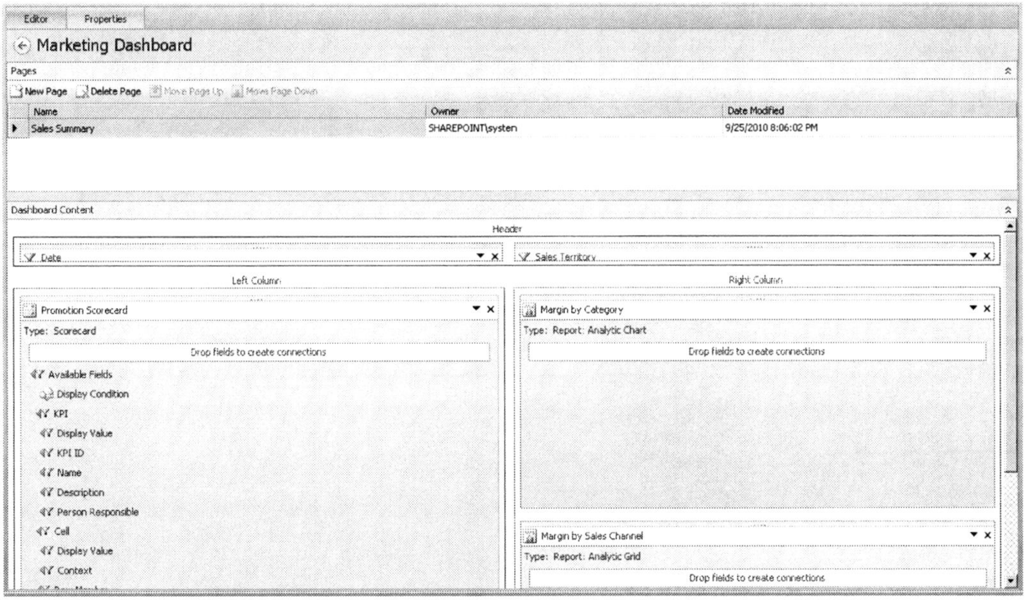

*Figure 17–84. The dashboard page with components*

The components are now on the page (Figure 17–84), but they are not integrated with one another. By dragging fields from one component to another, data is passed to synchronize or filter data throughout, or between, dashboard pages. The behavior we want is as follows:

- When a date range is selected in the filter, it should be applied to all components.

- When a Sales Territory is selected in the filter, it should be applied to all components.

- When the user clicks on a row or cell in the scorecard on the left, the reports on the right should be filtered to display data only for that promotion.

Now we will create the connections to create this behavior

- Hover over the Date filter. A panel will drop down showing all of the fields that are available from this filter. Drag Member Unique Name and drop it onto the scorecard.

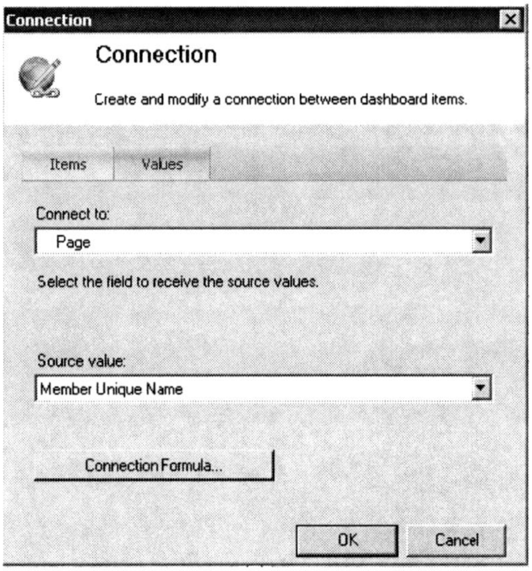

*Figure 17–85.* *Creating connections between dashboard items*

- The default connection is to Page, which refers to the scorecard's overall filter (Figure 17–85). Click OK.

- Drag and drop the same field from the Date filter onto the two report components. The reports will default the connection to the Date Fiscal background field that is specified in the reports.

- From the Sales Territory filter, drag the Member Unique Name field to the scorecard. Again, Page is the connection field.

- Drag and drop the same field from the Sales Territory filter onto the two report components. When the connection dialog appears, select Sales Territory for the "Connect to" field (Figure 17–86).

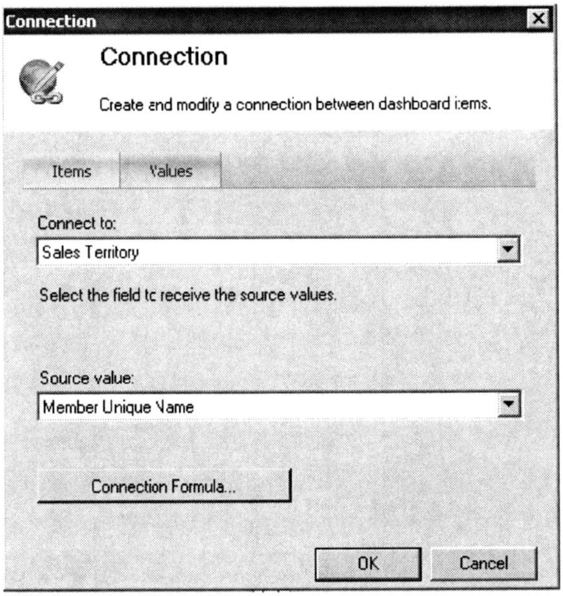

*Figure 17–86. Connecting to the Sales Territory filter*

- From the Promotion Scorecard, drag Row Member ➤ Member Unique Name onto each report. Verify that the connection dialog shows that the field is connected to the Promotion field (Figure 17–87).

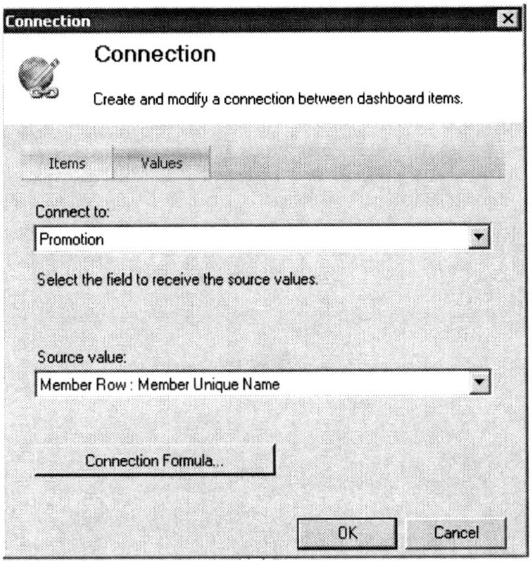

*Figure 17–87. Connecting to the Promotion field*

- The dashboard is now complete (Figure 17–88). Save the dashboard and the workspace.

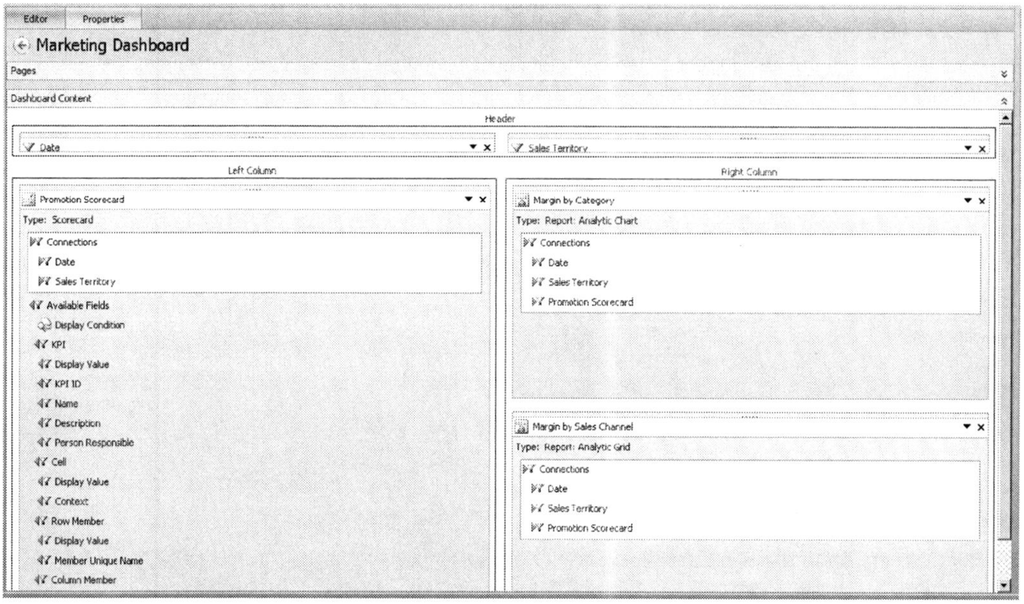

**Figure 17–88.** *The completed dashboard*

# Deploying the Solution to SharePoint, and Exploring

We are now ready to deploy our dashboard and start analyzing data. Remember that the dashboard we created in the previous section is only the definition for a dashboard. That definition is stored in our PerformancePoint Content list. When we deploy the dashboard, the definition is converted into a folder of ASPX pages that implement our dashboard.

Note that PerformancePoint uses Silverlight controls to render some of the UI controls. Now would be a good time to download and install the latest version of Silverlight from www.microsoft.com/silverlight.

- Open the Marketing.ddwx file in Dashboard Designer.

- Right-click on the Marketing Dashboard item and select Deploy to SharePoint… as shown in Figure 17–89.

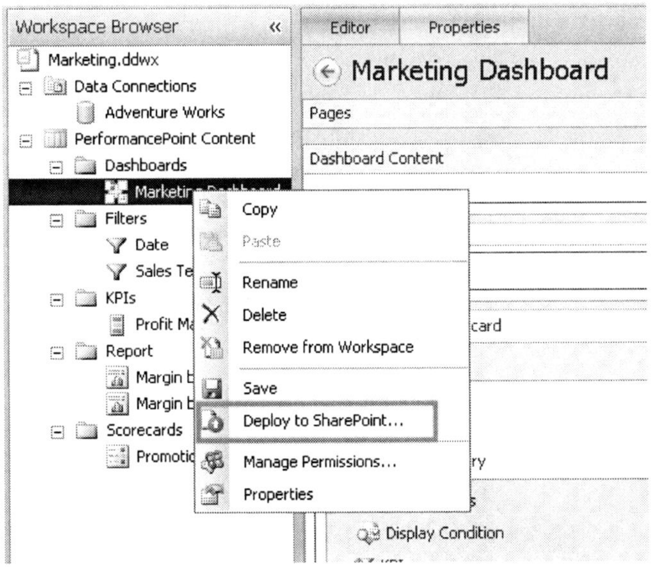

*Figure 17–89. Deploying to SharePoint*

- Since this is the first time we've deployed the dashboard, Dashboard Designer will prompt for a destination location for the dashboard.

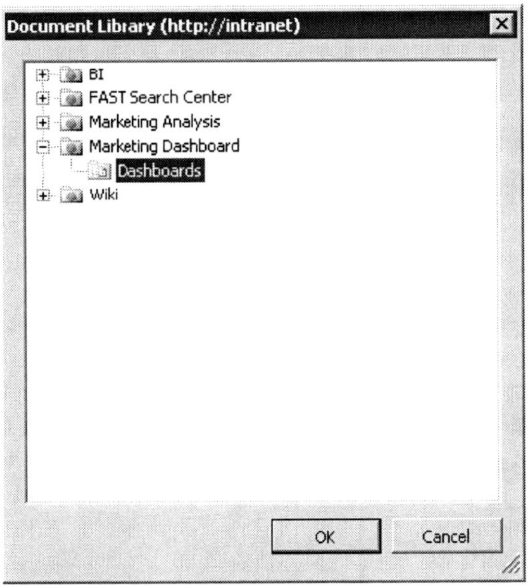

*Figure 17–90. Putting the dashboard in the Dashboards library*

- Select the Dashboards document library in the BI Center site (Figure 17–90) and click OK.

- After a few seconds, a web browser window will open to the Sales Summary page of the dashboard (Figure 17–91).

- Select a time period in the Date filter that contains data. The scorecard and both reports are filtered accordingly.

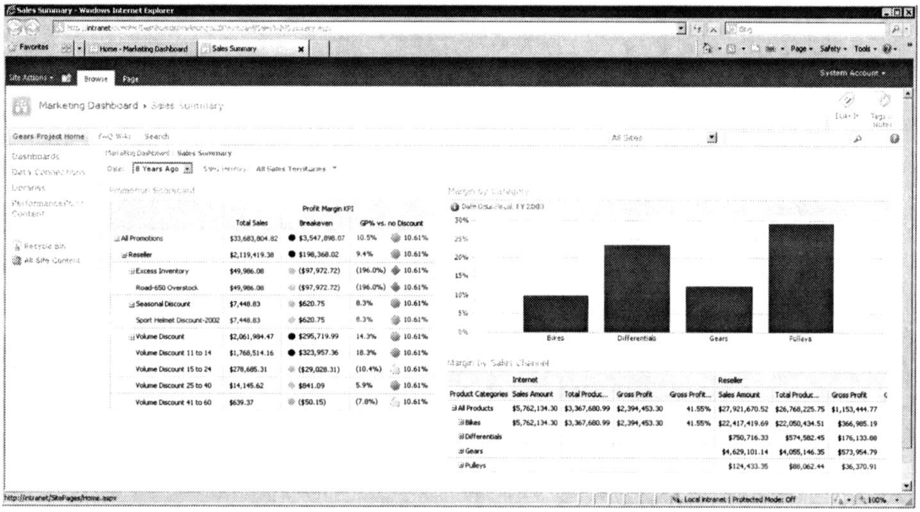

*Figure 17–91. The Sales Summary page*

- Select a Sales Territory. Notice the text displayed in the Information Window above the "Margin by Category" chart (Figure 17–92).

Margin by Category

ⓘ Date Date.Fiscal: **FY 2003**, Sales Territory: **United States**

30%

*Figure 17–92. Text in the information window*

- Close the web browser and open a new window to view the dashboard. Note that the filter values selected in the previous session are remembered (Figure 17–93).

Marketing Dashboard : **Sales Summary**

Date: | 8 Years Ago ▼ |    Sales Territory:    United States ▼

*Figure 17–93. Values from the previous session are remembered.*

- Click on a row on the scorecard. Note the changes that occur on the reports to the right (Figure 17–94).

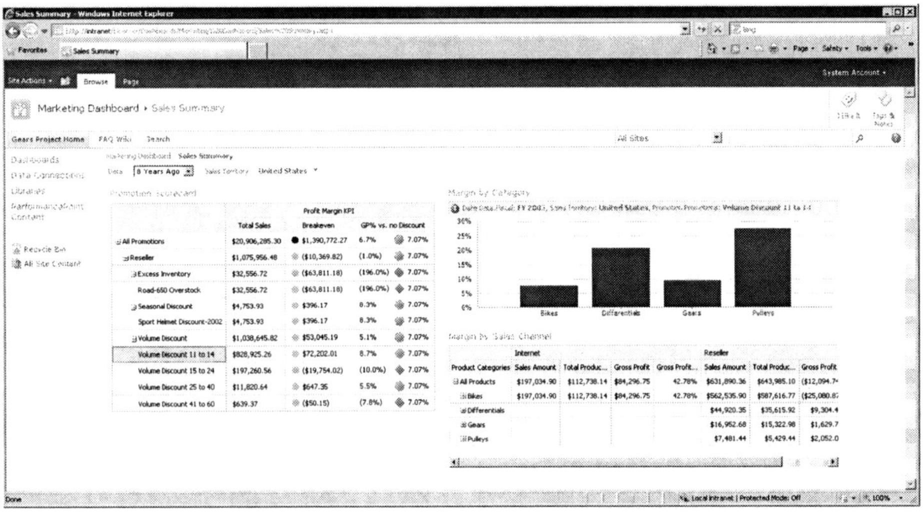

*Figure 17–94. Click a row on the scorecard to modify the reports*

- Right-click on one of the cells in the Margin by Sales Channel report and select Show Details. A window is displayed containing all of the data that went into that cell. This data can also be exported to Excel for further analysis (Figure 17–95).

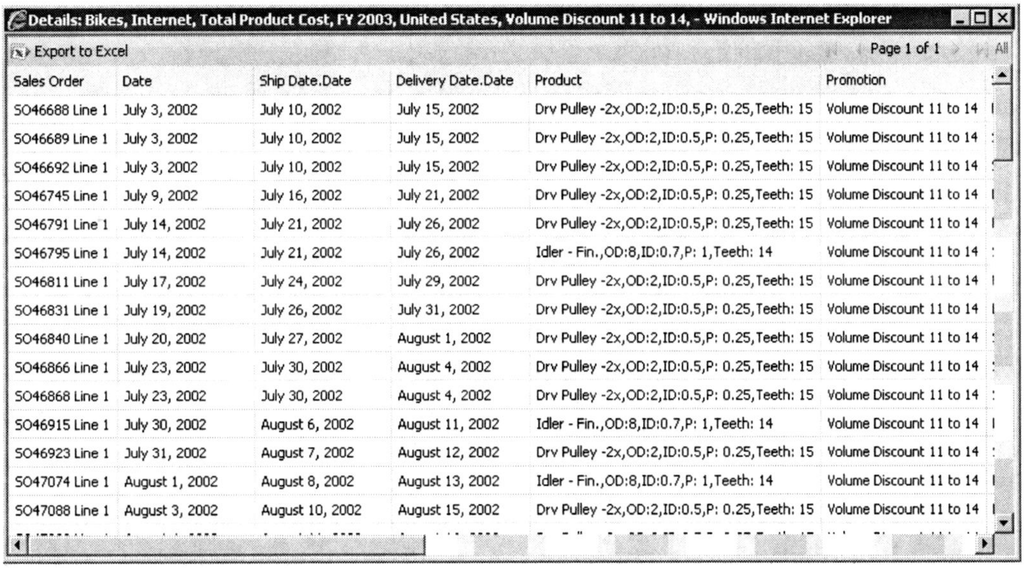


| Sales Order | Date | Ship Date.Date | Delivery Date.Date | Product | Promotion |
|---|---|---|---|---|---|
| SO46688 Line 1 | July 3, 2002 | July 10, 2002 | July 15, 2002 | Drv Pulley -2x,OD:2,ID:0.5,P: 0.25,Teeth: 15 | Volume Discount 11 to 14 |
| SO46689 Line 1 | July 3, 2002 | July 10, 2002 | July 15, 2002 | Drv Pulley -2x,OD:2,ID:0.5,P: 0.25,Teeth: 15 | Volume Discount 11 to 14 |
| SO46692 Line 1 | July 3, 2002 | July 10, 2002 | July 15, 2002 | Drv Pulley -2x,OD:2,ID:0.5,P: 0.25,Teeth: 15 | Volume Discount 11 to 14 |
| SO46745 Line 1 | July 9, 2002 | July 16, 2002 | July 21, 2002 | Drv Pulley -2x,OD:2,ID:0.5,P: 0.25,Teeth: 15 | Volume Discount 11 to 14 |
| SO46791 Line 1 | July 14, 2002 | July 21, 2002 | July 26, 2002 | Drv Pulley -2x,OD:2,ID:0.5,P: 0.25,Teeth: 15 | Volume Discount 11 to 14 |
| SO46795 Line 1 | July 14, 2002 | July 21, 2002 | July 26, 2002 | Idler - Fin.,OD:8,ID:0.7,P: 1,Teeth: 14 | Volume Discount 11 to 14 |
| SO46811 Line 1 | July 17, 2002 | July 24, 2002 | July 29, 2002 | Drv Pulley -2x,OD:2,ID:0.5,P: 0.25,Teeth: 15 | Volume Discount 11 to 14 |
| SO46831 Line 1 | July 19, 2002 | July 26, 2002 | July 31, 2002 | Drv Pulley -2x,OD:2,ID:0.5,P: 0.25,Teeth: 15 | Volume Discount 11 to 14 |
| SO46840 Line 1 | July 20, 2002 | July 27, 2002 | August 1, 2002 | Drv Pulley -2x,OD:2,ID:0.5,P: 0.25,Teeth: 15 | Volume Discount 11 to 14 |
| SO46866 Line 1 | July 23, 2002 | July 30, 2002 | August 4, 2002 | Drv Pulley -2x,OD:2,ID:0.5,P: 0.25,Teeth: 15 | Volume Discount 11 to 14 |
| SO46868 Line 1 | July 23, 2002 | July 30, 2002 | August 4, 2002 | Drv Pulley -2x,OD:2,ID:0.5,P: 0.25,Teeth: 15 | Volume Discount 11 to 14 |
| SO46915 Line 1 | July 30, 2002 | August 6, 2002 | August 11, 2002 | Idler - Fin.,OD:8,ID:0.7,P: 1,Teeth: 14 | Volume Discount 11 to 14 |
| SO46923 Line 1 | July 31, 2002 | August 7, 2002 | August 12, 2002 | Drv Pulley -2x,OD:2,ID:0.5,P: 0.25,Teeth: 15 | Volume Discount 11 to 14 |
| SO47074 Line 1 | August 1, 2002 | August 8, 2002 | August 13, 2002 | Idler - Fin.,OD:8,ID:0.7,P: 1,Teeth: 14 | Volume Discount 11 to 14 |
| SO47088 Line 1 | August 3, 2002 | August 10, 2002 | August 15, 2002 | Drv Pulley -2x,OD:2,ID:0.5,P: 0.25,Teeth: 15 | Volume Discount 11 to 14 |

*Figure 17–95. Exporting data to Excel*

- Right-click on one of the cells in the Margin by Sales Channel report and select Decomposition Tree. A window is displayed that allows the user to decompose the results in the cell in any way needed to discern patterns (Figure 17–96).

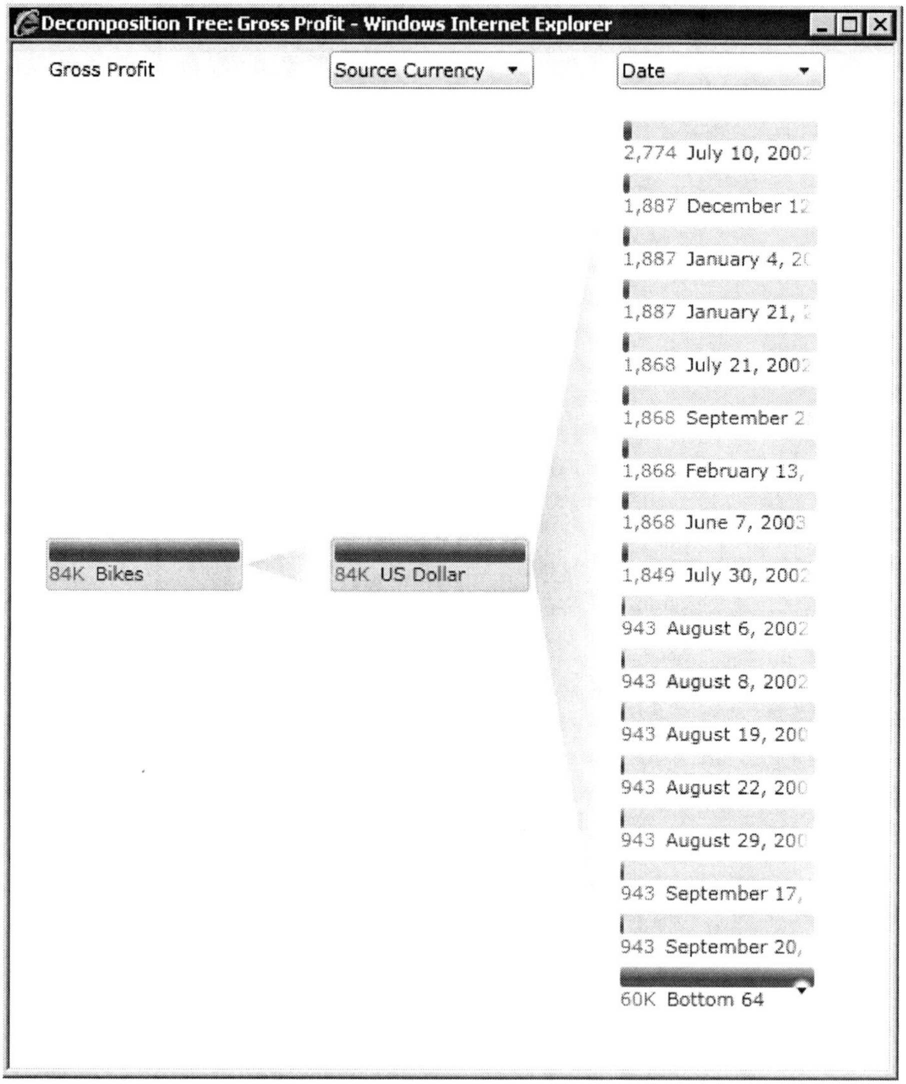

**Figure 17–96.** *Decomposing a cell*

# Advanced Report Types

Now let's extend our sample dashboard to include data from two external sources: Excel and Visio. The data will be integrated using the Excel Services and Strategy Map report types, respectively.

**PROBLEM CASE**

Extend the marketing dashboard to allow users to analyze data by sales territory and promotion hierarchy.

*Solution:*

We will add two additional pages to our dashboard, one using Excel Services reports and another using a Strategy Map report.

# Create an Excel Services Report

Microsoft Excel is one of the most widely used packages for doing numerical analysis. As a file-based desktop application, however, it is limited in its ability to reach a large audience and integrate with other solutions. As we saw in Chapter 5, SharePoint Server 2010 incorporates Excel Services to address these issues by creating a server environment for storing, processing, and delivering Excel content. With PerformancePoint Services, we have the opportunity to leverage Excel's analytical abilities and familiar user interface to integrate rich reports into our PPS solutions.

In this section, we will create a simple Excel Services spreadsheet and deploy it to SharePoint. Then, we will integrate the elements of that spreadsheet into our existing dashboard as a pair of new reports on a new page. The new page will allow us to view a grid and a chart with a breakdown of our sales figures by Sales Territory.

- Launch Excel 2010 and create a new blank workbook.

- On the ribbon menu, select Data ➤ From Other Sources ➤ From Analysis Services.

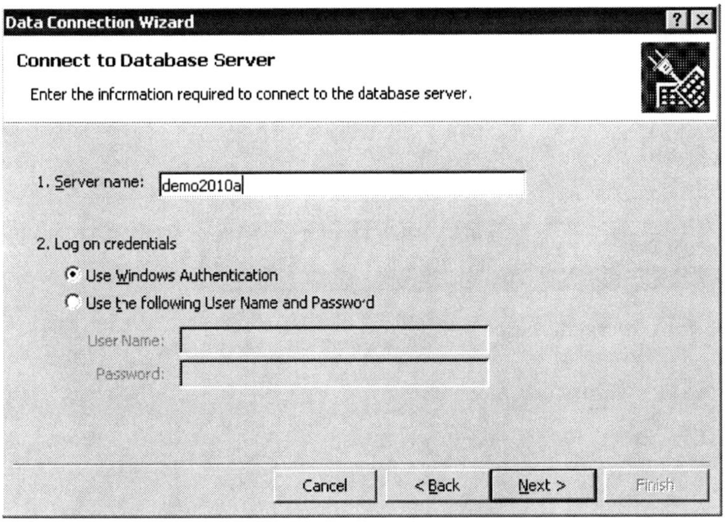

*Figure 17–97. Selecting the database server to connect to*

- Enter the name of the SSAS server containing the Adventure Works DW database as shown in Figure 17–97.

- Click Next.

- Select the Adventure Works DW database.

- Select the Adventure Works cube.

- Click Next.

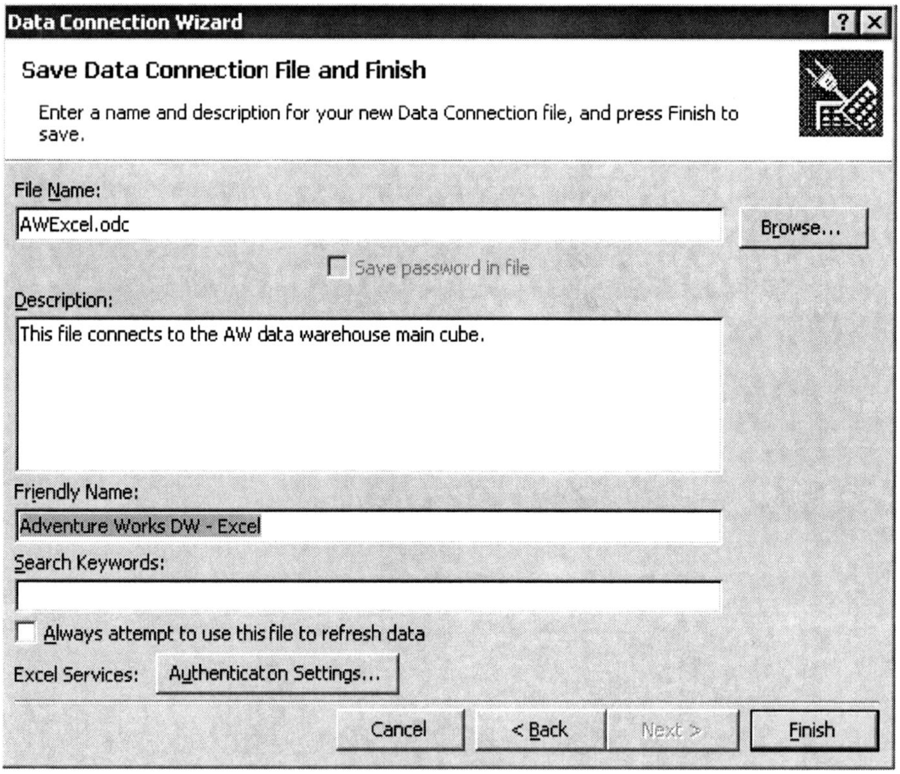

*Figure 17–98. Entering a name for the data connection file*

- Enter "AWExcel.odc" for the File Name (Figure 17–98).

- Enter "Adventure Works DW – Excel" for the Friendly Name.

- Click Finish.

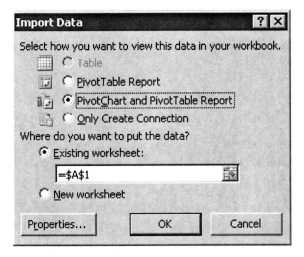

*Figure 17–99. Choosing how to view data in the workbook*

- Select PivotChart and PivotTable Report (Figure 17–99) and click OK.

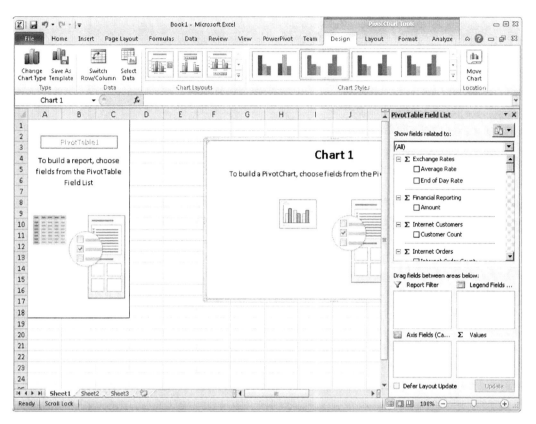

*Figure 17–100. The Pivot Table Field List*

- From the Pivot Table Field List (Figure 17–100), drag the fields listed in Table 17–5 into the indicated panel at the lower right of the Excel window.

*Table 17–5. Pivot Table Fields*

| Field | Panel |
|-------|-------|
| Date ➤ Fiscal ➤ Date.Fiscal | Report Filter |
| Promotion ➤ Promotions | Report Filter |
| Sales Territory ➤ Sales Territory | Axis Fields |
| Sales Summary ➤ Sales Amount | Values |

- The spreadsheet should now look like the image in Figure 17–101.

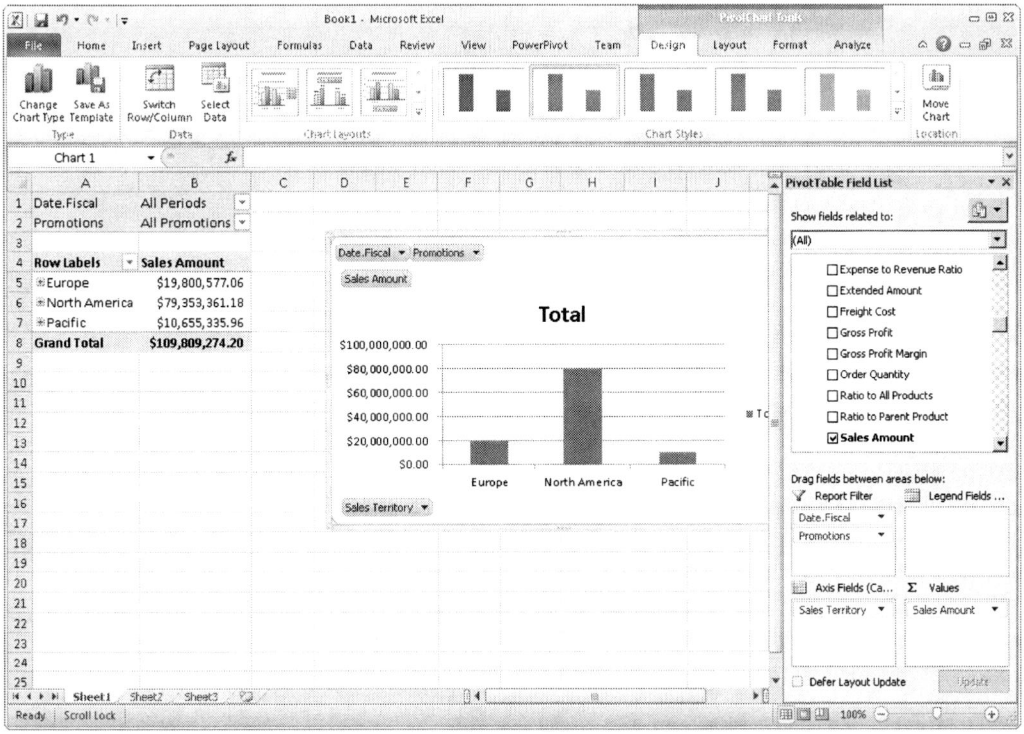

*Figure 17–101. The pivot chart*

- Right-click on the chart and change the chart type to Pie.

- Right-click on the chart title and select Delete.

- From the ribbon menu, select PivotChart Tools ➤ Layout ➤ Data Labels ➤ Best Fit (Figure 17–102).

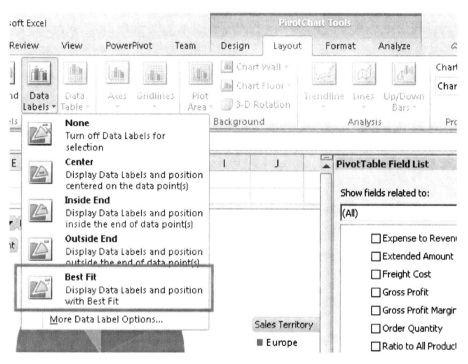

*Figure 17–102. Displaying data labels*

- From the ribbon menu, select PivotChart Tools ➤ Layout ➤ Properties. Enter "SalesChart" into the Chart Name box (Figure 17–103).

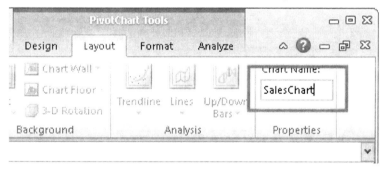

*Figure 17–103. Entering the chart name*

- Click on one of the cells in the PivotTable.

- From the ribbon menu, select PivotTable Tools ➤ Options ➤ PivotTable. Enter "SalesTable" into the PivotTable Name box (Figure 17–104).

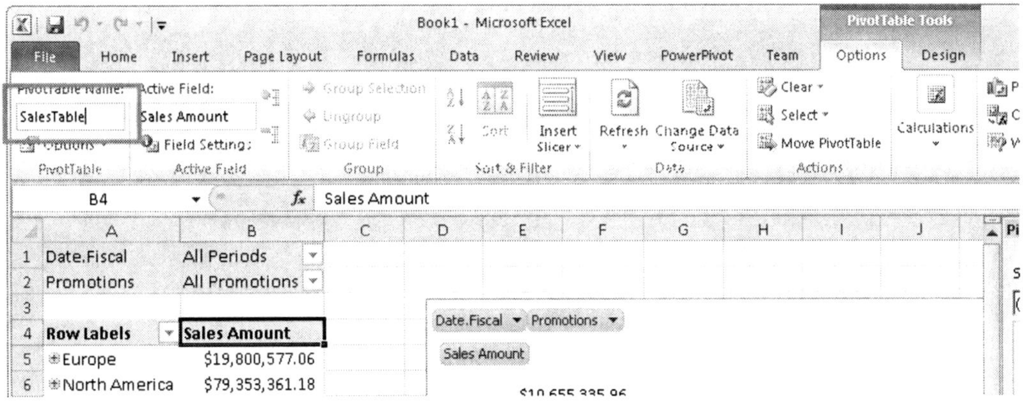

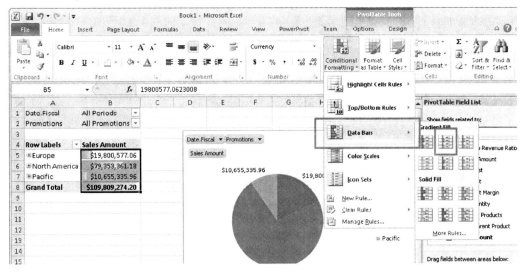

*Figure 17–104. Entering the name of the pivot table*

- Select the "Sales Amount" column cells on the PivotTable.

- Select Home ➤ Styles ➤ Conditional Formatting ➤ Data Bars and select one of the options shown (Figure 17–105).

*Figure 17–105. Selecting a style for the data bars*

- Click on cell B1. This should be the All Periods value for the Date.Fiscal filter. Be sure to select the value cell (B1), not the label cell (A1).

- Type "Date" into the name box and press Enter (Figure 17–106).

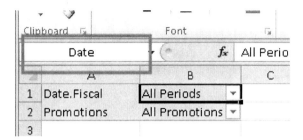

***Figure 17–106.** Setting up conditional formatting for the Date filter*

- Click on cell B2. This should be the All Promotions value for the Promotions filter. Be sure to select the value cell (B2), not the label cell (A2).

- Type Promotions into the name box and press Enter.

    The Excel spreadsheet is now ready to be published to SharePoint. For simplicity, we will store it in the Dashboards library in our BI Center site (though it could be stored in any location trusted by Excel Services). First, we'll create a copy of the data connection we're using.

- From the ribbon menu, select Data ➤ Connections ➤ Properties.

- Select the Definition tab (Figure 17–107).

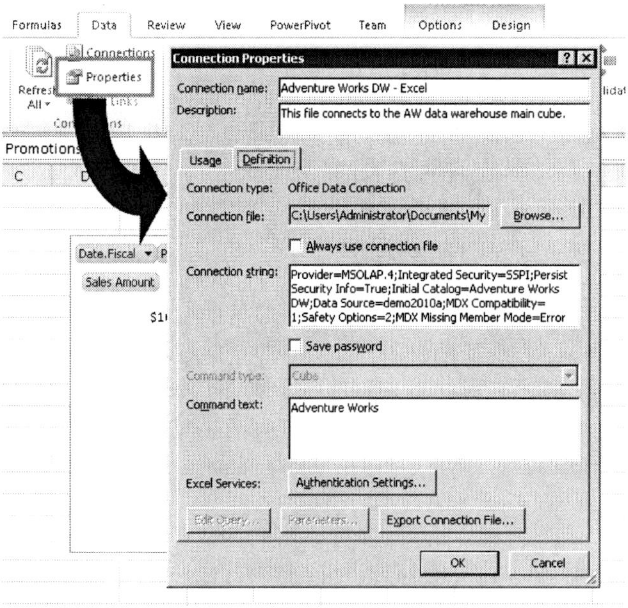

***Figure 17–107.** Copying the data connection*

- Click the Export Connection File… button.

- In the File Save dialog, navigate to the Data Connections library in the BI Center site.

- Set the file name to "AW for Excel" and click Save (Figure 17–108).

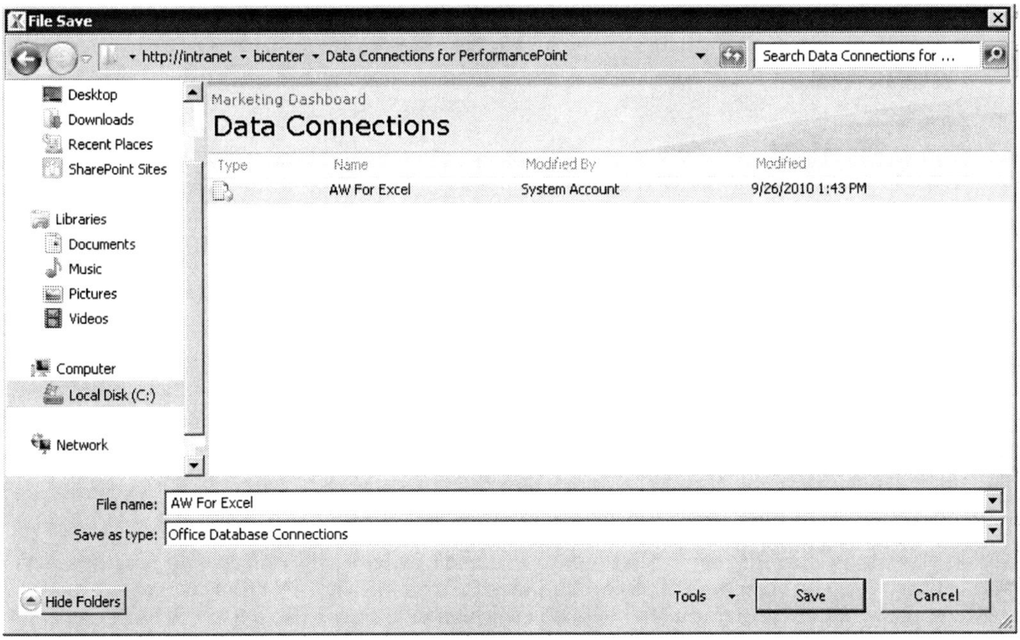

*Figure 17–108. Naming the data connection file*

- Select Office Data Connection File as the Content Type and click OK (Figure 17–109).

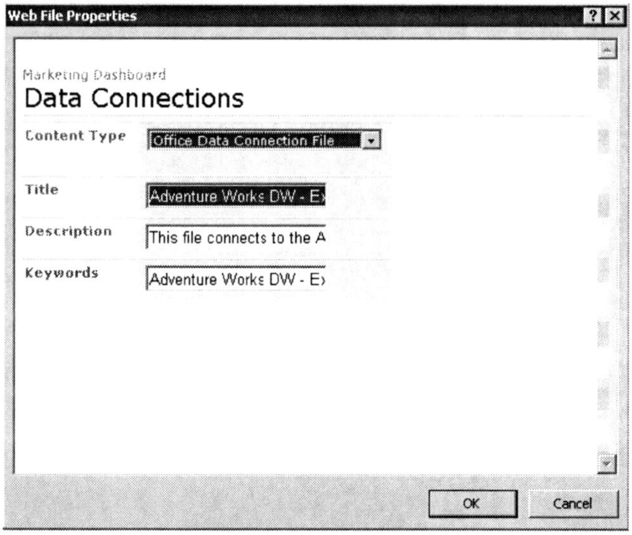

*Figure 17–109. Selecting the content type of the data connection file*

- Click Cancel to dismiss the Connection Properties dialog.

Before we publish the spreadsheet to SharePoint, we need to identify the objects and parameters to expose to Excel Services. The objects we'll use are the SalesChart and SalesTable objects. We will declare the Date and Promotions cells as parameters, which PerformancePoint will use to pass in dashboard filter selections.

- From the ribbon menu, select File ➤ Save & Send ➤ Save to SharePoint.

- Click the Publish Options button.

- Select Items in the Workbook from the drop-down list (Figure 17–110).

- Check the SalesChart and SalesTable items.

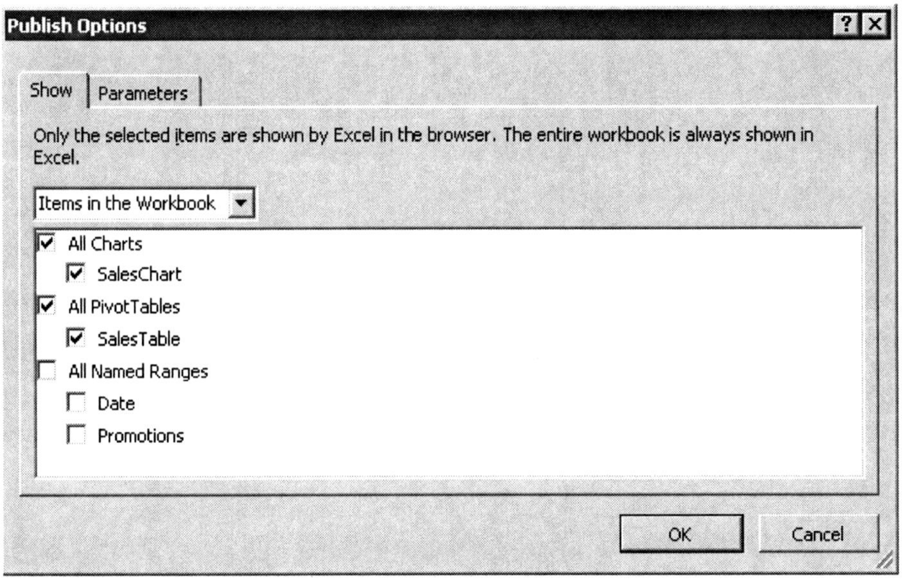

*Figure 17–110. Choosing the items that will be displayed in the browser*

- Switch to the Parameters tab (Figure 17–111).

- Click the Add button.

- Check both available parameters and click OK.

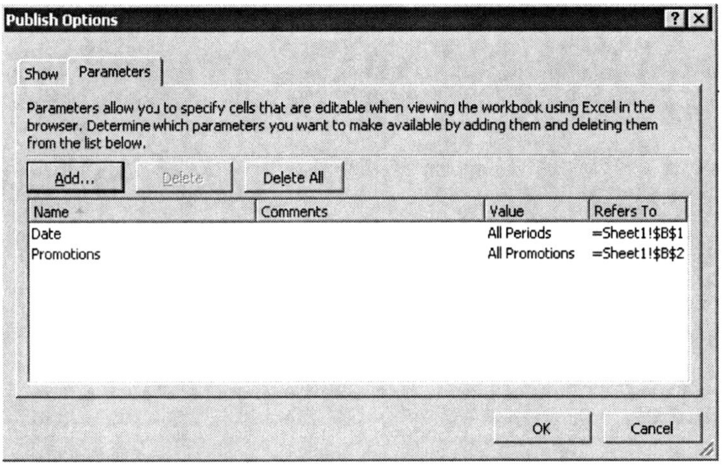

*Figure 17–111. Adding parameters*

- Click OK.

- If the Dashboards library is not shown under Locations (Figure 17–112), select Browse for a location to add it.

*Figure 17–112. Saving to SharePoint*

- Double-click the location to publish the file to SharePoint.
- Enter the file name "AWExcelRpt" in the Save As dialog and click Save.
- Select Document as the content type and click OK.
- The spreadsheet will be displayed in a new browser window.
- Close the new browser window and Excel.

Now that we have a spreadsheet published to SharePoint, we will add the PivotTable and PivotChart as reports in a new page on our dashboard.

- Open the Marketing.ddwx file in Dashboard Designer.
- Right-click on the PerformancePoint Content list and select New ➤ Report.
- Select the Excel Services template and click OK.
- Set the name of the report to "Sales Table".
- Enter the URL for the BI Center site in the "SharePoint site" box on the report editor (Figure 17–113).
- Select the Dashboards library.
- Select "AWExcelRpt.xls" file for the workbook.
- Select "SalesTable" for the item name.

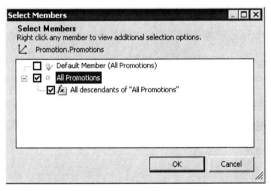

**Figure 17–113.** *Adding a new Sales Table report*

- Note that the Dashboard Designer has already identified the Workbook Parameters: Date and Promotions.

- Copy and paste the Sales Table report in the Workspace Browser.

- Rename "Sales Table – Copy" to "Sales Chart."

- Select SalesChart from the Item name drop-down on the Sales Chart report editor.

- Save both reports and the workspace file.

- Right-click on the PerformancePoint Content list and select New ➤ Filter.

- Select the Member Selection filter template and click OK.

- Select Adventure Works for the data source and click Next.

- Press Select Dimension… and choose Promotion.Promotions.

- Click OK.

- Press Select Members… and select All Promotions and all of its descendants (Figure 17–114).

**Figure 17–114.** *Selecting the All Promotions member*

- Click OK to move to the next screen (Figure 17–115).

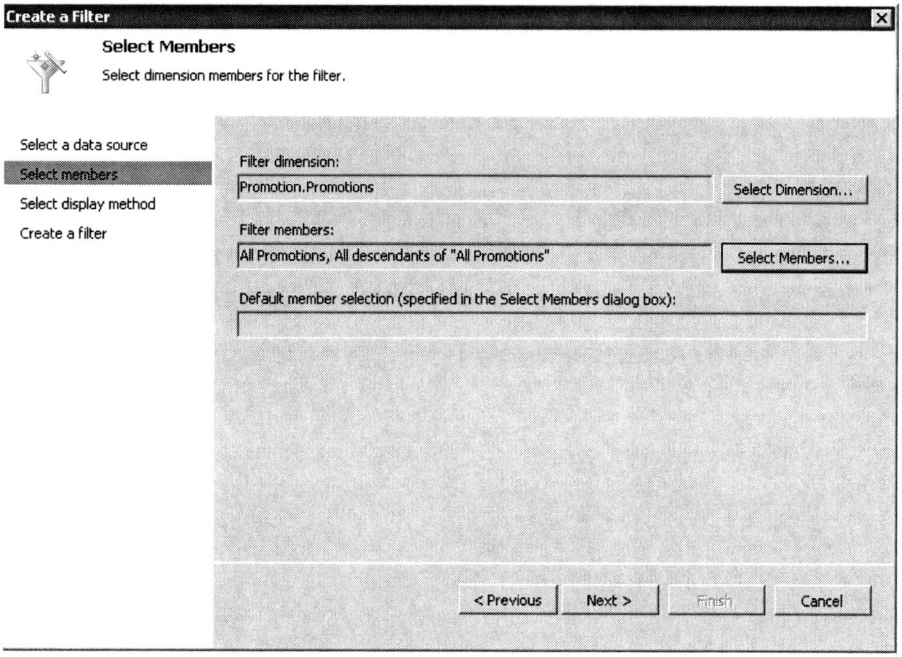

**Figure 17–115.** *Creating a filter*

- Click Next.
- Select Tree and click Next.
- Name the new filter Promotion.

We now have the new filter and reports created for our new page. Next we'll create the new dashboard page and deploy the dashboard.

- Select the Marketing Dashboard in the Workspace Browser.
- Click New Page in the dashboard editor and select the default template.
- Name the page "Sales by Promotion".
- From Details, drag the Date and Promotion filters into the header of the new page.
- From Details, drag the Sales Table report into the left column zone.
- From Details, drag the Sales Chart report into the right column zone.
- Add the connections shown in Table 17–6 to the page.

*Table 17–6. Connections for the Dashboard*

| Get Values From | Send Values To | Connect To | Source Value |
|---|---|---|---|
| Date Filter | Sales Table | Date | Member Unique Name |
| Promotion Filter | Sales Table | Promotions | Member Unique Name |
| Date Filter | Sales Chart | Date | Member Unique Name |
| Promotion Filter | Sales Chart | Promotions | Member Unique Name |

The dashboard page should now resemble the image in Figure 17–116..

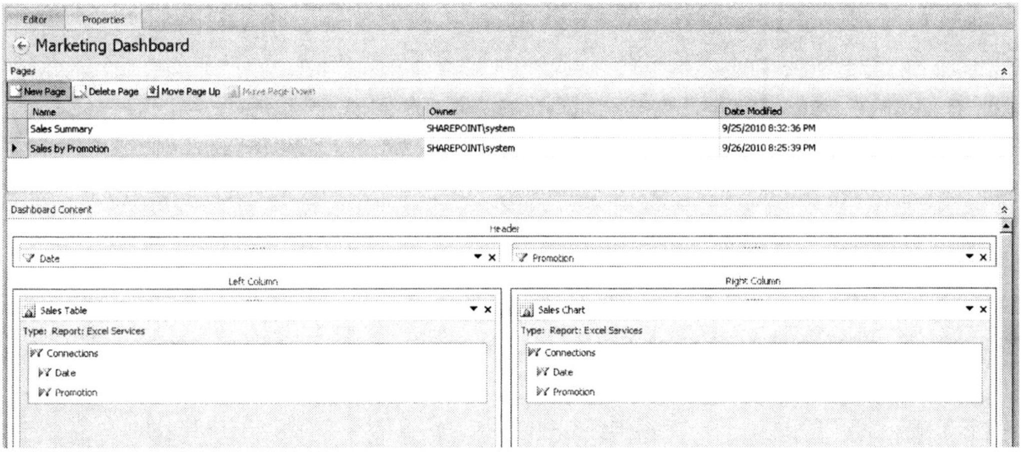

*Figure 17–116. The dashboard page*

- Right-click the Marketing Dashboard and select Deploy to SharePoint….
- When the browser window opens, click on the Sales by Promotion link.

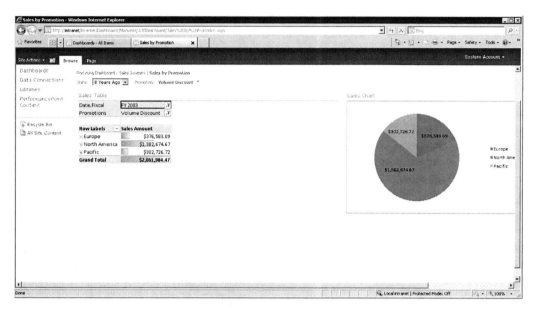

***Figure 17–117.*** *Excel reports displayed in the browser*

Notice that all of the formatting from Excel is displayed on the dashboard, including the pie chart and data bars (Figure 17–117). Now any changes made to the Excel spreadsheet will automatically be reflected in the dashboard. This allows users who are more comfortable with Excel to author reports that can be integrated with the rest of a PerformancePoint solution.

## Create a Strategy Map Report

Microsoft Visio is a powerful desktop visualization tool. As we saw in Chapter 2, the Visio Services component in SharePoint Server 2010 allows Visio diagrams to be brought to life with real data. With PerformancePoint Services, we can take that integration one step further. A Visio diagram can be created that visually represents the KPIs on a scorecard. Those KPIs can then be connected to the Visio diagram to create a graphical representation of the status of the enterprise. In PerformancePoint, this type of report is called a *strategy map.*

In this section, we will create a simple Visio diagram that we'll deploy to PerformancePoint as a Strategy Map report. The term "strategy map" refers to a particular type of diagram often used in conjunction with the "balanced scorecard" methodology. While this feature in PerformancePoint is ideally suited for implementing that type of map, any Visio diagram can be used as long as it contains only simple shapes that don't involve sets or groupings within Visio.

---

■ **Note** Readers who are not familiar with Visio or Visio Services should review Chapter 2 before proceeding with the rest of this section.

---

- Launch Visio 2010 and create a new blank diagram using the Basic Diagram (US Units) template.

- Create a diagram with a set of simple shapes that looks something like the image in Figure 17–118. The precise details of the diagram are not important.

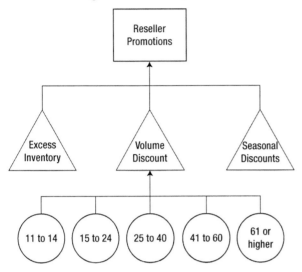

*Figure 17–118. A simple Visio diagram*

- Save the file with the file name Promotion Tree.vsd anywhere on your local computer.

- Close Visio.

- Open the Marketing.ddwx file in Dashboard Designer.

- Right-click on the PerformancePoint Content list and select New ➤ Report.

- Select the Strategy Map template from the Select a Report Template dialog and click OK.

- Select the Promotion Scorecard as the scorecard for the strategy map (Figure 119). The Strategy Map report uses a scorecard as a data source instead of a normal data source object.

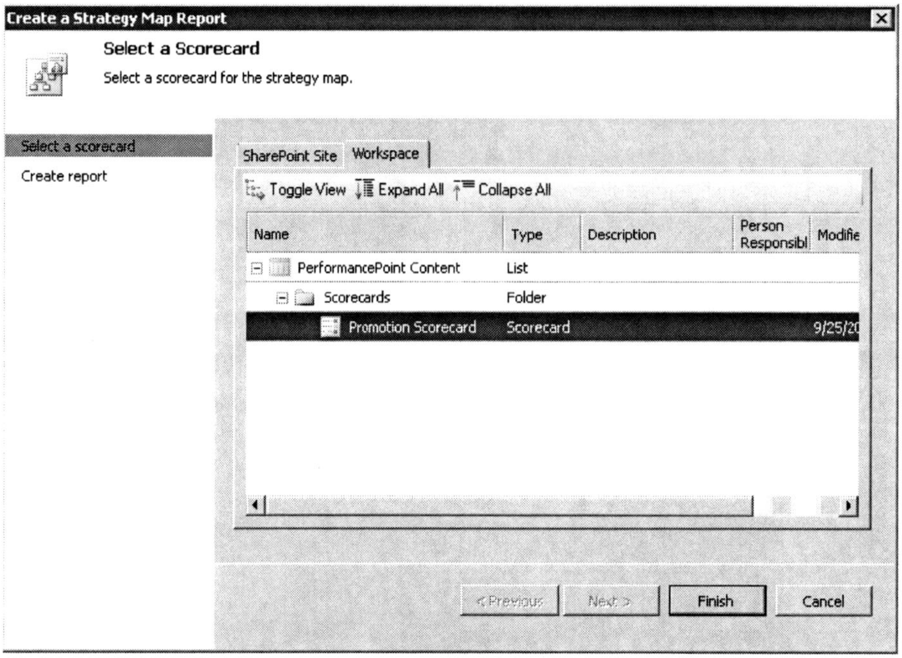

*Figure 17–119. Creating a strategy map report using the Promotion Scorecard*

- Click Finish.

- Name the new report Promotion Map.

- From the ribbon menu, select Edit ➤ Report Editor ➤ Edit Strategy Map (Figure 17–120).

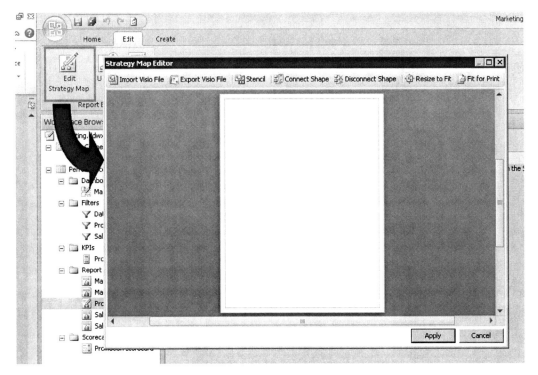

*Figure 17–120. The Strategy Map Editor*

- Click the Import Visio File button.
- To connect the Reseller Promotions shape to the scorecard, click on the shape and then on the Connect Shape button as shown in Figure 17–121.

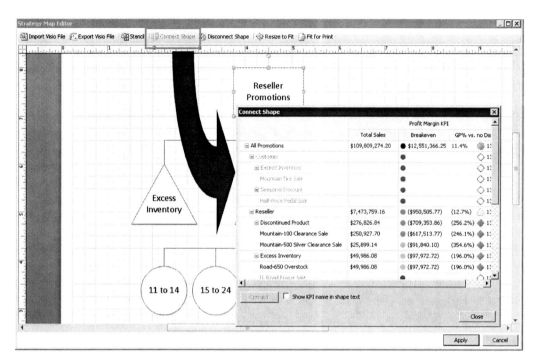

**Figure 17–121.** *Connecting the Reseller Promotions shape to the scorecard*

- The Connect Shape dialog shows a view of the underlying scorecard. Select the cell at the intersection of the Reseller row and the GP% vs. no Discount column.

- Ensure that the "Show KPI name in shape text" checkbox is not selected and click the Connect button.

- Click Close and the Reseller Promotions shape will now be colored the same as the KPI.

- Repeat steps 14 though 117 for each of the other shapes on the diagram. When complete, the diagram should look like the image in Figure 17–122. Your colors may vary depending on the filters that are active in your environment. The important thing is to connect the proper shape to the correct KPI.

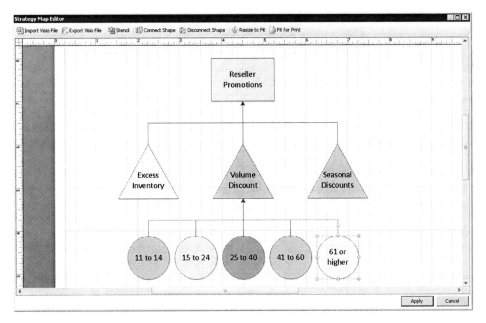

*Figure 17–122. The Visio diagram with all shapes connected to the scorecard*

- Drag the cursor over the diagram to select all of the shapes.
- Right-click one of the shapes and select Data ➤ Edit Data Graphic…
- Click the New Item… button.
- On the New Item dialog, select the options indicated in Table 17–7 and shown in Figure 17–123.

*Table 17–7. Options for the Shapes*

| Field | Value |
| --- | --- |
| Display ➤ Data Field | Status |
| Display ➤ Displayed as | Text |
| Position ➤ Use default position | unchecked |
| Position ➤ Horizontal | Center |
| Position ➤ Vertical | Below Shape |
| Details ➤ Label Position | Not Shown |
| Details ➤ Border Type | None |

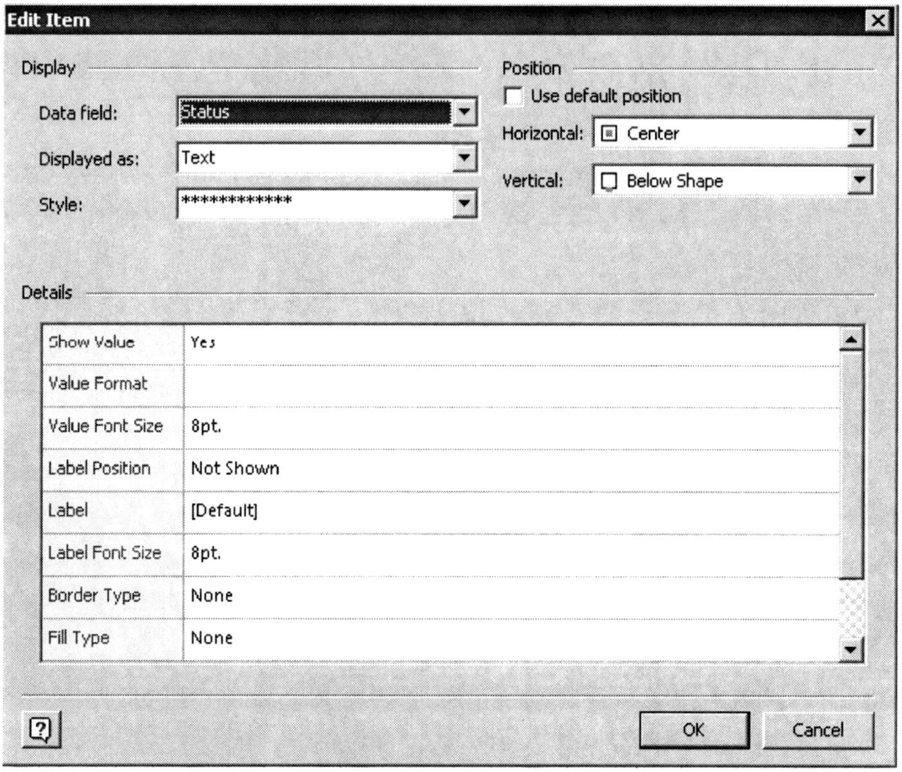

*Figure 17–123. Values for the data graphic*

- Click OK to create the Data Graphic.
- Click OK to save Data Graphics.
- Answer "Yes" to "Do you want to apply this data graphic to the selected shapes?"
- Now the map should look something like Figure 17–124.

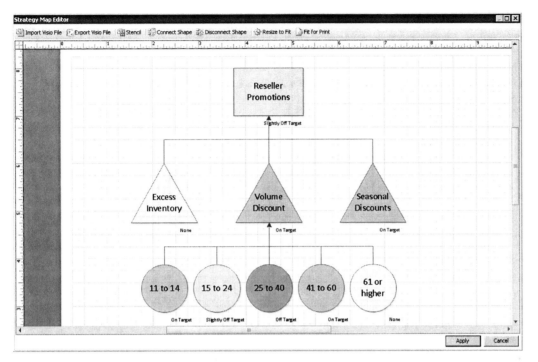

*Figure 17–124. The shapes with the data graphic applied*

- Click Apply.
- Save the Promotion Map report and the workspace.
- Select the Marketing Dashboard in the Workspace Browser.
- Add a new page to the dashboard with the default template.
- Name the page "Promotion Map."
- Add the components in Table 17–8 to the zones of the new page.

*Table 17–8. Components for the New Page*

| Component | Zone |
| --- | --- |
| Date Filter | Header |
| Sales Territory Filter | Header |
| Promotion Scorecard | Left Column |
| Promotion Map Report | Right Column |

- Create the connections shown in Table 17–9.

*Table 17–9. Connections for the New Page*

| Get Values From | Send Values To | Connect To | Source Value |
|---|---|---|---|
| Date Filter | Promotion Scorecard | Page | Member Unique Name |
| Sales Territory Filter | Promotion Scorecard | Page | Member Unique Name |
| Date Filter | Promotion Map Report | Page | Member Unique Name |
| Sales Territory Filter | Promotion Map Report | Page | Member Unique Name |

- The dashboard should now look like Figure 17–125.

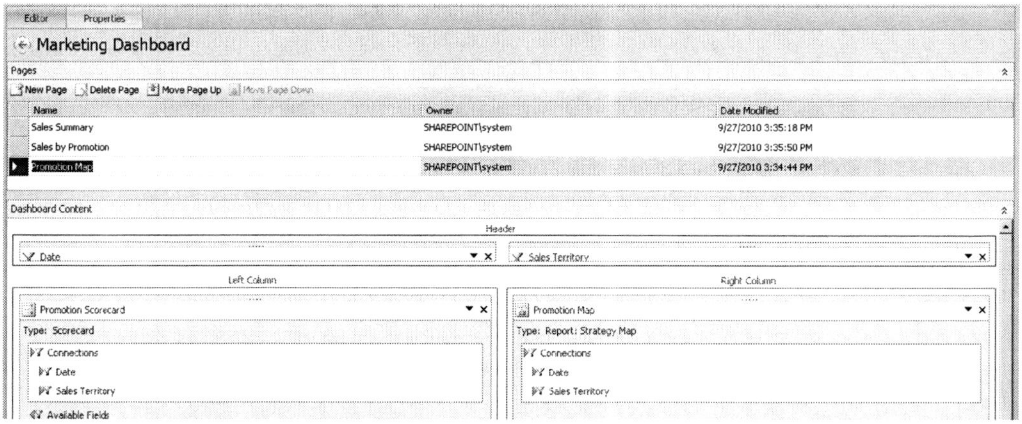

*Figure 17–125. The Marketing Dashboard*

- Save the dashboard and workspace.
- Deploy the dashboard to SharePoint.

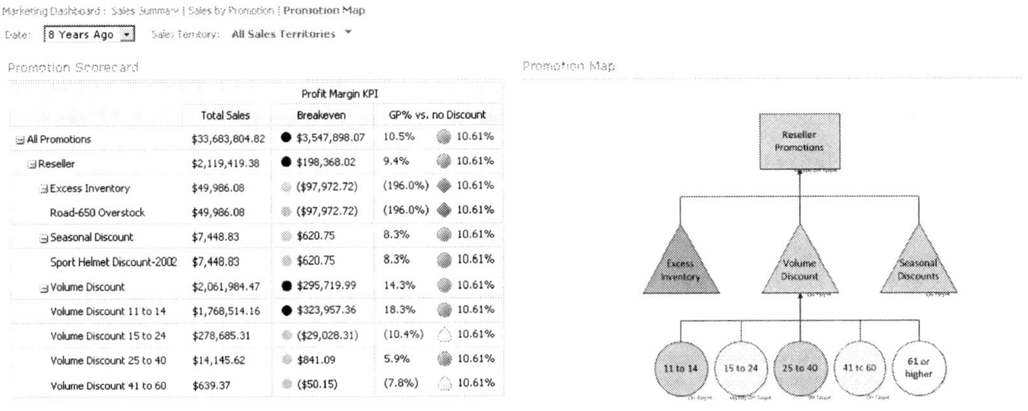

*Figure 17–126. Trying out the strategy map*

Try selecting different values for the Date and Sales Territory filters (Figure 17–126). Both the scorecard and the map are updated simultaneously. There are several features of the map to note:

- The end user can zoom in and out as desired by right-clicking on the map.

- By holding Ctrl and clicking on a shape, users can select that shape. Right-clicking a selected shape provides the option to view a detailed list of KPI properties.

- While it is common to display the scorecard associated with a strategy map on the same page, it's not required. The scorecard is still an active part of the dashboard even when it's not visible on the current page. Therefore, you could remove the scorecard from this page and the only effect would to be to hide it. The strategy map would still function correctly.

There is an important limitation when using strategy maps that can be handled with a little additional planning. In our example, if we select a different date range and sales territory, we may see rows on the scorecard that don't appear on the map, or we may see rows on the scorecard disappear due to a lack of data. These shapes still appear on the map, but they don't show a color. When we connect shapes to the scorecard, that connection is static. We can't change that association as needed to fit how the scorecard is filtered. We also can't add shapes as new rows appear in the scorecard.

There are different strategies for handling such situations. One way is to include every possible shape on the map. You could also limit the filtering of the page to prevent unwanted rows from appearing in the scorecard. Regardless, the shapes on the map and how they are associated are fixed at runtime.

Strategy maps are a versatile way to add visualization to your solution. They can be used to provide a user-friendly means of interpreting your key performance indicators.

# Summary

In this chapter, we have explored PerformancePoint Service as outlined in Figure 17–127, including:

- The components of the PerformancePoint Services architecture.

- How to configure PerformancePoint Services using both Central Administration and PowerShell commands.

- How to enable the features of PerformancePoint Services within a SharePoint site and deploy the Business Intelligence Center.

- How to use Dashboard Designer to author and deploy a dashboard and its supporting components to SharePoint 2010.

- How to integrate PerformancePoint Dashboards with diagrams using Visio Services and spreadsheets using Excel Services.

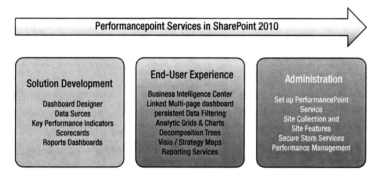

*Figure 17–127. PerformancePoint Services Road Map*

# CHAPTER 18

# Public-Facing SharePoint Sites

"Can we use SharePoint for our public-facing site? What benefit is there for us if we do?"

These are questions I get all the time in the field, usually coming from customers who have already had some level of exposure to SharePoint. Organizations have been adopting SharePoint and it's been spreading throughout their business areas, gaining a lot of traction with users. People like what it is doing for them, so the progression to looking at it for public-facing web content is a fairly natural one.

Having said that, the decision to use SharePoint for a public-facing site is one that is usually met with a lot more scrutiny from a business. An organization's public web site is very important to them; it's how a very large portion of people will get their first impression of the organization—and that first impression may be the difference between them looking further in to your business and potentially becoming a client, or simply moving on to the next web site their search engine has returned to them. There is a lot riding on a public-facing sites so the decision to use SharePoint, or any other technology, will need to be a well thought out one . The measure of success will ultimately be around how well the site is able to deliver real value for the organization, be it through gaining customers, increasing exposure, improving access to information, or any combination of these and other factors.

Using SharePoint on the Internet is not a new concept. Microsoft knows that the product is used this way and they have a licensing model that supports this. In fact, organizations such as Ferrari, AMD, and the United Nations have public-facing sites that are running on SharePoint (see Figure 18-1). SharePoint is used across many different industries including health, technology, education, and government; it's also used for sites based in countries all around the globe. There are literally thousands of sites that are driven by SharePoint and the number continues to grow every day.

**Figure 18-1.** *The Ferrari web site runs on SharePoint technology*

# What to Expect From This Chapter

I could easily fill a whole book with all the topics that could be covered when discussing how to do a public-facing site with SharePoint. Alas, I have only one chapter, so I will cover some high level concepts that I have found to be keys to success when delivering these kinds of sites with SharePoint.

Ideally, after reading this chapter you will have a good idea of the potential hurdles and issues you may need to address when you start a project to build a public-facing site. With that information in mind, you can dive deeper and make sure you are armed with all the information you need to provide a successful web site project with SharePoint.

# Getting Started

When an organization comes to me to talk about using SharePoint on the Internet, one of the first questions I will get is "Who else is doing it?" Organizations will often spend time looking for similar businesses and organizations that are also using SharePoint for their public-facing sites, which is a perfectly valid thing to do. People naturally feel safer knowing that what they are doing has already been done by someone else, and adoption of SharePoint for Internet sites is no exception. Luckily, there is a fantastic resource to help you find other SharePoint sites: www.WssDemo.com. Run by Ian Morrish of Microsoft, its sole purpose is to list all of the public-facing web sites running on SharePoint. You're able to view lists and sort and filter by industry, country, the version of SharePoint, and even a rating that scores the site on its quality. There is an excellent Pivot View of all the sites in the list at www.wssdemo.com/livepivot/. It's well worth a look before you begin any public-facing SharePoint venture.

# Why SharePoint?

When kicking off a project to build a public-facing web site, people will often have a lot of great ideas for content and design, but the decision about what technology to use to deliver the content is sometimes left up in the air. Will you use a content management system of some sort, or will you have a solution custom built? What current solutions meet your requirements? How much do these systems cost, both up front and longer term? To help make the decision to use SharePoint for a public-facing site, you will need to understand what makes it a good choice for your organization.

As mentioned, many organizations are using SharePoint internally for a range of uses. This internal use is often a driver for using the same technology for public web sites. When an organization invests in implementing SharePoint, a wide range of elements are put in place alongside SharePoint that help make sure it's successful. Hardware and infrastructure; disaster recovery plans; internal skills relating to administration, development, and end user training are just some of the examples of how organizations invest around the SharePoint platform, and this existing investment can translate out to a reduced investment when it comes to using the same SharePoint technology for the public site.

## Leveraging Existing Infrastructure

Hardware and infrastructure requirements will always be included in an assessment of a solution to use for your site, and organizations that are already using SharePoint may find that they don't need to provision as much to get their public site up and running. An example here is a business that already has extranet sites set up. If a SharePoint farm has already been provisioned for external use, it might be possible that this same farm could be reused and extended a little to accommodate a public-facing web site (this would require that the extranet farm was purchased with the SharePoint for Internet sites license, however). In this case, common services may be shared across the farm (such as managed metadata, Visio services, and even user profiles) which will mean you don't end up duplicating the resources required to run these services on a second farm.

Even if an existing farm can't be reused, there are still potential benefits to be had around infrastructure if SharePoint is used. Your organization may have existing SQL servers that are capable of providing database functionality to a new farm, again translating to less hardware required for the new farm. Other hardware and software investments relating to your existing SharePoint deployment may also be used for your new farm, including monitoring tools like Systems Centre Operations Manager (SCOM) or other third party products that relate to SharePoint infrastructure. When comparing SharePoint to other platforms for your public site, it's important that more than just the direct requirements of the software be taken into consideration. This can be one of the reasons that SharePoint can start to look like a more attractive option for the public site.

## Acknowledging Existing Skill Sets

Another area of heavy investment is training. From the staff managing the infrastructure through to the end users working with the system every day, there is a range of training and skills that are necessary to ensure success of a SharePoint project, this it's likely that a much smaller investment is needed to reuse the platform for a public site. Conversely, using a different application to drive the public site would mean introducing a whole new second range of skills specific to the other system, which will cost money and time to implement.

Moreover, existing infrastructure skills related to SharePoint can also be reused. Having the skills within your organization to maintain and manage your SharePoint farms can be critical to keeping your environments running smoothly and supporting a quick turnaround when things go wrong. Using SharePoint for the public site as well as internally means the same skills will apply to how it can be managed and monitored, even if configurations between farms are different.

Some organizations also have in-house development expertise and can create their own customizations for SharePoint. There is a bit of a learning curve to get up to speed in effectively creating custom code for SharePoint, and organizations will often invest in their people by sending them on training courses. Being able to use these skills for a public web site as well as internal development means a greater return on the organization's investment in training .

The last element that is not to be overlooked is end user training. This is very important, particularly in a large organization with a wide range of content authors. The reality is that having to learn one system is far easier than learning two. So if you have already made an investment in training your organization to use SharePoint for internal content, your staff will be able to adapt quite easily when using the public web site to publish content. This will mean less effort to produce training materials, less information for users to remember about how to create and manage content, and no need to have your help desk or support areas deal with users on two separate systems.

## Content is King

Now that you have made the decision to use SharePoint as the platform for your public-facing site and you're happy with your technology choice, you are free to focus on what will make up your site: content. Your choice of technology will always have some effect on how you plan to implement your content (not as much on the content itself) and SharePoint is no exception. By utilizing the features that SharePoint provides relating to web content management (WCM), you can deliver a compelling web presence that makes it easy to author content, manage, and maintain. Features such as workflow, search, content types, and metadata are common features that relate to how content is maintained, so appropriate planning around how to take advantage of these features is key to taking advantage of your investment in SharePoint.

## Workflows

One of the great features that SharePoint offers is a powerful workflow engine integrated into the platform, Based on Windows Workflow Foundation in .NET 3.5, it allows you to execute and track various processes against the content you put in to your SharePoint site, such as individual pages or documents. The most common example of workflow in a SharePoint WCM-based site is an approval workflow. SharePoint provides a basic version of out of the box, as shown in Figure 18-2; you can also create customized processes using SharePoint Designer 2010 or Visual Studio 2010.

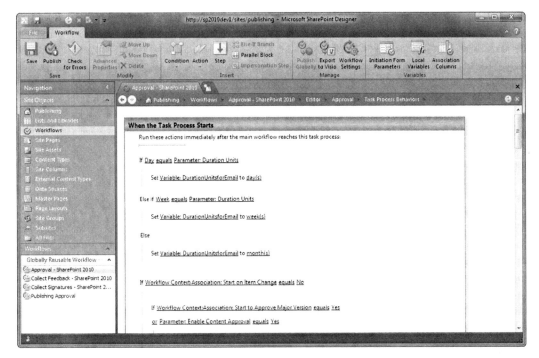

*Figure 18-2. The workflow designer in SharePoint Designer 2010*

The goal of the approval workflow is simple: to get an appropriate person to say that the content is approved before it goes to the general public. Nothing too complicated there. The reason this is such a useful concept for a public-facing site, though, is when you start to have the discussion around distributed content authoring. What this means is that you can begin to introduce people who normally wouldn't be responsible for the web site to editing content on the site—such as allowing specific sections or branches within the organization the rights to manage their own content. While these business areas will almost always have a solid grasp on their business and the information that needs to be conveyed through the site, they may not know how to write for the web, design standards for the site, web accessibility standards, etc. Having a good approval process in place here will help ensure that the content that hits the web site meets all of your organizational standards—and still allows you the flexibility to distribute the content authoring beyond the central team responsible for the web site.

To ensure the success of distributed authoring, appropriate thought will need to go in to planning your content approval process. Not only will you need to ask questions about who will be editing which sections of your site, but you need to know who will be approving the content also. Will there be one central team who approves it? Will managers from each section approve the content for their parts of the web site? Will you combine the two and have managers approve content and then have a web content team approve the web-specific elements of the page like accessibility and other elements? There is no one-size-fits-all approach; the answers to these questions will vary from organization to organization. What is important is that you ask the questions and document the process so you know exactly what you are implementing and why you are implementing it.

Of course, workflow can be used for much more than content approval. Other common uses in the WCM space include managing scheduled reviews of content, approving removal of content from the site, or gathering feedback on a specific piece of content on the site.

## Content Types and Metadata

Content types in SharePoint allow you to identify various types of content and what metadata you associate with your content. Quite often you will see many custom content types in use within your internal SharePoint sites. There are plenty of good reasons to adopt content types in a public-facing SharePoint site (or any SharePoint WCM site) as well. By using content types appropriately, you can better categorize your content and make it easier to work with for both internal users as well as the general public.

When you provision a WCM site (which are the site templates that incorporate the publishing features; the publishing portal is an example of one of these), SharePoint provisions a number of content types that are designed to allow you to work with web-page–style content; these are the enterprise wiki page, article page, and welcome page. Each of these content types inherits from the System Page content type, which SharePoint identifies as a content page.

When planning content types for a public-facing site, you will always need to plan for your web content pages to inherit from the system page content type. From there you can add whatever other information you would like to see on the screen. Where this information appears on the page is determined through the use of page layouts, so the two of these are very closely linked. I'll discuss page layouts in more detail later in the chapter.

## Reusable Content

A frequent requirement of content management systems is the ability to easily and quickly update pieces of content across the site. SharePoint allows you to do this through a feature called *reusable content*. This allows content authors to create pieces of text (or HTML) that can be inserted into content pages without the authors needing to retype them, as shown in Figure 18-3. This is important to be aware of and something to include in your user training as it will make maintaining content simpler, especially across a large site.

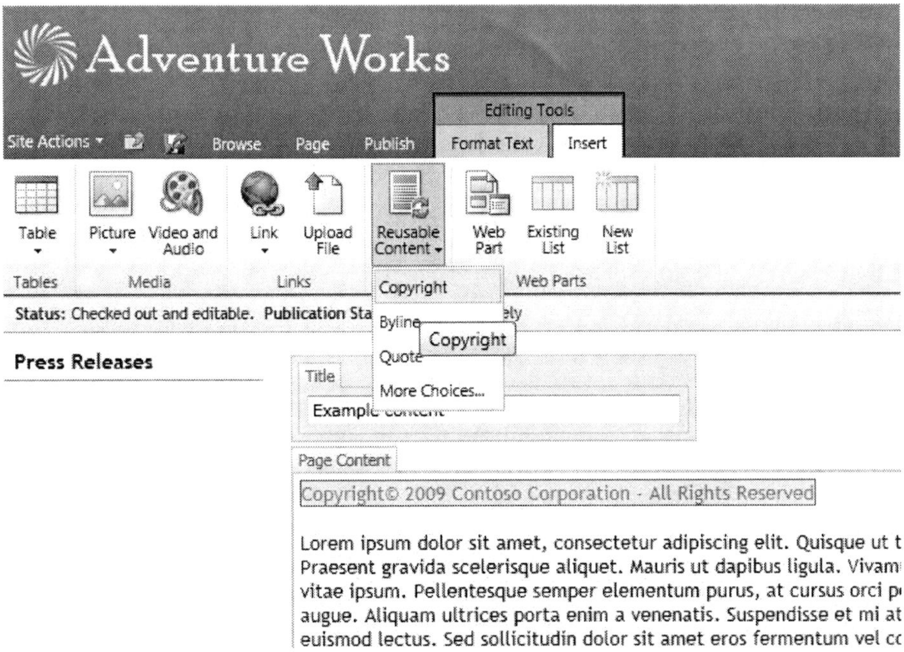

*Figure 18-3. Inserting reusable content into a publishing page of a SharePoint 2010 site*

All reusable content is stored in a list at the root of your site collection, and you are given options to control how it is used, such as if the item should appear in the drop-down menu on the ribbon and if the content should be in HTML or plain text. The more important piece of metadata here is a field called Automatic Update. When a piece of content has this option selected, you are able to make changes to the item in the list and have the change reflected across the entire site wherever it was inserted. If this option is not selected, changing the item will only affect future uses of the content.

This Automatic Update option is what really drives the need to plan for how reusable content will be implemented across your publishing site. Being able to insert text, such as the name of your company, an address, or a disclaimer message, is a great use of reusable content that should be automatically updated. There are also examples of things that you may not want to see updated, such as specific copyright or other legal notices; this type of content may need to be inserted from a predefined piece of text to get wording right, but once on the page it should not be changed.

Having the ability to automatically update sections of content across the entire site collection is incredibly powerful and can be a massive time saver (especially on a large site). For this reason, planning what items should be in this list is of key importance. The second element is ensuring that the content authors all know about this option and are actually using it. If an author manually types in a piece of text that is driven from the list, it won't be included in any automatic updates.

# Maintaining an Image

Your public-facing site says a lot about your organization, so the look of the end result is important. From my own experience, this is one of the biggest concerns businesses have about using SharePoint for their public sites—they don't want it to look like SharePoint and often are convinced that this isn't easily possible. Hopefully, you have looked at `www.WssDemo.com` after I mentioned it earlier and you know that this isn't the case!

## Style Guide Ideas

When discussing the look and feel of your public site, one thing often gets overlooked is a good style guide. Traditionally a style guide covers things like fonts, colors, location of content on specific types of pages, etc. A style guide for SharePoint should also cover what page layouts are required (including what content type they will be linked to), what elements are included on the page, and any CSS specific elements within the page layout. It should also include master page details including layout, what controls are on the page, and key style components. The goal as far as these elements go is to give a good overview of how the design is implemented in SharePoint, so that when someone needs to make changes to it later there is a solid guide as to how it was put together the first time around.

You will also want to cover things such as colors for text and backgrounds, which fonts will be used and where. The key for this as far as a SharePoint-specific site is concerned is that you don't just use plain text and headings. You need to consider SharePoint specific elements as well, such as headers on Web Parts, fonts and colors in out-of-the-box controls like date pickers and list views, just to name a few.

## Driving Content Rules Through Page Layouts

One of the best things about page layouts is not just the predefined templates for where content should go on a page, but the incredible level of control over what the content should look like based on where on the page you put it (see Figure 18-4). Say you have a page layout with your main content area in a column down the right hand side. Its background color is different than the background color for special notes. In the main content area, it's okay for authors to use any formatting that is appropriate for delivering the information on the page, but in that side column you only want plain text with minimal formatting. This can be achieved by customizing the page layout.

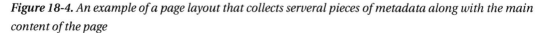

*Figure 18-4. An example of a page layout that collects serveral pieces of metadata along with the main content of the page*

When you are editing a page layout in SharePoint designer, you can right-click on any rich HTML area where your users can enter text and select Properties. This will bring up a window that will display a wide range of options about what can and can't be done within that specific HTML area. The lengthy list of options includes controlling what the user can do with fonts (sizes, types, bold and italic, colors, etc.); whether content such as images, tables, or hyperlinks (both internal and external) can be added; and whether specific HTML elements (such as headings or lists) can be used in the area. This is an incredibly powerful feature when you start to look at design integrity and it should not be overlooked. You can lock areas through the page layouts, which means that have complete control over what your public audience sees.

You can further protect the integrity of your designs by controlling what page layouts are available to users in the first place. This will prevent them from simply selecting another layout and doing whatever they want with it. Site administrators have the option to select which page layouts can be used within a particular site. This becomes useful when you begin to plan out where your page layouts should be used within your site. For example, you might have some page layouts that are used for news pages and you can change the settings to only allow these layouts in the news sub site. You might then have a page layout for product information pages; again, you can limit those to use in that section of the site only. These options can be set manually or they can be set in the web template that is used to create the site, which ensures that new sites will follow the rules you have defined for your content.

Seeing the control you can implement within your page layouts and your site settings, you can probably now see why it is important that these SharePoint-specific elements are recorded in your style guide. The style guide should be the first and last stop for anything to do with what your web site looks like. When put together well, it makes a fantastic document to use as a reference later on, especially when you are introducing new authors to the site.

## Attracting Attention from the World Wide Web

The ultimate goal of your public-facing site is to get people to come to it and use it. In the case of intranet and extranet solutions built on top of SharePoint, this is a given—users will know where your site is because it's part of their job to go there to get information, submit forms, share documents, etc. For your public-facing site, though, things are very different. The people you want to come to your site might not even know you exist, let alone that you have a web site. So how do your users find you in the first place? In a very large number of cases, the answer is simple: search engines.

Search engines such as Bing and Google are constantly crawling the Internet for content to add to their indexes, and from search engines like these users will find all sorts of public-facing content every minute of every day. This raises the discussion of search engine optimization (SEO) and what you can do with your SharePoint sites to give them the best chance of being discovered by users who are searching. There are many, many books on search engine optimization, so I cover only a few general points and how they can be implemented within SharePoint.

One of the first things to look at when preparing any public-facing site for SEO is how the site looks in a plain text view. This is important because this is exactly how your site is seen by search engines; this is why your HTML markup is important. A great way to do this is with a text-only browser such as Lynx (http://lynx.isc.org/). This will allow you to see the text on your page and how it appears structurally based on elements such as headings and lists. This sort of view will help you understand how a search engine will treat your content (things such as the order items appear in, if text is a heading, what images appear as based on their alt tags and other markup, etc.) and as such, what will be placed in the index.

When planning your master pages and page layouts in a SharePoint site, it is always a good idea to create some test pages to run through this sort of treatment to ensure the markup that is going to be containing all the content in your site is being interpreted correctly. This also helps highlight the importance of correct use of HTML when preparing your content. If your page has invalid markup, it may not be interpreted correctly, which may cause problems with how your page is indexed. Having correct markup also helps make your page more generally accessible to anyone who is trying to view your site (such as a visually impaired person who relies on a text-to-speech engine such as Jaws to read your content to them).

There are other things you can do to help direct a search engine crawler around your web site, such as putting robots.txt and SiteMap.xml files into your sites root directory. Robots.txt is a list of paths that you want to tell search crawlers not to index; this is very useful if you have a section of your site that is archived and not designed to be found by external searches (usually because you want the external searches to only refer to the current content rather than the archived content). SiteMap.xml is a way to list all of the pages on your site and provide additional information such as when the page was last modified, how important the page is, and how frequently the page is updated. Both of these files play a critical role in giving external crawlers the best possible information about your site, so you will want to include them in your SharePoint site.

There are a few ways you can go about inserting these files. You could just open SharePoint Designer to the root site collection in a web application and simply upload the files to the site (as the files need to exist outside of a document library, you need to use SharePoint Designer to get them in the right place). This is fine, and the crawlers will see them and act on them, but you will find yourself with the problem of keeping them up to date, especially if your site is larger and its structure changes a fair bit. Fortunately, the SharePoint community has some great ideas on how to resolve this; a couple of the better solutions I have found were published by Waldek Mastykarz on his blog. He has created solutions to help dynamically generate these files and they are well worth a look; see http://blog.mastykarz.nl/generating-robots-txt-files-mavention-robots-txt/ and http://blog.mastykarz.nl/mavention-xml-sitemap-sharepoint-2010-server/.

# Helping Your Users Find Their Content

External search engines are just one entry path to your web site. There's one other very important search engine you need to worry about: your own! While external search engines can help users find content on your site, having a site specific-search engine is just as important. Also, SharePoint offers various navigation controls that provide other ways for your users to navigate around your site.

## Customizing the Search Experience

Having your internal search engine provide effective results to your users is a great way to improve the chances of your users finding content on your site. Adding things such as search scopes and advanced search pages will also improve the standard search functionality, but there are other ways you can take advantage of your search indexes. Through the APIs you can query data in the search indexes and take advantage of what SharePoint knows about your content to improve the user experience while browsing your site.

### Search Scopes

There are numerous ways you can use search to improve the user experience on your site beyond simply indexing your content and providing a search box. The first option to look at for extending this functionality is to provide search scopes to accompany your search box. A search scope is a way of allowing someone to search for a subset of content in the index, which is defined by creating a set of rules to control what content gets included in the scope and what is excluded. Some examples of how you could use scopes include having one to search just products on your site or just recent news and announcements. You might have a scope for recently published content, for archived content, for a specific department's content, or even for documents rather than web pages (see Figure 18-5).

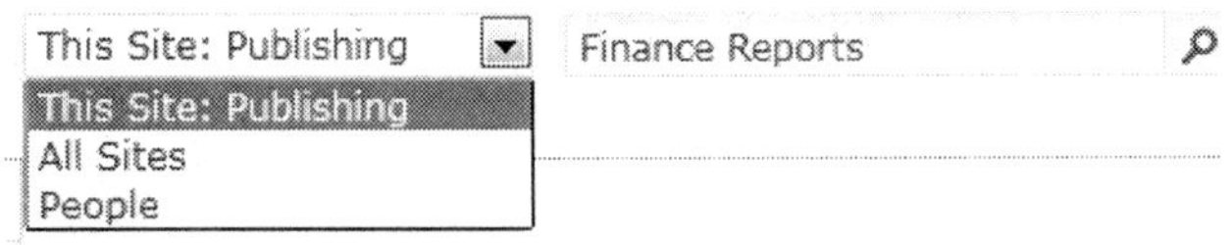

**Figure 18-5.** *The search scope drop-down*

The rules for search scopes allow you to include or exclude content from a scope based on three types of rules: URLs (all content at a specific path in the site), metadata (all content where property X = Y) or all content (include everything and then filter out with an exclude rule). Looking at these rule types you can start to see why things such as information architecture are just as important for a public SharePoint site as they are for an internal one. Having an appropriate site structure will let you make use of the URL-based rules, and appropriate content types and metadata will let you get the most from the metadata rules. In fact, you can even create a rule to filter based purely on content type, which is great for something like news pages. You might have a news page layout and content type that is used all over your site, with each area having their own news announcements that get rolled up and displayed at the top level site. You could search all the news items by simply creating a scope for ContentType = 'News Page'. This sort of thing can make finding content much easier for your end users and your content authors alike.

## Advanced Searches

Offering an advanced search page is a great way to provide power users of your site the ability to easily find content they want, especially if you have a large site. SharePoint provides an advanced search Web Part that can easily be inserted on a page (see Figure 18-6). But to really add value to your search experience, some consideration needs to go into how the advanced search will be used and what your users will be likely to look for on your site.

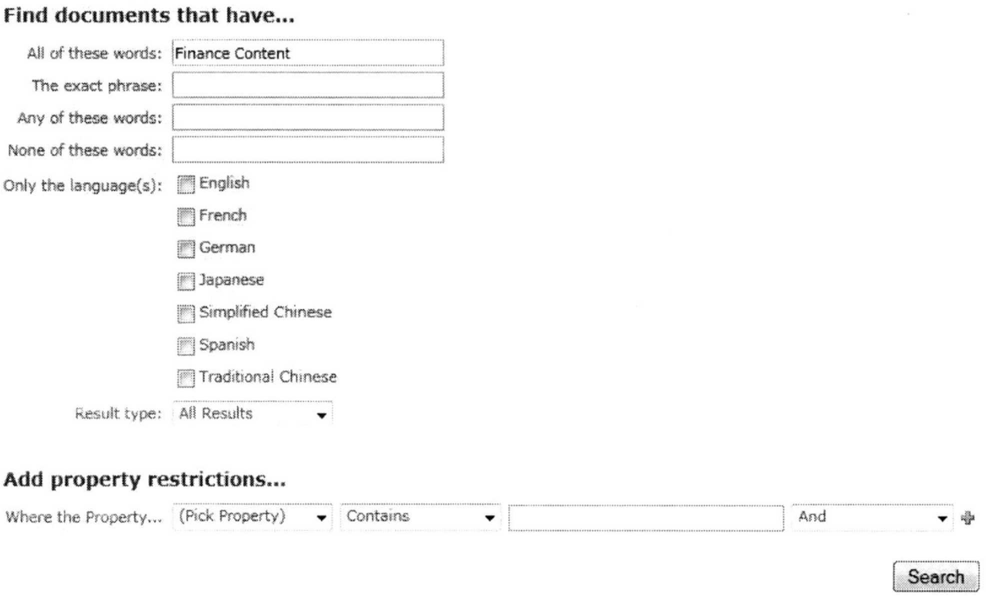

**Find documents that have...**

| | |
|---|---|
| All of these words: | Finance Content |
| The exact phrase: | |
| Any of these words: | |
| None of these words: | |

Only the language(s):
- English
- French
- German
- Japanese
- Simplified Chinese
- Spanish
- Traditional Chinese

Result type: All Results

**Add property restrictions...**

Where the Property... (Pick Property) ▼  Contains ▼ [                    ] And ▼ ✚

Search

*Figure 18-6.* *The standard advanced search Web Part*

The advanced search Web Part lets you control what options the user is presented with when they browse to the page. The text boxes (all words, exact phrase, any words, none of these words), inclusion of scopes, languages, file types, and specific properties are all controlled through the Web Part Properties window.

Properties for the advanced search Web Part are primarily driven through an XML document stored in the Web Part properties. This XML is broken up into a few key sections that control what info is displayed on the screen. There are several sections of this XML that control the appearance of the advanced search Web Part, including what languages are shown, what properties are available to refine the searches, and what document formats users can search for.

## Programmatically Working with Search

An often overlooked element of SharePoint's search service is the ability to access it programmatically. When a custom Web Part is created it will often need to query a large amount of data in a site, which can take up a lot of resources and time. The same data could possibly be retrieved from the search index, resulting in much lower resource usage and quicker results. The tradeoff here is that the data returned is not "live" as such and will only be as current as your search index.

The main benefit to taking this approach for querying data is performance. Due to the way that SharePoint stores and works with your data, querying across a wide scope (such as an entire site collection or perhaps even multiple site collections) can be a very resource-intensive task that will take some time to complete. Placing code like this on a public-facing site that could potentially be hit by many users at the same time could cause big performance problems for you. By choosing to query the search index instead of the live data, results can be returned much quicker, which will help ensure your farm doesn't have performance issues trying to deliver this type of content.

Assembling a call to the search service application in SharePoint 2010 is an incredibly simple task. The following code demonstrates this:

```
var proxy = (SearchServiceApplicationProxy)
SearchServiceApplicationProxy.GetProxy(SPServiceContext.GetContext(SPContext.Current.Site));
var query = new KeywordQuery(proxy)
{
        ResultsProvider = Microsoft.Office.Server.Search.Query.SearchProvider.Default,
        QueryText = "My Search Terms"
};
query.ResultTypes |= ResultType.RelevantResults;
var searchResults = query.Execute();
```

The process here is to first get the `SearchServiceApplicationProxy` object. (All service applications will allow you to interact with them through a proxy. The proxy will determine which service application instance your code should interact with based on the associations of the current web application). Once you have the proxy object, it's simply a matter of creating a `KeywordQuery` object. This allows you to define the settings for your query, including the results provider type and the actual query itself. Once the settings are defined, just call the `Execute` method and then parse the result set (which is a `ResultTableCollection` object, which can easily be loaded into a DataTable and then parsed).

# Navigation Options for SharePoint Sites

It may sound incredibly obvious but having reliable and simple navigation on your public site is an incredibly important factor to its success. If users find your site difficult to use, they will quickly move on. For this reason, it's important that you know your options for navigation on your SharePoint site so that you can choose the ones that will best suit your site.

## Main (Global) Navigation

The most obvious place to start with navigation is the main navigation menu that runs across the top of the default master page in SharePoint 2010. This is referred to as the global navigation menu. It is generally used to provide a consistent menu across your entire site, so it will have the same content no matter where you are within the site. When looking at a master page for your SharePoint 2010 site, the global navigation menu appears inside the `<asp:ContentPlaceHolder>` element with an ID value of `PlaceHolderHorizontalNav`.

## Quick Launch Navigation

The quick launch navigation is the common name given to the list of links that runs down the left side of the standard SharePoint 2010 master page. The key differentiator between these links and the global navigation used across the top of the master page is that the quick launch links will usually be specific to the part of the site you are currently browsing in. For example, while in the Products section of your site you might see links related to products appear in the quick launch, but the global navigation will still show exactly the same set of links as it would anywhere in the site.

This is important to know as it can play a key factor in how you plan your navigation controls on the site. Having the global navigation provides a good overview of the structure of your site, and the quick launch allows users to quickly dive deeper into your content based on the pages they chose from the global navigation. It provides a simple way to drill down to content without necessarily having to put everything into the top navigation (which can easily become overly cluttered if not planned appropriately).

## Table of Contents Web Part

The table of contents Web Part is another great example of how navigation can be provided on a SharePoint site. The best way to describe what this Web Part does is to think of it like a site map of sorts. It can display all of your sites and sub sites in a list that your users can browse through. This is a great thing to have on a public site for two reasons. First, it's a dynamic site map that users can browse to find content. Second, search engines like it. These crawlers will essentially start at the home page in your site and will look at every page that is linked to from there. Having a site map page that links to large portions of your site will help ensure that search crawlers find your pages and index them. This way you know that the pages on the site map are not likely to become orphaned or lost from your site due to someone inadvertently changing navigation settings or removing links.

## Breadcrumbs

Breadcrumbs let users know what part of your site they are currently looking at and allow them to browse back up the hierarchy. Breadcrumbs usually look something like Home > sub site 1 > sub site 2 > my page, with each of the individual sites mentioned being a hyperlink back to those sites. SharePoint has a couple of ways of implementing this sort of link trail, and there is one on most standard master pages.

If you look at one of the standard SharePoint master pages, just to the right of the site actions menu, you will see a small folder icon; if selected it will show you the breadcrumb for the page you are currently viewing. The control is the <SharePoint:PopoutMenu> control, which includes the <asp:ContentPlaceHolder> for the PlaceHolderTitleBreadcrumb element.

Within these controls is the ListSiteMapPath control, which is what will actually display the breadcrumb inside the small popup window that appears when the folder icon is selected. It has a range of settings that can control how it is displayed. It is worth noting that the appearance of the control here is different between the standard v4.master page and the nightandday.master page that the publishing sites will use by default. The standard one shows a hierarchy that runs over multiple lines, indenting at each level, while the nightandday.master page shows it in a single line separated by a > character. The other difference is that the control v4.master will also show you what current library or list you are within, whereas the nightandday.master version will just show you which site you are currently in (see Figure 18-7). This difference is controlled through the SiteMapProviders setting and is something that needs to be considered when implementing breadcrumb (and all navigation) controls.

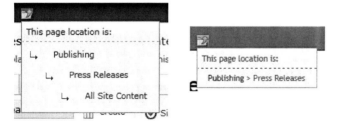
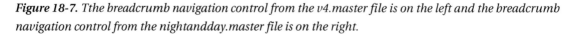

*Figure 18-7. Tthe breadcrumb navigation control from the v4.master file is on the left and the breadcrumb navigation control from the nightandday.master file is on the right.*

# Navigation Providers

Navigation options are more than just the navigation controls themselves; they're the properties for specifying data sources. These tell SharePoint where it should look specifically to get the data it needs to render a specific navigation control. Therefore it's important to understand the differences between the various options as this may help you get the data you want out of a control that doesn't show it the way you like by default. All of the options for providers are all listed in the web.config file and in Table 18-1.

*Table 18-1. Standard SharePoint Navigation Providers*

| Navigation Provider | Description |
| --- | --- |
| SPNavigationProvider | Provides a base class for SharePoint Foundation site-map providers that are specialized for SharePoint site navigation. |
| SPSiteMapProvider | Provides the SiteMapNode objects that constitute the global content portion of the breadcrumb, which represents objects in the site hierarchy. |
| SPContentMapProvider | This class provides the SiteMapNode objects that constitute the content portion of the breadcrumb, where "content" refers to the lists, folders, items, and list forms composing the breadcrumb. |
| SPXmlContentMapProvider | Provides methods and properties for implementing an XML-based site map provider for a Microsoft SharePoint Foundation site. |
| ExtendedSearchXmlContentMap Provider | Provider for navigation in Extended Search pages. |
| AdministrationQuickLaunch Provider | QuickLaunch navigation provider for the central administration site. |
| SharedServicesQuickLaunch Provider | QuickLaunch navigation provider for shared services administration sites. |
| GlobalNavSiteMapProvider | CMS provider for Global navigation. |
| CombinedNavSiteMap Provider | CMS provider for Combined navigation. |
| CurrentNavSiteMapProvider | CMS provider for Current navigation. |
| CurrentNavSiteMapProviderNo Encode | CMS provider for Current navigation; no encoding of output. |
| GlobalNavigation | Provider for MOSS Global Navigation. |
| CurrentNavigation | Provider for MOSS Current Navigation. |

| | |
|---|---|
| `SiteDirectoryCategoryProvider` | Site Directory category provider. |
| `MySiteMapProvider` | MySite provider that returns areas and based on the current user context. |
| `MySiteLeftNavProvider` | MySite Left Nav provider that returns areas and is based on the current user context. |
| `MySiteSubNavProvider` | MySite Sub Nav provider that returns areas and is based on the current user context. |

The default master pages in SharePoint use various combinations of these to create various navigation elements on the page. The `SPNavigationProvider` is used as a default navigation provider that is overridden through the use of delegate controls in specific types of sites. The `CurrentNavigation` provider is used to drive the left navigation, and `GlobalNavigation` is used in publishing sites as the default for the global navigation menu. When I spoke about breadcrumbs previously, the difference between the look of the two different master pages was based on two different settings for the data sources.

## What to Tell the Developers

Developing for SharePoint has always required that developers learn a little more than they would for a typical ASP.NET project, and a lot of the same hurdles that need to be jumped will also be present in a public-facing site. This is where the line gets drawn between content, configuration, and development.

## What to Look for in a Developer

Most people who have worked on SharePoint specific projects will tell you that you really do need developers with SharePoint-specific development skills. This is quite true and valid for most SharePoint projects, but when you start to talk about working with public-facing web sites you will generally need a bit more as just "general SharePoint development" skills won't cut it for a high quality public-facing site.

Working on a public-facing SharePoint site is a very different project than most standard internal SharePoint projects. Developers need to be more aware of how to develop for the Web rather than taking the approach of "let's just make it work," which is common on internal projects.

On an internal project you know your users, you know their browsers (usually), and you know what operating systems they are running. This makes development much easier as bugs that fall outside of that scope can easily be written off. This is not the case with a public site, and developers need to be prepared to work through issues such as using HTML, CSS, and JavaScript across platforms plus load times and performance on expected connection speeds.

Also developers (and the technical architects) need to plan how version control will be handled. When you're working on an internal environment, you will probably know when new releases will occur, but this isn't the case with a public-facing web site. Developers need to consider the fact that any downtime on a public web site is time that potential customers are not able to interact with the business. You should have an appropriate infrastructure in place to support a minimal or no down time scenario when deploying solutions.

# Separating Content From Development

SharePoint by its very nature allows for non-technical users to create mash-up– style applications by easily adding Web Parts to pages and configuring the settings to suit their needs. Creating dashboards is a great example of this. In an intranet or team-based collaborative environment, this is a great way to deliver functionality without having to roll through a full development cycle. When it comes to a public-facing site, however, there should be more scrutiny over how these types of changes are rolled out.

Looking back to what was said earlier in this chapter about the importance of a public-facing site, this is a big reason for why this line around exactly what is content on your site and what isn't needs to be drawn. This site could be the front door to your entire business; any problems with the site it can reflect on your organization. Therefore, when you are adding functionality to the site, there needs to be appropriate levels of planning to ensure that it won't adversely affect the site or cause errors for users as they browse. There is a very good reason most change control processes involve one or more pre-production environments to test and validate any type of solution before letting it go live. This is to ensure the stability of the environment after the change, that no other functionality is affected by the change, that the change can be rolled back if need be, etc.

Likewise, in many SharePoint deployments, any edits a user makes will exist solely in the production-related environments, with snapshots of content taken back to pre-production environments as often as required to ensure that when testing is done, it's done with a close image of what the current site looks like.

To apply a change management process to the site, there must be a clear separation between what is treated as content and what requires a configuration change or development process. You need to understand what is okay for a content author to do directly to the production site because it's content, and what will require appropriate documentation and testing through the pre-production environments.

There are plenty of scenarios where this line is easy to draw. When a user edits the text of a page or inserts an image, this is clearly to be treated as content; likewise a change to a custom developed control will to go through a testing process before being deployed to production. But what about scenarios that aren't so clear cut? What happens when a user wants to change the configuration of Web Parts on a page? When a user wants to change templates for new sites? When master pages or page layouts need to change? When workflows need to be modified? Or when search settings needing to be modified? These are all things that can be driven through the browser when a user has appropriate permissions; therefore you need to know what should and shouldn't be handled through the browser as content, and what should go through a change process.

# Considerations for what Needs Change Control

One of the key differentiators for assessing what is content and what is not is documentation. When a user updates the text on a specific page, there is likely to be no documentation about that change (outside of a simple approval workflow process). However, if a developer is writing a new control that will be embedded into pages on the site, there should be some documentation about this change. What does the control do? How is it deployed and retracted? What impact does it have on existing functionality? How was it written and what would a new developer need to know to pick up the code and make changes later?

One of the reasons that you do this type of documentation for your changes is to meet the requirements of an organization's disaster recovery plan. In the event that a SharePoint farm has to be rebuilt from nothing due to catastrophic failure, any custom solutions that are deployed to the server will need to be redeployed to the new environment, and there will need to be appropriate instruction on how to do this. Another example could be that a component needs to be changed and the original developer has left the company. The new developer will need documentation to be able to quickly pick up on the existing solution and make the required changes.

Now consider those elements in regards to things that a user could change through the browser. What if the farm is lost and needed to be rebuilt. Would the Web Part customizations restore correctly or would settings need to be adjusted to account for changing internal IDs of various elements? What if a content author put together a complex set of Web Parts on a page and paired that up with some SharePoint Designer-based workflows, only to move on six months later? Would the next content author understand what was done so they could continue to maintain the site? The answers might vary based on your users and your individual backup/restore processes but the reality is that you might not know. This is why it is important to identify functionality that is added to the site instead of just content that is added to the site, and then include it in an appropriate application lifecycle management process.

## Playing Nice in the Sandbox

Sandbox solutions are a new concept for SharePoint 2010. Basically they allow a site collection administrator to upload a solution (WSP package) to their site and allow it to run. This empowers users to upload their own solutions to the site without having to involve IT staff. Given what I have just been saying around having a clear line between content that is managed through the browser and custom development, the whole concept of sandbox solutions raises some interesting issues.

Sandbox solutions are a great concept for anyone who is working in a hosted environment where you might not have control over the server to deploy traditional farm solutions. You get the ability to just upload them through the browser, turn them on, and off you go. This improved flexibility does come with some pretty big tradeoffs, though. A sandbox solution is limited to a very small list of elements that can be deployed through features, and all code is executed in a separate process to the main SharePoint processes, which has more limitations on what can be done. (For example, a sandbox solution can't connect to a web service from the server; anything involving web services must be run from the client side through either JavaScript or Silverlight).

Now that you have this new ability to deploy solutions this way, care needs to be taken to ensure that your plans about content and development remain separated but intact. This does not necessarily mean that you should rule out the use of sandbox solutions at all. (In fact, where possible all custom development should be targeted to the sandbox so that if it ever needed to run in a sandbox environment it could.) It does mean that a decision needs to be made about whether or not you will allow sandbox solutions and who will be responsible for them. You also need to decide whether a sandbox solution will require some sort of change control process. For example, a sandbox solution might not need the full process required of a traditional deployment, but it might have an approval workflow for just the production environment so that there is some record of who wanted the solution, why it was put in as a sandbox solution, and where it originated from. Everything that will run within the sandbox process should also run well as a farm solution, so if someone wants to deny approval to a solution packaged as a sandbox solution, it could be handled as a farm solution and deployed as such.

One of the biggest problems with sandbox solutions in a public-facing SharePoint site is the limitations around the API for custom development. In a SharePoint WCM site, there is a set of functionality specific to the content management features of SharePoint and this library can't be used in the sandbox. This means that if you want to work with the SharePoint site-specific features in code, you with either be blocked or you will need to implement a number of workarounds that may not meet your initial requirements exactly. In many cases, this limitation is a show stopper for sandbox solutions.

Once sandbox solutions are deployed, they must be monitored. Administrators are able to set limits on what resources a solution can consume before it is effectively shut down, so these should be set appropriately to ensure that non–administrator-approved code can't cause undue performance problems for the rest of the farm. Coming back to the fact that internal and external SharePoint sites are different, shutting down an intranet might be an appropriate way to deal with the situation, but if it's your public-facing site and it suddenly shuts down because you have hit a resource quota limit, then you are without your site (or at least a subset of its functionality). Depending on your business requirements, this might be something that can be managed, but more often than not this is another show stopper for public-facing sites and sandbox solutions.

The bottom line is that sandbox solutions can provide a great way to push solutions in as a user-based action, but appropriate planning and thought needs to be done before this allowed (if at all). Decisions need to be made as to whether the improved flexibility in deployment is worth the increased risk of downtime and the limitations put on developers. If you have a good style guide and a plan for your corporate image, there may actually be very little need to have this increased flexibility. Everything going onto the site should be approved from both a design and technical perspective, thus you can safely avoid dealing with sandbox solutions all together.

## What about SharePoint Designer?

SharePoint Designer is another tool that needs to be accounted for in a plan for a public-facing SharePoint site. SharePoint Designer is a free download, so unless the PCs in your organization prevent users from installing it, it's possible that a user could get access to your sites with this tool and you wouldn't know about it.

Luckily, SharePoint 2010 provides some options to limit access to sites through SharePoint Designer; these should be factored into a plan for a public site. Through central administration it's possible to disallow access to SharePoint Designer all together, or to just prevent users from changing the URL structure, editing master pages and page layouts, or from detaching pages from the site definition.

### Impact of Editing Content with SharePoint Designer

One of the options for restricting SharePoint Designer access is to prevent pages from being detached from the site definition. This is a process commonly referred to as *un-ghosting the page* (with the page being referred to as *ghosted* before that point). While a page is ghosted, any requests to load the page will result in the page being retrieved from SharePoint's cache, which is created when the application pool is loaded; this makes it load very quick. When a page is modified through SharePoint Designer, it will un-ghost the page, resulting in a copy of the page being stored in the content database for the web application, which will impact the load time slightly.

The bigger issue with un-ghosting of content is how changes to the file in the site definition are handled. When site definitions and web templates are deployed via a WSP package, SharePoint deploys the files to the file system and loads them in to a cache when the application pool is loaded. Let's assume that someone modifies one of these pages through SharePoint Designer for a specific web application while leaving it as-is for a second web application. Now when the WSP package is updated and the page is changed, the second web application will see the changes immediately as it is still ghosted and referring to the cache, but the first web application, which un-ghosted the page, will still be referring to its own version that is now in the content database. This means that if files that are part of a site definition are modified through SharePoint Designer, it can impact any upgrade processes for these solutions. For this reason, it is important to limit what SharePoint Designer can do in a production environment, as well as who can use it.

## The Accessibility Argument

Customers always ask, "How accessible is SharePoint?" Government agencies, in particular, often need to meet levels-of-accessibility requirements for their sites to ensure that as many citizens as possible can access their content. Rules such as those specified by the section 508 legislation in the United States and the Web Content Accessibility Guidelines (WCAG) written by the World Wide Web Consortium (W3C) are often used to mark a measurable level of accessibility.

When SharePoint 2010 was released, Microsoft made many improvements to accessibility and claimed it was W3C WCAG 2.0 Level AA compliant out of the box. For those who are unfamiliar with the work of the W3C, they have published two major releases of their guidelines (more commonly referred to as WCAG); these are rules that specify what needs to be done for a site to be classed as levels A, AA and AAA for accessibility. The AA rating was a bit of a big deal, as anyone who had worked with SharePoint 2007 for public-facing sites may have run into trouble meeting the rules specified in the WCAG documentation. To back up this claim, Microsoft released a number of conformance statements that relate to its products, shown in Table 18-2.

*Table 18-2. Conformance Statements for SharePoint Products and Technologies*

| Product | Links |
| --- | --- |
| SharePoint Foundation 2010 | http://technet.microsoft.com/en-us/library/ff852105.aspx |
| | http://technet.microsoft.com/en-us/library/ff852106.aspx |
| SharePoint Server 2010 | http://technet.microsoft.com/en-us/library/ff852107.aspx |
| | http://technet.microsoft.com/en-us/library/ff852108.aspx |
| Office Web Applications | http://technet.microsoft.com/en-us/library/ff852098.aspx |
| | http://technet.microsoft.com/en-us/library/ff852097.aspx |

The most important thing to remember when discussing the W3C guidelines is that they are just guidelines—and as such are open to a very wide level of interpretation. Some groups out there interpret the rules differently than Microsoft. There is no W3C validator to ensure that content meets the guidelines; the validators and tools that exist in the marketplace for this purpose are all based on a specific group or organization's interpretation of the guidelines. For this reason, you can take a SharePoint site and run it through a number of different validators; you'll find that it's level AA complaint in some, while it fails some tests in others.

It is also important to mention that Microsoft make the claim of level AA accessibility for a completely out-of-the-box deployment. The second you customize anything (such as master pages, Web Parts, style sheets, web content etc.) the compliance statement no longer applies; you are on your own to ensure that you continue to meet these guidelines. This is important for your developers to understand as they need to ensure custom components meet the guidelines (if satisfying this requirement is important to your business). Moreover, your end users need to be trained on how to create accessible content for the web. Earlier in the chapter I made the claim that content is what makes up a SharePoint site, it is why people head to your site, and as such, it needs to be accessible. There are a number of mistakes that users can make when writing content for the web that make it less accessible to end users who are using assistive technologies; these sorts of things need to be kept in mind during the content creation and approval process.

There is also an argument to be made as to how much value comes from meeting these types of guidelines in the first place. Yes, if you are a government body you may be legally required to do so based on the legislation in your country. I have seen many cases where people thought they followed the guidelines (coming back to the point around interpretation) and ended up with a site that was still difficult to navigate with a screen reader. In other words, the guidelines are a good place to start for making content accessible, but there is certainly no guarantee that ticking all of those boxes will translate to a perfectly accessible site.

If you are really serious about delivering accessibility to people with disabilities and you're not just looking to tick a box with your site, I recommend finding an organization in your country that deals with assisting people with disabilities and engage them for their input. In Australia, this would be an organization such as Vision Australia; I'm sure there are similar groups all over the world. These groups are often staffed by people with disabilities, and they can sit down with you and work through your site to provide you with feedback that is directly relevant to your site and the assistive technologies in question. This will give you a far more practical set of tasks to implement on your site to make it accessible, as opposed to you taking your best guess at interpreting the guidelines.

# Summary

In this chapter I have covered some of the reasons you would use SharePoint for a public site, as well as some of the elements that have helped me ensure success with these types of projects. If you make sure that your plans for a public site cover all of the topics I've mentioned in this chapter, you will have an effective and easy-to-maintain site. Remember that content is king. In reality, the very large majority of what SharePoint is made up of is just content—so with a well-designed SharePoint deployment behind you, you are helping to ensure that the content of your site will always be at its best. I hope this chapter has helped. All the best for your projects.

# CHAPTER 19

# Claims-Based Authentication in SharePoint 2010

This chapter is indented to give the reader an overview of the new claims-based authentication method available in SharePoint 2010. The claims world beyond SharePoint is large and varied. This chapter will not teach you everything there is to know about dealing with claims in SharePoint. This chapter will discuss when to use claims authentication, some of the most common steps to implementing it, and how to avoid some of the common pitfalls with working with claims. While not every possible scenario is covered, it should serve as a good foundation to help you avoid some of the common pitfalls.

Topics covered:

Understanding Claims in SharePoint 2010

Implementing SAML token-authentication in SharePoint 2010

Installing Active Directory Federation Services 2.0

Configuring Your Federation Server

Configure SharePoint 2010 for Claims Authentication

Enabling claims in your SharePoint Web Application

## Understanding Claims in SharePoint 2010

In order to understand how claims work in SharePoint 2010, you must first understand how security works in SharePoint in general.When a user logs in to SharePoint, they can utilize several different authentication mechanisms.However, SharePoint essentially only sees two:classic mode and claims mode.

Classic mode is the legacy Windows authentication option based on an individual's Active Directory identity using NTLM or Kerberos.This is your first and best option when working in a pure Windows environment.

However, in many environments, classic mode may not be a viable option.This could be for a plethora of reasons, and I will discuss some of the determining factors on when to use classic mode versusclaims mode later in this chapter.For starters,Table 19-1 looks at how SharePoint categorizes each of the different authentication methods.

*Table 19-1.Different Authentication Methods*

| Method | Examples |
| --- | --- |
| Windows | • NTLM |
| | • Kerberos |
| | • Anonymous |
| | • Basic |
| | • Digest |
| Forms-based authentication | • Lightweight Directory Access Protocol (LDAP) |
| | • Microsoft SQL Server database or other database |
| | • Custom or third-party membership and role providers |
| SAML token-based authentication | • Active Directory Federation Services (AD FS) 2.0 |
| | • Third-party identity provider |
| | • Lightweight Directory Access Protocol (LDAP) |

If you're familiar with SharePoint 2007 authentication options, you will notice a new one: SAML token-based authentication.This is where claims come in to play.SharePoint 2010 utilizes the Window Identity Foundation (WIF) framework to implement claims aware applications (http://msdn.microsoft.com/en-us/security/aa570351.aspx).

WIF supports a variety of standards such as WS-Federation, WS-Trust, and the SAML protocol.This is the first dirty little secret about claims in SharePoint 2010.At the time of this writing, SharePoint 2010 only supports SAML 1.1.Thus, while this is a limiting factor (as SAML 2.0 is the latest standard), it's important to understand it when looking at your options for claims providers.Be sure they support (provide) SAML 1.1 tokens.As a side note, WIF is also the framework utilized for identity management in the cloud.So, if you are interested in learning more about cloud computing, particularly in the identity management space, WIF is a great place to start.And experience with SAML tokens in SharePoint will be helpful.

There are some important terms to understand when dealing with claims-based authentication, as they are sometimes confused.A *SAML token* is essentially a cookie added to your browser that validates your identity and contains claims.*Claims* can be a variety of things from just your username or e-mail to specific information such as the organization to which you belong.This is where the real power of SAML token authentications (a.k.a. claims-based authentication) comes in to play.Assuming your claims provider sends additional information along, you can take advantage of that information for security trimming, customized branding, etc.This will require close coordination with the claims provider to determine what is available when planning your application.

## Deciding When to Use SAML Token-Based Authentication

Today there are a plethora of authentication options available in both the enterprise and on the Internet. SharePoint (like other Microsoft products) would prefer you use classic (Windows) authentication.However, you may choose to go with claims authentication for business or technical reasons.  Some reasons to consider using SAML token-based authentication include the following:

- Your Active Directoy environment is inadequate (missing trusts or serving non-Windows users).

- You already have a claim provider in place and wish to take advantage of it.

- You will be working with partners external to your organization (or other third-party identity providers).

- You have custom identity requirements that can't easily be addressed in Active Directory.

The industry is obviously moving towards claims, so the day may come when your enterprise may require that your application be claims aware (much like Kerberos has been in the past).The information in this chapter can help you meet that requirement.

# Implementing SAML Token-Authentication in SharePoint 2010

If you are spearheading the first SAML token-authentication project for your company (which is often the case with SharePoint), you may find the entire process frustrating.Unlike classic authentication, which is well known and easily understood, SAML token-authentication requires a great deal of communication between your team and the remote team providing the token.

The first thing you will need to do is identify the Security Token Service (STS) you wish to use.Active Directory Federation Services (AD FS) 2.0 is the most commonly used STS in Windows environments and will be the STS I will use throughout this chapter.

There are essentially two sides to any STS relationship: the identity provider and the relying party.The identity provider issues tokens that can contain one or more claims.As mentioned earlier, claims can be a number of different things from name to telephone number to the organization to which you belong.It's up to the identity provider to determine what information they want to expose as a claim.The relying party is the other side of the exchange.For the purposes of this chapter, it's a SharePoint 2010 web application.

The steps required to implement SAML token-based authentication are as follows:

1. The identity provider creates and exports a token-signing certificate.This certificate is known as the Import Trust Certificate.You will need to copy this certificate into your SharePoint 2010 farm.

2. Coordinate with the identity provider to identify the identity claim.The identity claim is the unique identifier for the user.This is often a user name or e-mail address.You will need it later when mapping claims in SharePoint.

3. Define additional claims to be mapped.If you don't specifically map a claim, it will be ignored and thus won't be available for reference in code.I highly recommend mapping all the claims available even if you're not planning to use them.Better to have it and ignore it, than to need it later and have to re-configure your STS.

4. Import the token-signing certificate (created in step 1) using the SP-PowerShell utility.This will create a new authentication provider within

SharePoint.There are actually several steps to this process, and this is where most people get in to trouble.I will discuss this process in detail later in the chapter.For now, it is important to understand that this is where you specify the identity claim and other claims you plan to use in SharePoint.In addition, you create a realm.Realms are ways to associate a SAML token-based authentication provider with a SharePoint web application.Thus, you can have a single provider associated with several SharePoint web applications simply by creating additional realms.

5.  Add an entry to the STS to associate the relying party and the identity provider.This is essentially a URI entry, so it can be done before the SharePoint web application is created. Note that when you do create the web application (in the next step), it must match the URI entered in the STS.

6.  Create a new SharePoint web application.The new authentication provider you created in the previous steps will appear as an option in the drop-down menu when you check claims mode in Central Administration.If it doesn't, you made a mistake.

SharePoint will only allow one token-signing certificate to be assigned to a farm, and keep in mind this certificate is generated by the identity provider.This is where AD FS comes in handy.If you put AD FS between the organization you are trying to work with and your SharePoint farm, from SharePoint's perspective AD FS is the identity provider (and thus providing a token-signing certificate).The nice thing is that AD FS can also establish relationships with other identity providers, thereby allowing SharePoint to interact with multiple identity providers while only requiring one token-signing certificate (from AD FS).In effect, you are shifting identity management to AD FS.It doesn't matter where the person is coming from, as long as they have a valid token.

If you worked with the SSO provider in SharePoint 2007, you should recognize how much of a quantum leap this is for external identity management in SharePoint 2010.Gone are the days of web application extensions for user mapping and mucking with your `web.config` files.A couple of PowerShell commands and a check box and you're in business!

Well, at least that's what it looks like from SharePoint's perspective.As you will see, enabling SAML token-based authentication in SharePoint is relatively easy.Building out the infrastructure to support claims aware applications is where the real work is.

---

■ **Note** The People Picker (when adding a new user) can't search or validate a user from the SPTrustedClaimProvider class (your identity provider).This is important to understand because it will appear as though the user has been validated when, in fact, it's just the people picker blindly accepting the user (because it can't search to validate).In order to provide that kind of functionality, you will need to create a custom claims provider that implements search and name resolution.Information about how to do this is available on TechNet at `http://technet.microsoft.com/en-us/library/gg602072.aspx`.The good news is if you do create a custom claims provider, you can use any claim you want (such as a phone number), so you're not just limited to user name.

---

# Before You Attempt to Install AD FS

Before attempting to install AD FS, there are a few things you need to do first.

1. Acquire appropriate certificates.

2. Ensure the AD FS Server is visible.

# Certificates Required for Operating an AD FS Server

There are essentially two certificates necessary to operate an AD FS environment.Table 19-2 describes the certificate types.

*Table 19-2. Certificate Types*

| Certificate Type | Description |
| --- | --- |
| Token-signing certificate | This is an X509 certificate that is used to associate public/private key pairs to digitally sign all security tokens.You can have multiple token-signing certificates (managed in the AD FS 2.0 Management snap-in), but only one primary signing certificate may be used at a time. |
| Service communication certificate | The service communication certificate is used to secure web services traffic via Secure Sockets Layer (SSL) communication with web clients and/or other federation servers. This is the same certificate that a federation server uses as the SSL certificate in Internet Information Services (IIS). |
| Token-decryption certificate | This is an additional certificate for decrypting older tokens.It's not necessary for your initial setup of AD FS but may become necessary as older certificates expire |

For specific information about about using SSL certificates, see IIS 7.0: Configuring Secure Sockets Layer in IIS 7.0 (http://go.microsoft.com/fwlink/?LinkID=108544) and IIS 7.0: Configuring Server Certificates in IIS 7.0 (http://go.microsoft.com/fwlink/?LinkID=108545).

AD FS 2.0 uses the Secure Hash Algorithm (SHA) for digital signatures.SHA 1 or SHA 256 are both supported.I highly recommend using SHA 256 as it is much more secure and most modern software supports it.However, if you are communicating with older systems, be aware that SHA 1 is supported but other hash methods are not supported.You can switch the hash algorithm you are using in the Advanced tab when you set up your partnerships.

Also, while AD FS 2.0 will support self-signed certificates, this is not recommended (except *maybe* in a development environment).Using self-signed certificates in a production environment could potentially allow a malicious user in an account partner organization to take control of federated servers in a resource partner organization.For self-signed certificates to work, they must be added to the trusted root certificate store of another federation server, which can leave that server open to attack.

Assuming you took my advice and requested certificates from a Certificate Authority (CA) appropriate to your needs (public or private), the next thing you need to do is store those certificates in the appropriate certificate store.You have the following two options here:

- Import the certificates to the personal store using the Certificates MMC snap-in.

- Import the service communication (SSL) certificate with the IIS Manager snap-in and assign it to the default web site.

## Understanding Token-Signing Certificates

Token-signing certificates are used to sign the SAML tokens your AD FS server will be issuing to SharePoint.This is the most important piece of your AD FS infrastructure.It is used by partner organizations to ensure that tokens received are from a valid source and that they haven't been modified.

Token-signing certificates utilize a Public Key Infrastructure (PKI) to validate the sender and the contents.Each certificate contains a cryptographic private key and public key.A security token is signed using the private key.When a partnership is established in AD FS, the public key is used to validate the authenticity of the encrypted token.

Since each token is digitally signed by the account partner, the resource partner can verify that it was indeed issued by the account partner.Digital signatures are validated by the public key portion of a partner's token-signing certificate. Once the signature is verified, the resource federation server generates its own security token for its organization and signs it.Once the web server receives a valid token (signed by the resource federation server), it allows the appropriate access to the client.

During the setup process for AD FS 2.0 you will be asked for a token-signing certificate.You may be tempted to use the same certificate you used for the service communication certificate (SSL).**Don't do it!**This is against PKI best practices.If the private key is compromised for either use, your entire system is compromised.

## Understanding Service Communication Certificates

Service communication certificates are used to ensure the federation server's identity to a client.This is similar to an SSL certificate and is set up in much the same way.For service communication certificates to work, they must meet the following criteria:

- The certificate must include the server authentication enhanced key usage (EKU) extension.

- The certificate revocation lists (CRLs) must be accessible for all the certificates in the PKI chain, and the root CA must be trusted by the clients.

- **Most important:**The subject name used in the service communication certificate must match the Federation Service name in the properties of the Federation Service.If you set your properties wrong, you will not be able to establish a trust with anybody.

## Installing Active Directory Federation Services 2.0

The first step in installing Active Directory Federation Services (AD FS) 2.0 is downloading it.A common misconception about AD FS 2.0 is that it is built in to the operating system as was AD FS 1.X.While future versions of Windows will likely have it, as of the time of this writing, you still need to download it.The download is available from Microsoft at `http://go.microsoft.com/fwlink/?LinkId=151338`.

**Note** This section not intended to be a comprehensive guide to installing and configuring AD FS.Federation Services is an entire book unto itself.My intent here is a quick overview of the components involved in AD FS to give you some context for when you are building a lab or production environment.If you want a deep dive in AD FS, a good place to start is the AD FS 2.0 deployment guide on TechNet at`http://technet.microsoft.com/en-us/library/adfs2-deployment-guide(WS.10).aspx`.

Another caveat of AD FS is that it can't be installed on the same server as SharePoint.This is because SharePoint can run its own Secure Token Service (STS) and certain SharePoint Services may use components of the STS in the background.AD FS running on the same box could create a conflict.Thus, it is not a supported configuration.

The installation is pretty straightforward.Specific steps are available at `http://technet.microsoft.com/en-us/library/dd807096(WS.10).aspx`.

**Note** There is a pretty long list of prerequisites that need to be installed for AD FS 2.0 to work properly.As always, it's best to ensure your server is fully patched before attempting to install new software to make sure there are no prerequisite problems.The AD FS 2.0 installer will check for these prerequisites, and download and install them if needed.This, of course, infers that your Federation Server has access to the Internet.

# Configuring Your Federation Server

Once you have installed AD FS 2.0, the next thing you will need to do is configure it.The most common way to get to the configuration wizard is through the Start menu (Start ➤ Administrative Tools ➤ AD FS 2.0 Management) and then click on the AD FS 2.0 Federation Server Configuration Wizard link on the Overview page or Actions pane.Another option is to go to the executable itself (located in the folder you choose to install it in), which is `C:\Program Files\Active Directory Federation Services 2.0\FsConfigWizard.exe` by default.

At this point you have a couple of decisions to make.The first is if you want to operate a standalone server or a federation server farm.There are a variety of reasons to choose a farm.One important thing to note is if you choose to install as a standalone server, the NETWORK SERVICE account will automatically be chosen for you.This can be nice in a lab environment, as the NETWORK SERVICE account already has a Service Principle Name (SPN) established within Active Directory.However, using the NETWORK SERVICE account is not a recommended practice for use in production as it may open up your federation server to attack.In addition, if you ever do want to scale your AD FS implementation from a standalone instance to a farm, you will need a service account anyway.

The next step in configuring you AD FS server is choosing your Federation Service name and ensuring it is associated to the right SSL certificate.By default, this is the SSL certificate assigned to the default website, assuming a certificate has been assigned at all.If a certificate has not been assigned, then a list of available certificates is generated from amongst the certificates in the personal certificates store.

Once you have established the service account and certificate, the next thing you will need to do is configure your AD FS configuration database.If the install program detects an already existing configuration database, it will delete it.You will be prompted, but be careful as there is no way (though the installer) to save an existing database.It will delete it.

If you are creating or adding a federation server to a farm, there are some additional steps asking if the server will be the primary server (or where the primary server is if you're adding a new server to the farm).

In any case, the last steps are the Ready to Apply Settings page and the results page.However, you're not quite done yet.All the wizard really does is create a configuration database, and in the case of a farm, establish the relationships between federation servers in the farm.

Once you complete the configuration wizard, you still need to add a few certificates to your AD FS infrastructure before you can begin to utilize it.The first certificate to add is your token-signing certificate.

---

■ **Note** You may have noticed the Token-Decrypting and Service Communications certificate options in the certificates node.By default, these two certificates use the SSL certificate assigned in IIS.This is the place to go if you need to change them for some reason.

---

## Adding a Token-signing Certificate

To add a token-signing certificate, follow these steps.

1.  Choose StartäAll ProgramsäAdministrative Tools ä AD FS 2.0 Management.

2.  In the console tree, double-click Service, and then click Certificates.

3.  In the Actions pane (to the right), click the Add Token-Signing Certificate link.

4.  In the Browse for Certificate file dialog box, navigate to the certificate file that you want to add, select the certificate file, and then click Open.

You should now see your certificate listed under the token-signing certificates node.

## Understanding Identity Providers (AD FS Account Partners)

Now that you have AD FS installed and your certificates are set up, you need to establish an identity provider trust.In AD FS this is call the account partner.This is the organization providing the authentication you will use in your SharePoint environment.There are essentially three types of account partner trusts you can establish in AD FS.

• Provide your own Active Directory users with access to your own claims-aware application.

• Provide your Active Directory users with access to other organizations' applications.

• Provide users in another organization access to your claims-aware application.

In the first case above, you may be thinking, "Why would I ever want to use AD FS to provide access to my own users?"Think about scenarios involving applications that sit on your perimeter, such as an expense reporting system where users may be inside or outside of the corporate firewall.With an ADFS implementation, it doesn't matter where you are authenticated from; once you have a token, you're good to go.So from the application perspective, you only need to deal with one authentication mechanism.

The second case is the first case where you are truly crossing organizational lines.In this scenario you have users on your Active Directory implementation that wish to access resources on another organization's infrastructure.In this case, you are using AD FS to provide authentication information to a claims-aware application at the remote organization.Essentially you are passing their Active Directory identity via a token.

The third case is what you will most likely see with your SharePoint implementation.It's the scenario where you have another identity provider generating a token to AD FS that you can use in SharePoint for identity management.While the first case may apply to SharePoint also, this is where you must use AD FS.The first case is a preference, but you can still use classic mode (Windows) authentication if you want to.

Keep in mind that AD FS is not just about federating with other Active Directory implementations.In the second and third cases mentioned previously, either the party providing the authentication token or the party accepting the token may not be Active Directory implementations.AD FS can manage identities from a variety of sources."AD" may be in the name, but the real beauty of AD FS is its ability to federate with non-Active Directory implementations.

Once you know the scenario, the next thing to think about is which design is best for your particular case.Microsoft has two categories for Single-Sign-On (SSO): a Federated Web SSO Design or just a Web (without the Federated qualifier) SSO Design.The difference between *Federated* Web SSOand Web SSO is essentially if you have a configured "federated" trust between two distinct organizations, then it's a Federated Web SSO.If the users are coming in as individual users from a credential store (Active Directory, LDAP, or SQL), and you are using AD FS to generate a token, then it's a Web SSO.When looking for additional documentation, just keep in mind the difference between *Federated* Web SSO and just Web SSO is that there is a federated trust between two distinct organizations.

## Adding a Claims Provider Trust Manually

You may get lucky and work with a mature claims provider that can provide you with metadata to import your trust relationship information.But most likely you will have to create the trust manually.To do that, take the following steps:

1. Choose StartäAll ProgramsäAdministrative Tools ä AD FS 2.0 Management.

2. Expand the AD FS 2.0\Trust Relationships node, and right-click Claims Provider Trusts, and then click Add Claims Provider Trust.This willopen the Add Claims Provider Trust Wizard.

3. On the Welcome page, click Start.

4. On the Select Data Source page, click "Enter claims provider trust data manually," and then click Next, as shown in Figure 19-1.(This is where you could also import a provided configuration file.)

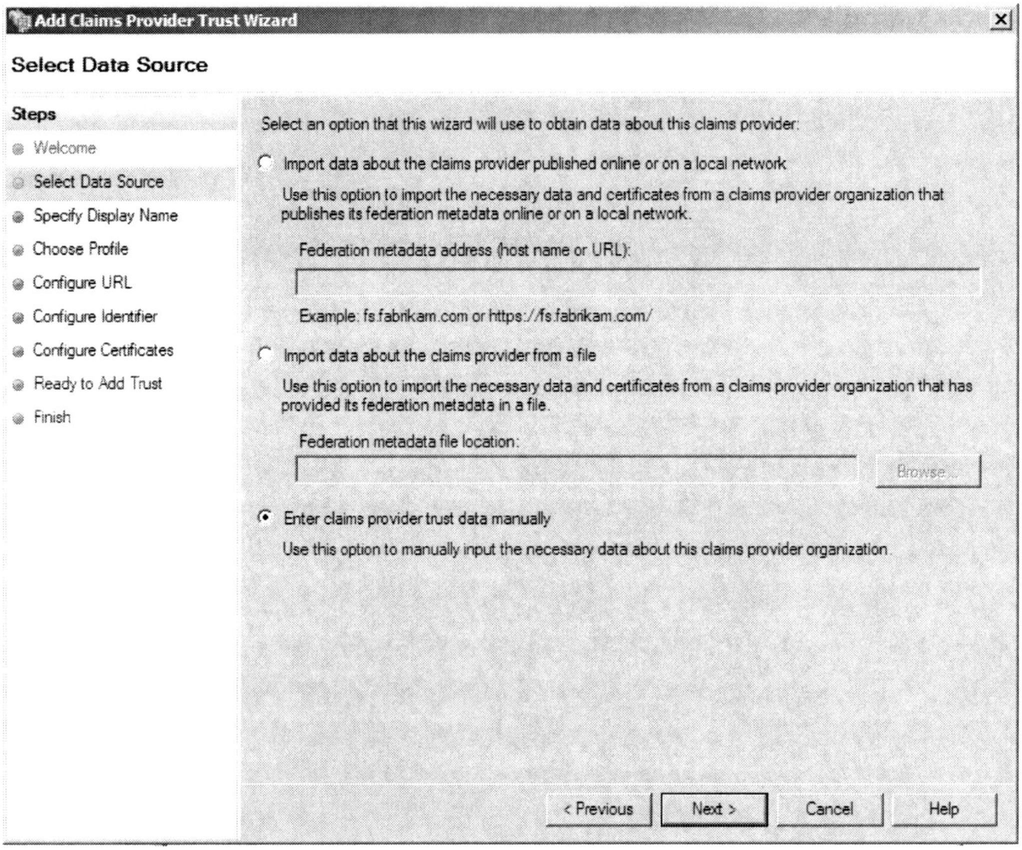

*Figure 19-1. Entering the data source*

5.  On the Specify Display Name page, type a name appropriate to your organization, as shown in Figure 19-2. Under Notes type a description for this claims provider trust, and then click Next.

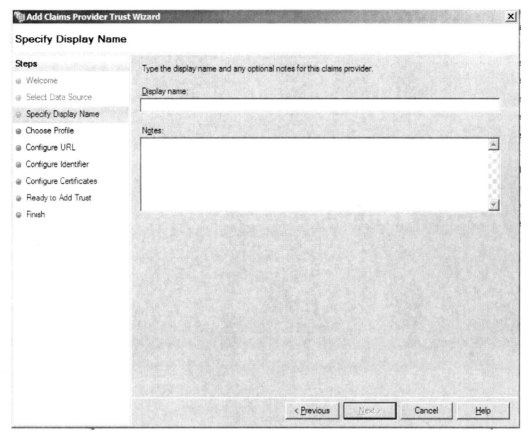

*Figure 19-2. Entering the display name and any important notes*

6.  On the Choose Profile page, choose the AD FS profile you will be importing from, as shown in Figure 19-3.

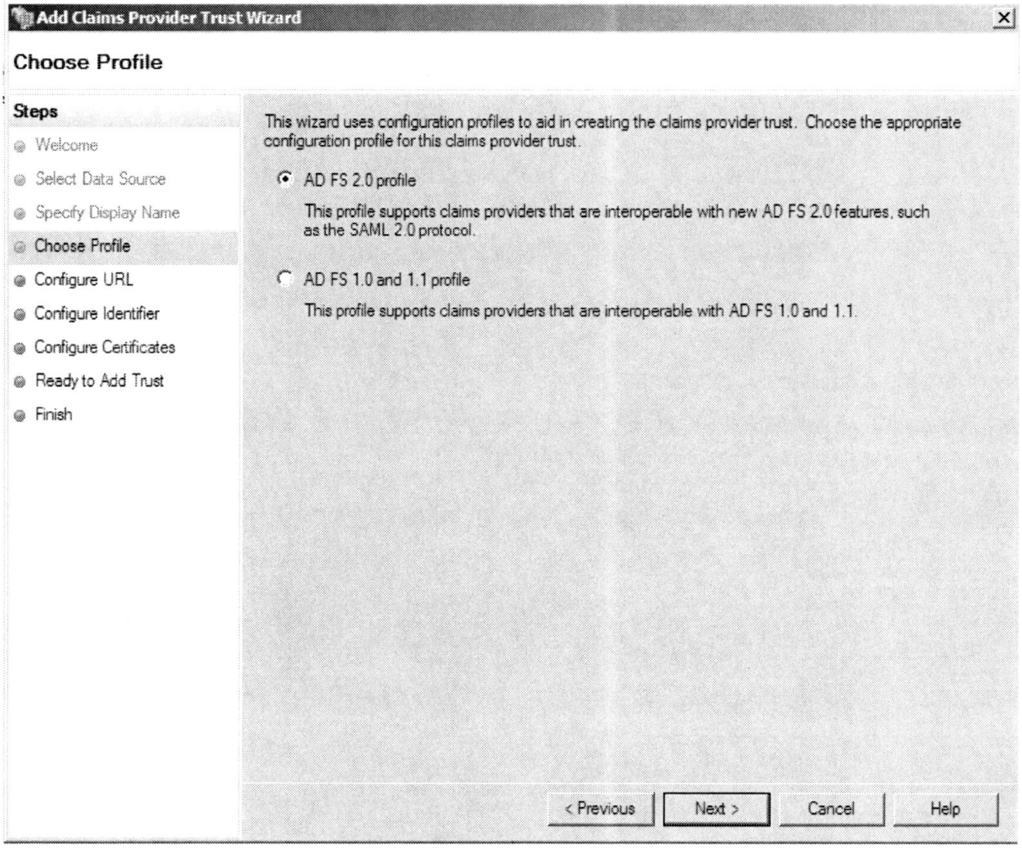

*Figure 19-3. Pick one of the two choices for AD FS profile.*

---

■ **Note** SharePoint requires a AD FS 2.0 profile on the other end, but for this section it is the profile you are getting the identity from, so it can be AD FS 1.1.

---

At this point the next steps you take diverge a little bit depending on if you choose to import an AD FS 1.1 profile or AD FS 2.0 profile.The wizard will ask for specific information regarding the implementation you choose to import.This is information you should be able to get from the identity provider.

- If you choose AD FS 2.0 profile, you will be taken to the Configure URL page where you will be shown a couple of checkboxes, as shown in Figure 19-4.

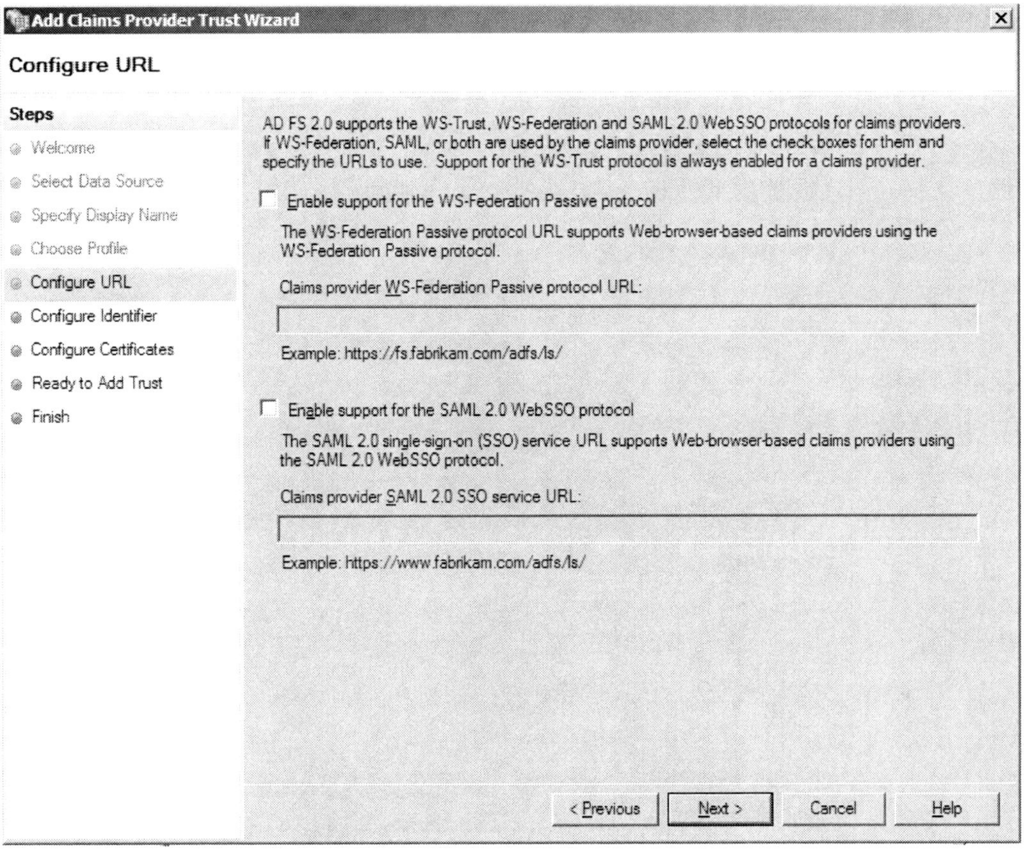

**Figure 19-4.** *Two options for AD FS 2.0*

- *Enable support for the WS-Federation Passive protocol*: This is if your account partner supports the WS-* protocols (usually a Microsoft tool).

- *Enable support for the SAML 2.0 Web SSO protocol*: For other vendors supporting the SAML SSO protocol.

- If you choose AD FS 1.0 and 1.1 profile, your only option is WS-Federation Passive protocol, as you can see in Figure 19-5.

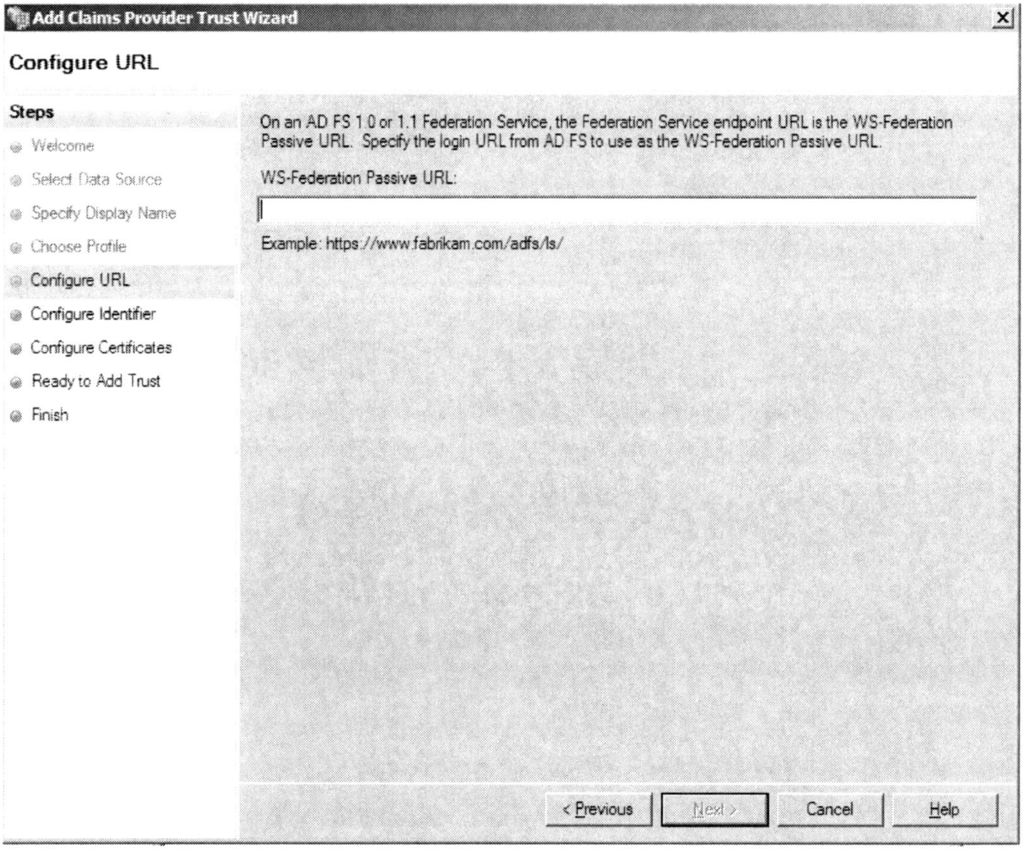

*Figure 19-5. Only one option is available for AD FS 1.0 and 1.1*

7. On the Configure Identifier page, under Claims provider trust identifier, type the appropriate identifier, and then click Next.

8. On the Configure Certificates page, click Add to locate a certificate file (that you got from the identity provider) and add it to the list of certificates, and then click Next.

9. On the Ready to Add Trust page, click Next.

10. On the Finish page, click Close. This action automatically displays the Edit Claim Rules dialog box.

# Understanding Claims Rules in AD FS

Claims rules are at the very heart of what AD FS is about.This is where the real work is done.Up to this point you have essentially established certificate-based trusts between account partners and relying partners.Now you need to apply logic to the claims (attributes) that are passed between the partners.You can actually setup claims rules on either end of the communication.Say, for example, an organization is publishing a claim of Social Security Number.(No one should be dumb enough to publish information like that, but let's say they are.)If you control your AD FS environment, you have a few options.

- Filter the claim to something less specific (e.g. the last four digits) either at the account partner integration point or relying partner integration point.

- Allow the claim through.

- Block the claim either at the account partner integration point or relying partner integration point.

You can see the power of claims now.Perhaps you could make a rule for just accounting personnel (based on an organization claim) or only managers.Depending on what claims are published, you may be able to do some very powerful stuff before the tokens even get to SharePoint (assuming you have access to the AD FS environment).Table 19-3 is a list of the claims available to you in AD FS 2.0.

*Table 19-3. Claims Available in AD FS 2.0*

| Name | Description | URL |
|------|-------------|-----|
| E-Mail Address | The e-mail address of the user | `http://schemas.xmlsoap.org/ws/2005/05/identity/claims/emailaddress` |
| Given Name | The given name of the user | `http://schemas.xmlsoap.org/ws/2005/05/identity/claims/givenname` |
| Name | The unique name of the user | `http://schemas.xmlsoap.org/ws/2005/05/identity/claims/name` |
| UPN | The user principal name (UPN) of the user | `http://schemas.xmlsoap.org/ws/2005/05/identity/claims/upn` |
| Common Name | The common name of the user | `http://schemas.xmlsoap.org/claims/CommonName` |
| AD FS 1.x E-Mail Address | The e-mail address of the user when interoperating with ADFS 1.1 or ADFS 1.0 | `http://schemas.xmlsoap.org/claims/EmailAddress` |
| Group | A name of group to which the user belongs | `http://schemas.xmlsoap.org/claims/Group` |
| AD FS 1.x UPN | The UPN of the user when interoperating with AD FS 1.1 or ADFS 1.0 | `http://schemas.xmlsoap.org/claims/UPN` |
| Role | A user's role | `http://schemas.microsoft.com/ws/2008/06/identity/claims/role` |

| Name | Description | URL |
|------|-------------|-----|
| Surname | The surname of the user | http://schemas.xmlsoap.org/ws/2005/05/identity/claims/surname |
| PPID | The private identifier of the user | http://schemas.xmlsoap.org/ws/2005/05/identity/claims/privatepersonalidentifier |
| Name Identifier | The SAML name identifier of the user | http://schemas.xmlsoap.org/ws/2005/05/identity/claims/nameidentifier |
| Authentication Method | The method used to authenticate the user | http://schemas.microsoft.com/ws/2008/06/identity/claims/authenticationmethod |
| Deny Only Group SID | The deny-only group SID of the user | http://schemas.xmlsoap.org/ws/2005/05/identity/claims/denyonlysid |
| Deny only primary SID | The deny-only primary SID of the user | http://schemas.microsoft.com/ws/2008/06/identity/claims/denyonlyprimarysid |
| Deny only primary group SID | The deny-only primary group SID of the user | http://schemas.microsoft.com/ws/2008/06/identity/claims/denyonlyprimarygroupsid |
| Group SID | The group SID of the user | http://schemas.microsoft.com/ws/2008/06/identity/claims/groupsid |
| Primary group SID | The primary group SID of the user | http://schemas.microsoft.com/ws/2008/06/identity/claims/primarygroupsid |
| Primary SID | The primary SID of the user | http://schemas.microsoft.com/ws/2008/06/identity/claims/primarysid |
| Windows account name | The domain account name of the user in the form of <domain>\<user> | http://schemas.microsoft.com/ws/2008/06/identity/claims/windowsaccountname |

As you can see, there are quite a few options. Most organizations are not going to use or publish every one of these claim types. In fact, in my experience, most organizations generate very few claims. Some of this is because people don't fully understand the power of claims. Some of it is because they are fearful of publishing too much information.

**A best practice when providing claims is to publish as much information as possible**. This where claims can become a very powerful alternative to other authentication methods. The more information you publish about your users within the claim, the more dynamic of a solution your trusted partners can create. **Break out of the User ID and Password paradigm**. With claims you can do MUCH more than just authenticate people. Also, keep in mind this information is not going out to anybody; it's going only to trusted partners.

For each claim you want to let through, follow these steps:

1.  Click on Add Rule.

2.  In the Claim rule template drop-down, choose Transform an Incoming Claim (as shown in Figure 19-6), and click Next.

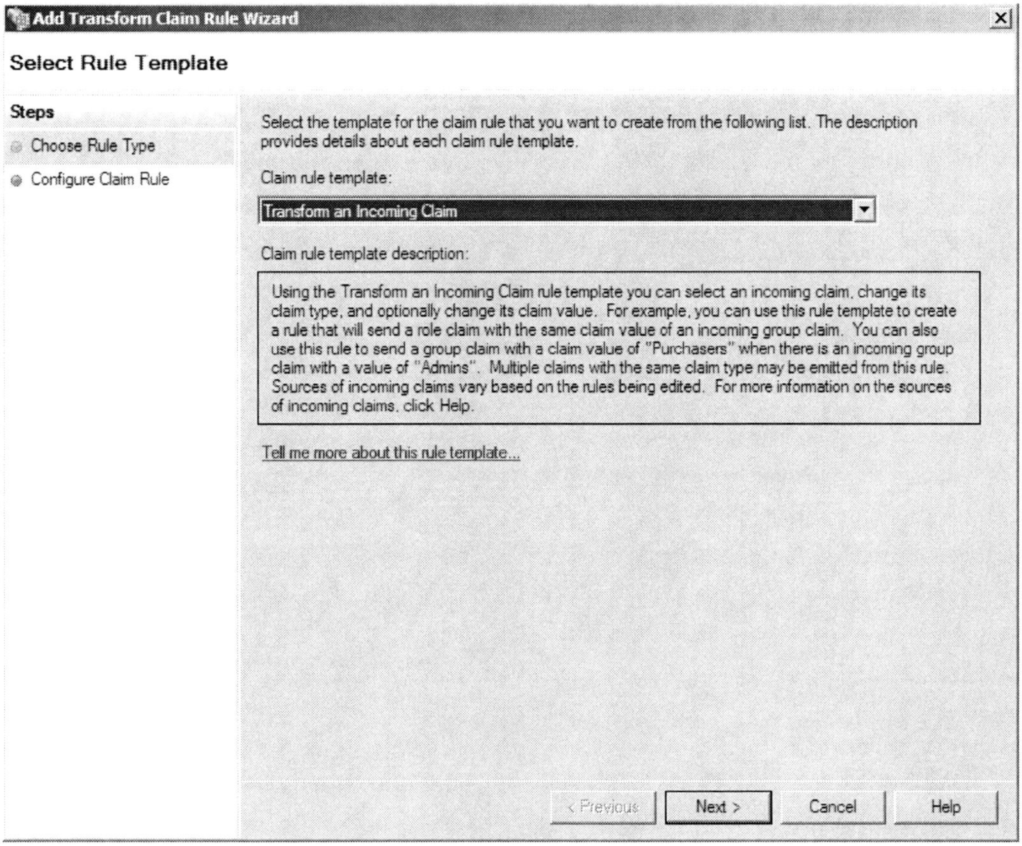

*Figure 19-6. Selecting to transform an incoming claim*

3.  Enter the following values in the Add Transform Claim Rule wizard shown in Figure 19-7:

| Name | Value |
| --- | --- |
| Claim Rule Name | *Name appropriate to the claim* |
| Incoming claim type | *Choose the appropriate claim type* |

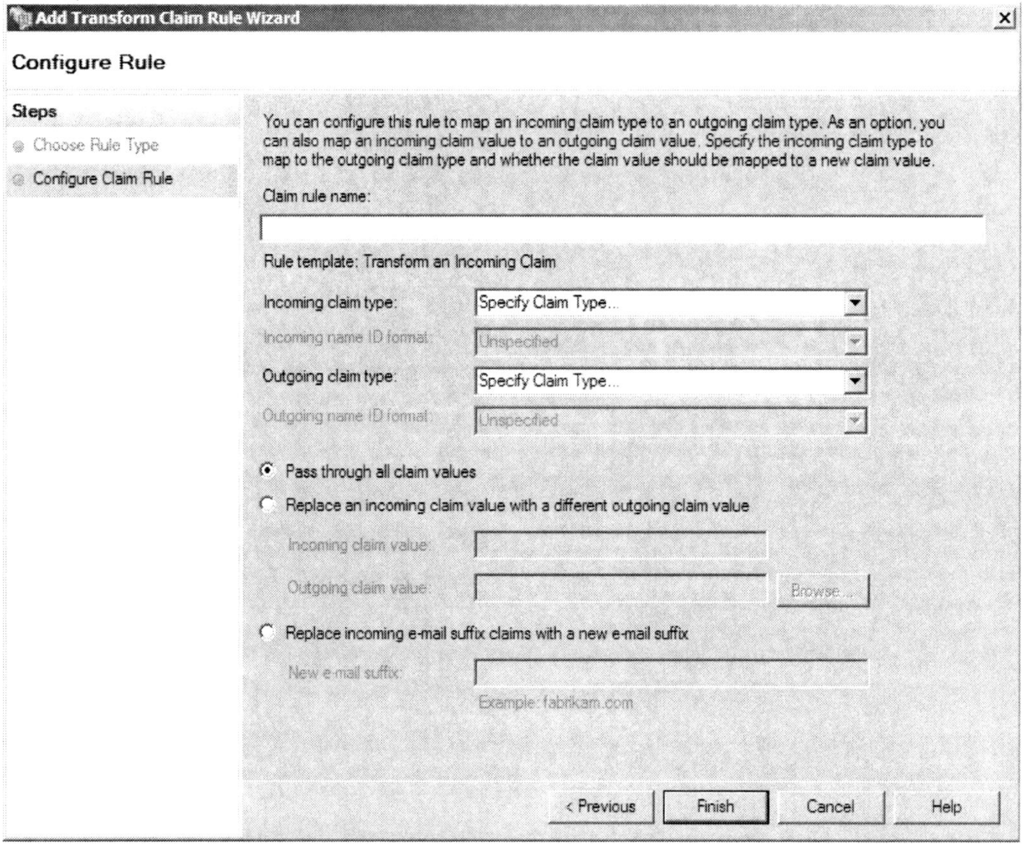

*Figure 19-7. Entering the claim rule name and type*

4. Check on the Pass through all claim valuesradio button, and then click Finish.

Repeat these steps as necessary to add all the claim types available.

# Configuring AD FS Relying Party

The other half of an AD FS configuration is adding the Relying Party trust.This is where you will add your SharePoint environment.Much like adding an Account Partner, the steps are relatively trivial; it's understanding them that is more complex.

Steps to add a Relying Party Trust, follow these steps:

1. Choose StartäAll ProgramsäAdministrative Tools ä AD FS 2.0 Management.

2. Open the AD FS 2.0\Trust Relationships node, right-click Relying Party Trusts, and then click Add Relying Party Trust.This will openAdd Relying Party Trust Wizard.

3. On the Welcome page, click Start.

4. On the Select Data Source page, click "Enter data about the relying party manually," and then click Next. Unfortunately SharePoint doesn't publish a relying party metadata document for consumption by AD FS 2.0. It would be great if they did. It would make our lives much easier. As a result, when setting up SharePoint you need to choose the option to Enter Relying Party Data Manually.

5. On the Specify Display Name page, type a name appropriate to your organization. Under Notes, type a description for this claims provider trust, and then click Next.

6. On the Choose Profile page, choose AD FS 2.0 profile and click Next. SharePoint 2010 expects an AD FS 2.0 profile. If you choose the AD FS 1.1 profile, SharePoint won't be able to recognize the SAML token, and all the configuration of AD FS you have done up to this point will be for naught.

7. On the Configure Certificate page, click Next. This is for decryption certificates, which you don't need on an initial setup.

8. On the Configure URL page, click Next. You won't need either of these options to work with SharePoint.

9. On the Configure Identifiers page, in the Relying Part trust identifier text box, enter the URL of your SharePoint website, click Add, and then click Next.

10. On the Choose Issuance Authorization Rules page, select "Permit all users to access this relying party," and then click Next, as shown in Figure 19-8. This doesn't override SharePoint's permission sets. It is simply whether AD FS users are authenticated through by default or not.

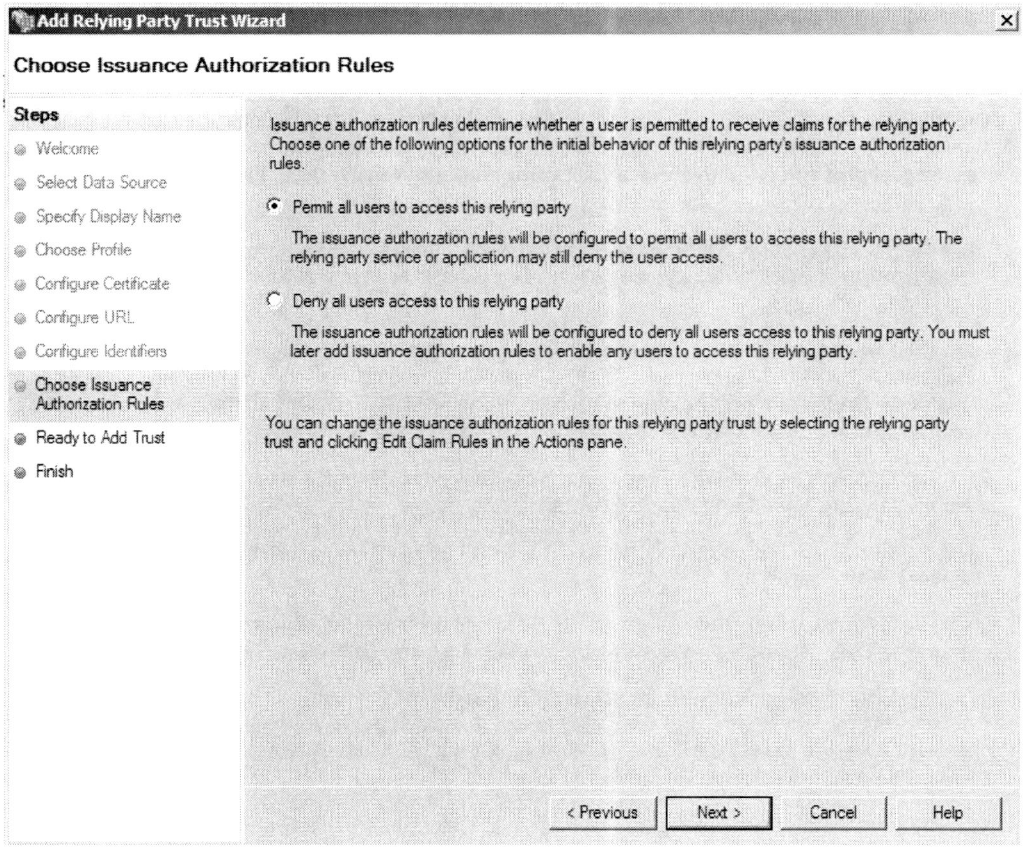

***Figure 19-8.*** *Creating issuance authorization rules*

11. On the Ready to Add Trust page, review the settings, and then click Next.

12. On the Finish page, click Close. This action automatically opens the Edit Claim Rules wizard.

This is the point where you may want to add some filtering to your claims. However, most of the time, you will probably just let everything through.

13. Click on Add Rule.

14. In the Claim rule template drop-down, choose Pass Through or Filter an Incoming Claim, and click Next.

15. Enter the following values in the Add Transform Claim Rule Wizard:

| Name | Value |
|------|-------|
| Claim Rule Name | *Name appropriate to the claim* |
| Incoming claim type | *Choose the appropriate claim type* |

16. Check on the "Pass through all claim values"radio button, and then click Finish.

Repeat these steps as necessary to add all the claim types available.

# Configuring SharePoint 2010 for Claims Authentication

Now that you (finally) have the AD FS environment setup and the necessary trusts established,the next step is to configure SharePoint to accept the SAML token you will be receiving from AD FS.One trend you may have noticed in other Microsoft products is the move towards PowerShell for scripting administrative tasks.The SharePoint team has joined that party.If you have managed to avoid learning PowerShell through the years (as I have), the time has come to bite the bullet.With regard to configuring your SharePoint Server for claims authentication, PowerShell is your only option.There is no GUI for configuring the SPTrustedClaimProvider class.This point of confusion for some people because they see a checkbox when creating a new SharePoint web application and think that is all they need to do—and they quickly find out that it's more complicated than that.Furthermore, there is no migration path in to claims (from 2007 OR 2010).You either start in claims or you don't.Thus, if you're looking to upgrade some kind of single sign-on solution from SharePoint 2007 to 2010 and you want to go to claims, you will quickly discover you are in trouble.

To open SharePoint PowerShell navigate to Start➤Microsoft SharePoint 2010 Products➤SharePoint 2010 Management Shell. The following sections are executed in the SharePoint Management Shell (PowerShell) command window.

# Adding the Token-Signing Certificate to SharePoint

The first thing you need to do to establish the claims trust is to add the token-signing certificate to the SharePoint certificate store.*If you are in a PKI environment, you will need to add a certificate from each Certificate Authority (CA) in the certificate chain until you get to the root CA. A common mistake is to add just the certificate from the closest CA (and not map to the root CA).*

For **each** certificate in your certificate chain, starting with the one you are sending to the AD FS server, execute the following command in SharePoint Management Shelll:

```
$root = New-Object System.Security.Cryptography.X509Certificates.X509Certificate2↩
("Location of your .cer file")
New-SPTrustedRootAuthority -Name "Token Signing Certificate Name" -Certificate $root
```

# Adding a Trusted Identity Provider to SharePoint

The next thing you need to do is add the claim mappings to SharePoint.This is yet another opportunity to limit the claims that will be available to you.However, you can't filter claims here.Note that the following commands need to be executed in the same PowerShell window; you are essentially creating a list of variables and then referencing the variables in a final command at the end.While it is possible to just run a single giant command, I find it easier to work with variables.

For **each** claim you wish to bring in from AD FS, execute the following commands in SharePoint Powershell:

```
$Claim1 = New-SPClaimTypeMapping -IncomingClaimType "URL of the claim type you are
mapping"↵
 -IncomingClaimTypeDisplayName "Claim Type Display Name" –SameAsIncoming
```

Example:

```
$Claim1 = New-SPClaimTypeMapping -IncomingClaimType "http://schemas.xmlsoap.org/↵
emailaddress" -IncomingClaimTypeDisplayName "v1EmailAddress" –SameAsIncoming
```

Repeat for each claim until you have all your claims mapped.

Once you have all your claims mapped, the next thing to do is create a new SPTrustedIdentityTokenIssuer. This is essentially the mapping that SharePoint uses to accept SAML tokens. It has the following list of required fields. If you wish to know more about all the options you can see them at http://msdn.microsoft.com/en-us/library/ff607628.aspx

- *ClaimsMappings:*Used to map claims on the SAML token to SharePoint.

- *Description:*Description of the new identity provider.

- *Identifier Claim:*Specifies which claim type will be used as a unique identity in SharePoint

- *Name:*The name of the new identity provider.

- *Realm:*This is essentially the web application you are mapping the claims to (written as a URL).

- *SignInUrl:*The sign-in URL your users will need to be redirected to if they don't have a SAML token.

Ok, time to put it all together.

```
$ap = New-SPTrustedIdentityTokenIssuer -Name "The name you want displayed to users"↵
 -Description "Description for the Identity provider" -Realm "URL for your SharePoint↵
 Web Application -ImportTrustCertificate $cert -ClaimsMappings $Claim1, $Claim2 etc↵
-SignInUrl "Your sign-in URL"-IdentifierClaim $Claim1.InputClaimType
```

Example:

```
$ap = New-SPTrustedIdentityTokenIssuer -Name "My SSO" -Description "My ADFSv2 Federated↵
 Identity" -Realm "http://SomeURL.com" -ImportTrustCertificate $cert –ClaimsMappings↵
 $Claim1, Claim2 –SignInUrl "https://SomeURL.com/adfs/ls" signinurl –IdentifierClaim↵
 $Claim1.InputClaimType
```

# Enabling Claims in Your SharePoint Web Application

Now that you have established a trust identifier, the last thing you need to do is enable claims authentication in your web application. To do this, go to the Central Administration site for your SharePoint Farm and take the following steps:

1.  Choose Manage Web Applications, and then choose the web application from the list you wish to make claims aware.

2. On the ribbon, click on the Authentication Providers button.

3. Choose the appropriate zone for your web application.

4. Scroll down to the Authentication Types section.Uncheck Integrated Windows Authentication if it is checked (default).

5. Check Trusted Identity Provider, and then check the name of your identity provider below.

You can now add site collections to your web application with users that are authenticated based on claims.This also implies that your site collection administrators must use claims authentication.

Congratulations! You have created a claims aware web application in SharePoint 2010!

## Validating Your Claims are Working

The last step in any project such as this is to test it.All you need to do is open a web browser and browse to your web application.You should see the sign-in page you are using (or a generic one if you are using Active Directory) prompting you for credentials.Once you enter a valid credential set, you should be redirected to the home page of your root site collection.

## Chapter Summary

You now have the tools you need to implement claims authentication in SharePoint. While specific implementations can vary widely, the fundamentals presented in this chapter remain the same. The first thing you need to do is determine if claims authentication is the right solution for your particular project. Once the decision is made, the next thing you need to do is establish a trust with an identity provider (by exchanging certificates). The typical implementation for this is to use Active Directory Federation Services; however, anything that can provide a valid SAML token could be utilized. Once the trust is established, you just need to make a few configuration changes to SharePoint and you're on your way.

Claims authentication provides a whole new paradiam for how identity management can be utilized within SharePoint (or any other claims-aware application). Consider the scenario where your application natively supports role-based access control based on a department claim type, so as users change departments, their access changes automagically. Such capabilities are why claims have received rapid industry adoption. The skills you learn in this chapter will carry you a long way into the future. Good luck!

# Index

## ■ S

CPSIA information can be obtained at www.ICGtesting.com
Printed in the USA
LVOW050940180312

273578LV00001B/8/P